Jump Right In!
PREMIUM MEDIA SITE ACCESS CODE

Improve your grade with hands-on tools and resources!

- Master key terms and vocabulary
- Prepare for exams by taking practice quizzes

And for even more tools, you can access the following Premium Resources using your Access Code. Register now to get the most out of *Jump Right In!*

- *Objective Videos:* Review key concepts and skills covered in each objective*
- *Diving Deeper Videos:* Take students deeper into chapter content*

*Access code required for these premium resources

Your Access Code is:

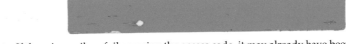

Note: If there is no silver foil covering the access code, it may already have been redeemed, and therefore may no longer be valid. In that case, you can purchase online access using a major credit card or PayPal account. To do so, go to **www.pearsonhighered.com/jump**, select your book cover, click on "Buy Access" and follow the on-screen instructions.

To Register:

- To Start you will need a valid email address and this access code.
- Go to **www.pearsonhighered.com/jump** and scroll to find your text book.
- Once you've selected your text, on the Home Page, click the link to access the Student Premium Content.
- Click the Register button and follow the on-screen instructions.
- After you register, you can sign in any time via the log-in area on the same screen.

System Requirements

Windows 7 Ultimate Edition; IE 8
Windows Vista Ultimate Edition SP1; IE 8
Windows XP Professional SP3; IE 7
Windows XP Professional SP3; Firefox 3.6.4
Mac OS 10.5.7; Firefox 3.6.4
Mac OS 10.6; Safari 5

Technical Support

http://247pearsoned.custhelp.com

D1403740

Photo credits: Goodluz/wrangler/Elena Elisseeva/Shutterstock

2nd Edition

Jump Right In!

Essential Computer Skills
Using Microsoft® Office 2013

2nd Edition

Jump Right In!

Essential Computer Skills
Using Microsoft® Office 2013

Jean Andrews, PhD

Joy Dark

Jill West

PEARSON

Boston   Columbus   Indianapolis   New York   San Francisco   Upper Saddle River
Amsterdam   Cape Town   Dubai   London   Madrid   Milan   Munich   Paris   Montréal   Toronto
Delhi   Mexico City   São Paulo   Sydney   Hong Kong   Seoul   Singapore   Taipei   Tokyo

Executive Editor: Jenifer Niles

Team Lead, Project Management: Laura Burgess

Senior Project Manager: Marilyn Lloyd

Program Manager: Emily Biberger

Development Editor: Shannon LeMay-Finn

Editorial Assistant: Melissa Davis

Director of Product Marketing: Maggie Waples

Director of Field Marketing: Leigh Ann Sims

Field Marketing Managers: Brad Forrester & Joanna Sabella

Marketing Coordinator: Susan Osterlitz

Senior Operations Specialist: Maura Zaldivar

Interior and Cover Design: Jonathan Boylan

Cover Photo: Courtesy of Shutterstock® Images

Associate Director of Design: Blair Brown

Digital Media Editor: Eric Hakanson

Director of Media Development: Taylor Ragan

Media Project Manager, Production: John Cassar

Full-Service Project Management: Lynn Steines/S4Carlisle Publishing Services

Composition: S4Carlisle Publishing Services

Credits and acknowledgments borrowed from other sources and reproduced, with permission, in this textbook appear in the end matter.

Library of Congress Cataloging-in-Publication Data

Andrews, Jean
   Jump right in!: essential computer skills using Microsoft Office 2013 / Jean Andrews.—Second Edition.
      pages cm
   Includes index.
   ISBN-13: 978-0-13-342550-5
   ISBN-10: 0-13-342550-9
   1. Microsoft Office.   2. Microsoft Windows (Computer file)   3. Business—Computer programs.   4. Microcomputers.   5. Computer literacy.   I. Title.
   HF5548.4.M525A53 2014
   005.5—dc23

                                                                                    2014002118

10 9 8 7 6 5 4 3 2 1
V011

ISBN-10:   0-13-342550-9
ISBN-13: 978-0-13-342550-5

Contents at a Glance

Videos

Contents

ix

About the Authors

Jean Andrews, PhD, has more than 30 years of experience in the computer industry, including more than 13 years in the college classroom and three years in public schools. She has worked in a wide variety of businesses and corporations designing, writing, and supporting applications software; managing an IT help desk; and troubleshooting wide area networks. She has written a variety of books on software, hardware, and the Internet. She lives in northwest Georgia.

Joy Dark has worked in the IT field as a help desk technician providing first-level support for a company with presence in 29 states, a second-tier technician in healthcare IT, and an operations specialist designing support protocols and structures. As a teacher, Joy has taught online courses with the Stride Center in California using the first edition of *Jump Right In!* and has taught English as a Second Language in the United States and South America. She has helped write several technical textbooks with Jean Andrews, her mother, and Jill West, her sister. Joy lives in Dalton, Georgia, with her Doberman dog.

Jill West brings a unique variety of experience in writing, business, and education to the development of her innovative educational materials. She has taught multiple ages and content areas using a flipped classroom approach, distance learning, and educational counseling. Jill's résumé includes service with a nonprofit agency to inner city disadvantaged populations, on-the-job training with a law firm, ten years working with Jean Andrews in textbook development, and multiple entrepreneurial ventures. Jill used the first edition of *Jump Right In!* to teach a hybrid online course at the high school level, and she was instrumental in piloting a flipped classroom program for learning support level courses at North Georgia Technical College. Her insights into the art of self-teaching provide students with effective tools for taking ownership of their own learning. Jill and her husband Mike live in the hills of northwest Georgia where they homeschool their four children.

Acknowledgments

From Jean Andrews:

Thank you to all the Pearson folks who made this book possible. Shannon LeMay-Finn, Jenifer Niles, Marilyn Lloyd, Lynn Steines, Joyce Nielson, and Elizabeth Lockley; it's been a pleasure working with you. Thank you to the many editors, designers, and managers who gave so much to make a book we can all be proud of. It was truly a team effort.

As a family of educators and technicians, Joy, Jill and I decided to tackle writing this book as a mother-and-two-daughters author team. It's been awesome! Thank you, Jill and Joy, for your great ideas, long hours, and dedication to excellence. You've made this work fun!

From Joy Dark:

Thank you to everyone at Pearson who dedicated so much time and effort in this edition. I'm going to miss our Monday morning calls! Thank you to Jill West for digging in while keeping me focused. Thank you to Jean Andrews for your guidance and wisdom. Your direction is always appreciated. Finally, thank you to all my family who encourage me in everything I do.

From Jill West:

To my husband, Mike: Thank you for bringing me chocolate while I work. And homemade mochas. And ice cream. And smoothies. Thank you for the freedom you pour into my dreams, and the solid ground you put under my feet every day. You're a source of life for our family, as you fill our home with the love of God for each of us.

To my kids, Jessica, Sarah, Daniel, and Zack: Thank you for hugs throughout the day, yellow flowers, hand-colored pictures, and rubber band bracelets. Your gifts help keep us connected through the long hours of my working.

To my mom and Joy: Thank you for embracing me on this new level of our journey together. I love building this dream with you.

To my husband, Mike: Thank you for the chocolate.

To our Pearson team: Y'all rock. I have so enjoyed working with a team of professionals with such high standards and resourceful solutions to every challenge we faced.

To my husband, Mike: Did I mention the chocolate? And the mochas. Seriously—if we ever retire, I look forward to opening that little coffee shop we've dreamed about so often!

Dedication

This book is dedicated to the glory of God.

Introduction

Jump Right In! Essential Computer Skills Using Microsoft Office 2013 was written to be the best tool in the market today to prepare you to be a skilled and knowledgeable computer user. Computers are everywhere, and we all need to know how to use them, how to take care of them, how to buy one, and what to do when they don't work.

Microsoft Office 2013 is the most popular personal productivity software on the market today. It is a suite of applications including Microsoft Word, PowerPoint, Excel, Access, OneNote, and Outlook. This book teaches you how to use these applications to help you perform the most common personal and business tasks. You learn to use Word to create documents including a flyer, business letter, résumé, and research paper. OneNote is used to collect and organize your research notes. You use PowerPoint to create dynamite presentations. Excel is a great tool to manage tables of text, numbers, and calculations. Outlook is used to manage email, and Access can be used to manage a database. Each project you work on is one that you actually might encounter in the real world. You learn not only how to use the application, but also how the application can help you solve a problem in your professional, personal, or academic career.

Knowing how to take care of a computer to keep it secure and running well and knowing what to do when things go wrong are just as important as knowing how to use a computer. Several chapters in the book are devoted to help you become a confident computer owner. You learn all the technical knowledge you need to make the best buying or upgrading decisions and how to secure your computer and keep it maintained and running smoothly. You learn how to fix the most common computer problems, such as an Internet connection that doesn't work, a virus infection, or a missing or corrupted data file. By the end of this course, expect your family and friends to be impressed at how confident you are at solving common computer problems.

Although these are all important computer skills, the most important computer skill of all is how to teach yourself a computer skill. Computer hardware and software are constantly changing and improving. In the computer world, what you learn today won't carry you through tomorrow. This book is designed to help you teach yourself a computer skill. Rather than provide the step-by-step, paint-by-number approach to learning a computer skill, this book encourages you to tinker, poke around, and explore on your own with minimum direction. You learn to teach yourself using the web or help tools that each application or Windows makes available to you. The more you can figure out on your own, the better prepared you will be to teach yourself a computer skill after you complete this course. However, know that each activity in the chapter has a complete step-by-step solution available *if you need or want it.*

A Note to Instructors

As instructors, we are always looking for the best tools to help our students. This book is designed to be just that because it allows you to teach the way you want to teach and allows students to learn the way they want to learn. This book works especially well in a flipped classroom because it encourages students to learn at their own pace and to use its resources on demand.

You can easily tailor this book and the accompanying materials to each student's needs. Some students might need to step through each solution to each On Your Own activity. Other students need more of a challenge. For these students, you can encourage them to skip directly to the Chapter Mastery Project. After they have completed the projects at the end of the chapter, they can use any extra time to tutor slower students in your class. Most students will fall somewhere in the middle: They might be able to skip directly to the Chapter Mastery Project on some chapters but not others. They will rely on the solutions occasionally but will not always need them. They might start the Chapter Mastery Project, get stuck, and turn back to the chapter to complete the tasks there. Because students can use a variety of methods as they choose, everyone can work at the pace he or she is comfortable and the entire class can be successful. Your guidance to help each student find the method that works best for him or her will be crucial to the student's success.

The freedom to try, explore, make mistakes, and try again is one of the best learning experiences we can provide our students. This learning style is more in keeping with the real world and what our students will most certainly encounter when they leave our classrooms. The very best experience we can provide them in this course is this process of learning to teach themselves a computer skill.

Skills Learned in This Book

In reexamining the computer skills needed for the 21st century, it becomes evident that change is needed. We need less of the history of computing and details about Microsoft Office and more about other related computer skills, such as using the Windows operating system; exploring the Internet; and buying, maintaining, and securing a personal computer. The content in this book is about a 50-50 split between Microsoft Office applications and these other valuable hands-on computer skills.

Hardware, Software, and Internet Requirements

To successfully complete the activities in this book, you need access to the following equipment and software:

> A personal computer using Windows 8 with the 8.1 update applied and Microsoft Office 2013, including the Word, PowerPoint, OneNote, Outlook, Excel, and Access applications
> Internet access, using either a wired or wireless connection
> A USB port on the computer
> A USB flash drive is desirable but not required
> A printer is desirable but not required

Jump Right In
and Learn How to Teach Yourself Computer Skills!

One main goal of this book is to prove to you that you really don't need a textbook to learn a computer skill. It is our hope that after working through a few chapters, you will agree. Think of this book as a diving board. It's a jumping-off point to a lifetime of teaching yourself how to use, maintain, buy, and fix computers. Pick the learning path that works best for you.

Explore, experiment, and follow the path that works for you.

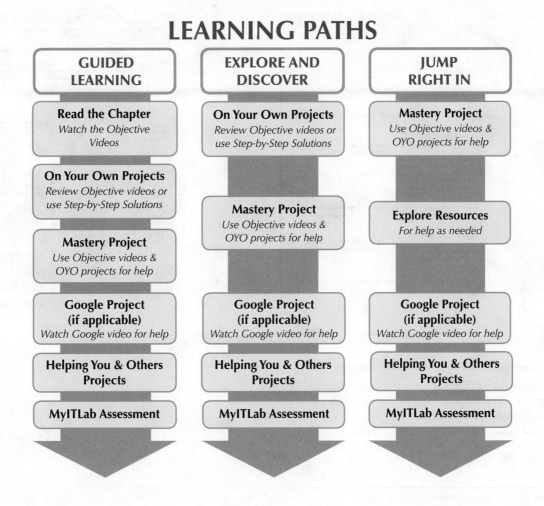

LEARNING PATHS

GUIDED LEARNING	EXPLORE AND DISCOVER	JUMP RIGHT IN
Read the Chapter *Watch the Objective Videos*	**On Your Own Projects** *Review Objective videos or use Step-by-Step Solutions*	**Mastery Project** *Use Objective videos & OYO projects for help*
On Your Own Projects *Review Objective videos or use Step-by-Step Solutions*	**Mastery Project** *Use Objective videos & OYO projects for help*	**Explore Resources** *For help as needed*
Mastery Project *Use Objective videos & OYO projects for help*		
Google Project (if applicable) *Watch Google video for help*	**Google Project (if applicable)** *Watch Google video for help*	**Google Project (if applicable)** *Watch Google video for help*
Helping You & Others Projects	**Helping You & Others Projects**	**Helping You & Others Projects**
MyITLab Assessment	**MyITLab Assessment**	**MyITLab Assessment**

What's New in the Second Edition

> **Completely Updated content** covering Windows 8.1 and Office 2013. (Windows 7 chapters are available as well.)
> **New Objective/On Your Own videos** walk students through the steps of each *On Your Own* project.
> **New Dive Deeper videos** take students further into content not covered in each chapter.
> **New Mastery Projects** that provide a comprehensive project covering all of the skills taught in the chapter.
> **NEW Google doc projects** allow students to apply their knowledge in a non-Microsoft Office environment—the way they will have to do it in the real world.

JUMP RIGHT IN: If you already know the material in a chapter or want to test the waters as an independent investigator and learner, you are encouraged to jump directly to the Chapter Mastery Project.

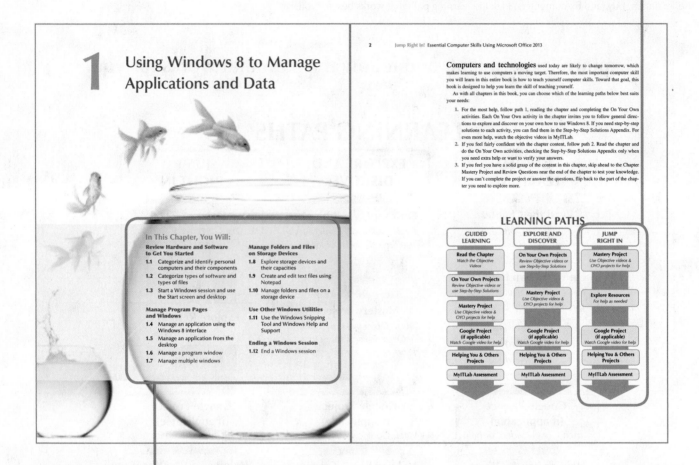

CHAPTER OBJECTIVES: Each chapter begins with a list of concepts you will learn or tasks you will complete as you work your way through the chapter.

On Your Own

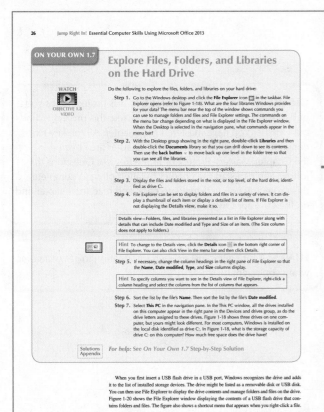

ON YOUR OWN: More than 120 On Your Own projects give you hands-on practice to apply what you are learning. All On Your Own projects are explained in videos.

STEP-BY-STEP SOLUTIONS APPENDIX: Try to do each On Your Own activity with the minimal directions given in the activity. If you need help, turn to the step-by-step solution for the activity in the *Step-by-Step Solutions Appendix*.

Chapter Mastery Projects

> CHAPTER 1: Using Windows 8 to Manage Applications and Data   35
>
> - > A library is a group of folders. Windows default libraries are the Documents, Music, Pictures, and Videos libraries.
> - > Notepad is used to create and edit text files.
> - > Two methods to copy or move a folder or file are the drag-and-drop operation and the commands on the shortcut menus. These commands include Copy, Cut, and Paste.
> - > To rename a folder or file, use the Rename command on the shortcut menu of the file or folder.
> - > Use the Safely Remove Hardware and Eject Media icon in the taskbar before you remove a USB flash drive from your computer.
>
> Using Other Windows Utilities
>
> - > Use the Windows Snipping Tool to capture an area of the Windows screen and store the snip in a file.
> - > You can use Windows Help and Support to find information and links to videos on how to use Windows.
>
> Ending a Windows Session
>
> - > Before you step away from a computer, end the Windows session using one of the options on the user account menu, the Power menu in the Settings charm, or the menu that appears when you right-click the Start button on the desktop. These options can include Lock, Sign out, Sleep, Shut down, Restart, and Hibernate.
>
> ### CHAPTER MASTERY PROJECT
>
> Now it's time to find out how well you've mastered the content in this chapter. If you can do all the steps in this mastery project without looking back at the chapter details and can answer all the review questions following this project, you have mastered this chapter. If you can complete the project by finding answers using Windows Help and Support, you've proven that you're well on your way to teaching yourself essential computer skills.
>
> Hint All the key terms in the chapter are used in this mastery project. If you find a word you don't know, glance through the chapter and find that key term.
>
> If you find you need a lot of help doing the project and you have not yet read the chapter or done the activities, drop back and start at the beginning of the chapter, watch the videos, review the step-by-step solutions as you work through the On Your Own activities, and then return to this project.
>
> Tip If you need help completing this part of the mastery project, review the "Hardware and Software to Get You Started" and the "Managing Program Pages and Windows" sections in the chapter.
>
> Follow these steps to start a Windows 8 session:
>
> Step 1. Power up your computer and sign on. Practice moving from the Start screen to the Windows desktop and back to the Start screen using the Windows key, the charms bar, and the Start button on the Windows desktop.
>
> Step 2. Open (launch) the News app and the Sports app. Practice changing the sizes of the two pages. Open the Weather app. How many pages are displayed? Switch to the third page. Close all open apps.
>
> Step 3. The Paint program is included with Windows and is used to create freehand graphics. Open the **Paint** program.

CHAPTER MASTERY PROJECT: This project helps you pull together all your new skills. Complete this project to find out whether you have mastered the chapter. All the key terms, concepts, and skills covered in the chapter are covered in the Chapter Mastery Project or in the Review Questions that follow. You can start the chapter by attempting to complete this project. If you get stuck, go back and read the chapter and do the On Your Own activities.

HINTS: A hint gives just enough information to get you going when you might be stuck.

Are Your Learning to Teach Yourself?

After you successfully complete the Chapter Mastery Project and the Review Questions, you are asked to rate yourself as to how independent a learner you are. Rate yourself by how much help you needed from the On Your Own activities and the solutions in the *Step-by-Step Solutions Appendix*. As you progress from one chapter to the next, try to depend less and less on the solutions so that toward the end of the book you can truly say, "I can teach myself a computer skill!"

>
> 23. Where do you need to position your pointer or cursor to move a window?
> 24. What appears in a window when the window is resized so that everything cannot display?
> 25. After minimizing a window, how do you restore the window to the desktop?
> 26. When you have three program windows open, how many of these windows can be the active window? How do you use the program icon in the taskbar to make a window the active window?
> 27. A program uses portions of RAM when it's running. What might happen to your computer performance if you have several windows open at the same time?
> 28. Windows and other software are installed on a hard drive installed inside the computer case. What is another name for this hard drive? What drive letter is usually assigned to this drive?
> 29. What are four units of measure used to measure the capacity of a storage device? Which unit is large enough to hold only a single character? Which capacity is larger, 500 GB or 0.5 TB?
> 30. What are the four libraries on your hard drive?
> 31. What does a white triangle in the navigation pane of File Explorer indicate? What happens when you right-click in the white space of the right pane of File Explorer? What happens when you double-click a folder in the right pane of File Explorer?
> 32. In File Explorer, which key can you hold down to select nonsequential files in a list? Which operation results in a file being deleted from its original location and placed in a new location: copy and paste or cut and paste? When you copy or cut a file, where is the file temporarily stored?
> 33. When taking a snip of your screen, what is the default file extension that Windows assigns the file that is saved using the Windows Snipping Tool?
> 34. Before you can safely remove a USB flash drive that you have written on, what should you do?
> 35. List the steps to use the Recycle Bin to recover a file you accidentally deleted from the hard drive. If you need help finding the answer, refer to Windows Help and Support.
> 36. When a laptop or netbook has been asleep for some time and the battery is getting low, what might it do to conserve power?
>
> ### Becoming an Independent Learner
>
> Answer the following questions about becoming an independent learner:
>
> 1. To teach yourself to use Windows 8, why is it better to rely on Windows Help and Support when you need answers rather than rely on this book?
> 2. The most important skill learned in this chapter is how to teach yourself a computer skill. Rate yourself at Level A through E on how well you're doing with this skill. What is your level?
>   - Level A: I was able to successfully complete the Chapter Mastery Project with the help of only a few of the On Your Own activities in the chapter.
>   - Level B: I completed all the On Your Own activities and the Chapter Mastery Project without referring to any of the solutions in the Step-by-Step Solutions Appendix.
>   - Level C: I completed all the On Your Own activities and the Chapter Mastery Project by using just a few of the solutions in the Step-by-Step Solutions Appendix.
>   - Level D: I completed all the On Your Own activities and the Chapter Mastery Project by using many of the solutions in the Step-by-Step Solutions Appendix.
>   - Level E: I completed all the On Your Own activities and the Chapter Mastery Project and had to use all the solutions in the Step-by-Step Solutions Appendix.
>
> To continue toward the goal of teaching yourself computer skills, if you're not at Level A, try to move up one level on how you learn in Chapter 2.

INDEPENDENT LEARNER sections help you get better at learning about computers.

Projects to Help You and Others

At the end of each chapter are three "Projects to Help You" in your professional, personal, and academic careers. Depending on what you want to accomplish, you might want to complete one or all of these projects. For several chapters, the first Project to Help You uses a Google Drive. This Google Drive project coaches you as you teach yourself how to use this powerful online tool.

No matter what you are doing in your life, always look for opportunities to give back. The last project in each chapter is a project to help another. Find an apprentice who wants to learn about computers—perhaps a neighbor, younger brother, uncle, grandmother, or friend. The best learning happens as you teach someone else. Help this person learn what you have learned in the chapter. For the best experience, teach someone older or younger than you and encourage this person to stick it out with you through the entire course.

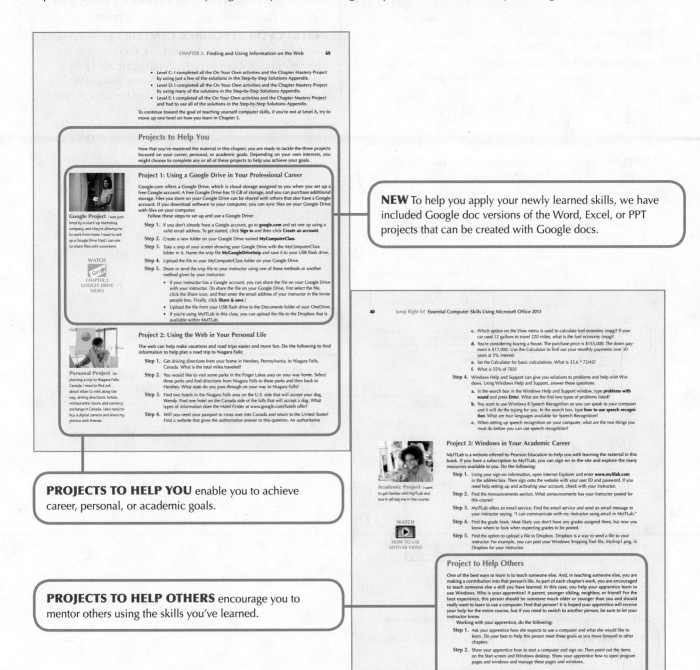

NEW To help you apply your newly learned skills, we have included Google doc versions of the Word, Excel, or PPT projects that can be created with Google docs.

PROJECTS TO HELP YOU enable you to achieve career, personal, or academic goals.

PROJECTS TO HELP OTHERS encourage you to mentor others using the skills you've learned.

Help Along the Way

Provides a fully digital learning experience including all of the resources for the book, the interactive etext, and auto-graded versions of the Mastery Projects and related simulation training for Office Application chapters. For more information, visit www.myitlab.com.

COMPANION WEBSITE: Visit the companion website at www.pearsonhighered.com/jump for sample files used in chapter projects, Chapter Review Quizzes, Objective Videos, and Diving Deeper Videos. Watch a video to see how to do an activity that might be difficult, requires hardware you don't have, or requires a permission in Windows that is not available on your school lab computer.

INSTRUCTOR RESOURCE CENTER: Online Instructor Resources include Annotated Solutions, Capstone Project, Chapter Answers, Data Files, End-of-Chapter, Instructor Manual, PowerPoint Presentations, Prepared Exams by Project and Chapter, Scorecards, Scripted Lectures, Syllabus Template, Test Bank, and a Test-Out Exam.

TIPS: A tip gives information that can help you with the current activity or might be useful in a later situation.

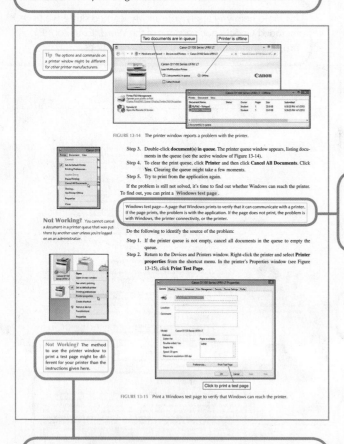

KEY TERMS: Key terms are defined in a key term box as you encounter them in the text. The boxes are easy to spot on the page, which makes them easy to find when you're skimming a chapter.

NOT WORKING?: These boxes tell you what to check or try when something is not working.

Wrapping Up the Chapter

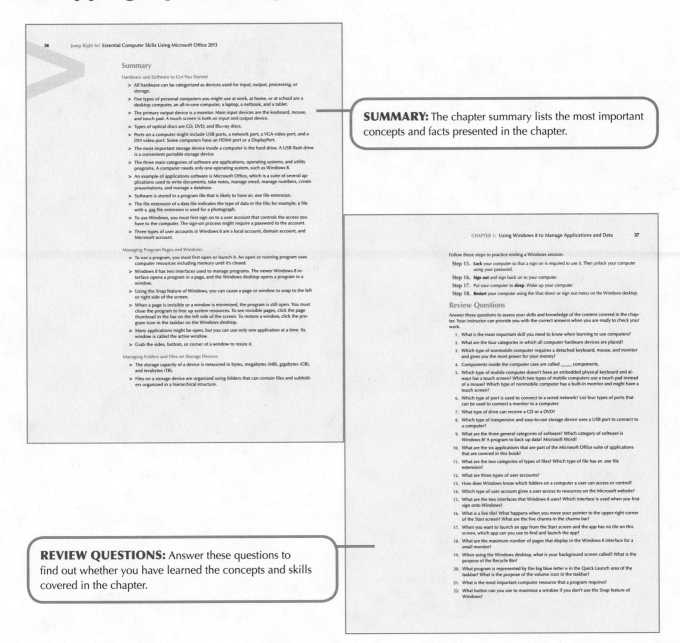

SUMMARY: The chapter summary lists the most important concepts and facts presented in the chapter.

REVIEW QUESTIONS: Answer these questions to find out whether you have learned the concepts and skills covered in the chapter.

Companion Website

Visit our website and register this book at **http://www.pearsonhighered.com/jump/** for convenient access to any updates, downloads, or errata that might be available for this book. The website contains all the sample files you'll need to do many of the activities and projects in the book. For your convenience, you might want to download these sample files to your USB flash drive. An activity in Chapter 2 shows you how.

1 Using Windows 8 to Manage Applications and Data

In This Chapter, You Will:

Computers and technologies used today are likely to change tomorrow, which makes learning to use computers a moving target. Therefore, the most important computer skill you will learn in this entire book is how to teach yourself computer skills. Toward that goal, this book is designed to help you learn the skill of teaching yourself.

As with all chapters in this book, you can choose which of the learning paths below best suits your needs:

1. For the most help, follow path 1, reading the chapter and completing the On Your Own activities. Each On Your Own activity in the chapter invites you to follow general directions to explore and discover on your own how to use Windows 8. If you need step-by-step solutions to each activity, you can find them in the Step-by-Step Solutions Appendix. For even more help, watch the objective videos in MyITLab.
2. If you feel fairly confident with the chapter content, follow path 2. Read the chapter and do the On Your Own activities, checking the Step-by-Step Solutions Appendix only when you need extra help or want to verify your answers.
3. If you feel you have a solid grasp of the content in this chapter, skip ahead to the Chapter Mastery Project and Review Questions near the end of the chapter to test your knowledge. If you can't complete the project or answer the questions, flip back to the part of the chapter you need to explore more.

LEARNING PATHS

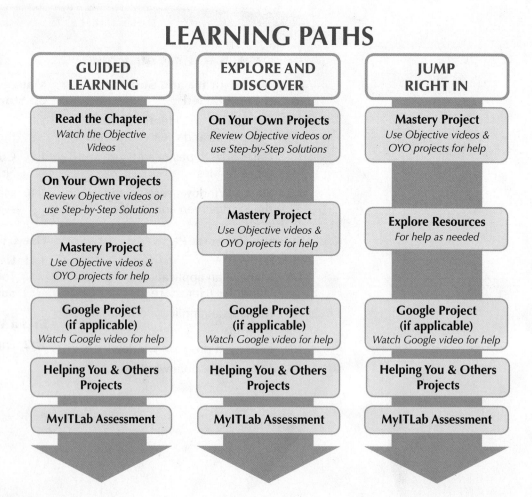

GUIDED LEARNING	EXPLORE AND DISCOVER	JUMP RIGHT IN
Read the Chapter *Watch the Objective Videos*	**On Your Own Projects** *Review Objective videos or use Step-by-Step Solutions*	**Mastery Project** *Use Objective videos & OYO projects for help*
On Your Own Projects *Review Objective videos or use Step-by-Step Solutions*	**Mastery Project** *Use Objective videos & OYO projects for help*	**Explore Resources** *For help as needed*
Mastery Project *Use Objective videos & OYO projects for help*		
Google Project (if applicable) *Watch Google video for help*	**Google Project (if applicable)** *Watch Google video for help*	**Google Project (if applicable)** *Watch Google video for help*
Helping You & Others Projects	**Helping You & Others Projects**	**Helping You & Others Projects**
MyITLab Assessment	**MyITLab Assessment**	**MyITLab Assessment**

No matter which path you choose, complete the chapter by working through the Helping Yourself and Helping Others projects to apply the chapter skills to new situations. And as you work your way through the chapter, remember that the most important computer skill is how to teach yourself a computer skill. By the time you've finished the chapter, you'll have discovered just how independent and resourceful a self-learner you can be.

Hardware and Software to Get You Started

Let's begin by exploring the hardware and software you'll use in this book.

WATCH

OBJECTIVE 1.1
VIDEO

Objective 1.1: Categorize and Identify Personal Computers and Their Components

All hardware can be categorized as devices used for input, output, processing, or storage (see Figure 1-1). In this part of the chapter, we'll look at several types of computers and common input, output, and storage devices. In Chapter 14, we'll examine the central processing unit (CPU), which is the main device used for processing.

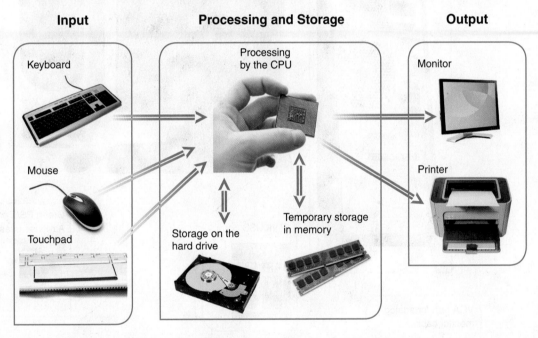

FIGURE 1-1   Computer devices are used for input, output, processing, or storage.

In this book, a key term box like the following provides an easy and quick reference to new computer terms.

> **monitor**—The primary output device for a computer.
>
> **keyboard**—The primary input device for a computer.
>
> **mouse**—An input device used to move a pointer on the computer screen and to perform other operations.
>
> **hard drive**—The most important storage device inside a computer, used to store both software and data until you need them.

Desktop Computers

One type of personal computer you might use at work, home, or school is a **desktop computer** . Figure 1-2 shows some ports and devices you might find on a desktop computer. If you're using a desktop computer for this course, locate each device on your computer that is labeled in the figure. In later chapters, you'll learn about many other hardware devices used on computers, but these are enough to get you started.

> **desktop computer**—A computer that sits on or under a desk with an attached monitor, keyboard, and mouse.

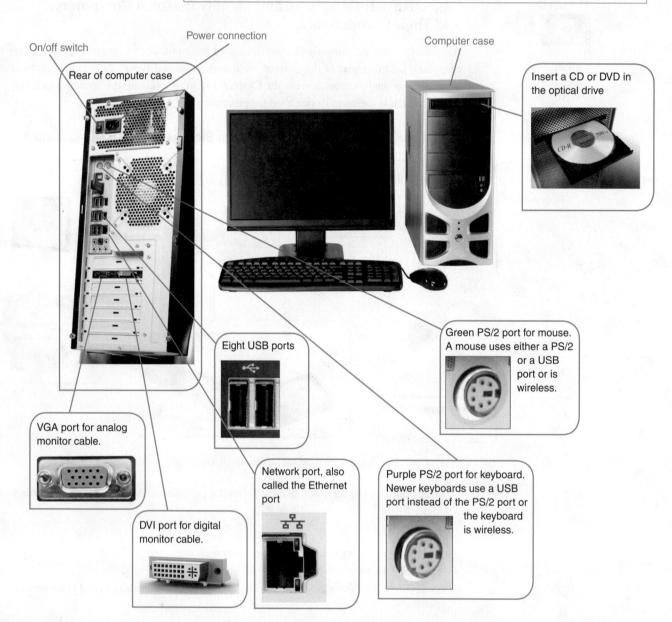

FIGURE 1-2 A desktop computer has input and output devices attached to ports and an optical drive.

All computers need a keyboard or **touch screen** for input and a monitor for displaying output. Desktop computers use a mouse, which you use to move the pointer on the monitor screen and select items on the screen. A desktop computer has a heavy **computer case** and is the least portable of all computers. A desktop is also the best buy to get the most power.

Touch screen

> **touch screen**—A screen that receives touch input. You can control the computer by moving your fingers over the screen. A touch screen is both an output and an input device and is used on some netbooks, laptops, and all-in-one computers.
>
> **computer case**—The large box of a computer that contains the main components. Components installed inside the computer case are called *internal components*. Components outside the case are called *external components* or *peripherals*.

Laptops and Netbooks

Types of computers that are more portable than a desktop are a **laptop** (see Figure 1-3) and a **netbook** (see Figure 1-4). A laptop and a desktop computer are likely to have an **optical drive**, but a netbook doesn't usually have one.

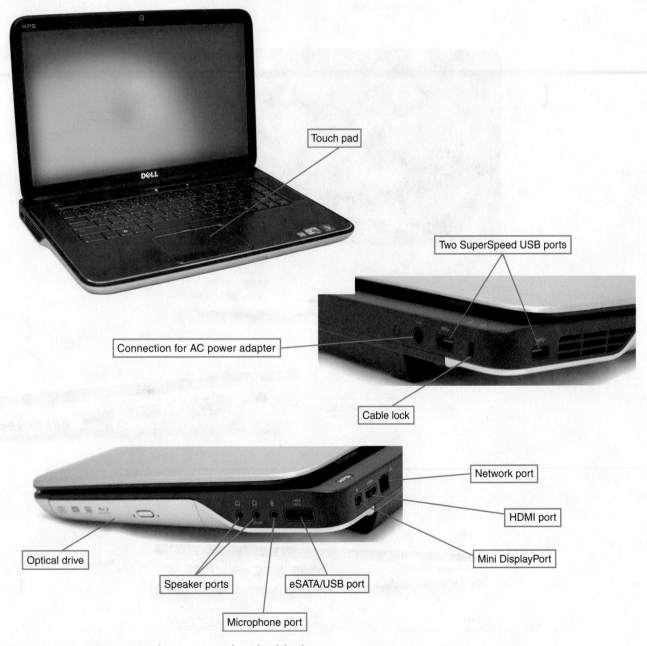

FIGURE 1-3 A Blu-ray/DVD drive opens on the side of this laptop.

> **laptop**—A portable computer small enough to hold in your lap. Sometimes called a notebook.
>
> **netbook**—A small, light, inexpensive portable computer that is powerful enough for only general computer use.
>
> **optical drive**—A type of drive that can read (and often write on) an optical disc. Optical discs include CD, DVD, and Blu-ray discs. The three discs look the same, but a Blu-ray disc holds more data than a DVD, which holds more data than a CD.

Laptops and netbooks use a **touch pad** to move the pointer on the screen. If you don't like to use a touch pad, you can connect a USB or wireless mouse to your laptop or netbook. If you're using a laptop or netbook for this course, locate all the items on your computer that are labeled in Figure 1-3 or Figure 1-4.

> **touch pad**—The small pad with two buttons near the keypad on a laptop or netbook. You use the pad to move a pointer on the monitor screen, and you use the left and right buttons to perform other operations.

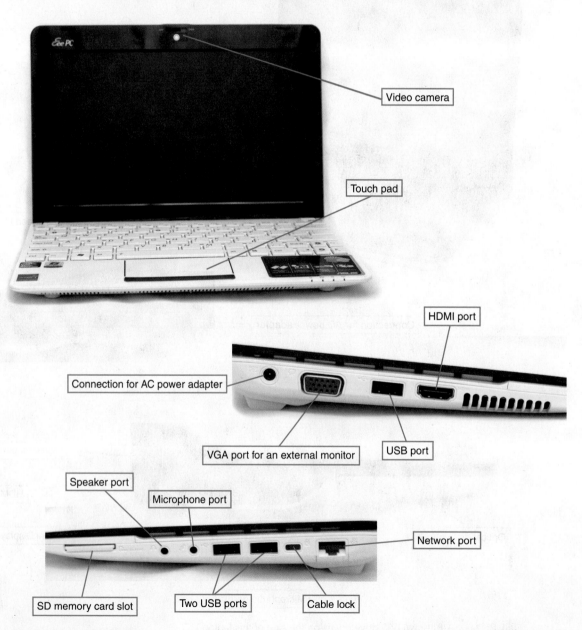

FIGURE 1-4   A netbook computer has a smaller screen size than a laptop and no optical drive. It might have a touch screen.

All-in-One Computers

A fourth type of computer is an **all-in-one computer** (see Figure 1-5). It uses a mouse and keyboard for input, and the monitor is built into the computer. Some all-in-one computers have a touch screen for input. If you're using an all-in-one for this course, find the items on your computer that are labeled in Figure 1-5.

> **all-in-one computer**—A computer that sits on a desk and has the monitor and computer case built together. A keyboard and mouse are attached. Some all-in-one computers have a touch screen.

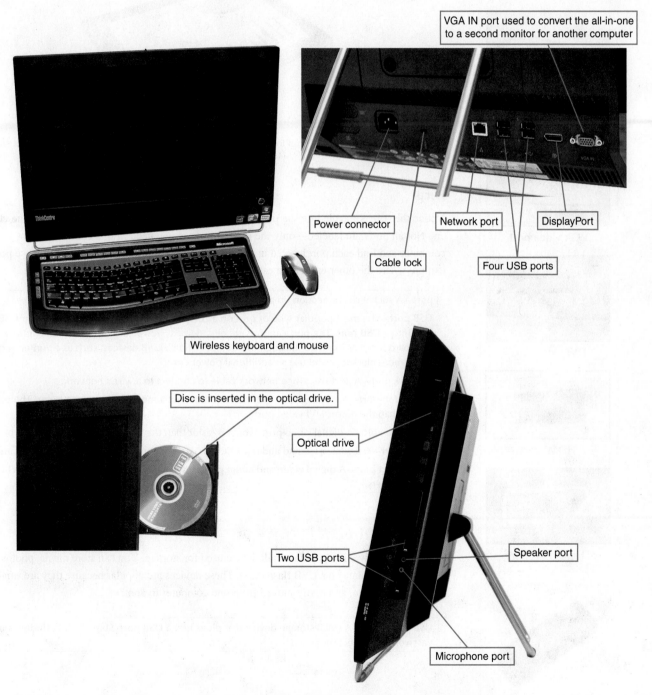

FIGURE 1-5 An all-in-one computer might have multitouch display and a wireless mouse and keyboard.

USB port

Network port

VGA video port

DVI video port

HDMI port

DisplayPort port

USB flash drive

Tablets

A fifth type of personal computer is a **tablet** (see Figure 1-6). A tablet uses a touch screen for input and output and might have only a few buttons, such as a power button or a volume button. A tablet might have one USB port and is mostly dependent on the web for access to its data.

> **tablet**—A small personal computer used mainly for games, communicating with others on the Internet, and light productivity. Tablets rely primarily on a touch screen for input and output.

FIGURE 1-6 A tablet relies on a touch screen for input and has few hardware buttons and slots.

Ports

Notice the **ports** labeled on the photos of the desktop, laptop, netbook, and all-in-one computers. Not all ports are labeled—only the important ones you need in this course. Look at your own computer and find each port labeled in the photos. Identify the cables connected to these ports and explore where the other end of the cable is attached.

> **port**—A socket or connection on a computer used to connect a cable or external device.
>
> **USB port**—The most popular type of port on a computer. You can plug a USB cable or USB device into a USB port. The port can provide electricity to power the device. For example, a USB keyboard receives its power through the USB port. Some USB devices, such as a printer, require much more electricity and use an additional power cord.
>
> **network port**—A port used for a network cable to connect to a wired network.
>
> **VGA video port**—An analog video port used to connect a monitor to the computer. The port is slower than the newer DVI video port.
>
> **DVI video port**—A digital video port, which is faster than the older analog or VGA video port.
>
> **HDMI port**—A digital video and audio port, often used to connect to home theater equipment.
>
> **DisplayPort port**—A digital video and audio port that is expected to replace VGA and DVI ports on computers.

USB Flash Drives

A **USB flash drive** is a popular small device used for storage. You can store music, photos, documents, and other data on a USB flash drive. These devices are popular because they are small, easy to use, inexpensive, and easily moved from one computer to another.

> **USB flash drive**—A small storage device that plugs into a USB port. Some USB flash drives use a password to protect their data.

Tip In the key terms, you'll notice some initials such as USB and VGA. USB stands for *Universal Serial Bus*, and VGA stands for *Video Graphics Adapter*. To keep things simple in this book, we're not explaining the meanings of initials unless the meaning is really important. If you want to know the meanings, see the Glossary available on the www.pearsonhighered.com/jump website and in MyITLab. In Chapter 2, you learn how to download the Glossary to your computer.

WATCH

OBJECTIVE 1.2
VIDEO

Objective 1.2: Categorize Types of Software and Types of Files

Let's quickly explore some software and files you'll use when you work with your computer.

Software

Software is a group of instructions a computer can follow to do a job. Software is also called a **program** . The three main categories of software are **applications** , **operating systems** , and **utility programs** .

> **software**—A group of instructions that a computer can follow to do a job. Three general types of software are applications, operating systems, and utility programs.
>
> **program**—Another name for software.
>
> **application**—A type of software designed with a specific purpose in mind, such as drawing pictures, editing video, creating documents, or playing a game. Examples of applications software include Microsoft Office, QuickBooks (used by accountants and bookkeepers), and AutoCAD (used by architects). Applications are sometimes called apps.
>
> **operating system (OS)**—Software that manages a computer. It controls other software, hardware, and data and receives user input.
>
> **utility program**—A program that helps the operating system and might not need user interaction to work. An example of a utility program is software used to back up important data.

In this course, you'll learn to use these six **Microsoft Office** applications:

> **Microsoft Word** is a word processing application used to create documents that can include text, color, pictures, drawings, and other graphics.
> **OneNote** is used to hold and organize notes, including content taken from the web. It's a great tool when keeping class notes or doing a research paper.
> **Outlook** manages email, contacts, and calendars.
> **PowerPoint** is used to create slides for a presentation. Slides can contain text, graphics, color, video, and sound.
> **Excel** is used to manage rows and columns of numbers, text, and calculations in a worksheet.
> **Access** is used to manage large amounts of data in a database.

> **Microsoft Office**—Personal productivity software including software for creating and editing documents, notes, email, presentations, worksheets, and databases.

An operating system, such as Windows 7 or Windows 8, is the most important software installed on a computer because the operating system controls everything the computer does. It controls all the hardware devices, all the applications, and all the data. When you want the computer to do something, such as print a letter, you must tell the operating system what you want, and it sees that the job gets done. Because all the work you do with a computer is done by way of the operating system, it's important that you understand how to use it. That's why learning to use **Windows 8** is the first thing covered in this book.

> **Windows 8**—The latest operating system sold by Microsoft for personal computers. A computer can have many applications installed on it, but it needs only one operating system. The latest update for Windows 8 is Windows 8.1.

Software such as the Windows 8 operating system and the Microsoft Office applications are installed in a computer on the hard drive. The hard drive permanently holds both software and data until you need them. Figure 1-7 shows a 3.5-inch hard drive used inside a desktop computer and a smaller 2.5-inch hard drive used inside a laptop. The storage capacity of a hard drive determines how much software you can install on the computer. You'll learn about the storage capacity of hard drives later in the chapter.

FIGURE 1-7 A 3.5-inch hard drive is used in a desktop computer, and a smaller 2.5-inch hard drive is used in a laptop.

Files

Data or software is stored in a file , and the file is assigned a name such as MyData25.txt. A file that holds data is called a data file , and a file that stores software is called a program file .

> file—A collection of data or software in a computer stored under a single name. Two general types of files are data files and program files.
>
> data file—A file that contains data. Examples of data files are files that contain a photograph, business letter, list of names and addresses, or video.
>
> program file—A file that contains a program. Complex software, such as Windows 8 and Microsoft Office 2013, uses many program files to hold all the software.

Two examples of program files are

> The file **OneNote.exe** holds the OneNote application, which is one of the Microsoft Office applications and is used for taking notes.
> The file **WordPad.exe** holds the WordPad application, which is used to create documents.

Notice the period in the name of each file. The letters to the left of the period are called the filename (OneNote and WordPad). The period and the letters to the right of the period are called the file extension. Both upper- and lowercase letters and numbers are used in file names and file extensions.

The **file extension** tells you something about what type of data or program is contained in the file. A file extension of .exe identifies the file as a program file.

> **file extension**—The part of a file name including the last period and the letters following the last period that identifies what kind of program or data is contained in the file.

Here are two examples of data files:

> The file **Wendy.jpg** holds a photograph of a dog.
> The file **LetterToDave.docx** holds the letter I wrote last week to a business associate.

The .jpg file extension identifies the file as a file containing a photo. The .docx file extension identifies the file as a document file created by Microsoft Word.

Now that you know a little about hardware, software, and files, you're ready to use Windows 8.

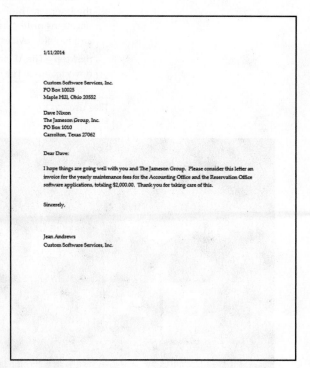

1/11/2014

Custom Software Services, Inc.
PO Box 10025
Maple Hill, Ohio 20552

Dave Nixon
The Jameson Group, Inc.
PO Box 1010
Carrolton, Texas 27062

Dear Dave:

I hope things are going well with you and The Jameson Group. Please consider this letter an invoice for the yearly maintenance fees for the Accounting Office and the Reservation Office software applications, totaling $2,000.00. Thank you for taking care of this.

Sincerely,

Jean Andrews
Custom Software Services, Inc.

WATCH

OBJECTIVE 1.3 VIDEO

Objective 1.3: Start a Windows Session and Use the Start Screen and Desktop

When you first turn on your computer, you might need to sign in (log on) to Windows using a specific **user account** and password. This user account can be a **local account**, **domain account**, or **Microsoft account**.

> **user account**—Information that tells Windows what degree of control a user has over a computer, including what **folders** on the hard drive the user can access and the user's preferences such as the colors used on a screen.
>
> **folder**—A location on a storage media (for example, a hard drive or USB flash drive) that can contain files or other folders called subfolders.
>
> **local account**—A user account that applies only to the one computer.
>
> **domain account**—An account that applies to all the computers that a corporation or school manages. Domain accounts are managed from a centralized computer on the corporate or school network.
>
> **Microsoft account**—An account kept by Microsoft that is set up using an email address and password on the Microsoft website. The account can be used to synchronize data, settings, and apps on any Windows 8 computer with that kept on the Microsoft website.

No matter what type of user account you're using, the account must have already been set up by the person responsible for the computer. If only one user account is set up on the computer and this account doesn't require a password, Windows skips the sign-on screen and automatically signs you in to that account.

Windows 8 provides two ways for you to do your work: the Start screen and the Windows desktop . When you first start a Windows 8 session, the Start screen appears (see Figure 1-8).

> Start screen—The Windows screen used to start applications and access Windows features and the Internet. The Start screen is new with Windows 8 and uses tiles, or squares, to represent applications or features on the screen. The interface is designed to work well with touch screens and mobile devices.
>
> desktop—The Windows screen where you work with applications, utility programs, and Windows features. The Windows desktop is used in Windows 8 and all previous versions of Windows.

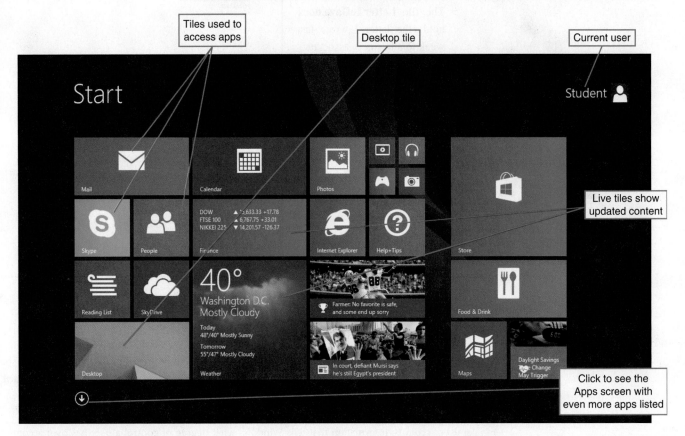

FIGURE 1-8   Use the Windows 8 Start screen to open applications and work with Windows features.

To get to the Windows desktop, you can click or tap the **Desktop** tile on the Start screen or press the Windows key on the keyboard. The Windows desktop is shown in Figure 1-9. To return to the Start screen, press the Windows key again or click the Start button in the lower-left corner of the desktop. Another way to get to the Start screen is to use the charms bar , shown in Figure 1-9. No matter what you're doing in Windows, when you move your mouse to the upper-right or lower-right corner of the screen, the charms bar appears. On the charms bar, click the **Start** charm to return to the Start screen.

> click—To select an item on the computer screen by quickly pressing and releasing the left button on the mouse or laptop touch pad. For a touch screen, you can tap the item on the screen.
>
> tap—Using a touch screen, quickly touch an item on the screen to select it.
>
> Start button—The Windows flag icon in the lower-left corner of the Windows desktop. Click or tap it to return to the Start screen.
>
> charms bar—A group of icons on the right side of the Windows screen that appears when you move the pointer to the upper-right or lower-right corner of the screen. Click a charm to access this Windows feature.

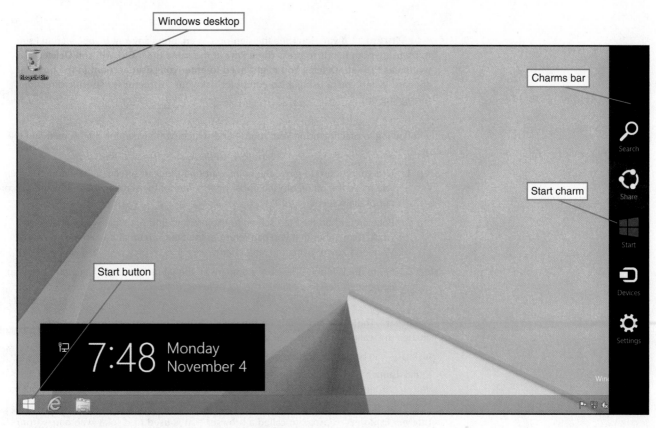

FIGURE 1-9 Use the Windows desktop to work with applications and Windows features.

Start a Windows Session

Power up your computer and sign in to Windows 8. You might be required to enter a user account and/or password on the Windows sign-on screen shown in Figure 1-10. If you don't know the Windows password in your computer lab, ask your instructor. After sign-on, the Windows 8 Start screen appears (refer back to Figure 1-8).

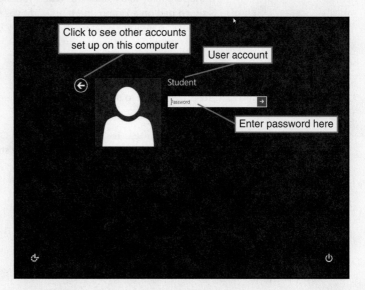

FIGURE 1-10 The Windows sign-on screen determines which user account is in use.

> **Not Working?** If you don't see the sign-on screen, press any key. If you still don't see it, try using both hands to press three keys at the same time: **Ctrl**, **Alt**, and **Delete** (also written as **Ctrl+Alt+Delete**). You might need to enter your user account in the box that appears. When you're using a lab computer, ask your instructor for specific directions for signing on.

Do the following to practice using your mouse and switching between the Start screen and the desktop:

Step 1. Use your mouse to move the pointer around the Start screen. What happens when you move the pointer to the upper-right corner of the screen? To the lower-right corner of the screen?

Step 2. Poke around on the Start screen to explore and find out what works and doesn't work. Remember that you can return to the Start screen at any time by pressing the Windows key or using the Start charm.

Step 3. Go to the Windows desktop. Compare all the items labeled in Figure 1-11 to your computer's desktop. Here is the list of items you need to identify on the desktop:

> **wallpaper**—The color or pattern on the desktop. You'll learn later in the book how to change the wallpaper to suit your own tastes.
>
> **taskbar**—The bar at the bottom of the screen that includes Quick Launch icons.
>
> **Quick Launch icon**—An icon on the left side of the taskbar used to start a program that you use often. The two Quick Launch icons that normally appear in the taskbar are Internet Explorer 🄴 and File Explorer 📁.
>
> **Internet Explorer**—A program called a browser that is used to display web pages from the Internet.
>
> **File Explorer**—A program used to manage the files and folders stored on your computer. In previous versions of Windows, File Explorer was called Windows Explorer.
>
> **volume icon**—The icon in the taskbar used to control sound. Click it and then move the bar up and down to control the volume.
>
> **Recycle Bin**—The Windows trashcan in the upper-left corner of the desktop. Files deleted from the hard drive are stored in the Recycle Bin in case you change your mind and want them back.
>
> **pointer**—The movable icon 🔍 on the desktop that allows you to point to a position on the screen or to a command. When you move the mouse or move your finger over the touch pad on a laptop, the pointer moves on the screen. The shape of the pointer can change to indicate what work is currently in progress. The pointer is sometimes called the **cursor**.
>
> **cursor**—Another name for the pointer.

Step 4. Return to the Windows 8 Start screen.

> **Not Working?** Try to do each On Your Own activity without help. But remember, the Step-by-Step Solutions Appendix has the step-by-steps if you need them.

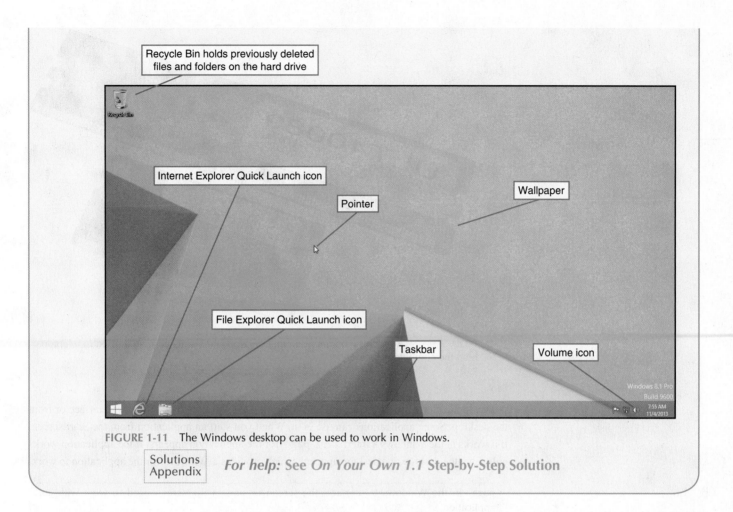

FIGURE 1-11   The Windows desktop can be used to work in Windows.

Solutions
Appendix

For help: See *On Your Own 1.1* Step-by-Step Solution

Managing Program Pages and Windows

Now that you're familiar with starting a Windows session, the Start screen, and the Windows desktop, let's explore some applications and their pages and windows.

Objective 1.4: Manage an Application Using the Windows 8 Interface

WATCH

OBJECTIVE 1.4
VIDEO

To use any program, including an application, you must first start it. When you start a program, the operating system assigns to the program the resources the program needs to do its work. Starting a program is sometimes called *launching a program*, and a program that has been started is called an **open program**.

> **open program**—A program that has been started. Open programs need computer resources to work, and these resources are assigned to the program when it starts. An open program is also called a *running program*.

The most important computer resource a program requires is memory. **Memory**, also called **RAM**, is temporary storage a program uses to do its work. A computer's memory is kept on small boards inside the computer case. Figure 1-12 shows one board (called a *memory module*) that fits in a desktop computer and a smaller module that fits in a laptop. The amount of memory a computer has determines how many applications you can have open at the same time. If you don't have much memory installed, opening three or four applications at one time can cause your computer to run slower.

> **memory**—The temporary storage used by programs when they're running. Also called *RAM*.
> **RAM (random access memory)**—Another name for memory.

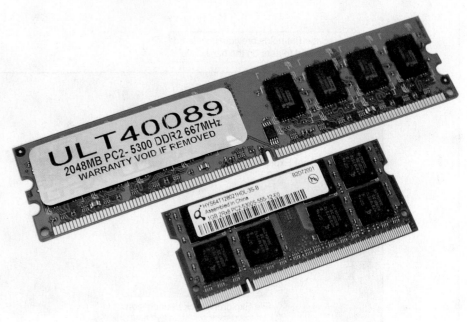

FIGURE 1-12   A memory module used in a desktop and a smaller module used in a laptop hold the computer's memory.

An application (also called an app) in Windows 8 can work in the Windows 8 interface or from the desktop. Some applications can use both. When you start an application from the Start screen, if it works in the Windows 8 interface, a **page** for the application appears. If the application works only from the desktop, the desktop appears, which provides a **window** for the application to work.

---

page—In the Windows 8 interface, the screen or part of the screen used to work with an application.

window—A rectangle on the desktop that Windows has assigned to a program. You can use the window to work with the program. You can change the size of a window.

Here's how to manage applications using the Windows 8 interface:

> To open an application that appears on the Start screen, click the application tile. If the application works in the Windows 8 interface, the application page opens. You can use the page to work with the application.

> If the application tile isn't showing, move your pointer to the far-right side of the screen to see more tiles. You can also use the scrollbar at the bottom of the screen to scroll left or right.

> Another way to see a list of apps is to click the down arrow near the bottom of the Start screen. The Apps screen appears, showing all apps installed on the system. Click one to open it.

---

right-click—Quickly press the right button on the mouse or the laptop touch pad. On a touch screen, press and hold on the screen until a menu or item appears.

> Still another way to find an app is to use the Search app. From the Start screen, type the first few letters of the application. The Search app opens and displays a list of apps. Click the app you want to open. For example, Figure 1-13 shows the apps that appear when you type the letter p.

Not Working? This book assumes you are using Windows 8.1, the latest update of Windows 8. If you're using Windows 8 without the 8.1 update, you won't see the down arrow on your Start screen. To get to the Apps screen, **right-click** anywhere on the Start screen and then click the All apps button in the bottom-right corner of the screen.

FIGURE 1-13   On the Start screen, when you type letters, the Search app opens to help you find an application.

> To close an application and its page, move your pointer to the top of the screen. Your pointer changes to a hand. **Press and drag** the hand to the bottom of the screen. The page moves to the bottom of the screen and then the page and app close.

> **press and drag**—Hold down the left mouse button at the same time you move the mouse. This press-and-drag action can sometimes be used to select items and move them on the screen. For a touch screen, swipe across the screen.

> You can open as many apps as you like, but with most monitors, only two pages can display at the same time. To move a page from the entire screen to the left or right side of the screen, move your pointer to the top of the screen. The pointer becomes a hand. Press and drag the hand to the left or right side of the screen. The page **snaps** to that side of the screen.

> **snap**—The Windows feature that uses a press-and-drag motion to allow a page or window to fill the left or right side of a screen or fill the entire screen. Large monitors can snap up to four pages on a screen.

> When you open the next application, its page snaps to the other side of the screen.
> To change the sizes of the two pages, press and drag the bar between the two pages (see Figure 1-14).

Not Working? To snap pages, your screen resolution must be at least 1024 × 768. The screen resolution is the number of dots across the screen and down the screen available for Windows to use. You'll learn more about screen resolution in Chapter 13.

Drag bar to left or right to resize the two pages

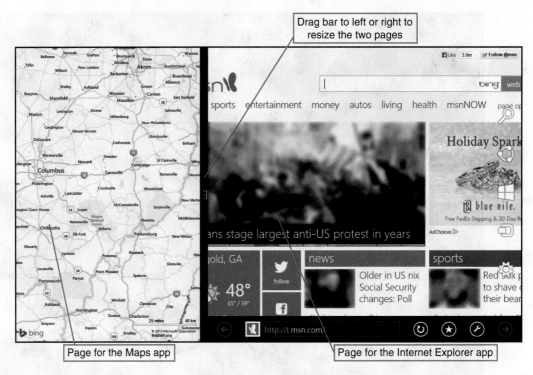

Page for the Maps app

Page for the Internet Explorer app

FIGURE 1-14 Two pages appear side by side in the Windows 8 interface.

> To switch between several open pages, move your pointer to the upper-left corner of the screen and drag it down the left side. A bar showing **thumbnails** of other open apps appears (see Figure 1-15). Click the thumbnail you want to view.

thumbnail—A small picture or icon of a page, file, folder, or other item.

Bar on left side of screen shows all open apps

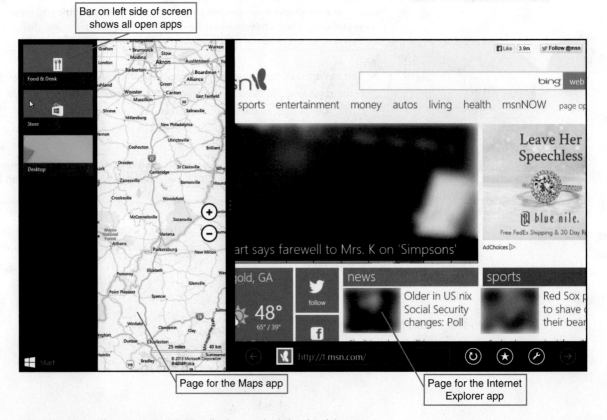

Page for the Maps app

Page for the Internet Explorer app

FIGURE 1-15 All open apps appear in the bar on the left side of the screen.

ON YOUR OWN 1.2

Manage Apps in the Windows 8 Interface

WATCH

OBJECTIVE 1.4
VIDEO

WATCH

CHAPTER 1
DIVING DEEPER
VIDEO

Solutions
Appendix

Do the following to learn to manage apps that use the Windows 8 interface:

Step 1. On the Start screen, open the **Maps** app. Snap the apps page to the right side of the screen.

Step 2. Several apps, such as the Weather app, use **Live Tiles**. Open the **Weather** app. Both app pages should appear on the screen.

> **Live Tiles**—Tiles that continually display real-time information available from the Internet.

Step 3. Practice changing the sizes of the two pages.

Step 4. Open the **Photos** app. Which two pages now appear on the screen? Switch to the third open app.

Step 5. Close all three apps and return to the Start screen. How do you close an app?

For help: See *On Your Own 1.2* Step-by-Step Solution

WATCH

OBJECTIVE 1.5
VIDEO

Objective 1.5: Manage an Application from the Desktop

When you use the Start screen to open an application that works only from the desktop, the desktop appears and displays a window for the application. What goes inside a window is determined by the program. But every window has some common elements that Windows 8 determines. In the following instructions, you start Paint, a freehand drawing program. The goal here is not to learn to use Paint but rather to learn to use Windows 8 to manage a program window. The skills you learn here can be applied to any window, not just the Paint window.

ON YOUR OWN 1.3

Start a Program That Uses the Desktop

WATCH

OBJECTIVE 1.5
VIDEO

Now let's start a program that uses the desktop:

Step 1. Using the Start screen, open the **Paint** app. The desktop and the Paint window appear, as shown in Figure 1-16.

Step 2. Notice in Figure 1-16 that the Paint icon is in the taskbar. When a program is running, you see its **program icon** in the taskbar to indicate that the program is open. Look at Figure 1-16 and find the following items labeled in the figure on your own computer screen. New terms used in the figure are explained here.

program icon—A small picture that represents a program. When a program is open, the program icon appears in the taskbar.

title bar—The bar at the top of a window. The name of the program displays in the title bar.

minimize button—Most title bars have three buttons on the right side. You use the minimize button ⊟ to make the window disappear from the desktop. Sometimes you might want to get a program window out of your way so that you can work with other programs but don't want to close the first program. Minimizing the window gets it off the desktop, but the program is still open.

maximize button—One of the three buttons on the right side of the title bar. Use the maximize button ⬜ to make the window fill the entire screen (except the taskbar can still be seen). When a window is maximized, the button changes to the restore button ⧉. Use the restore button to return the window to its previous size.

close button—One of the buttons on the right side of the title bar. Use the close button ✕ to close a program. When you finish using a program, you close it. When a program closes, it releases back to the computer the memory it was using to hold data. All data that wasn't saved to a storage device is lost when the program is closed.

scrollbar—A vertical or horizontal bar on the right side or bottom of a screen, window, or part of a window used to scroll through the screen or window.

Every Windows 8 window contains these common elements. The scrollbar might or might not display in your Paint window, depending on the size of the window.

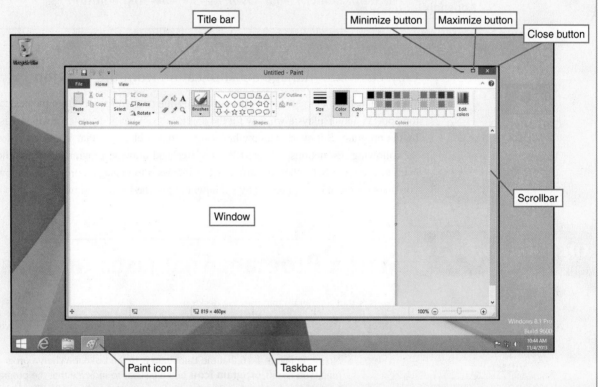

FIGURE 1-16 The Paint application provides a window for drawing freehand.

Solutions Appendix

For help: See *On Your Own 1.3* **Step-by-Step Solution**

A program window has a lot of other text, buttons, and other tools specific to the program you're using. The Paint window that you now have open is a great tool for freehand drawing. If you like, take a few moments to experiment with this program. To draw in the Paint window, press and drag your pointer. Have some fun playing with the colors, brushes, and shapes in the Paint window.

WATCH

OBJECTIVE 1.6
VIDEO

Objective 1.6: Manage a Program Window

Next let's look at how to change the position and size of a program window on the screen.

ON YOUR OWN 1.4

Move a Window

WATCH

OBJECTIVE 1.6
VIDEO

When you drag a window to the top of the screen, it maximizes, or fills, the entire screen. When you drag a window to the far left or far right of the screen, it snaps to the left or right side of the screen.

Manage the Paint window by doing the following:

Step 1. Maximize the window by dragging the window to the top of the screen.

> **Hint** To drag a window, position your pointer in the title bar at the top of the window. Then press and drag the title bar.

Step 2. Restore the window to its previous size by dragging it downward on the screen.

Step 3. Snap the window to the right side of the screen by dragging it to the right.

Step 4. Snap the window to the left side of the screen by dragging it to the left.

Step 5. Click the **minimize** button to minimize the window.

Step 6. Notice that the Paint icon is still in the taskbar. When you see the Paint icon, you know the application is still open even if the window is not visible. Click the **Paint** icon in the taskbar to restore the window.

Solutions
Appendix

For help: See *On Your Own 1.4* Step-by-Step Solution

ON YOUR OWN 1.5

Resize and Close a Window

WATCH

OBJECTIVE 1.6
VIDEO

You can **resize** a window by pressing and dragging the side, bottom, or corner of a window.

> resize—Change the size of a window.

Do the following to resize and close the Paint window:

Step 1. Practice resizing the window by changing first the height and then the width of the window. Then change both the height and the width at the same time.

> **Hint** When your pointer is on the side or bottom of a window, it changes to a double arrow.

Step 2. Resize the Paint window so that a scrollbar appears on the right side of the window. Use the scrollbar to scroll through the window.

Step 3. To close the **Paint** window, click the red **X** in the upper-right corner of the window ⟨ × ⟩. If you've drawn on the window, Paint asks whether you want to save your work. Click **Don't Save**. The Paint window closes. When you close a window, you're closing the program.

Solutions
Appendix

For help: See *On Your Own 1.5* Step-by-Step Solution

WATCH

OBJECTIVE 1.7
VIDEO

Objective 1.7: Manage Multiple Windows

Most productivity work is done from the Windows desktop. Sometimes you might want to work with two or more open windows at the same time. You may have many windows open, but only one is the active window . When you click a program icon in the taskbar, the window it represents becomes the active window.

> **active window**—The window you're currently using. Some Windows 8 programs such as File Explorer or Paint have a red X close button ✕ when they are the active window.

ON YOUR OWN 1.6

WATCH

OBJECTIVE 1.7
VIDEO

Manage Multiple Windows

Do the following to practice managing multiple open windows:

Step 1. Using the **Start screen**, open the **Paint** program. Use the Quick Launch icon in the taskbar to open **File Explorer** 📁.

Step 2. Move the windows so that the File Explorer window overlaps the Paint window. Then click anywhere on the Paint window to make it the active window, causing it to come to the foreground. For some programs, the active window has a red close button.

Step 3. Use the taskbar to make the File Explorer window the active window. How can you use the taskbar to make a window the active window?

Step 4. Close both windows.

Solutions Appendix

For help: See *On Your Own 1.6* Step-by-Step Solution

You now know how to handle multiple application pages in the Windows 8 interface and windows using the desktop. Be aware, however, that an open app uses memory, a computer resource. The more apps you have open, the more memory you have tied up. Having many apps open at the same time can slow down a computer because Windows doesn't have all the memory it needs to work.

Hiding app pages from view or minimizing windows doesn't solve the problem of a slow computer. Even when an app page is hidden or a window is minimized, the program is still tying up memory. To free up memory, you must close the app page or window.

Tip We all like to have more than one app open at the same time. Just don't overdo it unless you have a lot of memory installed on your computer.

Managing Folders and Files on Storage Devices

Next let's look at how data and programs are stored in a computer and how to manage these storage devices.

Objective 1.8: Explore Storage Devices and Their Capacities

WATCH

OBJECTIVE 1.8
VIDEO

Suppose you use your computer to write a business letter. The letter you type is stored as data in a data file. Two popular places to store data files in a computer are on the hard drive and on a USB flash drive.

A hard drive installed inside the computer case is called a local disk . Some computers have more than one local disk. A local disk holds the Windows operating system and all the applications software installed on the computer. In most cases, there's still plenty of extra room for data files.

> **local disk**—A hard drive installed inside the computer case.

How much software and data can you store on a hard drive? The storage capacity for a hard drive is measured in **gigabytes** or **terabytes** . Here are the units used to measure storage capacity:

> **byte**—One unit of storage that can store one letter, number, or other character. For example, the word "hello" needs 5 bytes to store it.
> **megabyte (MB)**—About 1 million bytes.
> **gigabyte (GB)**—Roughly 1,000 megabytes, or about 1 billion bytes.
> **terabyte (TB)**—Roughly 1,000 gigabytes, or about 1 trillion bytes.

Tip To do all the activities in this part of the chapter, you need a USB flash drive. Some schools and colleges don't allow USB flash drives to be used with lab computers. If you're working in a lab, ask your instructor whether using flash drives is allowed. If you're not able to use flash drives in the lab, you can still use them with your home computer.

The hard drive on the one-year-old computer I'm now using has a capacity of 579 GB. A computer that is five years old might have a hard drive that holds about 150 GB. The latest computers use hard drives that hold upward of 3 TB. A USB flash drive has much less storage capacity—for example, 2 GB to 128 GB. But a USB flash drive is much easier to move from computer to computer.

So where on a hard drive or USB flash drive will you put that data file holding your business letter? A file on a drive is stored in a folder, and the folders are organized like branches on an upside-down tree. A folder can contain files and other folders, called subfolders. The top level of a storage device is called the root and can contain both folders and files. Figure 1-17 shows File Explorer displaying the folders and subfolders on a USB flash drive and a diagram of the folder tree on the drive.

> **root**—In Windows, the top level of the folder tree on a storage device. The root contains folders and files.

In File Explorer, you can use the left pane, called the **navigation pane** , to find drives, folders, and libraries. Click a white triangle beside a drive, folder, or library to show its details. Click the black triangle to hide the details.

> **navigation pane**—The pane on the left side of a window—for example, the File Explorer window—that can be used to navigate through the contents displayed in the window.

A library is a group of one or more folders. You use the right pane to view the contents of a device, folder, or library. A scrollbar might be provided to scroll through the contents in a pane if the window is too small to show all the contents.

> **library**—A group of one or more folders. Windows provides four libraries named Documents, Music, Pictures, and Videos to store these types of data on the hard drive.

Figure 1-18 shows the four libraries provided by Windows, which display when you first open File Explorer. Notice in the figure the elements of the File Explorer window that you can use to manage libraries, folders, and files.

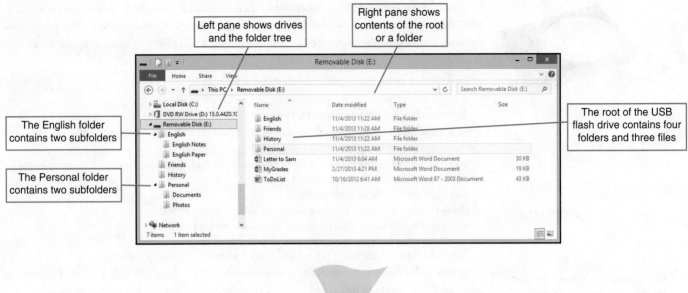

Left pane shows drives and the folder tree

Right pane shows contents of the root or a folder

The root of the USB flash drive contains four folders and three files

The English folder contains two subfolders

The Personal folder contains two subfolders

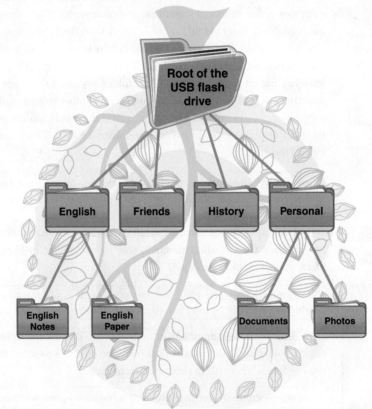

FIGURE 1-17 On a storage device, the root, each folder, and subfolder can contain files.

Each hard drive, flash drive, optical drive, or other drive installed in a computer is assigned a drive letter. You can see the drive letter followed by a colon listed in the Devices and drives group of File Explorer. For example, in Figure 1-18, the installed drives are C:, D:, and E:. When you first insert a flash drive in a USB port or a CD or DVD in the optical drive, Windows might display the AutoPlay **dialog box**, like the one in Figure 1-19. If so, you can ignore the dialog box and it will quickly disappear.

> **dialog box**—A rectangle used to display information and provide menu choices. The difference between a dialog box and window is that a window can be resized and a dialog box has only one size.

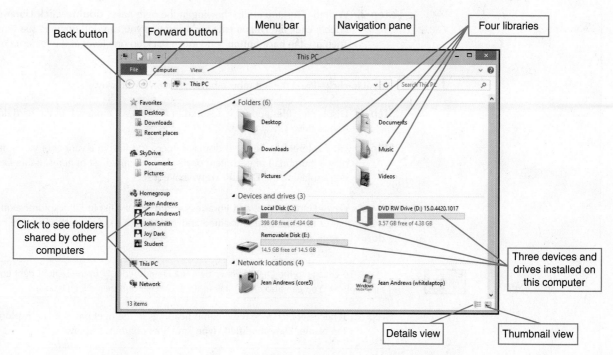

FIGURE 1-18   Using File Explorer, you can manage libraries, folders, and files on your computer.

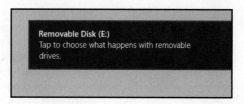

FIGURE 1-19   The AutoPlay dialog box might appear when you first connect a storage device to your computer.

ON YOUR OWN 1.7

Explore Files, Folders, and Libraries on the Hard Drive

WATCH

**OBJECTIVE 1.8
VIDEO**

Do the following to explore the files, folders, and libraries on your hard drive:

Step 1. Go to the Windows desktop and click the **File Explorer** icon 📁 in the taskbar. File Explorer opens (refer to Figure 1-18). What are the four libraries Windows provides for your data? The menu bar near the top of the window shows commands you can use to manage folders and files and File Explorer settings. The commands on the menu bar change depending on what is displayed in the File Explorer window. When the Desktop is selected in the navigation pane, what commands appear in the menu bar?

Step 2. With the Desktop group showing in the right pane, **double-click** Libraries and then double-click the **Documents** library so that you can drill down to see its contents. Then use the **back button** ⊙ to move back up one level in the folder tree so that you can see all the libraries.

> **double-click**—Press the left mouse button twice very quickly.

Step 3. Display the files and folders stored in the root, or top level, of the hard drive, identified as drive C:.

Step 4. File Explorer can be set to display folders and files in a variety of views. It can display a thumbnail of each item or display a detailed list of items. If File Explorer is not displaying the **Details view**, make it so.

> **Details view**—Folders, files, and libraries presented as a list in File Explorer along with details that can include Date modified and Type and Size of an item. (The Size column does not apply to folders.)

> **Hint** To change to the Details view, click the **Details** icon ▦ in the bottom right corner of File Explorer. You can also click View in the menu bar and then click Details.

Step 5. If necessary, change the column headings in the right pane of File Explorer so that the **Name**, **Date modified**, **Type**, and **Size** columns display.

> **Hint** To specify columns you want to see in the Details view of File Explorer, right-click a column heading and select the columns from the list of columns that appears.

Step 6. Sort the list by the file's **Name**. Then sort the list by the file's **Date modified**.

Step 7. Select **This PC** in the navigation pane. In the This PC window, all the drives installed on this computer appear in the right pane in the Devices and drives group, as do the drive letters assigned to these drives. Figure 1-18 shows three drives on one computer, but yours might look different. For most computers, Windows is installed on the local disk identified as drive C:. In Figure 1-18, what is the storage capacity of drive C: on this computer? How much free space does the drive have?

Solutions
Appendix

For help: See *On Your Own 1.7* Step-by-Step Solution

When you first insert a USB flash drive in a USB port, Windows recognizes the drive and adds it to the list of installed storage devices. The drive might be listed as a removable disk or USB disk. You can then use File Explorer to display the drive contents and manage folders and files on the drive. Figure 1-20 shows the File Explorer window displaying the contents of a USB flash drive that contains folders and files. The figure also shows a shortcut menu that appears when you right-click a file.

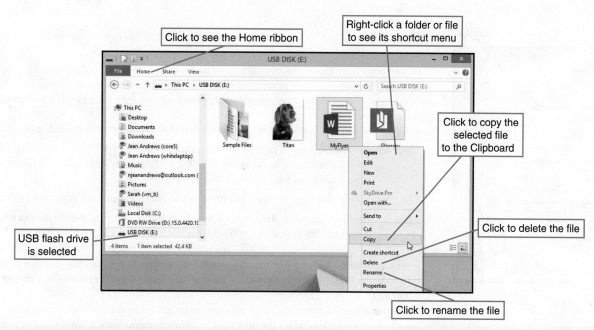

FIGURE 1-20   Folders and files can be managed using the File Explorer menu or a folder or file shortcut menu that appears when you right-click the folder or file.

WATCH

OBJECTIVE 1.9 VIDEO

Objective 1.9: Create and Edit Text Files Using Notepad

The Notepad program is a great tool for creating and editing text files, and a USB flash drive is useful for storing the files you create. In this part of the chapter, you learn to use both.

ON YOUR OWN 1.8

Create and Edit Text Files Using Notepad

WATCH

OBJECTIVE 1.9 VIDEO

To use Notepad to create a text file and store it on a USB flash drive, follow these steps:

Step 1. If necessary, plug in your USB flash drive in a USB port.

Step 2. Open Notepad and use it to create a text file that contains two lines of text showing your name and the name of this class. Save the file to your USB flash drive, naming the file **MyText1**. Figure 1-21 shows the Notepad window after you save the file. What file extension does Notepad assign the file?

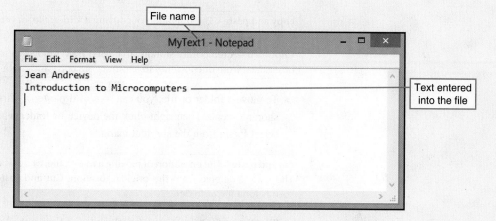

FIGURE 1-21   Notepad shows the filename in the title bar of the window.

MyText2 Properties

General | Details

MyText2

Type of file: Text Document (.txt)

Opens with: 📄 Notepad   Change...

Location: E:\

Size: 66 bytes (66 bytes)

Size on disk: 16.0 KB (16,384 bytes)

Created: Today, November 5, 2013, 1 minute ago

Modified: Today, November 5, 2013, 1 minute ago

Accessed: Today, November 5, 2013

Attributes: ☐ Read-only   ☐ Hidden   ☑ Archive

OK   Cancel   Apply

Step 3. Close the file. Use File Explorer to verify the text file is stored at the location you selected.

One way to open a file is to double-click it in File Explorer. When you open a data file, you view its contents. The program used to create the file is normally used to open the file, but this isn't always the case. For example, when you open a photograph file, Windows opens a picture viewer so you can view the file.

Follow these steps to open the MyText1 text file, edit the file, and save it under a new name:

Step 4. Use File Explorer to open the **MyText1** file. Then add a third line of text that contains today's date. Save the file again, this time naming it **MyText2**. Save the file to the same location as the first file. Close the file.

Step 5. Use File Explorer to verify that the two text files are stored on your USB flash drive.

Step 6. Windows identifies a file type by the file extension. Display the file **Properties box** to find out the file extension for the **MyText2** file. What is the file extension?

> **Properties box**—A dialog box that displays the properties of a folder, file, or other item. To view the Properties box, right-click the item and select **Properties** from the **shortcut menu**.
>
> **shortcut menu**—A menu that appears when you right-click an item. The options listed in a shortcut menu depend on the item itself. A shortcut menu is sometimes called a drop-down menu.

Solutions Appendix

For help: See *On Your Own 1.8* Step-by-Step Solution

WATCH

OBJECTIVE 1.10
VIDEO

Objective 1.10: Manage Folders and Files on a Storage Device

Folders are a great way to organize files on a removable storage device, such as a USB flash drive. For example, you might want to keep your files in three folders on your flash drive: Computer Class, English Class, and Sample Files. Here are some useful tips when working with folders and files on a storage device:

> To copy a folder or file, you can **copy and paste** it. First, right-click the item and click **Copy** on the folder or file's shortcut menu (refer to Figure 1-20). Windows temporarily places the item and its contents in the Windows **Clipboard**. Then right-click the device or folder where you want to place the item and select **Paste** from the shortcut menu.

> **copy and paste**—The operation of copying a folder, file, or other item in a new location without deleting it from the original location.
>
> **Clipboard**—A temporary storage area used by Windows to transfer data (folders, files, text, or other data) from one location to another. The copy-and-paste operations use the Clipboard.

> To move a folder or file, you can **cut and paste** it. First, use the **Cut** option on the item's shortcut menu. Then right-click the device or folder where you want to place the item and select **Paste** from the shortcut menu.

> **cut and paste**—The operation of moving a folder, file, or other item from one location to another. The item is deleted from the original location. Cut and Paste are commands on the shortcut menus for a file or folder.

> To delete a folder or file, select the item and press the **Delete** key. You can also use the **Cut** command or the **Delete** command on the folder or file's shortcut menu.

> Another way to copy or move a folder or file is to **drag and drop** the item to its new location. This method works well when you have two File Explorer windows open. When you drag and drop a folder or file to another location on the same storage media, Windows *moves* the item. When you drag and drop the item from one storage device to another, Windows *copies* the item.

> **drag and drop**—The operation of copying or moving a folder, file, or other item from one location to another by holding down, dragging the item, and releasing the left mouse button. To copy (not move) an item, hold down the Ctrl key as you drag and drop.

> To rename a folder or file, use the **Rename** command on the item's shortcut menu.
> To create a folder, click **Home** in the File Explorer menu bar and then click **New folder** (see Figure 1-22). The folder is created in the currently displayed folder. It is named New folder, but the name is selected so that you can type a new name. Notice you can also use the Home **ribbon** to copy, move, delete, and rename selected files or folders.

> **ribbon**—The area at the top of a window that contains groups of commands. Click a menu item to display its ribbon.

Tip File Explorer has the Quick Access Toolbar, which is a shortcut for a few of the more common tasks on the Home ribbon. Find the Quick Access Toolbar on the left side of the title bar on the File Explorer window as labeled in Figure 1-22.

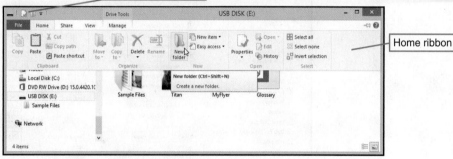

FIGURE 1-22   Use the Home ribbon to create a new folder.

ON YOUR OWN 1.9

Manage Folders and Files on a USB Flash Drive

WATCH

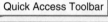

OBJECTIVE 1.10 VIDEO

Let's use your USB flash drive to practice creating, deleting, renaming, and copying folders and files:

Step 1. If necessary, plug in your USB flash drive in a USB port. Create a folder named **Computer Class** on your flash drive.

Step 2. Create a subfolder named **Data** in the Computer Class folder. Then delete the **Data** folder.

Step 3. Create a folder named **History Class** at the root level of the USB flash drive. Rename the **History Class** folder to **English Class**.

Step 4. Use the copy-and-paste operation or the drag-and-drop operation to copy the two text files, **MyText1** and **MyText2**, that you created in On Your Own 1-8 from the root of the USB flash drive to the **Computer Class** folder.

Step 5. Move (don't copy) the **MyText1** file from the root of the flash drive to the **English Class** folder. Verify that the file is no longer in the root of the flash drive.

Step 6. Rename the **MyText2** file in the root of the flash drive to **MyClass**.

Step 7. Delete the **MyText1** file in the Computer Class folder.

Solutions Appendix

For help: See *On Your Own 1.9* Step-by-Step Solution

You now know how to copy, move, delete, and rename folders and files. Here are two more tips when you want to copy and paste multiple files:

> If you want to copy multiple files in a list, click the first file in the list to select it. Hold down the **Shift** key and click the last file in the list. All the files in the list are selected. Then right-click anywhere in the list and select **Copy** from the shortcut menu (see Figure 1-23). All files selected are copied to the Clipboard. You can now use one **Paste** command to copy all the files to a new location.

> If you want to copy multiple files that are not together in the same list, click one file to select it. Then hold down the **Ctrl** key while you click other files.

After you write files to your USB flash drive, don't unplug the drive immediately because the write operation might not be finished. To be certain it's safe to unplug the flash drive, click the up arrow on the right side of the Windows taskbar and click the **Safely Remove Hardware and Eject Media** icon. In the list that appears, click the item to eject your USB flash drive. It is now safe to unplug the flash drive from the USB port.

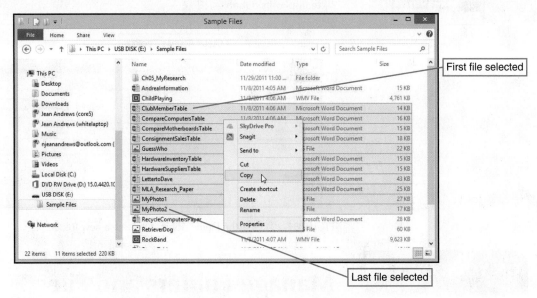

FIGURE 1-23 Multiple selected files can be copied to the Clipboard.

Using Other Windows Utilities

WATCH

OBJECTIVE 1.11 VIDEO

Besides File Explorer and Internet Explorer, two other programs included in Windows are the Windows Snipping Tool and Windows Help and Support.

Objective 1.11: Use the Windows Snipping Tool and Windows Help and Support

Tip The Windows Snipping Tool doesn't work in the Windows 8 interface. To take a screen capture of your entire screen while in the Windows 8 interface, press **Win+Print Screen**. (Hold down the **Win** key as you press the **Print Screen** key.) Then look for the capture file in the Screenshots folder in the Pictures library.

You can use the Windows Snipping Tool to capture a screenshot or **snip** of your desktop. The tool can be useful when you need to document your work in Windows. Your instructor might ask you to create a snip of your Windows screen to show you've done the work as assigned. You can store a snip in a file.

> **snip**—A capture of part or all of the Windows desktop that can be stored in a file. You can use the Windows Snipping Tool to take a snip.

ON YOUR OWN 1.10

Capture a Screen Snip Using the Windows Snipping Tool

WATCH

▶

OBJECTIVE 1.11 VIDEO

Open File Explorer and view the contents of the root of your USB flash drive. Then take a snip of this part of your Windows desktop. Save the snip to your USB flash drive or another location specified by your instructor. Name the file **MySnip1**. By **default**, Windows uses the **PNG file** format to save the file.

> **default**—The choice made by software that applies until someone changes it.
>
> **PNG file**—A file with a .png file extension that contains a graphic. The file has a smaller file size than other types of graphics files.

| Solutions Appendix |

For help: See *On Your Own 1.10* Step-by-Step Solution

When you're learning to use any software, look for a help feature in the software that you can use to get help when you need it. Windows offers Windows Help and Support. To open this program, return to the **Start screen**, begin typing **help and support**, and then click **Help and Support** in the list that appears. The Windows Help and Support window opens on the desktop (see Figure 1-24). To find information, type words in the Search box and press **Enter**.

FIGURE 1-24   Use Windows Help and Support to teach yourself about Windows.

Ending a Windows Session

WATCH

OBJECTIVE 1.12
VIDEO

Next let's look at how to end a Windows session before you step away from your computer.

Objective 1.12: End a Windows Session

When you finish using a computer, you have options as to what you do before you step away. Several of these options are listed in the key terms that follow.

shut down—To completely stop all computer operations. All windows are closed, and the computer is powered down. If you plan to be away from your computer for at least until the next day, you should shut down Windows and turn off the power to the computer.

sign out—To close all your open programs and then close access to your user account in Windows.

lock—Close access to your user account in Windows without closing the open programs. Use this option if you're stepping away from your computer for just a few moments and don't want other people to see the work on your desktop while you're away. To unlock your computer, you have to sign back on.

restart—To sign off your account and any other users who also might be signed on and close Windows. Windows then loads again, and you can sign back on the system. Some program installations require you to restart the system before the installation completes.

sleep—To save all work and put the computer in a mode that uses a low level of power. Any open windows remain open. If you plan to be away from your computer for more than a few minutes but not all day, you can put the computer to sleep. Later, when you press a key on the keyboard or move the mouse, the computer resumes just where you left off.

hibernate—To save your current Windows session and all your work to the hard drive and then power down the system. Later when you press the power button, Windows reloads any open applications and documents. Hibernation is used on laptop and netbook computers to conserve power. When a laptop computer is put to sleep for a long time and the battery is getting low, the laptop automatically goes into hibernation. Desktop computers and many laptops don't normally show the hibernate option on the Shut down menu.

ON YOUR OWN 1.11

End a Windows Session

WATCH

OBJECTIVE 1.12
VIDEO

Before you step away from a computer, you need to end the Windows session. Practice each of these methods:

Step 1. To close all open windows and close access to your user account, **Sign out** of Windows. You can see the Sign out option when you click your user account on the Start screen (see Figure 1-25a). How do you sign back on?

Step 2. Put the computer to **Sleep** to conserve power. To find the Sleep option, click the **Settings** charm, and then click **Power** (see Figure 1-25b). The options available on the Power menu depend on how your computer is configured. How do you wake up the computer?

(a)   (b)

FIGURE 1-25 Options to end a Windows session: (a) Sign out, and (b) Sleep and Shut down.

Step 3. To shut down the computer, stopping all computer operations in an orderly manner, you can use the Power options on the Settings charm or you can use the Windows desktop. Go to the Windows desktop and right-click the **Start** button. On the menu that appears, point to **Shut down or sign out** (see Figure 1-26). In the submenu that appears, click the **Shut down** option. The computer performs an orderly shutdown.

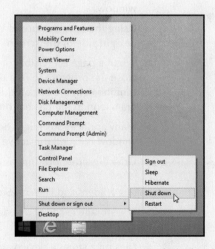

FIGURE 1-26 Right-click the Start button to see a menu of Windows tools, including Shut down or sign out options.

Solutions
Appendix

For help: See *On Your Own 1.11* Step-by-Step Solution

Summary

Hardware and Software to Get You Started

> All hardware can be categorized as devices used for input, output, processing, or storage.

> Five types of personal computers you might use at work, at home, or at school are a desktop computer, an all-in-one computer, a laptop, a netbook, and a tablet.

> The primary output device is a monitor. Main input devices are the keyboard, mouse, and touch pad. A touch screen is both an input and output device.

> Types of optical discs are CD, DVD, and Blu-ray discs.

> Ports on a computer might include USB ports, a network port, a VGA video port, and a DVI video port. Some computers have an HDMI port or a DisplayPort.

> The most important storage device inside a computer is the hard drive. A USB flash drive is a convenient portable storage device.

> The three main categories of software are applications, operating systems, and utility programs. A computer needs only one operating system, such as Windows 8.

> An example of applications software is Microsoft Office, which is a suite of several applications used to write documents, take notes, manage email, manage numbers, create presentations, and manage a database.

> Software is stored in a program file that is likely to have an .exe file extension.

> The file extension of a data file indicates the type of data in the file; for example, a file with a .jpg file extension is used for a photograph.

> To use Windows, you must first sign on to a user account that controls the access you have to the computer. The sign-on process might require a password to the account.

> Three types of user accounts in Windows 8 are a local account, domain account, and Microsoft account.

Managing Program Pages and Windows

> To use a program, you must first open or launch it. An open or running program uses computer resources including memory until it's closed.

> Windows 8 has two interfaces used to manage programs. The newer Windows 8 interface opens a program in a page, and the Windows desktop opens a program in a window.

> Using the Snap feature of Windows, you can cause a page or window to snap to the left or right side of the screen.

> When a page is invisible or a window is minimized, the program is still open. You must close the program to free up system resources. To see invisible pages, click the page thumbnail in the bar on the left side of the screen. To restore a window, click the program icon in the taskbar on the Windows desktop.

> Many applications might be open, but you can use only one application at a time. Its window is called the active window.

> Grab the sides, bottom, or corner of a window to resize it.

Managing Folders and Files on Storage Devices

> The storage capacity of a device is measured in bytes, megabytes (MB), gigabytes (GB), and terabytes (TB).

> Files on a storage device are organized using folders that can contain files and subfolders organized in a hierarchical structure.

> A library is a group of folders. Windows default libraries are the Documents, Music, Pictures, and Videos libraries.

> Notepad is used to create and edit text files.

> Two methods to copy or move a folder or file are the drag-and-drop operation and the commands on the shortcut menus. These commands include Copy, Cut, and Paste.

> To rename a folder or file, use the Rename command on the shortcut menu of the file or folder.

> Use the Safely Remove Hardware and Eject Media icon in the taskbar before you remove a USB flash drive from your computer.

Using Other Windows Utilities

> Use the Windows Snipping Tool to capture an area of the Windows screen and store the snip in a file.

> You can use Windows Help and Support to find information and links to videos on how to use Windows.

Ending a Windows Session

> Before you step away from a computer, end the Windows session using one of the options on the user account menu, the Power menu in the Settings charm, or the menu that appears when you right-click the Start button on the desktop. These options can include Lock, Sign out, Sleep, Shut down, Restart, and Hibernate.

CHAPTER MASTERY PROJECT

Now it's time to find out how well you've mastered the content in this chapter. If you can do all the steps in this mastery project without looking back at the chapter details and can answer all the review questions following this project, you have mastered this chapter. If you can complete the project by finding answers using Windows Help and Support, you've proven that you're well on your way to teaching yourself essential computer skills.

> **Hint** All the key terms in the chapter are used in this mastery project or in the review questions. If you find a word you don't know, glance through the chapter and find that key term.

If you find you need a lot of help doing the project and you have not yet read the chapter or done the activities, drop back and start at the beginning of the chapter, watch the videos, review the step-by-step solutions as you work through the On Your Own activities, and then return to this project.

> **Tip** If you need help completing this part of the mastery project, review the "Hardware and Software to Get You Started" and the "Managing Program Pages and Windows" sections in the chapter.

Follow these steps to start a Windows 8 session:

Step 1. Power up your computer and sign on. Practice moving from the Start screen to the Windows desktop and back to the Start screen using the Windows key, the charms bar, and the Start button on the Windows desktop.

Step 2. Open (launch) the News app and the Sports app. Practice changing the sizes of the two pages. Open the Weather app. How many pages are displayed? Switch to the third page. Close all open apps.

Step 3. The Paint program is included with Windows and is used to create freehand graphics. Open the **Paint** program.

Step 4. Maximize the **Paint** window by using Snap and the press-and-drag action. Then restore the window to its original size.

Step 5. Move the **Paint** window so that it snaps to the right side of your monitor screen. Now snap the window to the left side of the screen.

Step 6. Use the minimize button to minimize the **Paint** window. Restore the window. Resize the **Paint** window by changing first the height and then the width of the window. Then change the height and width at the same time.

Step 7. Close the **Paint** window by using the close button.

Step 8. Open the **Paint** window. Use the Quick Launch icon in the taskbar to open **File Explorer**. Practice making each window the active window. Close both windows.

> **Tip** If you need help completing this part of the mastery project, review the "Managing Folders and Files on Storage Devices" section in the chapter.

Follow these steps to manage folders and files:

Step 9. Using File Explorer, display the This PC window. Then display the folders in the root of the hard drive.

Step 10. Insert a USB flash drive in your computer. Use Notepad to create a text file named **MyInfo1** that contains your name and phone number. Save the file to your USB flash drive and close the file. Use File Explorer to open the file and add to the text file your mailing address. Then save the file to your USB flash drive, naming it **MyInfo2**. Close the file.

Step 11. Display the file **Properties** dialog box (also called the Properties box) of the **MyInfo1** file. Close the dialog box.

Step 12. To use your USB flash drive to practice creating, renaming, moving, opening, and closing files and folders, do the following:

  a. If File Explorer is showing thumbnails of files, change the view to Details view. Sort the files in the root of your USB flash drive by **Date modified**.

  b. If you have not already done so, use the Home ribbon in File Explorer to create a folder named **Computer Class** on your USB flash drive. In the Computer Class folder, create a subfolder named **Data**.

  c. Create a folder named **History Class** at the root of the USB flash drive. Rename the History Class folder to **English Class**.

  d. Copy the **MyInfo1** file to the **Computer Class** folder on the flash drive using a copy-and-paste operation or a drag-and-drop operation.

  e. Move the **MyInfo1** file from the **Computer Class** folder to the **English Class** folder using a cut-and-paste operation or a drag-and-drop operation.

  f. In the English Class folder, rename the **MyInfo1** file to **MyContact**. Then delete the **MyContact** file.

  g. Delete the **Data** folder in the Computer Class folder.

> **Tip** If you need help completing this part of the mastery project, review the "Using Other Windows Utilities" section in the chapter.

Follow this step to take a snip of your screen:

Step 13. Use the Windows Snipping Tool to take a capture of the File Explorer window and save the snip to the USB flash drive or another location given by your instructor. Name the snip file **MySnip2**. The Snipping Tool automatically assigns a .png file extension.

Step 14. Submit to your instructor the MyInfo2 file you created in Step 10 and the MySnip2 file you created in Step 13. If you're using MyITLab in this course, you can put the files in your Dropbox in MyITLab. If you're not using MyITLab, ask your instructor how he wants you to submit the files.

> **Tip** If you need help completing this part of the mastery project, review the "Ending a Windows Session" section in the chapter.

Follow these steps to practice ending a Windows session:

Step 15. **Lock** your computer so that a sign on is required to use it. Then unlock your computer using your password.

Step 16. **Sign out** and sign back on to your computer.

Step 17. Put your computer to **sleep**. Wake up your computer.

Step 18. **Restart** your computer using the Shut down or sign out menu on the Windows desktop.

Review Questions

Answer these questions to assess your skills and knowledge of the content covered in the chapter. Your instructor can provide you with the correct answers when you are ready to check your work.

1. What is the most important skill you need to know when learning to use computers?

2. What are the four categories in which all computer hardware devices are placed?

3. Which type of nonmobile computer requires a detached keyboard, mouse, and monitor and gives you the most power for your money?

4. Components inside the computer case are called _____ components.

5. Which type of mobile computer doesn't have an embedded physical keyboard and always has a touch screen? Which two types of mobile computers use a touch pad instead of a mouse? Which type of nonmobile computer has a built-in monitor and might have a touch screen?

6. Which type of port is used to connect to a wired network? List four types of ports that can be used to connect a monitor to a computer.

7. What type of drive can receive a CD or a DVD?

8. Which type of inexpensive and easy-to-use storage device uses a USB port to connect to a computer?

9. What are the three general categories of software? Which category of software is Windows 8? A program to back up data? Microsoft Word?

10. What are the six applications that are part of the Microsoft Office suite of applications that are covered in this book?

11. What are the two categories of types of files? Which type of file has an .exe file extension?

12. What are three types of user accounts?

13. How does Windows know which folders on a computer a user can access or control?

14. Which type of user account gives a user access to resources on the Microsoft website?

15. What are the two interfaces that Windows 8 uses? Which interface is used when you first sign onto Windows?

16. What is a live tile? What happens when you move your pointer to the upper-right corner of the Start screen? What are the five charms in the charms bar?

17. When you want to launch an app from the Start screen and the app has no tile on this screen, which app can you use to find and launch the app?

18. What are the maximum number of pages that display in the Windows 8 interface for a small monitor?

19. When using the Windows desktop, what is your background screen called? What is the purpose of the Recycle Bin?

20. What program is represented by the big blue letter e in the Quick Launch area of the taskbar? What is the purpose of the volume icon in the taskbar?

21. What is the most important computer resource that a program requires?

22. What button can you use to maximize a window if you don't use the Snap feature of Windows?

23. Where do you need to position your pointer or cursor to move a window?

24. What appears in a window when the window is resized so that everything cannot display?

25. After minimizing a window, how do you restore the window to the desktop?

26. When you have three program windows open, how many of these windows can be the active window? How do you use the program icon in the taskbar to make a window the active window?

27. A program uses portions of RAM when it's running. What might happen to your computer performance if you have several windows open at the same time?

28. Windows and other software are installed on a hard drive installed inside the computer case. What is another name for this hard drive? What drive letter is usually assigned to this drive?

29. What are four units of measure used to measure the capacity of a storage device? Which unit is large enough to hold only a single character? Which capacity is larger, 500 GB or 0.5 TB?

30. What are the four libraries on your hard drive?

31. What does a white triangle in the navigation pane of File Explorer indicate? What happens when you right-click in the white space of the right pane of File Explorer? What happens when you double-click a folder in the right pane of File Explorer?

32. In File Explorer, which key can you hold down to select nonsequential files in a list? Which operation results in a file being deleted from its original location and placed in a new location: copy and paste or cut and paste? When you copy or cut a file, where is the file temporarily stored?

33. When taking a snip of your screen, what is the default file extension that Windows assigns the file that is saved using the Windows Snipping Tool?

34. Before you can safely remove a USB flash drive that you have written on, what should you do?

35. List the steps to use the Recycle Bin to recover a file you accidentally deleted from the hard drive. If you need help finding the answer, refer to Windows Help and Support.

36. When a laptop or netbook has been asleep for some time and the battery is getting low, what might it do to conserve power?

Becoming an Independent Learner

Answer the following questions about becoming an independent learner:

1. To teach yourself to use Windows 8, why is it better to rely on Windows Help and Support when you need answers rather than rely on this book?

2. The most important skill learned in this chapter is how to teach yourself a computer skill. Rate yourself at Level A through E on how well you're doing with this skill. What is your level?
   - Level A: I was able to successfully complete the Chapter Mastery Project with the help of only a few of the On Your Own activities in the chapter.
   - Level B: I completed all the On Your Own activities and the Chapter Mastery Project without referring to any of the solutions in the Step-by-Step Solutions Appendix.
   - Level C: I completed all the On Your Own activities and the Chapter Mastery Project by using just a few of the solutions in the Step-by-Step Solutions Appendix.
   - Level D: I completed all the On Your Own activities and the Chapter Mastery Project by using many of the solutions in the Step-by-Step Solutions Appendix.
   - Level E: I completed all the On Your Own activities and the Chapter Mastery Project and had to use all of the solutions in the Step-by-Step Solutions Appendix.

To continue toward the goal of teaching yourself computer skills, if you're not at Level A, try to move up one level on how you learn in Chapter 2.

Projects to Help You

Now that you've mastered the material in this chapter, you're ready to tackle the three projects focused on your career, personal, or academic goals. Depending on your own interests, you might choose to complete any or all of these projects to help you achieve your goals.

Project 1: Windows in Your Professional Career

Career Project I need help recovering a file I accidentally deleted, and I want to annotate a snip.

Most successful professionals are constantly learning about new technologies as they arise. Knowing how to teach yourself computer skills is essential for keeping up with all these new technologies. Do the following to teach yourself about some features of Windows that weren't covered in the chapter:

Step 1. When you delete a folder or file on your hard drive, Windows moves the item to the Recycle Bin. To open it, double-click the **Recycle Bin** icon on your desktop.

Step 2. Use Windows Help and Support to teach yourself about Windows. To open Windows Help and Support, use the **Search** charm and type **help** in the search box. In the list of apps, click **Help and Support**.

Step 3. Using the Help and Support window, get help about the **Recycle Bin**. Use information provided by Windows Help and Support to complete the following:

   a. List the steps to recover a file that has been deleted and you can see is in the Recycle Bin.

   b. List the steps to empty the Recycle Bin. Emptying the Recycle Bin can free up some space on your hard drive.

Step 4. Recall that the Windows Snipping Tool can be used to capture a screen shot or snip of your screen. The tool can be extremely useful when writing instructions to users on how to use software. Using Windows Help and Support, find out how to annotate a snip.

Step 5. Take a snip of part of your Windows screen showing the Help and Support window in step 3. Use the highlighter tool to highlight an area of the snip. Use the red pen to write on the snip. Save the snip to your USB flash drive, naming the file **MySnip3**.

Step 6. Using File Explorer, create a new folder named **Snips** on your USB flash drive. Move the MySnip3 file to this new folder.

Step 7. Send the file to your instructor. If you're using MyITLab, you can place the file in your Dropbox. If you're not using MyITLab, ask your instructor how he or she wants you to submit the file.

Project 2: Windows in Your Personal Life

Personal Project I want to use the Windows Calculator to find the fuel economy of my car, and I want to use Speech Recognition software in Windows 8.

Learning to use computers in your personal life is a moving target because what you want to do with a computer changes as your needs change. In addition, hardware and software are constantly changing. To keep up with all this change, you need to learn to teach yourself computer skills. Do the following to learn to use some features of Windows that were not covered in the chapter:

Step 1. Windows offers the Calculator program, which you can use to convert numbers and dates and do calculations. Open the **Calculator** program.

Step 2. Use Windows Help and Support to learn about the Calculator. To open the Windows Help and Support window, go to the **Start screen** and type **Help**. Then click **Help and Support**.

Step 3. To find help, type **Calculator** in the search box near the top of the Windows Help and Support window and press **Enter**. Using information provided by Windows Help and Support, answer these questions using the Calculator:

   a. How do you set the Calculator to perform Unit conversion? What is 29 degrees Celsius converted to degrees Fahrenheit?

   b. Switch the Calculator to perform a Date calculation. How many days are there from January 10, 2014, to April 1, 2015?

   c. Which option on the View menu is used to calculate fuel economy (mpg)? If your car used 12 gallons to travel 220 miles, what is the fuel economy (mpg)?

   d. You're considering buying a house. The purchase price is $155,000. The down payment is $17,000. Use the Calculator to find out your monthly payments over 30 years at 5% interest.

   e. Set the Calculator for basic calculations. What is 55.6 * 72/45?

   f. What is 55% of 783?

Step 4. Windows Help and Support can give you solutions to problems and help with Windows. Using Windows Help and Support, answer these questions:

   a. In the search box in the Windows Help and Support window, type **problems with sound** and press **Enter**. What are the first two types of problems listed?

   b. You want to use Windows 8 Speech Recognition so you can speak to your computer and it will do the typing for you. In the search box, type **how to use speech recognition**. What are four languages available for Speech Recognition?

   c. When setting up speech recognition on your computer, what are the two things you must do before you can use speech recognition?

Project 3: Windows in Your Academic Career

Academic Project I want to get familiar with MyITLab and how it will help me in this course.

MyITLab is a website offered by Pearson Education to help you with learning the material in this book. If you have a subscription to MyITLab, you can sign on to the site and explore the many resources available to you. Do the following:

Step 1. Using your sign-on information, open Internet Explorer and enter **www.myitlab.com** in the address box. Then sign onto the website with your user ID and password. If you need help setting up and activating your account, check with your instructor.

Step 2. Find the Announcements section. What announcements has your instructor posted for this course?

Step 3. MyITLab offers an email service. Find the email service and send an email message to your instructor saying, "I can communicate with my instructor using email in MyITLab."

Step 4. Find the grade book. Most likely you don't have any grades assigned there, but now you know where to look when expecting grades to be posted.

Step 5. Find the option to upload a file to Dropbox. Dropbox is a way to send a file to your instructor. For example, you can post your Windows Snipping Tool file, MySnip1.png, in Dropbox for your instructor.

WATCH

**HOW TO USE
MYITLAB VIDEO**

Project to Help Others

One of the best ways to learn is to teach someone else. And, in teaching someone else, you are making a contribution into that person's life. As part of each chapter's work, you are encouraged to teach someone else a skill you have learned. In this case, you help your apprentice learn to use Windows. Who is your apprentice? A parent, younger sibling, neighbor, or friend? For the best experience, this person should be someone much older or younger than you and should really want to learn to use a computer. Find that person! It is hoped your apprentice will receive your help for the entire course, but if you need to switch to another person, be sure to let your instructor know.

   Working with your apprentice, do the following:

Step 1. Ask your apprentice how she expects to use a computer and what she would like to learn. Do your best to help this person meet these goals as you move forward to other chapters.

Step 2. Show your apprentice how to start a computer and sign on. Then point out the items on the Start screen and Windows desktop. Show your apprentice how to open program pages and windows and manage these pages and windows.

Step 3. Explain the purpose of File Explorer to manage folders and files. Make sure your apprentice understands the purpose of

- File Explorer
- Folders
- Files
- Storage devices including the hard drive, a USB flash drive, and an optical drive

Step 4. Show your apprentice how to use Notepad to create a text file on her USB flash drive and how to edit that file. Watch and coach as your apprentice works. Don't do it for her.

Step 5. Show your apprentice how to use Windows Help and Support. Based on the goals of your apprentice, suggest other skills in this chapter you think would be useful to her and suggest investigating these skills using Windows Help and Support.

Step 6. Help your apprentice learn each skill but encourage her to discover on her own. Remind your apprentice that teaching yourself a computer skill is the most important computer skill to know.

Step 7. Ask your apprentice to evaluate how the tutoring session went. Briefly describe her response.

Step 8. Use Notepad to create a text file that contains the answers to the following questions. Send the file to your instructor. If you're using MyITLab in this course, you can put the file in your Dropbox in MyITLab. If you're not using MyITLab, ask your instructor how he or she wants you to submit the file. Here are the questions:

1. Who is your apprentice?
2. What goals did your apprentice list in step 1?
3. Which was easier for your apprentice to learn, using pages in the Windows 8 interface or using windows on the desktop?
4. How well do you think your apprentice understands the purpose of each of the four items listed in step 3?
5. Based on the goals of your apprentice, what other skills in this chapter did you suggest your apprentice investigate? List these skills.
6. Briefly describe how your apprentice evaluated the tutoring session.
7. Did you enjoy the experience? What might you do differently the next time you tutor your apprentice?

2 Finding and Using Information on the Web

In This Chapter, You Will:

Getting News on the Web

2.1 Use Internet Explorer to surf the web

2.2 Manage multiple web pages in a single IE window

2.3 Customize Internet Explorer

Searching for Other Information on the Web

2.4 Use a search engine to find information on the web

2.5 Perform Google advanced searches and find images, videos, directions, and translations

Using Applications and Storing Data in the Cloud

2.6 Describe cloud computing and download files from the web

2.7 Use OneDrive to store your data

Conducting Business Safely on the Web

2.8 Apply several methods to stay safe while doing business on the web

2.9 Use antivirus software to protect your computer against malware

2.10 Download and install software from the web

2.11 Switch Windows 8 sign on to a Microsoft account

You have probably already used the Internet and the web to find information, store data, shop, and make a purchase. Regardless of your previous experiences, this chapter can take you deeper to understand more about what's available on the Internet and the web and how to use these amazing tools more effectively.

As with all chapters in this book, you can choose which of the learning paths below best suits your needs. No matter which path you choose, as you work your way through the chapter, remember the most important computer skill is how to teach yourself a computer skill. Therefore, this chapter is designed to help you teach yourself how to find and use information on the web.

LEARNING PATHS

GUIDED LEARNING	EXPLORE AND DISCOVER	JUMP RIGHT IN
Read the Chapter *Watch the Objective Videos*	**On Your Own Projects** *Review Objective videos or use Step-by-Step Solutions*	**Mastery Project** *Use Objective videos & OYO projects for help*
On Your Own Projects *Review Objective videos or use Step-by-Step Solutions*	**Mastery Project** *Use Objective videos & OYO projects for help*	**Explore Resources** *For help as needed*
Mastery Project *Use Objective videos & OYO projects for help*		
Google Project (if applicable) *Watch Google video for help*	**Google Project (if applicable)** *Watch Google video for help*	**Google Project (if applicable)** *Watch Google video for help*
Helping You & Others Projects	**Helping You & Others Projects**	**Helping You & Others Projects**
MyITLab Assessment	**MyITLab Assessment**	**MyITLab Assessment**

Getting News on the Web

Let's begin this chapter about using the web by examining the difference between the Internet and the web. Then we'll discuss how to use Internet Explorer to get news off the web.

Objective 2.1: Use Internet Explorer to Surf the Web

The **Internet**—a vast network of computers all over the world—is the transportation system computers can use to serve up the news in web pages. A **web page** is a document that contains text and perhaps graphics, sound, animation, or video, to be displayed on a computer screen by a **browser**. The collection of all web pages available on the Internet is called the **World Wide Web**, or just the **web**.

> **Internet**—A global network of networked computers that's used to receive and serve up untold amounts of data and provide us with powerful ways to communicate. When you use a computer connected to the Internet, your computer is also part of the Internet.
>
> **web page**—A document that can include text, graphics, sound, animation, and video. The document is written using a group of rules collectively called the Hypertext Markup Language (HTML). The document is called a hypertext document and is designed to be displayed by a browser.
>
> **browser**—A program that searches or browses web pages.
>
> **World Wide Web or web**—A collection of web pages made available by computers connected to the Internet. The World Wide Web is one of many applications that the Internet supports.

Internet Explorer

If your computer is connected to the Internet, you can use Internet Explorer (IE) to find information on the Internet. Internet Explorer, Version 11, is the browser included in Windows 8 with the Windows 8.1 update applied. When you start IE from the Start screen, it opens as a page using the Windows 8 interface. When you start IE from the desktop, it opens as a window.

WATCH

OBJECTIVE 2.1
VIDEO

Tip The Internet and the web are similar to a transportation system that supports the delivery of cargo. For example, the road system (the Internet) in our country is used by the postal system (World Wide Web) to deliver the mail (web pages).

Not Working? This chapter assumes that the computer you're using is a Windows 8 computer with the Windows 8.1 update applied, and the computer is connected to the Internet. If you have a problem with the connection, Chapters 12 and 13 cover how to connect a computer to the Internet and what to do when the connection fails.

ON YOUR OWN 2.1

Use Internet Explorer

WATCH

OBJECTIVE 2.1
VIDEO

In this activity, you'll use Internet Explorer from the Start screen and also from the desktop. Do the following to get the news using Internet Explorer:

Step 1. Go to the Windows 8 Start screen and open **Internet Explorer**. An Internet Explorer page opens and displays the **home page** (see Figure 2-1).

> **home page**—The web page that appears when you first open a browser.

Step 2. Click a **link** on your home page to drill down to another web page. Click a link on the new page that displays.

> **link**—Text or graphic on a web page that points to another web page. When you mouse over a link, the pointer changes to a hand 👆. When you click the link, the browser requests and displays the other web page. A link is also called a *hyperlink*.

Step 3. To return to the previous web page, click the left arrow in the black pane at the bottom of the screen (see Figure 2-1). If you don't see the black pane, right-click anywhere on the page to make it appear.

> **Tip** You can also move your pointer to the left edge of the screen. When you do, a left arrow appears on the left edge. Click the arrow to return to the previous page.

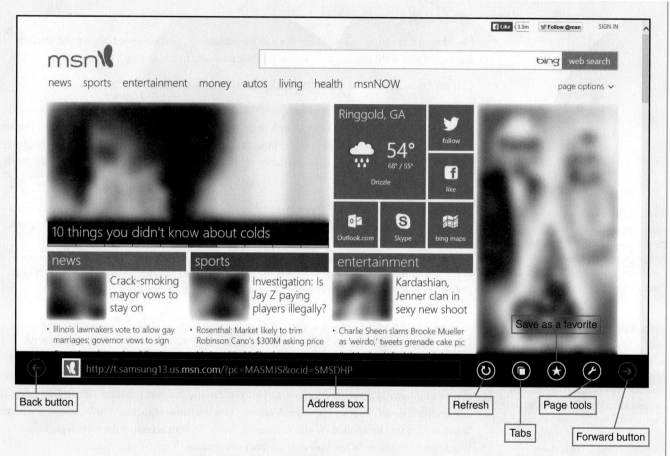

FIGURE 2-1   Internet Explorer using the Windows 8 interface displays a web page.

You can type the address of a web page in the **address box** of Internet Explorer. The address of a web page is called the **Uniform Resource Locator (URL)**.

> **address box**—The area of a browser that contains the URL or address of the web page currently displayed.
>
> **Uniform Resource Locator (URL)**—The address of a web page, for example, www.cnn.com or cnn.com/business.

Do the following to enter a URL:

Step 4.   Using the IE address box, go to the **www.cnn.com** news site. Click a link on that page.

Step 5.   Use the left and right arrows to revisit previously viewed pages. As you move from one page to the next, notice how the URL in the address box changes.

> **Hint**   To enter a new URL in the address box, select the current URL and replace it with a new one. Three ways to select all the text in the address bar are to (1) press and drag your pointer over all the text, (2) click anywhere in the address box and then press **Ctrl+A**, and (3) triple-click in the address box.

Do the following to use Internet Explorer from the Windows desktop:

Step 6.   Go to the Windows desktop and click the **Internet Explorer** icon in the taskbar. The Internet Explorer window opens (see Figure 2-2).

> **Not Working?**   The instructions and figures used in this chapter are for Windows 8 and Internet Explorer 11. To find out what version of IE you have, click the **Tools** button in the upper-right corner of the Internet Explorer window and then click **About Internet Explorer**. If you're using a different version of IE, some IE features described in the chapter might work differently on your computer.

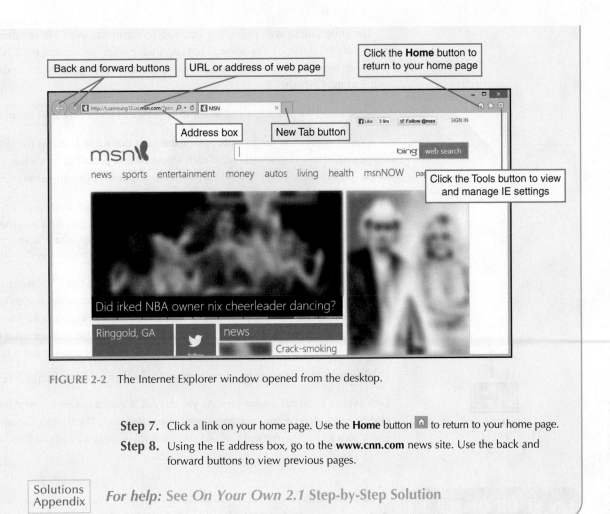

Back and forward buttons

URL or address of web page

Click the **Home** button to return to your home page

Address box

New Tab button

Click the Tools button to view and manage IE settings

FIGURE 2-2 The Internet Explorer window opened from the desktop.

Step 7. Click a link on your home page. Use the **Home** button 🏠 to return to your home page.

Step 8. Using the IE address box, go to the **www.cnn.com** news site. Use the back and forward buttons to view previous pages.

Solutions Appendix

For help: See *On Your Own 2.1* Step-by-Step Solution

Web Servers and Clients

A computer that makes web pages available to other computers is called a web server because it serves up web pages. When you first open your browser, the browser sends a URL over the Internet to a web server that holds your home page (see Figure 2-3). The web server locates the requested page and sends the page to your browser. A computer that requests and receives a web page or other content is called a client computer or just a client .

---

web server—A computer that stores and serves up web pages.

client—A computer or software that requests and receives content from other computers or other software. A browser such as Internet Explorer is an example of client software.

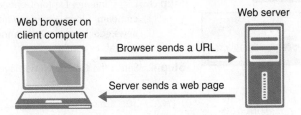

Web browser on client computer

Web server

Browser sends a URL

Server sends a web page

FIGURE 2-3 A client computer sends a URL to a web server, which returns the requested web page.

The collection of web pages that one web server makes available is called a **website** . For most websites, entering the **www** is not required. Earlier you visited the CNN news website at www.cnn.com. You could have entered only **cnn.com** in your address box, and the browser would still find the CNN site.

> **website**—All the web pages that one web server stores and makes available to the web.

Every computer on the Internet has a name, and that name is called the **domain name** . The domain name can have several parts, each separated by a period, as in www.cnn.com. The last part of the domain name (such as .com) is called the **top-level domain name** .

> **domain name**—The name of a computer on the Internet, which consists of letters and periods.
>
> **top-level domain name**—The ending of a domain name that identifies the type of organization that owns the domain name. Common top-level domain names are .com (commercial), .edu (educational), .org (nonprofit), .gov (government), .info (information), and .museum (museums).

Suppose your browser sends out the URL of www.cnn.com. The CNN server receives the request and serves up its home page (also called the default page) at the server because no specific page was requested. To request a specific page on a server, the browser adds a slash and the name of the requested page following the domain name of the server. For example, if the browser sends the URL www.cnn .com/business, the CNN server responds with the web page on the server that is named business.

Objective 2.2: Manage Multiple Web Pages in a Single IE Window

Let's explore some other news sites. As you do, you'll learn a few tricks about Internet Explorer, including how to keep several web pages open at the same time. The Internet Explorer window displays a web page in a tab on the window, and you can have as many tabs as you like—one for each page.

WATCH

OBJECTIVE 2.2
VIDEO

ON YOUR OWN 2.2

Manage Multiple Web Pages Using IE Tabs

WATCH

OBJECTIVE 2.2
VIDEO

Let's see how you can have several web pages open at the same time. We begin by using IE from the Start screen:

Step 1. Using Internet Explorer opened from your Start screen, navigate to the CNN news site at **cnn.com**. Open a new tab and go to **news.yahoo.com**. Open a third tab and go to **news.google.com**. Open a fourth tab and go to **foxnews.com**. Practice moving from one tab to another.

Step 2. Select the **Google News** page and then close that tab.

> **Hint** To open a new tab using IE in the Windows 8 interface, right-click anywhere on the current page except on a graphic. In the black pane that appears at the bottom of the screen, click the new tab button ⊕ in the upper-right corner.

Do the following to manage multiple web pages in IE using the desktop:

Step 3. Using Internet Explorer opened on the desktop, navigate to the CNN news site at **cnn.com**. Open a new tab and go to **news.yahoo.com**. Open a third tab and go to **news.google.com**. Open a fourth tab and go to **foxnews.com**. Practice moving from one tab to another.

Step 4. Select the **Google News** page and then close that tab.

Solutions
Appendix

For help: See *On Your Own 2.2* Step-by-Step Solution

WATCH

OBJECTIVE 2.3
VIDEO

Objective 2.3: Customize Internet Explorer

During an Internet Explorer session, you can use the back and forward buttons to step through pages you just visited. If you want to save a web page address so that you can easily return to it even after you've closed Internet Explorer or restarted your computer, add the web page address to your **Favorites** . You can also use the **Internet Options dialog box** to customize IE, including changing the home page that IE displays when you first launch the browser.

WATCH

CHAPTER 2
DIVING DEEPER
VIDEO

> **Favorites**—A list of web page addresses saved by Internet Explorer so you can easily revisit the page.
>
> **Internet Options dialog box**—A box used to customize Internet Explorer. To open it, click the **Tools** icon ⚙ in the upper-right corner of the IE window and then click **Internet options**.

ON YOUR OWN 2.3

WATCH

OBJECTIVE 2.3
VIDEO

Solutions
Appendix

Save a Favorite and Change Your IE Home Page

To add a web page to your Favorites using IE in the Windows 8 interface, click the Favorites button ⭐ in the black pane at the bottom of the page and then click the **Add to favorites** button ⭐ that appears on the black pane. To customize Internet Explorer, do the following:

Step 1. Using Internet Explorer opened from the Start screen, navigate to **news.google.com**. Add the page to your Favorites list. Revisit the Google News site by using your Favorites list.

Step 2. Using Internet Explorer opened from the desktop, add **foxnews.com** to your Favorites list. Revisit the site by using your Favorites list.

Step 3. Change your home page to your favorite website. For example, if you want to get the latest sports scores each time you open Internet Explorer, change your home page to **espn.go.com**. When you change your home page using the Internet Options box in IE on the desktop, the change also applies to IE opened from the Start screen.

For help: See *On Your Own 2.3* Step-by-Step Solution

Searching for Other Information on the Web

Next, let's look at how to use Google.com, which is a search engine, as well as explore some other popular websites.

WATCH

OBJECTIVE 2.4
VIDEO

Objective 2.4: Use a Search Engine to Find Information on the Web

The easiest way to find information on the web is to use a **search engine** . Google.com and Bing.com are the two most popular search engines, with Google being more popular than Bing.

> **search engine**—A website that finds information on the web.

To make it easier for you to use a search engine, Internet Explorer allows you to enter your **search string** in the IE address box. Unless you change your Internet Explorer settings, it uses the Bing search engine to search for the information.

> **search string**—The text you type in the address box of a browser or in the search box of a search engine website such as Google or Bing that is used by the search engine to find information on the web. The text is not case sensitive, meaning that you can type either lowercase or uppercase letters and get the same results.

ON YOUR OWN 2.4

WATCH

OBJECTIVE 2.4
VIDEO

Use a Search Engine

Two ways to use a search engine are to first go to the search site and then use its search box or to enter your search string directly in the Internet Explorer address box. Use both methods to find information on the web:

Step 1. Using Internet Explorer opened either from the Start screen or the desktop, go to **google.com**. To find out the weather in Seattle, Washington, enter **seattle weather** as the search string in the search box. If the instant search feature of Google is on, results appear even as you type. (This feature is called *autosuggest* or *autocomplete*.) Use this autosuggest feature of Google to select **seattle weather** to get the weather in Seattle, Washington.

Step 2. How many results are in the **hit list** that appears? Drill down to one of these web pages found by Google.

> **hit list**—The list of web pages found by a search engine.

Step 3. Now practice searching using the Internet Explorer address box. Search for how to change the oil in a car. Which search engine is the default search engine used by the IE address box?

Solutions
Appendix

For help: See *On Your Own 2.4 Step-by-Step Solution*

As you use a search engine, you'll notice a few sites that tend to reappear frequently depending on the type of information you're searching:

> **wikipedia.org** contains more than 3 million articles written by volunteers around the world on all kinds of topics. It's the most popular **wiki** on the web. Wikipedia gets its name from *wiki* and *encyclopedia*.

> **wiki**—A website where many people freely contribute and collaborate about a topic of common interest.

> **ask.com, about.com, ehow.com, wisegeek.com**, and **howstuffworks.com** frequently pop up when you search on how to do something, how something works, or what something is.
> **eBay.com** and **craigslist.org** are the two most popular sites individuals use to sell goods and services online.
> **facebook.com** is a social networking site where you can keep up with your friends and let them know what is happening in your life. Google and Facebook are the two most popular websites on the web. Facebook is often used by businesses, public figures, and organizations. When you search on a person's name, his or her Facebook page might appear in the hit list.

social networking—Interaction between people who share a common interest. Facebook.com and twitter.com are the two most popular social networking websites.

> **youtube.com** is the most popular website for sharing videos.
> **maps.google.com** and **mapquest.com** are the two most popular sites for finding driving directions and maps.
> **wordpress.com** and **blogger.com** are popular blogging websites where you can post a blog .

blog—Short for *weblog*; an online diary or journal used to express your thoughts, opinions, and activities.

WATCH

OBJECTIVE 2.5
VIDEO

Objective 2.5: Perform Google Advanced Searches and Find Images, Videos, Directions, and Translations

Google, Bing, and other search engines present web page hits to you ordered according to how well the search engine determines the page matches your search string. This order is called the page rank . In addition, a website can pay Google to put its pages first. These paid-for hits are called **sponsored links** . In Google, sponsored links are marked with the word *Ads* (see Figure 2-4).

page rank—The order of importance assigned to a list of pages found in a search by a search engine.

sponsored link—A link displayed at the top of a search engine hit list because the owner of the web page has paid for this favored position. Sponsored links provide income for Google and other search engine sites.

Sponsored links are listed first in search results

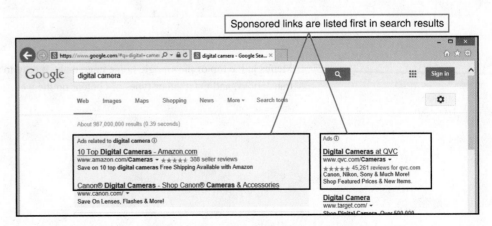

FIGURE 2-4 Sponsored links are listed at the top of the hit list or in the right column.

A search engine can find and list millions of hits. Fortunately, you're likely to find what you're looking for on the first page or two of hits because of how well the search engine orders the results. However, you can limit the results or number of hits, called the **hit count**, to help zero in on what you need by performing more advanced searches.

> hit count—The number of hits resulting from a search by a search engine.

The goals of using advanced searches are to reduce the hit count and to cause the most important hits to appear near the top in page rank. Advanced searches can be formed to

> Limit the search by how recently the page was last updated
> Search for the exact words you typed or similar words or exclude certain words
> Limit the country where the web page is stored
> Limit the search to specific websites

Both Google and Bing offer tips and tutorials for building advanced searches. On the Google page that displays the results of a search, click the tools icon ✿ and then click **Advanced search** to find these tools.

ON YOUR OWN 2.5

WATCH

OBJECTIVE 2.5 VIDEO

Perform Google Advanced Searches

Use the Google search engine to perform the following advanced searches:

Step 1. Search for information on how a search engine works, limiting the search only to the **wikipedia.org** site.

> Hint Use the **site:** option in the search string.

Step 2. Limit the results of the preceding search to content updated in the past 24 hours.

Step 3. Try a new search for an exact group of words. To search for the exact group of words, use double quotation marks around words in the search string. Search for the exact string like this: **"who invented google earth"**.

Step 4. Try a search where you want to exclude a word from the results. To not include a word in a search, put a minus sign in front of the word. Search for an apartment near **Emory University** but eliminate **luxury** apartments from your search.

Solutions Appendix

For help: See *On Your Own 2.5* Step-by-Step Solution

Menus at the top of the Google home page make it easy to find images, maps, videos, directions, translations, and many other types of content on the web.

ON YOUR OWN 2.6

WATCH

OBJECTIVE 2.5
VIDEO

Find Images, Videos, Directions, and Translations

Let's use the menus on the Google search page to find images, videos, driving directions, and translations:

Step 1. Find images about Hurricane Sandy.

Step 2. Find videos showing you how to make a homemade pizza.

Step 3. Go to **maps.google.com** and find driving directions from Baltimore, Maryland, to Newark, New Jersey. How many miles is the trip?

Step 4. Go to **translate.google.com** and find a translation into Spanish for the text, "Good morning. Welcome to my home."

Solutions
Appendix

For help: See *On Your Own 2.6 Step-by-Step Solution*

WATCH

OBJECTIVE 2.6
VIDEO

Using Applications and Storing Data in the Cloud

Have you heard of cloud computing? In this section, we'll explore cloud computing and learn how to use OneDrive, which is free online data storage in the cloud.

Objective 2.6: Describe Cloud Computing and Download Files from the Web

In the last chapter, you learned how to install and use an application on your computer. You also learned to store data files to local storage devices such as a USB flash drive or the hard drive. With cloud computing , the application is installed on a computer somewhere on the Internet and the data files are also stored on a remote computer on the Internet (in the cloud). Windows 8 has many features that make cloud computing easy to use.

> **cloud computing**—Applications and data stored on remote computers on the Internet. Most cloud applications and data are accessed using a browser.

The advantages of cloud computing are that you don't need to buy the application, and the data is always available from whatever computer you use as long as that computer has access to the Internet. It's also easy to share the data with other users on the Internet. Here are some popular websites that provide free cloud computing, including online apps and online data storage:

> **Flickr.com** lets you store and share photos. You can use the applications on the site to crop, fix, and edit the photos; attach notes and tags to them; and print them.

> **Shutterfly.com** is a popular site to store and share photos. Using the applications on the site, you can make cards, stationery, calendars, and even books with your photos.

> Google Drive at **drive.google.com** lets you upload any type file to its free file storage. Using personal software applications on the site, you can edit documents, worksheets, presentations, drawings, and forms. You can also work with a team as several people contribute to a work.

> **Live.com** (called Windows Live) is similar to Google Drive. It includes **OneDrive** , a storage location for files, and scaled-down versions of Microsoft Office personal applications (including Word, Excel, PowerPoint, and OneNote).

Tip   *OneDrive used to be called SkyDrive.*

> **OneDrive**—A personal storage location on the live.com website where you can upload and save any type of file.

Another free cloud storage site is the companion website that accompanies this book. The site contains several resources to help you in this class, including some sample files used in activities and projects in this book. If you have a subscription to MyITLab, you can also find these and other resources in MyITLab on the web.

WATCH

OBJECTIVE 2.6 VIDEO

ON YOUR OWN 2.7

Download Files from the Web

The sample files that we use throughout this book are stored on the book's companion website in a **compressed folder**.

> **compressed folder**—A folder that is compressed to conserve space on a storage device and to make download and upload times shorter.

Do the following to download the sample_files folder from the companion website:

Step 1. Using Internet Explorer, go to **www.pearsonhighered.com/jump**. On that page (see Figure 2-5), click **Companion Website** on the left side of the page.

Step 2. Download the sample_files compressed folder to your computer.

Step 3. Uncompress the folder and store its contents on your USB flash drive. What is the file name and file extension of the compressed folder?

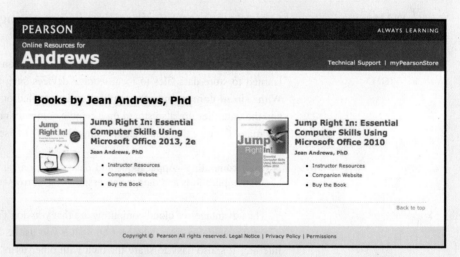

FIGURE 2-5 The companion website for this book offers sample files, which we use in activities and projects in the book.

> **Tip** You can create your own compressed folder. To do so, right-click in the white space of the right pane of File Explorer, point to **New** in the shortcut menu, and click **Compressed (zipped) Folder**. You can then name the compressed folder.

Solutions Appendix

For help: See *On Your Own 2.7* Step-by-Step Solution

WATCH

OBJECTIVE 2.7
VIDEO

Objective 2.7: Use OneDrive to Store Your Data

OneDrive, available on live.com, is a quick and easy way to store a file in the cloud and share it with others. For example, some instructors prefer that you send your homework to them by posting your file on your OneDrive and giving your instructor access to your OneDrive. You can access your OneDrive using Internet Explorer. Later in the chapter, you will learn how to sign on to a Windows 8 computer using your Microsoft account. When you do that, you can access your OneDrive using File Explorer or the SkyDrive app on the Windows 8 Start screen. (OneDrive used to be called SkyDrive, and the Windows 8 app is still called the SkyDrive app.)

ON YOUR OWN 2.8

WATCH

OBJECTIVE 2.7
VIDEO

Set Up and Use OneDrive

Your OneDrive is automatically created when you sign up for a Microsoft account, also called a Windows Live ID, on the live.com website. You can use your own email address, or, if you would rather, you can create a new email address when you set up your Microsoft account.

Do the following to set up your personal OneDrive and post a photo to it:

Step 1. If you don't already have a Microsoft account, go to **signup.live.com** and create one. After you've created the account, sign out and then sign back in to get access to your account online resources including Outlook, People, Calendar, and OneDrive. What folders are automatically put in your OneDrive? What is the maximum storage capacity of your OneDrive?

> Tip   *OneDrive used to be called SkyDrive. Some Microsoft apps still use the SkyDrive name.*

Step 2. Upload the document file LettertoDave from the sample_files folder on your USB flash drive to the Documents folder on your OneDrive.

Step 3. Your instructor might want access to your OneDrive so you can post homework files there. If requested by your instructor, share the Documents folder on your OneDrive with your instructor using his or her email address. Have Windows Live send a notification to your instructor that contains a link to the file in your OneDrive Documents folder.

Step 4. Before you step away from a computer, be sure to sign out of your Microsoft account so the next user doesn't have access to your account. Sign out of the Microsoft account now.

Solutions
Appendix

For help: See *On Your Own 2.8* Step-by-Step Solution

Conducting Business Safely on the Web

Using the web to do business is convenient and can save you time. In this section, we'll explore how to stay safe while doing business on the web and how to purchase, download, and install software from the web.

WATCH

OBJECTIVE 2.8
VIDEO

Objective 2.8: Apply Several Methods to Stay Safe while Doing Business on the Web

The web is a great tool, but it can also be dangerous. Stay safe as you do business on the web by following these safety precautions:

> **Do business only with trustworthy sites.** Never give personal information such as your date of birth or credit card information to a website unless you trust that site. If you're not

sure if the site is trustworthy, you can use Google to search for reviews about the site. For example, to find reviews about www.buy.com, enter **www.buy.com reviews** in the Google search box and press **Enter**.

> **Download free data or software only from sites you trust.** Some sites offer free music, videos, games, or other software just so they can install **adware** or other malicious software on your computer during the download. Before you download anything from a website, read some reviews about the site.

---

adware—Software that runs on your computer to display pop-up ads when you surf the web. Adware can be annoying and slow down a system.

> **Use only secured transmissions.** Before you enter personal information on a website, make sure the site is using **HTTPS** to protect your information when it is in route from your computer to the web server.

HTTPS—A group of rules (called a protocol) used to transfer data securely to a website. The data is coded (said to be encrypted) so that it cannot be read if intercepted by thieves. HTTPS stands for Hypertext Transfer Protocol Secure.

You know the data is protected if you see the padlock to the right of the address bar. Also notice the http:// that usually appears to the left of the web page address is written as https:// (see Figure 2-6).

FIGURE 2-6 Notice the https:// and the padlock, which indicate your personal data is protected during transmission to this secured website.

Tip To protect your online accounts, use a different password for each online account.

> **Use a strong password for each online account.** Before you can pay a bill or manage your bank account online, you must set up an online account at the company's website. Most retail sites require you set up an account before you can buy online. Use a **strong password** for each online account. If you write down the password, keep it in a safe place.

---

strong password—A password that includes a mix of uppercase and lowercase letters and numbers and that is not easy to guess. Don't include the name of your pet or child or your date of birth in a password. Examples of strong passwords are UtPp93ej and dUh427Yq.

> **Keep a record of important transactions.** When you do banking or business, you need a record of the transaction in case the bank or business makes a mistake and overcharges or charges you for something you didn't buy. Many retail sites email you a receipt. Just in case

that email doesn't arrive, you might want to save or print the web page showing the transaction so you have a record of it.

Saving a web page to your USB flash drive, OneDrive, or hard drive is more convenient than printing the page. If the web page isn't too complicated, Internet Explorer saves the page to a file using the **MHT file format**, which uses the .mht file extension. (Web pages that contain a lot of graphics or other elements are saved to an HTML file and accompanying folder.)

> **MHT file format**—A file format by Microsoft used to save and email web pages. The file has an .mht file extension and is viewed using a browser. MHT stands for Multipurpose HyperText.

> **Use antispyware.** To protect against **spyware**, install and run **antispyware** software on your computer.

> **spyware**—Software running on your computer without your knowledge that is trying to steal personal information you type on your computer.
> **antispyware**—Software designed to catch and prevent spyware from stealing your personal data.

> **Use antivirus software.** Besides spyware, another type of malicious software is a **virus**. Every computer needs **antivirus software** running on it to protect it from viruses and other types of malicious software or **malware**. Windows 8 includes Windows Defender, which is antispyware and antivirus software.

> **virus**—Software running on your computer without your knowledge that is trying to corrupt Windows, applications, or your data installed on your computer.
> **antivirus software**—Software designed to discover and remove a virus that might have infected your computer. Most antivirus software also searches for spyware.
> **malware**—Any type of malicious software that intends harm, such as a virus, spyware, or adware.

> **Use PayPal, which is a convenient and safe way to pay for purchases online.** You can set up a **PayPal** account at www.paypal.com and connect the account to your bank account, debit card, or credit card. Then when you make an online purchase, you enter the PayPal account and password rather than give the retail site your banking or credit card information. Then PayPal charges the transaction to your bank account, debit card, or credit card. You can also put money directly into your PayPal account.

> **PayPal**—An online money account at paypal.com used for shopping and paying bills online without having to share your banking information with a retail or business site.

Tip Some sites, such as epinions.com, consumersearch.com, and shopping.yahoo.com, specialize in product reviews. Amazon.com also keeps reviews about its products. Many customers post videos about products on youtube.com. To find more reviews, enter the product followed by the word **reviews** in the Google search box.

> **Compare prices and read online reviews about products or services before you make a buying decision.** To compare prices, enter a product in the Google search box and click **Shopping**. You can then sort the list by price or review score (see Figure 2-7). To read some reviews about a product, click the stars assigned a product by those who reviewed it.

> **Learn to identify an authoritative source.** As you search for reviews about a product, know that some reviews might give wrong information about a product. The website of the product manufacturer is considered the **authoritative source** regarding facts about its own products (for example, product warranty, prices, and features).

Tip In Chapter 12, you'll learn even more ways to stay safe and secure your computer and its data.

> **authoritative source**—A source that is considered the final word on a matter. For example, the authoritative website about an MP3 player is the website of the manufacturer. A website that reviews the MP3 player is not considered authoritative.

Some companies offer online chat sessions to help customers with their questions. For example, as you browse the Dell.com website looking for a new computer, the *How can we help you today?* box might pop up. Click **Chat with Dell Now** to begin a **chat** session online with a customer service representative. This person can answer your questions.

> **chat**—An Internet service that allows two or more people to communicate in text online.

Choose how to sort your results here

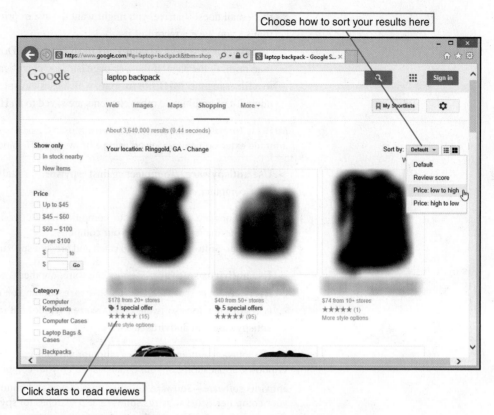

Click stars to read reviews

FIGURE 2-7   Google Shopping results show images and prices.

Print and Save a Web Page

It's a good idea to keep a record of all your online business or banking transactions. Saving a web page is convenient, but some people prefer a printed record. To practice printing and saving a web page, do the following:

WATCH

OBJECTIVE 2.8 VIDEO

Step 1. Go to **paypal.com** and print this web page. If you don't have access to a printer, display the **Print preview** of the page. A page might be disorganized when it prints, but all the important text does print. What two items print at the bottom of each page?

Step 2. Go to **wellsfargo.com** and save the page as a data file to your USB flash drive or other location given by your instructor. To verify you have saved the page, close your browser and then display the saved web page. What is the file extension of the file you saved?

Solutions Appendix

For help: See *On Your Own 2.9* Step-by-Step Solution

WATCH

OBJECTIVE 2.9 VIDEO

Objective 2.9: Use Antivirus Software to Protect Your Computer against Malware

When you're using the Internet, it's important to make sure that your computer is running antivirus software so it is protected against malware.

ON YOUR OWN 2.10

WATCH

OBJECTIVE 2.9
VIDEO

Check Windows Defender Settings

Windows 8 automatically runs Windows Defender in the background to check for viruses and spyware. To make sure Defender is running, open the **Windows Defender** app, which opens on the Windows desktop. Make sure that real-time protection is turned on (see Figure 2-8). If you made a change, be sure to save it before you close the window. Which tab in the Windows Defender window controls real-time protection?

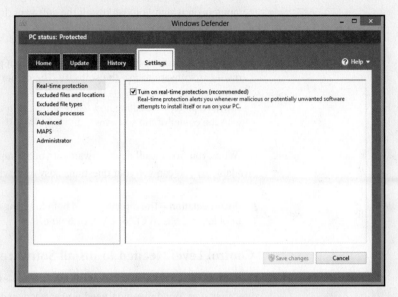

FIGURE 2-8 Windows Defender is set to run in the background to protect the computer against malware.

Solutions Appendix

For help: See *On Your Own 2.10* Step-by-Step Solution

WATCH

OBJECTIVE 2.10
VIDEO

Objective 2.10: Download and Install Software from the Web

Unless you're using software in the cloud, the software must be installed on your computer before you can use it. Windows 8 includes several applications, such as Internet Explorer, and you can install other applications, such as Microsoft Office 2013. Let's find out how.

Commercial Software, Freeware, or Shareware

Software can come on CD or DVD in a box (see Figure 2-9), you can use Internet Explorer to download software from the web, or you can use the Store app on the Start screen to download apps from the Windows Store. Software can be purchased (called commercial software), can be free (called **freeware**), or might be offered on a trial basis without cost or for a small donation (called **shareware**). Some manufacturers also allow you to rent or subscribe to software for an agreed-to time period.

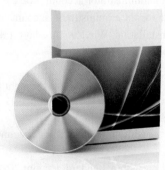

FIGURE 2-9 Software purchased on CD or DVD is called boxed software.

> **freeware**—Software that is free.
> **shareware**—(1) Software that is offered free on a trial basis. If you decide to continue using the software after the trial period is over, you must purchase the software. (2) Software provided by the owner for a small donation.

Freeware and shareware are usually downloaded from a website or from the Windows Store. Shareware that is downloaded on a trial basis locks itself when the trial period expires so that you can't use it. After you purchase the software, it unlocks.

Software License Agreement and Software Documentation

When you purchase software, you don't actually own the software. You own a license to use the software according to the agreed-to terms of use. The first time you use the software, you are asked to accept the terms of the **Software License Agreement** . This agreement includes the number of computers on which you can install the software. Installing the software on more computers than you have agreed to is called **software piracy** .

> **Software License Agreement**—An agreement that gives permission for someone other than the owner of software to use the software. The owner of the software retains the copyright, which is the right to copy it.
> **software piracy**—Installing and using software in a way that violates the agreement you made with the owner of the software.

When you first install new software on your computer, make sure you have the **documentation** available so you can get your questions answered when learning to use the software.

> **documentation**—The directions and help for using a product, which can be provided in a printed booklet, in a file on CD or DVD, or online.

Control Level Needed to Install Software

To protect the computer, Windows doesn't allow every user to install software. Recall that when you first start Windows, you need a user account to sign on. The account is assigned a level of control, which determines what power the user has over the computer. The two most common levels of control are

> An **administrator account** , which has full control over the computer.
> A **standard account** , which has less control and can't install software.

> **administrator account**—A type of Windows user account that has the most control over a computer.
> **standard account**—A type of Windows user account that has limited control over a computer.

If Windows skips the sign-on screen when you first start Windows, taking you directly to the Start screen, the computer has only one user account set up, and that account is an administrator account. In this situation, you have full control of the computer.

If you sign on to Windows using an account that is not an administrator account, you can still install software. However, you must provide the password for an administrator account at the beginning of the installation process. When you begin the installation, Windows displays a **User Account Control (UAC) dialog box** , such as the two shown in Figure 2-10:

> **User Account Control (UAC) dialog box**—A dialog box used to verify the user has the right to perform a Windows operation and gives the user the opportunity to stop the operation.

> The box on the left appears when the user is logged on with an administrator account. To continue the installation, click **Yes**.
> The box on the right appears when the user is logged on with a standard account. To continue, type the password for an administrator account and click **Yes**.

Tip *Computers in school labs might be configured so that you can't install software and you will not be able to complete the following activity. In this situation, watch the Objective 2.10 Video to see the installation.*

FIGURE 2-10   The User Account Control dialog box protects against unauthorized software installations (a) when the user is an administrator and (b) when the user is a standard user.

ON YOUR OWN 2.11

WATCH

OBJECTIVE 2.10
VIDEO

Install and Use an App from the Windows Store

Windows 8 can find and download software (apps) from the Windows Store. Many of these apps are free. Do the following to install and use a free app from the Windows Store:

Step 1. From the Start screen, open the **Store** app and search for a free app. You can use the scrollbar at the bottom of your window to scroll through the categories of apps, or you can use the Search charm to search for a particular app.

Step 2. Install and use the app. If you're not already signed in with a Microsoft account, you must enter your account and password before the app installs.

Solutions
Appendix

For help: See *On Your Own 2.11* Step-by-Step Solution

WATCH

OBJECTIVE 2.11
VIDEO

Objective 2.11: Switch Windows 8 Sign On to a Microsoft Account

In this chapter, you've learned how to use OneDrive and the Windows Store. Both tools require you have a Microsoft account and provide the email address and password to the account. As you work with Windows 8 and the Internet, it's convenient to sign in to Windows 8 using your Microsoft account so that Windows can provide the account information any time it is requested by a website or app.

Switch Windows 8 Sign On to Your Microsoft Account and Use Your OneDrive

WATCH

OBJECTIVE 2.11 VIDEO

You can switch your local user account to a Microsoft account so that you can sign in to Windows using your Microsoft account email address and password.

> **Tip** When switching Windows 8 sign in to a Microsoft account, Windows gives you the opportunity to designate the computer as a trusted device so that you can change the account settings on the computer without proving you are the owner of the account. Don't designate a computer as a trusted device unless you own the computer or trust all its users. You don't want others to get access to your Microsoft account by way of a trusted device.

Do the following:

Step 1. From the Start screen, open the **Settings** charm and click **Change PC settings**. Then click **Accounts**. If necessary, click **Your account**. In the right pane, click **Connect to a Microsoft account** (see Figure 2-11). Follow directions on screen to make the switch. When asked if you want to receive a code to make the computer a trusted device, skip this step by clicking **I can't do this right now**.

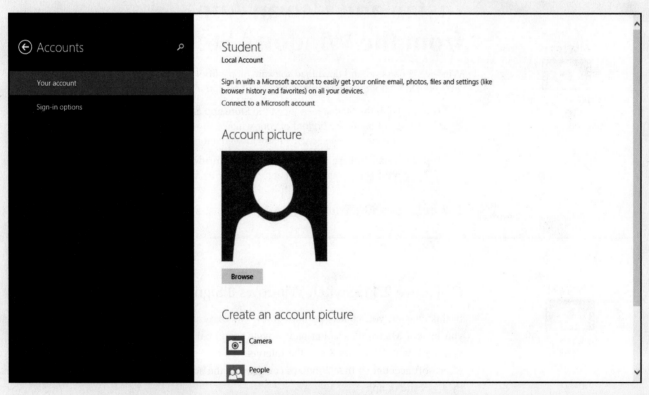

FIGURE 2-11   Switch Windows 8 from a local account to a Microsoft account.

Step 2. Sign off Windows 8 and sign back on. What are the steps to signing off Windows 8? What information about your Microsoft account appears on the sign-on screen? What information is required to sign in?

Step 3. Now that you have signed on to the computer with a Microsoft account, you can conveniently access your OneDrive using the SkyDrive app on the Start screen and File Explorer on the desktop. Open the SkyDrive app on the Start screen and verify you can see the LettertoDave file stored in your OneDrive Documents folder.

Step 4. Use SkyDrive in the navigation pane of File Explorer to view the contents of your OneDrive in the right pane of File Explorer. Use File Explorer to upload the GuessWho photo from the sample_files folder on your USB flash drive to the Pictures folder on your OneDrive. Use the SkyDrive app to verify you can see the GuessWho photo on your OneDrive.

Solutions Appendix

For help: See *On Your Own 2.12* Step-by-Step Solution

Summary

Getting News on the Web

> The Internet is a network of computers connected globally. Some of these computers make web pages available to other computers and are collectively called the World Wide Web or the web.

> A web page is built using HTML and is called a hypertext document.

> Internet Explorer is a browser that is part of Windows and is used to explore the Internet. IE can work in the Windows 8 interface or from the desktop.

> Every web page available on the Internet has an address called its URL.

> A client computer requests and receives content from a server. A web server provides web pages to clients.

> Every computer on the Internet has a domain name assigned to it. The ending of the domain name, called the top-level domain name, identifies the type organization that owns the domain name.

> You can use the tabs in an Internet Explorer window to keep several web pages open so you can easily move back and forth between them.

> Save a web page address (URL) to your Favorites to easily revisit it later.

> You can use the Internet Options dialog box to change Internet Explorer's default settings including the home page.

Searching for Other Information on the Web

> Search engines such as Google and Bing are used to find information on the web.

> A search string is entered into a search box on a search website to locate information. Websites that match the search are called a hit list and are displayed on a results page. The list is ordered by how closely the site content matches the search string.

> Wikipedia.org is the most popular wiki on the web. Sites that explain how things work include ask.com, about.com, ehow.com, wisegeek.com, and howstuffworks.com. Two popular sites for finding driving directions and maps are maps.google.com and mapquest.com.

> Facebook.com is the most popular social networking site on the web. Youtube.com is the most popular site for distributing videos. A blog site such as wordpress.com and blogger .com is used for personal journaling that you can share with family and friends.

> One measure of performance for a search engine is how well it orders the pages in the hit list so that close matches to your search appear at the top of the list. This order is called the page rank.

> Use advanced searches with a search engine to reduce the number of results and zero in on your search. Advanced searches can limit the search to a certain website, limit the age of the content, search for exact words, and exclude words.

> You can use a search engine to find images, videos, directions, maps, translations, and many other types of content on the web.

Using Applications and Storing Data in the Cloud

> Cloud computing lets you use applications and storage space made available by remote computers on the web.

> Sites that provide cloud computing include flickr.com (for storing and editing photos), shutterfly.com (for storing photos and making documents with them), and drive.google .com and live.com (for storing and editing documents, worksheets, presentations, drawings, and forms).

> You can use OneDrive on live.com to store and share data files.

> Internet Explorer and some Windows apps on the Start screen can be used to access applications and download and upload files on the web.

Conducting Business Safely on the Web

> Follow these precautions to ensure you're safe when conducting business on the web:

>> Do business only with trustworthy sites. Read online reviews of a site if you are not familiar with it.

>> Download free software, music, videos, and other data only from sites you trust because some downloads might include adware and other malware.

>> Use an HTTPS secure transmission to transmit your personal data to a web server and use strong passwords to protect your online accounts.

>> Run antispyware and antivirus software on your computer to protect it and your identity from malware and thieves. Windows Defender is antispyware and antivirus software included in Windows 8.

>> Use shopping features of a search engine and online reviews to find the best products and prices online.

>> Keep a record of every online purchase in the event the site overcharges you or makes other mistakes. The record can be a web page saved to your local storage device, a printed web page, or a receipt sent to you by email.

> When Internet Explorer saves a not-too-complicated web page, it uses the MHT file format.

> Freeware, shareware, and commercial software can be downloaded from the web or installed from the Windows Store. The Windows Store is new to Windows 8.

> Two levels of control assigned to Windows user accounts are the administrator account and standard account. The administrator account has the most control of a computer.

> The User Account Control (UAC) dialog box is used to verify the user has the right to perform an operation or gives permission to perform it.

> You can configure Windows 8 to sign in using your Microsoft account so that Windows can provide the account information any time it is requested by a website or app. When you use a Microsoft account to sign in to Windows, your OneDrive can be accessed using the SkyDrive app and the SkyDrive group in File Explorer.

CHAPTER MASTERY PROJECT

Now it's time to find out how well you've mastered the content in this chapter. If you can do all the steps in this mastery project without looking back at the chapter details and can answer all the review questions following this project, you've mastered this chapter. If you can complete the project by finding answers on the web, you've proven that you understand its power and value.

> **Hint** All the key terms in the chapter are used in this mastery project or in the review questions. If you encounter a word you don't know such as *wiki*, enter **define: wiki** in the Internet Explorer address box. The word is defined in the chapter, but it's more fun to find the definition on the web.

If you find you need a lot of help doing the project and you have not yet read the chapter or done the activities, drop back and start at the beginning of the chapter, watch the videos, review the step-by-step solutions as you work through the On Your Own activities, and then return to this project.

> **Tip** If you need help completing this part of the mastery project, review the "Searching for Other Information on the Web" section in the chapter.

Follow these steps to use Google.com to search for information on the web:

Step 1. Open Internet Explorer and go to **Google.com**. Search for information on how the Internet works, limiting the search only to the Wikipedia.org site. What is your search string? Limit the hit count by excluding the word "architecture" from the search results. What is your search string?

Step 2. Limit the hit count of the preceding search to content updated in the past 24 hours. Next, remove the time limitation from the search.

Step 3. Use Google Translate to translate into Spanish: "The food was delicious. Thank you." Listen to the translation.

Step 4. Use the Internet Options dialog box to change your home page to **news.google.com**.

> Tip If you need help completing this part of the mastery project, review the "Using Applications and Storing Data in the Cloud" section in the chapter.

Do the following to download the sample_files folder from this book's companion website:

Step 5. Use Internet Explorer to go to **www.pearsonhighered.com/jump** and follow links to download the sample_files.zip folder. Store the compressed folder on your USB flash drive and uncompress the folder. Take a look at the files in the folder.

If you have not already set up a Microsoft account with OneDrive, follow these steps:

Step 6. Using the live.com site, create a Microsoft account using your email address. If you don't have an email address, get one using the live.com site.

Step 7. Using your browser, upload the **AndreaInformation** document file in the sample_files folder on your USB flash drive to the Documents folder on your OneDrive. Your instructor might want access to your OneDrive so you can post homework files there. If requested by your instructor, use the **Sharing** command to share the Documents folder on your OneDrive with your instructor using his or her email address. When you do so, an email message is sent to your instructor with a link to the folder.

Step 8. You can have OneDrive send a new email message to your instructor at any time to inform him or her a new file has been posted to your Documents folder. Post any file to your Documents folder and send a second email message to your instructor with a link to the file.

Step 9. To see a list of all people with whom you have shared a OneDrive folder, view the details pane for the folder. First, open the folder and then click the **Show or hide the details pane** icon. You might have to then click Sharing.

Step 10. To have OneDrive provide you a link to any folder on your OneDrive, first select the folder, share the folder, and then, on the Share page, click **Get a link**.

Step 11. Return to **live.com** and save the web page to your Favorites in IE.

> Tip If you need help completing this part of the mastery project, review the "Conducting Business Safely on the Web" section in the chapter.

Windows Defender is embedded in Windows 8 to provide real-time protection against spyware, viruses, and other malware. Follow this step to verify Windows Defender settings:

Step 12. Open the Windows Defender app. Make sure real-time protection is turned on. Then close the app.

Follow these steps to practice shopping online:

Step 13. Use the Google Shopping feature to search for a GPS navigator or some other electronic device you would like to buy. Did sponsored links appear at the top of the search results? Change the page rank to sort the products first by relevance and then by price from low to high. Search for product comparisons. Besides price, what other information is provided to help you decide on a product? Select a device to review. Use Google.com to find images of the device.

Step 14. Open a new Internet Explorer tab and find online reviews about the selected device. Find a video review of the device. Did you find a site that you would consider an authoritative source about the device?

Step 15. Open a third tab in IE to compare prices for the selected device. Select a retail site that offers the device at a reasonable price. Do you see a way to open a chat session on the site so you can ask questions about the product or the purchase?

Step 16. Open a fourth tab and find online reviews about this retail site so that you can decide whether the site is trustworthy. Close this fourth tab.

Follow this step to print a web page and save the page to a data file:

Step 17. Visit **target.com** and click **my account**. Print this web page. If you don't have access to a printer, display the preview of the printed page. Save the page to your USB flash drive, hard drive, or another location given by your instructor. What is the name and file extension of the file? Close your browser and then open the saved file.

Do the following to install a free app from the Windows Store and to switch your local account to your Microsoft account on your Windows 8 computer:

Step 18. Search the Windows Store for a free app and install it. Then use the app. Does the app provide documentation to help you learn to use it?

Step 19. Use the Settings charm to set up your Microsoft account on your computer. Sign off Windows and then sign back onto Windows using your Microsoft account.

Step 20. Use the SkyDrive app on the Start screen to view the file(s) in your Documents folder on your OneDrive. Use File Explorer to upload the Wendy photo file in the sample_files folder on your USB flash drive to the Pictures folder on your OneDrive. (Note that OneDrive is called SkyDrive in File Explorer.)

Review Questions

Answer these questions to assess your skills and knowledge of the content covered in the chapter. Your instructor can provide you with the correct answers when you're ready to check your work.

1. What is the most important skill you need to know when learning to use computers?

2. All the computers connected together in the world's largest global network are called the _____. Some of these computers provide web pages for distribution and these computers and web pages are called the _____. All the web pages stored on one of these computers are called a(n) _____.

3. A trucking company is to the roads system as the World Wide Web is to the _____. A cargo package is to a trucking company as a _____ is to the World Wide Web.

4. A web page is written using what set of rules?

5. A web page is stored and served up by a _____ to a _____ computer.

6. Internet Explorer is included in Windows 8. List the steps to find out which version of Internet Explorer you're using.

7. What is the full URL used in the Internet Options dialog box to make the Google search site the home page for Internet Explorer? What is the domain name for this site? What is the top-level domain name for this site?

8. When you click a link on a web page, what does your browser do?

9. What type of organization uses a URL that ends in .org? In .com?

10. Using Internet Explorer in the Windows 8 interface, how can you display a second web page in your browser without closing the first page?

11. Using IE from the desktop, how can you display a second web page in your browser without closing the first page?

12. What type of website is the best choice to use if you want to keep a journal of your six-week trip to Europe so that your friends and family can read about your adventures each day?

13. Which box in the Internet Explorer window can be used to receive a search string that is then used by a search engine to find information on the web?

14. What site is the most popular wiki on the web?

15. If you wanted to let your friends know what you were doing each day in a brief sentence or two, would you most likely use a blogging site or a social networking site, such as Facebook?

16. What is the purpose of the **site:** text added to a search string?

17. Search for a list of the top smartest dog breeds but exclude hits that include the word "poodle." What is your search string?

18. What two types of services do computers in the cloud offer?

19. What is the name of the personal cloud computing service offered by Windows Live? Offered by Google?

20. What are three programs you can use to post files to your OneDrive using Windows 8 when you sign on with a Microsoft account?

21. When comparing online reviews about a product you're considering to buy, what site is most likely to offer a video review? What are the two most popular sites used to find driving directions?

22. For most retail sites, what must you do before you can purchase from the site?

23. If the web page is not too complicated, what file format does Internet Explorer use to save the web page?

24. After downloading free music from the web, you notice pop-up ads appear as you surf the web. What type of malware got installed when you downloaded the music? In the future, how can you find out whether a website is safe to use?

25. When you purchase a license to use software, do you really own the software? Where are your specific rights to the software described? What term is used to describe using software in a way that violates the rights of those who actually own the software?

26. Retail sites ask for personal information such as your email address and credit card number, and this information needs to be protected while in transit. What two items can you look for in the Internet Explorer address box to verify the information is protected in transit? What security protocol is used to transmit the data?

27. Which website can you use to pay for an online purchase so you don't have to reveal financial information to a retail site?

28. Why is it important to print or save a record of an online transaction?

29. Before you can pay a bill online to a utility company, what must you do first?

30. Is sally1972 a strong password to use for your online banking account? Why or why not?

31. Installing software requires administrator rights. If you're not signed on to Windows using an administrator account, what must you enter before you can complete the installation? What dialog box is used to enter this information?

Becoming an Independent Learner

Answer the following questions about becoming an independent learner:

1. To teach yourself to use Internet Explorer, do you think it's best to rely on the chapter or on Windows Help and Support when you need answers?

2. To teach yourself to construct advanced Google searches, do you think it's best to rely on the chapter or on the help features available on the Google website?

3. The most important skill learned in this chapter is how to teach yourself a computer skill. Rate yourself at Level A through E on how well you are doing with this skill. What is your level?

   - Level A: I was able to successfully complete the Chapter Mastery Project with the help of only a few of the On Your Own activities in the chapter.

   - Level B: I completed all the On Your Own activities and the Chapter Mastery Project without referring to any of the solutions in the Step-by-Step Solutions Appendix.

- Level C: I completed all the On Your Own activities and the Chapter Mastery Project by using just a few of the solutions in the Step-by-Step Solutions Appendix.
- Level D: I completed all the On Your Own activities and the Chapter Mastery Project by using many of the solutions in the Step-by-Step Solutions Appendix.
- Level E: I completed all the On Your Own activities and the Chapter Mastery Project and had to use all of the solutions in the Step-by-Step Solutions Appendix.

To continue toward the goal of teaching yourself computer skills, if you're not at Level A, try to move up one level on how you learn in Chapter 3.

Projects to Help You

Now that you've mastered the material in this chapter, you are ready to tackle the three projects focused on your career, personal, or academic goals. Depending on your own interests, you might choose to complete any or all of these projects to help you achieve your goals.

Project 1: Using a Google Drive in Your Professional Career

Google Project I was just hired by a start-up marketing company, and they're allowing me to work from home. I need to set up a Google Drive that I can use to share files with coworkers.

WATCH

CHAPTER 2
GOOGLE DRIVE
VIDEO

Google.com offers a Google Drive, which is cloud storage assigned to you when you set up a free Google account. A free Google Drive has 15 GB of storage, and you can purchase additional storage. Files you store on your Google Drive can be shared with others that also have a Google account. If you download software to your computer, you can sync files on your Google Drive with files on your computer.

Follow these steps to set up and use a Google Drive:

Step 1. If you don't already have a Google account, go to **google.com** and set one up using a valid email address. To get started, click **Sign in** and then click **Create an account**.

Step 2. Create a new folder on your Google Drive named **MyComputerClass**.

Step 3. Take a snip of your screen showing your Google Drive with the MyComputerClass folder in it. Name the snip file **MyGoogleDriveSnip** and save it to your USB flash drive.

Step 4. Upload the file to your MyComputerClass folder on your Google Drive.

Step 5. Share or send the snip file to your instructor using one of these methods or another method given by your instructor:

- If your instructor has a Google account, you can share the file on your Google Drive with your instructor. (To share the file on your Google Drive, first select the file, click the Share icon, and then enter the email address of your instructor in the Invite people box. Finally, click **Share & save**.)
- Upload the file from your USB flash drive to the Documents folder of your OneDrive.
- If you're using MyITLab in this class, you can upload the file to the Dropbox that is available within MyITLab.

Project 2: Using the Web in Your Personal Life

The web can help make vacations and road trips easier and more fun. Do the following to find information to help plan a road trip to Niagara Falls:

Step 1. Get driving directions from your home in Hershey, Pennsylvania, to Niagara Falls, Canada. What is the total miles traveled?

Step 2. You would like to visit some parks in the Finger Lakes area on your way home. Select three parks and find directions from Niagara Falls to these parks and then back to Hershey. What state do you pass through on your way to Niagara Falls?

Step 3. Find two hotels in the Niagara Falls area on the U.S. side that will accept your dog, Wendy. Find one hotel on the Canada side of the falls that will accept a dog. What types of information does the Hotel Finder at www.google.com/hotels offer?

Step 4. Will you need your passport to cross over into Canada and return to the United States? Find a website that gives the authoritative answer to this question. An authoritative

Personal Project I'm planning a trip to Niagara Falls, Canada. I need to find out about sites to visit along the way, driving directions, hotels, restaurants, tours, and currency exchange in Canada. I also need to buy a digital camera and share my photos with friends.

answer is an answer given by someone with authority. In this case, look for a website with a .gov URL, which means the site is hosted by the government.

Step 5. How much will it cost for an adult to take the *Maid of the Mist* boat ride up near the bottom of the falls? What is the authoritative website for ticket price information regarding the *Maid of the Mist*? Find a photo of the *Maid of the Mist* near the falls. How many decks does the boat make available for customers?

Step 6. You plan to take $400 in U.S. currency into Canada. How much is that in Canadian currency? What is Canadian currency called?

Step 7. When you are vacationing, it's interesting to know the history behind the area. Who was the first person to go over the falls and live to tell about it? What year did it happen?

Do the following to record and share the trip with friends and family:

Step 8. Shop for a digital camera to use on your trip. Save a web page to your USB flash drive that shows the camera and its price on a retail site that you would trust to make the purchase. Save another web page to your flash drive that contains a review of the camera.

Step 9. Sign up for a shutterfly.com account and post one photo to the site. Share your site on Shutterfly with your instructor, a class member, friend, or family member. If you don't have your own photo to post to the site, you can use the MyPhoto1.jpg photo in the sample_files folder that you downloaded earlier in the chapter from the www.pearsonhighered.com/jump website.

Project 3: Using the Web in Your Academic Career

Academic Project I want to purchase and install on my computer the Microsoft Office applications I'll use in this course. I expect to use these apps for my entire academic career. What are the options offered by Microsoft for Office and can I get a student discount?

In this course, you learn to use the Microsoft Office software. Microsoft offers several editions of Office, and students can get a discount for some of these editions. Search the Microsoft websites to answer these questions about Microsoft Office:

Step 1. Go to **www.microsoftstore.com** and search for the Office Suites. Answer these questions about the eight editions offered on the site:

1. Microsoft gives the options to buy or rent the software. Which two editions can you rent for one year? How many computers can use one subscription to an edition?

2. Which edition can you rent for four years? How much does a four-year subscription cost? Which applications are included in this edition?

3. The Office Home and Student 2013 edition is purchased and not rented. List the four applications that are included in this edition. How much does the edition cost? What is the most important advantage of purchasing software rather than renting it?

4. Which applications are included in Office Professional 2013 but are not included in Office Home and Business 2013?

Step 2. A subscription to Office 365 includes extra OneDrive storage, use of Skype to make voice calls over the web, and access to Office on Demand. To find out about Office on Demand, search for and watch the video "Use Office on any PC with Office on Demand." Then answer these questions:

1. When you use Office on Demand on a computer in a library, hotel business center, or other public place, is the version of Office you have purchased installed on the computer? Do you have access to all the applications and features of Office for which you have subscribed?

2. After using Office on Demand and before you step away from a public computer, why is it important to sign off your OneDrive or Microsoft account?

Step 3. Microsoft makes it easy for students to find the discounted edition of Office by offering the web site www.theultimatesteal.com. Go to **www.theultimatesteal.com**. Which edition of Office is offered on this site?

Step 4. If you're using a computer in your school computer lab, the software is already installed. However, you might need to install Microsoft Office on your home computer or laptop. The Office 365 University edition is offered to students who have an email address assigned by their school. This address will end in .edu—for example, yourname@example.edu. If you plan to purchase or subscribe to an edition of Microsoft Office, go ahead and buy and install the software now so that you're ready to use it when you start Chapter 3.

Project to Help Others

One of the best ways to learn is to teach someone else. And, in teaching someone else, you are making a contribution into that person's life. As part of each chapter's work, you are encouraged to teach someone else a skill you have learned. In this case, you help your apprentice learn to use the web.

Working with your apprentice, do the following:

Step 1. Ask your apprentice how he expects to use the web to find information, shop, do banking, or pay bills. Describe what your apprentice wants to learn. Do your best to help this person meet these goals.

Step 2. Coach your apprentice as he uses Internet Explorer to surf the news on a news website. Try not to touch the keyboard or mouse. Let your apprentice do all the work.

Step 3. Help your apprentice set his home page to a site of his choice. What is that site? If your apprentice doesn't have a specific site in mind, use Google as the home page.

Step 4. Coach your apprentice to find images and videos of a topic that interests him.

Step 5. Ask your apprentice about something he would like to understand better, such as how something works. Coach your apprentice to find that information.

Step 6. Coach your apprentice to do a Google search on his own name and that of his close friends and family.

Step 7. Ask your apprentice what service or product he might need. If your apprentice does not have ideas on how to find information about the product online, use these:

   a. Find an auto mechanic in the area that gets good reviews.

   b. Find a restaurant in the area that gets good reviews and that he has not yet tried.

   c. Shop for a new television or camera.

Step 8. Ask your apprentice to evaluate how the tutoring session went. Briefly describe his response.

Step 9. Use Notepad to create a text file that contains answers about the tutoring session and send the file to your instructor. If you're using MyITLab, you can post the file in Dropbox in MyITLab. On the other hand, your instructor might prefer you post the file to your OneDrive. Here are the questions:

   1. Who is your apprentice?

   2. In step 4, what topic did your apprentice use to find images and videos on the web?

   3. In step 5, what topic did your apprentice use to better understand?

   4. In step 6, what information did your apprentice find about himself and others?

   5. Briefly describe how the apprentice evaluated the tutoring session.

   6. How do you think the session went? How would you like to improve it next time?

3 Creating Documents with Microsoft Word

In This Chapter, You Will:

From inviting friends to a birthday party to posting a flyer in the school hallways about an upcoming club meeting, most of us find it necessary to make short and simple documents. These documents contain little text, an attention-grabbing photo or graphic, and background color for impact.

In this chapter, you'll learn to use Microsoft Word, a word processing application that is one of the applications included in Microsoft Office. In particular, you'll learn how to use Word to make three one-page documents with text, graphics, and color: a checklist for a camping trip, a jazz concert announcement, and a thank you note. In later chapters, you'll learn more about Word.

As with all chapters in this book, you can choose which of the learning paths below best suits your needs. No matter which path you choose, as you work your way through the chapter, remember that the most important computer skill is how to teach yourself a computer skill. Therefore, this chapter is designed to help you teach yourself how to create documents.

LEARNING PATHS

GUIDED LEARNING	EXPLORE AND DISCOVER	JUMP RIGHT IN
Read the Chapter *Watch the Objective Videos*	**On Your Own Projects** *Review Objective videos or use Step-by-Step Solutions*	**Mastery Project** *Use Objective videos & OYO projects for help*
On Your Own Projects *Review Objective videos or use Step-by-Step Solutions*		**Explore Resources** *For help as needed*
Mastery Project *Use Objective videos & OYO projects for help*	**Mastery Project** *Use Objective videos & OYO projects for help*	
Google Project (if applicable) *Watch Google video for help*	**Google Project (if applicable)** *Watch Google video for help*	**Google Project (if applicable)** *Watch Google video for help*
Helping You & Others Projects	**Helping You & Others Projects**	**Helping You & Others Projects**
MyITLab Assessment	**MyITLab Assessment**	**MyITLab Assessment**

Entering Text and Saving the Document

In this part of the chapter, you'll learn how to use the Word window and Word Help, how to enter and edit text in a Word document, and how to save and open the document.

Objective 3.1: Create and Edit a Word Document

WATCH

OBJECTIVE 3.1
VIDEO

Microsoft Word is a popular word processing program that allows you to enter text and add graphics to documents. Using Word, you can easily format the text and change the layout of the text and graphics to make the document attractive. After you create a document, you can save the document for later use, print the document, and modify it.

> **Microsoft Word**—A word processing application included in the Microsoft Office suite of applications. Word is used to create documents that can include text, color, pictures, drawings, and other graphics. You can use Word to make documents such as letters, invitations, term papers, flyers, invoices, and resumes. Several editions of Microsoft Office have been published. This book uses Microsoft Office 2013.

Tip In this book, we use these Microsoft Office 2013 applications: Word, OneNote, PowerPoint, Excel, and Access. If you're purchasing and installing Microsoft Office 2013, make sure you purchase a version that includes all these applications.

In this chapter, you create three documents, all designed to show you different features of Word. Follow along on your computer to create the documents, but don't worry about getting the details of each document perfect. To get the most out of the chapter, focus on learning to use Word's tools—experiment with the tools explained in this chapter or try other tools you see at the top of the Word window.

ON YOUR OWN 3.1

Create a Blank Document and Use the Word Window

WATCH

OBJECTIVE 3.1
VIDEO

Create the Checklist Document: Part 1 of 8

In On Your Own 3.1 through On Your Own 3.8, you'll build the Checklist document. Let's begin by learning about the Word window and Word help:

Step 1. Open **Microsoft Word 2013** and start with a new blank document. Maximize the window.

Step 2. Compare Figure 3-1 to your Word window and identify all the items labeled in Figure 3-1 on your Word window. As you mouse over a button, you will see a bubble appears that describes the tool.

> **Not Working?** More than one version of Microsoft Word exists. In this book, we are using Word 2013. If you're using a different version, such as Word 2010, your window might not look the same as the one shown in Figure 3-1.

Step 3. Make sure the **rulers** above the document area and along the left side of the document are displayed. Make sure the Word **ribbon** is pinned to (stays put on) the Word window.

> **rulers**—Bars along the top and left side of a document that measure and mark page margins, tab positions, indents, and other organizational items on the page. Press and drag an item on the rulers to change its position.
>
> **ribbon**—In Office applications, the area across the top of the application window that contains groups of commands. Click a tab above the ribbon to switch to a new ribbon.

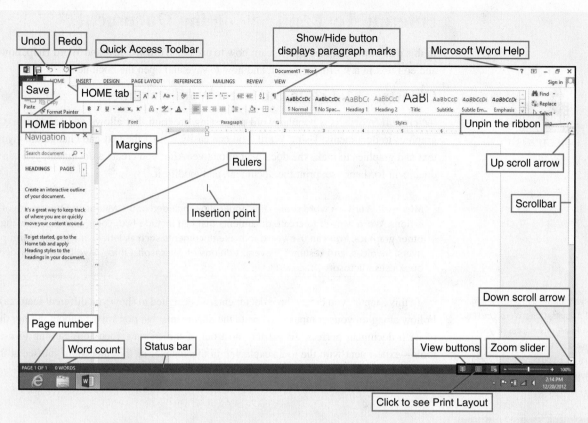

FIGURE 3-1   The Word 2013 window displays a blank document.

Step 4. Use the status bar at the bottom of the Word window to make sure **Print Layout** view is selected.

> **Hint** Word has a built-in Help window that gives directions to use all the Word features. You access Help by clicking the **Microsoft Word Help** button **?** in the top-right corner. As an independent learner, you can use this Help feature to teach yourself about Word.

Step 5. Locate the **insertion point**, which shows where your text will appear when you start typing.

> **insertion point**—The blinking vertical bar | that marks where characters will appear when you type.

Step 6. Recall that OneDrive used to be named SkyDrive. Word uses both names in Word Help and on Word screens. Use the Word Help window to find out how Word works with OneDrive or SkyDrive. What website does Word use when it searches for information in Word Help?

Solutions Appendix   *For help:* See *On Your Own 3.1* Step-by-Step Solution

The first step to creating a document is to enter text. If you aren't an expert at typing, don't worry. Word makes it easy to edit what you type. As you read through this section, follow along on your computer. Don't be afraid to experiment as you are introduced to new features of Word.

The first document you'll build is a checklist someone could use when taking a group of kids camping. Figure 3-2 shows the finished document, which includes a graphic, a checklist for campers, and a line for the parent or guardian signature.

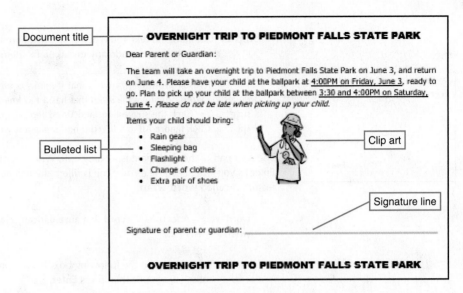

Document title —— **OVERNIGHT TRIP TO PIEDMONT FALLS STATE PARK**

Dear Parent or Guardian:

The team will take an overnight trip to Piedmont Falls State Park on June 3, and return on June 4. Please have your child at the ballpark at <u>4:00PM on Friday, June 3</u>, ready to go. Plan to pick up your child at the ballpark between <u>3:30 and 4:00PM on Saturday, June 4</u>. *Please do not be late when picking up your child.*

Items your child should bring:

Bulleted list ——
- Rain gear
- Sleeping bag
- Flashlight
- Change of clothes
- Extra pair of shoes

—— Clip art

—— Signature line

Signature of parent or guardian: _____

OVERNIGHT TRIP TO PIEDMONT FALLS STATE PARK

FIGURE 3-2   This document uses a bulleted list and clip art.

ON YOUR OWN 3.2

Enter and Edit Text

WATCH

▶

OBJECTIVE 3.1
VIDEO

Create the Checklist Document: Part 2 of 8

In this activity, you'll type the first lines of text into your Checklist document. To advance to a new line, press **Enter**. Don't worry about the size or position of the text on the page; you'll format the text later. If you make a mistake as you enter text, use these tips to edit the text:

- To delete what you just typed, press the **Backspace** key.
- To move the insertion point to a new location, click somewhere in the text. You can also use your arrow keys to move the insertion point. Then press the **Backspace** key to delete text to the left of the insertion point.
- To insert new text, click where you want the text. Then type the new text.
- You can also select large amounts of text and delete or replace the selected text. Use the press and drag operation to select text. The selected text is highlighted in gray. To delete highlighted text, press **Delete**. To replace selected text, just start typing. Whatever you type replaces the text that was highlighted in gray.
- To deselect text that you have selected, click somewhere off the selected text.
- To select and highlight one word, double-click the word. What you type next replaces that word. Or you can press **Delete** to remove the word.
- To select all the text in a sentence, triple-click anywhere in the sentence.
- To undo what you have just done, click the **Undo** button ↺ found on the **Quick Access Toolbar** at the top-left corner of the Word window.

> **Quick Access Toolbar**—In Office applications, a group of commands in the title bar that include Save and Undo.

To continue making the Checklist document you started in On Your Own 3.1, do the following:

Step 1.   Move the Zoom slider so that the size of the document is set to 100%. This size makes it easier to see what you're typing. Type the following text in the blank document, pressing **Enter** after each line:

> Overnight Trip to Piedmont Falls State Park
> Dear Parent or Guardian:

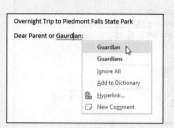

Step 2. Compare the text you typed to the text here and make sure you typed everything correctly. If you made any mistakes, fix them now.

> **Hint** Microsoft Word flags a word that it thinks is misspelled by drawing a wavy red line under the word. Right-click a word that has a red line to see a shortcut menu with spelling suggestions. Click the suggestion, and Word replaces the misspelled word with the correct spelling. Click **Ignore All** to tell Word not to flag this word again.

The next part of the document is a paragraph. When typing a paragraph, you don't have to press Enter as you type, because as one line is filled, the text automatically spills to the next line. This feature is called **word wrap**.

> **word wrap**—A feature of Word that automatically causes text to flow to a new line when a line is full.

Step 3. Type the text in the following box. Do not press Enter until you finish typing the entire paragraph. Then press **Enter**.

> The team will take an overnight trip to Piedmont Falls State Park on June 3, and return on June 4. Please have your child at the ballpark at 4:00PM on Friday, June 3, ready to go. Plan to pick up your child at the ballpark between 3:30 and 4:00PM on Saturday, June 4. Please do not be late when picking up your child.

Solutions Appendix

For help: See *On Your Own 3.2* Step-by-Step Solution

WATCH

OBJECTIVE 3.2
VIDEO

Objective 3.2: Save, Locate, and Open a Document

After you invest your time in a document, it's important to save that file even before you're finished. Be sure to save every few minutes and after you make any major changes. The first time you save a file, you need to specify the name of the document and the location it should be saved. In Word 2013, the default file extension of a document file is **docx** .

> **docx**—The file extension that Word 2013 uses for document files.

ON YOUR OWN 3.3

Save, Close, and Open a Document

WATCH

OBJECTIVE 3.2
VIDEO

Create the Checklist Document: Part 3 of 8

As you work on a document, you can save it on your computer's hard drive, a USB flash drive, the OneDrive that you set up in Chapter 2, or another location given by your instructor, such as a server in the computer lab.

Here's how to save the Checklist document to a USB flash drive or your computer's hard drive:

Step 1. With the document still open, click the **FILE** tab and click **Save**. Because this is the first time you've saved the document, the Save As window appears (see Figure 3-3).

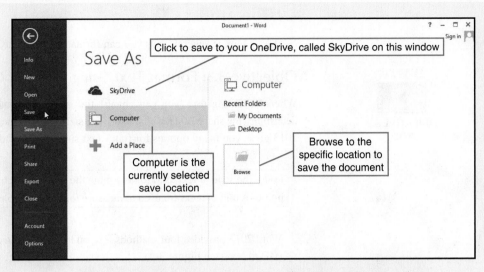

FIGURE 3-3   The Save As window lets you decide where to save the document.

Step 2.   With **Computer** selected, you can select the Documents library or the Windows Desktop, or you can click Browse to point to a different location. Make your choice, and the Save As window appears.

Step 3.   Name the document **Checklist**. Do not change the file type. Click **Save**. After the document is saved, Word returns you to the document window.

> **Tip**   If you want to verify where you've saved a document, click the FILE tab. The file name and location appear under Info. To return to the document window, click the left arrow.

OneDrive used to be called SkyDrive and is still called SkyDrive in Microsoft Office windows. To save the document to your OneDrive (also called SkyDrive) on the web, do the following:

Step 4.   Click the **FILE** tab, click **Save**, and click **SkyDrive**. If you are not already signed in, sign in to your Microsoft account.

Step 5.   Name the document **Checklist** and save it to the Documents folder on your OneDrive. Note that you've signed in to your OneDrive using your Microsoft account, so you don't need to sign in again during this Windows session.

After you save a document the first time, Word does not require you to give the document name or save location again. Instead, the document is saved with the original name and in the same location.

You can use any one of the following three methods to save a document after it has been saved the first time. Do the following to practice resaving the document:

Step 6.   Click the **FILE** tab and click **Save**. The document saves again.

Step 7.   Press **Ctrl+S**. The document saves again.

Step 8.   Click the **Save** button 🖫 on the Quick Access Toolbar. The document saves again.

As you work, save your document about every five minutes or after making significant changes. To practice closing and reopening your document, do the following:

Step 9.   Close the **Word** window.

Step 10.   Open the **Checklist** document again.

> **Tip**   Before removing your USB flash drive, don't forget to use the Safely Remove Hardware and Eject Media icon in the taskbar.

> **Tip**   Before stepping away from your computer, you can use the Word window to sign out of OneDrive. To do so, click the **FILE** tab and click **Account**. On the Account window, click **Sign out**. You can also use the Account window to sign in to OneDrive.

Solutions
Appendix

For help: See On Your Own 3.3 Step-by-Step Solution

Formatting Text

Next let's look at several ways you can format text to make it more attractive and interesting.

WATCH

OBJECTIVE 3.3
VIDEO

Objective 3.3: Format Text Using the Font Group Formatting Tools

When formatting text, you can change the size, color, and font of the text. The font used determines the shape of each character. The size of text is measured in a unit called a point. Word 2013 gives you many options for fonts, text size, colors, and other special features.

> font—The style of text used to determine the shape of each character.
>
> point—A unit of measure used to measure font size; 72 points equal 1 inch.

Word 2013 provides four methods for you to format text. All four methods can be found on the HOME ribbon (see Figure 3-4).

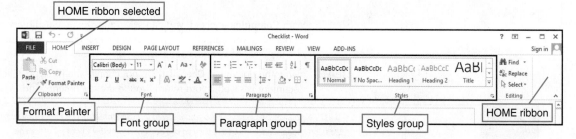

FIGURE 3-4   Text formatting is done using the tools on the HOME ribbon.

> **Font group.** Tools in the Font group allow you to change the size and font of the selected text. You can also underline, bold, italicize, and strikethrough your text. You can change the color of text and apply other special features. Figure 3-5 shows some formatting that was done using the Font group.

> ## The font and size of this text is Arial Black 14 point.
>
> The font and size of this text is Times New Roman 10 point.
>
> The color of this text is red.
>
> This text is highlighted in yellow.
>
> THIS SENTENCE USES UPPERCASE, AN OPTION UNDER CHANGE CASE.
>
> This <u>word</u> is underlined. This ~~word~~ has strikethrough applied.
>
> **THIS SENTENCE USES TEXT EFFECTS.**
>
> Water can be written as H_2O and needs a subscript, which is a small character below the baseline.

FIGURE 3-5   Font, size, and other formatting features available in the Font group are applied to selected text.

> **Paragraph group.** Select one or more paragraphs and use the Paragraph tools to format the selected paragraphs. You can left-justify , right-justify , justify , center, create a bulleted or numbered list, and sort or indent paragraphs.

> **left-justify**—To align text with the left side of the document. Left-justify is the default setting for text in Word.
> **right-justify**—To align text with the right side of the document.
> **justify**—To align text with both the left and right sides of the document.

> **Styles group.** Select the text and apply a style. A **style** is a shortcut for formatting. Examples of style names are Heading 1 and Heading 2. When you apply a style to selected text, all the formatting features assigned to that style are applied. You learn to use styles in Chapter 5.

> **style**—A predetermined set of formatting features that have been assigned a name and can be applied to text.

> **Format Painter.** Use the **Format Painter** tool ✨ to duplicate formatting already applied to other text in the document.

> **Format Painter**—A tool used in Office applications to duplicate text formatting already applied in the document. The tool is handy when applying the same formatting to different parts of a document.

Let's learn to use the Font group. All of the Font tools on the HOME ribbon are labeled in Figure 3-6. To format text using the Font tools, you first select the text and then use a Font tool to format it. As you slowly move your mouse over a tool, a bubble appears that describes the tool.

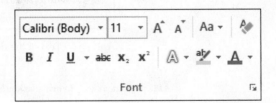

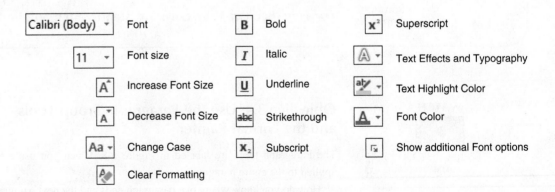

FIGURE 3-6   The tools in the Font group are used to format text.

> **Hint** As you format text, to undo what you have just done, click the **Undo** button ↺ found on the Quick Access Toolbar.

A down arrow **A** ˅ beside a tool indicates you have options within the tool that you can select. For example, when you click the down arrow next to the Font Color tool, a palette of colors appears from which you can choose.

ON YOUR OWN 3.4

Format Text Using the Font Tools

WATCH

OBJECTIVE 3.3
VIDEO

Create the Checklist Document: Part 4 of 8

Let's move on to the next phase of creating our Checklist document. First, you need to format the text that you've entered so far in the document:

Step 1. Format all the text in the document in **Tahoma, 12 point**. A good size for text in the body of a document is 12 point.

> **Hint** To select all the text in a document, press **Ctrl+A**.

Step 2. Select the title and format it as **Arial Black**, **14** points, **Uppercase**.

Step 3. Underline the text **4:00PM on Friday, June 3**.

Step 4. Underline the text **3:30 and 4:00PM on Saturday, June 4**.

Step 5. Format the last sentence in the paragraph in **Italic**.

Step 6. Your document should now look like the one shown in Figure 3-7. Check your document for errors and save it.

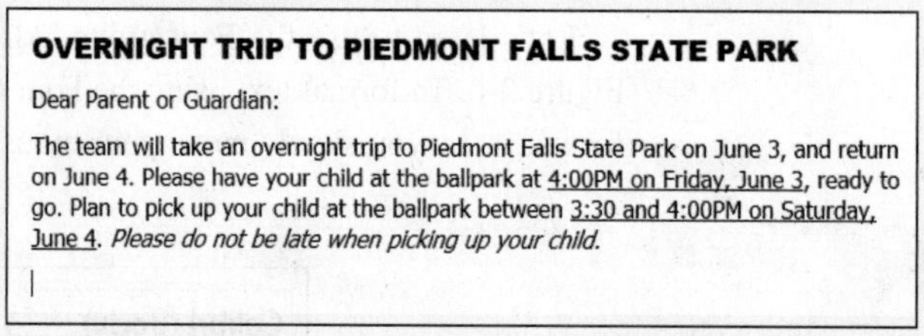

OVERNIGHT TRIP TO PIEDMONT FALLS STATE PARK

Dear Parent or Guardian:

The team will take an overnight trip to Piedmont Falls State Park on June 3, and return on June 4. Please have your child at the ballpark at <u>4:00PM on Friday, June 3</u>, ready to go. Plan to pick up your child at the ballpark between <u>3:30 and 4:00PM on Saturday, June 4</u>. *Please do not be late when picking up your child.*

FIGURE 3-7   Text in the document is formatted using the Font tools.

> **Tip** If you don't like a format that you just applied, click the **Undo** button ↶ to undo the formatting.

> Solutions
> Appendix

For help: See *On Your Own 3.4* Step-by-Step Solution

WATCH

OBJECTIVE 3.4
VIDEO

WATCH

CHAPTER 3
DIVING DEEPER
VIDEO

Objective 3.4: Use the Paragraph Group Tools and the Format Painter

The Paragraph tools are labeled in Figure 3-8. When you use a Paragraph tool, formatting is applied to the entire paragraph.

How do you know where one paragraph ends and the next paragraph begins? A paragraph ends when you press the Enter key as you type. The special character created when you pressed the Enter key is called a **hard return**. The positions of hard returns in a document are displayed using a **paragraph mark**. If you want to see where the hard returns are in a document, display the paragraph marks by clicking the **Show/Hide** button ¶ in the Paragraph group. Click the button again to hide the marks.

> **hard return**—The nonprinting character created in a document when you press the Enter key that marks the end of a paragraph. Hard returns are indicated by the paragraph mark.
>
> **paragraph mark**—A nonprinting character ¶ that can be displayed in a document to show the hard returns that mark the ends of paragraphs.

Bullets	Sort	Justify
Numbering	Show/Hide	Line and Paragraph Spacing
Multilevel List	Align Left	Shading to color background
Decrease Indent	Center	Borders around paragraphs or tables
Increase Indent	Align Right	Show more Paragraph Settings

FIGURE 3-8   Tools in the Paragraph group apply formatting to the entire paragraph.

ON YOUR OWN 3.5

Create a Bulleted List and Use the Format Painter

WATCH

OBJECTIVE 3.4
VIDEO

Create the Checklist Document: Part 5 of 8

Now we'll move on to the next part of creating our Checklist document. In this part, you will center text using the Center paragraph tool, create a bulleted list, and use the Format Painter to duplicate existing formatting. When you're finished, your document will look like the one shown in Figure 3-9.

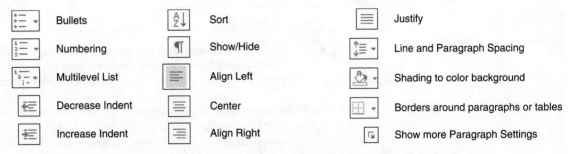

OVERNIGHT TRIP TO PIEDMONT FALLS STATE PARK

Dear Parent or Guardian:

The team will take an overnight trip to Piedmont Falls State Park on June 3, and return on June 4. Please have your child at the ballpark at 4:00PM on Friday, June 3, ready to go. Plan to pick up your child at the ballpark between 3:30 and 4:00PM on Saturday, June 4. *Please do not be late when picking up your child.*

Items your child should bring:

- Rain gear
- Sleeping bag
- Flashlight
- Change of clothes
- Extra pair of shoes

Signature of parent or guardian: _____

OVERNIGHT TRIP TO PIEDMONT FALLS STATE PARK

FIGURE 3-9   The document title is centered and a bulleted list and signature line are added.

Step 1. Center the document title.

Step 2. Position your insertion point at the end of the document.

> **Hint** To quickly move your insertion point to the end of a document, press **Ctrl+End.** (Hold down the **Ctrl** key while you press the **End** key.) To move your insertion point to the top of a document, press **Ctrl+Home**.

Step 3. Type the following text, pressing **Enter** after each line of text:

> Items your child should bring:
> Rain gear
> Sleeping bag
> Flashlight
> Change of clothes
> Extra pair of shoes

Step 4. Practice using the **Format Painter** by formatting this new text the same as the title line, which is **Arial Black, 14 point, Centered**. Then use the Format Painter to change the formatting of the new text to **Tahoma, 12 point**.

> **Hint** Use the Format Painter to copy formatting from one place in a document to another place. First, select text, a paragraph, or a graphic that has the formatting you want to copy. Then click the **Format Painter** . The pointer changes to a paintbrush . Whatever text you select next will be formatted the same as the original text.

Step 5. Change the last five lines of text to a bulleted list by using the **Bullets** button in the Paragraph group.

Step 6. At the end of the document, drop down two lines and add the signature line, formatting it as **Tahoma, 12 point**.

> Signature of parent or guardian: _____

Step 7. Drop down two more lines and add the flyer title again. Rather than retyping the title, you can copy and paste the title. Make sure the formatting for the title at the bottom of the page is the same as the title at the top of the page.

> **Hint** To copy text, select the text and then click **Copy** on the HOME ribbon. The text is copied to the Windows Clipboard. Position your insertion point where you want the copied text, and click **Paste** on the HOME ribbon. You can also use the Cut and Paste operations to move selected text.

Step 8. The text in the document is now finished. Save the document.

Solutions Appendix

For help: See *On Your Own 3.5* Step-by-Step Solution

Adding Graphics to a Document

Next let's look at how to add graphics to a document.

Objective 3.5: Use Clip Art and Pictures in a Document

Graphics, including photographs, shapes, and clip art , add impact to your documents. So let's add clip art to the document to see how this improves the overall look.

WATCH

OBJECTIVE 3.5 VIDEO

> **clip art**—A cartoon or other drawing that can be inserted into a document. Microsoft Office Online provides much clip art for documents. You can also add your own clip art to a document.

You can use Word to insert graphics, including clip art, into documents using one of two methods:

> An **inline graphic** is tied to text and moves with the text if the text changes position. When the text moves, so does the graphic. This method is the default method for Word.

> A **floating graphic** stays where you put it on the page and text flows around it. To change an inline graphic to a floating graphic, use the Wrap Text command on the FORMAT ribbon.

---

inline graphic—A graphic that moves with the text as the text changes position.

floating graphic—A graphic that stays in a fixed position on the page even when the text around it is changed.

ON YOUR OWN 3.6

Insert Clip Art into a Document

WATCH

OBJECTIVE 3.5
VIDEO

Create the Checklist Document: Part 6 of 8

If you're connected to the Internet, you can use Word to find clip art, photos, and other graphics on the Office.com website and on the web. When inserting clip art into your document, use the INSERT ribbon to insert an Online Picture. Then you might need to move, resize, or format it.

> **Tip** To delete a picture or other object, first select it by clicking the object and then press **Delete**.

To continue creating your Checklist document, let's insert clip art of a camper into the document:

Step 1. Position your insertion point at the end of the line **Items your child should bring:**

Step 2. On the INSERT ribbon, click **Online Pictures** and search for **camp** clip art. Find the clip art of the camp leader shown earlier in Figure 3-2, and it will be inserted at your insertion point. Don't worry about its exact position.

> **Not Working?** If you don't see a list of clip art, you might not have Internet access. If you don't find the clip art used in the chapter, substitute another.

Step 3. The clip art has been inserted as an inline graphic. Use the **Wrap Text** button on the FORMAT ribbon to change the graphic to a floating graphic so that you have more control of its position in the document. For example, the **Square** selection provides a clean boundary around the graphic.

> **Hint** When you select a graphic, the FORMAT tab appears on the Word window. Click the **FORMAT** tab to format a graphic. You can use tools on this ribbon to change a graphic to meet your needs, such as changing it from inline to floating, adding shadow effects, adjusting the brightness or contrast, or recoloring it.

Step 4. When an object is selected, you can see the **sizing handles**. Use the sizing handles to **resize** and/or move the graphic so that it is below the paragraph and to the right of the bulleted list, as shown earlier in Figure 3-2.

> **sizing handle**—In Office applications, this is a white circle or square on the boundaries of a clip art, shape, or other object that is used to resize the object. To resize an object without changing its proportions, you might need to hold down the **Shift** key as you drag a corner sizing handle.

> **Hint** To move an object, first select it. With your pointer showing four-directional arrows ✛, press and drag the object to move it.

Step 5. Save the document.

Solutions
Appendix

For help: See On Your Own 3.6 Step-by-Step Solution

Finishing Up and Printing Your Document

You're just about done with your Checklist document, so now let's learn how to finish up a document and print it.

Objective 3.6: Verify Document Properties and Print the Document

Every document created in Word has certain properties, including the size of the document file, the date created, the author of the document, and the document location. You can find properties in the Info group on the FILE tab (see Figure 3-10).

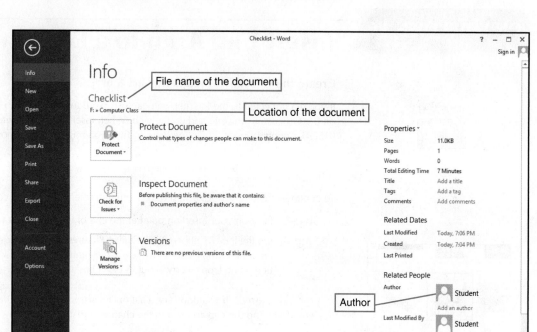

FIGURE 3-10   The Info group on the FILE tab shows the document's author and other file properties.

Change Document Properties

Create the Checklist Document: Part 7 of 8

Your instructor is likely to require you to submit your work electronically instead of printing it. If you're asked to email a document to your instructor or post it to a OneDrive or other location, be sure to verify that you are listed as the document author. Do the following to verify the properties of the Checklist document:

Step 1. Use the FILE tab to display the document properties. Which group on the FILE tab lists the author of the document? What is the size of your Checklist.docx document?

Step 2. If you are not the author, change the document properties so that you're listed as the author. Then save the document.

> **Hint** To change the document author, begin by right-clicking the name of the author.

Solutions
Appendix

For help: See *On Your Own 3.7* Step-by-Step Solution

When you print a document, you decide the number of copies to print, which printer to use, what pages to print, and other printing settings. A printout of a document is also called a **hard copy**.

> **hard copy**—Another name for a printout.

ON YOUR OWN 3.8

Verify Page Count and Print a Document

WATCH

▶

OBJECTIVE 3.6
VIDEO

PAGE 1 OF 1   104 WORDS

Create the Checklist Document: Part 8 of 8

To print the Checklist document you've been working on, follow these steps:

Step 1. The document should have only one page. Look in the bottom-left corner of the Word window for the page number including the total number of pages in the document. If your document has more than one page, you need to go back and fix the problem. Perhaps text or a blank line has spilled over to a second page. Use the paragraph marks to make sure you don't have extra lines.

> **Not Working?** If you can't see the page number on the status bar at the bottom of the Word window, right-click the status bar and check **Page Number**.

Step 2. Save the document. You should get in the habit of always saving the document before printing it.

Step 3. Click the **FILE** tab and click **Print**. The Print window appears (see Figure 3-11). Using this window, you can select the number of copies, the printer, and the pages to print as well as other print settings. Select your printer and click **Print**.

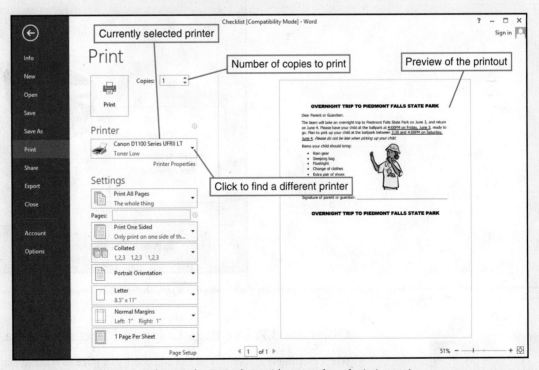

FIGURE 3-11   The Print window on the FILE tab provides a number of printing options.

> **Not Working?** If your printer is not working, go to Chapter 13 to find out how to troubleshoot a printer problem.

Step 4. You're now finished with the Checklist document, so you can close it.

Solutions
Appendix

For help: See *On Your Own 3.8* Step-by-Step Solution

Using Page Color, Text Boxes, Shapes, and WordArt

When creating documents in Word, you might want to have more control over where text is placed on the page and add special effects, such as decorative letters, shapes, and color. In this section, we'll look at how to create text boxes, apply WordArt effects, and create shapes. As you read, follow along at your computer. Together, we'll make the *Jazz in the Park* document shown in Figure 3-12. This document is an ad about a jazz concert that is intended to be included in an email sent to all students and faculty. Because we don't intend to print the ad, we're free to use background color, which doesn't really print well but can improve an email message.

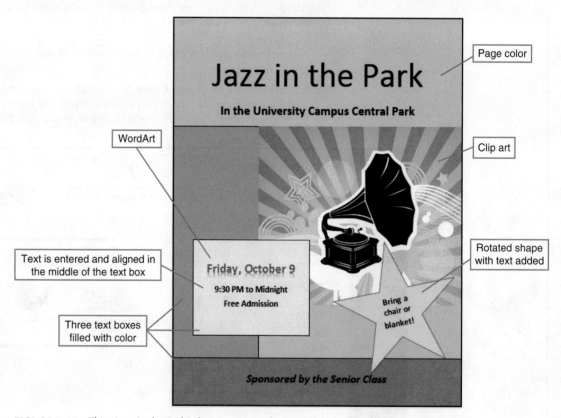

FIGURE 3-12   This "Jazz in the Park" document uses three text boxes, page color, WordArt, clip art, and a shape.

WATCH

OBJECTIVE 3.7
VIDEO

Objective 3.7: Use Page Color and Text Boxes in a Document

When creating documents, you can add color to a page to make it stand out more. You can also use text boxes to keep text together and give you more control over where the text is placed on a page. For example, the *Jazz in the Park* document shown in Figure 3-12 uses text boxes to position color and text on the page.

The first thing to do when creating text boxes is to insert the text box, then you can add text, format, move, resize, or rotate the box.

ON YOUR OWN 3.9

Add Page Color and a Text Box

WATCH

OBJECTIVE 3.7
VIDEO

Create the JazzConcert Document: Part 1 of 5

To build the document shown in Figure 3-12, we first add the title, subtitle, and page color. Next we'll add a text box to put more color on the page. When you complete this On Your Own activity, your document should look like Figure 3-13.

FIGURE 3-13 The "Jazz in the Park" document has page color, text, and a text box.

Let's get started:

Step 1. Open a new blank Word document.

Step 2. Set the Page Color to a medium orange. **Orange, Accent 2, Lighter 40%** works well.

> **Hint** The Page Color command is on the DESIGN ribbon in the Page Background group.

Step 3. Type two lines of text:

> Jazz in the Park
>
> In the University Campus Central Park

Step 4. Format the first line of text to **Calibri (Body)** font, **72 point**. Format the second line to **Calibri (Body)**, **26 point**, and **Bold**.

Step 5. Center both lines on the page.

> **Tip** When a document is printed, page color does not print, but fill color in a text box or shape does print.

Step 6. Save the document to your USB flash drive, hard drive, OneDrive, or other location given by your instructor. Name the document **JazzConcert**.

Step 7. Create the text box on the left side of the page in Figure 3-13. Fill it with a dark orange color. **Orange, Accent 2** works well.

> **Hint** To insert a text box in a document, on the **INSERT** ribbon, click **Text Box** and click **Draw Text Box**. Draw the box in the document. You can then add text in the box and move, resize, and format the box.

>

> **Not Working?** The colors for text boxes and other shapes that we use in this chapter might not be the same as those provided by Word on your computer. If so, use colors close to the ones we suggest.

Step 8. Save the document.

Solutions Appendix

For help: See *On Your Own 3.9* Step-by-Step Solution

Tip *When designing an ad or other document, start with a great graphic. Then design the entire document around the graphic.*

We're now ready to add the gramophone clip art to the document. The colors and shapes in this clip art were the inspirations that led to the overall design of the *Jazz in the Park* ad.

ON YOUR OWN 3.10

Insert Clip Art and a Text Box into a Document

WATCH

▶

OBJECTIVE 3.7 VIDEO

Create the JazzConcert Document: Part 2 of 5

In this activity, you add the gramophone clip art and a second text box to the JazzConcert document you just started. At the end of this activity, your document will look like Figure 3-14.

FIGURE 3-14   The "Jazz in the Park" document has clip art and a third text box inserted.

Do the following:

Step 1. Use the **INSERT** ribbon to insert an online picture, searching for **gramophone**. The clip art you're searching for is shown in Figure 3-14.

Step 2. Format the clip art as a floating graphic. Move and resize the clip art so that it's aligned at the top of the vertical text box, as shown in Figure 3-14. Save your document.

Step 3. Create a second text box, positioning it along the bottom of the page. Fill it with a red color.

Step 4. In this red text box, enter this text:

Sponsored by the Senior Class

Step 5. Format this text as **Calibri (Body)** font, **24 point**, **bold** and **italic**. **Center** the text in the text box. **Align** the text in the text box in the middle of the box.

Solutions Appendix   *For help:* See *On Your Own 3.10* Step-by-Step Solution

WATCH

OBJECTIVE 3.8 VIDEO

Objective 3.8: Use Shapes in a Document

The star in the *Jazz in the Park* ad is one of many shapes that Word offers. After you insert a shape, you can move, resize, and rotate it. You can also format the shape and add text inside the shape. Here are some tips to help you when using a shape in a document:

> Hold down the Shift key as you resize a shape to keep it in proportion.
> To rotate a shape or other object, select it, and then press and drag the   **rotation handle** .
> To add text inside a shape, right-click it and click **Add Text** in the shortcut menu that appears.
> To format a shape with color or other special effects, use the FORMAT ribbon, which appears when a shape is selected.

rotation handle—In Office applications, a white or green circle on the boundary of a picture, shape, or text box that is used to rotate the object. Drag the rotation handle in the direction you want to rotate the object.

ON YOUR OWN 3.11

Add a Shape to a Document

WATCH

OBJECTIVE 3.8 VIDEO

Create the JazzConcert Document: Part 3 of 5

Let's continue building the *Jazz in the Park* document. Do the following to insert a star and format it, adding text inside the star:

Step 1. On the INSERT ribbon, in the Illustrations group, click the Shapes button, and select the **5-Point Star**. Your pointer changes to a cross **+**. Press and drag to draw the star on the document.

Step 2. If necessary, move the star to the correct position (refer to Figure 3-12). Rotate the star so that it points to the upper left of the document.

Step 3. Add the following text inside the star:

Bring a chair or blanket!

Step 4. Make the font color of this text **Black** and **Bold** the text. Size the text **18 point**.

Hint To format the text inside a shape, first select the text. When the text is selected, the box around the shape is a dotted line. To format the shape, first select the shape. When the shape is selected, the box around the shape is a solid line (see Figure 3-15).

>

A solid line for a selected shape

A dotted line for selected text inside a shape

FIGURE 3-15   (a) The shape is selected and ready for formatting, and (b) the text inside the shape is selected and ready for formatting.

> **Tip** If a shape or text box is rotated, it returns to the original, upright position when you add or edit the text. When you click off the object, it returns to the rotated position.

Step 5. Change the fill color of the star to **Yellow**.

Step 6. Save your document.

Solutions Appendix

For help: See *On Your Own 3.11* Step-by-Step Solution

As you layer text boxes, clip art, and shapes in a document, the object on top is the one that displays. Here are some tips to help you change the layering order and select objects:

> To change the layering order of objects, click an object to select it. Then click the **FORMAT** tab. Click **Bring Forward** to bring the object forward one layer. Click **Send Backward** to send the object behind an object. If you have several objects layered, you might have to click **Bring Forward** several times to bring an object to the front of several layered objects.

> If you're having trouble selecting an object, on the FORMAT ribbon, click **Selection Pane**. A list of shapes in the document appears. Select one from the list.

WATCH

OBJECTIVE 3.9 VIDEO

Objective 3.9: Use WordArt in a Document

WordArt is used to add special effects to text. For the most impact, don't overdo WordArt. Use a little WordArt in a document to add emphasis to only the most important text.

ON YOUR OWN 3.12

Add WordArt to a Document

WATCH

OBJECTIVE 3.9 VIDEO

Create the JazzConcert Document: Part 4 of 5

Do the following to add a text box with WordArt to the *Jazz in the Park* document:

Step 1. Look back at Figure 3-12 and create the text box shown in the ad to hold the date and time information about the concert. Fill the text box with a light orange. **Orange, Accent 2, Lighter 80%** works well.

Step 2. Enter the following text in the text box:

> Friday, October 9
>
> 9:30 PM to Midnight
>
> Free Admission

Step 3. Format the first line of text as **WordArt**. As for the fill color of the text, **Gold, Accent 4, Darker 50%** works well. Also apply a **Reflection** and **Bold** the text. Increase the size of the text so as to add emphasis but not so large as to cause word wrap. For this ad, **26 point** works well.

Step 4. Format the last two lines of text in **Calibri (Body), 18 point**, **bold**.

Step 5. Center all the text in the text box. Align the text in the middle of the text box.

Step 6. The document is finished. Take a moment to look back at Figure 3-12. Correct any problems you see with your work and save the document.

Solutions Appendix

For help: See *On Your Own 3.12* Step-by-Step Solution

WATCH

OBJECTIVE 3.10
VIDEO

Tip When building a document, you should save the file as a Word document before saving it as a PDF file to make sure you have your changes saved in each file type.

Objective 3.10: Save a Word Document as a PDF File

Your instructor expects you to post or send your documents as Word documents so that she can view and edit them using Microsoft Word. However, if you are sending a document to your friends or posting it to a website, you might want to save the document using the **PDF file** format. Word 2013 can create, read, and edit PDF files, although earlier editions of Microsoft Word can only create a PDF file and not read or edit it.

> **PDF file**—A type of file first created by Adobe Systems used to distribute documents over the Internet and on CD or DVD. Because a PDF file can be read by many applications, it is said to have a universal file format. PDF stands for Portable Document Format.

Most computers have software installed to read a PDF file, and if they don't, you can download the reading software free. This free software enables your computer to read the PDF file, but you can't edit the document without additional software.

ON YOUR OWN 3.13

Save a Document as a PDF File

WATCH

OBJECTIVE 3.10
VIDEO

Create the JazzConcert Document: Part 5 of 5

Do the following to save the *Jazz in the Park* document as a Word document and also as a PDF file:

Step 1. Save the document as usual. Then save the document again, this time as a PDF file. Save the file to the same location you previously saved the Word document file.

> **Hint** To save a document using a different file type, use the Save As command and change the file type in the *Save as type* field in the Save As window.

Step 2. The JazzConcert document is finished. Close all windows.

Step 3. If you saved the files to your hard drive, a USB flash drive, or another local storage device, open **File Explorer** in Windows 8 or **Windows Explorer** in Windows 7 and verify that you have saved two files: the Word document file and the PDF file. Open the PDF file. Can you edit this file?

Step 4. If you saved the files to your OneDrive, go to your OneDrive and verify that both files are saved to your OneDrive folder.

Solutions Appendix

For help: See *On Your Own 3.13* Step-by-Step Solution

Using Templates as Shortcuts to Great Documents

It's good to know the mechanics of building a document step-by-step, but in this part of the chapter, you learn some shortcuts to save time and produce some dazzling results.

Objective 3.11: Use Word Templates and Honor Copyrights

A **template** is a document that already has the look and feel you want and includes places where you can add your own text and graphics. Microsoft Word offers many templates for a variety of purposes, such as business cards, calendars, certificates, and invitations.

> **template**—In Office applications, a document designed for a specific purpose that already has elements included and places for you to add your own content.

To see some templates, click **New** on the FILE tab (see Figure 3-16). To find more templates, you can use the search box at the top of the window or drill down into the categories of templates listed under the search box.

WATCH

OBJECTIVE 3.11 VIDEO

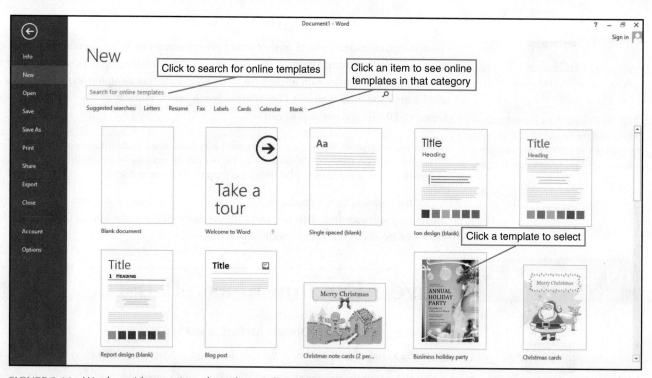

FIGURE 3-16 Word provides a variety of templates to fit a wide range of document types and uses.

ON YOUR OWN 3.14

Use a Thank You Note Template

WATCH

OBJECTIVE 3.11
VIDEO

Create the ThankYou Document

In this activity, you'll use a template to create a thank you note. The completed document is shown in Figure 3-17.

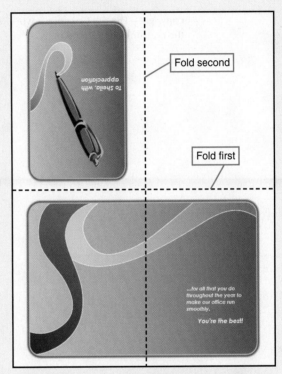

FIGURE 3-17   You can use a Word template to create a thank you note.

To use a template, you start by selecting the template. Let's get started:

Step 1.   In Word 2013, click the **FILE** tab and then click **New**. Take a few moments to drill down into the various categories of templates to see what's available. You can also use the Filter by pane on the right. Locate the **Administrative professional thank you card (quarter-fold)** template, which is in the Business group of the Cards templates. Find the one that looks like the document in Figure 3-17. Create a new document using this template.

> **Not Working?** Word searches for templates online. If you don't see many templates, make sure you're connected to the Internet.

Step 2.   In the new document, change the text **With appreciation** to **To Sheila, with appreciation**. Use the same text formatting.

Step 3.   Verify that the author name for your Word document is correct. Save the document, naming it **ThankYou**. Print the document. Fold the printed page in a quarter fold.

Solutions Appendix

For help: See *On Your Own 3.14* Step-by-Step Solution

Sometimes you can't find a template to meet your needs, and you must design your own documents. To find sample designs for a document, try searching the web. For example, to find a great design for a flyer to advertise music lessons, use Google to search on **great flyer designs music lessons**. Search for **Images**.

Document designs generally are not protected by copyright , and you can use these ideas to design your own documents. But the graphics and photos used in a document might be copyrighted. Honor the rights of others; don't copy their work and distribute it to others without the permission of the owner.

> **copyright**—The right to copy a work, which belongs to the creator of the work or to someone the creator has given the right.

Summary

Entering Text and Saving the Document

> Microsoft Word is a word processing program that allows you to enter, edit, and format text and insert graphics into a document.

> Word's Help feature is a good way to research Word's features and to solve problems when you get stuck using Word.

> The insertion point in Word shows where text will be entered when you type.

> The Quick Access Toolbar has commonly used commands such as save, redo, and undo.

> Word automatically wraps text to the next line so you don't have to worry about typing off the page. This feature is called word wrap.

> Word 2013 uses the .docx file extension for document files. You can save a document to the hard drive, another local storage device, or a OneDrive (also called a SkyDrive). You should save your work every five minutes or so to avoid losing information.

Formatting Text

> The four types of formatting tools available on the HOME ribbon are the Font group, the Paragraph group, the Styles group, and the Format Painter.

> You can format text to change its size, font, color, or other features, including bold, uppercase, underline, and italics.

> The Show/Hide button is used to toggle between showing and hiding the hard returns and other nonprinting characters in a document.

Adding Graphics to a Document

> A graphic, such as clip art, in a document can be inline or floating. An inline graphic moves with the text, whereas a floating graphic stays put on the page.

> When an object is selected, sizing handles and a rotation handle appear. Use them to resize and rotate the object. Press and drag an object to move it.

Finishing Up and Printing Your Document

> You can view a document's properties in the Info group on the FILE tab. The properties include the name and location of the document, the document author, and the date and time the file was created and modified.

> Print a document using the **Print** command on the FILE tab. The printer used and printer settings can also be controlled in this window.

Using Page Color, Text Boxes, Shapes, and WordArt

> Page color adds impact to a document and is useful when the document is not printed.

> A text box can be positioned anywhere and can contain text, fill color, borders, and graphics.

> Shapes are inserted using the INSERT ribbon and can be resized, reshaped, moved, rotated, and filled with color and text.

> Graphics and text can be layered in a document. Use the **Bring Forward** and **Send Backward** commands to change the layering order.

> WordArt is a fun way to add special effects to text. For the most impact, don't use too much WordArt in a document.

> Word files can be saved as PDF files using the Save As command on the FILE tab.

> PDF files save the formatting of the original document and are useful when emailing documents to others or posting them on the web.

Using Templates as Shortcuts to Great Documents

> Templates are good shortcuts to well-designed documents, and Word offers many templates available from the Office.com site.

> When designing a document, search the web for great document designs but don't copy the works of others.

CHAPTER MASTERY PROJECT

WATCH

INTRO TO GRADER PROJECTS VIDEO

Now it's time to find out how well you have mastered the content in this chapter. If you can do all the steps in this mastery project without looking back at the chapter details and can answer all the review questions following this project, you have mastered this chapter. If you can complete the project by finding answers using the Word Help window, you have proven that you can teach yourself Microsoft Word.

> **Hint** All the key terms in the chapter are used in this mastery project or in the review questions. If you encounter a key word you don't know, such as *font*, enter **define:font** in the Internet Explorer address box. You can also search for the word using the Word Help window.

If you find you need a lot of help doing the project and you have not yet read the chapter or done the activities, go back and start at the beginning of the chapter, watch the videos, review the step-by-step solutions as you work through the On Your Own activities, and then return to this project.

By following the steps in this mastery project, you'll create the document shown in Figure 3-18.

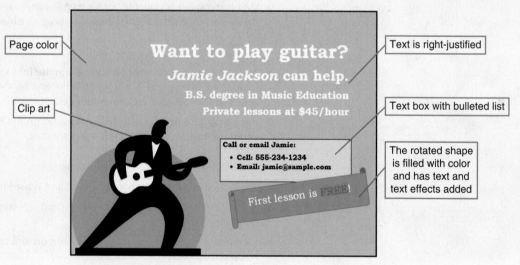

FIGURE 3-18 This document uses text, a text box, a bulleted list, a shape, clip art, and WordArt.

> **Tip** If you need help completing this part of the mastery project, review the section "Entering Text and Saving the Document" in the chapter.

Follow these steps to enter text in a document:

Step 1. Open **Microsoft Word** and create a new blank document. On the PAGE LAYOUT ribbon, click **Orientation** and then click **Landscape**. The document is now oriented in Landscape view. Verify that the rulers are showing on the document window, the ribbon is pinned to the window, and the Print Layout view is selected.

Step 2. Type the following four lines of text, placing a hard return after each line. If you make any mistakes, move your insertion point to the mistake and correct it. When you're done, make sure your insertion point is on a new line of text at the end of the document.

> Want to play guitar?
> Jamie Jackson can help.
> B.S. degree in Music Education
> Private lessons at $45/hour

Step 3. Save the document file to your USB flash drive, hard drive, OneDrive, or other location given by your instructor. Name the document **GuitarLessons**.

> **Tip** If you need help completing this part of the mastery project, review the section "Formatting Text" in the chapter.

Follow these steps to format the text you have already typed into the document:

Step 4. Right-justify all the text in the document and format the text as **Bookman Old Style** font.

- Format the first line of text as **48 point**, **bold.**
- Use the **Format Painter** to copy the formatting of the first line to the second line.
- Change the point size of the second line to **36 point**.
- Format **Jamie Jackson** in the second line in **italics**.
- Format the last two lines of text in **26 point**, **bold**.

Step 5. Save the document using the **Save** button in the Quick Access Toolbar. Close the document and reopen it.

> **Tip** If you need help completing this part of the mastery project, review the section "Adding Graphics to a Document" in the chapter.

Do the following to add clip art to the document:

Step 6. Insert the clip art of a guitar player into the document. Change the graphic from an inline graphic to a floating graphic. Position the clip art as shown earlier in Figure 3-18. Use sizing handles to resize the graphic to about the size shown in the figure.

> **Not Working?** If you can't find the clip art used here, substitute another.

Step 7. Save the document using **Ctrl+S**.

> **Tip** If you need help completing this part of the mastery project, review the section "Using Page Color, Text Boxes, Shapes, and WordArt" in the chapter.

Do the following to add page color, a text box, and a shape to the document:

Step 8. Make the page color of the document a gray color. **White, Background 1, Darker 25%** works well. Format all the text in the document as **White**.

Step 9. Insert a text box to the right of the clip art, as shown in Figure 3-18. Make the shape fill color a light blue. **Blue-Gray, Text 2, Lighter 80%** works well. Type the following text into the text box:

> Call or email Jamie:
> Cell: 555-234-1234
> Email: jamie@sample.com

Step 10. Format the text in the text box as **Bookman Old Style**, **18 point**, **bold**. Make the last two lines in the text box a bulleted list. The text in the text box should be left-justified.

Step 11. Insert a Horizontal Scroll shape into the document. Make the shape fill color a medium blue. **Blue-Gray, Text 2, Lighter 40%** works well. Use the rotation handle to rotate the scroll, as shown in Figure 3-18. Type the following text into the scroll:

First lesson is free!

Step 12. Format the scroll text as **Bookman Old Style**, **26 point**. Center the text in the scroll. Align the text in the middle of the scroll.

- Format the word **free** using WordArt. Make the Text Fill to be **Red**. Make the Text Effects to be an orange glow. **Orange, 18 pt glow, Accent color 2** works well.
- Change the word **free** to all uppercase using the command in the Font group on the HOME ribbon.
- Make sure the scroll is layered on top of the text box, not beneath it. If necessary, use the **Bring Forward** or **Send Backward** commands to change the layering of the objects.

Step 13. Save the document using the **Save** command on the FILE tab.

> Tip   If you need help completing this part of the mastery project, review the section "Finishing Up and Printing Your Document" in the chapter.

Do the following to finish up the document and save it as a PDF:

Step 14. Verify that the document is a one-page document. If the document has more than one page, fix the problem. Use the paragraph marks to make sure you don't have extra lines in the document. Verify that the document properties show you as the author of the document. If necessary, change the document author to your name.

Step 15. Save the document as a Word document. Save the document as a PDF file.

Step 16. This document is not designed to be printed in hard copy. Display a Print Preview of the document.

Review Questions

Answer these questions to assess your skills and knowledge of the content covered in the chapter. Your instructor can provide you with the correct answers when you are ready to check your work.

1. What is the icon for Help in Word?
2. What keys do you press to quickly save a Word document that has been saved before?
3. What file extension does Word 2013 use for its documents?
4. What group on the HOME ribbon has the formatting command to make text bold?
5. When referring to formatting, what is a style?
6. What group on the HOME ribbon includes several styles and can provide a shortcut to formatting text?
7. Where is the Quick Access Toolbar located?
8. If you make a mistake positioning or resizing the graphic, how can you undo your change?
9. What is word wrap?
10. What key do you press to end a paragraph?
11. What is the difference between an inline graphic and a floating graphic?
12. How do you find the sizing handles on an object?
13. What are the steps to copy text from one location in a document to another?
14. Which operations would you use to move text from one location to another?

15. On what ribbon of the Word window can you find Page Color?

16. Which tab on the Word window do you click to change the author of a document?

17. What file format should be used to email a document to someone who might not have Microsoft Word installed on his or her computer?

18. When you add a graphic into a document, when do you need to use Send Backward?

19. If you are having trouble selecting an object in a document, how can you get a list of objects from which you can select one?

20. Where does Word store most of its templates?

21. If you can't find a template that you can use for a document design, what is one way to find designs you can use?

22. Sometimes you might find a great photo or graphic that you want to use in a document you create. Why should you not use a photo or other graphics that you find on the web in a document you plan to distribute to others?

23. What keys do you press to select all the text in a document?

Answer the following questions about the Guitar Lessons document you created in the Chapter Mastery Project:

24. Why would printing the Guitar Lessons flyer present a problem?

25. In creating the Guitar Lessons flyer, you did not use the word wrap feature of Word. Why was the feature not used?

Becoming an Independent Learner

Answer the following questions about becoming an independent learner:

1. To teach yourself to use Microsoft Word, is it best to rely on the chapter or on Word Help when you need answers?

2. The most important skill learned in this chapter is how to teach yourself a computer skill. Rate yourself at Level A through E on how well you're doing with this skill. What is your level?
   - Level A: I was able to successfully complete the Chapter Mastery Project with the help of only a few of the On Your Own activities in the chapter.
   - Level B: I completed all the On Your Own activities and the Chapter Mastery Project without referring to any of the solutions in the Step-by-Step Solutions Appendix.
   - Level C: I completed all the On Your Own activities and the Chapter Mastery Project by using just a few of the solutions in the Step-by-Step Solutions Appendix.
   - Level D: I completed all the On Your Own activities and the Chapter Mastery Project by using many of the solutions in the Step-by-Step Solutions Appendix.
   - Level E: I completed all the On Your Own activities and the Chapter Mastery Project and had to use all of the solutions in the Step-by-Step Solutions Appendix.

To continue toward the goal of teaching yourself computer skills, if you're not at Level A, try to move up one level on how you learn in Chapter 4.

Projects to Help You

Now that you've mastered the material in this chapter, you're ready to tackle the three projects focused on your career, personal, or academic goals. Depending on your own interests, you might choose to complete any or all of these projects to help you achieve your goals.

Google Project I'm not ready to buy Microsoft Office for my home computer. Is there free online software I can use to create simple documents at home?

Project 1: Beyond Office: Using Google Drive to Create a Document

In Chapter 2, you set up a Google Drive and stored a file in it. Google Drive also includes a word processing application that you can use to create documents on your Google Drive. Because the Google Drive software is in the cloud on the Google website, you don't have to install it on your computer—and it's free. However, it doesn't have all of the functionality that Word has.

As an independent learner, you can teach yourself how to use Google Drive software. Let's use it to create the document shown in Figure 3-19. As you work on a document, Google automatically saves it to your Google Drive. After the document is finished, you can share it with others who also have a Google account, and you can download it to your computer.

Follow these steps to enter text in the document, format the text, and add clip art:

WATCH

CHAPTER 3
GOOGLE DRIVE
VIDEO

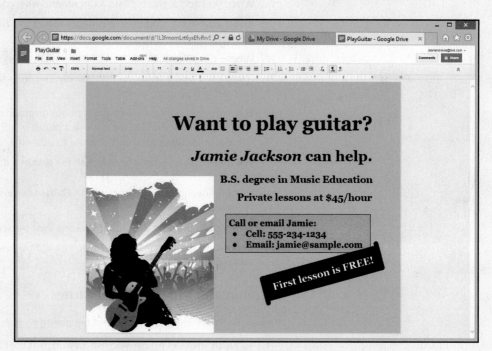

FIGURE 3-19   This document is created using free cloud software at Google Drive.

Step 1.   Go to Google.com, sign in, and access the Google Drive you set up in Chapter 2. Create a new document. Orient the Page setup using **Landscape**, and make the page color of the document a gold color.

Step 2.   Type the following four lines of text, placing a hard return after each line. Because of the way Google manages graphics on a page, it's best to keep pressing **Enter** until your insertion point reaches the bottom of the page.

> Want to play guitar?
> Jamie Jackson can help.
> B.S. degree in Music Education
> Private lessons at $45/hour

Step 3.   Right-justify all the text in the document and format the text as **Georgia** font.

- Format the first line of text as **48 point, bold**.

- Format the second line of text as **36 point, bold**.

- Format **Jamie Jackson** in the second line in **italics**.

- Format the last two lines of text in **24 point, bold**.

- Change spacing between lines (called line spacing) to **1.5**.

Step 4.   Upload to your Google Drive the GuitarPlayer graphic in the sample_files folder on your USB flash drive. Then insert the image in the document. Change the image from an *In line* image to a *Wrap text* image so that you have more control over where the image is placed on the page. Resize and position the image as shown earlier in Figure 3-19.

Do the following to add a text box and a shape to the document:

Step 5. Insert a text box to the right of the graphic, as shown in Figure 3-19. Make the shape fill color orange. Make the line color **Black**. Type the following text into the text box:

> Call or email Jamie:
> Cell: 555-234-1234
> Email: jamie@sample.com

Step 6. Format the text in the text box as **Georgia, 18 point, bold**. Make the last two lines in the text box a bulleted list. The text in the text box should be left-justified.

Step 7. Insert a Horizontal Scroll shape (Google callout) into the document. Make the shape fill color black and make the text white. Type the following text into the scroll:

> First lesson is FREE!

Step 8. Format the scroll text as **Georgia, 24 point, bold**. Center the text in the scroll. Align the text in the middle of the scroll. Use the rotation handle to rotate the scroll as shown in Figure 3-19. Make sure the scroll is layered on top of the text box, not beneath it. The document is now finished and stored on your Google Drive.

Do the following to share and download the document. You'll download the document as a Microsoft Word document and a PDF:

Step 9. Name the document **PlayGuitar**. Verify the document is a one-page document. If the document has more than one page, fix the problem.

Step 10. Share the Google doc with your instructor. To do that, you'll need to know your instructor's email address for his or her Google account.

Step 11. Download the Google doc as a Microsoft Word document to your USB flash drive, hard drive, or another location given by your instructor. Download the document again, this time as a PDF file. Open the Microsoft Word file. Notice that spacing and graphic placement might need adjusting in Word. Open the PDF file. Notice that the .jpg file is not included in the document.

Project 2: Using Word in Your Personal Life

The most important computer skill is how to teach yourself a computer skill. Microsoft Word has many features not covered in the chapter. In this project, create a one-page document advertising a business you are starting. The business can be for anything you like, perhaps a hobby or business you enjoy. Business ideas might be golf lessons, tutoring, pet sitting, or babysitting. Don't forget to put your contact information in the document.

Include these features and elements in the document:

> Text that uses WordArt.

> **Hint** To insert WordArt or SmartArt into a document, go to the INSERT ribbon and click **SmartArt** or **WordArt**.

> A photo, which can be a picture of yourself or any other photo that can help advertise your business. If you don't have a photo, use the MyPhoto1.jpg photo in the sample_files folder on the www.pearsonhighered.com/jump website or in MyITLab.

> **Hint** To insert a photo in a document, click **Pictures** on the INSERT ribbon. In the Insert Picture dialog box that appears, locate your photo and then click **Insert**.

Name the document **MyBusiness**. After you finish the document, print it.

Personal Project I'm starting up a pet-sitting business. I want to post a flyer in the neighborhood park where people walk their dogs.

Academic Project I need to create a calendar that shows my class schedule and all the due dates for important assignments.

Project 3: Word in Your Academic Career

Word offers several templates that can help you plan your schedule, homework assignments, or events. To see these templates, on the FILE tab, search for **Planners** templates. Select a template that will be useful to you in your academic career. Download the template and fill it in. Name the document **MyPlanner**. After you finish the document, print it.

Project to Help Others

One of the best ways to learn is to teach someone else. And, in teaching someone else, you are making a contribution to that person's life. As part of each chapter's work, you are encouraged to teach someone a skill you have learned. In this case, help your apprentice learn to use Microsoft Word.

When helping others learn, don't do the work for them. Coach and instruct. Show them how to find information for themselves. Help them be as independent a learner as possible.

Working with your apprentice, do the following:

Step 1. Ask your apprentice what type of one-page document she might like to create. Examples are a flyer, business card, certificate, invitation, meeting agenda, schedule, or permission slip.

Step 2. Help your apprentice create the document. Will a template help? If you can find a template that suits your purpose, show your apprentice how to download and use the template. If you can't find a template, help your apprentice create the document from a new blank document.

Step 3. Ask your apprentice to evaluate how the tutoring session went. Briefly describe her response.

Step 4. Print the document that your apprentice created and bring it to class.

Step 5. Use Notepad to create a text file that contains answers about the tutoring session and send the file to your instructor. If you are using MyITLab, you can post the file in Dropbox in MyITLab. On the other hand, your instructor might prefer that you post the file to your OneDrive. Here are the questions:

1. Who is your apprentice?

2. What kind of document did your apprentice create?

3. Did your apprentice create a document starting with a blank document or a template?

4. Briefly describe how the apprentice evaluated the tutoring session.

5. How do you think the session went? How would you like to improve it next time?

4 Using OneNote to Research Online

In This Chapter, You Will:

Select Your Research Topic and Prepare to Take Research Notes

4.1 Examine how to choose an appropriate research topic

4.2 Prepare OneNote to collect research notes

Explore the Topic and Its Subtopics

4.3 Find general information and subtopics about a topic

4.4 Capture images and graphics into your OneNote research

Dig Deeper to Find the Best Sources

4.5 Identify information for a Works Cited list

4.6 Decide whether content is credible

4.7 Find primary sources and authoritative websites

4.8 Find books and scholarly journal articles online

4.9 Use your school library's website for research

Evaluate Your Research and Organize Your Research Notes

4.10 Evaluate your research by asking important questions

4.11 Use OneNote to organize, print, and export your research notes

The web has changed the way we research. Because the web offers many credible and authoritative sources, including books and professional journals, it's possible to do all of your scholarly or academic research on a topic without ever walking through the doors of a library. In this chapter, you'll learn how to use the web to research important topics. In Chapter 5, you'll learn how to use Microsoft Word to create a research paper. If you know about the many shortcuts discussed in this chapter, you can find the best sources quickly, saving much time.

As with all chapters in this book, you can choose which of the learning paths below best suits your needs. No matter which path you choose, as you work your way through the chapter, remember the most important computer skill is how to teach yourself a computer skill. Therefore, this chapter is designed to help you teach yourself how to use OneNote to research online.

LEARNING PATHS

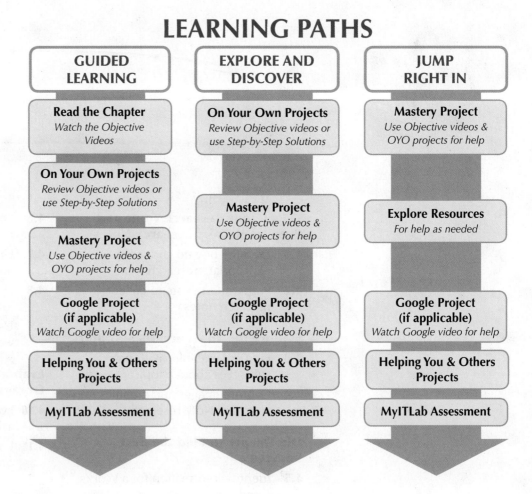

GUIDED LEARNING	EXPLORE AND DISCOVER	JUMP RIGHT IN
Read the Chapter *Watch the Objective Videos*	**On Your Own Projects** *Review Objective videos or use Step-by-Step Solutions*	**Mastery Project** *Use Objective videos & OYO projects for help*
On Your Own Projects *Review Objective videos or use Step-by-Step Solutions*		**Explore Resources** *For help as needed*
Mastery Project *Use Objective videos & OYO projects for help*	**Mastery Project** *Use Objective videos & OYO projects for help*	
Google Project (if applicable) *Watch Google video for help*	**Google Project (if applicable)** *Watch Google video for help*	**Google Project (if applicable)** *Watch Google video for help*
Helping You & Others Projects	**Helping You & Others Projects**	**Helping You & Others Projects**
MyITLab Assessment	**MyITLab Assessment**	**MyITLab Assessment**

Selecting Your Research Topic and Preparing to Take Research Notes

Researching and writing on a topic are important skills used by students and employees. In this part of the chapter, you learn how to choose an appropriate research topic, how to use OneNote to collect your research, and about the four phases of research.

WATCH

OBJECTIVE 4.1
VIDEO

Objective 4.1: Examine How to Choose an Appropriate Research Topic

In a research and writing class, your instructor might ask you to select your topic. For example, suppose an instructor gives you the research and writing assignment shown in Figure 4-1. First, let's focus on selecting the topic so that it fits the criteria given in the assignment.

Mr. Greg Chen
English 102

Research Paper Assignment

Requirements for the research paper:
- The body of the paper must be a minimum of 400 words and no more than 600 words
- Select a topic that is current
- Include at least one example of a primary source
- Use the MLA style guide to format the paper
- No more than 20% of the paper can be direct quotes

Required sources:
- One or more books
- One or more scholarly journal articles
- One or more web sites
- One or more newspapers or reputable news web sites

Deliverables:
- Your research notes including your outline
- The research paper

FIGURE 4-1   This research paper assignment lists required types of sources and allows you to select the topic.

When deciding on a good topic for a research paper, keep these tips in mind:

> The topic should be of interest to you. Pick a hot topic that is exciting and that you want to learn about it.

> The topic should give you the opportunity to offer your own opinions or solutions.

> The paper should offer a solution to a problem or help someone.

> The topic should lend itself well to the source requirements. For example, books come out about two years after an event. If you must use a book as a source, recent events will not work unless you can include historical or background information about the event, which you can find in a book.

Tip As you search the web for research topics, you might find a so-called paper mill site. This type of site offers to write a research paper for you or offers research papers for sale. Avoid **plagiarism**! Most schools have an academic code of honor that says you will not present other works as your own and you will not do others' work for them. Breaking the honor code can lead to failing a class or being expelled from school. In addition, technology today helps instructors detect when papers come from such sites.

> The topic should not be so obscure or narrow that you will not find enough sources.
> The topic should not be so broad that the number of sources will overwhelm you or make it difficult for you to adequately cover it in the number of required pages.
> You should choose a topic that your instructor likes and approves.

The web can help you find a good topic. Here are some tips:

> Do a Google search on "research topics."
> Get more specific. For example, search for "political research topics" or "autism research topics."

Don't settle for the first ideas you find. Browse a bit until you find a topic that truly sparks your interest and fits the criteria given earlier.

As you search for general information and subtopics, if you decide your topic is too broad, change your topic to one of its subtopics. If you decide your topic is too narrow, use it as a subtopic in a broader topic.

> **plagiarism**—Presenting someone else's ideas or words as your own.

Suppose you're considering the adventure of volunteering for the Peace Corps, and you want to find out about the requirements and how to apply. You also want to know about the benefits of serving and what it's like to serve. You can use this topic about the Peace Corps for your research and writing assignment. You'll need to find credible information, collect your research in organized notes, and compose a paper from that information. In this chapter, we use the Peace Corps as our research topic and OneNote to collect our research.

Objective 4.2: Prepare OneNote to Collect Research Notes

Microsoft Office **OneNote** is a great application for taking notes because it's easy to grab content from your browser into OneNote. In OneNote, notes are kept in notebooks. Just as with physical notebooks, a OneNote notebook has sections, and each section has one or more pages, as shown in Figure 4-2.

> **OneNote**—A Microsoft Office application used to hold and organize notes, including content taken from the web. OneNote keeps content in notebooks. Notebooks are divided into sections. Sections can have one or more pages.

WATCH

**OBJECTIVE 4.2
VIDEO**

Tip In this chapter, we cover only some of the features of OneNote. Use the OneNote Help feature to learn more about the application.

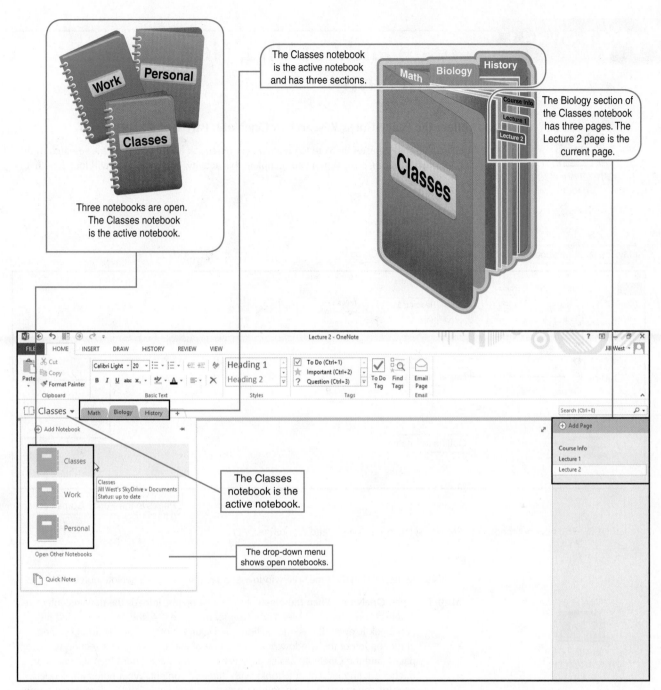

FIGURE 4-2 A OneNote notebook is organized like a physical notebook: A notebook has sections, and each section has pages.

ON YOUR OWN 4.1

Create and Set Up a New Notebook in OneNote

WATCH

OBJECTIVE 4.2
VIDEO

Collect the Peace Corps Research in OneNote: Part 1 of 9

In this activity, you'll use OneNote to create a new notebook and set it up for the research in this chapter on the Peace Corps. When you complete this activity, your notebook will look like that in Figure 4-3.

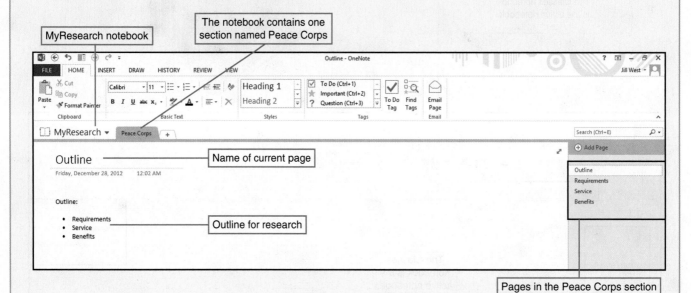

FIGURE 4-3   The new notebook contains one section, four pages, and an outline.

WATCH

CHAPTER 4
DIVING DEEPER
VIDEO

Let's start by examining the OneNote window and creating a new OneNote notebook:

Step 1. Open **OneNote**. When the OneNote window opens, it loads the most recently used notebook on your computer. For example, in Figure 4-4, the notebook titled Jill's Notebook is open. It has one section titled Quick Notes, which is listed on the tab at the top left of the window next to the title of the notebook. This section has two pages, and the OneNote Basics page is the current page. Your OneNote window might contain different notebooks with different content. What notebook is open on your computer? To open another notebook, you can click the drop-down arrow beside the currently open notebook.

Step 2. Create a new notebook, naming the notebook **MyResearch**. Save it to your USB flash drive, hard drive, OneDrive, or another location given by your instructor. As you work, OneNote automatically saves your notebook to this device each time you make changes in the notebook.

> **Hint** To create a new notebook, start by clicking the **FILE** tab.

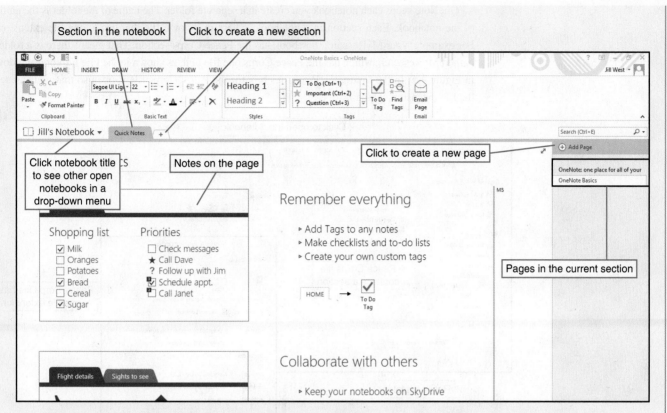

FIGURE 4-4   The OneNote window is used to manage notebooks, sections, pages, and notes.

Do the following to set up your new notebook for research in this chapter:

Step 3.   The notebook has only one section named *New Section 1*. Rename the section **Peace Corps**.

Step 4.   The first page of this section is named *Untitled page*. Rename the page **Outline**.

> **Hint**   To rename a page, type the name of the page in the text field at the top left of the page. The name showing in the page tab changes as you type.

Step 5.   You can keep research about each subtopic on its own subtopic page. Create three new pages, naming them **Requirements**, **Service**, and **Benefits**. You can add new pages later for other subtopics. As you research, keep your research notes organized by putting research about a particular subtopic on its page.

> **Hint**   To add a new page, click **Add Page** on the right side of the OneNote window.

Step 6.   Return to the Outline page and type an outline that has three subtopics: **Requirements**, **Service**, and **Benefits**. Refer back to Figure 4-3 to see the outline.

> **Hint**   To type on a page, click anywhere on the page to create an insertion point and start typing.

Step 7.   Later, as you search the web using Internet Explorer, you can switch back and forth between OneNote and Internet Explorer by clicking the program icons in the taskbar. For now, close OneNote.

Solutions
Appendix

For help: See On Your Own 4.1 Step-by-Step Solution

OneNote keeps each notebook you create in a separate folder. The name of the folder is the name of the notebook. Each section in a notebook is kept in its own file that has a .one file extension. For example, your MyResearch notebook has the Peace Corps section. That means there is a folder named MyResearch, which has the Peace Corps.one file in it, as shown in the File Explorer window in Figure 4-5. In the figure, the Properties box for the Peace Corps file is open so that you can see the file extension, which is .one.

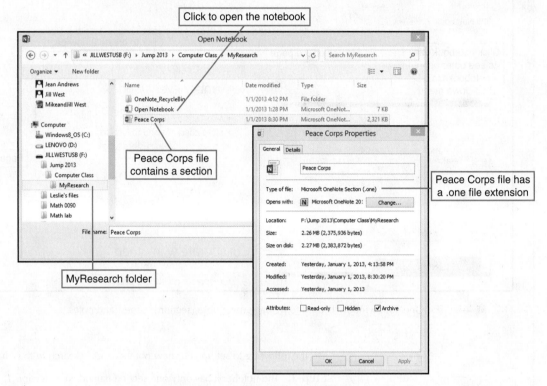

FIGURE 4-5   A OneNote notebook is a folder, and a section is a .one file.

Not Working? This screen shot shows File Explorer in Windows 8. Windows Explorer in Windows 7 will look a little different, but the same information is available.

One way to open a notebook is to double-click the **Open Notebook** file, which is shown in Figure 4-5.

You're now ready to start your research. An expert researcher uses a four-phase process when researching a topic:

Phase 1.   Explore general information and subtopics about the topic.
Phase 2.   Dig deeper to find the best sources.
Phase 3.   Evaluate where your research is taking you and ask penetrating questions.
Phase 4.   Organize your research notes.

In this chapter, we'll follow this four-phase approach as we research the Peace Corps.

Research Phase 1: Exploring the Topic and Its Subtopics

In the first phase of research, you explore your topic by finding general information and subtopics about it.

Objective 4.3: Find General Information and Subtopics about a Topic

Your goal at this stage of research is to explore the topic without going too deep into the details. General information might include definitions of technical terms, background, controversies about the topic, unsolved problems, and key players. A research paper is typically divided into subtopics, so you'll also be looking for these subtopics during this initial phase of research.

WATCH

OBJECTIVE 4.3
VIDEO

Tip At this stage of research, don't pay too much attention to the sources of information. If you do find something interesting, however, be sure to bookmark it so you can return to the website later. In the next phase of research, you focus on finding authoritative and credible sources that you can use in your research paper.

Tip Wikipedia.org articles are written by anyone who wants to contribute to them. Because the articles are not always written by recognized experts, most instructors do not allow Wikipedia.org to be cited as a source for a research paper. However, Wikipedia.org is a great place to look for general information about a topic for the first phase of your research. The site can also lead you to authoritative sources you'll need for the second phase of research.

As you search for general information, look for answers to these questions:

> Can I explain the topic in one short paragraph?
> What are the issues and who are the experts?
> When and where did important events happen?
> What are people saying who are directly involved?
> What are people saying who are analyzing the topic?
> What problems are not yet solved?
> Who is responsible for solving these problems?

Websites can help you find general information and subtopics:

> Use Google.com *autosuggest* to find subtopics. Google *related searches* can help you broaden a topic. Google *related people* or *videos* can provide additional perspectives. You learn to use all these tools in On Your Own activities in this part of the chapter.
> Use Wikipedia.org to find general information, subtopics, an outline, and links to other content.
> Use a **clustering search engine** to find subtopics.

> **clustering search engine**—A search engine that specializes in sorting hits by subtopics. Examples are carrot2.org, yippy.com, and iboogie.com.

ON YOUR OWN 4.2

WATCH

OBJECTIVE 4.3 VIDEO

peace corps	
peace corps	
peace corps **jobs**	
peace corps **wiki**	
peace corps **application**	

Searches related to **peace corps**

peace corps requirements	peace corps jobs
peace corps alternatives	peace corps blogs
americorps	peace corps wiki
peace corps history	peace corps headquarters

Find Preliminary Research and Subtopics about Your Topic

Collect the Peace Corps Research in OneNote: Part 2 of 9

Let's use Google autosuggest and Google related searches to find ideas for subtopics or ideas to broaden a topic that is too narrow. Do the following:

Step 1. Open your MyResearch notebook. Use Google.com in Internet Explorer to search on the phrase **peace corps**. Choose two subtopics that Google autosuggest offers to complete the search string and add those subtopics as pages in your OneNote notebook.

Step 2. The related searches list at the bottom of the Google results page can help you broaden a topic if your current topic is too narrow. Choose a broader topic from the related searches list and add it as a page in your OneNote notebook.

To use Wikipedia.org to find general information and subtopics about the Peace Corps, do the following:

> **Tip** You could use the search utility on the Wikipedia.org site rather than a Google search, but a Google search usually gives better results.

Step 3. Search for information about the Peace Corps, limiting your Google search only to the **Wikipedia.org** site.

Step 4. Find an article on the Peace Corps that gives a good overview and definition of the Peace Corps. Bookmark the article in Internet Explorer **Favorites**.

>

Step 5. From within the article you found in step 4, find the paragraph that best defines and/or provides an overview of the Peace Corp. Copy the paragraph onto the Outline page of the Peace Corps section of your OneNote notebook.

> **Hint** To copy a paragraph in your browser into OneNote, press and drag to select the paragraph. Right-click on the selection. In the shortcut menu that appears, click **Send to OneNote**, as shown in Figure 4-6. The Select Location in OneNote dialog box appears. Select the OneNote page to receive the paragraph and click **OK**.

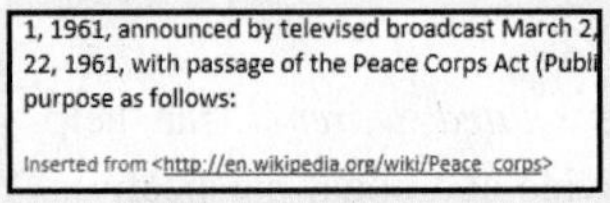

1, 1961, announced by televised broadcast March 2,
22, 1961, with passage of the Peace Corps Act (Publi
purpose as follows:

Inserted from <http://en.wikipedia.org/wiki/Peace_corps>

Step 6. Notice that OneNote inserts the source URL of the paragraph below the text. Use the highlighting feature of OneNote to highlight an important sentence in this paragraph.

Step 7. Most Wikipedia articles include an outline, and this outline can help you make sure you haven't overlooked an important subtopic. Find the outline in the Peace Corps article. Besides the subtopics already identified, add two more subtopics suggested by the outline in the Wikipedia article.

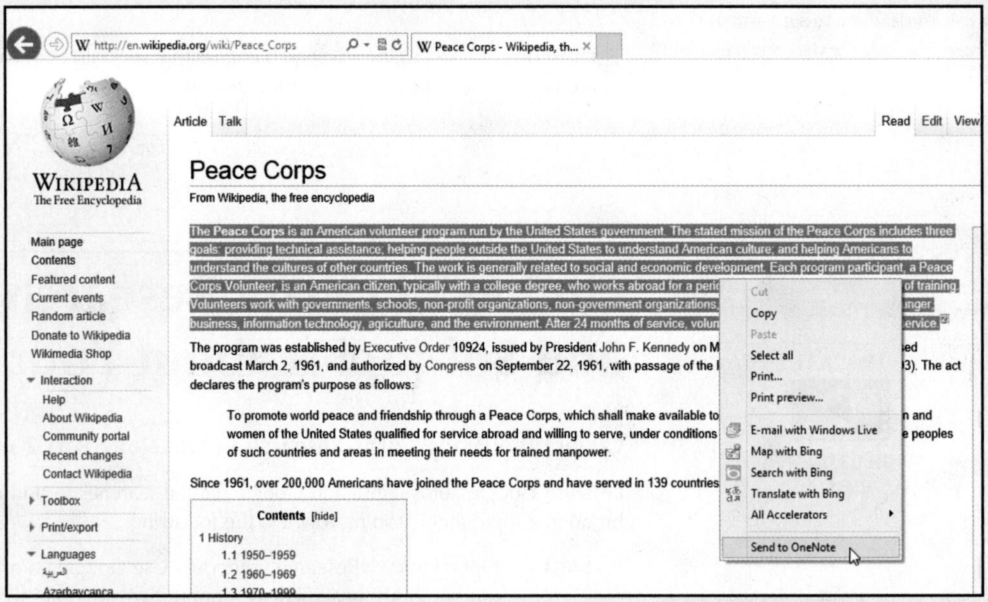

FIGURE 4-6   Selected text in Wikipedia.org is ready to be copied into OneNote.

Next use a clustering search engine to find subtopics:

Step 8. Go to the **carrot2.org** site and search for information about the Peace Corps. What are some subtopics that the search identified? Add one more subtopic to your OneNote notebook.

> **Tip** As you find general information and subtopics about a topic, develop your outline on the Outline page of OneNote. Don't forget to bookmark the sites that offer useful information. If content looks really good, you can go ahead and copy it into OneNote.

Solutions Appendix

For help: See *On Your Own 4.2* **Step-by-Step Solution**

WATCH

OBJECTIVE 4.4
VIDEO

Objective 4.4: Capture Images and Graphics into Your OneNote Research

Google provides multiple options for customizing your search. As you learned in Chapter 2, you can limit the search to sites with images. When you find images or other graphics in your search, you can import a copy of those images into your OneNote notebook using the OneNote Screen Clipping tool.

ON YOUR OWN 4.3

WATCH

OBJECTIVE 4.4
VIDEO

Use the OneNote Screen Clipping Tool

Collect the Peace Corps Research in OneNote: Part 3 of 9

The Screen Clipping tool is available on the INSERT ribbon of OneNote. Let's use the tool to import an image into your OneNote notebook:

Step 1. Use Google to search for images about the Peace Corps. Be sure to search for the exact text "Peace Corps."

Step 2. Use the OneNote Screen Clipping tool to copy some of the image results into the Outline page in your OneNote notebook.

For help: See On Your Own 4.3 Step-by-Step Solution

Solutions
Appendix

Research Phase 2: Digging Deeper to Find the Best Sources

After you're familiar with a topic and have an outline, you're ready to dig deeper. The next step is to find authoritative and scholarly research about the topic. Here's where the web can make this part of research easy and fun.

WATCH

OBJECTIVE 4.5
VIDEO

Objective 4.5: Identify Information for a Works Cited List

As you search for sources to use in your research paper, know that the source must be listed in the Works Cited list of the paper. Figure 4-7 shows an example of a Works Cited page. The information provided in a Works Cited list should enable others to find the source if they want to verify what you've written or learn more about the topic.

> Works Cited—The list of all sources used to write a research paper. The Works Cited list is at the end of the paper and is also called the Bibliography or References. List all your sources even if you don't include a direct quote from the source.

> Witt 3
>
> Works Cited
>
> Banerjee, Dillon. *The Insider's Guide to the Peace Corps: What to Know Before You Go.*
>
> Berkeley: Ten Speed Press, 2009. Web. 6 Jan. 2013. <http://books.google.com>.
>
> Nichols, Christopher. "Peace Corps volunteer from Taunton still helping friends in Africa."
>
> *Taunton Daily Gazette* 8 Dec 2012. Web. 1 Jan. 2013.
>
> *Peace Corps.* n.d. Web. 28 Dec. 2012. <http://www.peacecorps.gov>.
>
> Plante, Thomas G., Katy Lackey, and Hwang Jeong Yeon. "The Impact of Immersion Trips on
>
> Development of Compassion Among College Students." *Journal of Experiential*
>
> *Education* 32.1 (2009): 28-43. *EBSCO.* Web. 28 Dec. 2012.
>
> *Waid's World.* 7 August 2011. Web. 30 Dec 2012. <http://waidsworld.wordpress.com>.

FIGURE 4-7   This sample Works Cited page lists all sources used in the research paper.

Table 4-1 lists the information you need for each type of source. If you find a book or article online rather than in print, in addition to the information listed in Table 4-1, include this information about the online source:

> Name of website or online database
> URL of the website
> Date you accessed the website

As you find sources, record the **citation** information in OneNote. Later, you will use it to build your Works Cited list. In Chapter 5, you learn how to arrange and format a Works Cited list.

---

citation—Brief text inside parentheses within the body of a research paper that gives credit to another source. If the source uses page numbering, include the page or pages where you found the information. Also called *parenthetical documentation*.

WATCH

OBJECTIVE 4.6
VIDEO

Tip When you're researching a project in a class, your instructor might prefer that you use only your school library's website because the library might attempt to use only credible resources.

Objective 4.6: Decide Whether Content Is Credible

As you research, you'll find websites, books, and journal articles that might not be credible sources. Some websites present false information or facts that aren't verified, and a website might be intentionally lying. A good researcher knows how to weed out bad sources from the good ones. When searching the web, you must therefore decide whether the content you find is credible.

When deciding whether content is credible, consider the following questions:

> What is the type of website and who owns it?
> What are others saying about the source?
> Is the author of the work credible?
> Are there opposing views?

The next sections explain the reasons behind each question.

What Is the Type of Website, and Who Owns It?

Websites that have a top-level domain name of .gov or .edu belong to the government or to educational institutions. Content from these sites is usually considered credible and appropriate for research papers.

The owner of a website is usually listed at the bottom of its home page. If you want to find out more, go to the website **whois.net** and enter the domain name of the website in the search box. Whois.net returns the person or organization that owns the domain name unless the owner's name is blocked for privacy. If you don't recognize the owner's name, do a Google search to find out more about the owner.

TABLE 4-1   Information about a Source Needed for a Works Cited List

Type of Source	Required Citation Information
Book*	• Author or authors (up to four authors) • Book editor (if applicable) • Title, including subtitle • Publisher • City of publication (only one city required) • Latest copyright year (year published) • Volume number (if applicable)
Journal or magazine article*	• Author or authors (up to four authors) • Article title • Journal or magazine title • Volume number • Issue number (if applicable) • Date published (month, day, year) • Pages that the article spans (for example, 72–73) or first page of the article if it jumps pages (for example, 72+)
Newspaper article*	• Author or authors (up to four and might be omitted) • Article title • Newspaper title • Date published (month, day, year) • Pages that the article spans or first page of article if it jumps pages
Website content, including text and images	• Author or authors (up to four and might not be available) • Title of work (might not be available) • Title of website • Date of publication of the work (if known) • Date you accessed the source • URL (optional)
Interview	• Name of person interviewed • Date of interview

*Note: If you find a book or article online rather than in print, in addition to the information listed above, include in the Works Cited list the name of the website or online database, the website URL, and the date you accessed the website.

What Are Others Saying about the Source?

Use Google to search for reviews about the source. For example, to find reviews about the website soyouwanna.com, use this search string in Google:

soyouwanna.com website reviews

To limit the hits to sites other than soyouwanna.com, use this search string:

soyouwanna.com website reviews -site:soyouwanna.com

You can also search for reviews about magazines, books, or journals. Amazon.com is a great place to look for reviews about a book. For example, Figure 4-8 shows a book on the Amazon .com site. From this page, you can read customer reviews, a biography of the author, and some pages in the book.

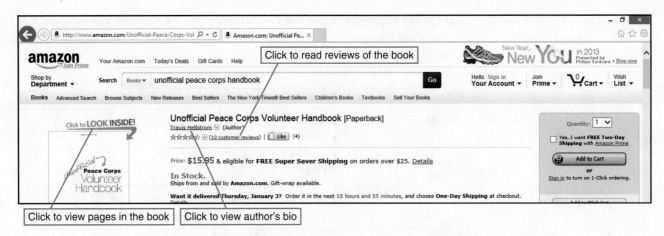

FIGURE 4-8   Amazon.com provides book reviews written by customers and a biography of the author.

Is the Author of a Work Credible?

You can find information about the author on the web. Ask these questions about the author:

> What are others saying about the author? To find out, enter the name of the author in a Google search box and follow some links.

> Is the author considered an expert on the topic? What are the author's credentials?

> Does the author's name appear with the website? Does the author not want to be associated with the website? If so, suspect the credibility of the work.

> Is contact information about the author published? If not, the author might be trying to avoid confrontation or honest discussion about a topic.

> Do others quote the author in their own works?

Are There Opposing Views?

Many websites take sides on an issue and fail to present opposing views. Ask these questions when considering how the author handles opposing views:

> Is a website presenting only one side of an issue? If so, the site might be biased. A biased site sometimes presents the facts in a slanted way so as to make a point. What are the opposing views?

> Is the site giving opinions without backing these opinions with facts?

> Are there glaring omissions that indicate that the author does not want you to consider other facts or opinions?

> Is the site attacking the character of those who disagree with its position? Biased authors tend to do that.

As you search for authoritative content about your topic, be sure to ask yourself if each source you are about to use is credible.

Objective 4.7: Find Primary Sources and Authoritative Websites

Notice in the original assignment in Figure 4-1 that the instructor asks you to use at least one primary source in your paper. In research, **primary sources** are sources that provide *firsthand* accounts by someone who is directly involved in an activity or event. Note that this person may

WATCH

**OBJECTIVE 4.7
VIDEO**

Tip When you browse the web for news sites, be sure to verify the news site is a reputable one. If you're not sure the site is reputable, do a Google search to get reviews of the site.

> **primary source**—In research, a source that provides firsthand content by someone who is directly involved in an activity or event. This person might not be an expert about the topic. For example, an interview, Facebook post, or blog by someone who experienced Hurricane Sandy is a primary source.

Tip As you search the archives of newspaper sites, you might find an article that you can't view unless you pay a fee or subscribe to the site. For example, **newspaperarchive.com** is a subscription website that offers a great database of 200 years of historical newspaper articles. Your school library or a public library near you might subscribe to the site. Later in the chapter, you'll learn about accessing information paid for by your school.

or may not be an expert about the topic. Newspaper articles often include quotes from people involved in an event that make for good primary sources. Such articles can also provide excellent insight into how people view an event or activity.

Today, most newspapers provide searchable online *archives* of all their content. The Google News site (**news.google.com**) is a great starting point for locating newspaper articles. In addition, some websites, like the one shown in Figure 4-9, let you search a wide range of newspaper archives to find information.

In addition to newspapers, *blogs* written by those directly involved in an event can be excellent sources when you're searching for firsthand experiences about a topic.

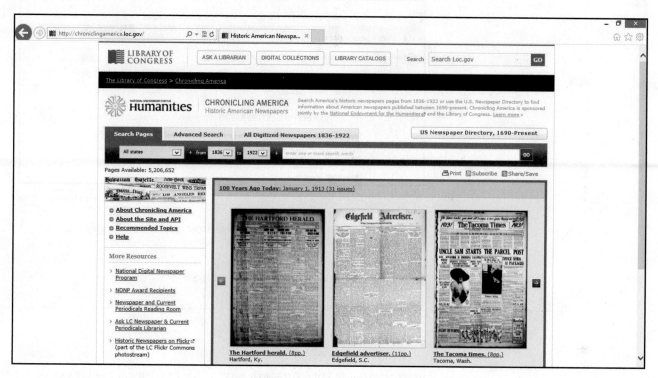

FIGURE 4-9 Chroniclingamerica.loc.gov archives many old newspaper issues and serves as a newspaper database.

ON YOUR OWN 4.4

Find Online Newspaper Articles and Blogs

WATCH

OBJECTIVE 4.7
VIDEO

Collect the Peace Corps Research in OneNote: Part 4 of 9

Suppose you want to find newspaper articles about how Peace Corps volunteers have made a difference in other countries. Do the following:

Step 1. Go to the Google News site (**news.google.com**) that you bookmarked in Chapter 2. Search for an article about how Peace Corps volunteers have made a difference. What search string did you use that located a good article? Figure 4-10 shows the results of one search with an article at the top that fits the criteria. The article is named *Peace Corps volunteer from Taunton still helping friends in Africa*. What is the title of the article you found?

Step 2. Copy a paragraph from the article you found into OneNote. Put the text on the Service page in OneNote. Highlight text in the paragraph that you think is most useful.

>

If you find a quote by someone directly involved, that quote can serve as a primary source.

Step 3. Include on the page in OneNote all the information you need to cite the article later in your Works Cited list. For an online newspaper article, you need the author, article title, newspaper title, date published, URL, and date you accessed the site.

Step 4. Find a blog written by someone in the Peace Corps in the past year. Copy text into the Benefits or Service page of OneNote and make sure you have all the citation information you need.

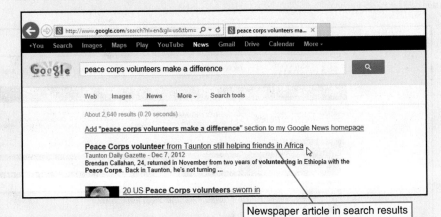

FIGURE 4-10   Google News provides newspaper articles that can give valuable insight as to how people view an event or activity.

Solutions Appendix

For help: See *On Your Own 4.4* Step-by-Step Solution

Primary sources can bring a research paper to life by reporting real-life experiences about a topic. In addition to these firsthand experiences, most papers should include what the experts have to say. Contributions by experts who are not directly involved in the event or topic are called **secondary sources** and usually include explanations, an analysis, and conclusions.

> **secondary source**—In research, a source that provides secondhand knowledge about an event or topic and usually includes an analysis and conclusions. Good secondary sources are written by the experts on a topic. For example, an analysis of Hurricane Sandy written by a weather scientist is a secondary source.

So how can you find the experts? Although Wikipedia.org is not itself an authoritative site, it can lead you to the experts and authoritative sources. Wikipedia.org articles sometimes include sections titled References, Further reading, and External links, which can provide links to authoritative websites and other secondary sources.

ON YOUR OWN 4.5

Use Wikipedia.org to Locate Authoritative Content

WATCH

OBJECTIVE 4.7
VIDEO

Collect the Peace Corps Research in OneNote: Part 5 of 9

Let's see how Wikipedia.org can help you find authoritative sources and content. Do the following:

Step 1. Return to the Peace Corps article in Wikipedia.org that you bookmarked earlier. Does the article contain sections titled Further reading or References?

Step 2. Look near the bottom of the article to find a list of **External links** (see Figure 4-11).

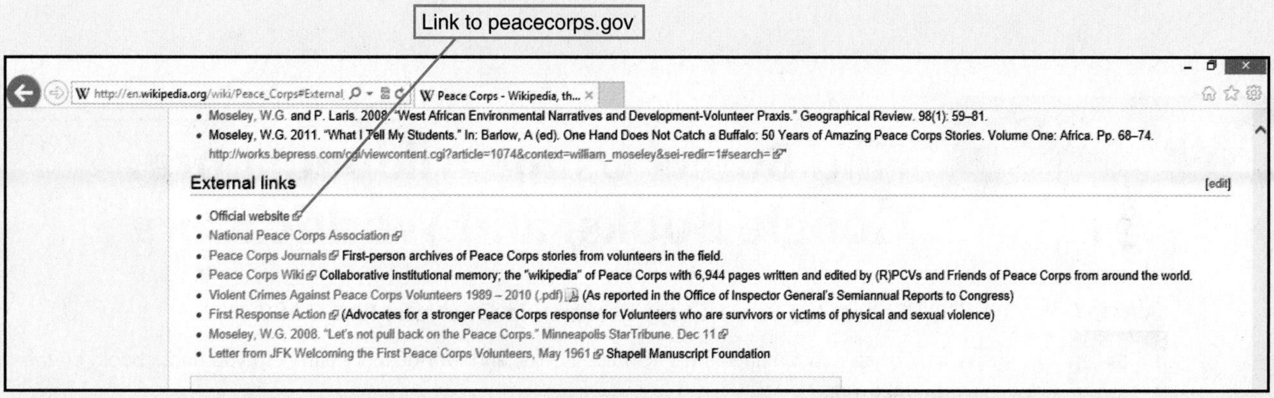

Link to peacecorps.gov

W http://en.wikipedia.org/wiki/Peace_Corps#External   W Peace Corps - Wikipedia, th... ×

- Moseley, W.G. and P. Laris. 2008. "West African Environmental Narratives and Development-Volunteer Praxis." Geographical Review. 98(1): 59–81.
- Moseley, W.G. 2011. "What I Tell My Students." In: Barlow, A (ed). One Hand Does Not Catch a Buffalo: 50 Years of Amazing Peace Corps Stories. Volume One: Africa. Pp. 68–74. http://works.bepress.com/cgi/viewcontent.cgi?article=1074&context=william_moseley&sei-redir=1#search=

External links   [edit]

- Official website
- National Peace Corps Association
- Peace Corps Journals First-person archives of Peace Corps stories from volunteers in the field.
- Peace Corps Wiki Collaborative institutional memory; the "wikipedia" of Peace Corps with 6,944 pages written and edited by (R)PCVs and Friends of Peace Corps from around the world.
- Violent Crimes Against Peace Corps Volunteers 1989 – 2010 (.pdf) (As reported in the Office of Inspector General's Semiannual Reports to Congress)
- First Response Action (Advocates for a stronger Peace Corps response for Volunteers who are survivors or victims of physical and sexual violence)
- Moseley, W.G. 2008. "Let's not pull back on the Peace Corps." Minneapolis StarTribune. Dec 11
- Letter from JFK Welcoming the First Peace Corps Volunteers, May 1961 Shapell Manuscript Foundation

FIGURE 4-11   The External links section of a Wikipedia.org article can lead you to authoritative sources and content.

Step 3. The first item listed in the External links section shown in Figure 4-11 is *Official website*, which links to www.peacecorps.gov. Go to **www.peacecorps.gov** and bookmark this site. The website's top-level domain (.gov) indicates that it is a government website.

Step 4. Browse the **peacecorps.gov** site to find answers to the following questions. When you find what you need, copy the text into the Requirements page of OneNote and highlight the most important parts of that text:

    a. Who is eligible to serve in the Peace Corps? How long is the commitment? What types of jobs might a volunteer perform?

    b. How long does the application process take? What are the steps in the application process?

Step 5. Make sure you have the information in OneNote that you will later need to cite the source in your Works Cited list of your research paper. Information you need to collect about a website includes the author(s) (if available), the title of the work (if available), the title of the website, and the date of publication of the work (if known). In addition, OneNote automatically records the URL and the date you accessed the site.

Solutions
Appendix

For help: See *On Your Own 4.5* Step-by-Step Solution

WATCH

OBJECTIVE 4.8
VIDEO

Objective 4.8: Find Books and Scholarly Journal Articles Online

Most instructors require you use at least one book for a research source. Recall that some Wikipedia .org articles have a Further reading section where you can find books about the topic. Google Books (books.google.com) is a powerful tool used to locate books on any topic. The site offers online pages of many books so that you can use content from the book without having to locate the book in a library.

Sometimes Google Books presents a book that appears to be useful for your research, but the pages in the book are not available. In this situation, you can

> Search other websites for the book pages online. Amazon.com often includes pages in a book that you can search.

> Search the Worldcat.org website, which contains a catalog of almost all the books ever printed. Use it to find a library near you that has the book. Google Books contains links to the Worldcat.org site.

ON YOUR OWN 4.6

Find Books Using Wikipedia.org, Google Books, and Worldcat.org

WATCH

OBJECTIVE 4.8
VIDEO

Collect the Peace Corps Research in OneNote: Part 6 of 9

To see how Wikipedia.org, Google Books, and Worldcat.org can help you find a book, do the following:

Step 1. Return to the Wikipedia.org article about the Peace Corps that you bookmarked. Look in the **Further reading** section and find a book about serving in the Peace Corps. Figure 4-12 shows one book, *So, You Want to Join the Peace Corps: What to Know Before You Go,* by Banerjee Dillon.

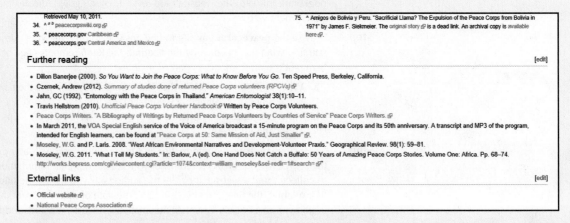

FIGURE 4-12   The Further reading section of a Wikipedia.org article can lead you to good books about the topic.

Step 2. Use **Google Books** to search for books about the Peace Corps. Select one book that describes preparations for Peace Corps service and gives text online. Copy into OneNote some text from the book.

> **Not Working?** If you don't find the book text at Google Books, try Amazon.com. If you still can't find the book text, try a different book.

Step 3. Include the citation information for the book in OneNote. Include the author, title, publisher, city of publication, and year of copyright. Also include the name of the website. (OneNote automatically collects the URL and date you accessed the site.)

Step 4. Use the **Worldcat.org** website to find a library near you that holds the book you found in step 1. Which library did you find?

Solutions Appendix

For help: See *On Your Own 4.6* Step-by-Step Solution

You can also find scholarly journals in print and on the web. Google Scholar (scholar.google .com) is a great shortcut for web research. Google Scholar returns hits for scholarly research, including books and articles in scholarly journals. By clicking these links, you can sometimes find enough scholarly research so that you don't need to go to a library searching for printed books and journals.

> **scholarly journal**—A publication that is published periodically (for example, monthly) and written by experts. The publication is addressed to other experts and professionals. Articles in a scholarly journal are **peer reviewed** and are considered among the best types of sources when doing academic research. An article in a scholarly journal often begins with an **abstract** of the article. Some scholarly journals can be found online.
>
> **peer reviewed**—When people with a similar background and knowledge about a subject read a work and verify the work is accurate. This review by peers happens before the work is published.
>
> **abstract**—An overview of a journal article that can be used to find out what the article covers and the conclusions made in the article.

A little explanation is needed about how journals and journal pages are numbered (see Figure 4-13):

> A journal has a **volume number**, which is the number of years the journal has been published. For example, if a journal has been published for nine years, all the journals published in the ninth year will be labeled as Volume 9 or Volume IX when Roman numerals are used.

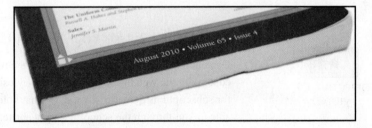

FIGURE 4-13   A journal has a volume number and might have an issue number.

> **volume number**—The number of years a journal has been published. Roman numerals are sometimes used for volume numbers.

> An **issue number** is used only if each journal published in a year starts over at page 1. For example, suppose four journals are published in the sixth year and each journal starts with page 1. An article on pages 45–46 of the fourth journal is identified as Volume 6, Issue 4, pages 45–46.

> **issue number**—The number assigned a journal when each journal published in a single year restarts at page 1.

> If the pages in the journals don't start over at page 1 during the year, no issue number is needed. For example, if an article is found on pages 756–757 in the fourth journal of the sixth year, the article is identified as Volume 6, pages 756–757. In this case, an issue number is not needed to locate the article.

ON YOUR OWN 4.7

WATCH

OBJECTIVE 4.8
VIDEO

Use Google Scholar to Find a Journal Article

Collect the Peace Corps Research in OneNote: Part 7 of 9

Now let's use Google Scholar to find a journal article about the Peace Corps and collect that information into OneNote:

Step 1. Use Google Scholar at **scholar.google.com** to search on **Peace Corps volunteer benefits**. Locate one journal article about the topic.

Step 2. Copy the abstract of the article into the Benefits page of OneNote.

Step 3. Include in OneNote all information you need to cite the article in the Works Cited list of your research paper. Citation information for a journal article includes the author, title of the article, journal title, volume number, issue number (if applicable), date published, and the pages the article spans or first page if the article jumps pages.

Some websites allow you to view the abstract free, but you must pay to see the full article. Sometimes an abstract of an article is all you need. If you need to see the full article, know that your school pays for subscriptions to many journals. Rather than pay for the article yourself, use your school library website to locate and view the article.

Solutions Appendix

For help: See On Your Own 4.7 Step-by-Step Solution

WATCH

OBJECTIVE 4.9
VIDEO

Objective 4.9: Use Your School Library's Website for Research

Content that search engines can locate on the web is called the *free web*. The deep web includes content on the web that you cannot find by using search engines. For example, your school pays for subscriptions to many databases that hold scholarly research and makes that research available to you through the school library website. The school provides access to this deep web data to students, faculty, and other patrons.

> **deep web**—Content on the web that cannot be found by search engines. Most content on the web is in the deep web and includes content that can be accessed only when you pay for the service.
>
> **database**—A collection of data about a topic that is organized so that the data can be searched and retrieved quickly.

Not Working? If you aren't able to access one of these sites using a school computer lab, your school might have blocked the website.

Table 4-2 lists several websites that provide excellent content for research on various topics. Some of these sites hold content that is not free. You might be able to access this content through your school library's website. Follow links on your school library's site that will take you to the other sites. When you arrive at the other site, you'll have access to the content your school has subscribed to.

TABLE 4-2   Websites That Hold Specialized Databases Useful for Research

Website	Description
eric.ed.gov	The Education Resources Information Center (ERIC) database, owned by the U.S. Department of Education, contains scholarly articles about education.
www.apa.org/pubs/databases	American Psychological Association (APA) databases are about behavioral sciences.
www.nlm.nih.gov	Several databases, including the popular PubMed/MEDLINE database, are owned by the U.S. National Library of Medicine (NLM) and are about medicine and health care.
www.oyez.org	The Oyez database, owned by the Oyez Project, is about the U.S. Supreme Court and its work.
www.fedstats.gov	This federal website contains statistics from more than 100 federal agencies.
www.usa.gov	This site provides general government data and statistics.
www.bls.gov	U.S. Bureau of Labor Statistics (BLS) provides economic data, tools, and calculators.
www.bls.gov/bls/other.htm	This BLS web page lists links to websites of international statistical agencies.
infomine.ucr.edu	INFOMINE, owned by the Regents of the University of California, contains scholarly research on a variety of topics.
www.ipl2.org	Internet Public Library (IPL), a public service site hosted by Drexel University and other colleges and universities, holds works on many topics; a chat service is manned by volunteers.
www.worldcat.org	WorldCat is the world's largest library catalog; use it to find almost any library holdings on the planet.

ON YOUR OWN 4.8

WATCH

OBJECTIVE 4.9
VIDEO

Explore Your School Library's Website

Collect the Peace Corps Research in OneNote: Part 8 of 9

When you become a student at a school or university, you're assigned a user ID and password that you can use to access the school library's website. If the library has paid for access to databases, they're available to you after you've logged in.

> **Not Working?** If you're not a student, you can apply for a library card at a public library in your area. This card gives you a user ID and password that you can use to access the public library's website and its holdings.

To use your school library website, do the following:

Step 1. Log on to your school's website using the user ID and password assigned by your school. If you're not sure of the website or your login information, ask your instructor.

Step 2. Explore the online databases that your library provides. Try to find the journal article you found using Google Scholar earlier in the chapter. Can you find the article? Can you view the full text of the article?

Step 3. Some journal databases give you the citation information for an article. If you can find the article, does the website give you this citation information already prepared for a Works Cited list? If so, copy this information into OneNote on the same page as the article abstract.

Solutions
Appendix

For help: See *On Your Own 4.8* Step-by-Step Solution

Research Phases 3 and 4: Evaluating Your Research and Organizing Your Research Notes

After you've found the required sources, you're ready for the third and fourth phases of research.

WATCH

OBJECTIVE 4.10
VIDEO

Objective 4.10: Evaluate Your Research by Asking Important Questions

Before you consider your research complete, verify that you have found all your required sources and perhaps a few extra. It's always better to have extra research than not enough research. Then you're ready for the third phase of research. Pause and ask yourself these questions:

> What have I learned from my research?
> Where is my research taking me?
> What are my lingering questions?
> Will my research satisfy my reader?

As you consider these questions, you might want to change your outline for your research paper. Or you might find that you need to do additional research on one subtopic. Perhaps you've discovered a new direction that you want to explore and you still have questions unanswered. Keep researching until your questions are answered and you believe that your research will satisfy your reader.

WATCH

OBJECTIVE 4.11
VIDEO

Objective 4.11: Use OneNote to Organize, Print, and Export Your Research Notes

After your research is finished, take time to organize your research notes before you start writing your research paper. Organizing research notes in OneNote is easy. Using OneNote, you can move content from one page to another, and you can move, rename, and delete pages. Your instructor might require a digital version of your research notes. If your instructor has OneNote installed on his or her computer, you can give him or her the .one file. Recall that a .one file contains one section of a OneNote notebook. Your instructor can double-click the file to open it.

Your instructor in another class might not have OneNote. In this case, you can **export** the data from OneNote to an .mht file containing all the pages in a section. Recall from Chapter 2 that an .mht file is a web page file that can be viewed in Internet Explorer.

> **export**—To copy data used by a program such as OneNote into a file format that can be used by another program, such as Internet Explorer.

ON YOUR OWN 4.9

Organize, Print, and Export Your Research in OneNote

WATCH

OBJECTIVE 4.11
VIDEO

Collect the Peace Corps Research in OneNote: Part 9 of 9

Now that your research is done, you're ready to use OneNote to organize, print, and export your research. Do the following:

Step 1. Make sure your outline in OneNote is complete and organized. This outline will guide you when you're writing your research paper. Add several lines to your outline based on your research about the Peace Corps in this chapter.

Step 2. Practice copying or moving a note container box from one page to another page in OneNote.

> **Hint** OneNote stores all notes in note *container boxes*. Click a container box to select it. To move a box on the page, press and drag the gray bar at the top of the box (see Figure 4-14). Right-click a container to see a shortcut menu to copy, cut, paste, or delete the container.

FIGURE 4-14 The pointer changes to a four-headed arrow as you move a note container box on the page.

Step 3. Delete any pages you created in the Peace Corps section that you didn't use to hold research.

Step 4. If you have access to a printer, print the entire Peace Corps section of your OneNote notebook.

Step 5. Create an .mht file containing all the pages in the Peace Corps section of your OneNote notebook.

> **Hint** To create an .mht file with OneNote, select the **FILE** tab, click **Export**, and then click **Section**. In the Select Format area, click **Single File Web Page (*.mht)**.

Solutions Appendix

For help: See *On Your Own 4.9* Step-by-Step Solution

Summary

Selecting Your Research Topic and Preparing to Take Research Notes

> When selecting a research topic, pick a topic that is of interest to you and your instructor, gives you the opportunity to offer your own opinions and solutions, offers a solution to a problem or helps someone, lends itself well to the source requirements, and is not so broad as to overwhelm you or so narrow that you cannot find enough sources.

> OneNote is a Microsoft Office application designed to hold and organize notes, including content taken from the web. OneNote keeps notes in notebooks, sections, and pages.

> Create a section in a OneNote notebook for each research topic. Keep each subtopic on its own page in the section.

> The four phases of research are to (1) explore general information and subtopics about the topic, (2) dig deeper to find the best sources, (3) evaluate where your research is taking you and ask penetrating questions, and (4) organize your research notes.

Research Phase 1: Exploring the Topic and Its Subtopics

> Wikipedia.org is a great place to start to find general information about a topic.

> A clustering search engine can help you find subtopics about a topic.

> The OneNote Screen Clipping tool is used to copy images and graphics into OneNote.

Research Phase 2: Digging Deeper to Find the Best Sources

> Each source you use to write a research paper must be cited in the paper. The citation includes enough information for someone to locate the work.

> When you are deciding whether content is credible, ask these questions: What is the type of website, and who owns it? What are others saying about the source? Is the author of a work credible? Are there opposing views?

> Current newspapers and those available in online archives can give insights into how people view an event or activity. Blogs can be excellent primary sources if written by people directly involved in an event or activity.

> Although Wikipedia.org is not considered an authoritative source, a Wikipedia article can lead you to authoritative information and sources.

> The government uses the .gov top-level domain name, and educational institutions use the .edu top-level domain name. These sources are generally considered to be authoritative and credible.

> Wikipedia.org, Google Books, Amazon.com, and Worldcat.org are useful websites when searching for books.

> A peer-reviewed scholarly journal is one of the best sources for authoritative research. Google Scholar can help you find abstracts of journal articles online free.

> Your school library subscribes to many databases containing scholarly research. You can access this information through your school library's website.

Research Phases 3 and 4: Evaluating Your Research and Organizing Your Research Notes

> Before your research is done, evaluate where your research is going and ask yourself if you have unanswered questions or if your reader might have unanswered questions.

> Use OneNote to organize research by building an outline and making sure all research notes are placed on the right pages of OneNote according to the subtopics being researched.

> You can export your OneNote research into an .mht file to be viewed by Internet Explorer.

CHAPTER MASTERY PROJECT

Now it's time to find out how well you have mastered the content in this chapter. If you can do all the steps in this mastery project without looking back at the chapter details and can answer all the review questions following this project, you have mastered this chapter.

> **Hint** All the key terms in the chapter are used in this mastery project or in the review questions. If you encounter a word you don't know, such as *primary source*, enter **define:primary source** in the Internet Explorer search box. The word is defined in the chapter, but it's more fun to find the definition on the web.

If you find you need a lot of help doing the project and you have not yet read the chapter or done the activities, go back and start at the beginning of the chapter, watch the videos, review the step-by-step solutions as you work through the On Your Own activities, and then return to this project.

> **Tip** If you need help completing this part of the mastery project, review the section "Selecting Your Research Topic and Preparing to Take Research Notes" in the chapter.

Suppose your instructor gives you this research and reporting assignment:

Find out about mentoring. What are some best practices when being mentored or being a mentor? What should a mentee know and practice to get the most out of the experience? What are the benefits of mentoring? Put your research in writing and be sure to include your sources.

To prepare to research this topic, do the following to create a notebook in OneNote and set it up for research:

Step 1. Open **OneNote**. If you have not already created a notebook named **MyResearch**, do so now. Save the notebook to your USB flash drive, hard drive, OneDrive, or other location given by your instructor.

Step 2. Create a new section in the notebook named **Mentoring**. Create four pages in this section named **Outline**, **Mentee Tips**, **Mentoring Benefits**, and **Best Practices**. Close the notebook and reopen it.

Step 3. On the Outline page, type the paragraph from above detailing the assignment. Create the following outline on the **Outline** page of OneNote:

Outline:

- Tips to maximize being mentored
- Benefits of being a mentor
- Best practices of mentoring

> **Tip** If you need help completing this part of the mastery project, review the section "Research Phase 1: Exploring the Topic and Its Subtopics" in the chapter.

Follow these steps to find general information and subtopics about mentoring:

Step 4. Find three topics that Google autosuggest offers that might be considered additional subtopics to the mentoring topic and add them as pages to your notebook. Find two topics that Google related searches offers that might broaden the mentoring topic and add them as pages to your notebook.

Step 5. Create a search string in Google that searches for information about mentoring and limits the search to the Wikipedia.org site. What search string did you use? Choose a good Wikipedia article about mentoring. Bookmark the article in Internet Explorer Favorites. Does the Wikipedia article have an outline? If so, choose some subtopics to add to your notebook.

Step 6. Use a clustering search engine such as **carrot2.org** to find subtopics and general information about mentoring. Add these subtopics and any useful information to your notebook.

Step 7. Use Google Images to search for images or graphics related to your topic. Use the OneNote Screen Clipping tool to copy at least one image into your notebook.

> **Tip** If you need help completing this part of the mastery project, review the section "Research Phase 2: Digging Deeper to Find the Best Sources" in the chapter.

As you search for authoritative and scholarly research, keep in mind that you must keep a record of each source you plan to use in your research paper so that you can build a Works Cited list at the end of your paper. Follow these steps to find authoritative content:

Step 8. Return to the Wikipedia article on mentoring that you bookmarked earlier or find another Wikipedia article about mentoring. Look in the **External links** section of the article and search for a website that discusses benefits of mentoring. Copy the text into the Mentoring Benefits page of OneNote. In OneNote, highlight important text. Include in OneNote the information you need for the Works Cited list.

Step 9. Decide whether the website you used in step 8 is credible. These questions about the site can help you decide:

a. What is the top-level domain name of the site?

b. Who owns the website?

c. Does the website list an author? If so, who is the author? What are others saying about this author?

d. Try to find a review about this website on another site. What search string did you use to search for this review?

Step 10. Find a newspaper or magazine article online that lists tips for the mentee. Copy the tips into the Mentee Tips page of OneNote. Highlight text in OneNote that you think is important. Include on the page in OneNote all the information you need to cite the article later in your Works Cited list. See Table 4-1 for a list of citation information.

Step 11. To make sure you have a primary source in your research, find a blog written by a mentee or a mentor about his or her mentoring experiences. Copy the text into the Mentoring Benefits page of OneNote. Highlight important text and include the information you will later need to cite the source.

Step 12. Using Google Books, find a book about best practices in a mentoring relationship. View the pages of the book. Find one paragraph that describes a best practice. Copy the paragraph into the Best Practices page of OneNote. Highlight an important sentence in the paragraph. Include the citation information for the book in OneNote. See Table 4-1 for a list of citation information. Use Worldcat.org to find a library near you that has the book. What library did you find?

Step 13. Use Google Scholar to find a peer-reviewed article in a scholarly journal about any subtopic on mentoring. Copy the abstract of the article into the appropriate page of OneNote. Include in OneNote all information you need to cite the article, including the volume number and the issue number if applicable, in the Works Cited list of your research paper. See Table 4-1 for a list of citation information. Can you read the full text of the article? Some websites provide the article abstract free and charge a fee to read the full article.

Step 14. Sign on to your school's website using your user ID and password. Choose an appropriate online database provided by your library. Try to find the journal article about mentoring that you found using Google Scholar. Does the library site provide the article? Can you read the full text of the article? Does the site give you the citation information for the article? If so, copy the citation information into OneNote on the same page as the article abstract.

Tip If you need help completing this part of the mastery project, review the section "Research Phases 3 and 4: Evaluating Your Research and Organizing Your Research Notes" in the chapter.

Follow these steps to use OneNote to organize, print, and export your research:

Step 15. On the Outline page of OneNote, expand your outline so that it better reflects what you have learned from your research about mentoring.

Step 16. Copy or move note containers to different pages to best organize your research information. Delete any unused pages.

Step 17. If you have access to a printer, print the **Mentoring** section of your OneNote notebook.

Step 18. Export your research to a file that someone can use without OneNote; create an .mht file of your research about mentoring. View the file using Internet Explorer.

Review Questions

Answer these questions to assess your skills and knowledge of the content covered in the chapter. Your instructor can provide you with the correct answers when you are ready to check your work.

1. What is the most important skill you need to know when learning to use computers?

2. What are three factors to consider when choosing a research topic?

3. Why is OneNote a good application to use when taking research notes? Give two reasons.

4. How does OneNote store a notebook on a USB flash drive: in a file or in a folder?

5. If a research topic is kept in a section of a OneNote notebook, where should each subtopic be kept?

6. What are the four phases of research?

7. Why is Wikipedia.org not considered an authoritative source on a research topic?

8. How can a clustering search engine such as carrot2.org help you research a topic?

9. What are three names for the page(s) in a research paper that lists the sources used in the paper?

10. When you cite a book, what additional information must be included in the citation to indicate that you found the book online?

11. Which is the best choice as a firsthand source (primary source) about the 2010 Gulf of Mexico oil spill: a blog or Wikipedia.org? Which is most likely to be the best secondary source: a Wikipedia.org article or a website with a .gov top-level domain name?

12. Which website can help you find a library near you that holds a book you need?

13. What is the advantage of a peer review of a journal article?

14. What is an overview of a journal article called?

15. If a journal has printed on its front Volume 8, Issue 3, how many years has the journal been published?

16. If you have answered all your questions about a topic during your research, what one last question should you ask before your research is done?

17. In which of the first two phases of research is it acceptable to use content taken from Wikipedia.org? In which of the first two phases is it not acceptable to use Wikipedia content? Explain your answer.

18. As you use the web to search for ideas for a research topic, you might stumble onto a paper mill site. What is the purpose of a paper mill site, and why are papers sold on these sites considered plagiarism?

19. What file extension is assigned to a section in a OneNote notebook?

20. What four questions should a researcher ask that indicate the research is compete?

21. What is the final phase of research that should happen before you start writing?

Becoming an Independent Learner

Answer the following questions about becoming an independent learner:

1. To teach yourself to research using the web, do you think it is best to rely on the chapter or on the web when you need answers?

2. To teach yourself to use OneNote, do you think it's best to rely on the chapter or on the OneNote Help feature?

3. The most important skill learned in this chapter is how to teach yourself a computer skill. Rate yourself at Level A through E on how well you're doing with this skill. What is your level?

   - Level A: I was able to successfully complete the Chapter Mastery Project with the help of only a few of the On Your Own activities in the chapter.
   - Level B: I completed all the On Your Own activities and the Chapter Mastery Project without referring to any of the solutions in the Step-by-Step Solutions Appendix.
   - Level C: I completed all the On Your Own activities and the Chapter Mastery Project by using just a few of the solutions in the Step-by-Step Solutions Appendix.
   - Level D: I completed all the On Your Own activities and the Chapter Mastery Project by using many of the solutions in the Step-by-Step Solutions Appendix.
   - Level E: I completed all the On Your Own activities and the Chapter Mastery Project and had to use all of the solutions in the Step-by-Step Solutions Appendix.

Regardless of how you did it, the good news is you completed the work. Congratulations! To continue toward the goal of teaching yourself computer skills, if you're not at Level A, try to move up one level on how you learn in Chapter 5.

Projects to Help You

Now that you've mastered the material in this chapter, you're ready to tackle the three projects focused on your career, personal, or academic goals. Depending on your own interests, you might choose to complete any or all of these projects to help you achieve your goals.

Project 1: Research in Your Professional Career

When preparing for a career in computer technologies, recognize that employers are looking for three general qualifications: degrees, certifications, and experience. Certifications in information technology (IT) are provided by several organizations. Three major organizations that offer IT certifications are Microsoft, CompTIA, and Cisco.

Use the web to answer these questions about IT certifications offered by Microsoft, CompTIA, and Cisco:

> How valuable are certifications in the IT industry?

> What are two entry-level certifications offered by Microsoft that a person might need when supporting Windows 8 and Microsoft Office applications at a small business?

> What is the most popular CompTIA certification? Describe what the certification covers and what types of IT jobs might require this certification.

> What types of certifications does Cisco offer? What is the entry-level certification offered by Cisco? What types of IT jobs might require Cisco certifications?

> If someone is planning a career in IT and wants to start out as a desktop support technician, what are the two most important certifications you would recommend?

Using the web, research answers to these questions and others that might arise during your research. Save your research in your **MyResearch** notebook in OneNote. Create a new

Career Project I want a job in information technology (IT), and I've noticed that job postings are asking for IT certifications. What are these certifications, when do I need them, and who offers them? What are people saying about which certifications are the best to have? How can I find all these answers on the web?

section for the research, naming the section **IT Certifications**. Include these sources found on the web:

> One or more websites that give credible content

> One or more books

> One or more magazine articles

> One or more newspapers, reputable news websites, or blogs

Include in OneNote all the citation information you need to prepare a Works Cited list for a research paper.

Project 2: Research in Your Personal Life

Using the web for research can apply to many areas of your life. Suppose, for example, that you or a close family member are considering adopting a child. You might have these questions:

> Is it best to do a domestic adoption or an international adoption? What are the pros and cons of each? What countries offer children for adoption, and which countries are the best to use?

> How long will an adoption take, and about how much will it cost?

> What emotional or social challenges might an adopted child have later in life, and what can the adoptive parents do to help overcome these challenges?

Using the web, research answers to these questions and other questions that might arise during your research. Save your research in your **MyResearch** notebook in OneNote. Create a new section for the research, naming the section **Adoption**. Include these sources:

> One or more websites that give credible content

> One or more books

> One or more scholarly journal articles

> One or more newspapers, reputable news websites, or blogs

Include in OneNote all the citation information you need to prepare a Works Cited list for a research paper.

Project 3: Research in Your Academic Career

You can rely heavily on the web for the research you will do during your academic career. Suppose, for example, that you are majoring in law enforcement and you need to understand the functions of INTERPOL—not the rock band, but the International Criminal Police Organization. You might have these questions:

> What is the INTERPOL organization? When and why was it formed, and who manages and regulates it?

> What does INTERPOL do? In what areas does it assist local, state, federal, and foreign law enforcement agencies?

> What are the limitations and constraints of INTERPOL?

Using the web, research answers to these questions and others that might arise during your research. Save your research in your **MyResearch** notebook in OneNote. Create a new section for the research, naming the section **INTERPOL**. Include these sources:

> One or more websites that give credible content

> One or more books

> One or more scholarly journal articles

> One or more newspapers, reputable news websites, or blogs

Include in OneNote all the citation information you need to prepare a Works Cited list for a research paper.

Personal Project

My brother and his wife are considering adopting a child. They've asked me to help them research domestic and international adoptions and find a good book on the topic. They want to know what problems an adopted child might have later in life. I need to use the web to do this research.

Academic Project I'm majoring in law enforcement, and my English composition teacher has assigned a research paper. My law enforcement adviser has suggested I write the paper on INTERPOL. I have to find websites, books, journal articles, and newspaper articles about INTERPOL. Can I do all that research on the web?

Project to Help Others

One of the best ways to learn is to teach someone else. And, in teaching someone else, you are making a contribution into that person's life. As part of each chapter's work, you are encouraged to teach someone a skill you have learned. In this case, you help your apprentice research a topic using the web.

Working with your apprentice, do the following:

Step 1. Ask your apprentice what topic interests him that he would like to know more about. If your apprentice does not have a research topic, suggest one.

Step 2. Show your apprentice how to set up a new OneNote notebook for his research and create a section for the research topic.

Step 3. Coach your apprentice to use Google autosuggest and Google related searches to learn about the topic. Encourage your apprentice to find links to the topic and to bookmark these links.

Step 4. Find one website, such as Wikipedia.org, that gives general information about the topic. Show your apprentice how to copy content into OneNote from this website.

Step 5. Watch and coach as your apprentice continues his research on the topic to find authoritative and credible sources. Be sure to point out how to use Google Books to view pages in a book and to use Google search strings to find blogs, newspaper articles, and magazine articles about the topic.

Step 6. Help your apprentice decide whether each source is credible.

Step 7. Ask your apprentice if he is satisfied with the research. What lingering questions does he still have? Help your apprentice find answers to these questions.

Step 8. Use Word to create a file that contains your answers to the following questions about the tutoring session. Name the file **Chapter 4 Tutoring** and send the file to your instructor. If you are using MyITLab, you can post the file in a Dropbox assignment or email the file in MyITLab. On the other hand, your instructor might prefer that you post the file to your OneDrive or email the file using your school email. Here are the questions:

1. Who is your apprentice?
2. In step 1, what is the topic that your apprentice chose to research?
3. In step 7, what lingering questions does your apprentice still have?
4. Briefly describe how your apprentice evaluated the tutoring session.
5. How do you think the session went? How would you like to improve it next time?

5 Writing Research Papers Using Word Templates and Tools

In This Chapter, You Will:

In Chapter 4, you learned to use the web for research. In this chapter, you learn to use the many tools of Microsoft Word to organize and format your paper.

When learning to use any application such as Word, you'll always be learning something new. It's impossible to cover all the features of Word in this book, and Microsoft occasionally updates Microsoft Office applications. As with all chapters in this book, you can choose which of the learning paths below best suits your needs. No matter which path you choose, as you work your way through the chapter, remember the most important computer skill is how to teach yourself a computer skill. Therefore, this chapter is designed to help you teach yourself how to create documents using Word templates and tools.

LEARNING PATHS

GUIDED LEARNING	EXPLORE AND DISCOVER	JUMP RIGHT IN
Read the Chapter *Watch the Objective Videos*	**On Your Own Projects** *Review Objective videos or use Step-by-Step Solutions*	**Mastery Project** *Use Objective videos & OYO projects for help*
On Your Own Projects *Review Objective videos or use Step-by-Step Solutions*		
Mastery Project *Use Objective videos & OYO projects for help*	**Mastery Project** *Use Objective videos & OYO projects for help*	**Explore Resources** *For help as needed*
Google Project (if applicable) *Watch Google video for help*	**Google Project (if applicable)** *Watch Google video for help*	**Google Project (if applicable)** *Watch Google video for help*
Helping You & Others Projects	**Helping You & Others Projects**	**Helping You & Others Projects**
MyITLab Assessment	**MyITLab Assessment**	**MyITLab Assessment**

Preparing to Write Your Research Paper

Let's start by exploring formatting guidelines for research papers as well as how to appropriately cite the sources you use in your paper. We'll also examine how to use a Word template to help with this formatting and how to use the research you collected in OneNote to create your paper.

Objective 5.1: Use MLA Guidelines to Cite Sources Appropriately in a Research Paper

WATCH

OBJECTIVE 5.1 VIDEO

Several formatting guidelines are used for research papers. The two most popular are the Modern Language Association (MLA) guidelines and the American Psychological Association (APA) guidelines. The **MLA guidelines** are used for literary papers. The **APA guidelines** are used for scientific or technical papers. When you're writing a research paper for an English class, most likely your instructor will require the MLA guidelines.

> **MLA guidelines**—The rules for formatting a research paper developed by the Modern Language Association (MLA). The MLA guidelines, also called the MLA style, are used primarily in literary, philosophy, and history papers. See www.mla.org for details.
>
> **APA guidelines**—The rules for formatting a research paper developed by the American Psychological Association (APA). The APA guidelines, also called the APA style, are used primarily in social science, education, political science, technical, and scientific papers. See www.apastyle.org for details.

Tip When writing a paper for another class, your instructor might require formatting that varies from the MLA guidelines covered in this chapter. Always follow the guidelines given by your instructor.

In this chapter, we'll use the MLA guidelines to organize and format a research paper about the Peace Corps using the research notes we took in Chapter 4. The completed paper is shown in Figure 5-1. The MLA guidelines include rules for page margins, heading information, paragraph formatting, citation formatting, a Works Cited page, and many more formatting details you'll learn about as you build the paper in this chapter.

When You Need Permission to Use a Source

As you write papers, keep in mind you must take care to avoid plagiarism. Recognize that the author owns the *copyright* to his or her work. Copyright laws state that you must not copy, publish, or sell another person's work without first getting permission from that person to do so. However, there is an exception to this law called **fair use**.

> **fair use**—According to the copyright laws posted at www.copyright.gov, fair use allows "reproduction by a teacher or student of a small part of a work to illustrate a lesson."

Fair use includes using a source in a research paper written by a student if you only present that paper to your instructor and don't publish it. In this limited situation, you don't need to ask permission from an author to use his or her work. Note, however, that you're still required to give the author credit for his or her work.

When and How to Document a Source

If you use information from a website, journal, book, or other source in your paper, you must document the source in two ways:

> **In a citation.** Include a citation following the sentence or paragraph in your paper where you use information from the source. A citation is enclosed in parentheses and includes enough information that the reader can identify the source in the Works Cited list. We'll discuss how to create citations later in the chapter.

Citations

restroom, paint the dorms, and rid the dorms of fleas (Nichols). As you help others to change, expect that you will change, too. Expect to grow in compassion, courage, and leadership skills (Plante 28-43). You can also learn the language and culture of another country. When you come

> **On the Works Cited page.** The Works Cited page gives enough details about your sources so the reader can locate a source. We'll build a Works Cited list later in the chapter.

Document all sources even if you don't use a direct quotation from a source.

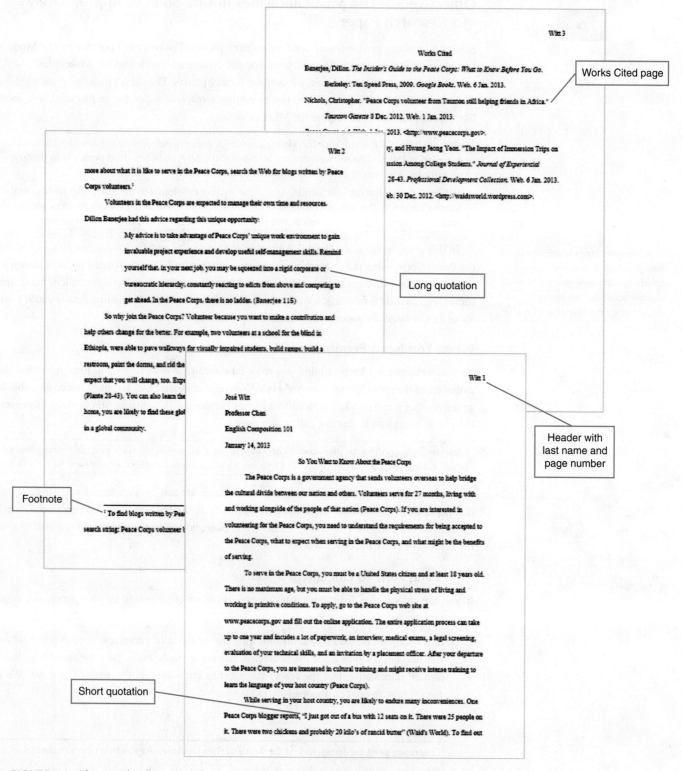

FIGURE 5-1   The completed paper on the Peace Corps includes short and long quotations, a header, a footnote, and a Works Cited page.

How to Handle Direct Quotations

Your paper can include a small amount of **direct quotations**, although it is important to not use too many direct quotations, as the work will no longer seem like your own thoughts.

> **direct quotation**—A repetition of someone's exact words. In research papers, always give credit to a person you quote.

You handle direct quotations in a research paper in two ways (see Figure 5-2):

> A quotation that is four or fewer lines is written in the text inside quotation marks.

> A quotation five lines or more starts on a new line and is indented one inch from the left margin.

Always include where the quotation came from by inserting a citation at the end of the sentence or paragraph. Figure 5-2 shows a short and a long quotation. The short quotation was taken from a blog, and the long quotation was taken from a book.

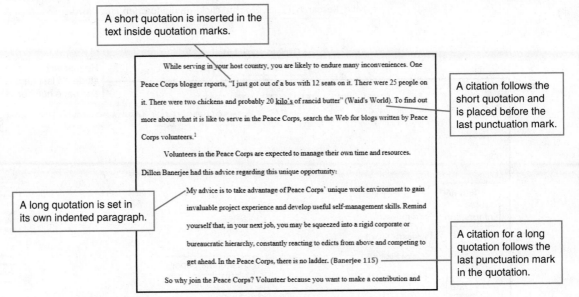

A short quotation is inserted in the text inside quotation marks.

A citation follows the short quotation and is placed before the last punctuation mark.

A long quotation is set in its own indented paragraph.

A citation for a long quotation follows the last punctuation mark in the quotation.

FIGURE 5-2 A direct quotation can be in line within the text or set off as an indented paragraph.

How to Paraphrase Text

As a writer, you must also learn to **paraphrase**. By writing information in your own words, you avoid using too many direct quotations in your papers.

> **paraphrase**—To rewrite text written by someone else in your own words.

Here are some steps you can follow to paraphrase effectively:

Step 1. Carefully read the source text.

Step 2. Cover up the source so you can't see the text.

Step 3. Write the information in your own words without peeking at the source.

Step 4. After you finish writing in your own words, look back at the source to verify you have all the facts correct.

WATCH

OBJECTIVE 5.2
VIDEO

Objective 5.2: Set Up a Research Paper Using an MLA Template

Microsoft Word offers several templates for research papers using either the MLA or the APA guidelines. These templates have most of the formatting done for you using custom-made styles and other Word settings applied to the template and are a great shortcut when preparing a research paper.

ON YOUR OWN 5.1

Create a Document Using an MLA Template

WATCH

OBJECTIVE 5.2 VIDEO

Create the Peace Corps Paper: Part 1 of 9

Do the following to create a document using an MLA template and examine the document. Note that you must be connected to the Internet to find Office 2013 templates.

Step 1. Create a new document in Microsoft Word using the **MLA style research paper** template. Identify on your screen the items labeled in the document shown in Figure 5-3.

> **Not Working?** If you can't find the MLA style research paper template in the Word templates, a substitute document is available. Look in the sample_files folder available at www.pearsonhighered.com/jump or in MyITLab for the Word document named MLA_Research_Paper. Double-click the file to open it in Word.

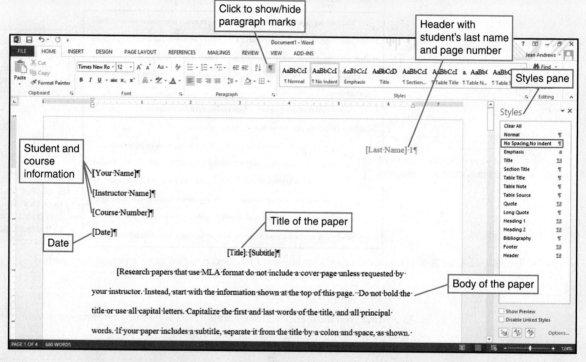

FIGURE 5-3 You can use an MLA research paper template provided by Word when writing a research paper.

> **Tip** When to use a hard return is important in MLA guidelines. Displaying the paragraph marks as you edit the document can help you get the hard returns right.

Step 2. MLA guidelines require specific formatting for the paper, and much of this formatting has been done for you using custom-made styles and other Word settings applied to the template. If you weren't using the template, you would have to manually apply these settings. To see the list of styles used, make sure the Styles pane is showing on the right (see Figure 5-3).

> **Tip** Recall that a style in Word is a predetermined set of formatting that has been assigned a name and can be applied to text.

> **Hint** To view the Styles pane, click the More arrow in the lower-right corner of the Styles group on the HOME ribbon. To apply a style, select the text and then click the style in the Styles group or Styles pane. To view or modify a style, right-click it and select **Modify** from the shortcut menu.

Step 3. Verify the following list of MLA formatting requirements on the first page of the paper:

- The paper has a **header** that contains a last name and page number. There is one space between the name and the page number, and the header is right-aligned. MLA guidelines require page numbers in a header, although Word allows you to also put page numbers in a **footer**.

> **header**—The area at the top of a page in a Word document. Text inserted in the header repeats on every page in the document.
>
> **footer**—The area at the bottom of a page in a Word document. Text inserted in the footer repeats on every page in the document.

- The header, your name and course information, date, and title of the paper are double-spaced with no bold, italics, quotation marks, all capital letters (also called all caps), or underlining.
- Your name, course information, and date are left-aligned. The title is centered.
- The current date is required below the course number. The Date Picker, which is a **Content Control**, is used to make sure the date is entered correctly. When you pick a date, you click the **[Date]** area and then select a date from the drop-down calendar that appears.

> **Content Control**—A container placed in a document that controls the type of content that can be entered into the area. Content Controls are used in a form, template, or document to control user entries.

- Page margins are 1 inch on the top, left, bottom, and right sides of the page.

Step 4. The Normal style can be used to format each paragraph in the body of the paper. MLA guidelines require a paragraph to be aligned left, double-spaced, and no extra spacing before or after the paragraph. The first line of the paragraph is indented 0.5 inches. Verify the first paragraph has the **Normal** style applied. Verify this style uses the MLA guidelines for paragraph formatting.

Step 5. Save the document to your USB flash drive, hard drive, OneDrive, or other location given by your instructor. Name the document **PeaceCorpsPaper**.

As you work on your paper, don't forget to save often.

| Solutions Appendix | *For help:* See *On Your Own 5.1* Step-by-Step Solution |

WATCH

OBJECTIVE 5.3 VIDEO

WATCH

DIVING DEEPER VIDEO

Objective 5.3: Use Research Stored in OneNote to Create a Research Paper

Normally, you would open your own OneNote notebook, but to make things easier in this chapter, we provided a notebook with research notes in the Ch05_MyResearch subfolder on the www.pearsonhighered.com/jump website or in MyITLab.

In the creative writing stage of making a research paper, you would paraphrase your research as you write your paper. This chapter does not cover this creative writing process. Instead, we have provided for you the text for the paper.

ON YOUR OWN 5.2

Open the OneNote Notebook to View Research Notes and Text for the Paper

WATCH

OBJECTIVE 5.3
VIDEO

Create the Peace Corps Paper: Part 2 of 9

Let's use OneNote to find the research and text we've provided for the paper:

Step 1. Locate the Ch05_MyResearch folder in the sample_files folder available at www.pearsonhighered.com/jump or in MyITLab. In Chapter 2, recall you downloaded the sample_files folder to your USB flash drive.

Step 2. Double-click the **Peace Corps** file in the Ch05_MyResearch folder. The OneNote notebook opens with the Peace Corps section selected. To save you typing time, we created the text for the research paper for you. You can find the text on the Text for Research Paper page, as shown in Figure 5-4.

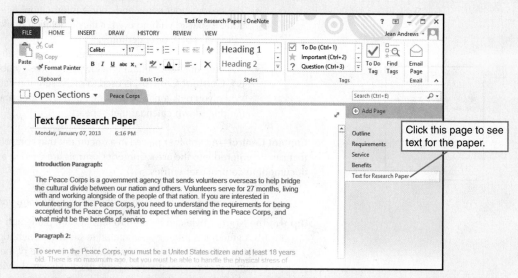

FIGURE 5-4   The text for the research paper used in this chapter can be found in the OneNote section file named Peace Corps in the Ch05_MyResearch folder.

Step 3. Leave the OneNote window open so you're ready to copy research and text from the OneNote window into the Word window as you build the paper.

Solutions Appendix

For help: See *On Your Own 5.2* Step-by-Step Solution

Writing and Formatting Your Paper

Tip The Word template we're using already has page numbers inserted. However, if you need to insert page numbers in a document, click the **INSERT** tab and click **Page Number**.

Now that you have your research paper document prepared from the Word MLA template and your OneNote research notes ready, you're ready to start writing your paper. In this section, we'll look at how to format your paper headings and text, including citations, quotations, and footnotes, all using MLA guidelines.

WATCH

**OBJECTIVE 5.4
VIDEO**

Objective 5.4: Use MLA Guidelines to Format the Paper Headings and Other Elements

As noted above, a research paper using the MLA guidelines begins with a header, student and course information, the date, and the title of the paper, as shown in Figure 5-5.

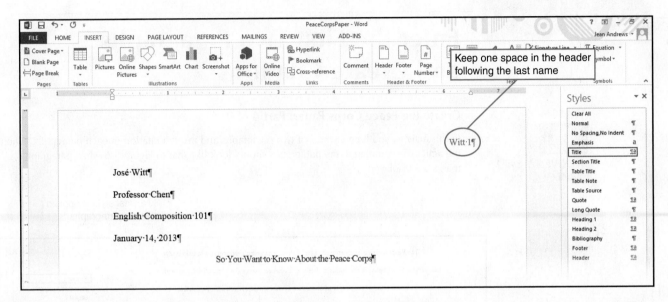

FIGURE 5-5   The first page contains a header, student and course information, the date, and the title of the paper. (Your date will be different from the one shown here.)

ON YOUR OWN 5.3

Enter a Header, Student and Course Information, a Date, and a Paper Title

WATCH

**OBJECTIVE 5.4
VIDEO**

Create the Peace Corps Paper: Part 3 of 9

To enter a header, student and course information, a date, and the paper title to your paper, do the following:

Step 1.   Enter the information shown in Figure 5-5. The paper is by José Witt, written for Professor Chen's English Composition 101 class. The title of the paper is "So You Want to Know About the Peace Corps." Use your current date for the paper. Don't forget to edit the existing header.

> **Hint** To edit an existing header, double-click it. To return to the document, double-click somewhere in the document. If you need to create a new header in a document, click the **INSERT** tab and click **Header**.

> **Hint** To insert the Latin letter "é" in "José Witt," use the **Symbol** command on the INSERT ribbon.

Step 2.   Delete all the text in the paper following the title down through the end of the paper, including the Works Cited page, and save the document.

**Solutions
Appendix**

For help: See *On Your Own 5.3 Step-by-Step Solution*

WATCH

OBJECTIVE 5.5
VIDEO

Objective 5.5: Format a Paragraph and Create a Website Citation

You're now ready to build the body of the paper. The first two paragraphs in the paper use information taken from the website www.peacecorps.gov. The paragraphs also include two citations needed to give credit to this source.

ON YOUR OWN 5.4

Enter the First Two Paragraphs and Create Citations

WATCH

OBJECTIVE 5.5
VIDEO

Create the Peace Corps Paper: Part 4 of 9

In this activity, you'll enter the first two paragraphs and insert a citation in each paragraph. When the activity is completed, the paragraphs should look like that in Figure 5-6 when paragraph marks are displayed.

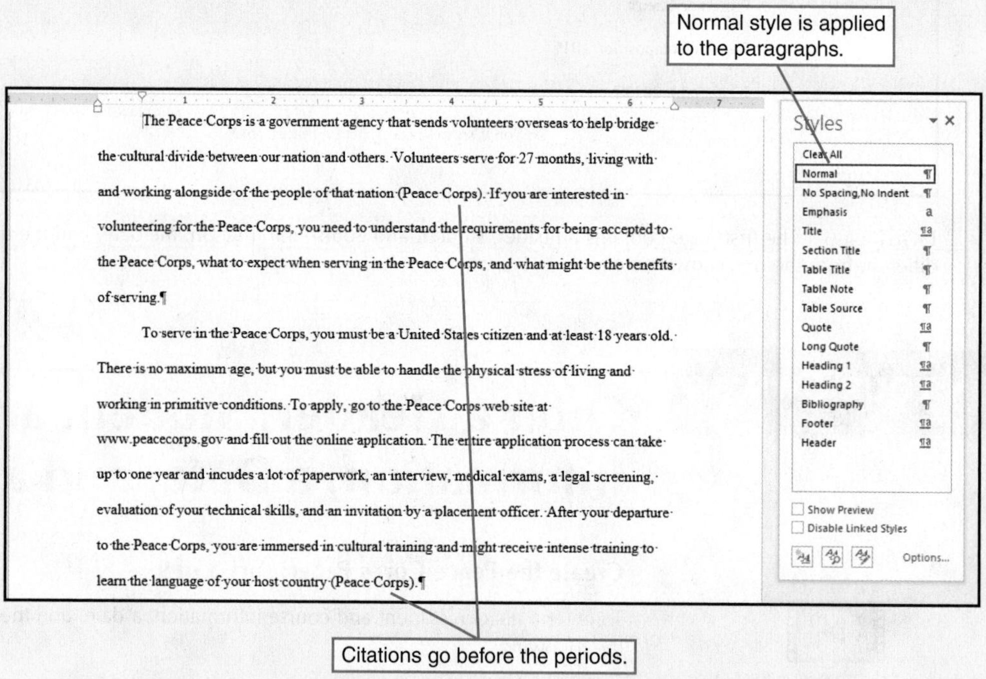

Normal style is applied to the paragraphs.

The Peace Corps is a government agency that sends volunteers overseas to help bridge the cultural divide between our nation and others. Volunteers serve for 27 months, living with and working alongside of the people of that nation (Peace Corps). If you are interested in volunteering for the Peace Corps, you need to understand the requirements for being accepted to the Peace Corps, what to expect when serving in the Peace Corps, and what might be the benefits of serving.¶

To serve in the Peace Corps, you must be a United States citizen and at least 18 years old. There is no maximum age, but you must be able to handle the physical stress of living and working in primitive conditions. To apply, go to the Peace Corps web site at www.peacecorps.gov and fill out the online application. The entire application process can take up to one year and incudes a lot of paperwork, an interview, medical exams, a legal screening, evaluation of your technical skills, and an invitation by a placement officer. After your departure to the Peace Corps, you are immersed in cultural training and might receive intense training to learn the language of your host country (Peace Corps).¶

Styles

Clear All
Normal ¶
No Spacing,No Indent ¶
Emphasis a
Title ¶a
Section Title ¶
Table Title ¶
Table Note ¶
Table Source ¶
Quote ¶a
Long Quote ¶
Heading 1 ¶a
Heading 2 ¶a
Bibliography ¶
Footer ¶a
Header ¶a

☐ Show Preview
☐ Disable Linked Styles

Options...

Citations go before the periods.

FIGURE 5-6   The first two paragraphs have citations from the same Peace Corps website.

Tip   MLA guidelines require one space following each sentence in a paragraph.

To save you time in this chapter, we have done all the writing for you. To enter the two paragraphs, do the following:

Step 1. Copy the Introduction Paragraph from the Text for Research Paper page in OneNote into the Word document. Apply the **Normal** style to the paragraph, as shown in Figure 5-6.

Step 2. Following the second sentence in the paragraph, insert a citation from the Peace Corps website. Insert the citation before the period at the end of this sentence. The citation information can be found in OneNote on the Requirements page. To cite this website, you need the name of the web page, date the site was accessed, and the URL. Include **http://** at the beginning of the URL. In addition, you will enter **Web** as the Medium for the source to indicate it was found online. If you use the same source for another citation later in the paper, you don't have to enter the source information again.

> **Hint** To insert a citation, position the insertion point, click the **REFERENCES** tab, and make sure the **MLA Seventh Edition** style is used for the citation.

> **Hint** Months should be spelled out in the text but are abbreviated in sources and the Works Cited list except for May, June, and July. Always use a period following the abbreviation. For example, February is written as Feb. (with the period).

Step 3. Copy Paragraph 2 from the Text for Research Paper page in OneNote into the Word document. Remove the hyperlink in the text, and apply the **Normal** style to the paragraph. Add a citation for the Peace Corps website at the end of this paragraph.

> **Hint** If you find a mistake in the information you entered for a source, click a citation in the body of the paper that uses that source. Then click the down arrow on the right side of the citation box. Click **Edit Source** from the drop-down menu that appears. In the Edit Source dialog box, make your changes and click **OK**.

| Solutions Appendix | *For help:* See *On Your Own 5.4* Step-by-Step Solution |

WATCH

OBJECTIVE 5.6
VIDEO

Objective 5.6: Create and Format a Blog Citation and a Footnote

In the next activity, you'll create a citation for a blog and add a footnote. A footnote in a paper can be used to add extra information that does not fit into the body of the paper. To insert a footnote in a Word document, click the **REFERENCES** tab and click **Insert Footnote**. Word automatically assigns a number to each footnote in a document and places the footnote near the bottom of the page.

> footnote—Text placed near the bottom of the page that contains comments about the main text. If the document has a footer, the footnote appears above the footer.

---

[1] To find blogs written by Peace Corps volunteers, use Google.com and the following search string: Peace Corps volunteer blogs.

ON YOUR OWN 5.5

Enter More Text, a Blog Citation, and a Footnote

WATCH

OBJECTIVE 5.6
VIDEO

Create the Peace Corps Paper: Part 5 of 9

In this activity, you'll enter the third paragraph, a citation for a blog, and a footnote. When this activity is completed, the paragraph and the footnote should look like that in Figure 5-7. This figure does not display paragraph marks so that you can better see the footnote details. Also, your paragraph will flow from page 1 to page 2.

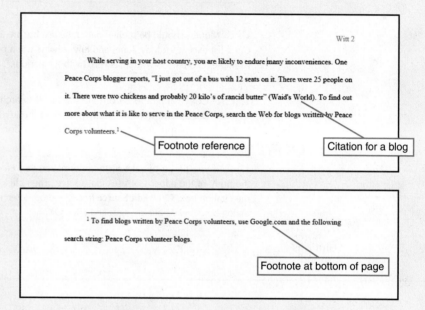

FIGURE 5-7   The third paragraph of the paper has a citation and a footnote.

Do the following:

Step 1.   Copy Paragraph 3 from the Text for Research Paper page in OneNote into the Word document. Apply the **Normal** style to the paragraph.

Step 2.   Insert a citation following the direct quotation from the blog Waid's World. The entry on the blog was made on August 7, 2011. You can find the details for the citation information on the Service page of OneNote (see Figure 5-8).

> **Hint** A citation for a direct quotation with quotation marks is inserted after the final quotation mark and before the period.

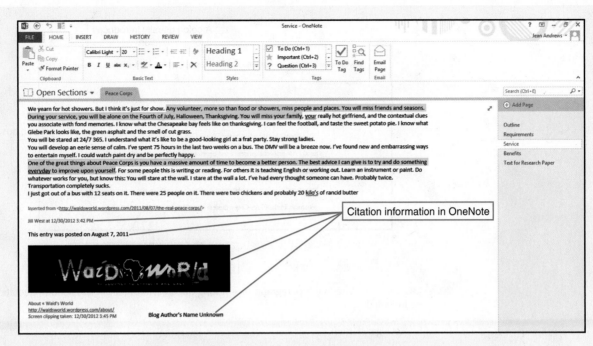

FIGURE 5-8 Entry and citation information are shown for the Waid's World blog.

Step 3. Add a footnote at the end of the paragraph. Enter this text for the footnote:

> To find blogs written by Peace Corps volunteers, use Google.com and the following search string: Peace Corps volunteer blogs.

Step 4. Apply the **Normal** style to the footnote.

Solutions Appendix

For help: See *On Your Own 5.5* Step-by-Step Solution

WATCH

OBJECTIVE 5.7 VIDEO

Objective 5.7: Format a Long Quotation and a Citation for a Book Accessed Online

It's now time to format a long quotation and create a citation for a book. The book was first published in print and then posted online. To indicate a printed work is accessed online, you cite the work as though it is printed and also enter **Web** as the Medium.

ON YOUR OWN 5.6

Enter More Text, a Long Quotation, and a Book Citation

WATCH

OBJECTIVE 5.7 VIDEO

Create the Peace Corps Paper: Part 6 of 9

In this activity, you'll insert the fourth paragraph, including a long quotation, and add a citation for a book. When the activity is completed, the fourth paragraph and the indented long quotation should look like that in Figure 5-9.

>

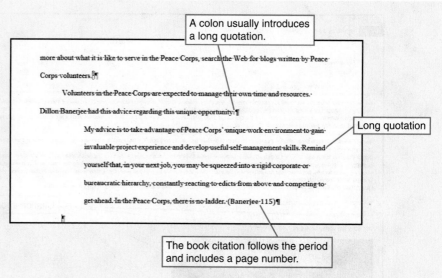

A colon usually introduces a long quotation.

Long quotation

The book citation follows the period and includes a page number.

FIGURE 5-9   The fourth paragraph uses a long quotation from a book. The long quotation must be indented.

Let's get started:

Step 1. Copy Paragraph 4 from the Text for Research Paper page in OneNote into the Word document. Apply the **Normal** style to the paragraph.

Step 2. The paragraph contains a long quotation that needs to be set in its own indented paragraph. Insert a hard return following the colon in the text **Dillon Banerjee had this advice regarding this unique opportunity:**

Step 3. Format the quotation using the **Quote** style.

> Tip   The Quote style in our template does not indent the first line of a long quotation, which follows MLA guidelines for long quotations of one paragraph or less. If the long quotation had been two or more paragraphs, we would use the Long Quote style, which indents the first line of each paragraph for long quotations according to MLA guidelines.

Step 4. Following the quotation, insert the citation from the book *The Insider's Guide to the Peace Corps: What to Know Before You Go*. You can find the citation information for the book on the Service page of OneNote. Because we found the book online, enter **Web** in the Medium field for the citation.

> Hint   A citation for a long quotation is inserted at the end of the quotation following the last punctuation mark in the quotation.

> Hint   When entering the author's name in a citation, enter the last name first, followed by a comma, and then the first name.

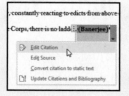

Step 5. A book citation requires a page number. In the OneNote research, the page number is 115. Insert the page number in the citation.

> Hint   To insert a page number in a citation, first create the citation without the page number and then edit the citation.

Solutions Appendix

For help: See *On Your Own 5.6 Step-by-Step Solution*

WATCH

OBJECTIVE 5.8
VIDEO

Objective 5.8: Create Newspaper and Journal Article Citations

Now you're ready to create a citation for a newspaper that was accessed online and a journal article also accessed online.

ON YOUR OWN 5.7

Enter the Conclusion Paragraph and Two More Citations

WATCH

OBJECTIVE 5.8
VIDEO

Create the Peace Corps Paper: Part 7 of 9

The conclusion paragraph needs citations for a newspaper article and a journal article. When this activity is completed, the conclusion paragraph should look like that in Figure 5-10.

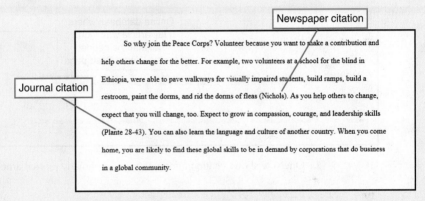

Newspaper citation

Journal citation

So why join the Peace Corps? Volunteer because you want to make a contribution and help others change for the better. For example, two volunteers at a school for the blind in Ethiopia, were able to pave walkways for visually impaired students, build ramps, build a restroom, paint the dorms, and rid the dorms of fleas (Nichols). As you help others to change, expect that you will change, too. Expect to grow in compassion, courage, and leadership skills (Plante 28-43). You can also learn the language and culture of another country. When you come home, you are likely to find these global skills to be in demand by corporations that do business in a global community.

FIGURE 5-10   The conclusion paragraph contains citations for a newspaper article and a journal article.

Do the following:

Step 1. Copy the Conclusion Paragraph from the Text for Research Paper page in OneNote into the Word document. Apply the **Normal** style to the paragraph.

Step 2. Insert a citation following the third sentence in the paragraph. The information was taken from the *Taunton Gazette* newspaper article titled "Peace Corps volunteer from Taunton still helping friends in Africa" by Christopher Nichols. You can find the citation information on the Service page of OneNote.

Step 3. Insert a citation for the journal article following the sentence "Expect to grow in compassion, courage, and leadership skills." The journal article is titled "The Impact of Immersion Trips on Development of Compassion Among College Students" in the *Journal of Experiential Education*. The citation information is on the Benefits page of OneNote and is shown in Figure 5-11.

> **Hint** When a work has more than one author, enter the primary author's name with last name first, followed by first name. Other authors follow with first name first and separated by a comma. For example, Stone, Tammy D., Elizabeth Anderson, and Rachel Davis.

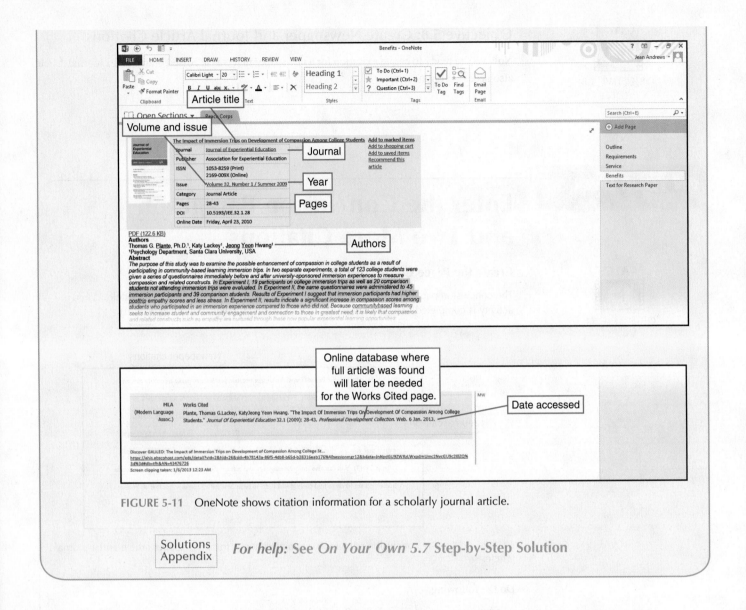

FIGURE 5-11   OneNote shows citation information for a scholarly journal article.

Solutions
Appendix

For help: See *On Your Own 5.7* Step-by-Step Solution

Creating the Works Cited Page

The body of the paper is finished. You're now ready to create the Works Cited page. The Works Cited page contains one entry for each source used to write the paper.

WATCH

OBJECTIVE 5.9
VIDEO

Objective 5.9: Create a Works Cited Page Following MLA Guidelines

To have Word generate a Works Cited list using all the sources you've identified in the paper, first create a new page at the end of the document. Then on the REFERENCES ribbon, click **Bibliography** and click **Works Cited**. The list generated by Word for the Peace Corps paper is shown in Figure 5-12. Word puts the Works Cited title at the top of the list, and entries are sorted alphabetically. Notice in the list the two extra sources. These two sample sources were in the original template and must be deleted.

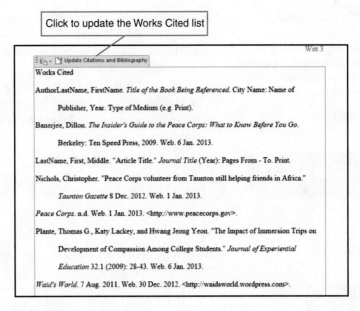

FIGURE 5-12   The Works Cited page generated by Word needs editing.

The list might not completely follow MLA guidelines, so you need to carefully check it:

> Be sure the Works Cited title is centered on the page.
> Check to be sure each Works Cited entry follows the proper MLA guidelines. Table 5-1 shows the guidelines for each type of Works Cited entry used in the Peace Corps paper.

TABLE 5-1   Format for Entries in the Works Cited List

Source	Format
Blog	Author (if known). Title of Web Site. Date published (if known). Web. Date accessed. <URL (optional)>.
Book accessed online	Author. Title of Book. City of Publication: Publisher, Year. Online Database. Web. Date accessed.
Journal accessed online	Author. "Title of the Article." Title of the Journal Volume number. Issue number (Year): Pages. Online Database. Web. Date accessed.
Newspaper article accessed online	Author. "Title of the Article." Title of the Newspaper Date published. Web. Date accessed.
Website with no author	Title of Web Site. Title of Web Page (if known). Date published. Web. Date accessed. <URL (optional)>.

Hint The Works Cited list is inserted in a document inside a container box. To have Word regenerate the list, select the container and click **Update Citations and Bibliography** at the top of the container. But be aware that any edits you manually made to the list are lost when Word updates it.

Tip MLA guidelines no longer require the URL of a website in the Works Cited list. Some instructors still require them. For complete MLA guidelines that apply to a Works Cited list, see www.mla.org or ask your instructor or librarian.

> Note that when a printed work is found on the web, you must add to the end of the Works Cited entry the following:
> > The title of an online database set in italics and followed by a period (if the title is not available, it can be omitted)
> > The word **Web** followed by a period
> > The date accessed followed by a period
> When any other work is found on the web, insert before the date accessed the word **Web** followed by a period.

ON YOUR OWN 5.8

Create a Works Cited Page

WATCH

OBJECTIVE 5.9
VIDEO

Create the Peace Corps Paper: Part 8 of 9

In this activity, you'll create the Works Cited page. When the activity is completed, the page should look like that in Figure 5-13.

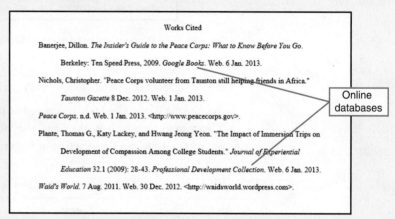

FIGURE 5-13   The Works Cited page is generated by Word and then changes were made.

Do the following to create a Works Cited page:

Step 1. To view the list of sources in your paper and correct any errors, start by clicking **Manage Sources** on the REFERENCES ribbon. Delete the two extra sources included in the original Word template so that you have a total of five sources.

Step 2. Create a **page break** following the last paragraph in the document. Insert a Works Cited list. Make any changes necessary so that the list complies with MLA guidelines.

---------Page Break---------¶

page break—A mark in a document that indicates a new page. To insert the mark, click the **Page Break** button on the INSERT ribbon or press **Ctrl+Enter**. When you click **Show/Hide**, the Page Break mark displays on the screen along with other formatting symbols.

Hint If you need to correct errors in the source information used to generate the Works Cited list, click **Manage Sources** on the REFERENCES ribbon. Correct the source information and then have Word update the Works Cited page. Remember: Any edits you made to the Works Cited page are lost and must be made again.

Step 3. Two printed works in the list were found online in databases. Make these changes:

    a. Insert the name of the online database in the Plante, Thomas G. entry before the date:

Professional Development Collection. Web. 6 Jan. 2013.

    b. Insert the name of the online database in the Banerjee, Dillon entry before the date:

> *Google Books.* Web. 6 Jan. 2013.

Step 4. Save your work.

| Solutions Appendix |

For help: See *On Your Own 5.8* Step-by-Step Solution

Revising and Proofing Your Paper

Next, let's learn about a few handy tools to help you revise and clean up your paper.

Objective 5.10: Use Word Tools to Revise and Proof Your Paper

WATCH

OBJECTIVE 5.10
VIDEO

Now that you've entered all your text into the paper and have formatted it, go back and read your paper from start to finish and revise it as needed. You'll also want to check the paper for errors. Word offers tools to help you revise your writing and find mistakes.

Use Synonyms Provided by Word

As you write, you might appreciate the built-in **thesaurus** offered by Word. Right-click a word and point to **Synonyms** from the shortcut menu. A list of **synonyms** appears (see Figure 5-14). Click one to substitute it for the original word. In the shortcut menu, click **Thesaurus**. The Thesaurus pane shows a longer list of synonyms from which you can choose. Another way to open the Thesaurus pane is to select a word and click **Thesaurus** on the REVIEW ribbon.

> **thesaurus**—A list of synonyms.
>
> **synonym**—A word similar to another word. For example, a synonym for *interesting* is *stimulating*, which is, well, a more stimulating word.

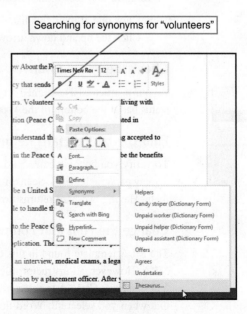

FIGURE 5-14   Word offers synonyms and access to a thesaurus with even more synonyms.

Search for Text

Suppose you need to search your paper for specific text. First, click **Find** on the HOME ribbon. The Navigation pane appears and snaps to the left side of the window. Enter text you want to find in the search box at the top of the Navigation pane. Instances of the text are highlighted in the document and also display in a list in the Navigation pane (see Figure 5-15).

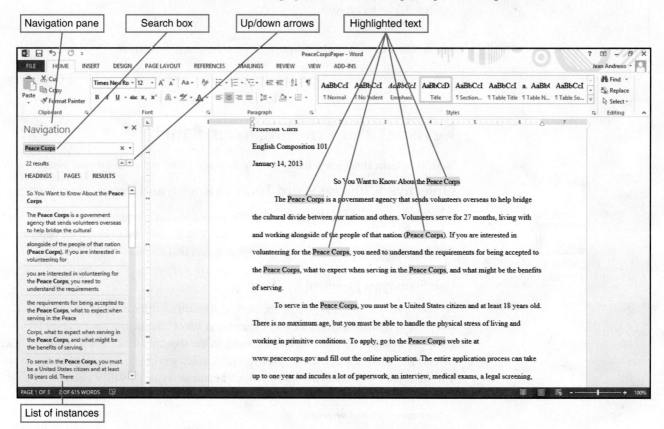

FIGURE 5-15   Search results are highlighted in the document and listed in the Navigation pane.

To move to places in the document where the text was found, you can

> Click one of the items listed in the Navigation pane.
> Click the up and down arrows above the list to step through the list.

Check the Word Count

If your instructor has assigned a minimum or maximum number of words in the paper, check the status bar at the bottom of the Word window for the number of words in the document.

Find Unwanted Hard Returns

To verify you have no extra hard returns, use the Show/Hide button ¶ on the HOME ribbon to display paragraph marks. Scan through the document looking for unwanted hard returns and delete them. Having two hard returns next to each other is most likely a problem.

Change the Font and Font Size

The MLA template found in this chapter uses Times New Roman, 12 point, which is allowed in MLA. However, an instructor might require a different font or font size, such as Arial, 11 point. You can press **Ctrl+A** to select all text in the document and change it to Arial, 11 point. But know that when you select all, Word does not include headers, footers, and footnotes in the selection. You have to select these items individually to change the font and font size.

Check for Grammar and Spelling Errors

Word draws a wavy green or blue line under any word or phrase that it thinks has a grammar error. If you see one of these lines, right-click the text to see a fix offered by Word in the shortcut menu (see Figure 5-16). Click the fix to make the correction. If you know the grammar is correct as it is, click **Ignore Once**.

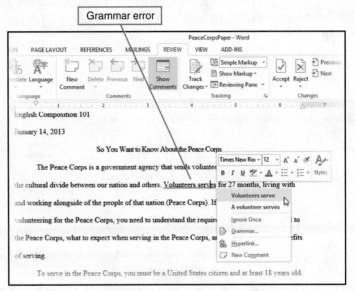

FIGURE 5-16   Word identifies a possible error in grammar and offers a fix.

Not Working? If you don't think Word is checking for all grammar errors, click the **FILE** tab and click **Options**. In the Word Options dialog box, select **Proofing** on the left. Then click **Settings**. In the Grammar Settings dialog box (see Figure 5-17), check the grammar options you need. Then click **OK** to close each box.

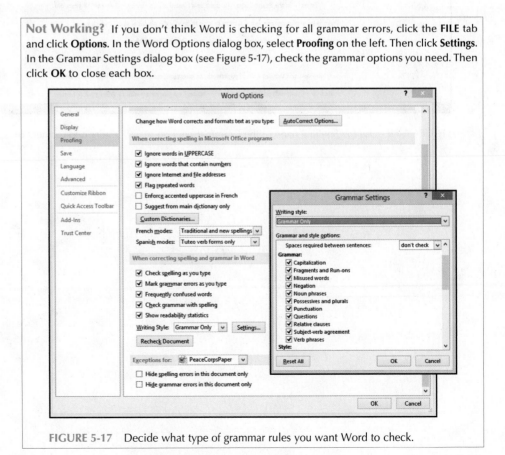

FIGURE 5-17   Decide what type of grammar rules you want Word to check.

Recall from Chapter 3 that Word identifies misspelled or unfamiliar words with a wavy red underline. You can scroll through the paper looking for these red lines and correct any spelling errors.

Another way to check a paper for all spelling and grammar errors is to click **Spelling & Grammar** on the REVIEW ribbon. The Spelling pane or Grammar pane appears in turn on the right (see Figure 5-18). Use each pane to work your way through the entire document as it searches for each spelling or grammar error. You can close the last pane when you're done.

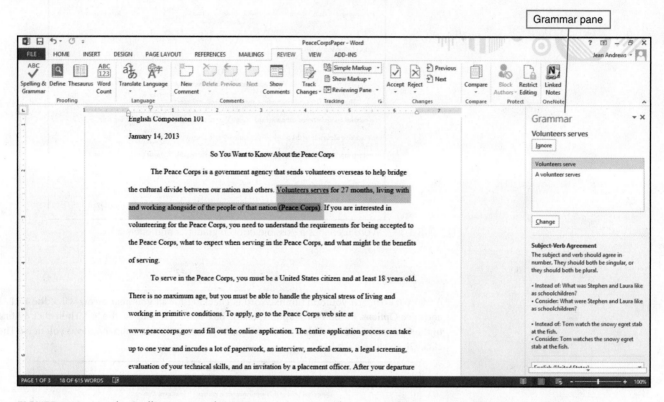

FIGURE 5-18   Use the Spelling pane or the Grammar pane to search an entire document for spelling or grammar errors.

ON YOUR OWN 5.9

WATCH

OBJECTIVE 5.10
VIDEO

Revise and Proof Your Paper

Create the Peace Corps Paper: Part 9 of 9

After you check the paper for errors and make revisions, don't forget to make sure the document properties show you as the author of the document. You're then ready to print the document. To practice revising and proofing a paper, do the following:

Step 1. In the third sentence of the paper, find a synonym for **interested** using the **Thesaurus** pane. If you change the word, use the Undo button to undo your change.

Step 2. Search the paper for the text **Peace Corps**. Step through several instances of the text.

Step 3. Use the status bar to determine the word count.

Step 4. Use the Show/Hide button on the HOME ribbon to display paragraph marks in the paper.

Step 5. Change the font for the entire paper from Times New Roman to **Arial**. When you're done, use the Undo button to return the paper back to **Times New Roman**.

Step 6. Misspell a word in the first sentence of the paper. Use the Spelling pane to check the paper and find and correct the error. Save your work.

Solutions Appendix

For help: See *On Your Own 5.9* Step-by-Step Solution

Summary

Preparing to Write Your Research Paper

> The two most popular guidelines for constructing and formatting research papers are MLA guidelines and APA guidelines. MLA is used for literary, philosophy, and history papers. APA is used for social science, education, political science, technical, and scientific papers. MLA guidelines are used in this chapter.

> In a paper, always give credit where credit is due. Copyright laws posted at copyright.gov apply to copying another person's works. An exception to copyright laws is fair use, which applies to papers written in a class and presented to an instructor.

> Document the sources you use with a citation and list the sources on a Works Cited page. Direct quotations and paraphrased text should always be cited in a paper.

> Word templates can be used to produce a research paper using MLA or APA guidelines. These templates might contain Content Controls to control how text is entered in a document and customized styles that follow MLA or APA guidelines. You can use the Styles pane to verify a style uses the correct MLA or APA guidelines.

> MLA requires a header containing your last name and page number.

> According to MLA, paragraphs in the body of the paper must be double-spaced and left-aligned and contain no extra spacing before or after the paragraph. The first line of the paragraph must be indented 0.5 inches. One space follows each sentence in the paragraph. Other MLA guidelines can be found at www.mla.org.

> Research stored in OneNote can be copied and pasted into a research paper.

Writing and Formatting Your Paper

> A page number can be inserted in the header or footer of a document using a command on the INSERT ribbon.

> A citation is added to a paper using the Insert Citation command on the REFERENCES ribbon. Types of works that are cited include websites, books, journal articles, newspaper articles, magazine articles, and blogs.

> Direct quotations in a paper can be formatted using the short or long quotation method.

> A footnote can be added to a paper using the Insert Footnote command on the REFERENCES ribbon.

Creating the Works Cited Page

> Insert a page break in a document using the Page Break command on the INSERT ribbon.

> Insert a Works Cited page in a paper using the Bibliography command on the REFERENCES ribbon. You might need to edit the page to conform to MLA guidelines or to add additional information.

Revising and Proofing Your Paper

> Word features used to revise a paper include synonyms, a thesaurus, word count, and a Find command to search for text.

> Use the spell-checking and grammar-checking features of Word to correct errors.

CHAPTER MASTERY PROJECT

Now it's time to find out how well you've mastered the content in this chapter. If you can do all the steps in this mastery project without looking back at the chapter details and can answer all the review questions following this project, you've mastered this chapter. If you can complete the project by finding answers using the Word Help window or the web, you've proven that you can teach yourself the content.

> **Hint** All the key terms in the chapter are used in this mastery project. If you encounter a key word you don't know, such as *citation*, enter **define:citation** in the Internet Explorer search box.

If you find you need a lot of help doing the project and you have not yet read the chapter or done the activities, drop back and start at the beginning of the chapter, watch the videos, review the step-by-step solutions as you work through the On Your Own activities, and then return to this project.

By following the steps in this mastery project, you'll create a research paper about mentoring. You did the research for this paper in the Chapter Mastery Project in Chapter 4. The completed paper is shown in Figure 5-19.

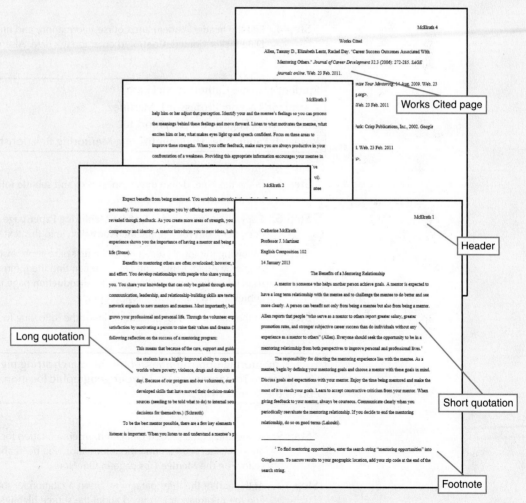

FIGURE 5-19   The completed paper on mentoring includes short and long quotations, a header, a footnote, and a Works Cited page.

> **Tip** If you need help completing this part of the mastery project, review the "Preparing to Write Your Research Paper" section in the chapter.

Do the following to prepare to write the research paper on mentoring:

Step 1. Locate the Ch05_MyResearch folder in the sample_files folder available at www.pearsonhighered.com/jump or in MyITLab. Using File Explorer (called Windows Explorer in Windows 7), drill down into the **Ch05_MyResearch** folder. In the folder, double-click the OneNote section file named **Mentoring**. A OneNote notebook opens with the Mentoring section selected. All the research you need for this project is found in this section.

Step 2. To save you time, we've done all the typing for the body of the paper for you. To see this text, select the **Text for Mentoring Paper** page in the Mentoring section of the notebook. Leave the OneNote window open so you're ready to copy information from OneNote into your Word document.

Step 3. Open a new document in Word using the **MLA style research paper** template. Save the document to your USB flash drive, hard drive, OneDrive, or another location given by your instructor. Name the document **MentoringPaper**.

> **Tip** If you need help completing this part of the mastery project, review the "Writing and Formatting Your Paper" section in the chapter.

Step 4. Edit the header, student and course information, and title of the document. Use the Date Picker Content Control to enter today's date. Also use the following information:

> Student's Name: Catherine McElrath
> Instructor's Name: Professor J. Martínez
> Course Title: English Composition 102
> Research Paper Title: The Benefits of a Mentoring Relationship

Step 5. In the title line, delete the colon, space, and subtitle following the title. Delete all the text in the rest of the document.

Step 6. Copy all the text on the **Text for Mentoring Paper** page in OneNote into the Word document. In Word, apply the **Normal** style to this text.

Step 7. Following the fourth sentence of the first paragraph, insert a citation for the journal article by Allen, Lentz, and Day. You can find the information you need about the source highlighted in yellow on the **Introduction** page in OneNote. Don't forget to use abbreviations for months as appropriate.

Step 8. At the end of the first paragraph, insert the following footnote:

> To find mentoring opportunities, enter the search string mentoring opportunities into Google.com. To narrow results to your geographic location, add your ZIP code at the end of the search string.

Step 9. At the end of the second paragraph, insert a citation for the article by Lakoski published on a website. You can find the information you need about the source highlighted in yellow on the **Mentee Tips** page in OneNote.

Step 10. At the end of the third paragraph, insert a citation for the blog entry by Stone. You can find the information you need about the source highlighted in yellow on the **Mentoring Benefits** page in OneNote.

Step 11. Edit the fourth paragraph as follows:

    a. Insert a second citation for the blog website by Stone at the end of the sentence "Through the volunteer experience, you gain personal satisfaction by motivating a person to raise their values and dreams."

    b. Use the **Quote** style to format the following text in the fourth paragraph as a long quotation:

> This means that because of the care, support and guidance of their online mentors, the students have a highly improved ability to cope in their very challenging worlds where poverty, violence, drugs and dropouts are the normal order of the day. Because of our program and our volunteers, our kids have practiced and developed skills that have moved their decision-making abilities from external sources (needing to be told what to do) to internal sources (making good life decisions for themselves).

    c. At the end of this long quotation, insert the citation for the blog by Schrauth. You can find the information for the citation highlighted in yellow on the **Mentoring Benefits** page in OneNote.

Step 12. Following the next-to-last sentence in the fifth paragraph, *When you have the opportunity, delegate authority and give permission to your mentee to explore . . . ,* insert a citation for the book by Shea. You can find the citation information highlighted in yellow on the **Best Practices** page.

> **Tip** If you need help completing this part of the mastery project, review the "Creating the Works Cited Page" section in the chapter.

Do the following to add the Works Cited page to your paper:

Step 13. Use the Manage Sources command on the REFERENCES ribbon to delete the two sample sources that were part of the original MLA template. You don't want these sample sources to appear in your Works Cited list.

Step 14. Insert a page break and then insert a Works Cited page. Center the title on the Works Cited page.

Step 15. Because the journal article and book were first published in print and then posted online, you need to add the additional web information to the Works Cited page. Make these changes:

    a. The journal article by Allen, Lentz, and Day was found on the Web in the **SAGE journals online** database on 23 Feb. 2011.

    b. The book by Shea was found on the Web in **Google Books** on 23 Feb. 2011.

Step 16. Add the text **Web.** to the Lakoski, Schrauth, and Stone entries.

> **Tip** If you need help completing this part of the mastery project, review the "Revising and Proofing Your Paper" section in the chapter.

Do the following to revise and proof the paper:

Step 17. Go back over the paper checking for spelling, grammar, or typing errors. Delete any extra hard returns.

Review Questions

Answer these questions to assess your skills and knowledge of the content covered in the chapter. Your instructor can provide you with the correct answers when you're ready to check your work.

1. Which guidelines—MLA or APA—are most likely to be required for a research paper in a history class? In a computer systems design class?

2. What are exceptions to copyright laws called that include reproducing a small part of a work in a research paper required by a teacher for a school assignment?

3. Using MLA guidelines, what punctuation marks are used to enclose a citation at the end of a sentence in a research paper?

4. What determines whether a direct quotation is written in line with the paragraph and enclosed in quotation marks or written in its own indented paragraph?

5. What is one website a school might use to scan research papers for plagiarism?

6. According to MLA guidelines, what information goes into the header of a paper?

7. On what ribbon of the Word window is the command to insert a citation in a document?

8. Why might a template contain a Date Picker Content Control rather than just mark the place the user should enter a date?

9. What information is included in the citation for a book shown in the body of the text?

10. On what ribbon of the Word window is the command to insert a footnote in a document?

11. When you are using a long quotation in a paper, the citation goes at the end of the quotation. Does the citation go before or after the last punctuation mark at the end of the quotation?

12. According to MLA guidelines, are titles in the Works Cited page underlined or placed in italics?

13. How does Word indicate a potential mistake in grammar?

14. What is the name of the pane on the Word window where search items are listed?

15. Suppose you want to change the font for an entire document. When you use Ctrl+A to select all the text in a document, is text in the headers, footers, and footnotes included in the selection?

16. You write a paper for an English class and have the opportunity to publish the paper on your school's website. Under fair use laws, can you put the paper on the site without getting permission from the authors of the works you use in the paper? Why or why not?

17. When you use a direct quotation that is four lines long, how do you format the quotation in your paper?

18. When you put text written by another in your own words, you are _____ the text.

19. According to MLA guidelines, what are the formatting rules that apply to the header, student and course information, date, and title of the paper?

20. What are the page margins for MLA guidelines?

21. What are the MLA guidelines that apply to a paragraph in a paper?

22. According to MLA guidelines, how wide is the left indent when formatting a long quotation?

23. When inserting a citation following a sentence in a paragraph, where does the citation go: before or after the last punctuation mark in the paragraph?

24. Suppose a source has two authors: Samuel Sandford and Emily Burton. How do you enter these authors' names in a citation?

25. After you enter a citation with its source information, how can you edit the citation?

26. After you enter a citation with its source information, how can you edit the source?

27. What does a wavy red line under a word indicate?

28. How can you find out the number of words in a document?

29. How do you use Word to find a more interesting word to use in place of "weird" in the sentence "The man had a weird look on his face"?

30. What are the steps to search for text in a document?

31. Which command on the HOME ribbon can you use to help you find unwanted hard returns in a document?

Becoming an Independent Learner

Answer the following questions about becoming an independent learner:

1. To teach yourself to use Microsoft Word to write papers, is it best to rely on the chapter or on Word Help when you need answers?

2. When you need help with the details of MLA guidelines, which source is the most authoritative: this chapter, the www.mla.org website, or a Wikipedia.org article about MLA?

3. The most important skill learned in this chapter is how to teach yourself a computer skill. Rate yourself at Level A through E on how well you are doing with this skill. What is your level?
   - Level A: I was able to successfully complete the Chapter Mastery Project with the help of only a few of the On Your Own activities in the chapter.
   - Level B: I completed all the On Your Own activities and the Chapter Mastery Project without referring to any of the solutions in the Step-by-Step Solutions Appendix.
   - Level C: I completed all the On Your Own activities and the Chapter Mastery Project by using just a few of the solutions in the Step-by-Step Solutions Appendix.
   - Level D: I completed all the On Your Own activities and the Chapter Mastery Project by using many of the solutions in the Step-by-Step Solutions Appendix.
   - Level E: I completed all the On Your Own activities and the Chapter Mastery Project and had to use all the solutions in the Step-by-Step Solutions Appendix.

To continue toward the goal of teaching yourself computer skills, if you're not at Level A, try to move up one level on how you learn in Chapter 6.

Projects to Help You

Now that you've mastered the material in this chapter, you're ready to tackle the three projects focused on your career, personal, or academic goals. Depending on your own interests, you might choose to complete any or all of these projects to help you achieve your goals.

Project 1: Writing Papers in Your Professional Career

Format a research paper using the MLA guidelines on how certifications can help you build a career in information technology (IT). All the research and the text for the paper are stored in the OneNote section file named Certifications in the Ch05_MyResearch folder in the sample_files folder available at www.pearsonhighered.com/jump or in MyITLab. Use the information to construct the paper complete with citations and the Works Cited page. The paper requires the following:

> **Four citations:** The position for each citation is marked and highlighted in yellow.

> **One footnote:** The position for the footnote is highlighted in blue.

> **A Works Cited page:** The page should include the four sources used for the four citations. Note that not all sources included in OneNote are used.

Career Project I'm planning my career in information technology (IT). I've read that getting a certification in IT might help me land a part-time job while I work toward a degree. I need to document what I've found.

Project 2: Writing Papers in Your Personal Life

Your friend Emily is posting far too much personal information on Facebook. You've tried to convince her to protect her privacy, but she's not listening. So you decide to write a paper about the topic. All the research and the text for the paper are stored in the OneNote Privacy file in the Ch05_MyResearch folder available at www.pearsonhighered.com/jump or in MyITLab. Use the information to construct the paper complete with citations and the Works Cited page using the MLA guidelines. The paper requires the following:

> **Five citations:** The position for each citation is marked and highlighted in yellow.

> **One footnote:** The position for the footnote is highlighted in blue.

> **A Works Cited page:** The page should include the five sources used for the five citations. Note that not all sources included in the OneNote Privacy section are used.

Project 3: Writing Papers in Your Academic Career

Your English professor is so impressed with your knowledge of creating research papers using MLA guidelines that she has asked you to help her grade research papers. One paper, named RecycleComputersPaper, can be found in the sample_files folder available at www.pearsonhighered.com/jump or in MyITLab. List 10 errors in the paper that fail to follow the MLA guidelines discussed in the chapter.

Project to Help Others

One of the best ways to learn is to teach someone else. And, in teaching someone else, you're making a contribution into that person's life. As part of each chapter's work, you're encouraged to teach someone else a skill you've learned. In this case, you help your apprentice learn more about Word.

Working with your apprentice, do the following:

Step 1. In previous chapters, you helped your apprentice learn about Word. Coach your apprentice to explore more of Word, looking for interesting tools and buttons she might like to learn about. Here are some ideas:

- Browse through the Word templates looking for documents to make.
- Insert shapes in a document to build a diagram or other graphic.
- Explore how to import a photo in a document. (On the INSERT ribbon, click **Online Pictures** or **Pictures**.) After you insert a picture, select it and use options on the FORMAT ribbon to jazz up the photo.
- Explore how to add a header or footer to a document.

Step 2. Use Word to create a document file that contains answers about the tutoring session and send the file to your instructor. If you're using MyITLab, you can post the file in Dropbox. On the other hand, your instructor might prefer you post the file to your OneDrive. Here are the questions:

1. Who is your apprentice?
2. What new skills using Word did you help your apprentice learn?
3. How do you think the tutoring session went? How would you like to improve it next time?

Personal Project I want to convince my friends they need to protect their privacy when using social networking sites like Facebook. If I put everything in writing, I think my paper might persuade them.

Academic Project My English teacher has asked me to help her grade research papers presented to her as Word documents. She wants me to make sure MLA guidelines are followed.

6 Communicating with Others Using the Internet

In This Chapter, You Will:

Communicate through Email

6.1 Understand how email works and how to use it

6.2 Manage email using a website

6.3 Use Microsoft Outlook to manage email

6.4 Follow best practices for email safety and etiquette

Explore Social Networking

6.5 Learn about online social networking

6.6 Build and enhance a social network using Facebook

6.7 Learn how businesses and public figures use Facebook pages

6.8 Use Twitter to know what's happening now

6.9 Stay LinkedIn with other professionals

6.10 Follow best practices for social networking

Present Yourself with Blogging

6.11 Create a blog and post to it

Communicate in Real Time with Text, Voice, and Video

6.12 Explore Instant Messaging, Internet voice, and streaming video

The Internet has forever changed the way we communicate. Email has replaced U.S. mail and interoffice memos as the preferred choice for personal and business communication. The Internet also supports social networking, blogging, and instant messaging on the web as well as voice communication.

In this chapter, you'll learn how to use the Internet to "get connected." As with all chapters in this book, you can choose which of the learning paths below best suits your needs. If you're already a savvy Internet user, consider jumping straight to the mastery project. No matter which path you choose, as you work your way through the chapter, remember the most important computer skill is how to teach yourself a computer skill. Therefore, this chapter is designed to help you teach yourself how to communicate using the Internet.

LEARNING PATHS

GUIDED LEARNING	EXPLORE AND DISCOVER	JUMP RIGHT IN
Read the Chapter *Watch the Objective Videos*	**On Your Own Projects** *Review Objective videos or use Step-by-Step Solutions*	**Mastery Project** *Use Objective videos & OYO projects for help*
On Your Own Projects *Review Objective videos or use Step-by-Step Solutions*	**Mastery Project** *Use Objective videos & OYO projects for help*	**Explore Resources** *For help as needed*
Mastery Project *Use Objective videos & OYO projects for help*		
Google Project (if applicable) *Watch Google video for help*	**Google Project (if applicable)** *Watch Google video for help*	**Google Project (if applicable)** *Watch Google video for help*
Helping You & Others Projects	**Helping You & Others Projects**	**Helping You & Others Projects**
MyITLab Assessment	**MyITLab Assessment**	**MyITLab Assessment**

Communicating through Email

WATCH

OBJECTIVE 6.1
VIDEO

Let's start by exploring exactly how email works and how you can use it either from a website or with email client software.

Objective 6.1: Understand How Email Works and How to Use It

As you probably know, email (short for "electronic mail") transfers messages from one computer to another. When you sign up for an email account, the organization assigns you an email address and requires you to select a password.

An email address has two parts that are separated by an at symbol (@) as in andrewsjean7@gmail .com. The first part (andrewsjean7) identifies the account, and the second part (gmail.com) is the domain name of the mail server the account uses. Two types of **mail servers** are used to manage email messages.

> **mail server**—A computer or software used to manage email. Two types of mail servers are the sender's mail server and the mailbox server. The mailbox server holds the mail until the recipient requests it.

A Three-Step Process

The process of sending and receiving email happens in three steps. Figure 6-1 shows the process when I send a message from my andrewsjean7@gmail.com account to my daughter Joy at joy.dark@yahoo.com:

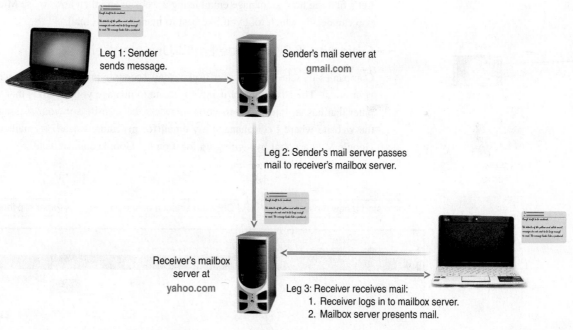

FIGURE 6-1 Sending and receiving email occurs in three steps.

1. My message goes from my computer to the gmail.com mail server.
2. The gmail.com mail server sends the message to the yahoo.com mailbox server.
3. The message sits on that mailbox server until Joy logs in to the mailbox server and receives the message.

Basic Email Functions

If you're first learning how to use email, you need to know how to do a number of basic functions:

> Open your **inbox** to view, print, and delete messages.

> **inbox**—A folder that contains email messages you've received.

> Create a new message and send it. If you start a message and aren't yet ready to send it, you can save it as a draft.
> Send a message to multiple recipients.
> Reply to a message that you receive. When you receive a message that's been sent to multiple recipients, you can choose to reply to all recipients. If you choose to reply to all, be sure to review the recipient list to make sure all should be included in your reply.
> Include a file with a message. The file is called an **attachment**. For example, you might want to email a photo to a friend.

> **attachment**—A file that is sent or received with an email message.

> Open an attachment you receive and save it to a storage location such as your USB flash drive.

Tools to Manage Email

The two types of tools used to manage email are:

> A website offered by your email provider (such as Gmail, which is offered by Google)
> Software installed on your computer, called an **email client**

> **email client**—Software installed on a computer used to manage email. One example of an email client is Microsoft Outlook. The software manages email messages, which can be stored on your hard drive.

Let's first see how to manage email using a website and then how to use Microsoft Outlook. Then you can decide which tool you like best to manage your email.

WATCH

OBJECTIVE 6.2
VIDEO

Objective 6.2: Manage Email Using a Website

Companies or schools that offer users email accounts provide websites where you can manage your email. The advantage of using a website to manage your email is that you can use any computer that has an Internet connection to access the website and your messages. Figure 6-2 shows the website where I can manage my email for my andrewsjean7@gmail.com account. I got the Google Mail account by signing up for it on the Google.com website.

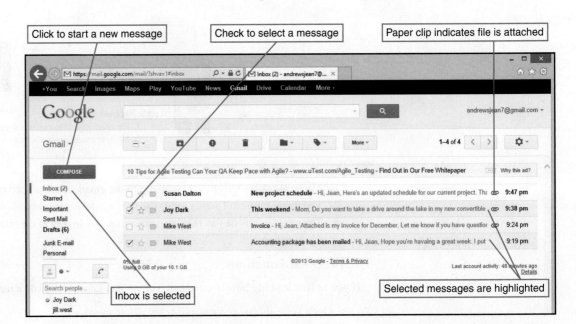

FIGURE 6-2 Email providers such as Gmail offer a website that you can use to manage your email.

ON YOUR OWN 6.1

WATCH

OBJECTIVE 6.2
VIDEO

Manage Email Using a Website

To do this activity, you must have an email account. In Chapter 2, you used an email account to set up a Microsoft account and OneDrive, so mostly likely you already have one. If you don't, you can open a free email account at gmail.com, live.com, mail.com, or yahoo.com.

Using the email account you used in Chapter 2 or another email account, do the following to use a website to manage email:

Step 1. Open Internet Explorer and go to the website of your email provider. For example, if your email address is andrewsjean7@gmail.com, enter **gmail.com** in your browser address box. Sign in to your email account. How many messages are in your inbox?

Step 2. If you have a message in your inbox, select the message to view it. Figure 6-3 shows a message using Gmail, but yours might look different. If you have access to a printer, print the message.

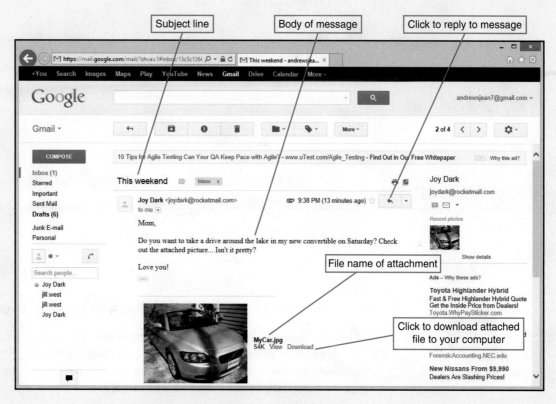

FIGURE 6-3   This email message includes an attached image.

Step 3. Next, write a message and send it to a friend in your class. Verify the message is in your Sent folder.

> **Hint** In a new message, be sure to include the email address of the receiver, a subject line, and the body of the message. Make sure the email address is entered correctly. An email message with an incorrect address might bounce back to you or end up in the wrong person's inbox.

Step 4. Are there messages in your inbox you need to delete? If so, delete them.

Step 5. Look in the deleted messages folder. Are the deleted messages there? How long deleted messages remain in this folder depends on your email provider.

Step 6. Write a second message and send it to two friends in your class. This time, include an attachment. The attachment can be any file such as a photo of yourself. If you don't have a file to attach, use the MyPhoto1 file in the sample_files folder available at www.pearsonhighered.com/jump or in MyITLab. (In Chapter 2, you downloaded the sample_files folder to your USB flash drive.)

> **Tip** When attaching a file to a message, always mention the attachment in the body of the message so the receiver knows to look for it.

Step 7. Ask a friend in your class to send an email message to you with an attachment. When you receive the attachment, open the file so you can view its contents. Then save the file to your USB flash drive or another location given by your instructor.

Step 8. Reply to your friend's message. Is the file your friend sent attached to the reply message?

> **Hint** When you reply to a message, attached files are not automatically included. When you forward a message, attached files are also forwarded by default.

> **Tip** When you attempt to open an attachment in an email message, know that your computer must have the software installed to open the file. For example, you need Adobe Reader, Adobe Acrobat, or similar software installed to be able to open a PDF file.

Solutions Appendix

For help: See *On Your Own 6.1* Step-by-Step Solution

WATCH
OBJECTIVE 6.3
VIDEO

Tip Why have more than one email account? I use one email account for business, family, and close friends. I use another account when I sign up for newsletters and other public emails so that the first account is better protected from **spam** and other abuse. Some companies assign email accounts to employees and expect these accounts not to be for personal use.

WATCH
CHAPTER 6
DIVING DEEPER
VIDEO

Objective 6.3: Use Microsoft Outlook to Manage Email

Microsoft Outlook is an email client—software installed on your computer to manage email. The advantages of using an email client such as Outlook are that the client can manage multiple email addresses and email can be stored on your local computer in case the website has a problem. Figure 6-4 shows the Microsoft Outlook application window set up to manage my gmail.com and live.com email accounts.

> **Microsoft Outlook**—One application in the Microsoft Office suite. It is used to manage email, appointments on a calendar, address lists, task lists, and notes.

> **spam**—Email you didn't ask for and don't want.

Gmail.com email account with folders

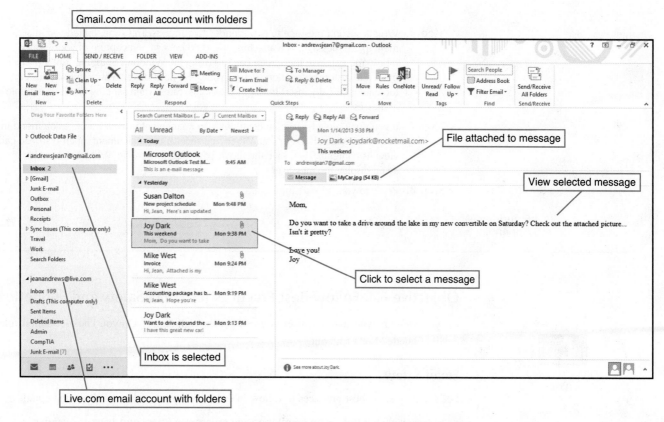

File attached to message

View selected message

Click to select a message

Inbox is selected

Live.com email account with folders

FIGURE 6-4   You can use an email client such as Microsoft Outlook to manage multiple email accounts.

ON YOUR OWN 6.2

Set Up and Use Outlook to Manage an Email Account

WATCH

OBJECTIVE 6.3
VIDEO

Before you can use Outlook to manage your email, you must tell it your email account information. This setup can happen when you open Outlook the first time, or you can set up an account later.

Do the following to set up an email account in Outlook:

Step 1. Open Microsoft Outlook 2013 and set up an email account. When the account is set up, the Outlook window shows the email account in the Folder Pane on the left side of the Outlook window.

> **Hint** To expand the Folder Pane, click the arrow above All Folders.

Step 2. Click **Inbox** under the email account to view messages in the inbox. Your screen should look similar to that in Figure 6-4 except only one email account might appear in the Folder Pane.

Earlier in the chapter, you used a website to manage email. You can perform the same tasks using an email client such as Outlook. Do the following:

Step 3. View the contents of your inbox. Sort messages in your inbox by date. Then sort messages by sender. If you have access to a printer, print a message.

Step 4. Write a message and send it to a friend in your class. Verify the message is in the Sent folder.

Step 5. Are there messages in your inbox you need to delete? If so, delete them. Look in the Trash or Deleted Items folder. Are the deleted messages there?

>

Step 6. Write a second message to two friends in your class. This time, include an attachment to the message. The attachment should be a screen capture of your Outlook Inbox. You can take the screen capture using the Windows Snipping Tool and save the file to a storage location such as your USB flash drive. What symbol does Outlook automatically insert between email addresses when sending email to multiple addresses?

Step 7. If you don't already have an email with an attachment in your inbox, ask a friend in your class to send one to you. When you receive the attachment, open it so you can view its contents. Then save the file to your USB flash drive. What do you click to again display the message?

Step 8. Reply to your friend's message.

Solutions Appendix

For help: See *On Your Own 6.2* Step-by-Step Solution

Objective 6.4: Follow Best Practices for Email Safety and Etiquette

WATCH

OBJECTIVE 6.4 VIDEO

Do you know how to avoid viruses you can get through email? Do you know common rules of email etiquette? Let's find out.

Email Safety

Let's look at some best practices to follow in order to stay safe when you're using email:

> **Never click a link in an email message unless you know and trust the sender.** By clicking a link in an email message, you can spread a virus to your computer.

> **Avoid viruses in email attachments.** Don't open an attachment unless you know and trust the sender. Also, set your antivirus software for real-time protection, which causes the software to scan all files and email attachments as they're downloaded. For Windows 8, Windows Defender is installed by default to protect your system. If you're using Windows 8, make sure Defender is set for real-time protection (see Figure 6-5). For Windows 7, you

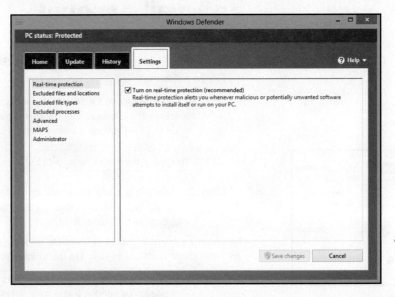

FIGURE 6-5 Windows Defender is set to run in the background to protect the computer against malware.

need to install antivirus software, such as Microsoft Security Essentials, and turn on real-time protection (see Figure 6-6). For more information about how to configure the software, see Chapter 2.

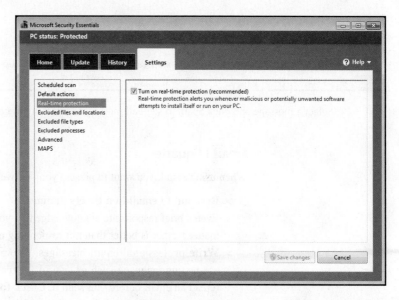

FIGURE 6-6   Microsoft Security Essentials is set to scan all downloaded files and attachments.

> **Never give personal information by email.** Email is not secure. Think of it like a postcard that anyone can read while in route. Never put your credit card information or other personal information in an email message.
> **Don't take the bait when thieves go phishing.** Phishing is an attempt to lure you into a scam. For example, you might receive an email offering you lots of money if you get involved in recovering millions for a Russian oil tycoon. Don't take the bait.

phishing (pronounced "fishing")—Attempts to trick you into giving private information by lying to you.

> **Beware of fake websites.** For example, you receive an email that appears to have come from your bank. You're asked to click a link in the message that takes you to a fake website. There you're asked to enter your logon account and password to your online banking site. This technique is a type of **social engineering** .

social engineering—Tricking people into giving private information to thieves.

> **Filter out spam.** Check the website of your email provider for a spam filter you can set to control spam. For example, Gmail automatically moves email it considers to be spam out of your inbox into your spam box. You can also select any message and click the **Report spam button** to mark it as spam (see Figure 6-7). In the future, messages from this same source are sent to your spam box.
> **Never forward chain email.** Chain email comes from a friend asking you to forward it to all your other friends. The original sender is often trying to clog up mail servers and find email addresses to be spammed.

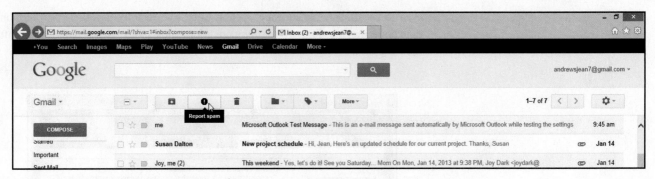

FIGURE 6-7   Select a message and click Spam to send all messages from this source to your spam box.

Email Etiquette

When using email, you want to present yourself well. Here are some good manners for using email:

> **Respond to email in a timely manner.** Respond to all professional emails within one day. Even a brief response to acknowledge that you received the message and are looking into the matter further is better than not responding or responding several days later.

> **Write professional email messages.** Use proper grammar and check your spelling. Don't use texting language such as "r u ok." Break your main thoughts into paragraphs. Always reread an email before you send it. Check for typos or bad sentence structure.

> **Be polite.** Never use all caps in email, which is like shouting. Stay positive and don't express anger in an email message because your tone might be misunderstood.

> **Use a subject line that summarizes the message.** Use short subject lines that are not too wordy or vague. Include enough information to make searching for specific emails easy.

> **Use CC and BCC features when appropriate.** The CC (carbon copy) feature allows you to send a copy of the message to someone other than the primary receivers. The BCC (blind carbon copy) is used to copy another person without others seeing that person's email address or knowing that person has been copied.

> **Protect the email addresses of your friends and coworkers.** Don't forward email messages to others that reveal the email addresses of your friends and coworkers unless you know it's okay to share that information.

> **Don't send large attachments in email.** Some mail servers won't receive large files as attachments, and the attachments might bog down the receiver's computer.

> **Don't email embarrassing or confidential information.** Keep private information private. Your email message might be forwarded to others you did not expect would receive it.

> **Know when email is not appropriate.** Never give bad or unpleasant news in an email. Be considerate and make a phone call instead. Also, complex conversations are best done over the phone and not by email. Email is intended to be brief and direct. If your email message is getting very long, it's probably time to pick up the phone or meet face to face.

Tip If you include someone in a BCC, when another receiver does a Reply All, the BCC email address will not receive the response.

Exploring Social Networking

Now let's turn our attention to social networking websites, such as Facebook, Twitter, and LinkedIn.

Objective 6.5: Learn about Online Social Networking

We all have a social network of friends, family, and business associates. The people in our network have their own networks that can broaden our network. Using websites for social networking makes it easy to stay connected and share our lives with others.

WATCH

OBJECTIVE 6.5
VIDEO

In the past, the web was used primarily to provide content to those who requested it. Today, many users contribute to content on the web. This second generation of how the web is used is called Web 2.0 . Online social networking is one example of Web 2.0.

> Web 2.0—The second generation of how the web is used. Content on the web is constantly changing as we all contribute to it.

The most popular **social networking sites** include the following:

> social networking site—A website designed for people and organizations to build a social network of friends, family, or business associates and share information with them.

> > **Facebook.com.** The most popular social networking website in the world
> > **Twitter.com.** A quick and easy way to send short messages of 140 or fewer characters to others
> > **LinkedIn.com.** Used mostly by professionals to maintain business contacts and to build a professional network

When using a Windows 8 computer, you can use the App Store to find social apps to place on your Start screen. For example, Facebook, Twitter, and LinkedIn have apps available for free in the App Store. However, note that the app might not have all the features provided by the full version used on websites.

Objective 6.6: Build and Enhance a Social Network Using Facebook

Facebook offers two types of accounts: a personal account and a business account. When you sign in to a personal Facebook account, the first thing you see is your Facebook Home page where you can see what's happening with your Facebook friends . By default, your Home page shows your News Feed , although you can choose to see other stuff, such as your friends' photos and your Facebook Messages . See Figure 6-8.

WATCH

OBJECTIVE 6.6
VIDEO

> Facebook Home page—A Facebook account page where the user can view his or her News Feed and other stuff shared by Facebook friends.
> Facebook friend—A Facebook user you've accepted into your network.
> News Feed—A column on your Home page that shows posts, comments, and tags made by your Facebook friends and businesses that you like. Facebook orders items in your News Feed by Top Stories or Most Recent.
> Facebook Messages—A private message between friends, which works similar to email. You can set your Facebook account to email your messages to a personal email address. You have to sign in to Facebook to reply to the message.

FIGURE 6-8   Use your Facebook Home page to find out what your Facebook friends are saying.

> **Note** Facebook is continually evolving. The organization of a Facebook page and how Facebook works change often. You might, therefore, find that current Facebook pages look different from those shown in the figures in this chapter.

No matter where you are in Facebook, the blue menu bar at the top of the Facebook window gives you access to your account. Click an icon in the menu bar to view your Friend Requests, Facebook Messages, and **Facebook Notifications** (see Figure 6-9). Use the search box in the menu bar to search for people, places, and things. Click your name to go to your **Facebook profile** page. Click **Home** in the menu bar to return to your Home page from anywhere in Facebook. Click the down arrow to view your activity logs, change your Facebook account settings, and log out of Facebook.

> **Facebook Notifications**—Notices of activity in your Facebook account such as when a friend comments on a post you made to her timeline or someone accepts your friend request.
> **Facebook profile**—A user's personal page on Facebook used to share status updates, personal info, photos, and a network of friends. When you sign up for a personal account, a Facebook profile is created for you, and you decide how much information on your profile page you share with others.

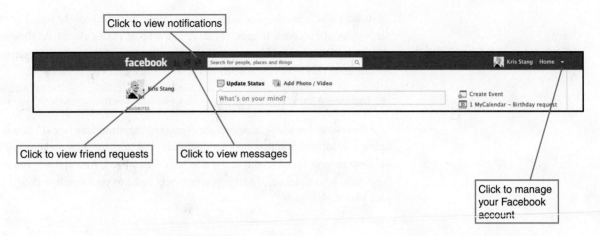

FIGURE 6-9   The menu bar at the top of the Facebook window gives access to pages in your Facebook account.

The menu bar always applies to your account even when you visit a friend's profile. For example, Kris Stang's Home page is showing in Figure 6-8. When Kris types Michael Blackwell in the search box, his profile page appears (see Figure 6-10). The menu bar at the top still applies to Kris Stang's account and she can click Home to return to her Home page.

FIGURE 6-10   A profile page shows a timeline and access to a person's friends and other stuff.

At the top of a profile page is the info area (information about the owner of the profile), links to the profiles of Facebook friends, photos, and a map of places visited. A **timeline** gives access to past events. When you visit a profile page of another user, you can click Message to leave a message for that user. This works even when this person is not your Facebook friend.

> **timeline**—A line on the profile page where you and your friends can write or post photos or videos.

All personal Facebook accounts are organized the same way (see Figure 6-11). Notice in the figure how information flows within your Facebook account. Any updates you make to your profile flow to your timeline and onward to your News Feed. Any updates you make to your News Feed go to your timeline. Updates you or others make to your timeline flow to the News Feeds of your Facebook friends.

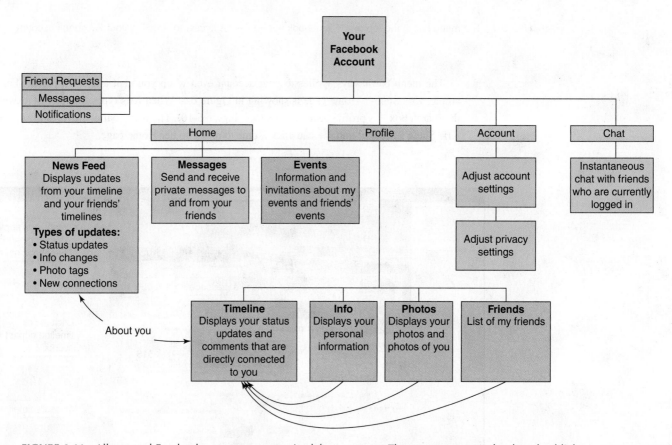

FIGURE 6-11   All personal Facebook accounts are organized the same way. The orange areas can be shared publicly.

Now that you know a bit more about how Facebook works, it's time to set up your own Facebook account. If you're already on Facebook, you can skip this activity.

ON YOUR OWN 6.3

Sign Up for Facebook and Build Your Profile

WATCH

▶

OBJECTIVE 6.6
VIDEO

Signing up for Facebook is free. Do the following to set up an account and build your profile:

Step 1. Open Internet Explorer, go to **facebook.com** and set up a Facebook account. If you like, you can skip the step to find friends because we cover finding friends in the next activity. In your profile, enter information about yourself, such as your high school, college or university, and employer.

> **Hint** If you get lost while building your profile, click the **Home** button at the top of the page.

Step 2. Post your **profile picture**. If you don't have a photo, use the GuessWho photo file in the sample_files folder available at www.pearsonhighered.com/jump or in MyITLab. (In Chapter 2, you downloaded the sample_files folder to your USB flash drive.)

> **profile picture**—A photo that always displays on the profile page and shows up when people are searching for you. Usually, this is a photo of the account owner.

Step 3. Add information you want to share, such as your education, work history, philosophy, activities and interests, and contact information. To complete the sign-up process, you'll need to respond to an email that Facebook sends to you.

Step 4. Edit your Privacy Settings to decide how much information you want to share and who can see it. Which privacy setting gives you the most privacy? What privacy settings are available under "Who can look me up?"

Step 5. Write something on your timeline.

Step 6. Look at your News Feed. Did your status update show up there? Order your News Feed by Top News and then by Most Recent.

> **Hint** If you need help using Facebook, type **help center** in the search box at the top of the Facebook window. The Help Center offers tons of help.

| Solutions Appendix | *For help:* See *On Your Own 6.3* Step-by-Step Solution |

As Facebook continues to evolve, so do the activities that show up on your News Feed. These activities might include the following:

> Updates written on your timeline
> Profile info changes
> Photo tags
> New connections with friends, businesses, and public figures
> Postings on a friend's timeline

ON YOUR OWN 6.4

Find Friends on Facebook

WATCH

OBJECTIVE 6.6
VIDEO

So now you need some Facebook friends. When you find someone you know on Facebook, you send that person a Friend Request and wait until he or she approves the connection. Use these three methods to find friends:

Step 1. Use the search box in the menu bar to search for your instructor's name or email address. When you find your instructor's profile, click **Add as Friend**. If your instructor responds to your Friend Request, you become Facebook friends.

> **Hint** Information about you that everybody can always see in Facebook is your name, gender, profile picture, user name, and network (list of friends). This is the information you can always count on to decide whether a person is someone you know.

Step 2. After you have at least one Facebook friend, Facebook sometimes suggests people you might know based on your current connections. To find people you know or to respond to a friend request, click the **Friend Requests** icon near the left side of the blue menu bar.

Step 3. Browse a friend's profile. Look at his or her list of friends. If you find a person you know, click **Add as Friend**.

Solutions Appendix

For help: See *On Your Own 6.4* Step-by-Step Solution

Facebook offers many ways to communicate with your friends. Figure 6-12 shows some of these ways. In the figure, the green dotted lines represent shared communication. The red dotted lines represent private communication between friends. The orange boxes represent pages that can be seen by others. If Privacy Settings are low, friends of friends or everybody might be able to see your profile and what you write on a friend's timeline.

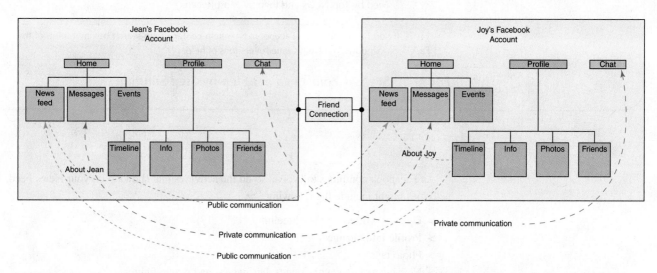

FIGURE 6-12   The red dotted lines represent private communication between friends, and the green dotted lines represent public communication among friends. The orange boxes represent pages that can be seen by others.

Chat and messages are the two private ways to communicate using Facebook. No matter where you are in Facebook, Chat is in the lower-left corner of your screen. A green dot beside a friend's name indicates the friend is online. When you click the name, you can begin an online chat session.

Messages work like email. To send a message, you can go to someone's profile page and click Message. If that person isn't currently logged in, a box appears that you can use to send your message. You can add other names in the To: field to send the message to other people on Facebook. If the person is logged in, a chat window opens instead of a message box. To view, create, and reply to your messages, click Messages in the left pane or click the Messages icon in the menu bar at the top of the Facebook window. The messages Inbox page that appears is shown in Figure 6-13.

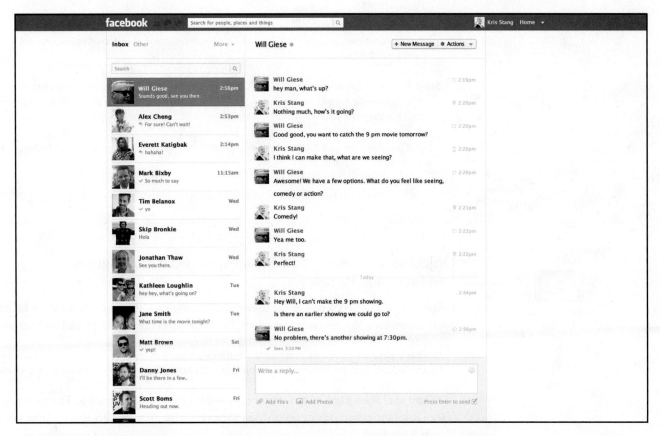

FIGURE 6-13 You can send a private message to a Facebook user and reply to messages you receive.

ON YOUR OWN 6.5

WATCH

OBJECTIVE 6.6
VIDEO

Explore Facebook in More Depth

Facebook enables you to do more than just connect with friends, of course. You can share on your timeline what you're doing or thinking and reply to friends' updates. You can post photos in albums, **tag** yourself and friends in photos, and comment on photos.

> **tag**—A link on a photo or in a status update to a Facebook user. Click the tag to see the user's profile.

To explore more of Facebook's features, do the following:

Step 1. Visit a friend's profile and look at his photos. Click **Like** on a photo you like. (You can also unlike the photo if you change your mind.)

> **Tip** Notice that you have the option to Like other items, such as shared links and status updates.

Step 2. Leave a comment on your friend's timeline. Include a tag to a friend in your comment so your tagged friend will be notified that you mentioned him or her.

> **Hint** To tag a friend's name as you're typing a comment or status update, start typing your friend's Facebook name. Select her name from the list that appears.

Step 3. Use the Chat box to chat with a Facebook friend who is currently online.

> **Tip** If you don't want your friends to know you're online, in the Chat box, click the **Options** icon, and then click **Turn Off Chat**.

Step 4. Go to someone's profile page and send a message to that person. If that person isn't currently logged in, a box appears that you can use to send a message. If the person is logged in, a chat window opens instead of a message box.

> **Tip** If your friend is logged in to Facebook using a mobile phone app, when you try to send a message, your friend can use the app to chat with you.

| Solutions Appendix | *For help: See On Your Own 6.5 Step-by-Step Solution* |

WATCH

OBJECTIVE 6.7 VIDEO

Objective 6.7: Learn How Businesses and Public Figures Use Facebook Pages

Individuals use a Facebook profile, but businesses, organizations, and public figures use a **Facebook page** to connect with consumers and clients. Facebook pages can be seen by all Facebook users.

> **Facebook page**—A page that represents a business, organization, or public figure on Facebook. A page contains information about the subject, posts, photos, videos, events, discussions, and links.

When you Like a page, as shown in Figure 6-14, your timeline reports it. The page you Like is then listed under your activities on your Facebook profile. You get later updates from that page in your News Feed.

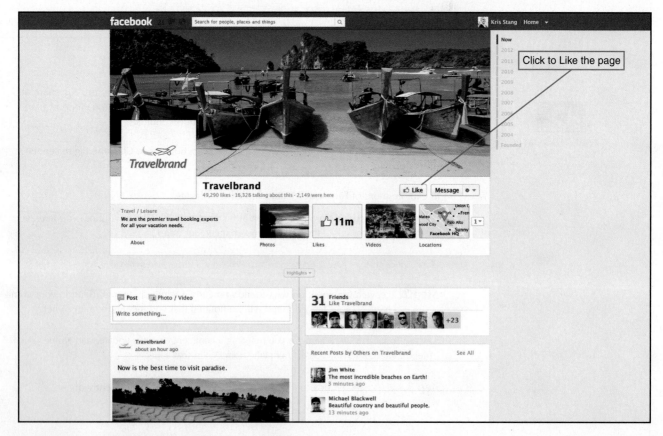

FIGURE 6-14 To Like a page, mouse over it and then click Like.

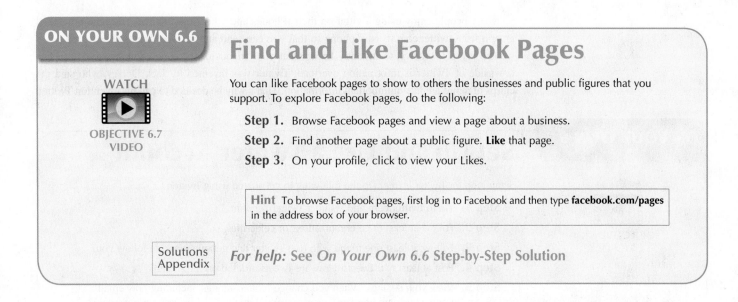

ON YOUR OWN 6.6

Find and Like Facebook Pages

WATCH

OBJECTIVE 6.7
VIDEO

You can like Facebook pages to show to others the businesses and public figures that you support. To explore Facebook pages, do the following:

Step 1. Browse Facebook pages and view a page about a business.

Step 2. Find another page about a public figure. **Like** that page.

Step 3. On your profile, click to view your Likes.

> **Hint** To browse Facebook pages, first log in to Facebook and then type **facebook.com/pages** in the address box of your browser.

Solutions Appendix

For help: See *On Your Own 6.6 Step-by-Step Solution*

WATCH

OBJECTIVE 6.8
VIDEO

Objective 6.8: Use Twitter to Know What's Happening Now

Twitter is a quick and easy way to send short messages of 140 or fewer characters to others. Sign up for Twitter at twitter.com and select Twitter accounts to follow. Then, whenever you log on to Twitter, you can read their **Tweets** or messages. You can send Tweets to whoever is following you (see Figure 6-15).

> **Tweet**—A short message (140 characters or less) sent to followers on Twitter.com. A Tweet can contain URL links to websites and images.

FIGURE 6-15 Send a quick Tweet to your followers about what's happening now.

Many people enjoy using Twitter on their iPhones and other smart phones. You can download an app from twitter.com to your phone so that you can send and receive Tweets at any time.

The joy of Twitter is to instantly know what your friends or those you admire are doing. The downside of Twitter is information overload. Twitter was invented by Jack Dorsey, who said the chirps of a bird are like unimportant information. That's why he decided to call his invention Twitter.

ON YOUR OWN 6.7

WATCH

OBJECTIVE 6.8 VIDEO

Set Up and Use a Twitter Account

Signing up for Twitter is free. Do the following to get started using Twitter:

Step 1. Go to **twitter.com** and set up a Twitter account.

Step 2. Follow at least three organizations or celebrities.

Step 3. Follow at least one friend who uses Twitter and get one friend to follow you.

Step 4. Post at least two Tweets. How are Tweets ordered on the screen?

Step 5. View your settings. When you change Twitter settings, including how email notifications are handled, what command do you click to save your changes?

Solutions Appendix

For help: See *On Your Own 6.7* Step-by-Step Solution

WATCH

OBJECTIVE 6.9 VIDEO

Objective 6.9: Stay LinkedIn with Other Professionals

LinkedIn.com is a social networking site used mostly by professionals to maintain business contacts. People build a network of connections on the site. These connections can be used to find a job, search for people to fill a job, or connect over a business opportunity (see Figure 6-16).

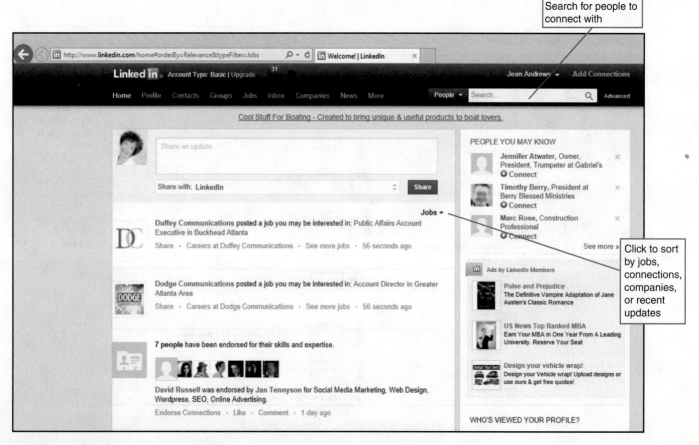

FIGURE 6-16 Make a connection in LinkedIn.

To get connected, go to linkedin.com and sign up for an account. After you sign up, find someone you know to connect to. LinkedIn provides suggestions on your LinkedIn home page (see Figure 6-17). When you click the link to connect, an email is sent to the person, who can accept or reject the connection. To see your list of connections, click **Contacts** and then click **Connections**.

Use LinkedIn to make professional contacts. For example, suppose I'm looking for a professional photographer, and Sarah Sambol, a technical writer, is one of my connections. I can see in my list of connections that Sarah has 77 connections. I can click her name to go to her Home page, where I can see her list of connections. I might find that photographer through Sarah's connections.

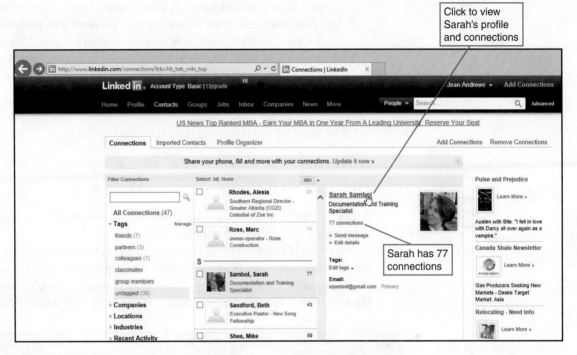

FIGURE 6-17   Find a new connection through your current connections in LinkedIn.

I can also post an update that I'm looking for a photographer, and my entire network of connections sees my post. The word gets out that there's a project available for a photographer. And so it goes to build a network of business and professional connections.

Objective 6.10: Follow Best Practices for Social Networking

WATCH

OBJECTIVE 6.10
VIDEO

Now that you know more about social networking sites, let's consider best practices when using them. Here are some tips for staying safe and presenting yourself well:

> **Understand your security settings on each social networking site you use.** Protect your privacy using these settings. Check your security settings occasionally to make sure the site has not changed the rules. When a site changes its rules, you might be more exposed than you expect. For Facebook, recall that you can view and change your security settings by clicking the **Tools** icon and then clicking **Privacy Settings**.

> **Be kind online.** Angry confrontations don't belong online. It's okay to express disagreements on Facebook, a blog, or other site, but write professionally when you do so. Anger online only makes you appear petty and unconvincing. Kind words turn away anger. Be gracious to others.

> **Pay attention to what you reveal about yourself.** To protect from thieves, never post online when you will be away from home. Never make public your date of birth, mother's maiden name, or other security questions that someone might use to steal your identity.

Tip If someone tags you in an embarrassing photo on his site, untag yourself.

Tip Remember this rule: *What you put online is forever.* If you later remove it, someone still has a record of it somewhere.

Most potential employers search for you online when you apply for a job. If an employer finds inappropriate photos, content about drugs and drinking, negative statements about previous employers or clients, or information that showed you lied on your application, you are unlikely to get the job.

> **Present yourself well.** Speaking of finding a job, employers are more likely to hire you if they find online that you can communicate well, that friends respond well to you, and that you generally have a positive outlook on life. Your online social networking sites are your opportunity to shine.

> **Use LinkedIn to focus only on your professional life.** Don't post comments about your personal life on LinkedIn. Generally limit your connections to people in your professional life.

> **Use good judgment when balancing your personal and professional life.** What might happen if you friended a boss, coworker, or client on Facebook? Would they know too much about your personal life that you don't want shared at work? Keeping personal and professional lives separated is difficult to do when we use social networking sites. Think before you share or connect online.

Presenting Yourself with Blogging

Blogging is for people who want to use the web to tell their story or share ideas. Let's find out how.

Objective 6.11: Create a Blog and Post to It

A blog, or weblog, is an online diary or journal. Many websites offer blog space. The two most popular blog sites are blogspot.com and wordpress.com.

The creator of a blog, called the *blogger*, posts text and photos and links to other sites. The creator can allow comments from others on the blog. Also, a group of people can together create a blog so the blog becomes a community blog. Corporations often use blogs to connect with their customers. Figure 6-18 shows a popular blog by Marc and Angel Chernoff at marcandangel.com.

WATCH

OBJECTIVE 6.11
VIDEO

FIGURE 6-18   Marc and Angel write a blog about practical tips for productive living.

Tip When creating your own blog, consider the design for your blog. To see some great designs for blogs, do a Google search on "great blog designs."

Is a blog a social networking site? Not really. A blog is a social medium. People come to your blog and make comments, but blogs are not used to build a network of blogs.

ON YOUR OWN 6.8

ON YOUR OWN 6.8

WATCH

OBJECTIVE 6.11
VIDEO

Create a Blog and Post to It

You can use blogging to tell your story online. Let's get started.

Step 1. Create a blog using blogspot.com, wordpress.com, or another free blogging site.

Step 2. Write on your blog an experience you had growing up that has influenced your life, a hobby you feel passionate about, or a review of your favorite movie. What is the name of your blog? What is the URL?

Step 3. So that your instructor can see your work in this and previous activities in the chapter, send an email to your instructor. Include in the email the link to your blog and attach to the email the screen capture file that you created in On Your Own 6.2, which shows your Outlook Inbox.

Solutions
Appendix

For help: See *On Your Own 6.8* Step-by-Step Solution

Communicating in Real Time with Text, Voice, and Video

You can use the Internet to communicate in real time using text, voice, and video. Figure 6-19 shows a video call in progress.

FIGURE 6-19   Real-time communication can happen in voice and video.

WATCH

OBJECTIVE 6.12
VIDEO

Objective 6.12: Explore Instant Messaging, Internet Voice, and Streaming Video

Now let's explore Instant Messaging, Internet voice, and streaming video.

Instant Messaging

Instant Messaging (IM), also called chat, is real-time communication in text over the Internet. Recall from Chapter 2 that businesses might offer a chat service on their websites. You can click a link on a web page to open a chat session with a customer service representative.

> **Instant Messaging (IM)**—Real-time communication in text on the Internet. Some IM software also includes the options to include voice and video. Also called *chat*.

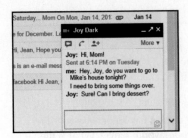

FIGURE 6-20 Some email clients offer a chat service.

Many websites offer chat services, including Facebook, Skype, Yahoo! Messenger, AIM, and Google Talk. If you have an account on these sites, you can chat with friends who have an account with the same service. Figure 6-20 shows the corner of my Gmail.com email window with a chat session open. You used Facebook Chat earlier in On Your Own 6.6.

Internet Voice Using VoIP

The technology used on the Internet for voice communication is called VoIP (Voice over Internet Protocol) . Companies that offer VoIP services include Skype, Vonage, Google, and many others. Skype is the most popular free VoIP service.

> **VoIP (Voice over Internet Protocol)**—A technology that allows voice communication over the Internet.

To use Internet voice, go to a website that offers the service and sign up for it. A service might cost you a fee. For example, you can sign up for a Skype account at no charge, and Skype-to-Skype calls are free. But you must pay for other types of calls, such as when calling landlines and cell phones. You need to download and install the Skype software.

To use Internet voice on your computer, you need a microphone and speaker. A good option for both is a headset .

> **headset**—A device that is both a microphone and speaker. It can use one USB port or two connectors that plug into the microphone and speaker ports on a computer.

Plugs in to microphone port

Plugs in to speaker port

Streaming Video

Many websites that offer chat and Internet voice also support streaming video . To communicate in live streaming video, each party needs a webcam and a microphone. You might need to first install the software that supports the webcam. This software is called a device driver .

> **streaming video**—Video that flows continually to your computer as you watch the video. The video might be live or might be streamed to you from a video file stored on a server, such as when you watch a video on YouTube. In the second situation, you're watching the video as the data is downloaded rather than downloading the entire file and then watching it.
>
> **webcam**—A video camera connected to your computer that can stream video to the Internet. Many laptops have built-in webcams, or you can plug an external webcam into a USB port.
>
> **device driver**—Software that supports a hardware device, such as a webcam or printer. When you purchase a device, the device drivers come on a DVD with the device or can be downloaded from the website of the device manufacturer.

You also need to install the streaming video software. Figure 6-21 shows the page at google.com/talk where you can download chat, voice, and video software from Google.

Web cam

Tip Most external webcams use a USB port. How to install a USB device is covered in Chapter 13.

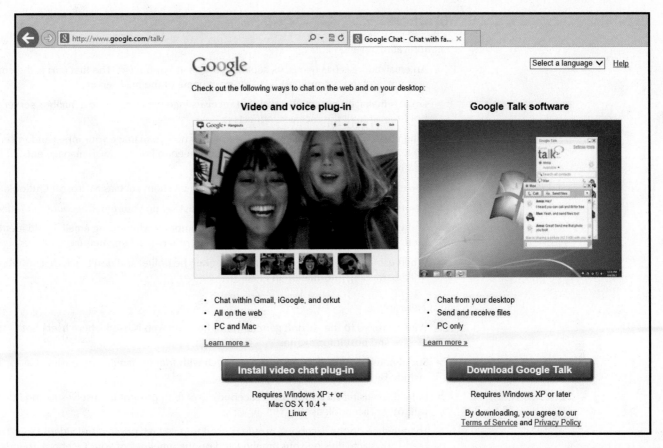

FIGURE 6-21   A chat session can include voice and video if both parties have a speaker, microphone, webcam, and installed software.

Summary

Communicating through Email

> An email address has two parts separated by an at symbol (@). The first part is the email account, and the second part is the domain name of the mail server.

> Email is managed by a mail server that receives incoming email and a mailbox server that holds email until the receiver requests it.

> When learning to use email, you need to know how to manage your inbox and to send, reply, forward, and delete messages. You also need to know how to manage email attachments.

> You can manage email using a website or an email client such as Microsoft Outlook.

> Before using Outlook to manage email, you must set up your email account in Outlook.

> Know how to protect your identity and your computer when using email. Avoid identity theft, viruses, phishing, spam, chain email, and other social engineering methods.

> When using email, respond in a timely manner, be polite, and don't include confidential or embarrassing information in email.

Social Networking

> Web 2.0 refers to the second generation of how the web is used where users both receive and post information.

> Social networking sites used to stay in touch with friends, family, and business associates include Facebook, Twitter, and LinkedIn.

> Individuals using Facebook use a Facebook profile to present themselves to and interact with other Facebook users.

> The timeline on the Facebook profile is used to post text, photos, and videos. Your News Feed shows activities on your timeline and on the timelines of your Facebook friends.

> Use the Facebook menu bar to access your Facebook Home page, profile, account settings, and other parts of your Facebook account.

> Use Facebook privacy settings to decide how much information about yourself and your activities are revealed to others.

> Businesses and public figures use Facebook pages rather than Facebook profiles used by individuals.

> Twitter is a quick and easy way to send Tweets, which are messages of 140 or fewer characters.

> An app is available for your smartphone to be able to receive and send Tweets using Twitter.

> LinkedIn.com is a social networking site used by professionals to build a network of professional contacts.

> When using social networking sites, use good security settings to protect your privacy, don't reveal inappropriate or confidential information, and present yourself well.

Presenting Yourself with Blogging

> A blog, or weblog, is an online diary or journal. Others can comment on your blog posts. You can post text, graphics, and links to other sites.

Communicating in Real Time with Voice, Text, and Video

> Instant Messaging (IM) or chat is real-time communication in text, voice, and video on the Internet.

> Voice communication on the Internet uses VoIP technology. Many providers, such as Skype, offer a free limited VoIP service.

> To use live streaming video over the Internet, you and your friend need a webcam to stream video as well as software installed on your computers.

CHAPTER MASTERY PROJECT

Now it's time to find out how well you've mastered the content in this chapter. If you can do all the steps in this mastery project without looking back at the chapter details and can answer all the review questions following this project, you've mastered this chapter. If you can complete the project by finding answers using the web, you've proven that you can teach yourself how to communicate with others using the web.

If you find you need a lot of help doing the project and you have not yet read the chapter or done the activities, drop back and start at the beginning of the chapter and then return to this project.

> **Hint** All the key terms in the chapter are used in this mastery project or in the review questions. If you encounter a key word you don't know, such as *Web 2.0*, enter **define: Web 2.0** in the Internet Explorer search box.

You need an email address to complete this project. In Chapter 2, you needed an email address to sign up for a OneDrive account. Use that email address or another address in this project.

> *Tip* If you need help completing this part of the mastery project, review the "Communicating through Email" section in the chapter.

Do the following to send and receive email using a website:

Step 1. Go to the website of your email provider and sign in to your email account. What is your account name? What is the domain name of your mail server? Open and view one message. If you have access to a printer, print the message.

Step 2. Write a message to a friend and send it. What is the email address of your friend?

Step 3. Delete the messages in your inbox you no longer need. Look in the folder for deleted messages. How many messages are there? How long will deleted messages stay in this folder?

Step 4. Write another message to a friend, this time attaching a Word document file to the message. If you don't have a file to attach, use the LetterToDave file in the sample_files folder available at www.pearsonhighered.com/jump or in MyITLab. (In Chapter 2, you downloaded the sample_files folder to your USB flash drive.)

Step 5. Ask a friend to send you a Word document as an attachment to an email message. When you receive the email, open the attachment. Then close the attachment and save it to your USB flash drive or another location given by your instructor. What is the name of the file you received from your friend? Forward your friend's message to another friend. Is the file your friend sent attached to the forwarded message?

Do the following to use Microsoft Outlook:

Step 6. Open Microsoft Outlook 2013 and set it up to use your email address to manage your email.

Step 7. Repeat steps 2 through 5, this time using Outlook rather than a website to manage email.

> *Tip* If you need help completing this part of the mastery project, review the "Exploring Social Networking" section in the chapter.

Do the following to set up and use Facebook:

Step 8. If you don't already have a Facebook account, sign up for one. View any notifications you have.

Step 9. Post a profile picture to your account. Write a status update on your timeline. Check your Privacy Settings. Who can see your status, photos, and posts? Adjust your privacy settings so you feel comfortable with what is revealed to others.

Step 10. View your News Feed. Is it ordered by Top Stories or Most Recent? Post a comment to your News Feed.

Step 11. Post a photo. If you don't have a photo to post, use one in the sample_files folder available at www.pearsonhighered.com/jump or in MyITLab.

Step 12. Use the search box to find a Facebook user that you know and then make a friend request. Use Facebook suggestions to find a friend and then make a friend request.

Step 13. Go to a friend's profile and browse his list of friends. Find someone you know and make a friend request. Find a photo in a friend's profile. Like the photo and tag someone in the photo you know. Send a private message to your friend. Use Facebook Chat to chat with a friend.

Step 14. Find a Facebook page for a public figure and Like that person.

Do the following to use Twitter:

Step 15. If you don't already have a Twitter account, sign up for one. Follow a public figure and at least one friend. Post a Tweet.

> **Tip** If you need help completing this part of the mastery project, review the "Present Yourself with Blogging" section in the chapter.

To start a blog, do the following:

Step 16. If you haven't already created a blog on blogspot.com, wordpress.com, or some other blogging site, do so now. What is the name of your blog? What is the URL?

Step 17. Write on your blog your experiences in this course. Which project did you enjoy the most?

To report to your instructor about this mastery project, do the following:

Step 18. Create a Word document and email the document to your instructor. In the document, include the following:

1. Your name and course information.
2. A screen capture of your Outlook Inbox taken using the Windows Snipping Tool.
3. The link to your Facebook profile. (With your Facebook profile showing in your browser, copy the URL in the browser address box and paste the URL into the document.)
4. The link to your Twitter page.
5. The link to your blog.

Review Questions

Answer these questions to assess your skills and knowledge of the content covered in the chapter. Your instructor can provide you with the correct answers when you're ready to check your work.

1. Which part of the email address SusieJones@sample.edu identifies the email account? The domain name of the mail server?

2. Where is an email message stored until the recipient requests it?

3. When you first open an email message you've received that has an attachment, is the attachment automatically opened?

4. How can having more than one email address help prevent spam from coming to the address you use for personal communication?

5. If you want to store all your email messages on your laptop, should you use a website or an email client to manage your email? Why?

6. When you delete a message in your email inbox, what happens to that message?

7. Why is it best not to click a link in an email message from a business or someone you don't know?

8. Why should you never include your credit card information in an email message?

9. Phishing is a type of _____ engineering. Describe phishing and explain how to avoid it.

10. When you send an email message with an attachment, does the attachment go to those who are listed under the CC feature of the message? What does CC stand for?

11. Why is online social networking called part of the Web 2.0?

12. Which is visible to other Facebook users, your News Feed or your Facebook profile?

13. Your timeline is on your Facebook _____ page, and your News Feed is on your Facebook _____ page.

14. When you find a Facebook user whom you want to be a friend, what two steps are needed to be friends on Facebook?

15. Using Facebook, a(n) _____ is when you identify a person in a photo.

16. Why is it important not to post embarrassing or confidential information on social networking sites such as Facebook?

17. What is the maximum length of a Tweet when using Twitter?

18. To use Twitter on your smart phone, what must you do first?

19. What is the primary purpose of LinkedIn?

20. Why is it not appropriate to post personal information on LinkedIn?

21. What are the two most popular blog sites?

22. Is a blog considered a social networking site? Why or why not?

23. What technology is used by Skype, Vonage, and other services to transmit voice over the Internet?

24. What is an example of a website that offers both IM and VoIP services?

25. What hardware device is needed to transmit video over the Internet so you can have a video chat session with a friend?

26. When you watch a video posted on YouTube, are you using VoIP, streaming video, chat, or a downloaded video file?

27. What two input devices are used during a video phone call using Skype?

28. What output device other than the monitor is used during a video phone call?

29. What type of software must be installed before you can use a webcam with any application?

Becoming an Independent Learner

Answer the following questions about becoming an independent learner:

1. To teach yourself to use the Internet for communication, do you think it's best to rely on the chapter or on the web when you need answers? Why?

2. The most important skill learned in this chapter is how to teach yourself a computer skill. Rate yourself at Level A through E on how well you are doing with this skill. What is your level?

    - Level A: I was able to successfully complete the Chapter Mastery Project with the help of only a few of the On Your Own activities in the chapter.
    - Level B: I completed all the On Your Own activities and the Chapter Mastery Project without referring to any of the solutions in the Step-by-Step Solutions Appendix.
    - Level C: I completed all the On Your Own activities and the Chapter Mastery Project by using just a few of the solutions in the Step-by-Step Solutions Appendix.
    - Level D: I completed all the On Your Own activities and the Chapter Mastery Project by using many of the solutions in the Step-by-Step Solutions Appendix.
    - Level E: I completed all the On Your Own activities and the Chapter Mastery Project and had to use all the solutions in the Step-by-Step Solutions Appendix.

To continue toward the goal of teaching yourself computer skills, if you're not at Level A, try to move up one level on how you learn in Chapter 7.

Projects to Help You

Now that you've mastered the material in this chapter, you're ready to tackle the three projects focused on your career, personal, or academic goals. Depending on your own interests, you might choose to complete any or all of these projects to help you achieve your goals.

Project 1: Communicating Online in Your Professional Career

Career Project I want to build a professional network using LinkedIn, and the business I work for part-time expects my email messages to look professional.

Do the following to build a LinkedIn network and improve your communication skills using email:

Step 1. If you don't already have a LinkedIn account, sign up for one. Try to expand your network of professionals to instructors, employers, and other friends also building a career in your chosen field. Ask an instructor or former employer to post a recommendation on your LinkedIn page. Post an update on the page about your plans to build a career.

Step 2. To improve your skills using email beyond what you learned in the chapter, do the following using the website of your email provider or using Outlook:

    a. In the chapter, you learned to attach a file to an email message. If the file contains a photo or other graphic, you can insert the file into the body of the email message. Compose an email message to your instructor and insert a picture in the body of the message.

    b. Format text in the email message to your instructor using bold, italic, font color, and other formatting tools.

    c. Find a stationery to use as the background for your email messages. Using Outlook, apply the stationery to the email message to your instructor.

    d. Include in the email the URL of your LinkedIn profile.

Step 3. Send the email to your instructor.

Project 2: Communicating on the Web in Your Personal Life

Personal Project I want to use Facebook and a blog to stay connected online with family and friends. I want to use Skype to talk for free with family members who live in another country.

The web is a great way to stay in touch with extended family and friends. Use the skills you learned in this chapter to build your relationships online. Do the following:

Step 1. Encourage older family members who don't use Facebook to sign up. Help a family member set up a Facebook account and find other family members to friend. Post a family photo to Facebook and tag the photo with the names of other family members on Facebook. Use the Windows Snipping Tool to take an snip of this photo and save the snip to your USB flash drive.

Step 2. Check the privacy settings on the Facebook account. Log off the account. Then do a Google search for your family member's name, searching on the Facebook.com site. What information can any visitors see about him or her even if he or she is not logged on to Facebook? Can they see his or her profile picture? His or her date of birth? How easy is it to find him or her on Facebook?

Step 3. In the chapter, you wrote a blog about an event in your childhood, a hobby, or a favorite movie. Ask a family member (spouse, sister, brother, child, grandparent, parent, aunt, or uncle) to comment on your blog. If this person doesn't know how to use the web and a blog, here's your chance to share what you've learned.

Step 4. Blog sites might offer privacy settings to allow everyone to access your blog, to block search engines from finding your blog, or to limit access to people you choose. What privacy settings are offered by your blog site? What settings are you currently using?

If you have a speaker, microphone, and access to a computer where you can install software, do the following to set up and use Skype:

Step 5. Go to skype.com and set up an account. You need to download and install the software on your computer.

Step 6. Find a friend or family member who has a Skype account and talk using Skype. Skype is a great way to talk with family and friends in other countries who use Skype because Skype-to-Skype calls are free. Use the Windows Snipping Tool to make an image snip of this conversation. Save the image snip to your USB flash drive.

Step 7. Use Word to create a file that contains your answers to the following questions about this project. Name the file **Chapter 6 Personal Project** and send the file to your instructor. If you're using MyITLab, you can post the file in a Dropbox assignment or email the file in MyITLab. On the other hand, your instructor might prefer you post the file to your OneDrive or email the file using your school email. Here are the questions:

1. Who in your family did you help create a Facebook profile? Include in the Word document the image snip you created in step 1.

2. In step 2, how secure is his or her Facebook profile?

3. In step 3, what is the URL of your blog where your family member commented?

4. In step 4, are anonymous comments allowed on your blog? Where do you change this setting?

5. In step 6, you created an image snip. Include that snip here.

Project 3: Communicating on the Web in Your Academic Career

Do the following to use the web for communication in your academic career:

Step 1. Select an instructor at your school who you like. Search the web for social networking sites that he or she uses. Does he or she write a blog? Does he or she have a profile on Facebook that is public? Is he or she on LinkedIn? Does he or she use Twitter? If he or she writes a blog that allows public comments, comment on his or her blog. Use the Windows Snipping Tool to make an image snip of your comment. Save the snip to your USB flash drive.

Step 2. Volunteer to build a Facebook page for a club at your school or a nonprofit organization. Do the following:

   a. Ask the leaders of the club or organization for permission and the correct information to post. Also ask for the email addresses of its members and associates and a graphic file of the logo. A photo or two will add interest to the page.

   b. Build the page and include the information, logo, and any photos you have. To find out how to set up a page for a business or other organization, search the Help Center in Facebook.

   c. Post a link to the page on your Facebook timeline and invite your friends to Like the page. Send an email message to the email addresses of the members of the organization and to your instructor announcing the page and asking them to Like it on Facebook.

Step 3. Use Word to create a file that contains your answers to the following questions about this project. Name the file **Chapter 6 Academic Project** and send the file to your instructor. If you are using MyITLab, you can post the file in a Dropbox assignment or email the file in MyITLab. On the other hand, your instructor might prefer you post the file to your OneDrive or email the file using your school or personal email. Here are the questions:

1. In step 1, on which social networking sites did you find an instructor at your school?

2. In step 1, what is the URL to your instructor's blog where you commented? Include in the Word document the image snip you made in step 1.

3. In step 2, what is the URL to the Facebook page you created?

Academic Project I want to see what my instructors are saying on the web. Also, my club wants to use Facebook to show pictures of our events and attract other members.

Project to Help Others

One of the best ways to learn is to teach someone else. And, in teaching someone else, you're making a contribution into that person's life. As part of each chapter's work, you're encouraged to teach someone else a skill you have learned. In this case, you help your apprentice learn more about communicating on the web.

Working with your apprentice, do the following:

Step 1. If your apprentice doesn't already use email, help him set up an email account and use it to send and receive email. Help him learn all the email skills presented in this chapter. If he already uses email, ask him if he has questions or wants to learn more.

Step 2. If your apprentice doesn't already have a Facebook account, help him set one up and use it. Keep working together until he understands Facebook, has several Facebook friends, and is comfortable building a social network using Facebook.

Step 3. Show your apprentice your blog and invite him to comment on one of your blog entries. Then show him how to set up his own blog. After he has posted to his blog, make a comment on his post.

Step 4. Does your apprentice want to learn to use Skype or another free Internet voice service? If so, help him set it up and use it.

Step 5. Use Word to create a file that contains your answers to the following questions about the tutoring session. Name the file **Chapter 6 Tutoring** and send the file to your instructor. If you're using MyITLab, you can post the file in a Dropbox assignment or email the file in MyITLab. On the other hand, your instructor might prefer you post the file to your OneDrive or email the file using your school or personal email. Here are the questions:

1. Who is your apprentice?
2. In step 2, what is the URL to your apprentice's Facebook profile page?
3. In step 3, what is the URL to your apprentice's blog?
4. How do you think the session went? How would you like to improve it next time?

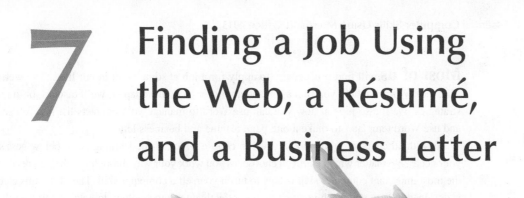

7 Finding a Job Using the Web, a Résumé, and a Business Letter

In This Chapter, You Will:

Explore Job-Hunting Strategies

7.1 Explore strategies to help you find a great job

7.2 Use Word tables to track contacts during a job search

Create and Send a Résumé

7.3 Use a résumé template and save the résumé for emailing or posting online

7.4 Email the résumé

Create and Send an Interview Follow-Up Letter

7.5 Know how to have a great job interview

7.6 Create a personal letterhead for all your business needs

7.7 Use a letter template to write an interview follow-up letter

7.8 Add an envelope to a letter

7.9 Email an interview follow-up letter

Most of us will find it necessary to apply for a job at some point in our lives. The web and Microsoft Word can help you find a job and apply for it. In this chapter, we'll discuss job-hunting strategies. We'll also look at how you can use Word to manage your contacts list in a job search and use Word templates to make a one-page résumé and business letter.

As with all chapters in this book, you can choose which of the learning paths below best suits your needs. No matter which path you choose, as you work your way through the chapter, remember the most important computer skill is how to teach yourself a computer skill. Therefore, this chapter is designed to help you teach yourself how to effectively use technology to help you find a job.

LEARNING PATHS

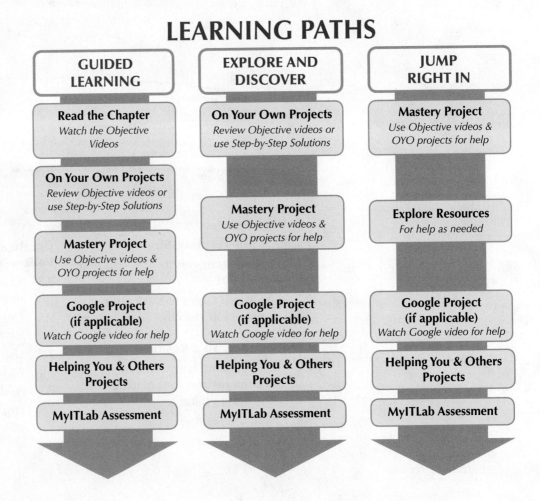

GUIDED LEARNING	EXPLORE AND DISCOVER	JUMP RIGHT IN
Read the Chapter *Watch the Objective Videos*	**On Your Own Projects** *Review Objective videos or use Step-by-Step Solutions*	**Mastery Project** *Use Objective videos & OYO projects for help*
On Your Own Projects *Review Objective videos or use Step-by-Step Solutions*	**Mastery Project** *Use Objective videos & OYO projects for help*	**Explore Resources** *For help as needed*
Mastery Project *Use Objective videos & OYO projects for help*		
Google Project (if applicable) *Watch Google video for help*	**Google Project (if applicable)** *Watch Google video for help*	**Google Project (if applicable)** *Watch Google video for help*
Helping You & Others Projects	**Helping You & Others Projects**	**Helping You & Others Projects**
MyITLab Assessment	**MyITLab Assessment**	**MyITLab Assessment**

Exploring Job-Hunting Strategies

Using a number of effective job-hunting strategies can help you more easily find the best job for you. It's also important to track your progress during a job search. We'll explore both in this section.

Objective 7.1: Explore Strategies to Help You Find a Great Job

WATCH

**OBJECTIVE 7.1
VIDEO**

Searching for a job can be hard work, and a good strategy makes work more effective. When searching for a job, keep these ten strategies in mind:

> **Know yourself.** Know your strengths and weaknesses. Know what will make you happy and satisfied. Your school might offer career and aptitude assessments. Take advantage of these opportunities to find out more about yourself.

> **Know what job will work for you.** Know what jobs you will be good at and will enjoy. When given the opportunity, be ready to explain what makes you unique and the best candidate for the job.

> **Work at finding a job.** Don't wait for the job to come to you. Use all the strategies in this chapter, work hard, and don't give up until you find your job.

> **Network with lots of people.** Let as many people as possible know that you're looking for a job. Use professional networking sites such as LinkedIn.com and TweetMyJobs.com and social networking sites such as Facebook.com. Tell your friends, family, neighbors, and former teachers that you're looking for a job. Most job openings are never advertised and are filled by a direct referral.

> **Communicate with real people.** Computers don't hire people; people hire people. Whenever possible, make personal contact with a real person. For example, after you post your résumé online, try to follow up with a personal phone call.

---

résumé—A document summarizing job experience and education for employers to use when deciding who to interview or hire for a job. The document should be brief and to the point.

> **Go to the top.** The higher the person is in the organization you talk with, the more likely you will be hired. Do your best to reach someone with authority and influence.

> **Know what companies want.** Most employers are hiring someone because they're trying to solve a problem. Ask enough questions to uncover what the problem is that needs to be solved. Then present yourself as the solution to the problem.

> **Be willing to settle for less.** Sometimes a temporary job that lasts only a few weeks or a part-time job is all you need to get your foot in the door. Be willing to take a job for less pay or less responsibility than you deserve. When working on this less-than-perfect job, always do your best even when you think no one is looking. As you prove yourself, people take notice and are more likely to offer you a better or more permanent job.

> **Keep good records.** Keep a list of contacts, what you sent the contact, and when you sent it. Include follow-up information. This list helps with your current job search and also can help you with future searches.

> **Use technology effectively.** In this chapter, you learn to effectively use technology to help you find a job. You learn to create a document for tracking contacts, create a résumé and email and post the résumé online, create an interview follow-up letter, and email the letter.

Using Web Resources

The web is also a valuable resource when you're looking for a job. For example, if you need to know how to best present yourself at a job interview, use Google.com to search the web for **tips for job interviews**.

Here are a few tips and websites to consider when looking online for a job:

> **Job search engines.** Some job search sites are Monster.com, Indeed.com, CareerBuilder.com, Dice.com (limited to jobs in technology), LinkUp.com, Glassdoor.com (posts jobs and what current employees say about a company), and SimplyHired.com. You can search for jobs in your area, and some of these sites allow you to post your résumé to the site.

> **Government jobs.** Find listings for jobs with the federal government at USAJOBS.gov. Also search your local and state government websites for job postings.

> **Large corporations.** Go to the websites of large corporations and look for job postings for the organization.

> **Local newspaper websites.** Check the classified ads sections of the website for your local newspaper for jobs in your area. Also look for jobs in the online classified ads on craigslist.org (see Figure 7-1).

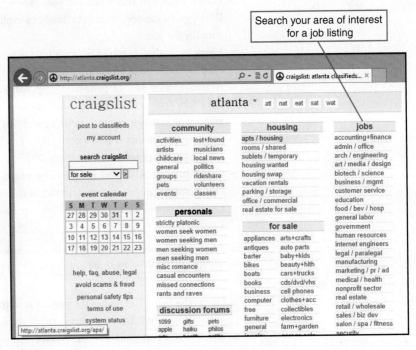

FIGURE 7-1   Craigslist.org offers job listings for specific areas.

> **Your school or university website.** Your school might post job openings in the area on its website. If you don't find postings there, check the student and alumni service department at your school for job openings and for help finding a job.

> **Job fairs.** Search the web for job fairs in your city and field. For example, do a Google search on **job fairs in Baltimore**. Your school website might also post announcements about job fairs in the area.

> **Recruiters.** Use a recruiter to help you find a professional job. Some recruiter sites are therecruiternetwork.com, theladders.com, headhunters.com, and job-hunt.org.

> **Networking sites.** Recall from Chapter 6 that LinkedIn.com and other professional networking sites can help you stay connected to professional friends and acquaintances who might be aware of a job that fits your needs.

Tip When attending a job fair, always take several copies of your résumé with you.

WATCH

OBJECTIVE 7.2
VIDEO

Objective 7.2: Use Word Tables to Track Contacts during a Job Search

Keeping good notes when job hunting helps to keep you on track. You can keep these notes in a handwritten notebook or a Word document. A **table** in a Word document can help keep notes organized.

> **table**—An element that can be inserted into a Word document and is made up of rows and columns. Tables are used to organize text and graphics.

You first insert a table in the document, and then you type text into the table. You can add new rows and columns to a table, and you can delete rows and columns you no longer need.

ON YOUR OWN 7.1

Create a Contacts Document Including Tables

WATCH

OBJECTIVE 7.2
VIDEO

In this activity, you'll create a document that uses tables to track your contacts when you're job hunting, as shown in Figure 7-2. In this document, you use one table for each contact. The document in Figure 7-2 has two contacts and a third table waiting for the next contact.

My Contacts	
Company	Sears
Name	Andy Knight
Title	Human Resource Manager
Phone	555-222-1234
Email	aknight@sample.com
Address	300 Valley Parkway, Lincoln, MI 50555
Actions	• Applied for job online on 9/30/2013 • Sent resume by email on 10/2/2013 • Followed up with phone call on 10/4/2013. Mr. Knight was not available, but Jessica, the receptionist, said to call back next week. • Plan to call again on October 11

Company	Macy's Inc.
Name	Sarah Smith
Title	Personnel Director
Phone	555-333-1234
Email	s.smith@sample.com
Address	1603 Commerce Way, Suite 200, Grand Rapids, MI 49500
Actions	• Applied for job online on 9/30/2013 • Called and left voice message on 10/5/2013. Call again tomorrow.

Company	
Name	
Title	
Phone	
Email	
Address	
Actions	

FIGURE 7-2   The contacts document uses one table for each contact.

To create the document, follow these steps:

Step 1. Create a new blank document in Word. Enter the title of the document and format it using the **Heading 1** style.

Step 2. Create one table with two columns. Enter the information in column 1, as shown in Figure 7-2 and also below. Resize the columns, as shown in Figure 7-2. Make two more copies of this table in the document.

> **Hint** Use the INSERT ribbon to insert a table. When a table is selected or the insertion point is inside a table, the TABLE TOOLS DESIGN tab and LAYOUT tab show up on the Word window. Use the LAYOUT ribbon to insert and delete rows and columns and format the table.

Step 3. Before you invest more time in the document, save it. Save the document to your USB flash drive, hard drive, OneDrive, or other location given by your instructor. Name the document **MyContacts**.

Step 4. Enter the following contact information for Andy Knight in the first table:

Company	Sears
Name	Andy Knight
Title	Human Resource Manager
Phone	555-222-1234
Email	aknight@sample.com
Address	300 Valley Parkway, Lincoln, MI 50555
Actions	• Applied for job online on 9/30/2013 • Sent resume by email on 10/2/2013 • Followed up with phone call on 10/4/2013. Mr. Knight was not available, but Jessica, the receptionist, said to call back next week. • Plan to call again on October 11

Step 5. Enter the following contact information for Sarah Smith in the second table:

Company	Macy's Inc.
Name	Sarah Smith
Title	Personnel Director
Phone	555-333-1234
Email	s.smith@sample.com
Address	1603 Commerce Way, Suite 200, Grand Rapids, MI 49500
Actions	• Applied for job online on 9/30/2013 • Called and left voice message on 10/5/2013. Call again tomorrow.

Step 6. Verify you are the author of the document, save your work, and close the document.

Solutions Appendix

For help: See On Your Own 7.1 Step-by-Step Solution

Creating and Sending a Résumé

After you've found a job opening, the next step is to apply. In most situations, an employer uses applicants' résumés to decide who will be interviewed for the job.

WATCH

OBJECTIVE 7.3
VIDEO

Objective 7.3: Use a Résumé Template and Save the Résumé for Emailing or Posting Online

Some companies ask you to email or upload your résumé to their website when applying for a job. Other companies require you to fill out an online form. You can also post your résumé on a job search site or carry it with you to a job fair or job interview.

WATCH

CHAPTER 7
DIVING DEEPER
VIDEO

Benefits of Using a Résumé Template

Because your résumé is likely to be an employer's first impression of you, writing a good one is an essential job-acquiring skill. A résumé template can help you create a dynamite résumé that can help you stand out as the best candidate for the job.

Although you can write your résumé without using a template, a résumé template can do the following:

> Provide a structure for the information in your résumé
> Give your résumé an appealing format
> Provide time-tested suggestions for what information to include on your résumé

Word provides many templates for résumés. A few are shown in Figure 7-3. Choose a résumé template that looks professional without clip art or too much color. If you choose a résumé template that targets the type of job you seek, the areas in the résumé are likely to work for you without a lot of changes.

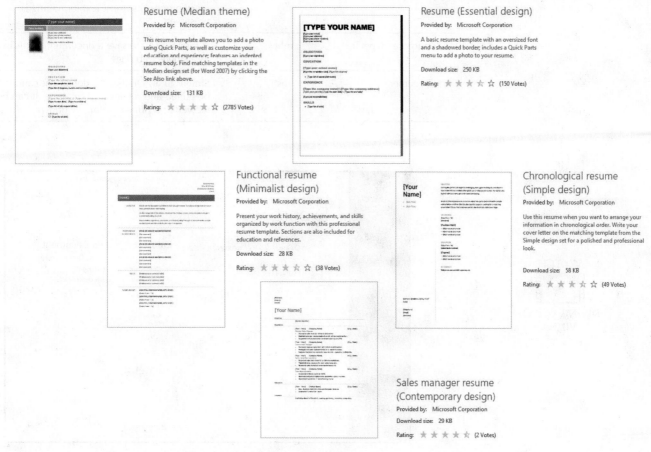

FIGURE 7-3 Templates make it easy to create professional résumés for any career.

Export the Word Document to a New Format

Job search sites and corporate websites sometimes allow you to upload your résumé. For example, to upload your résumé to the Indeed.com site, click **Post your resume** and follow the directions on-screen. If the website doesn't request a specific file format, use the PDF format. Although another computer might format or display a Word document differently than what appears on your screen, the PDF format keeps the document looking exactly as you intend. However, if a Word document is requested, use the .doc (not the .docx) file format so the file can be opened in older versions of Word. These and other common file formats are listed in Table 7-1.

One way to save a Word document in a new format is to click the **FILE** tab and then click **Export**. You can then save the document as a PDF or XPS document (see Figure 7-4) or click **Change File Type** to see other options. Recall from Chapter 3 that another way to save a document in a different format is to click the **FILE** tab and then click **Save As**. Then, in the Save As dialog box, change the file type.

TABLE 7-1   Common File Formats Supported by Word

File Format	File Extension	Description
Document	.docx	Current MS Word file format.
Word 97–2003 Document	.doc	Older MS Word file format.
Portable Document Format	.pdf	An image of a document that looks exactly like the print preview. Most computers have software installed to view a PDF file.
Plain Text	.txt	Text only; all formatting is lost.
Rich Text Format	.rtf	A format that can be edited by most word processors; most text formatting is preserved.
Multipurpose HyperText	.mht	A format used to save a document that is built as a single web page.
XPS Document	.xps	Similar to a PDF file, the document cannot be edited and retains its formatting. It can be viewed and printed within Windows.

WATCH

DIVING DEEPER
VIDEO

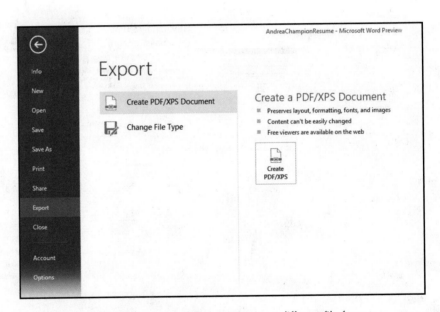

FIGURE 7-4   You can save a Word document using a different file format.

WATCH

OBJECTIVE 7.3
VIDEO

ON YOUR OWN 7.2

Create a Résumé Using a Résumé Template

Andrea Champion is looking for a seasonal retail job and has asked for your help creating a résumé. She has sent you her education and job experience in a Word document. You can find Andrea's information in the AndreaInformation document file in the sample_files folder available at www.pearsonhighered.com/jump or in MyITLab. (In Chapter 2, you downloaded the sample_files folder to your USB flash drive.) The completed résumé is shown in Figure 7-5 and is built using a Word template.

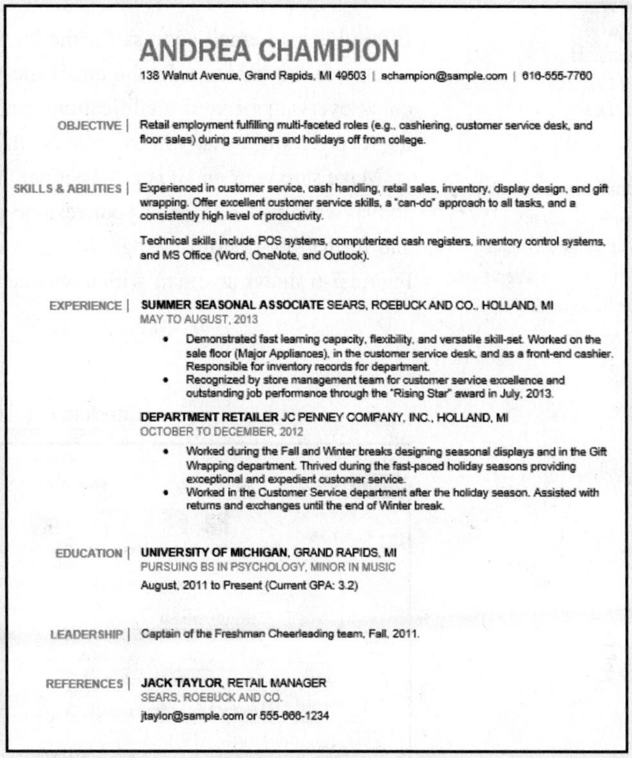

ANDREA CHAMPION

138 Walnut Avenue, Grand Rapids, MI 49503 | achampion@sample.com | 616-555-7760

OBJECTIVE | Retail employment fulfilling multi-faceted roles (e.g., cashiering, customer service desk, and floor sales) during summers and holidays off from college.

SKILLS & ABILITIES | Experienced in customer service, cash handling, retail sales, inventory, display design, and gift wrapping. Offer excellent customer service skills, a "can-do" approach to all tasks, and a consistently high level of productivity.

Technical skills include POS systems, computerized cash registers, inventory control systems, and MS Office (Word, OneNote, and Outlook).

EXPERIENCE | **SUMMER SEASONAL ASSOCIATE** SEARS, ROEBUCK AND CO., HOLLAND, MI
MAY TO AUGUST, 2013

- Demonstrated fast learning capacity, flexibility, and versatile skill-set. Worked on the sale floor (Major Appliances), in the customer service desk, and as a front-end cashier. Responsible for inventory records for department.
- Recognized by store management team for customer service excellence and outstanding job performance through the "Rising Star" award in July, 2013.

DEPARTMENT RETAILER JC PENNEY COMPANY, INC., HOLLAND, MI
OCTOBER TO DECEMBER, 2012

- Worked during the Fall and Winter breaks designing seasonal displays and in the Gift Wrapping department. Thrived during the fast-paced holiday seasons providing exceptional and expedient customer service.
- Worked in the Customer Service department after the holiday season. Assisted with returns and exchanges until the end of Winter break.

EDUCATION | **UNIVERSITY OF MICHIGAN**, GRAND RAPIDS, MI
PURSUING BS IN PSYCHOLOGY, MINOR IN MUSIC
August, 2011 to Present (Current GPA: 3.2)

LEADERSHIP | Captain of the Freshman Cheerleading team, Fall, 2011.

REFERENCES | **JACK TAYLOR**, RETAIL MANAGER
SEARS, ROEBUCK AND CO.
jtaylor@sample.com or 555-666-1234

FIGURE 7-5   The completed résumé for Andrea Champion uses the Basic resume template.

Tip It's hard for writers to catch their own errors. For this reason, always have another person carefully read your résumé, looking for errors.

Let's get started:

Step 1. Create a new document using a template. Word searches for templates online, so make sure you're connected to the Internet. In the **Resume** group of templates, select the **Basic resume** template.

Not Working? If you can't find the Basic resume template, open the BasicResume document in the sample_files folder available at www.pearsonhighered.com/jump or in MyITLab. (In Chapter 2, you downloaded the sample_files folder to your USB flash drive.)

Step 2. Using Figure 7-5 as your guide, replace the information that was in the résumé template with Andrea's information in the AndreaInformation document. (Note that the template has an area for COMMUNICATION that is not used in the final résumé.)

Hint The Basic resume template uses a table to build the résumé. The borders of the table are hidden. To see these borders so that you can more easily delete a row in the table, first select the entire table and then click the Borders icon ⊞ on the HOME ribbon.

Step 3. Save the résumé as a Word document and then as a PDF. Name the document and the PDF **AndreaChampionResume**. Close all windows.

Solutions Appendix   *For help:* See *On Your Own 7.2* Step-by-Step Solution

Tip Remember, computers don't hire people; people hire people. When applying for a job, do your best to find the name of a real person at the company. Then send your résumé to this person by email and follow up with a phone call.

Objective 7.4: Email the Résumé

If you have an email address for the human resource department or hiring manager, email your résumé to this address. In the email message, be sure to include the job you're applying for, a quick overview of your qualifications, and your contact information. In addition, you want to let the receiver know that your résumé is attached so it won't be missed.

Make sure your email is professional, includes a subject line, and doesn't have errors. As noted above, when possible, send your résumé as a PDF file so that it can be opened on any computer and formatting doesn't change. Make sure the PDF file name includes your first and last name. Figure 7-6 shows an email with a résumé ready to be sent by Andrea.

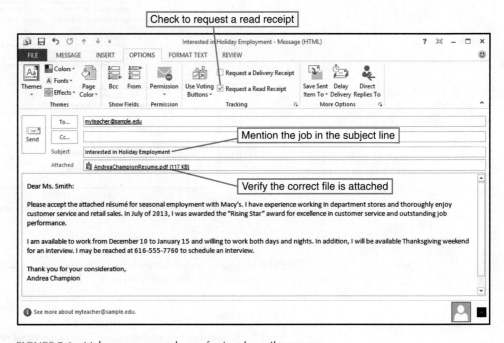

FIGURE 7-6   Make sure you send a professional email message.

Email a Résumé PDF

Remember that you're making your first impression with the email, so it is important that it's clear and doesn't have errors. Do the following to email the résumé to your instructor:

Step 1. Create the email subject line and body of the message. Here is the message:

> Dear Ms. Smith:
>
> Please accept the attached résumé for seasonal employment with Macy's. I have experience working in department stores and thoroughly enjoy customer service and retail sales. In July of 2013, I was awarded the "Rising Star" award for excellence in customer service and outstanding job performance.
>
> I am available to work from December 10 to January 15 and willing to work both days and nights. In addition, I will be available Thanksgiving weekend for an interview. I may be reached at 616-555-7760 to schedule an interview.
>
> Thank you for your consideration,
>
> Andrea Champion

Step 2. Verify that the email you typed is correct. Attach the résumé you created. Be sure to attach the PDF file and not the Word document file.

> **Hint** Windows identifies a PDF file as an Adobe Acrobat Document file.

Step 3. Request a read receipt. For Outlook, on the OPTIONS ribbon, click **Request a Read Receipt**. The read receipt will send you a message when the receiver opens the email and agrees to send the read receipt.

Step 4. Send the email message with the attachment to your instructor's email address.

Solutions Appendix   *For help:* See *On Your Own 7.3* Step-by-Step Solution

---

Tip In addition to emailing your résumé, also send the résumé by postal mail unless the job ad requests you not do that. This double reminder says to a potential employer that you're serious about the job.

WATCH

OBJECTIVE 7.5 VIDEO

Creating and Sending an Interview Follow-Up Letter

Based on your résumé, a company might select you for an interview. Following the interview, you can shine as the best candidate for the job by sending an interview follow-up letter.

Objective 7.5: Know How to Have a Great Job Interview

An interview can be nerve-racking, but if you follow these tips, you can have a successful interview:

> **Dress professionally.** You don't have a second chance to make a first impression, so make sure you dress professionally. A man might dress in a shirt and tie or suit, and a woman might choose a skirt or pants and a blazer. Be sure to freshly iron your clothes.

> **Arrive 10 minutes early.** Arriving early does more than show you're punctual; it also helps calm your nerves. You're more likely to be stressed if you have to rush to get to your interview on time.

> **Bring copies of your résumé.** Make sure you have several copies of your résumé to hand out to everyone at the interview. (You might be interviewed by several people.) You can also bring personal business cards that you print on your computer.

> **Hint** Business cards are easy to make using a Word Business card template. You'll need to print the cards on card stock paper that comes 10 cards to a sheet.

> **Greet with a handshake and make eye contact.** When you first meet the person or people interviewing you, look them in the eyes, smile, and shake their hand. Don't squeeze too hard, but don't be afraid to give a firm handshake. Continue to make eye contact throughout the interview.

> **Get the name and contact information for the primary interviewer.** Ask the person conducting the interview for a business card. You'll need the information later to follow up on the job, and it's always a good idea to have the name of the person interviewing you.

> **Ask questions during the interview.** Before the interview, research about the company and the position. Make sure you understand what problem the company needs solved and why it's looking to hire someone. Ask questions that show you're interested in the position and the company and are familiar with both. Make it clear that you're ready and able to solve the problem.

> **Ask when a decision will be made.** Don't leave the interview without finding out when the employer expects to make a hiring decision. Also ask whether it's okay if you check back later about the job.

> **Follow up after the interview.** Send a letter both by email and postal mail expressing your interest in the job. Sending both an email and a letter gives the interviewers two reminders of you.

WATCH

OBJECTIVE 7.6 VIDEO

Objective 7.6: Create a Personal Letterhead for All Your Business Needs

For all your business needs, your own personal letterhead or stationery can make you look especially professional, and Word **letterhead templates** can help.

> **letterhead template**—A design used for business letters which includes the name and contact information of a person or company.

ON YOUR OWN 7.4

WATCH

OBJECTIVE 7.6 VIDEO

Create a Personal Letterhead for Business Letters

When creating a personal letterhead document for writing business letters, choose a letterhead template that looks professional and reflects your taste. If your printer doesn't print in color, select a template that doesn't use color or that still looks good when printed in black and white. In this activity, you create a letterhead document for Andrea Champion. Figure 7-7 shows the finished document.

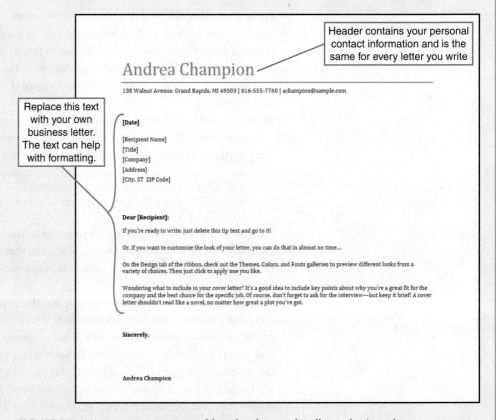

FIGURE 7-7   You can create a personal letterhead to use for all your business letters.

Do the following to create the letterhead document:

Step 1. Look in the **Letters** group of templates and limit the search to **Stationery**. Select the **Cover letter (blue)** template. Create a new Word document using this or another template.

> **Not Working?** If you can't find the Cover letter (blue) template, open the CoverLetter document in the sample_files folder available at www.pearsonhighered.com/jump or in MyITLab. (In Chapter 2, you downloaded the sample_files folder to your USB flash drive.)

Step 2. Replace the information at the top of the letterhead with Andrea's name, address, phone number, and email address. You can find Andrea's information in her résumé you created in the On Your Own 7.2 activity.

Step 3. If necessary, remove the hyperlink on the email address.

Step 4. Save the letterhead to your USB flash drive, hard drive, OneDrive, or other location given by your instructor. Name the document **AndreaChampionLetterhead**. Keep a copy of your letterhead so you can use it for all the letters you write.

Solutions Appendix

For help: See *On Your Own 7.4* Step-by-Step Solution

WATCH

OBJECTIVE 7.7
VIDEO

Objective 7.7: Use a Letter Template to Write an Interview Follow-Up Letter

Many of us dread having to write business letters, but Word templates can make it easy to write a great letter. A letter template contains the body of the letter that you can edit for your specific needs.

> letter template—A template that helps you write the body of a letter.

ON YOUR OWN 7.5

WATCH

OBJECTIVE 7.7
VIDEO

Create an Interview Follow-Up Letter

Create and Email the SarahSmith Letter: Part 1 of 3

Using the AndreaChampionLetterhead document created in the On Your Own 7.4 activity, write a follow-up letter for Andrea Champion after her interview. She interviewed with Macy's Department Store and met with Sarah Smith. The completed follow-up letter is shown in Figure 7-8.

>

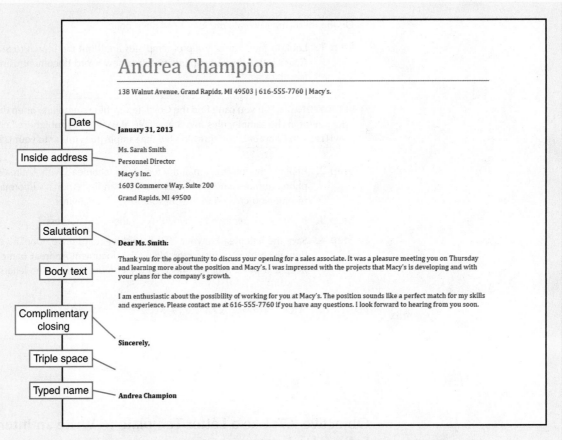

FIGURE 7-8   The follow-up letter thanks the interviewer for considering Andrea for the job.

Be sure to use the correct formatting and spacing for the letter as labeled in the figure. The parts of the letter identified in Figure 7-8 are defined next.

> **inside address**—The name and address of the receiver of the letter that appears a double space below the date.
>
> **salutation**—The greeting, such as Dear Mr. Jones:. Use a colon at the end of the salutation. Double-space below the salutation.
>
> **body text**—The reason you are writing. State your purpose in the first sentence. Always end the text with a closing call to action.
>
> **complimentary closing**—Complimentary text following the body text, such as Best regards, Sincerely, or Yours truly. End the closing with a comma and a triple space.

Do the following:

Step 1.   Open the **AndreaChampionLetterhead** document and save the document as **SarahSmith**. Save it to your USB flash drive, hard drive, OneDrive, or other location given by your instructor.

Step 2.   Enter today's date and address the letter to **Ms. Sarah Smith**. You can find her address in the contacts list shown earlier in the On Your Own 7.1 activity.

Step 3.   The salutation is **Dear Ms. Smith:**

Step 4.   To get ideas for writing the body of a letter, you can browse through letter templates to find a letter on your topic. Without closing the SarahSmith document, create a new document using the **Interview thank you letter** template. Copy the body of this letter into the Windows Clipboard.

Not Working? If you can't find the Interview thank you letter template, open the ThankYouForInterview document in the sample_files folder available at www.pearsonhighered.com/jump or in MyITLab. (In Chapter 2, you downloaded the sample_files folder to your USB flash drive.)

Step 5. Return to the SarahSmith letter and paste the text from the Interview thank you letter into the document. Edit the fields in the body text for Andrea's situation:

Thank you for the opportunity to discuss your opening for a sales associate. It was a pleasure meeting you on Thursday and learning more about the position and Macy's. I was impressed with the projects that Macy's is developing and with your plans for the company's growth.

I am enthusiastic about the possibility of working for you at Macy's. The position sounds like a perfect match for my skills and experience. Please contact me at 616-555-7760 if you have any questions. I look forward to hearing from you soon.

Step 6. The document is finished. Save and close it.

Solutions Appendix | *For help:* See *On Your Own 7.5* Step-by-Step Solution

---

WATCH

OBJECTIVE 7.8 VIDEO

Objective 7.8: Add an Envelope to a Letter

Word can produce a professional envelope for your business letter.

Tip When mailing your letter, sign it in blue or black ink. On a real job search, after mailing the letter, don't forget to record that action in your MyContacts document.

ON YOUR OWN 7.6

Add an Envelope to the SarahSmith Letter

WATCH

OBJECTIVE 7.8 VIDEO

Create and Email the SarahSmith Letter: Part 2 of 3

Add an envelope to the SarahSmith follow-up letter you created in On Your Own 7.5. Do the following:

Step 1. If necessary, open the SarahSmith letter. To create the envelope, click **Envelopes** on the MAILINGS ribbon. The Envelopes and Labels dialog box appears. Enter the Delivery address and Return address, as shown in Figure 7-9.

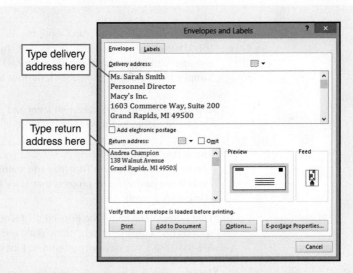

FIGURE 7-9   Microsoft Word can add a professional envelope to a document.

Step 2.   You can save the envelope in your document or immediately print it. To save it in your document, click **Add to Document**. Click **No** when you see the message "Do you want to save the new return address as the default return address?" The envelope is created as the first page of your document (see Figure 7-10).

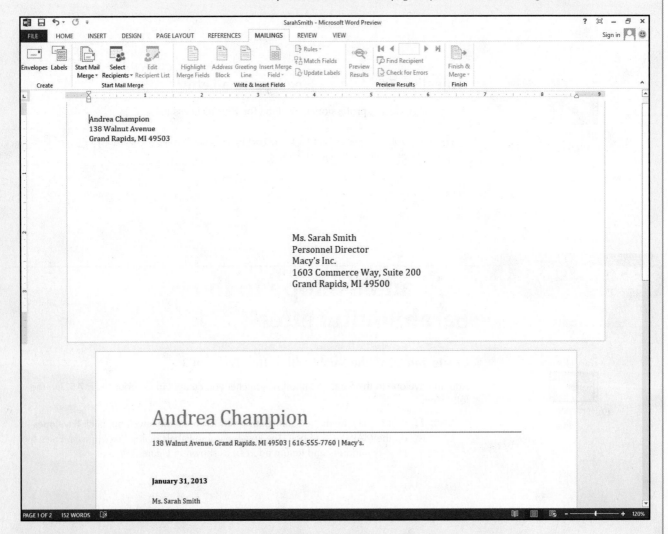

FIGURE 7-10   An envelope has been added as the first page of the document.

Step 3. If you have access to a printer, insert the envelope in your printer. Orient the envelope according to the instructions in your printer manual. Then click **Print**. The envelope prints first, followed by the letter.

| Solutions Appendix | *For help:* See *On Your Own 7.6* Step-by-Step Solution |

WATCH

OBJECTIVE 7.9
VIDEO

Objective 7.9: Email an Interview Follow-Up Letter

When you send a follow-up letter by postal mail and email, the employer gets two reminders of you. One reminder comes instantly from email, and one comes a few days later by postal mail. Don't attach the follow-up letter to an email message because the employer must take the extra time to open the attachment. To make it easier for the employer, copy and paste the letter into the email message.

Email the Follow-Up Letter

WATCH

OBJECTIVE 7.9
VIDEO

Create and Email the SarahSmith Letter: Part 3 of 3

The SarahSmith follow-up letter can be sent by email, as shown in Figure 7-11, when using Outlook.

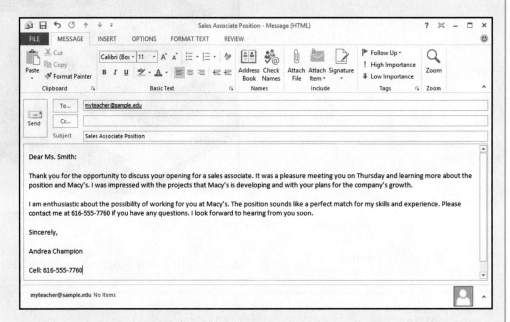

FIGURE 7-11   Send your follow-up letter by email.

Do the following to email the letter you created earlier:

Step 1. In Word, open the follow-up letter, **SarahSmith**. Select and copy the salutation, body, closing, and name into the Windows Clipboard.

Step 2. In Outlook, create a new email message and paste the letter into the body of the email. Check and correct any formatting problems. Add the subject line **Sales Associate Position**.

Step 3. Email the letter to your instructor.

Solutions
Appendix

For help: See *On Your Own 7.7* Step-by-Step Solution

After you have sent the letter by email, don't forget to record that action in your MyContacts document. In addition, a few days after the interview, call the employer and ask whether a decision has been made. Make a note of the phone call in your MyContacts document.

Summary

Exploring Job-Hunting Strategies

> Know your strengths and find a job that works for you. Work at finding a job and network with lots of people. Try to reach someone in an organization with authority and influence.

> Recognize that when a company is hiring someone, it is trying to solve a problem. Find out what the problem is and convince the employer you are the solution.

> Keep a list of contacts and the actions you've taken. The contacts list can help with your current and future job searches.

> Use a contacts document, a résumé, websites, email, and business letters to help find a job.

> Word tables are used to organize information. A table is the perfect tool to track each contact you make in your job search. Keep contact information current by adding each new action to the contacts document.

Creating and Sending a Résumé

> A résumé is an essential job-acquiring document to present your qualifications, skills, and education to a potential employer.

> Word offers résumé templates for a wide variety of job descriptions, experiences, and educational backgrounds. Use a résumé template to organize your information and give ideas as to what to include in the résumé.

> You can email a résumé, post it online, or mail it to potential employers.

> The best file format to use when emailing a résumé as an attachment is a PDF file.

Creating and Sending an Interview Follow-Up Letter

> Dress professionally for an interview, arrive early, and bring your résumé. Greet people with a handshake, a smile, and eye contact. Get the names of the people interviewing you. Ask questions that show you're interested in and familiar with the work.

> Never leave the interview without asking when a decision will be made and find out whether you can follow up with a phone call later regarding that decision.

> A letterhead template gives a design for a letter. Create your own personal letterhead document or stationery and use it for all your business letters.

> A letter template gives ideas for writing the letter.

> Word can be used to print an envelope with a mailing address and return address. You can also save the envelope to the document.

> Mail and email a follow-up letter after a job interview. Copy the text into the body of an email message so the employer doesn't have to take the time to open an attachment.

CHAPTER MASTERY PROJECT

Now it's time to find out how well you've mastered the content in this chapter. If you can do all the steps in this mastery project without looking back at the chapter details and can answer all the review questions following this project, you've mastered this chapter. If you can complete the project by finding answers using the Word Help window or the web, you've proven that you can teach yourself how to use technology to find a job.

> **Hint** All the key terms in the chapter are used in this mastery project or in the review questions. If you encounter a key word you don't know, such as *salutation*, enter **define:salutation** in the Internet Explorer search box.

If you find you need a lot of help doing the project and you have not yet read the chapter or done the activities, drop back and start at the beginning of the chapter and then return to this project.

> **Tip** If you need help completing this part of the mastery project, review the "Exploring Job-Hunting Strategies" section in the chapter.

Do the following:

Step 1. If you haven't already done so, create the MyContacts document, shown earlier in Figure 7-2.

Step 2. Copy and paste the third table so the document has four tables. In the third table, add a new contact for Charlie Jones, who is the personnel manager at Cook's Dry Cleaning. His phone number is 888-555-7777, and his email address is cjones@sample.com. You don't yet know his mailing address, but you have contacted him by email to ask whether you can send him your résumé. Save the document, naming it **MyContacts_MP**.

Step 3. You have decided to post your résumé on several job search sites. For each job search site, you need an online account and password. Create a new document with a table to keep track of this information. The table has three columns as shown:

Website	User Account	Password

Step 4. Save the document, naming it **WebsiteAccounts**. Because you're keeping passwords in the document, you need to password protect the document. Search Word Help to find out how to password protect a document. Then secure the document with a password.

Step 5. Close the document and open it. You must enter the password to open the document.

> **Tip** If you need help completing this part of the mastery project, review the "Creating and Sending a Résumé" section in the chapter.

What's the next job you expect to find? Will it be a part-time job while you're in school or a job after you graduate? Search for a job using the websites identified in the chapter or other websites. Pick a job that you think you might one day want to apply for. Answer these questions:

1. What job did you pick?

2. Where did you find the job?

Do the following to create your résumé that you might use when you apply for your next job:

Step 6. Select a résumé template in Word, keeping in mind your educational background and the job you're targeting. Save the résumé document to your USB flash drive, hard drive, OneDrive, or another location given by your instructor. Include your name in the filename—for example, **JeanAndrewsResume**.

Step 7. Enter your personal information and your education, skills, experience, and other information the résumé template suggests. Adjust the template fields and format the text as needed to fit your individual needs. Limit the résumé to one page.

Step 8. Save your résumé as both a Word document and a PDF.

Step 9. Create an email message with a subject line and body of the message to send the résumé to a potential employer. Pretend you're applying for the job you found earlier in this project and write an email message appropriate for that job. You can find ideas for the message in the On Your Own 7.3 activity in the chapter.

Step 10. Attach the PDF of your résumé to the email message and request a read receipt. Send the email to your instructor.

Be sure to save your résumé document so that it will be available in the future when you really are looking for a job.

> Tip If you need help completing this part of the mastery project, review the "Creating and Sending an Interview Follow-up Letter" section in the chapter.

Do the following to create your own personal letterhead:

Step 11. Select a letterhead template in Word that looks professional. Enter your personal contact information in the document.

Step 12. Save the document, naming it **MyLetterhead**. Print the document to make sure the colors look good when printed.

An employer might offer an informational interview to a promising job applicant to get to know you when no job is currently available. Pretend you have had an informational interview with a company that currently has no job openings. Do the following:

Step 13. Write an interview follow-up letter that thanks the person interviewing you and acknowledges there are no openings. As a guideline for writing the body text of the letter, search for an appropriate letter template. Which template did you use as a guide?

Step 14. Use today's date in the letter. For an inside address, make up a name, company, and address. For the salutation, don't forget to use a colon. For the complimentary closing, use **Best regards**. Make sure you use the correct spacing and formatting in the letter.

Step 15. Save the document, naming it **MyInterviewLetter**. Add an envelope to the letter. Be sure to include a return address. If you have access to a printer, print the envelope and the letter.

Step 16. Create an email message and copy the appropriate parts of the letter into the email message. Correct any problems with the text and the formatting of the message.

Step 17. Enter an appropriate subject line and send the email to your instructor. Don't forget to request a read receipt with the message.

Review Questions

Answer these questions to assess your skills and knowledge of the content covered in the chapter. Your instructor can provide you with the correct answers when you're ready to check your work.

1. List 10 job-hunting strategies presented in the chapter you should keep in mind when searching for the right job.

2. Why is it important to let family, friends, neighbors, and former teachers and business associates know you're looking for a job?

3. Why is it not enough to apply for a job using the web without communicating directly with people?

4. When you're applying for a job, why is it better to speak with someone who is influential at the company?

5. What are the benefits of keeping good records when searching for a job?

6. What is the purpose of a Word table?

7. What type of document is used by employers when deciding who to interview for a job?

8. What are three reasons presented in the chapter for using a résumé template when building your résumé?

9. Which file format is best to use when emailing a résumé to a potential employer? What are two reasons to use this format?

10. What is the file format used by a file that has a .docx file extension? .doc file extension? .pdf file extension? .txt file extension? .rtf file extension? .mht file extension? .xps file extension?

11. What is an Outlook read receipt?

12. List three websites that provide job search engines.

13. Which website do you use to find a job opening with the federal government?

14. Which websites can you use to find jobs in your local area?

15. What are eight tips presented in the chapter to help you have a good job interview?

16. What is the purpose of shaking hands and making eye contact when you first start the interview?

17. Why do you need the contact information of the person interviewing you?

18. Why is it important to ask questions about the job during an interview?

19. What one question should you always get answered at a job interview?

20. In what two ways should you always follow up with a potential employer after a job interview?

21. Explain the difference between a letterhead template and a letter template.

22. What type of information is contained in a letterhead? Is the body of the letter part of the letterhead?

23. Which punctuation mark is used at the end of the salutation for a business letter?

24. Which ribbon in Word is used to add an envelope to a letter?

25. Why is it not a good idea to attach a business letter to an email message?

26. Why is it important to both mail and email the interview follow-up letter?

27. After you've contacted a potential employer in any way, such as emailing an interview follow-up letter, what should you always do next?

Answer the following question about your work in the mastery project:

28. To protect your WebsiteAccounts document with a password, you first clicked the FILE tab and then clicked Info. Which command did you use next?

Becoming an Independent Learner

Answer the following questions about becoming an independent learner:

1. To teach yourself to use Microsoft Word to apply for a job, do you think it's best to rely on the chapter or on Word Help when you need answers?

2. The most important skill learned in this chapter is how to teach yourself a computer skill. Rate yourself at Level A through E on how well you are doing with this skill. What is your level?

   • Level A: I was able to successfully complete the Chapter Mastery Project with the help of only a few of the On Your Own activities in the chapter.

   • Level B: I completed all the On Your Own activities and the Chapter Mastery Project without referring to any of the solutions in the Step-by-Step Solutions Appendix.

   • Level C: I completed all the On Your Own activities and the Chapter Mastery Project by using just a few of the solutions in the Step-by-Step Solutions Appendix.

   • Level D: I completed all the On Your Own activities and the Chapter Mastery Project by using many of the solutions in the Step-by-Step Solutions Appendix.

   • Level E: I completed all the On Your Own activities and the Chapter Mastery Project and had to use all of the solutions in the Step-by-Step Solutions Appendix.

To continue toward the goal of teaching yourself computer skills, if you're not at Level A, try to move up one level on how you learn in Chapter 8.

Projects to Help You

Now that you've mastered the material in this chapter, you're ready to tackle the three projects focused on your career, personal, or academic, goals. Depending on your own interests, you might choose to complete any or all of these projects to help you achieve your goals.

Google Project *I want to use an app on Google Drive to create a résumé. Does Google Drive provide document templates that I can use for a great looking résumé?*

WATCH

CHAPTER 7
GOOGLE DRIVE
VIDEO

Project 1: Beyond Office: Using a Google Drive App to Create a Résumé

To use templates for documents you create in Google Drive, you must first connect a template app to your Google Drive. When you create a document, the app provides templates for your use. Let's use a template in Google Drive to create the résumé shown in Figure 7-12.

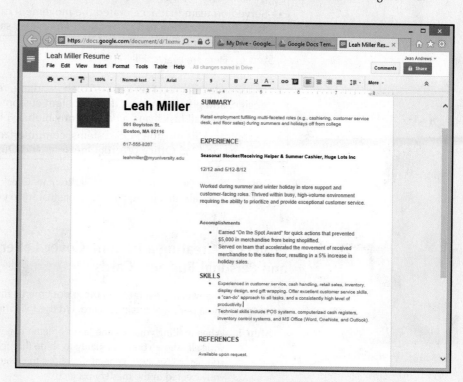

FIGURE 7-12   Use a template app and template in Google Drive to create a résumé.

Follow these steps:

Step 1. Sign in to your Google account and go to your Google Drive. Click **CREATE** and then click **Connect more apps**. Connect the **Drive Template Gallery** app to your Google Drive. Create a document using the **Resume – Standard** template.

Step 2. Here is the contact information used in the résumé:

Leah Miller
501 Boylston St. Boston, MA 02116
617-555-8267
leahmiller@myuniversity.edu

Step 3. Here is the summary statement:

Retail employment fulfilling multi-faceted roles (e.g., cashiering, customer service desk, and floor sales) during summers and holidays off from college.

Step 4. Here is Leah's experience:

> Seasonal Stocker/Receiving Helper & Summer Cashier Huge Lots Inc.
> 12/12 and 5/12-8/12
> Worked during summer and winter holiday in store support and customer-facing roles. Thrived within busy, high-volume environment requiring the ability to prioritize and provide exceptional customer service.

Step 5. Leah's accomplishments on the job are:

> - Earned "On the Spot Award" for quick actions that prevented $5,000 in merchandise from being shoplifted.
> - Served on team that accelerated the movement of received merchandise to the sales floor, resulting in a 5% increase in holiday sales.

Step 6. Here are Leah's skills:

> - Experienced in customer service, cash handling, retail sales, inventory, display design, and gift wrapping. Offer excellent customer service skills, a "can-do" approach to all tasks, and a consistently high level of productivity.
> - Technical skills include POS systems, computerized cash registers, inventory control systems, and MS Office (Word, OneNote, and Outlook).

Step 7. Name the document **LeahMillerResume**. Check your work to make sure the document looks like that in Figure 7-12. Note that some elements in the original template are not used.

Project 2: Creating a Résumé Cover Letter and Personal Business Cards

Personal Project I plan to apply for a job. I need to create a résumé and all the other documents that can help me land a great job.

Besides the all-powerful résumé, two other documents that can help you land a job are a résumé cover letter and a personal business card. Do the following to create these documents:

Step 1. When mailing your résumé, a cover letter can give you the opportunity to introduce yourself, allow your personality to shine through, and say something about the company. Use these general directions to create your cover letter to apply for the job you selected in the mastery project:

1. Use the personal letterhead that you created earlier in the chapter for a business letter.
2. Make the cover letter short, no more than three or four paragraphs on one page.
3. The first paragraph explains why you're writing. The second paragraph says why you're the best candidate for the job. Avoid repeating details about yourself that are in your résumé.
4. The last paragraph says you will follow up later with a phone call or email.
5. Type **Enclosure** below your name at the bottom of the letter.
6. Carefully check the letter for errors. Then ask a family member or friend to proofread your letter, checking for errors.

Step 2. Select a business card template that reflects your personality and career goals and use it to create your personal business card. A photo is a great way to help someone remember you. If you have a photo of yourself, create a business card that includes your photo. What Word template did you select?

Step 3. If you have access to a printer, print one sheet of business cards on regular paper. How many cards print to a page?

Step 4. Search the web for card stock paper that you could use to print your business cards. What website sells this paper? Is the paper intended for an inkjet printer or a laser printer? How many sheets come in a pack? How much does a pack cost?

Step 5. Email the cover letter and business card documents to your instructor.

Project 3: Using Academic Resources to Find the Right Job for You

Knowing yourself is the first step to finding the right job for you. Check with the academic advisers office at your school and find out what resources are available to help you learn about yourself. Use these resources to learn about yourself. This information can be invaluable when deciding what job you will like the most.

Create a Word document with the answers to the following questions and email the document to your instructor:

1. List the resources you found available at your school to help you learn about yourself and to help you find a job.

2. What aptitudes do you have that you would like to use on a job?

3. Describe your personality. Are you happier working on a team or working alone? Do you prefer to lead or follow? Do you like to work by a structured schedule or with plenty of freedom?

Project to Help Others

One of the best ways to learn is to teach someone else. And, in teaching someone else, you're making a contribution into that person's life. As part of each chapter's work, you're encouraged to teach someone else a skill you have learned. In this case, you help your apprentice learn to use the web and Word documents to find a job and to write letters.

Working with your apprentice, do the following:

Step 1. Ask your apprentice what her job goals are. If your apprentice plans to search for a job in the future, help her create her own résumé using a résumé template of her choice.

Step 2. Help your apprentice email the résumé using a professional email message. Have her email the résumé to you.

Step 3. Ask your apprentice what type of letter she might want to write in the near future. If she doesn't have an immediate need, suggest she write a letter of thanks to someone.

Step 4. Help your apprentice use a letterhead template and a letter template to create the letter.

Step 5. Use Word to create a document file that contains answers about the tutoring session and send the file to your instructor. If you're using MyITLab, you can post the file in Dropbox in MyITLab. On the other hand, your instructor might prefer you post the file to your OneDrive or email the file as an attachment. Here are the questions:

1. Who is your apprentice?

2. What new skills using Word did you help your apprentice learn?

3. How do you think the tutoring session went? How would you like to improve it next time?

Academic Project

I love what I'm studying, and I don't want to change my major. But the job market in my field is tough. I need to find out what job options are available for me. What academic resources can help me?

8 Using PowerPoint to Give a Presentation

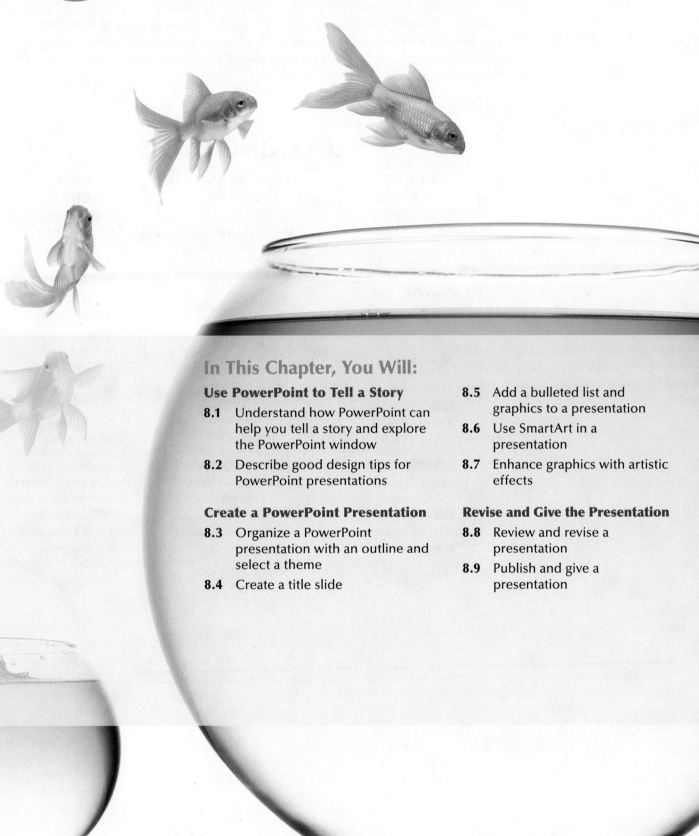

In This Chapter, You Will:

Use PowerPoint to Tell a Story

Create a PowerPoint Presentation

Revise and Give the Presentation

Most of us have sat through a slide presentation, and some of us have even given them. Microsoft PowerPoint is a popular program for creating such presentations, and in this chapter, we'll explore how to use PowerPoint.

As with all chapters in this book, you can choose which of the learning paths below best suits your needs. No matter which path you choose, as you work your way through the chapter, remember the most important computer skill is how to teach yourself a computer skill. Therefore, this chapter is designed to help you teach yourself how to create and design a basic PowerPoint presentation.

LEARNING PATHS

GUIDED LEARNING	EXPLORE AND DISCOVER	JUMP RIGHT IN
Read the Chapter *Watch the Objective Videos*	**On Your Own Projects** *Review Objective videos or use Step-by-Step Solutions*	**Mastery Project** *Use Objective videos & OYO projects for help*
On Your Own Projects *Review Objective videos or use Step-by-Step Solutions*		
Mastery Project *Use Objective videos & OYO projects for help*	**Mastery Project** *Use Objective videos & OYO projects for help*	**Explore Resources** *For help as needed*
Google Project (if applicable) *Watch Google video for help*	**Google Project (if applicable)** *Watch Google video for help*	**Google Project (if applicable)** *Watch Google video for help*
Helping You & Others Projects	**Helping You & Others Projects**	**Helping You & Others Projects**
MyITLab Assessment	**MyITLab Assessment**	**MyITLab Assessment**

Using PowerPoint to Tell a Story

WATCH

OBJECTIVE 8.1
VIDEO

Let's get started by exploring some of the basics of PowerPoint.

Objective 8.1: Understand How PowerPoint Can Help You Tell a Story and Explore the PowerPoint Window

Storytelling is one of the most effective means of communication. Microsoft **PowerPoint** is a powerful presentation tool to help you tell a story by using text, graphics, sound, and video. PowerPoint presentations are used by salespeople, executives, parents, children, physicians, auto mechanics, teachers, students, help-desk technicians, and others.

> **PowerPoint**—One of the applications included in the Microsoft Office suite of applications. PowerPoint is used to create slides that can include text, color, graphics, video, and sound. A PowerPoint presentation file has a .pptx file extension. Older versions of PowerPoint created presentation files with a .ppt file extension.

A presenter tells a story to an audience while stepping through the **slides** of the PowerPoint presentation. If the audience is more than two or three people, a projector can be used so that everyone in the room can see the presentation.

> **slide**—A page in a PowerPoint presentation. One slide at a time is viewed during a presentation.

Projector

Explore the PowerPoint Window

When you first open PowerPoint and use it to open a blank presentation, one slide, the **title slide** (see Figure 8-1), is created. To complete a presentation, you enter text or objects on this slide, create new slides, and add text and objects to these new slides. A presentation can also contain **speaker notes** about each slide to help you when giving the presentation.

> **title slide**—A slide that automatically includes text boxes for the title of the presentation and the subtitle.
> **speaker notes**—Text to help the speaker when giving the PowerPoint presentation. These notes don't appear on the slides, so they're not visible to the audience. Notes are typed in the notes pane at the bottom of the PowerPoint window.

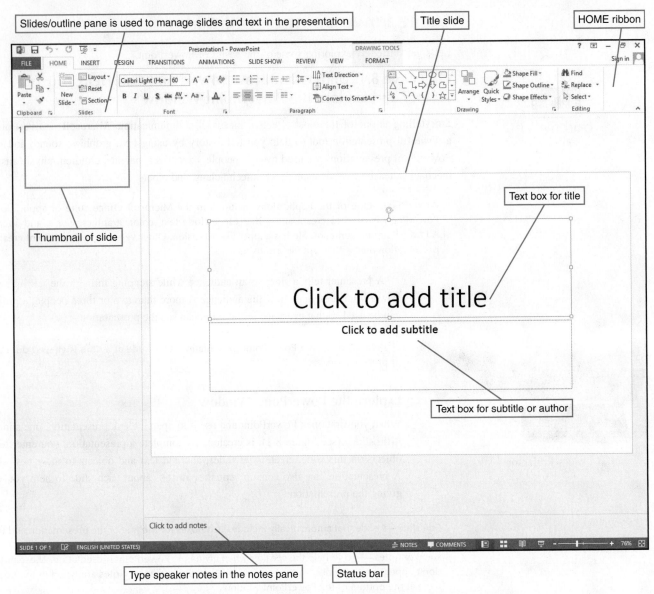

FIGURE 8-1   When you use PowerPoint to create a new blank presentation, a blank title slide is created.

You'll be happy to know that the PowerPoint window has many tools and ribbons that work the same as they do in the Word window. This makes it easy to learn a new Office application after you know how to use one Office application. Table 8-1 lists the purpose of each ribbon on the PowerPoint window.

TABLE 8-1   Main Purposes of PowerPoint Ribbons

Ribbon	Description
FILE	Save, print, close, or open a presentation.
HOME	Insert new slides and format text.
INSERT	Insert headers, footers, shapes, and other objects into an existing slide.
DESIGN	Change the background, colors, and **theme** of the presentation.
TRANSITIONS	Add **transitions** to your presentation. Transitions are covered in Chapter 9.
ANIMATIONS	Add **animation** to an object on a slide. Animation is covered in Chapter 9.
SLIDE SHOW	Start or customize a slide show.
REVIEW	Check spelling and compare two presentations.
VIEW	View your notes and the **slide master**, sort slides, and control PowerPoint windows.

> **theme**—In Office applications, a built-in design for a Word document, Excel worksheet, Outlook message, or PowerPoint presentation that includes colors, fonts, and effects. A theme can give your work in these applications a consistent look.
>
> **transitions**—A special effect that appears, such as a fading in or a rolling over, as one slide changes to the next slide.
>
> **animation**—A special effect that causes an object to move into or out of a slide or fade on the slide.
>
> **slide master**—A hidden slide. The text, color, objects, and formatting you place on this slide appear on all slides in the presentation.

Tip In this chapter, you learn about the basic tools of PowerPoint. More tools are covered in the next chapter. Don't wait until then to learn the tool if you see something that interests you. If you see a tool you think you'll like, try it out.

ON YOUR OWN 8.1

Explore the PowerPoint Window

When first learning about a new application, poke around in the application window and try out the tools. If you apply a change and don't like the results, use the Undo button ↺ in the Quick Access Toolbar at the top of the PowerPoint window. You can use the Help feature or the web to find answers to your questions.

So let's get started:

WATCH

OBJECTIVE 8.1
VIDEO

Step 1. Open **Microsoft PowerPoint 2013**, create a blank presentation, and maximize the window. Compare Figure 8-1 to your PowerPoint window and identify all the items labeled in Figure 8-1 on your window. As with Microsoft Word, when you mouse over a button, a bubble appears describing the tool.

> **Not Working?** If you don't see the notes pane at the bottom of your PowerPoint window, click **NOTES** in the status bar at the bottom of the window.

Step 2. Notice the title slide has two text boxes where you can type text or insert objects. Also take note of the left pane, which is the Slide/Outline pane. It contains a thumbnail for this slide, which shows the slide is blank.

Step 3. Check out the tools on each ribbon. What are some tools you found on these ribbons that are also on the Word ribbons?

Step 4. PowerPoint offers several slide layouts that have text boxes in various positions on the layouts to help you design your slides. To see a **gallery** of slide layouts, click the words "New Slide" on the HOME ribbon or click the down arrow to the right of New Slide (see Figure 8-2). Add a second slide that uses the **Comparison** layout. How many text boxes does this slide have?

gallery—In Office applications, a list of items from which you can choose that are displayed as pictures.

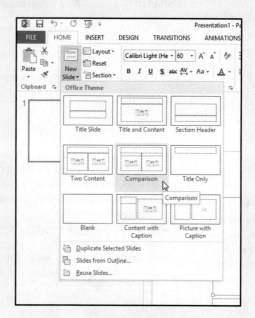

FIGURE 8-2   Choose a slide layout for a new slide.

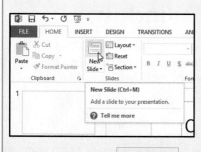

Step 5. On the HOME ribbon, click the **New Slide** icon above the words "New Slide" to add a new slide. Notice the new slide uses the same layout as the previous slide.

Step 6. An application's Help feature can help you learn about the application. Using PowerPoint Help, answer these questions:

- How do you apply a theme to a presentation?
- How do you add a slide number to each slide in a presentation?

Step 7. Close the presentation without saving your changes.

Solutions
Appendix

***For help:** See On Your Own 8.1* **Step-by-Step Solution**

Objective 8.2: Describe Good Design Tips for PowerPoint Presentations

When you're speaking to an audience, showing key words and graphics on a screen helps keep you and the audience focused on the topic. Be aware, however, that the design of the PowerPoint presentation can add to or distract from your story. Here are some tips for designing a professional-looking PowerPoint presentation:

> **Before you build your presentation, create an outline of what you want to say.** The outline helps you decide what goes on which slide and in what order.

> **Keep it simple.** A busy slide can distract the audience from what you're saying. Don't overdo video, animation, or audio. (Adding video, animation, and audio to a presentation is covered in Chapter 9.)

> **Aim for a few powerful slides.** Too many slides can overwhelm you and the audience and make you feel rushed.

> **Don't show all.** Plan to make some important points that are not on the slides. You don't want to be a robot reading from the screen. Let the slides back you up and not the other way around.

> **Pictures speak louder than words.** Engaging pictures tell a story far better than words do, and people remember them longer.

> **Use few words.** Limit text and bullet points to no more than six words per line and no more than six lines per slide. Avoid using full sentences unless you're quoting someone.

> **Use simple, large fonts.** Use a simple font, such as Arial, which is easy to read from a distance. Use large fonts (at least 28 points) so people sitting in the back of the room can easily read the slides.

> **Use contrasting colors that are easy to read.** A light font on a dark background is easiest to read from a distance.

> **Put the most important points first in your presentation.** If you must make several points, put the most important points first. If you run out of time when giving the presentation, you can skip the points on the last few slides.

Creating a PowerPoint Presentation

Now that you've explored PowerPoint, let's get started making a presentation. As we build it, notice how we applied the tips for good design.

Objective 8.3: Organize a PowerPoint Presentation with an Outline and Select a Theme

As noted above, the first step to creating a PowerPoint presentation is to make an outline, which is shown in Figure 8-3. The completed presentation that follows this outline has four slides, as shown in Figure 8-4. The rest of this section describes how to create the four slides. Follow along at your computer to create your own version.

Outline for What Motivates Us

A. What motivates us and why should we care?

    a. Title, author, and quote

    b. Motivated people tend to be happier and produce more than others

B. Others can motivate us

    a. Carrot in front of us, a stick behind us

    b. Reward

    c. Punishment

C. We can motivate ourselves from within

    a. Mastery: Opportunity to do something very well

    b. Independence: Right to make our own decisions (what, when, how, and with whom we do something)

    c. Contribution: Make a difference for others; the most significant motivator

D. How can you tell what motivates you?

    a. Look for where and when you find flow in your life

    b. Identify what type motivation you are experiencing when in this flow.

FIGURE 8-3   Use an outline to keep your presentation on track.

FIGURE 8-4   The presentation, "What Motivates Us," has four slides.

ON YOUR OWN 8.2

WATCH

OBJECTIVE 8.3
VIDEO

Choose a Theme

Create and Present the Motivation Presentation: Part 1 of 7

A PowerPoint theme sets the mood for the presentation with style, graphics, color, and fonts. To apply a theme to the presentation, do the following:

Step 1. Using PowerPoint, open a blank presentation.

Step 2. On the DESIGN ribbon, display the gallery of themes and then choose the **Slice** theme (see Figure 8-5). This theme best matches the mood for the last slide about attaining flow in our lives.

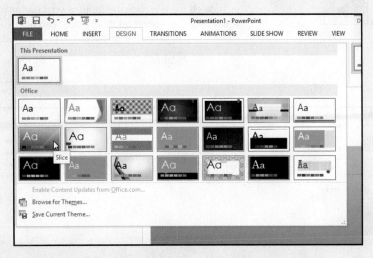

FIGURE 8-5   Select a theme for the presentation that complements the topic you are presenting.

Step 3. After you select a theme, you can customize it. Mouse over the Variants and see how the colors change on the title slide. Leave the theme color set to blue.

Step 4. Expand the Variants options. Mouse over other options to explore the other customizations you could choose but don't make any changes.

Step 5. PowerPoint records document properties just as Word does. Click the **FILE** tab and change the author to your name as you learned to do in Word.

Step 6. Save your presentation to your hard drive, USB flash drive, OneDrive, or another location given by your instructor. Name your presentation **Motivation** and leave the file type as PowerPoint Presentation. What file extension does PowerPoint assign to your presentation file?

Solutions
Appendix

For help: See *On Your Own 8.2* Step-by-Step Solution

WATCH

OBJECTIVE 8.4
VIDEO

Objective 8.4: Create a Title Slide

A good presenter has the PowerPoint presentation set up when the audience first walks into the room. As people come in, they see the title slide displayed until you begin your presentation. Include enough information on the title slide so your audience knows the purpose of the meeting and to give them something to think about before you start presenting.

ON YOUR OWN 8.3

WATCH

OBJECTIVE 8.4
VIDEO

Create the Title Slide

Create and Present the Motivation Presentation: Part 2 of 7

Include on the title slide the topic of your presentation, your name, and possibly your school or your company. A short quote or photo can help your audience focus on the topic. Figure 8-6 shows the title slide after this activity is completed.

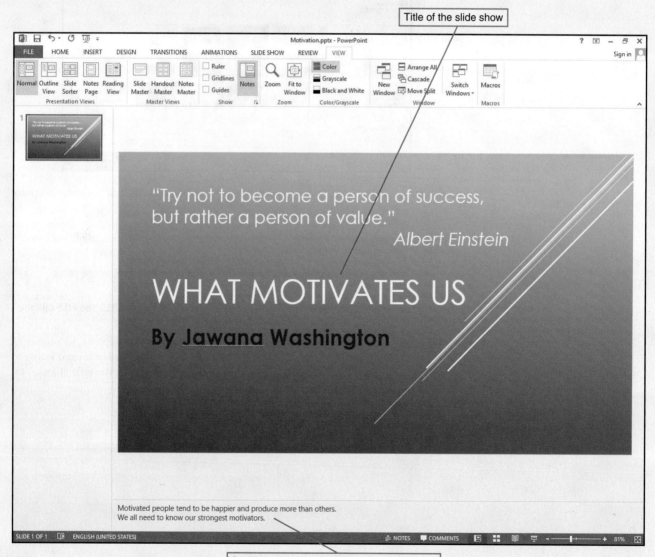

FIGURE 8-6 The title slide introduces the subject and the presenter.

Let's create the title slide:

Step 1. In the first text box, enter the title **What Motivates Us**. Increase the font size to fill the text box but still use only one line.

Step 2. In the second text box, enter the subtitle **By Jawana Washington**. Increase the font size to 40 points and make the text bold.

Step 3. You can delete text boxes you don't need, and you can insert new text boxes. Insert a text box for a quote at the top of the slide and add this quote by Albert Einstein:

> "Try not to become a person of success, but rather a person of value."
>
> Albert Einstein

Step 4. Increase the font size to **32** points. Right-justify and italicize Albert Einstein's name, as shown in Figure 8-6.

Step 5. If necessary, move or resize the text box so the quote is positioned as shown in Figure 8-6 and the line breaks right after the comma.

Step 6. In the notes pane labeled *Click to add notes*, enter the following speaker notes to remind you to mention why the presentation is important to the audience:

> Motivated people tend to be happier and produce more than others.
>
> We all need to know our strongest motivators.

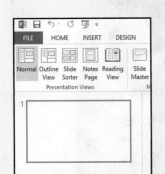

Step 7. Before you continue building the presentation, go to the VIEW ribbon and check out the Normal and Outline views. The Normal view shows a preview of the slides in your presentation. In the left pane of the Normal view, you can add new slides, select a slide, rearrange slides, copy slides, and delete slides. The Outline view shows the text in your presentation as an outline. As you build a presentation, you can use the Outline view to view and edit the text in the entire presentation.

> **Not Working?** If you don't see the Slide/Outline pane on your window, click **Normal** on the VIEW ribbon.

Step 8. View the slide as it will look in the slide show, return to Normal view, and then save your work. It's a good idea to view each slide as it will appear in the slide show and correct any errors you see before you move on to the next slide. What key do you press to end a slide show?

Solutions Appendix

For help: See *On Your Own 8.3* Step-by-Step Solution

Objective 8.5: Add a Bulleted List and Graphics to a Presentation

The next slide has a title, bulleted list, two clip art photos, and a shape. The content follows part B of the outline (refer to Figure 8-3). Text in the outline that is not on the slide is entered as notes for this slide.

ON YOUR OWN 8.4

Add a Slide with a Bulleted List and Graphics

WATCH

OBJECTIVE 8.5 VIDEO

Create and Present the Motivation Presentation: Part 3 of 7

Create the second slide. When this activity is completed, the slide will look similar to the one in Figure 8-7.

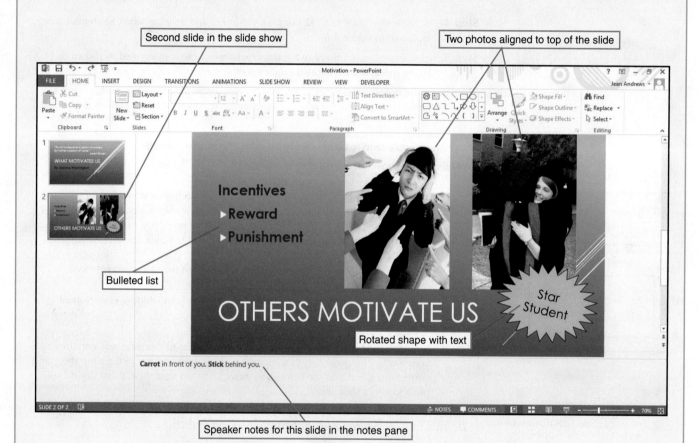

FIGURE 8-7　This slide uses two photographs and a shape to emphasize two key points.

Do the following:

Step 1. Add a new Title and Content slide and title it **Others Motivate Us**. Increase the font size to fill the text box but still use only one line.

Step 2. In the content text box at the top of the slide, enter the following text:

> Incentives
>
> Reward
>
> Punishment

Incentives
▶ Reward
▶ Punishment

The text is automatically formatted as a bulleted list. Delete the bullet on the first line. Set the font size for these three lines to **32** point and **Bold** the text.

Step 3. Use the INSERT ribbon to insert an Online Pictures photograph that speaks of punishment and will go in the top-center area of the slide. Resize and move the photo, as shown in Figure 8-7. Exact size and position are not important. When you're resizing the photo, be sure the photo proportions don't change.

> **Hint** When searching for an Online picture photo about how others motivate us, try searching on the text **punishment** or **graduate** to find images that will work. To find a photo on the web, enter your search string in the Bing Image Search box.

Not Working? The photos you find on the web will be different from the photos used in this chapter.

Step 4. Insert an Online Pictures photo about reward that will go in the top-right area of the slide. Resize and move the photo, as shown in Figure 8-7. Keep the proportions of the photo intact as you resize it.

Step 5. Insert a 24-point star shape. Change the Shape Fill color of the star to **Orange**. Position the star so it is slightly off the edge of the picture.

Step 6. Add the following text to the shape. Make the text black and **28** point.

> Star Student

Step 7. If necessary, increase the size of the star so the text fits inside the shape. Then rotate the star so that it looks like that in Figure 8-7.

Step 8. In the notes pane below the slide, enter the following speaker notes:

> Carrot in front of you. Stick behind you.

Step 9. Bold the key words **Carrot** and **Stick** so you will see them better when you glance at your notes during your presentation.

Step 10. Save your work.

Solutions Appendix

For help: See *On Your Own 8.4* Step-by-Step Solution

Objective 8.6: Use SmartArt in a Presentation

Microsoft offers **SmartArt** to help you organize text into artistic graphical containers. SmartArt is a shortcut to a professional-looking presentation.

> **SmartArt**—A feature of PowerPoint, Word, Excel, and Outlook that uses a graphical container for text and pictures.

The third slide (see Figure 8-8) uses SmartArt to present the three ways we motivate ourselves. The information in this slide comes from section C of the outline shown in Figure 8-3.

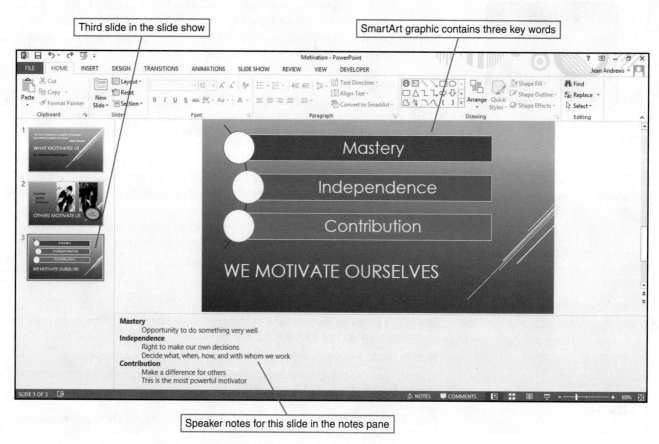

FIGURE 8-8   This slide uses SmartArt to visualize a list.

ON YOUR OWN 8.5

Add a Slide with SmartArt

Create and Present the Motivation Presentation: Part 4 of 7

Do the following to create the third slide, which is shown in Figure 8-8:

Step 1. Add a third slide. The title of this slide is **We Motivate Ourselves**. Increase the font size to fill the space.

Step 2. In the content text box of this slide, insert the SmartArt graphic named **Vertical Curved List**. If necessary, resize the SmartArt graphic to fit the empty space, as shown in Figure 8-8.

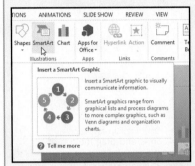

Step 3. In the three text boxes in the SmartArt graphic, insert the three words **Mastery**, **Independence**, and **Contribution**. Figure 8-9 shows the SmartArt inserted with the three words typed into the SmartArt text pane.

> **Tip** Most SmartArt graphics have three shapes used to hold three items. After you insert the SmartArt, you can select it and use the DESIGN ribbon to delete or add a shape. The DESIGN ribbon under SMARTART TOOLS shows up when SmartArt is selected.

Use the SmartArt text pane to edit the text   When the SmartArt is selected, the container box appears

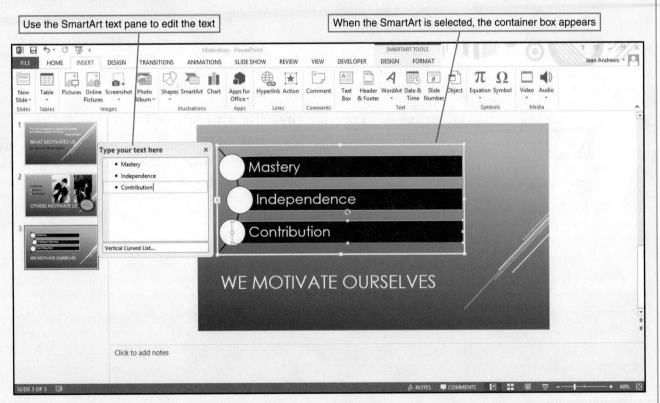

FIGURE 8-9   SmartArt provides a text pane you use to enter and format the text in the SmartArt graphic.

Step 4. It's best to use a large font size but not larger than the font size of the slide title. Apply the following formatting to the three words in the SmartArt:

    a. Increase the font size of the three words as necessary so they fill the space but don't make them larger than the slide title.

    b. Center the three words.

Step 5. To make the colors in the SmartArt a little more interesting, first select the SmartArt container box. Then click **Change Colors** on the DESIGN ribbon. Change the color scheme of the SmartArt to **Colorful - Accent Colors**.

Step 6. In the notes pane below the slide, add the following text to help you when giving the presentation. Make each of the motivators bold and indent the text under each motivator to make your notes easy to scan as you're speaking.

> **Mastery**
> > Opportunity to do something very well
>
> **Independence**
> > Right to make our own decisions
> > Decide what, when, how, and with whom we work
>
> **Contribution**
> > Make a difference for others
> > This is the most powerful motivator

Step 7. Save your work.

> **Hint** To increase the height of the notes pane on your window, press and drag the top of the notes pane.

Solutions Appendix

For help: See *On Your Own 8.5* Step-by-Step Solution

WATCH

OBJECTIVE 8.7
VIDEO

Objective 8.7: Enhance Graphics with Artistic Effects

The final slide displays during the conclusion of your presentation and when the audience is asking questions. Because your audience might see it for several minutes, it should make a strong point. The slide should suggest to the audience the next step you expect them to take. The information in this slide comes from section D of the outline shown in Figure 8-3.

ON YOUR OWN 8.6

WATCH

OBJECTIVE 8.7
VIDEO

Add the Final Slide with Artistic Effects

Create and Present the Motivation Presentation: Part 5 of 7

When this activity is completed, the final slide will look like that in Figure 8-10. The slide uses a photo that has artistic effects and color to add impact and interest.

The photo fills the entire slide and has artistic effects and color applied

The text box containing the title is in front of the photo

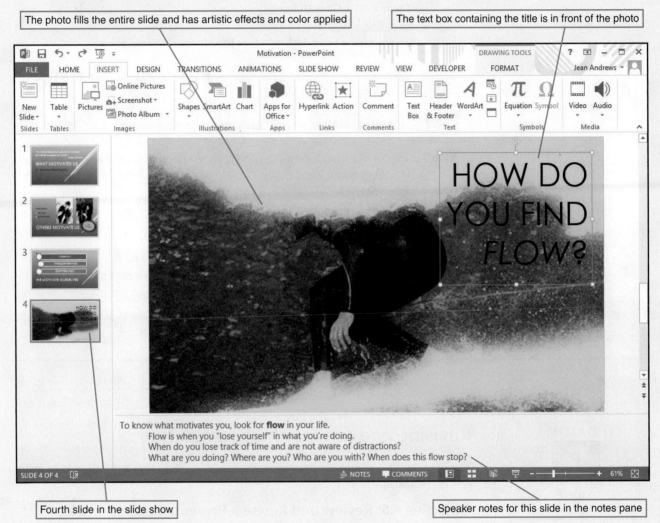

Fourth slide in the slide show

Speaker notes for this slide in the notes pane

FIGURE 8-10 The final slide should make a strong point for your audience and encourage thoughtful discussion and questions.

Let's create the slide:

Step 1. Insert a new slide using the Title Only slide layout. Add this title: **How Do You Find Flow?** Apply this formatting to the title text:

   a. Change the text color to Black. Right-justify the text. Set the font size to **66** points. Set the word **Flow** to italic.

   b. Resize the text box so text wrap causes the text to flow to three lines.

   c. Position the text box near the upper right corner of the slide, as shown in Figure 8-10.

Not Working? To find a photo on the web, enter your search string in the Bing Image Search box. The photo you find will be different than the one used here.

Step 2. Insert an Online Pictures photo of a surfer on a wave. You can use the words **riding a wave** in the Bing search box.

Step 3. Resize the photo so it fills the entire slide, covering even the title. Keep proportions the same as you resize and don't worry that the photo spills off the bottom or right side of the slide.

Step 4. Send the photo behind the title so that the title appears on top of the photo.

Step 5. To add interest, apply an artistic effect to the photo. The artistic effect used in Figure 8-10 is **Glow Diffused**.

> **Hint** With the photo selected, look for Artistic Effects on the FORMAT ribbon.

Step 6. Apply a color to the photo. The color used for the photo in Figure 8-10 is **Light Turquoise, Text color 2 Dark**.

> **Hint** With the photo selected, look for Color on the FORMAT ribbon.

Step 7. The last slide invites the audience to apply the presentation to their own lives. You can ask questions to encourage thought and discussion. Enter the following notes in the notes pane for this slide:

> To know what motivates you, look for **flow** in your life.
>
> Flow is when you "lose yourself" in what you're doing.
>
> When do you lose track of time and are not aware of distractions?
>
> What are you doing? Where are you? Who are you with? When does this flow stop?

Step 8. Save your work.

Solutions Appendix

For help: See *On Your Own 8.6* Step-by-Step Solution

WATCH

OBJECTIVE 8.8 VIDEO

FIGURE 8-11 Use the Outline view in the left pane to view and edit text in the presentation.

Revising and Giving the Presentation

You have finished creating a presentation, but you're not done yet. You still need to revise and give the presentation.

Objective 8.8: Review and Revise a Presentation

After you build the presentation, check it for errors. Here are some tips and tools that can help:

> **Check spelling.** The spell-checker in PowerPoint works as it does in Word. Misspelled words are underlined in red in the Normal view, but when the slide show is being viewed, the red spelling lines don't show. To check the spelling of all words in the presentation, click **Spelling** on the REVIEW ribbon.

> **View and edit text.** Editing text works as it does in Word. You can select and replace text, click an insertion point and type to add text, or use the Backspace or Delete key to delete text. If you need to view or edit a lot of text in the presentation, use the **Outline** view in the left pane (see Figure 8-11).

> **Move a slide.** You can use the Slide/Outline pane to move a slide in the presentation. Press and drag the slide to a new location.

> **Insert a new slide.** To insert a slide between two existing slides, right-click a slide in the left pane and select **New Slide** from the shortcut menu. The slide is inserted below the selected slide.

> **Delete a slide.** To delete a slide, right-click the slide in the Slide/Outline pane and click **Delete Slide** from the shortcut menu (see Figure 8-12).
> **Sort the slides.** If you need to reorder the slides, click **Slide Sorter** on the VIEW ribbon. In the Slide Sorter view (see Figure 8-13), press and drag thumbnails of the slides to new positions. Click **Normal** to return to Normal view.

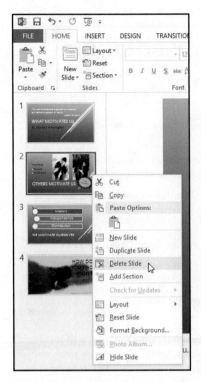

FIGURE 8-12 In the Slide/Outline pane, use the shortcut menu to delete, insert, or duplicate a slide.

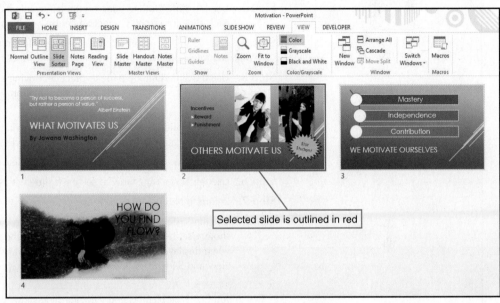

FIGURE 8-13 Use the Slide Sorter view to rearrange the order of slides.

> **Use the status bar buttons.** You can use the buttons in the status bar to switch quickly between Normal view, Slide Sorter view, Reading view, and the Slide Show (see Figure 8-14).

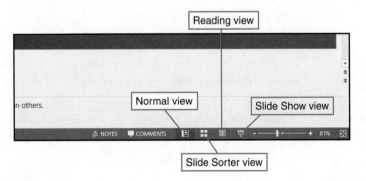

FIGURE 8-14 Use the status bar buttons to quickly switch between views.

ON YOUR OWN 8.7

WATCH

OBJECTIVE 8.8
VIDEO

Review and Revise the Presentation

Create and Present the Motivation Presentation: Part 6 of 7

To practice revising a presentation, do the following:

Step 1. Use the Slide/Outline pane on the left to select one slide after another and check each slide for errors. Correct any errors you find.

Step 2. Use the spell-checker to check the presentation for misspelled words and correct any misspellings.

Step 3. Use the Slide/Outline pane to practice moving a slide. For example, make the third slide the second slide in the presentation. Then return the slide to its original location.

Step 4. Go to the Slide Sorter view and practice moving a slide. Return the slide to its original location and then return to Normal view.

Step 5. Insert a new slide following slide 1. Then delete this blank slide.

Step 6. Use the Notes Page view to see each slide with speaker notes.

Step 7. Return to Normal view and save your work.

Step 8. Use the Slide Show button in the status bar to view your presentation as a slide show. Use the arrow keys to step though all the slides. Verify all the slides work well when displayed in this full-screen view. What is the difference between Reading view and Slide Show view?

> **Hint** If you find a problem as you view the slide show, press the **Escape** key to return to editing mode. After you make your changes, don't forget to save your work.

Solutions
Appendix

For help: See *On Your Own 8.7* Step-by-Step Solution

WATCH

OBJECTIVE 8.9
VIDEO

Objective 8.9: Publish and Give a Presentation

PowerPoint allows you to save the presentation as a **PowerPoint show** , which is the best file format to use when giving your presentation.

> **PowerPoint show**—A file format for a PowerPoint presentation that always opens as a slide show rather than in the Normal view used for editing. Speaker notes are not included in the file. A PowerPoint show has a .ppsx file extension.

Tip When someone asks for a digital copy of your presentation, give or email the PowerPoint show file. You can also save the presentation as a PDF, which can be viewed in a PDF reader.

You might want to print handouts for your audience so your audience has a record of the presentation and place to take notes as you speak. You can also print the Notes Pages of the presentation so you'll have the notes in your hand while presenting. On the other hand, when presenting with a projector, you can use an extended display. When you do that, the slide slow appears on the projector while you view the slides with notes on your monitor screen (see Figure 8-15).

FIGURE 8-15 Using an extended display, the left screen appears on the projector while the right screen appears on your monitor screen.

Tip To extend your display, first connect the projector or second monitor. Then in Windows, right-click the desktop and click **Screen Resolution**. In the Screen Resolution window, under *Multiple displays*, select **Extend these displays**.

WATCH

CHAPTER 8
DIVING DEEPER
VIDEO

Before giving the presentation, test it out. Here are some tips:

> If possible, set up your presentation in the same room where you'll be giving it. View the slides from the back of the room and make sure people in the back can read each slide. You might need to increase the font size, change the font color, or cut some text on a slide.
> Practice your presentation using the slides and your speaker notes. Time the presentation to make sure it's about right.
> Make an extra copy of the PowerPoint file just in case something happens to the original. Bring both copies with you when you make your presentation.

When giving the presentation, keep these tips in mind:

> Don't forget to turn off your cell phone before you start. Arrive early and set up the presentation before people arrive. You might need to dim the lights in the room so the presentation can be seen.
> If appropriate, meet each person at the door, shake hands, make eye contact, smile, thank each person for coming, and give each person your handout.
> Start strong. Your opening statement needs to catch the interest of your audience. Tell the beginning, middle, and end of your story in this opening statement while the first slide is displayed.
> Don't read the slides. If necessary, you can occasionally refer to your speaker notes. Keep your eyes on the audience and try to engage them. If you forget what to say next, you can pause and ask if there are any questions.
> At the end of your talk, summarize the beginning, middle, and end. Tell the audience what you want them to do as a next step. Thank them for participating.

ON YOUR OWN 8.8

Print the Presentation and Save as a PowerPoint Show

WATCH

OBJECTIVE 8.9
VIDEO

Create and Present the Motivation Presentation: Part 7 of 7

Click the **FILE** tab and do the following to explore ways to print a PowerPoint presentation:

Step 1. The print preview appears in Color, Grayscale (a blend of black and white), or Pure Black and White, depending on the printer selected. Display the print preview when the slides print in **Color**. Then show the print preview in **Grayscale**.

Step 2. You can produce handouts of the presentation for your audience. Display the print preview of the **3 Slides** option under Handouts (see Figure 8-16). What is the purpose of the lines in the right column of the handout? How many slides print to a page when using the Notes Pages option for printing slides?

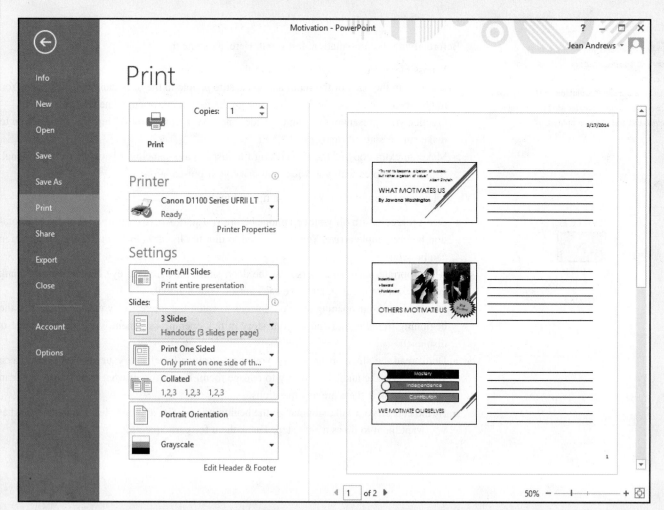

FIGURE 8-16 Three slides print to a page when you use the 3 Slides option for a handout.

Step 3. If you have access to a printer, print the notes pages and the handouts for your presentation.

Do the following to create and use a PowerPoint show:

Step 4. Click the **FILE** tab and use the **Save As** option to save the presentation as a PowerPoint show. Name the show **MotivationShow**. Close the PowerPoint window.

Step 5. Open File Explorer (In Windows 7, open Windows Explorer) and double-click the file **MotivationShow**. The show starts and the title slide appears. Use the down-arrow key to step to the next slide.

Step 6. Use the menu at the bottom of a slide to display thumbnails of all slides and jump to another slide in the show. End the show.

> **Tip** During a slide show, the menu at the bottom of a slide includes the annotation icon. You can use it to highlight text, draw on a slide, or point to important items during the slide show. These tools can make a presentation even more interesting to your audience.

Solutions Appendix

For help: See *On Your Own 8.8* **Step-by-Step Solution**

Summary

Using PowerPoint to Tell a Story

> A presenter can step through PowerPoint slides as he or she speaks to an audience to add key words, quotes, graphics, sound, and video to a presentation. For a large group, a projector can be used to project slides onto a large area.

> The PowerPoint presentation file can contain slides and speaker notes and has a .pptx file extension.

> Many of the tools and ribbons on the PowerPoint window are similar to those on the Word window. This similarity makes it easier to learn Office applications.

> When designing a PowerPoint presentation, keep to a few strong slides that use little text with simple and large fonts and make good use of graphics.

> When building a presentation, start with an outline to keep your slides on track and make sure you have covered all important points.

Creating a PowerPoint Presentation

> Organize your presentation by starting with an outline.

> A PowerPoint theme sets the mood for a presentation by using consistent style, colors, and fonts.

> The title slide shows the title and the author and should make a strong point about the presentation.

> Build a slide by selecting the best slide layout and then insert text and graphics. Text boxes are used to position text on the slide.

> SmartArt creates a graphical container to hold text and pictures.

> Artistic effects can improve the appearance of a graphic.

Revising and Giving the Presentation

> After you build the presentation, be sure to check it for errors, including spelling errors. You can move, delete, and insert slides and use the slide sorter to reorder slides.

> Handouts for your audience are printed one to nine slides to a page with and without write-on lines for note taking.

> The Notes Pages option for printing includes one slide to a page with speaker notes.

> A PowerPoint show has a .ppsx file extension and is used to view the slide show. This file is not used to edit the presentation and does not include speaker notes.

> When giving a presentation, tell the beginning, middle, and end of your story at the beginning of your presentation and again at the end. When you use this method, your audience is more likely to remember what you said because they heard it three times and saw the message on slides.

CHAPTER MASTERY PROJECT

Now it's time to find out how well you've mastered the content in this chapter. If you can do all the steps in this Mastery Project without looking back at the chapter details and can answer all the Review Questions following this project, you've mastered this chapter. If you can complete the project by finding answers using the PowerPoint Help window or the web, you have proven that you can teach yourself how to use PowerPoint.

> **Hint** All the key terms in the chapter are used in this mastery project or in the review questions that follow. If you encounter a key word you don't know, such as *gallery*, enter **define:gallery in PowerPoint** in the Internet Explorer search box.

If you find you need a lot of help doing the project and you have not yet read the chapter or done the activities, drop back and start at the beginning of the chapter, watch the videos, review the step-by-step solutions as you work through the On Your Own activities, and then return to this project.

> **Hint** If you need help completing this part of the mastery project, review the "Creating a PowerPoint Presentation" section in the chapter.

Build the four-slide presentation showing in Figure 8-17.

FIGURE 8-17 The PowerPoint presentation titled "Why Play?" has four slides.

To create the presentation, do the following:

Step 1. Use the Wisp theme with the Red color applied to it. Name the presentation **Play** and save it to your hard drive, USB flash drive, OneDrive, or another location given by your instructor. Click the **FILE** tab to verify that you are listed as the author of the presentation file.

Not Working? When searching for photos on the web for this project, you will not find the photos used here. Substitute other appropriate photos.

Step 2. Slide 1, the title slide, has text, a shape, and a photo. The text in the shape is black, 32 point, italic. The shape is flipped horizontally. To find an appropriate photo, use Online Pictures on the INSERT ribbon to search on **play guitar**. Be sure to increase the font size of the title and author.

In the notes pane, type these speaker notes for this slide:

> Play encourages imagination and innovation.
> Play is a great way to learn new skills.

Step 3. For Slide 2, choose the Title Only layout from the New Slide gallery. Enter the title and increase its font size as shown in Figure 8-17. Use Online Pictures to find a good photo, searching on **play beach**. Resize and position the photo to cover the entire slide. Apply the **Chalk Sketch** artistic effect to the photo. Move the title to its best position on the slide as shown in the figure.

In the notes pane, type these speaker notes for this slide:

Play is self-directed, open-ended, and fun.
Play focuses on the process rather than the product.

Step 4. Slide 3 uses the Title Only layout. Increase the font size of the title. The three interconnected circles are created with SmartArt. Using Online Pictures, search the web for a photo about play.

In the notes pane, type these speaker notes for this slide:

The opposite of play is depression (not work).

Step 5. Slide 4 uses the Title and Content layout. Increase the font size of the title and resize and rotate the text box. Move and resize the bulleted list. Use Online Pictures to search for two photos about **family play.** Apply the **Rotated, White** picture style to each photo.

In the notes pane, type these speaker notes for this slide:

How can you include play in learning to use computers in this course?

Hint If you need help completing this part of the mastery project, review the "Revising and Giving the Presentation" section in the chapter.

Using the "Why Play?" presentation, do the following:

Step 6. Check the presentation for misspelled words.

Step 7. View the presentation as a slide show and correct any problems you see.

Step 8. Use the VIEW ribbon to view the presentation as an outline.

Step 9. Return to Normal view. Using the Slide/Outline pane, move Slide 3 before Slide 2. View the slide show. Then use the Slide Sorter to return the slide to its original position.

Step 10. Insert a new slide following the title slide. Then delete the new slide.

Step 11. On the third slide, add a fourth ring to the SmartArt and insert the text **Enjoy Life** into this ring. Save your changes to the presentation.

Step 12. Save the presentation as a PowerPoint show, naming it **PlayShow**. Close the PowerPoint window. Using File Explorer (or in Windows 7, using Windows Explorer), locate the show and view the slide show by double-clicking the .ppsx file.

Step 13. Open the presentation file again and view handouts that print three to a page with write-on lines. If you have access to a printer, print these handouts.

Step 14. Submit the .pptx file to your instructor.

Review Questions

Answer these questions to assess your skills and knowledge of the content covered in the chapter. Your instructor can provide you with the correct answers when you're ready to check your work.

1. What components can PowerPoint slides add to a presentation you make?

2. A(n) _____ is a special effect that happens when a slide first displays. A(n) _____ is a special effect that happens when an object first displays.

3. If you need to put your company logo on every slide of a presentation, what type of slide is used to insert the logo?

4. Which is better, white text on a dark purple background or dark purple text on a white background? Why?

5. Which uses a stronger design, a slide that lists seven important points or one that shows one photo and one word? Why?

6. How do you organize a presentation before you start creating slides?

7. Which PowerPoint ribbon contains the option to add the slide number to each slide in the presentation?

8. What is the file extension for a PowerPoint presentation? For a PowerPoint show?

9. What is the first slide in a presentation called?

10. Where on the PowerPoint window do you type speaker notes that you don't want to appear on the slides?

11. Why should text on a slide use a font size of at least 28 points?

12. Which ribbon in PowerPoint is used to add clip art to a slide?

13. What PowerPoint tool provides predesigned graphical containers for text and pictures?

14. What happens to text on the slides when you edit the outline showing in the Slide/Outline pane?

15. When resizing a photo on a slide, how do you retain the proportions of the graphic?

16. How can you change the stacking order of objects on the slide when they overlap?

17. How can you see all the slides displayed as thumbnails on the screen so you can easily reorder the slides?

18. Why would you want to give your audience a handout of the presentation?

19. What is the maximum number of slides PowerPoint prints on one page of the handout?

20. Which key do you press to end a PowerPoint show?

21. During a PowerPoint show, how can you jump to a slide in the presentation that is not next to the current slide?

Becoming an Independent Learner

Answer the following questions about becoming an independent learner:

1. To teach yourself to use PowerPoint, do you think it's best to rely on the chapter or on PowerPoint Help or to explore tools on PowerPoint ribbons when you need answers?

2. The most important skill learned in this chapter is how to teach yourself a computer skill. Rate yourself at Level A through E on how well you are doing with this skill. What is your level?

   - Level A: I was able to successfully complete the Chapter Mastery Project with the help of only a few of the On Your Own activities in the chapter.
   - Level B: I completed all the On Your Own activities and the Chapter Mastery Project without referring to any of the solutions in the Step-by-Step Solutions Appendix.
   - Level C: I completed all the On Your Own activities and the Chapter Mastery Project by using just a few of the solutions in the Step-by-Step Solutions Appendix.
   - Level D: I completed all the On Your Own activities and the Chapter Mastery Project by using many of the solutions in the Step-by-Step Solutions Appendix.
   - Level E: I completed all the On Your Own activities and the Chapter Mastery Project and had to use all the solutions in the Step-by-Step Solutions Appendix.

To continue toward the goal of teaching yourself computer skills, if you're not at Level A, try to move up one level on how you learn in Chapter 9.

Projects to Help You

Now that you've mastered the material in this chapter, you're ready to tackle the three projects focused on your career, personal, or academic goals. Depending on your own interests, you might choose to complete any or all of these projects to help you achieve your goals.

Google Project I need to quickly create a simple presentation on a computer that doesn't have Office installed. Can Google Drive help me?

Project 1 : Beyond Office: Using Google Drive to Create a Presentation

The presentation app on Google Drive can be used to create presentations, but the app doesn't offer all the features you'll find in PowerPoint. In this project, you'll create the presentation shown in Figure 8-18.

> **Hint** If you need help learning to use Google Drive, open a new tab in your browser, go to google.com, and enter your question. You'll find many tips and steps on how to use Google apps.

WATCH

Google

CHAPTER 8
GOOGLE DRIVE
VIDEO

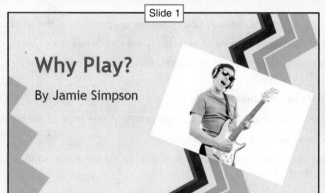

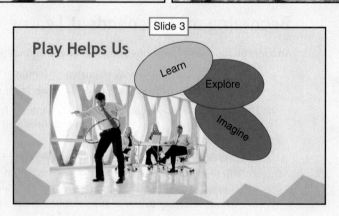

FIGURE 8-18   The Google Drive presentation about play has three slides.

Follow these steps to use Google Drive to create a presentation with three slides:

Step 1. Sign in to your Google account and go to your Google Drive. Create a presentation using the **Western** theme.

Step 2. On Slide 1, add this title and subtitle:

> Why Play?
> By Jamie Simpson

Step 3. On Slide 1, insert the ManPlaying image file in the sample_files folder on your USB flash drive. Rotate the image, as shown in Figure 8-18.

Step 4. On Slide 2, add the title **What Is Play?** Insert on the slide the Beach photo file in the sample_files folder on your USB flash drive. Make the photo fill the entire slide. Make sure the title is ordered in front of the photo.

Step 5. On Slide 3, add the title **Play Helps Us**. Insert on the slide the WorkPlay photo file in the sample_files folder on your USB flash drive.

Step 6. On Slide 3, add three shapes, each a different color, as shown in Figure 8-18. Put in the three shapes the words **Learn**, **Explore**, and **Imagine**, as shown in the figure.

Step 7. Name the presentation **Why Play**.

Project 2: Creating a Presentation about You

Build a PowerPoint presentation about yourself that follows this outline:

A. The title slide includes a title for the presentation and your name.

B. One activity you enjoy:

   a. What is it?

   b. Why do you enjoy it?

C. One or more family members you enjoy:

   a. His or her first name and relationship

   b. Something about him or her

D. One dream you have:

   a. What you want to do or where you want to go

   b. What is important to you about this dream

Personal Project I've been asked to speak about myself to a small group. I'd like to tell my story by showing photos of my family and talking about things I enjoy and want to do. How can PowerPoint help me do that?

The slide presentation needs to include four slides following these guidelines:

Step 1. Apply a theme to the presentation. Which theme did you use?

Step 2. On Slide 1, the title slide, include your name and a title for the presentation. What is the title of your presentation?

Step 3. Put a slide number on each slide of the presentation except the first slide.

Step 4. On Slide 2, include a shape and a clip art photograph. Use italic for at least one word on the slide.

Step 5. For Slide 3, use SmartArt. Bold at least one word on the slide.

Step 6. Slide 4 uses WordArt and a clip art photograph. Apply artistic effects, picture style, and/or color to the photo.

Step 7. Make sure you are listed as the author of the presentation file.

Step 8. Save the slides as a PowerPoint presentation and a PowerPoint show. Submit the presentation file to your instructor.

Project 3: Broadcasting a Presentation

Microsoft Office 2013 allows you to broadcast a PowerPoint presentation to remote viewers over the Internet. You must have a Microsoft account, which you created in Chapter 2. Broadcasting a slide show can work well if you're speaking to your audience on a conference phone line. Each member of the audience can listen on the phone and see the slide show in his or her web browser while you present it.

   Follow these steps to broadcast a presentation to someone in your class:

Academic Project My instructor in my online history class has assigned me the task of making a presentation to my online classmates. How can they see my PowerPoint presentation over the Internet?

Step 1. Open a presentation in PowerPoint that you created in this chapter. On the SLIDE SHOW ribbon, click **Present Online**. In the Present Online dialog box that opens, click **CONNECT**.

Step 2. PowerPoint displays a URL to your broadcast. Copy the URL into the Windows Clipboard. Paste the URL into an email message and email the message to your classmate.

Step 3. When your classmate receives the email message, he or she can click the link in the message. Internet Explorer displays the broadcast.

Step 4. When you're ready to start the slide show on your computer, click **START PRESENTATION**.

Step 5. Use Word to create a file that contains your answers to the following questions about the session. Name the file **Chapter8AcademicProject** and send the file to your instructor. If you're using MyITLab, you can post the file in a Dropbox assignment or email the file in MyITLab. On the other hand, your instructor might prefer that you post the file to your OneDrive or email the file using your school email. Here are the questions:

1. What information does the audience need to view the online presentation?
2. How does the presenter allow remote viewers to download the presentation?
3. If the audience moves to a different slide of the online presentation on their own, what do they click to return to where the presenter is in the online presentation?
4. How does the presenter end the online presentation?
5. How does the remote audience download a presentation?

Project to Help Others

One of the best ways to learn is to teach someone else. And, in teaching someone else, you're making a contribution into that person's life. As part of each chapter's work, you're encouraged to teach someone else a skill you have learned. In this chapter, help someone learn to use PowerPoint.

Working with your apprentice, do the following:

Step 1. Show your apprentice how to explore the PowerPoint window and demonstrate some of the tools on the PowerPoint ribbons. Open a presentation you've created to show your apprentice what PowerPoint can do.

Step 2. Ask your apprentice to create a presentation about himself, a family member, a recent vacation, a new job, or a hobby. Start by creating a short outline that lists the topics for three or four slides.

Step 3. Coach your apprentice as he builds each slide of the presentation. Encourage him to include clip art, photos, SmartArt, and other interesting elements to create well-designed and interesting slides.

Step 4. Ask your apprentice to present the slide show to a friend or family member.

Step 5. Use Word to create a file that contains your answers to the following questions about the tutoring session. Name the file **Chapter8Tutoring** and send the file to your instructor. If you're using MyITLab, you can post the file in a Dropbox assignment or email the file in MyITLab. On the other hand, your instructor might prefer that you post the file to your OneDrive or email the file using your school email. Here are the questions:

1. Who is your apprentice?
2. Which presentation that you created did you show your apprentice?
3. What is the subject of your apprentice's presentation?
4. Briefly describe how creating the outline of your apprentice's presentation helped to organize the presentation.
5. How do you think the session went? How would you like to improve it next time?

9 Adding Action and Sound to a PowerPoint Presentation

In This Chapter, You Will:

Add Video, Audio, and Animation to a Presentation

9.1 Use a slide master

9.2 Add video to a slide

9.3 Add audio and animation to a slide

9.4 Enhance a presentation with WordArt

9.5 Add animated graphics to a slide

Add Web Content and Transitions to a Presentation

9.6 Browse the web during a presentation

9.7 Enhance a presentation with transitions

In the last chapter, you learned the basics of creating a PowerPoint presentation. In this chapter, we'll add some bells and whistles and explore new tools. As you work on the chapter, don't be afraid to make mistakes. Remember the all-powerful Undo button is right there if you don't like the change you just made.

As with all chapters in this book, you can choose which of the learning paths below best suits your needs. No matter which path you choose, as you work your way through the chapter, remember the most important computer skill is how to teach yourself a computer skill. Therefore, this chapter is designed to help you teach yourself how to effectively use advanced tools in PowerPoint.

LEARNING PATHS

GUIDED LEARNING	EXPLORE AND DISCOVER	JUMP RIGHT IN
Read the Chapter *Watch the Objective Videos*	**On Your Own Projects** *Review Objective videos or use Step-by-Step Solutions*	**Mastery Project** *Use Objective videos & OYO projects for help*
On Your Own Projects *Review Objective videos or use Step-by-Step Solutions*		**Explore Resources** *For help as needed*
Mastery Project *Use Objective videos & OYO projects for help*	**Mastery Project** *Use Objective videos & OYO projects for help*	
Google Project (if applicable) *Watch Google video for help*	**Google Project (if applicable)** *Watch Google video for help*	**Google Project (if applicable)** *Watch Google video for help*
Helping You & Others Projects	**Helping You & Others Projects**	**Helping You & Others Projects**
MyITLab Assessment	**MyITLab Assessment**	**MyITLab Assessment**

Adding Video, Audio, and Animation to a Presentation

To learn how to add action and sound to a presentation, in this chapter, we'll create a presentation to help a professional musician speak to an audience of amateurs about taking a garage band on the road. The outline used to build the presentation is shown in Figure 9-1. The completed presentation is shown in Figure 9-2 and has four slides.

How to Get a Garage Band Out of the Garage and onto the Road

- Start with the press kit
    - Band bio and a professional photo
    - List of past gigs and future schedule
    - Song list
    - Equipment list (very important)
    - Publish a professional web site and Facebook presence
    - Business cards for all members
    - Make it clear who to contact
    - Put the press kit in a colorful envelope that stands out
    - Give out your business cards at gigs
- Get exposure by playing for free
    - Open mic nights
    - Volunteer to open for another band
    - Play at town fairs, county festivals, and city concerts
    - Play at Battle of the Bands in your area
    - Play at local restaurants for tips only
    - Post videos on YouTube.com
- What to do if opportunities are not coming your way
    - Change what you're doing until you find what works for you

FIGURE 9-1   An outline keeps us on track when creating a PowerPoint presentation.

Follow along at your computer as we build the presentation. As always, remember your goal is to learn how to use PowerPoint rather than to get the details on each slide right. Have some fun with it!

We begin by using the slide master to create the design for each slide in the presentation. The design can make or break a PowerPoint presentation. If you don't like the design we're using, feel free to try out your own design ideas.

WATCH

OBJECTIVE 9.1 VIDEO

Objective 9.1: Use a Slide Master

Recall from Chapter 8 that the slide master is a hidden slide. What you put on the slide master goes on all the slides in a presentation. For example, you can use it to put a company logo or text on all slides.

To access the slide master, click **Slide Master** on the VIEW ribbon. The Slide Master view displays, and the SLIDE MASTER ribbon is selected (see Figure 9-3). The SLIDE MASTER tab shows on the PowerPoint window as long as the Slide Master view is open. After you make your changes to the slide master, be sure to close the Slide Master view.

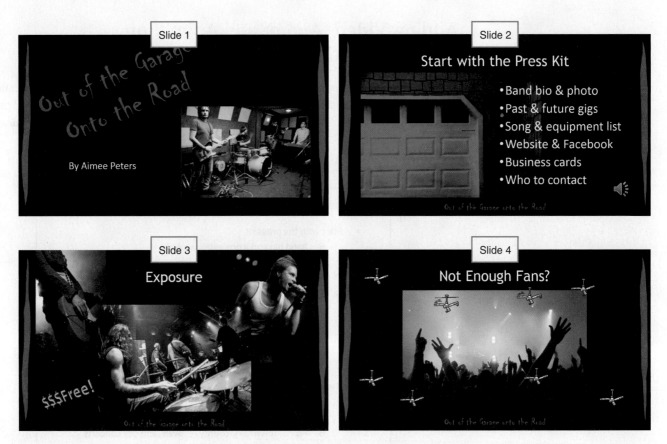

FIGURE 9-2 This presentation about garage bands has four slides and uses actions and sounds.

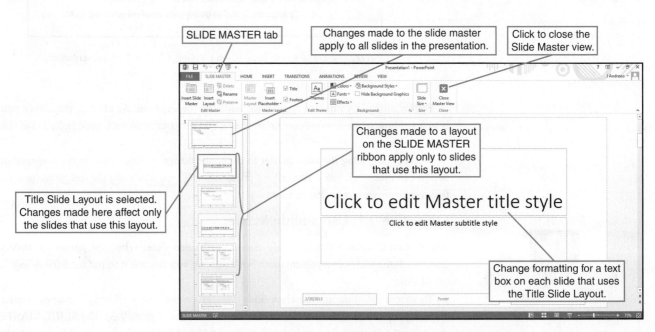

FIGURE 9-3 Changes made to the slide master apply to all slides. Changes made to a slide master layout apply only to that layout.

Here are some tips for using the slide master:

> Changes to the slide master apply to all slides in the presentation. Each type of layout has its own slide master layout that applies only to slides that use that layout.
> The text boxes provided on the slide masters are used only to format the text, not for entering the text. To change formatting for text on all slides, select a text box on the slide master and change the formatting for that text box.
> To place text on the slide masters, use the INSERT ribbon to insert a new text box. Do not put text in an existing text box on a slide master—remember these boxes are used only to format text.

Edit the Slide Master

WATCH

OBJECTIVE 9.1
VIDEO

Create the GarageBand Presentation: Part 1 of 7

If you plan to use a slide master when creating a presentation, edit the slide master first. When this activity is completed, the slide master should look like that in Figure 9-4.

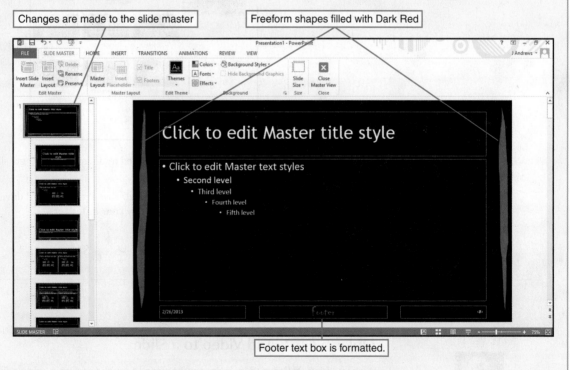

FIGURE 9-4 The slide master has background color, text formatting, and two graphics that create the design for the presentation.

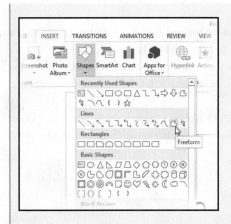

Open the Slide Master view and make these changes to the slide master:

Step 1. Use the **Freeform** shape to draw a jagged long shape like a flame or claw mark on each side of the master slide. Use Figure 9-4 as your guide but feel free to be creative with these shapes. Fill the shape with **Dark Red**. Change the Shape Outline to **No Outline**.

Step 2. To make the background color black and all text white, go to the SLIDE MAS-TER ribbon and change the Background Style to **Style 4**.

Step 3. Format the title text using the **Trebuchet MS** font and **44** points.

Step 4. Format the footer text using the **Chiller** font, **Dark Red**, and **32** points.

Step 5. Use the SLIDE MASTER ribbon to close the Master view. On the HOME ribbon, click the down arrow below the New Slide button and verify that all slide layouts use the design on the slide master (see Figure 9-5). If this is not the case, go back and correct any problems on the slide master.

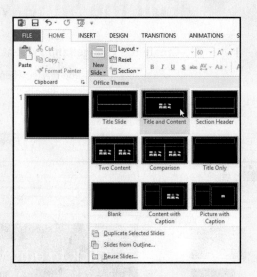

FIGURE 9-5   Changes to the slide master are applied to all layouts and new slides.

Step 6. Name the presentation file **GarageBand**. Save it to your hard drive, USB flash drive, OneDrive, or another location given by your instructor.

Solutions Appendix

For help: See *On Your Own 9.1* Step-by-Step Solution

WATCH

OBJECTIVE 9.2 VIDEO

Objective 9.2: Add Video to a Slide

A short video, called a video clip, can be added to a slide using a **video file** . Let's add a video clip to the title slide.

> **video file**—A file that contains audio and moving pictures. A video file might have an .mpeg, .avi, .mov, .mp4, or .wmv file extension.

ON YOUR OWN 9.2

Add Video to the Title Slide

WATCH

OBJECTIVE 9.2
VIDEO

Create the GarageBand Presentation: Part 2 of 7

When this activity is completed, the title slide should look like that in Figure 9-6 when the video clip is selected.

Do the following to create the title slide that contains a video:

Step 1. On the title slide, enter the title **Out of the Garage Onto the Road**. Format the text using the **Chiller** font, **80** point, **Dark Red**. Rotate, resize, and reposition the text box, as shown in Figure 9-6. Text wrap causes the title to fit on two lines.

FIGURE 9-6   The title slide includes a video clip that came from a video file.

Step 2. Enter the subtitle **By Aimee Peters**. Increase the font size to **32** point and align text to the middle of the text box. Move the text box down and to the left to make room for the video box.

Step 3. A video file named **RockBand** is located in the sample_files folder at www.pearsonhighered.com/jump, or you can access the file in MyITLab. (In Chapter 2, you downloaded the sample_files folder to your USB flash drive.) Insert the RockBand file on the slide and position the video box, as shown in Figure 9-6. On the VIDEO TOOLS FORMAT ribbon, add a dark red video border.

> **Hint** To insert a video file in a slide, click **Video** on the INSERT ribbon.

Step 4. To test the slide and the video, view it as a slide show. With the slide show running, click the Play button to play the video.

Step 5. Save your work.

> **Tip**   The video clip is now part of the .pptx file. A long video can make a .pptx file very large. You can use File Explorer (called Windows Explorer in Windows 7) to find out the size of a file.

Solutions
Appendix

For help: See *On Your Own 9.2* Step-by-Step Solution

260 Jump Right In! Essential Computer Skills Using Microsoft Office 2013

WATCH

OBJECTIVE 9.3
VIDEO

Objective 9.3: Add Audio and Animation to a Slide

You can add audio clips to a slide, and Microsoft Office clip art includes several short audio clips. You can use animation to cause objects (text boxes or graphics) to move into or out of a slide or fade on the slide.

ON YOUR OWN 9.3

Create the Second Slide with Audio and Animation

WATCH

OBJECTIVE 9.3
VIDEO

Create the GarageBand Presentation: Part 3 of 7

The second slide uses animation and an audio clip. When this activity is completed, the slide should look like that in Figure 9-7.

Animation is used to fade the garage door photo into the background.

Animation displays the items in the bulleted list one at a time.

Animation automatically plays the audio clip on the slide.

FIGURE 9-7   The second slide uses animated text and graphics and includes an audio clip.

Do the following to add a second slide to the presentation:

Step 1. Add a new slide using the **Two Content** slide layout. Title the slide **Start with the Press Kit**. Center the title in the text box.

Step 2. Add the footer text **Out of the Garage onto the Road**. The footer goes on every slide except the title slide.

> **Hint** To add a header or footer to a presentation, click **Header & Footer** on the INSERT ribbon.

> **Not Working?** If your footer is wrapping text to a second line, use the Slide Master to stretch out the text box size in the footer.

Not Working? *Photos on the Microsoft website and on the web change often. If you can't find a photo used in the chapter, substitute another appropriate photo.*

Step 3. Add a bulleted list to the text box on the right using the text shown in Figure 9-7. Increase the font size to **40** points.

Step 4. Insert the clip art photo of a garage door in the slide. To search for a photo on the web, use **garage door** in the Bing Image Search search box.

Step 5. Apply this formatting to the photo:

    a. Resize, crop, and position the photo, as shown in Figure 9-7. Send the photo behind the text box.

    b. Format the photo using the **Paint Strokes** artistic effect. Change the color of the photo to **Color Saturation 0%**.

Step 6. Search online for an audio clip of a revving car engine and insert it on the slide.

Step 7. Display the slide as a slide show. With the slide show displayed, click the audio button to play the engine sound. Return to Normal view and save your work.

Now let's add animation to the objects in the slide. Do the following:

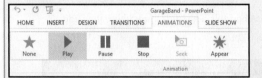

Step 8. Using the animation feature of PowerPoint, you can cause an audio clip to play without having to click the Play button on the slide. With the audio clip selected, click the **ANIMATIONS** tab and click **Play**.

Step 9. Run the slide show again. When you press the down arrow or click anywhere on the slide, the sound plays.

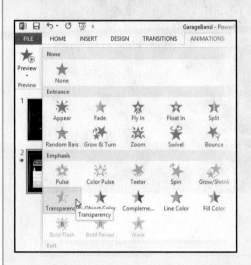

Step 10. We can use animation to cause the photo to fade into the background when the bulleted list appears. With the photo selected, display the Animation gallery on the ANIMATIONS ribbon. Select the **Transparency** animation in the Emphasis group.

Step 11. To animate each item in the bulleted list, apply the **Grow & Turn** animation to the bulleted list.

Step 12. View the slide as a slide show. As you click, the sound, photo, and text animations happen. Keep clicking the slide until all the items display. Then return to Normal view.

> **Hint** To change the order of objects that appear on a slide, click **Animation Pane** on the ANIMATIONS ribbon. Using the pane, you can change the order of animation.

Step 13. Enter these speaker notes as a bulleted list:

- Have a professional make the photo.
- Put the press kit in a large colorful envelope that stands out.
- Give your business cards out at your gigs. You never know who might receive one.

Solutions Appendix

For help: See *On Your Own 9.3* Step-by-Step Solution

WATCH

OBJECTIVE 9.4
VIDEO

Objective 9.4: Enhance a Presentation with WordArt

WordArt can add interest to a slide and is fun to create. Let's add some to our GarageBand presentation.

ON YOUR OWN 9.4

WATCH

OBJECTIVE 9.4
VIDEO

Create the Third Slide with WordArt

Create the GarageBand Presentation: Part 4 of 7

The third slide uses three photos and WordArt. When this activity is completed, the slide should look like that in Figure 9-8.

FIGURE 9-8   The third slide has three photos and WordArt.

Do the following to create the slide:

Step 1. Add the new slide using the **Title Only** layout. The title is **Exposure**. Center the title text.

Step 2. Use the Online Pictures command to search online for a photo of an **electric guitar**. Resize, crop, and position the photo so it fits in the area as shown in Figure 9-8. Align the photo with the top of the slide.

Not Working? When searching the web for photos, know you won't find the photos used in this chapter. Substitute other appropriate photos.

> **Hint** When searching for online pictures, click the **INSERT** tab and then click **Online Pictures**. In the Insert Pictures dialog box, you can search the Microsoft website by using the Office.com Clip Art search box. If you can't find a good picture, try using the Bing Image Search search box to extend your search to the web.

> **Hint** To cut off part of a photo (called *cropping the photo*), first select it and then click **Crop** on the FORMAT ribbon. Cropping handles appear as shown in Figure 9-9. Press and drag cropping handles to crop the photo.

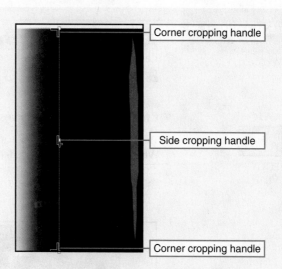

FIGURE 9-9   Press and drag cropping handles to crop a photo.

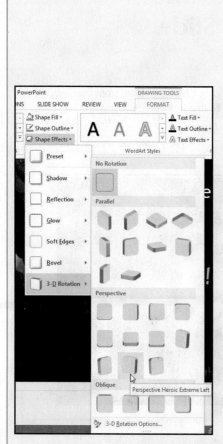

Step 3.   To find the photo of the soloist, search in the Online Pictures on **singer**. Resize and crop the photo as needed and align the photo with the top of the slide.

Step 4.   To find a photo for the center of the slide, search in the Online Pictures on **band**. Resize and crop the photo as needed, and position the photo near the center of the slide.

Step 5.   To insert the WordArt, click **WordArt** on the INSERT ribbon. Then select a WordArt fill style. The style **Fill - Gold, Accent 4, Soft Bevel** works well. The WordArt text is **$$$Free!**

Step 6.   To make the WordArt more interesting, select it and click **Shape Effects** on the FORMAT ribbon. In the 3-D Rotation group, click **Perspective Heroic Extreme Left**.

Step 7.   Move the WordArt text box to the lower-left area of the slide and rotate it, as shown in Figure 9-8.

Step 8.   View the slide as a slide show and check your work.

Step 9.   Enter these speaker notes that include a bulleted list and then save your work:

> Play for free:
> - Open mic nights
> - Volunteer to open for another band
> - Town fairs, county festivals, city concerts, Battle of the Bands
> - Play at restaurants for tips only

Solutions Appendix

For help: See *On Your Own 9.4* Step-by-Step Solution

WATCH

OBJECTIVE 9.5 VIDEO

Objective 9.5: Add Animated Graphics to a Slide

You already learned how to add PowerPoint animation to an object. You can also insert an animated graphic into a slide. You can find animated graphics in Office clip art that you access when you click Online Pictures on the INSERT ribbon. You can also find photos and animated graphics on the web.

Add Animated Graphics and a Screen Clipping to a Slide

WATCH

OBJECTIVE 9.5
VIDEO

Create the GarageBand Presentation: Part 5 of 7

This next slide uses animated graphics and a screen clipping that was copied from the web. When this activity is completed, the slide should look like that in Figure 9-10.

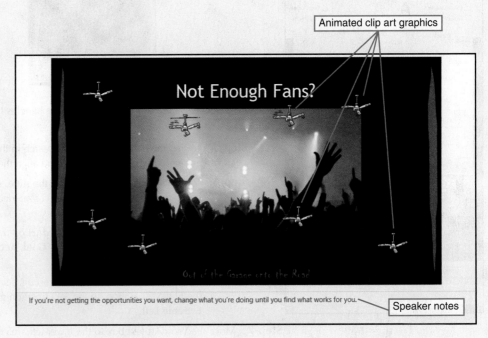

FIGURE 9-10   This fourth slide uses animated graphics and a screen clipping from the web.

Do the following:

Step 1. Add the new slide, using the **Title Only** layout. Add the slide title **Not Enough Fans?** Center the title text.

Step 2. To find the photo on the web, open **Internet Explorer** and go to my blog at **lifewithjean.wordpress.com**. Scroll down to the photo on that page. With the photo displaying in your browser window, use the **Windows Snipping Tool** to take a screen clipping of the photo.

WATCH

CHAPTER 9
DIVING DEEPER
VIDEO

> **Hint** How to use the Windows Snipping Tool is covered in Chapter 1. The Snipping Tool is available in Windows 8 and all Windows 7 editions except Windows 7 Starter used on netbooks.

Step 3. Return to PowerPoint and paste the photo onto the slide. Position and resize it, as shown in Figure 9-10.

> **Tip** Copying photos from the web into a PowerPoint presentation you create as a class assignment is covered under the fair use law and does not violate copyright laws. However, know that you must have permission from the owner to publish or sell these photos.

Step 4. To insert the fan graphic on the slide, open **Internet Explorer**, go to **office.microsoft.com** and search for a **fan** animation, as shown in Figure 9-11. Copy the animated graphic from the website and paste it to your slide. Copy and paste it multiple times over the slide.

Not Working? Microsoft
websites change often. If you can't find
the fan animated graphic used here,
substitute another animated graphic.
You will know a graphic is animated
because it moves on the Microsoft web
page.

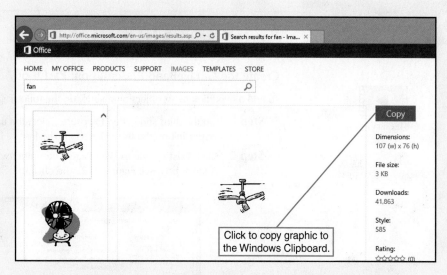

FIGURE 9-11   Search office.microsoft.com for animated graphics.

Step 5.   When you view the slide as a slide show, the fans turn. Correct any problems
you see.

> **Not Working?** If the fans do not turn when you run the slide show, most likely you
> selected a graphic from office.microsoft.com that is not animated. Go back and select
> another graphic.

Step 6.   Add the following speaker notes to the slide:

> If you're not getting the opportunities you want, change what you're doing until you
> find what works for you.

Step 7.   Save your work.

Solutions
Appendix   *For help: See On Your Own 9.5 Step-by-Step Solution*

Adding Web Content and Transitions to a Presentation

You've already learned how you can take a screen clipping from the web and put that clipping in
a presentation. In addition, PowerPoint lets you open Internet Explorer and browse the live web
during a presentation.

Objective 9.6: Browse the Web during a Presentation

WATCH

OBJECTIVE 9.6
VIDEO

One way for a garage band to get exposure is to play in Battle of the Bands. Suppose you want
to take your audience to the Battle of the Bands website to see where the next events are playing.
PowerPoint lets you do that without interrupting your slide show.

ON YOUR OWN 9.6

Embed a Link in a Slide

WATCH

OBJECTIVE 9.6
VIDEO

Create the GarageBand Presentation: Part 6 of 7

To add a hyperlink to an object on a slide, do the following:

Step 1. On the third slide titled Exposure, select the upper-right photo on the slide. Click **Hyperlink** on the INSERT ribbon. The Insert Hyperlink dialog box appears.

Step 2. Click **Existing File or Web Page**. Enter http://www.battleofthebands.com in the Address box (see Figure 9-12) and click **OK**.

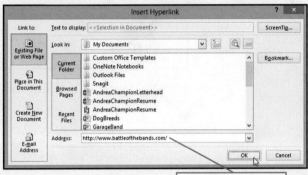

Enter URL of website.

FIGURE 9-12   Add a hyperlink to a slide by attaching the hyperlink to an object already on the slide.

> **Not Working?** If the link doesn't work, make sure the link begins with **http://**.

Step 3. Run the slide show. When you hover over the photo, you can see it is now a link. Click the photo. Internet Explorer opens and goes to the website. You can browse the site, play videos on the site, or go to other sites.

Step 4. When you're finished, close Internet Explorer. You return to the slide show. Return to Normal view and save your work.

Solutions
Appendix

For help: See *On Your Own 9.6* Step-by-Step Solution

WATCH

OBJECTIVE 9.7
VIDEO

Objective 9.7: Enhance a Presentation with Transitions

A transition is a special effect that happens when one slide changes to the next. For consistency, use the same style transition for all slides in a presentation.

ON YOUR OWN 9.7

Add Transitions to the Presentation

WATCH

OBJECTIVE 9.7
VIDEO

Create the GarageBand Presentation: Part 7 of 7

Let's add transitions to the slides:

Step 1. Before you add transitions to your presentation, view the entire slide show from beginning to end to make sure everything works as it should before we introduce something new.

Step 2. To add a transition to the first slide, select it and click the **TRANSITIONS** tab. Then click the More arrow to the right of the transitions to expand the options. The Transitions gallery appears (see Figure 9-13). Click a transition to see it. The last transition clicked is applied to the slide. Apply the Box transition to all slides in the presentation.

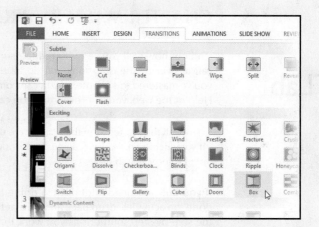

FIGURE 9-13   Transitions appear when one slide changes to the next.

Step 3. Save your work and view the entire slide show with transitions.

Solutions
Appendix

For help: See *On Your Own 9.7* Step-by-Step Solution

Summary

Adding Video, Audio, and Animation to a Presentation

> Text, graphics, formatting, and color on the slide master appear on all slides in the presentation.

> Video is added to a slide by inserting a video clip from a video file.

> Animated graphics can add interest to a presentation.

> Text and graphics can be animated so they move into or out of a slide or fade on the slide.

> Use the Animation pane to change the order of animation applied to objects.

> WordArt and the special effects applied to WordArt can add interest to a slide.

Adding Web Content and Transitions to a Presentation

> An object on a slide can be a link to the web. When you click the link, your browser opens to find the requested website.

> Know that adding a video file to a PowerPoint presentation can make the PowerPoint file very large.

> A transition is a special effect that happens when one slide changes to the next.

> For consistency, use only one style transition in a slide show.

CHAPTER MASTERY PROJECT

Find out how well you've mastered the content in this chapter by completing this project. If you can answer all the questions and do all the steps without looking back at the chapter details, you've mastered this chapter. If you can complete the project by finding answers using PowerPoint Help or the web, you've proven that you can teach yourself how to use PowerPoint.

> **Hint** All the key terms in the chapter are used in this mastery project or in the review questions. If you encounter a key word you don't know, such as *video file*, enter **define:video file** in the Internet Explorer search box.

If you find you need a lot of help doing the project and you have not yet read the chapter or done the activities, drop back and start at the beginning of the chapter, watch the videos, review the step-by-step solutions as you work through the On Your Own activities, and then return to this project.

> **Tip** If you need help completing this part of the mastery project, review the "Adding Video, Audio, and Animation to a Presentation" section in the chapter.

In this project, you build the PowerPoint presentation shown in Figure 9-14 about selecting a dog breed.

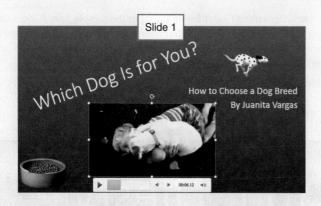

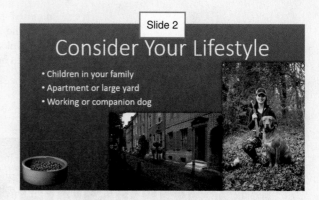

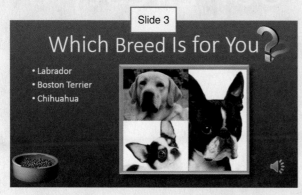

FIGURE 9-14   This presentation about selecting a dog breed has three slides and uses actions and sounds.

To build the presentation, follow these directions:

Step 1.   Open a blank presentation and make these changes to the slide master:

   a.   Insert an Online Pictures photo of a dog bowl, which will appear on all slides. Position the bowl in the lower-left corner of the slide and remove the background color from the photo.

Hint   Use the **Remove Background** button on the FORMAT ribbon to remove the background color from clip art. After you save your changes for the clip art, click the slide master in the left pane to return to the slide master.

---

   b.   Apply **Style 11** as the Background Style for the presentation.

Step 2.   Close the slide master and verify that the dog bowl appears on all slide layouts in the presentation.

Step 3.   Save your work, naming the file **DogBreeds**. Save the file to your hard drive, USB drive, OneDrive, or another location given by your instructor.

Step 4.   On the title slide, do the following:

   a.   Enter the title as WordArt, as shown on the first slide in Figure 9-14. The WordArt format is **Fill - White, Outline – Accent 1, Shadow**. Increase the font size of the title to **66** points. Resize and move the title text box and rotate it upward on the title slide.

   b.   Enter the subtitles. Right-justify the subtitles on the slide and increase the font size to **32** points.

   c.   Use Internet Explorer to go to **office.microsoft.com** and find an animated image of a dog and insert it on the title slide. Position and resize the dog animation above the subtitle, as shown in the title slide in Figure 9-14.

   d. Insert a video clip named **ChildPlaying** stored in the sample_files folder available on the www.pearsonhighered.com/jump website or in MyITLab. (In Chapter 2, you downloaded the sample_files folder to your USB flash drive.) Resize and position the video box in the lower portion of the slide.

Step 5. View the slide as a slide show to see the animation and view the video. Save your work.

Now let's create the second slide. The second slide is shown in detail in Figure 9-15.

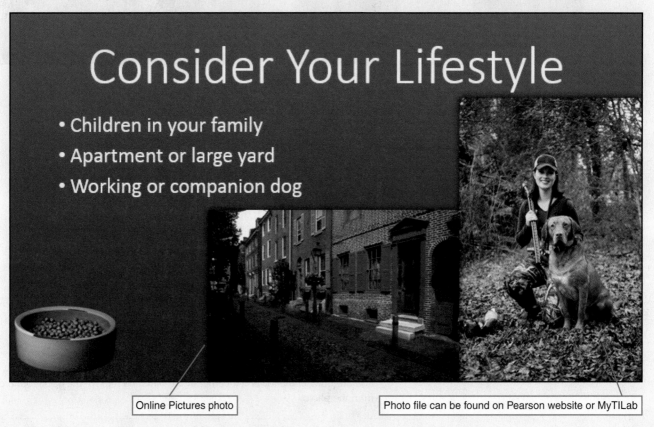

Online Pictures photo

Photo file can be found on Pearson website or MyTILab

FIGURE 9-15   The second slide has a bulleted list and two photos.

Step 6. To create the second slide, do the following:

   a. Enter the title and increase the font size of the title to fill the space. Center the title.

   b. Enter the bulleted list and increase the font size to **32** points. Resize and position the bulleted list text box so it fits on the left side of the slide.

   c. Insert an Online Pictures photo of apartments. Resize and align the photo with the bottom of the slide.

   d. Insert the photo, **RetrieverDog**, stored in the sample_files folder available on the www.pearsonhighered.com/jump website or in MyITLab. (In Chapter 2, you downloaded the sample_files folder to your USB flash drive.) Resize and align the photo with the bottom and right side of the slide.

   e. Format the two photos using the **Center Shadow Rectangle** picture style.

Step 7. View the slide as a slide show. Return to Normal view and save your work.

The third slide is shown in detail in Figure 9-16. The figure shows the Animation pane open so you can see the order that objects appear on the slide.

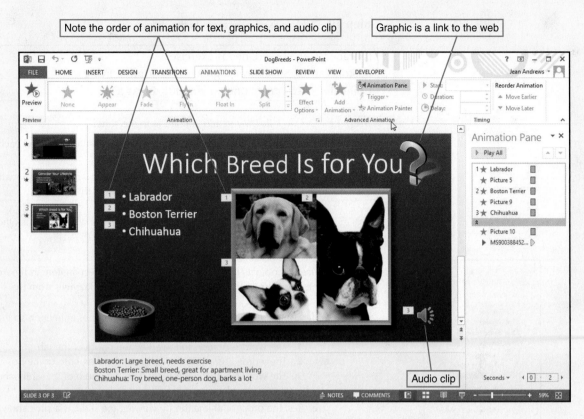

FIGURE 9-16   The third slide has three photos, audio, and a link to the web and uses animation.

Step 8.   To create the third slide, do the following:

a. Enter the text for the slide title and the bulleted list. Increase the font size of the title to fill the space. Center the text. Increase the font size of the bulleted list to **32** points.

b. Insert an Online Pictures graphic of a question mark at the end of the slide title.

c. Insert a **Rectangle** shape with a light blue color that will hold the three photos. Apply the **Preset 4** shape effect to the shape.

d. Go to my blog at **lifewithjean.wordpress.com** and take a screen clipping of the Labrador's head. Paste the clipping onto the slide. Resize, crop, and/or move the clipping so it fits in the upper-left corner of the rectangle.

e. Insert an Online Pictures photo of a Chihuahua and position and resize the photo.

f. Insert an Online Pictures photo of a Boston Terrier and position and resize the photo. If you use the photo we used on the Microsoft website, you must crop the right side to cut out the second dog in the photo. If needed, resize the rectangle shape to frame the three photos.

> **Hint**   When one photo is aligned with another, a dotted line appears to let you know they are aligned.

g. Insert an audio clip of a yappy dog on the bottom-right corner of the slide.

> **Hint**   To insert an audio clip, click Audio on the INSERT ribbon and then click Online Audio. Search for **barking dog.**

Step 9.   View the slide as a slide show and correct any problems you see. Be sure to test the audio and save your work.

Not Working? Microsoft websites change often. If you don't find the photos, graphics, or audio clips used here, substitute others.

Step 10. Add these speaker notes to the slide:

> Labrador: Large breed, needs exercise
> Boston Terrier: Small breed, great for apartment living
> Chihuahua: Toy breed, one-person dog, barks a lot

Step 11. Do the following to add animation to the slide:

    a. Apply the Fly In animation to the bulleted list text box and each of the three photos.

> **Hint** To change the order of animation, press and drag an item in the Animation pane to a new position. If you don't see an item, click the down arrows in the pane.

    b. Apply animation to the audio clip so it plays when you click the slide.

    c. Test the animation by viewing the slide as a slide show.

> **Hint** To cause two objects to appear at the same time, select an item in the Animation pane. Then click the down arrow to its right and select **Start with Previous** from the shortcut menu.

    d. Using the Animation pane, change the order of animation so that the objects appear in this order:

        1. The word *Labrador*, followed by the photo of the lab.

        2. The words *Boston Terrier*, followed by the photo of the Boston Terrier.

        3. The word *Chihuahua*, followed by the photo of the Chihuahua and the yappy dog audio playing.

    e. Test the order of animation by viewing the slide as a slide show.

    f. Change the animation of each photo so it appears at the same time the breed name appears.

    g. Include the audio clip with the Chihuahua name and photo so all three happen together.

Step 12. Test the order of animation by viewing the slide as a slide show. Don't forget to save your work.

> **Tip** If you need help completing this part of the mastery project, review the "Adding Web Content and Transitions to a Presentation" section in the chapter.

Do the following to add a link to the web to the third slide and add transitions to the presentation:

Step 13. Make the question mark a link to the website **www.akc.org/breeds**.

Step 14. Test the slide show and make sure the link works. Save your work.

Step 15. Add the Fly Through transition to each slide. View the slide show and make sure the transitions work. Save your work.

Review Questions

Answer these questions to assess your skills and knowledge of the content covered in the chapter. Your instructor can provide you with the correct answers when you're ready to check your work.

    1. Where can you make a change to a presentation, such as a formatting change, that applies to every slide in the presentation?

2. Where can you make a change that applies to every new slide that uses the Title Only slide layout?

3. Which view do you use to edit the size of the footer text box on every slide?

4. Which ribbon in the PowerPoint window can you use to add text to the header or footer text box?

5. What type of file uses a .wmv file extension?

6. Which ribbon in the PowerPoint window can you use to cause a bulleted list to pop or flow onto the screen one item at a time?

7. Which pane can you use to change the order that objects appear on a slide during a slide show?

8. Which ribbon in the PowerPoint window can you use to cut off or crop part of a photo already inserted on a slide?

9. Suppose you want a photo of a racecar for a PowerPoint slide you're preparing for a class assignment. You use Google to find the photo. What Windows tool can you use to copy the photo to a slide?

10. What law gives you the right to use a race car photo you found on the web in a PowerPoint assignment for a class?

11. What law is violated if you were to publish a PowerPoint presentation on the web that included photos you copied from a Google search but you did not contact the owner?

12. Which PowerPoint ribbon is used to turn an object on a slide into a link to the web? Which command on the ribbon is used?

13. Suppose you enter a URL of **www.google.com** to an object so that the object becomes a link to this website. When you run the slide show, you get an error. What is wrong with this URL?

14. Suppose you insert a video file into a PowerPoint presentation. When you email the .pptx file to a friend, do you need to also email the video file? Why or why not?

15. Which PowerPoint ribbon is used to make an audio clip play automatically when you click the slide during a presentation?

16. What is the size of the DogBreeds.pptx file?

Becoming an Independent Learner

Answer the following questions about becoming an independent learner:

1. To teach yourself to use PowerPoint, do you think it's best to rely on the chapter or on PowerPoint Help when you need answers?

2. The most important skill learned in this chapter is how to teach yourself a computer skill. Rate yourself at Level A through E on how well you are doing with this skill. What is your level?

   - Level A: I was able to successfully complete the Chapter Mastery Project with the help of only a few of the On Your Own activities in the chapter.
   - Level B: I completed all the On Your Own activities and the Chapter Mastery Project without referring to any of the solutions in the Step-by-Step Solutions Appendix.
   - Level C: I completed all the On Your Own activities and the Chapter Mastery Project by using just a few of the solutions in the Step-by-Step Solutions Appendix.
   - Level D: I completed all the On Your Own activities and the Chapter Mastery Project by using many of the solutions in the Step-by-Step Solutions Appendix.
   - Level E: I completed all the On Your Own activities and the Chapter Mastery Project and had to use all the solutions in the Step-by-Step Solutions Appendix.

To continue toward the goal of teaching yourself computer skills, if you're not at Level A, try to move up one level on how you learn in Chapter 10.

Projects to Help You

Now that you've mastered the material in this chapter, you're ready to tackle the three projects focused on your career, personal, or academic goals. Depending on your own interests, you might choose to complete any or all of these projects to help you achieve your goals.

Google Project Can I use Google Drive to create a presentation with a video, link to the web, and other cool features?

WATCH

CHAPTER 9
GOOGLE DRIVE
VIDEO

Project 1: Beyond Office: Using Google Drive to Create a Presentation

The presentation app on Google Drive offers a few tools to jazz up a presentation. Figure 9-17 shows the three slides in a presentation that include animation, transitions, and a YouTube video.
Follow these steps:

Step 1. Sign in to your Google account and go to your Google Drive. Create a new presentation using the **Steps** theme. Name the presentation **Dog Breeds**.

Step 2. On slide 1, enter the following title and subtitles. Rotate the title, as shown in slide 1 in Figure 9-17:

> Which Dog Is for You?
> How to Choose a Dog Breed
> By Juanita Vargas

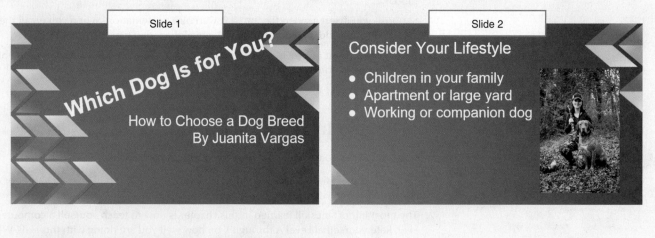

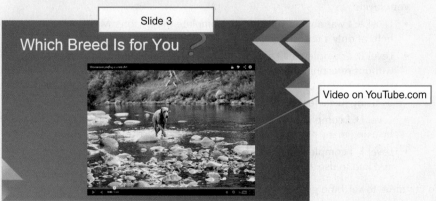

FIGURE 9-17 This Google Drive presentation about selecting a dog breed has three slides and uses animations and a YouTube video.

Step 3. On slide 2, enter the following text, making the last three lines a bulleted list, as shown in slide 2 in Figure 9-17:

> Consider Your Lifestyle
> Children in your family
> Apartment or large yard
> Working or companion dog

Step 4. On slide 2, insert the RetrieverDog photo file in the sample_files folder on your USB flash drive and also in MyITLab.

Step 5. On slide 2, apply a **Fly in** animation to each line in the bulleted list. Apply a **Spin** animation to the RetrieverDog photo.

Step 6. On slide 3, enter the following text:

> Which Breed Is for You

Step 7. Use WordArt to insert a question mark on slide 3. Format the question mark as **Comic Sans MS** and a red color. Make the question mark a link to the www.akc.org/breeds web page.

Step 8. Google Drive allows you to insert a video on the web in a slide. Insert a YouTube.com video of a dog at play. You can search on **Weimaraner playing in creek** or use a different YouTube.com video.

> **Hint** To insert a YouTube.com video in a slide, click **Insert** and click **Video**. In the Insert video box, enter a search string or a URL to a YouTube video and click **Insert**.

Step 9. Apply a **Cube** transition to all slides. View the slide show and make sure the transitions and animations work as they should. Also make sure the link to www.akc.org/breeds works and you can play the YouTube.com video.

Project 2: Using PowerPoint in Your Personal Life

Build a new PowerPoint presentation about any topic that interests you. Here are some possible topics:

> A car you want to sell
> A recent vacation or the next vacation you want to take
> The food you like best
> Who names the hurricanes

Step 1. Follow these guidelines:

    a. Put a text or a graphic on the slide master that appears on every slide in the presentation.

    b. Include at least three slides in the presentation.

    c. Include animated graphics on at least one slide.

    d. Use transitions.

    e. Use animation on one slide so that several objects appear on the slide in order.

Step 2. Send the PowerPoint presentation to your instructor. If you're using MyITLab, you can post the file in a Dropbox assignment or email the file in MyITLab. On the other hand, your instructor might prefer you post the file to your OneDrive or email the file using your school email.

Personal Project I want to learn to add action and sound to my PowerPoint presentations. To help me learn, I'd like to create a presentation about a topic that interests me and include sounds and photos.

Academic Project I've been asked to create a slide show to continually run on a computer in the lobby of the administration building. First, I must email it to some people for their approval.

Project 3: Using PowerPoint in Your Academic Career

Suppose you've been asked to create a PowerPoint presentation to continually run on a computer in the lobby of the administration building. You must email the presentation to others for approval. Do the following to teach yourself how to set up the presentation:

Step 1. Search the web or PowerPoint Help and find out how to make a self-running presentation continually run without user interaction. This is sometimes called *kiosk mode*. Test how to do this by continually running one of the presentations you created in this chapter.

> **Hint** Settings for videos are a little difficult to handle in a self-running presentation, so you need to first delete the videos from your presentation. For each slide that has a transition, go to the Timing group on the TRANSITIONS ribbon and uncheck **On Mouse Click**. Then check **After** and select the number of seconds you want each slide to show.

Step 2. A large PowerPoint file might be difficult to send by email. You can reduce the file size by creating a PowerPoint picture presentation. Search the web or PowerPoint Help to find out more about PowerPoint picture presentations.

Step 3. Convert one of the PowerPoint presentations you've built for this chapter to a PowerPoint picture presentation.

Step 4. Suppose the computer in the administration building lobby doesn't have PowerPoint installed. Research on the web or PowerPoint help to find out how you can publish your presentation as a video that can run without the PowerPoint application.

Step 5. The Office.com website offers many PowerPoint templates that you can use to quickly create a presentation. Do the following to explore these templates:

    a. On the FILE tab, click **New**. In the Available Templates and Themes pane, explore the available templates.

    b. Find and open a template to create a calendar.

    c. Find and open a template to create a certificate or award.

    d. When you're finished exploring the templates, close the presentations created by the templates without saving your changes.

Step 6. Answer the following questions about what you've learned:

    1. Describe the steps to format a PowerPoint presentation into kiosk mode.

    2. What is a PowerPoint picture presentation?

    3. How do you create a picture presentation?

    4. Can the receiver of a picture presentation edit the contents of a slide in the presentation?

    5. Are animated graphics animated when you view the slide show from a picture presentation?

    6. Do objects that have been animated by PowerPoint to appear in order on a slide work in a picture presentation?

    7. Do transitions work in a picture presentation?

    8. Can you watch a video that was inserted in a picture presentation?

    9. What are the steps to publish a PowerPoint presentation as a video? What is the file extension that PowerPoint assigns to the video file?

Project to Help Others

One of the best ways to learn is to teach someone else. And, in teaching someone else, you're making a contribution into that person's life. As part of each chapter's work, you're encouraged to teach someone else a skill you've learned. In this chapter, help someone learn to add sound and action to a PowerPoint presentation.

Working with your apprentice, do the following:

Step 1. Show your apprentice one of the slide shows you created in this chapter. Demonstrate animated graphics, animation added to a slide, video, audio, and transitions.

Step 2. Help your apprentice create her own PowerPoint presentation using the actions and sounds you demonstrated. What is the topic of her presentation?

Step 3. Ask your apprentice to briefly evaluate how the tutoring session went.

Step 4. Use Word to create a file that contains your answers to the following questions about the tutoring session. Name the file **Chapter 9 Tutoring** and send the file to your instructor. If you're using MyITLab, you can post the file in a Dropbox assignment or email the file in MyITLab. On the other hand, your instructor might prefer that you post the file to your OneDrive or email the file using your school email. Here are the questions:

1. Who is your apprentice?
2. Which presentation you created did you show your apprentice?
3. What is the subject of your apprentice's presentation?
4. Briefly describe how animated graphics—animation added to a slide, video, audio, and transitions to your apprentice's presentation—helped to emphasize key points in the presentation.
5. Briefly describe how your apprentice evaluated the tutoring session.
6. How do you think the session went? How would you like to improve it next time?

10 Managing Numbers and Text Using Excel

In This Chapter, You Will:

Understand How to Use Excel

10.1 Examine the Excel window and tools

Build a Worksheet with Titles, Headings, and Data

10.2 Enter and format titles and column headings

10.3 Enter data in a worksheet

10.4 Organize data in a worksheet

Add Calculations to a Worksheet

10.5 Use labels to make information easier to find

10.6 Use formulas and functions

10.7 Copy a formula that uses relative and absolute references

10.8 Calculate a percentage

Print a Worksheet

10.9 Format a worksheet for printing

We all find it necessary to occasionally track numbers and text. For example, you might need to keep track of money when making a budget for yourself, a business, or a club. You also might need to track scoring records for a softball team or track a list of classes and the grades you make in those classes. Pencil and paper might be your tools for the job, or a Word table might also work. If you learn to use Excel, however, you can track numbers and text and perform calculations on those numbers. In this chapter, you learn how to build and use Excel worksheets.

As with all chapters in this book, you can choose which of the learning paths below best suits your needs. No matter which path you choose, as you work your way through the chapter, remember the most important computer skill is how to teach yourself a computer skill. Therefore, this chapter is designed to help you teach yourself how to use Excel worksheets.

LEARNING PATHS

GUIDED LEARNING	EXPLORE AND DISCOVER	JUMP RIGHT IN
Read the Chapter *Watch the Objective Videos*	**On Your Own Projects** *Review Objective videos or use Step-by-Step Solutions*	**Mastery Project** *Use Objective videos & OYO projects for help*
On Your Own Projects *Review Objective videos or use Step-by-Step Solutions*		**Explore Resources** *For help as needed*
Mastery Project *Use Objective videos & OYO projects for help*	**Mastery Project** *Use Objective videos & OYO projects for help*	
Google Project (if applicable) *Watch Google video for help*	**Google Project (if applicable)** *Watch Google video for help*	**Google Project (if applicable)** *Watch Google video for help*
Helping You & Others Projects	**Helping You & Others Projects**	**Helping You & Others Projects**
MyITLab Assessment	**MyITLab Assessment**	**MyITLab Assessment**

Understanding How to Use Excel

To begin this chapter, let's look at how to use the Excel window and how to enter information into a new worksheet. Then we'll explore a workbook created using an Excel template.

Objective 10.1: Examine the Excel Window and Tools

WATCH

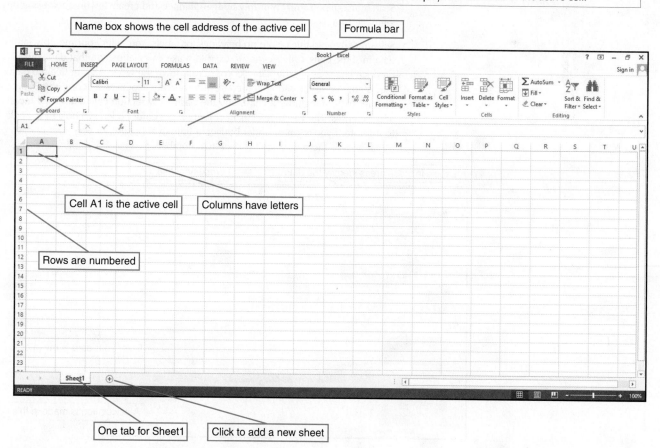

OBJECTIVE 10.1 VIDEO

Microsoft **Excel** is a **spreadsheet** program used to build a **worksheet** made up of columns and rows. An Excel data file contains one or more worksheets and is called a **workbook** .

> **Excel**—One of the applications included in Microsoft Office. It is a spreadsheet program used to manage text, numbers, and calculations in a worksheet. Excel 2013 files have an .xlsx file extension.
>
> **spreadsheet**—A type of software used to build and edit worksheets.
>
> **worksheet**—A group of columns and rows that can be used to manage text, numbers, calculations, charts, and graphics. Also called a sheet.
>
> **workbook**—A spreadsheet file that contains one or more worksheets. By default, an Excel workbook contains one sheet.

When you open the Excel program, you can create a blank workbook that has one worksheet (see Figure 10-1). Important items in the window are labeled in Figure 10-1 and defined as follows:

> **column**—A column in a worksheet is labeled by a letter (A, B, C, and so forth).
>
> **row**—A row in a worksheet is labeled by a number (1, 2, 3, and so forth).
>
> **cell**—The box where a column and row intersect. The cell is named by the column letter and row number, for example, A5 or G3.
>
> **name box**—A box that displays the cell address or name of the selected cell.
>
> **cell address**—The column and row coordinates for a cell.
>
> **formula bar**—The area on the Excel window that displays the contents of the active cell.

FIGURE 10-1 The Excel spreadsheet program opens a blank workbook with one worksheet.

Create a Worksheet and Use a Template and the Excel Window

WATCH

OBJECTIVE 10.1 VIDEO

In this activity, you get familiar with Excel without focusing on building a worksheet. Feel free to try new things and poke around. Do the following:

Step 1. Open Excel, create a blank workbook, and maximize the window. Then explore the window and its tools. Click each ribbon tab and look at the items on each ribbon. The tools on several of these ribbons work about the same as they do in Word and PowerPoint.

Step 2. Go to any cell on the worksheet and start entering numbers into some cells and text into other cells. Notice that, by default, the numbers are right-aligned, and the letters are left-aligned in the cell. When a cell is active, notice the cell address shows in the name box, and the contents of the cell shows in the formula bar. The active cell also has a heavy green border around it.

> **Hint** To make a cell the active cell, click the cell or use your arrow keys to move to the cell. Use the **Tab** key to move to the next cell in a row. Use the **Enter** key to move down one cell.

> **Not Working?** More than one version of Microsoft Excel exists. In this book, we're using Excel 2013. If you're using a different version, such as Excel 2010, your window might not look the same as the one shown.

Just as Word and PowerPoint have templates, so does Excel. Let's look at a template that can show you what Excel can do. Don't worry if you don't understand how this template is built. The idea is to see what Excel worksheets can do for you. Let's get started:

Step 3. On the FILE tab, click **New** and take a look at the different Excel templates. In the Search box, type **Family monthly budget planner** and create a workbook using this template (see Figure 10-2).

Several cells hold titles, column headings, or labels. You enter your monthly family data in some cells. Other cells are used to make calculations on that data and produce charts about the data. As you scroll down the worksheet, notice the data that is entered in the Monthly Income and Monthly Expenses sections; the Budget Planner section includes a chart, and the Cash Flow section calculates total income and expenses. The Variance cells in column F put color-coded symbols in the cells to indicate if you're on or under budget, a little over budget, or very over budget. (A variance is the difference between two numbers.)

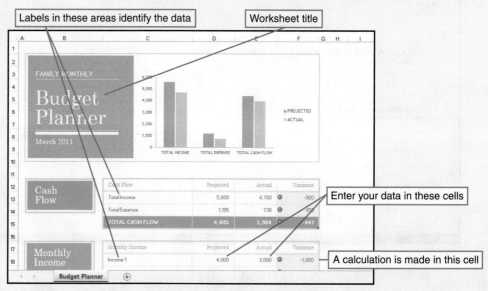

FIGURE 10-2   Enter values in a family monthly budget planner worksheet.

Step 4. Take a look at row 18. The Variance in cell F18 is a negative value, and the color code is red. Now change the value in cell E18 to **6000** and notice how the Variance in cell F18 changes. Change cell E18 to **100** and notice how the variances change and also how the chart at the top of the worksheet changes.

Why did these cells in column F change? Because the **formulas** entered into these cells reacted to the data you entered into the worksheet. If you're curious about these formulas, click a cell to see the formula in the formula bar above the worksheet. This template is a great example of how powerful an Excel worksheet can be in presenting information to a user and reacting to changes in data.

> **formula**—An equation in a cell used to perform a calculation or make a comparison. A formula always begins with an equals sign and can use numbers or cells. An example of a formula is =A10+5. In this example, 5 is added to whatever value is in cell A10. The result of the calculation goes in the cell that contains the formula.

Step 5. Notice this workbook has only a single worksheet named Sheet1. Create a new worksheet and then rename this new sheet **Budget Notes**. If you need help renaming a sheet, use Excel Help to find out how.

> **Not Working?** Click the **Help** button **?** in the top-right corner of the Excel window to access Excel Help.

Step 6. Close all the workbooks you have opened without saving them.

| Solutions Appendix | *For help:* See *On Your Own 10.1* Step-by-Step Solution |

Building a Worksheet with Titles, Headings, and Data

Now let's learn how to build a new worksheet that contains text, numbers, and calculations. In this part of the chapter, we'll use Excel to create a softball roster and to track the expenses that must be collected from each team member. The finished worksheet for Coach Stevens's softball team is shown in Figure 10-3. It contains a title, column and row headings, text, numbers, and calculations.

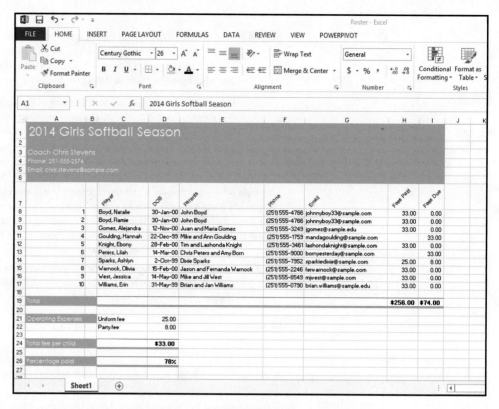

FIGURE 10-3   The Excel worksheet is used to keep a roster for a softball team.

Tip As you build this worksheet, remember the goal is to learn to use Excel. Don't worry about getting all the details of the worksheet correct. Focus on learning to use the tools of Excel.

Objective 10.2: Enter and Format Titles and Column Headings

The first step to creating the worksheet is to enter titles and column headings and format this text.

Enter Worksheet Titles and Headings

Create the Roster Workbook: Part 1 of 10

In this activity, you'll enter the text for the titles and column headings. When the activity is completed, the worksheet should look like that in Figure 10-4.

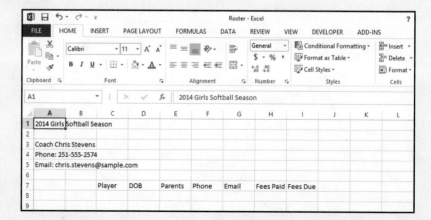

FIGURE 10-4   Titles and column headings are entered but not yet formatted.

Notice in the figure that cell A1 is the active cell. The content of cell A1 is the title **2014 Girls Softball Season**. When a cell is not wide enough to display the text in the cell, Excel handles the problem in this way:

- If adjacent cells to the right of the cell are empty, the displayed text spills over onto these cells. This is the case in Figure 10-4. Even though it appears that the titles are stored in more than one column, all the titles in the first five rows shown in the figure are stored in cells in column A and spill over onto adjacent empty cells.

- If adjacent cells to the right of the cell are not empty, Excel cuts off the text in the cell that is too narrow.

Do the following:

Step 1. Open a blank Excel workbook and enter the titles into cells in column A, as shown in Figure 10-4. Enter the column headings in cells in row 7.

Step 2. Click the **FILE** tab and verify you're the author of this workbook file. If you're not, change it. Changing a file's author works just as it does in Word.

Step 3. Save the workbook to your hard drive, USB flash drive, OneDrive, or other location given by your instructor. Name the workbook **Roster**.

> **Hint** Saving an Excel workbook file works the same way as saving a document in Word.

Solutions
Appendix   *For help:* See *On Your Own 10.2* Step-by-Step Solution

Formatting, styles, and themes work about the same way in Excel as they do in Word. The easiest way to format a cell or a group of cells is to use a **Cell Style**. Formatting can be applied before or after data is entered into the cells.

> **Cell Style**—Predetermined formatting that can be applied to a cell or group of cells. Cell Styles are found on the HOME ribbon.

ON YOUR OWN 10.3

Format Using Styles and Themes

WATCH

OBJECTIVE 10.2
VIDEO

Create the Roster Workbook: Part 2 of 10

In this activity, you format the titles and column headings for Coach Stevens's roster. When the activity is completed, the worksheet should look like that in Figure 10-5.

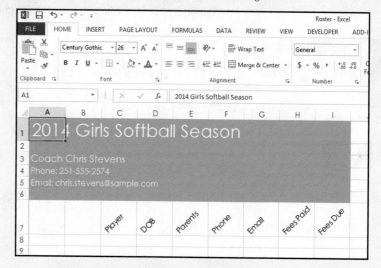

FIGURE 10-5   The softball roster has titles and column headings entered and formatted.

Do the following:

Step 1. To add background color to the top of the worksheet, apply a cell style to the block of cells A1 through I6. (A block or range of cells is written as A1:I6.) First, select these cells. Then, on the HOME ribbon, click **Cell Styles** and select **Accent 5**. (The cell color is now blue—later you'll change the color to orange.)

Step 2. To make the title of the roster stand out, increase the font size for cell A1 to **26** point. Increase the font size for the cell containing the coach's name to **14** point. Increase the font size for the phone and email cells to **12** point.

> **Hint** To select a block of cells (also called a range of cells), press and drag across the cells. As you do so, your pointer is a white cross, ✛ and selected cells are highlighted in a selection box.

Step 3. To tilt the column headings upward in row 7, select these cells and use the **Orientation** button ✎ on the HOME ribbon.

Step 4. A theme applies uniform formatting to an entire workbook. On the PAGE LAYOUT ribbon, click the **Themes** button, mouse over the different themes, and notice how the font and color on the worksheet change. Set the theme of the softball roster to **Mesh**.

Step 5. Save your work.

> Solutions Appendix

For help: See *On Your Own 10.3* Step-by-Step Solution

WATCH

OBJECTIVE 10.3
VIDEO

Objective 10.3: Enter Data in a Worksheet

The worksheet is now ready to receive the data for team members. In this section, you'll format the cells for team data and then enter that data. For numbers and dates, it's easier to first format the cells and then enter the data into the cells. The type of formatting to apply depends on what type of data the cell will hold. The following are examples of formatting options:

> A negative number can be formatted as −1234.10, (1234.10), or 1234.10. Accountants consider a number written in parentheses or in red to be a negative number.

> Currency might be formatted with none or two decimal places, for example, $1,234 or $1,234.10.

> A date might be formatted as 14-Mar-12 or March 14, 2012.

> A number, such as .34, can be formatted as a percentage: 34%.

> Ten digits can be formatted as a phone number, for example, (888) 555-1234.

ON YOUR OWN 10.4

Format Rows for Team Data and Add One Team Member

WATCH

OBJECTIVE 10.3
VIDEO

Create the Roster Workbook: Part 3 of 10

After you complete this activity, the rows for team data should be formatted and the first team member entered, as shown in Figure 10-6.

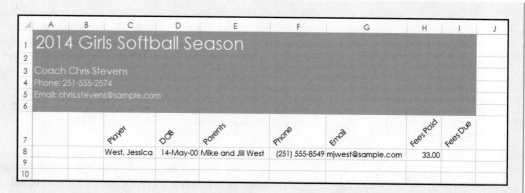

FIGURE 10-6   The rows for team data are formatted, and one team member is added.

To format Coach Stevens's roster, do the following to format the first row used for data, which is row 8:

Step 1.   Format cell **D8** to display the birthdate as day-month-year. First, select the cell. On the HOME ribbon, click **Format**. In the drop-down menu, click **Format Cells**. The Format Cells dialog box appears. Under Category, click **Date**. Click the **14-Mar-12** format, as shown in Figure 10-7.

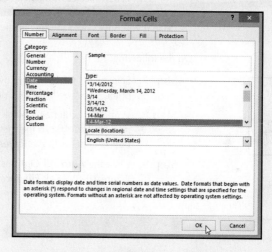

FIGURE 10-7   The Format Cells box provides options for formatting cells.

Step 2.   Format cell **F8** for a phone number.

> **Hint** The **Phone Number** option is found under the **Special** category in the Format Cells dialog box.

Step 3.   Format cells **H8** and **I8** for a **Number** with two decimal places displayed.

Now it's time to enter data into the row. With data entered, you can check the formatting for errors and adjust the column widths. Do the following:

Step 4.   Enter the following data for Jessica West into row 8:

Heading	Data
Player	West, Jessica
DOB	5/14/2000
Parents	Mike and Jill West
Phone	2515558549
Email	mjwest@sample.com
Fees Paid	33

> **Hint** When entering a date, use a slash or hyphen to separate the month/day/year. Excel then recognizes this data as a date. When entering numbers, don't enter the formatting symbols (for example, a comma or dollar sign). Enter only the digits and perhaps a decimal point. Excel does the rest.

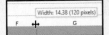

> **Tip** If you want to increase or decrease the width of a column, press and drag the vertical bar on the right side of the column letter.

Step 5. Notice not all the data for Jessica displays because the columns are too narrow. To fix this problem, first select cells C7:I8 (cells C7 through I8). Then click **Format** on the HOME ribbon and click **AutoFit Column Width** on the drop-down menu.

Step 6. Notice that Excel makes the email address in cell G8 a hyperlink. To remove the hyperlink, right-click on the cell and click **Remove Hyperlink** in the shortcut menu.

Next, you'll use the Excel **Auto Fill Options** tool to copy the formatting in row 8 to other rows for team data. To use the tool, you select the cells and then press and drag the **fill handle**.

Fill handle

> **Auto Fill Options**—An Excel tool that copies data, formatting, or a series of data into a range of cells. A series of data can be a series of numbers or a series of dates.
> **fill handle**—The small green square in the lower-right corner of a selection box. When you hover over the fill handle, your pointer changes to a black cross.

Do the following:

Step 7. Select cells **C8:I8**. Hover over the fill handle (green square) on the lower-right corner of the selection box. Your pointer changes to a black cross ✛.

Step 8. With the pointer as a black cross, press and drag the selection box down through row **18**. The data in the first row fills the selected rows, and the Auto Fill Options button appears in the lower-right corner of the fill box.

Step 9. Click the **Auto Fill Options** button. In the drop-down menu that appears (see Figure 10-8), click **Fill Formatting Only**. The copied data disappears, and the formatting is copied to the new selection.

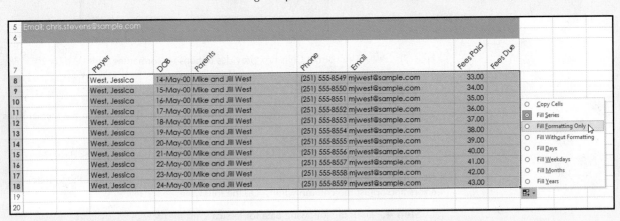

FIGURE 10-8 Use the Auto Fill Options tool to copy data, a series of data, or formatting to other cells.

> **Hint** Using the Auto Fill Options tool takes a little practice. If it doesn't work the first time, click the **Undo** button ↺ in the title bar and try again.

Step 10. Save your work.

Solutions Appendix *For help: See On Your Own 10.4 Step-by-Step Solution*

ON YOUR OWN 10.5

Copy Team Data from a Word Table and Edit the Data

WATCH

OBJECTIVE 10.3 VIDEO

Create the Roster Workbook: Part 4 of 10

All the data for each team member can be typed into the worksheet. However, to save you typing time, this data has been stored in a Word document in the sample_files folder available at www.pearsonhighered.com/jump or in MyITLab.

In this activity, you'll copy the team data in a Word document into your Excel worksheet. When the activity is completed, the worksheet should look like that in Figure 10-9.

FIGURE 10-9 The Roster worksheet has team data added.

Do the following:

Step 1. Open the Word document named **RosterTable** in the **sample_files** folder available at www.pearsonhighered.com/jump or in MyITLab. (In Chapter 2, you downloaded the sample_files folder to your USB flash drive.) Copy the team data in the RosterTable file into the Windows Clipboard. Paste the data into the Excel worksheet. When you paste the data, choose the option to **Match Destination Formatting**. By doing so, you retain the formatting in the worksheet.

Step 2. When you paste the data from the RosterTable into the worksheet, Jessica West is entered twice (one time from your data entry and one time from the table). To fix the problem, delete one of the rows containing her data.

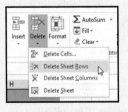

> **Hint** To delete a row, click somewhere in the row. Then click the drop-down arrow under **Delete** on the HOME ribbon. Click **Delete Sheet Rows**. Selected rows are deleted. Another way to delete a row is to right-click a row and select **Delete** from the shortcut menu.

Step 3. Widen the columns so that all the data displays. You can manually widen each column or use the AutoFit Column Width command.

> **Hint** When a date or number is too wide for a column, Excel displays the hash symbol (sometimes called the pound sign) several times (######) in the cell. Widen the column to see the data.

Step 4. Save your work.

Solutions Appendix

For help: See On Your Own 10.5 Step-by-Step Solution

Objective 10.4: Organize Data in a Worksheet

Organizing data in a worksheet makes the data easier to find and more meaningful. Let's look at two easy and effective ways of organizing data: sorting the data and adding row numbers.

ON YOUR OWN 10.6

Sort Data and Add Row Numbers

Create the Roster Workbook: Part 5 of 10

To help organize the data, sort the team members by name. To make the roster easier to use, add counting numbers in column A. When this activity is completed, the worksheet should look like that in Figure 10-10.

FIGURE 10-10 Players are sorted by name, and row numbers are added.

Do the following:

Step 1. To sort the rows, first select all the team data. To do so, select the range of cells **C8:H17**.

> **Hint** As you press and drag to select the cells, be sure not to accidentally grab the fill handle in the lower-right corner of a selection box. Doing so causes the cells to be copied, not selected. If you make a mistake, don't forget the handy Undo button at the top of your window.

Step 2. On the HOME ribbon, click **Sort & Filter**. Then click **Sort A to Z** in the drop-down menu. The data is sorted by the first column in the range of cells.

> **Tip** If you need to sort by more than one column or on a column other than the first column, select the cells to sort and click **Sort** on the DATA ribbon. The Sort dialog box appears and offers more sorting options.

Step 3. To enter counting numbers in column A, first type the number **1** in cell **A8**. You could continue typing each number, or you can let Excel do it for you. Use the Auto Fill tool to fill in counting numbers in column A down through cell **A17**.

Step 4. Narrow the column width of the first two columns, as shown in Figure 10-10.

Step 5. Save your work.

Solutions
Appendix

For help: See On Your Own 10.6 Step-by-Step Solution

WATCH

OBJECTIVE 10.5
VIDEO

Adding Calculations to a Worksheet

All the information collected for the softball team roster could have been kept in a Word table. However, we can get Excel to help us with the calculations. The ability to make calculations is one advantage that Excel offers over a Word table.

Objective 10.5: Use Labels to Make Information Easier to Find

Labels in a worksheet are put in cells to help identify the values or calculations in nearby cells. Labels help us to organize and make sense of data.

ON YOUR OWN 10.7

WATCH

OBJECTIVE 10.5
VIDEO

Enter Labels and Values for the Calculations

Create the Roster Workbook: Part 6 of 10

We want the worksheet to calculate for us the *Total fee per child* in cell D24 and the *Percentage paid* by the entire team in cell D26. Before we do that, let's put some labels on the worksheet to help identify these calculations. We'll also enter two values in cells D21 and D22 that will later be used to make the calculations. When the activity is completed, the worksheet should look like that in Figure 10-11.

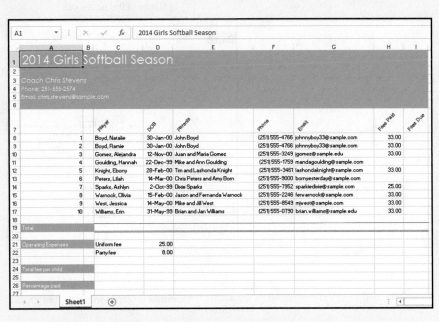

FIGURE 10-11   Labels and values for the calculations are entered.

Let's get started:

Step 1.   Enter the text in rows 19 through 26, as shown in Figure 10-12.

Step 2.   Format the cells as follows:

- Use the Format Painter to copy the formatting from cell A5 to cells A19, B19, A21, B21, A24, B24, A26, and B26.

- Apply the **Total** cell style to row 19 in cells C19:I19.

Step 3.   Resize column A so all text is visible.

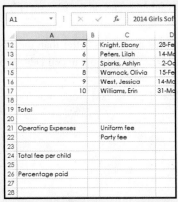

FIGURE 10-12   Enter the text for the calculation labels.

Step 4. In cell **D21**, enter **25**. In cell **D22**, enter **8**. Format both cells as **Number** with two decimal places.

Step 5. Save your work.

Solutions Appendix

For help: See *On Your Own 10.7* Step-by-Step Solution

WATCH

OBJECTIVE 10.6 VIDEO

Objective 10.6: Use Formulas and Functions

Excel does a calculation when you put a formula in a cell. Recall that a formula always begins with an equal sign and can use numbers or cells that contain numbers. A formula can contain $+$, $-$, $*$, and $/$ operators for addition, subtraction, multiplication, and division, respectively. Parentheses can be used for grouping, as in $=5/(5+30)$. The order of operations is the same as in math.

In our Roster workbook, cell D24 is to contain the total fee per child, which is the sum of the Uniform fee and the Party fee. Here are three ways to find this sum:

> **Using numbers.** Enter $=25 + 8$ in cell D24. Notice in Figure 10-13 that the sum 33 displays in cell D24. The formula bar shows the formula stored in the cell.

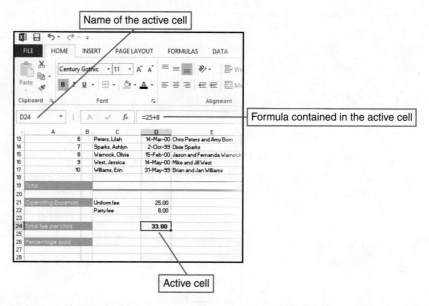

FIGURE 10-13 A formula is stored in a cell, but its calculated value displays on the worksheet.

> **Using cell addresses.** Enter $=D21+D22$ in cell D24. This method is better than the first method because if you change the values in cells D21 or D22, the formula in cell D24 automatically calculates a new sum.

> **Using a function.** Enter $=SUM(D21:D22)$ in cell D24. This method works not just for summing two cells but to sum an entire column of cells.

Tip To see a list of Excel functions, click **Insert Function** on the FORMULAS ribbon or search Excel Help on **Excel functions** (by category).

The last method uses the SUM **function** . Excel offers many functions to be used in formulas, such as the **SUM** , **AVERAGE** , **MAX** , **TODAY** , and **MIN** .

> **function**—A tool used in a formula to enhance what the formula can do. Parentheses and a colon are used to indicate a range of cells used by the function. For example, the SUM function is used in this formula: =SUM(D21:D40). The function sums the numbers in cells D21 through D40.
>
> **SUM function**—A function that sums a range of cells.
>
> **AVERAGE function**—A function that calculates the average for a range of cells.
>
> **MAX function**—A function that finds the largest value in a range of cells.
>
> **TODAY function**—A function that returns today's date. The date changes each day the workbook is opened. The function is written in a cell as **=TODAY( )**.
>
> **MIN function**—A function that finds the smallest value in a range of cells.

ON YOUR OWN 10.8

WATCH

OBJECTIVE 10.6 VIDEO

Enter Two Sums in the Worksheet

Create the Roster Workbook: Part 7 of 10

Accountants use a double line under a value to indicate it is the sum of a column of numbers. Excel provides a cell style named Total to format a sum in this way. In this activity, you'll enter two sums in the worksheet in cells D24 and H19. (Refer back to Figure 10-3.) Do the following to enter and format the first sum:

Step 1. Enter a formula in cell **D24** to calculate the sum of cells D21 and D22. Use cell addresses in the formula.

Step 2. Format cells **C24** and **D24** using the **Total** cell style. Format cell **D24** using **Currency** with **2** decimal places.

> **Not Working?** If you need to edit the formula in a cell, click the cell. The formula appears in the formula bar. Click in the formula bar to edit the cell.

You're now ready to put the sum of the Fees Paid column in cell H19. You can type the formula in cell H19, but an easier way is to use the **AutoSum** command.

> **AutoSum**—A command on the FORMULAS ribbon and the HOME ribbon of Excel that automatically inserts a function into a cell and defines the range of cells used in the function.

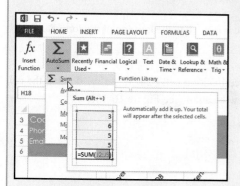

Do the following:

Step 3. Go to cell **H19**. On the FORMULAS ribbon, click the down arrow under AutoSum. In the drop-down list, click **Sum**. Excel inserts a SUM function in the cell. Excel also draws a selection box around cells above H19. You can adjust the selection box as necessary.

Step 4. Hover over a top corner of the selection box until your pointer changes to a double-headed arrow ☝. Press and drag this selection box to include all the cells in column H that are intended to contain numbers: cells **H8** through **H18** (see Figure 10-14). Press **Enter** to enter the formula into cell H19.

> **Not Working?** If you have trouble while using AutoSum, press the **Escape** key to cancel the operation. Delete the cell contents and try again.

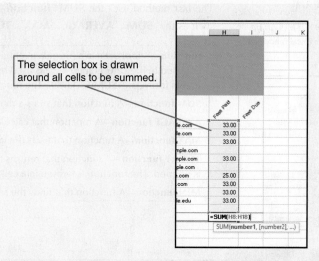

The selection box is drawn around all cells to be summed.

FIGURE 10-14 AutoSum inserts the SUM function and defines the range of cells to sum.

Step 5. Click cell **H19** to make it the active cell. Look in the formula bar to see the formula that AutoSum placed in the cell.

Step 6. Format cell **H19** using **Currency** with **2** decimal places. Adjust the column width to show the contents of the cell.

Solutions Appendix

For help: See *On Your Own 10.8* Step-by-Step Solution

WATCH

OBJECTIVE 10.7 VIDEO

Objective 10.7: Copy a Formula That Uses Relative and Absolute References

Sometimes a worksheet needs a column of calculations, such as the Fees Due column (column I). You can type a formula in each cell in the column. A quicker method is to type a formula in the first cell and copy this formula to other cells in the column.

When Excel copies a formula to a new cell, it automatically changes the cell addresses in the formula to adjust for the new location. This type of cell address in a formula is called a **relative reference** .

> **relative reference**—A cell address in a formula that is relative to the location of the formula. Also called a *relative address*.

For example, suppose we copy the formula in cell D24 to cell F24. When we do that, the cell addresses in the new formula are relative to the new location (see Figure 10-15).

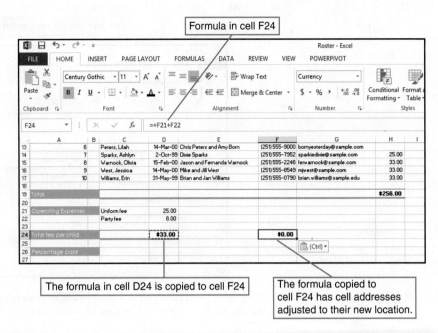

FIGURE 10-15   Using a relative reference, Excel changes a cell address in a formula when the formula is copied to a new location.

Hint To copy and paste a cell or range of cells, first press and drag to select the cells to be copied. Then click **Copy** on the HOME ribbon (or press **Ctrl+C**). Go to the new location and click **Paste** on the HOME ribbon (or press **Ctrl+V**).

In cell D24 in Figure 10-15, the two cell addresses in the formula are above cell D24. When this formula is copied to cell F24, the two cell addresses are adjusted to be those above cell F24. The new formula, therefore, uses cells F21 and F22.

If you don't want the cell address in a formula to change when the formula is copied, you must use an **absolute reference** . To do so, type a dollar sign ($) before the column letter and row number, as in $D$21.

---

absolute reference—A cell address in a formula that does not change when the formula is copied to a new location. Use $ in the address, for example, $D$21. Also called an *absolute address*.

For example, suppose a formula in cell D24 is =$D$21+D22. When this formula is copied to cell F24, the first address doesn't change, but the second address does change relative to its new location. The formula becomes =$D$21+F22, as shown in Figure 10-16.

The first cell address in the formula uses absolute referencing.

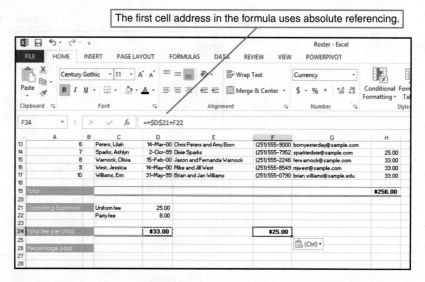

Tip To make typing easier when you're entering a cell address into a formula, press the F4 key to toggle the cell address from a relative address to an absolute address.

FIGURE 10-16 When you use an absolute reference, Excel doesn't change a cell address in a formula when the formula is copied to a new location.

ON YOUR OWN 10.9

WATCH

OBJECTIVE 10.7
VIDEO

WATCH

CHAPTER 10
DIVING DEEPER
VIDEO

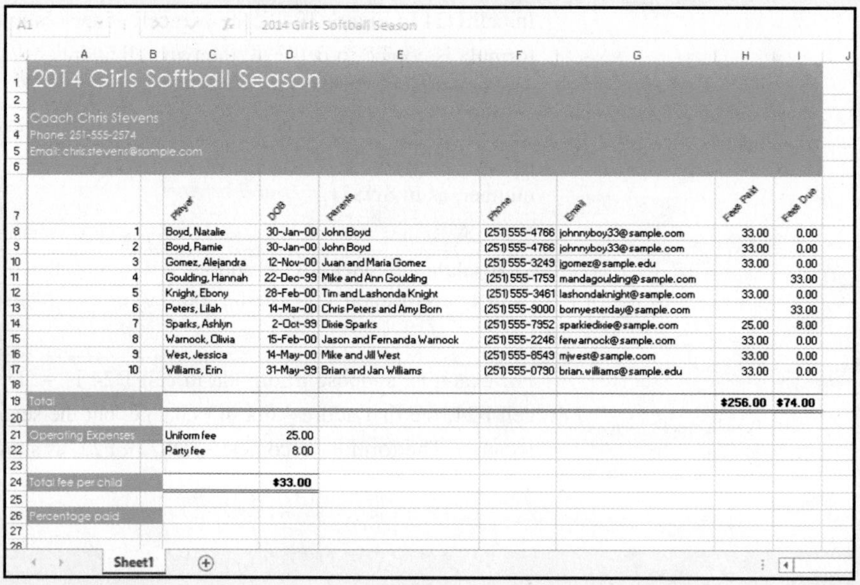

Calculate Fees Due

Create the Roster Workbook: Part 8 of 10

Our next task to build the worksheet is to enter formulas to calculate the Fees Due column (column I). You enter the formula for the first team member in cell I8 and then copy this formula to other cells in column I. When this activity is completed, the worksheet should look like that in Figure 10-17.

FIGURE 10-17 The Fees Due column is calculated and totaled.

Do the following to calculate the fees due and sum the fees due column:

Step 1. Enter a formula in cell **I8** that calculates Fees Due for the first team member. The formula is Total fees per child (cell **D24**) minus Fees Paid (cell **H8**). Use an absolute reference for cell D24 so this cell address does not change when the formula is copied. What formula did you use in this cell?

Step 2. Copy the formula into cells **I9** through **I17**.

Step 3. Use the **AutoSum** tool to put the sum of Fees Due into cell **I19**. What formula did AutoSum place in this cell?

Step 4. Use the Format Painter to copy the formatting in cell **H19** to cell **I19**.

Solutions Appendix

For help: See *On Your Own 10.9* Step-by-Step Solution

WATCH

OBJECTIVE 10.8 VIDEO

Objective 10.8: Calculate a Percentage

The last calculation on the worksheet is the percentage of total fees that have already been paid. A percentage is a part of a whole. It's calculated by dividing the part by the whole. A percentage is a fraction, and Excel can format the fraction as a percentage.

ON YOUR OWN 10.10

WATCH

OBJECTIVE 10.8 VIDEO

Calculate the Percentage Paid

Create the Roster Workbook: Part 9 of 10

Let's calculate the percentage paid. When you're finished with this activity, your worksheet should look like that shown earlier in Figure 10-3:

Step 1. Enter a formula into cell **D26** that calculates the percentage of total fees that have been paid. The total fees paid is in cell **H19**. The total fees is the sum of cells **H19** and **I19**.

Step 2. Format cells **C26** and **D26** using the **Total** cell style. Then format cell D26 using the **Percentage** cell format with no decimal places. Save your work.

Solutions Appendix

For help: See *On Your Own 10.10* Step-by-Step Solution

Printing a Worksheet

Next, let's look at how to format a worksheet to print the way you want it to print.

WATCH

OBJECTIVE 10.9 VIDEO

Objective 10.9: Format a Worksheet for Printing

When you print a worksheet, Excel assumes you want to print all cells that contain information. If you want to print less of the worksheet, you must specify a   **print area** .

print area—The range of cells in a worksheet to be printed.

Excel offers other print options that can be useful when printing large worksheets. These options are found on the PAGE LAYOUT ribbon.

ON YOUR OWN 10.11

WATCH

OBJECTIVE 10.9
VIDEO

Print the Worksheet

Create the Roster Workbook: Part 10 of 10

To print the worksheet, do the following:

Step 1. Click the **FILE** tab and click **Print**. Set the orientation to **Landscape**. To force the worksheet to print on a single page, click **No Scaling** and change to **Fit Sheet on One Page**. The print preview looks like that in Figure 10-18.

Step 2. If you have access to a printer, print the worksheet, which fits on a single page. Save your work and close the workbook.

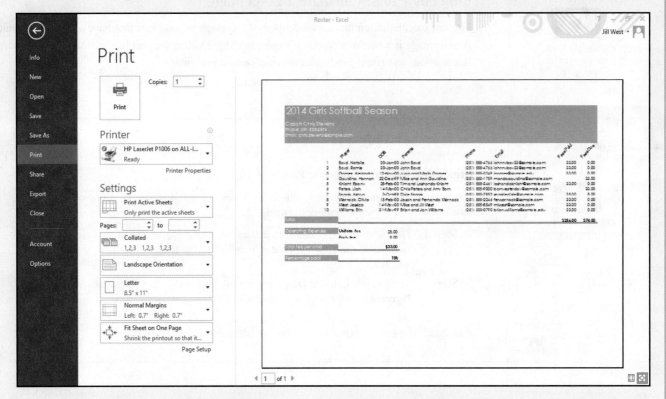

FIGURE 10-18   The worksheet prints on a single page.

Solutions Appendix

For help: **See** *On Your Own 10.11* **Step-by-Step Solution**

Summary

Understanding How to Use Excel

> Excel is a spreadsheet program used to build worksheets. Worksheets hold text, numbers, calculations, charts, and graphics.

> A workbook is an Excel file that can contain one or more worksheets. Excel 2013 workbook files have an .xlsx file extension.

> Columns and rows in a worksheet are addressed using letters and numbers. Each cell has an address using the column letter and row number, such as A25. The address of the selected cell displays in the name box at the top of the worksheet.

> Excel offers many templates you can use to create worksheets for a variety of purposes.

Building a Worksheet with Titles, Headings, and Data

> Begin a worksheet by entering titles and headings. Styles, themes, and other formatting can improve the appearance of a worksheet and make it easier to use.

> If a cell isn't wide enough for text to display and adjacent cells to the right are empty, Excel allows the data to display over the adjacent empty cells. If the adjacent cells to the right contain data, Excel doesn't display all the text in the narrow cell.

> If a cell is not wide enough for a number or date to display, Excel displays the hash symbol (#), also called the pound sign, several times in the cell.

> To widen a column to allow all data to be displayed, use the AutoFit Column Width command. You can also drag the vertical bar to the right of the column letter to change the column width.

> For numbers and dates, it's easier to format the cells intended for data before you enter the data. The Auto Fill Options tool or the Format Painter can be used to copy formatting in cells to other cells.

> The Auto Fill tool is used to copy formatting, data, or a series of data into a range of cells. A series of data can be a series of numbers or a series of dates.

> When pasting data into Excel from Word, use the Match Destination Formatting option to retain the formatting of the worksheet.

> Data can be sorted using the Sort & Filter command on the HOME ribbon.

Adding Calculations to a Worksheet

> Labels for calculations in a worksheet make the information more meaningful and easier to find.

> A formula in a cell is used to make a comparison or contains an equation used to make a calculation. A formula always begins with an equal symbol (=) and can contain arithmetic operators, including +, −, *, /, and parentheses for grouping.

> You can use numbers or cell addresses in a formula. If you use cell addresses, Excel automatically recalculates the formula when the contents of a cell address change.

> Functions enhance the power of a formula. Some Excel functions are SUM, AVERAGE, MAX, TODAY, and MIN. The (and) symbols and a colon are used by a function to indicate the range of cells used by the function.

> The AutoSum command on the FORMULAS ribbon inserts a function into a cell and defines the range of cells used by the function.

> Use a relative reference (also called a relative address) in a formula if you want the cell address to change when the formula is copied to a new location.

> Use an absolute reference (also called an absolute address) in a formula if you don't want the cell address to change when the formula is copied to a new location.

> A percentage is a part of the whole. To enter a percentage in a worksheet, enter in a cell the formula to calculate the fraction and format the cell as a percentage.

Printing a Worksheet

> When printing a worksheet, Excel prints all the cells that contain information unless you specify a print area.

> Options on the PAGE LAYOUT ribbon can be used to print a large worksheet.

CHAPTER MASTERY PROJECT

MyITLab®

Now it's time to find out how well you've mastered the content in this chapter. If you can do all the steps in this Mastery Project without looking back at the chapter details and can answer all the Review Questions following this project, you've mastered this chapter. If you can complete the project by finding answers using Excel Help or the web, you've proven that you can teach yourself how to use Excel to build a worksheet.

> **Hint** All the key terms in the chapter are used in this mastery project or in the review questions that follow. If you encounter a key word you don't know, such as *function*, enter **define:Excel function** in the Internet Explorer search box.

If you find you need a lot of help doing the project and you have not yet read the chapter or done the activities, drop back and start at the beginning of the chapter, watch the videos, review the step-by-step solutions as you work through the On Your Own activities, and then return to this project.

> **Tip** If you need help completing this part of the mastery project, review the "Understanding How to Use Excel" section in the chapter.

Let's practice creating a worksheet when using a template:

Step 1. Open the Excel spreadsheet program. Create a workbook using the **Loan amortization schedule** template. To find the template, type **Loan** in the Search box.

Step 2. Enter the following information about a loan:

- Loan amount: **120,000.00**
- Annual interest rate: **5%**
- Loan period in years: **30**
- Number of payments per year: **12**
- Start date of loan: **July 1, 2014**
- Rename the worksheet **30 year loan**. In the same workbook, create a second worksheet and rename it **Loan Notes**.

Step 3. Make sure you're the author of the workbook file. Save the workbook to your hard drive, USB flash drive, OneDrive, or other location given by your instructor. Name the workbook **Loan Schedule**. Then close the workbook file.

> **Tip** If you need help completing this part of the mastery project, review the "Building a Worksheet with Titles, Headings, and Data" section in the chapter.

In the remainder of this project, you create the worksheet shown in Figure 10-19. The worksheet tracks sales for a club fund-raiser selling citrus fruit. As you build the worksheet, don't forget to save your work often.

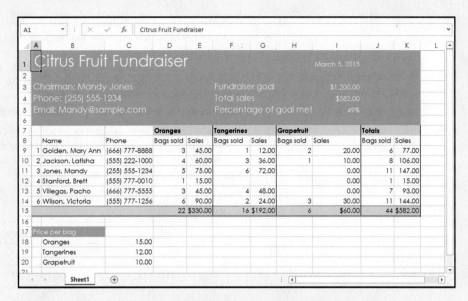

FIGURE 10-19 The worksheet tracks sales for a club fund-raiser.

First, we need to enter titles and headings at the top of the worksheet:

Step 4. Open a blank workbook file and apply the **Mesh** theme to the worksheet.

Step 5. Enter the titles and column headings at the top of the worksheet as follows:

Cell	Text
A1	Citrus Fruit Fundraiser
A3	Chairman: Mandy Jones
A4	Phone: (255) 555-1234
A5	Email: Mandy@sample.com
F3	Fundraiser goal
I3	1200
F4	Total sales
F5	Percent of goal met
D7	Oranges
F7	Tangerines
H7	Grapefruit
J7	Totals
B8	Name
C8	Phone
D8	Bags sold
E8	Sales

Step 6. Copy the text in cells D8 and E8 to cells F8 through K8, as shown in Figure 10-19.

Step 7. Make sure you're the author of the workbook file. Save the file to your USB flash drive, hard drive, OneDrive, or another location given by your instructor. Name the workbook file **CitrusFruitFundraiser**.

Step 8. Club member names and phone numbers are stored in a Word document named ClubMemberTable in the sample_files folder available at www.pearsonhighered.com/jump or in MyITLab. (In Chapter 2, you downloaded the sample_files folder to your USB flash drive.) Open the **ClubMemberTable** document. Copy the names and phone numbers to the Windows Clipboard. Paste the data into the worksheet beginning with cell B9. (When you paste, use the **Match Destination Formatting** option.) Select the names and phone numbers data and sort by Name in alphabetical order.

Step 9. Use the **AutoFit Column Width** tool to adjust the column widths so the text in rows 7 and 8 can be seen. Then adjust the column widths so the text in columns B and C can be seen. As you build this worksheet, adjust the column widths as necessary when a cell is too narrow to display its contents.

Step 10. Enter the Bags sold data as follows:

Cell	Number
D9	3
D10	4
D11	5
D12	1
D13	3
D14	6
F9	1
F10	3
F11	6
F12	0
F13	4
F14	2
H9	2
H10	1
H11	0
H12	0
H13	0
H14	3

Now we need to enter the Price per bag headings and data at the bottom of the worksheet:

Step 11. Enter the following headings and values:

Cell	Text or Number
A17	Price per bag
B18	Oranges
C18	15
B19	Tangerines
C19	12
B20	Grapefruit
C20	10

Tip If you need help completing this part of the mastery project, review the "Adding Calculations to a Worksheet" section in the chapter.

Next, you enter the calculations into the worksheet to determine number of bags sold and total sales. To make it easier for you, here are the formulas you'll need for steps 12 through 14, listed in no particular order:

=TODAY ()	=F9*$C$19	=SUM(D9:D14)
=H9*$C$20	=K15	=E9+G9+I9
=D9*$C$18	=D9+F9+H9	=I4/I3

Let's get started with the calculations:

Step 12. Enter the following calculations into the worksheet:

	Cell(s)	Calculation or Copy Action
1.	E9	Calculate the sales of Oranges for one club member. Use cells D9 and C18 in the formula. (The formula uses relative and absolute referencing.)
2.	E10:E14	Copy the formula in cell E9 to these cells.
3.	G9	Calculate Tangerine sales for one club member.
4.	G10:G14	Copy the formula in cell G9 to these cells.
5.	I9	Calculate the Grapefruit sales for one club member.
6.	I10:I14	Copy the formula in cell I9 to these cells.
7.	J9	Calculate the Total bags sold for Oranges, Tangerines, and Grapefruit for one club member.
8.	J10:J14	Copy the formula in cell J9 to these cells.
9.	K9	Calculate the Total Sales for Oranges, Tangerines, and Grapefruit for one club member.
10.	K10:K14	Copy the formula in cell K9 to these cells.
11.	D15	Use the AutoSum tool to calculate the Total in this column for all club members.
12.	E15:K15	Copy the formula in cell D15 to these cells.

Now enter the summary data near the top of the worksheet:

Step 13. Use the **TODAY** function to insert today's date in cell I1. Format the cell using the March 14, 2012 date format.

Step 14. In cell I4, enter a formula that puts the value of cell K15 in cell I4. In cell I5, enter a formula that calculates the percent of goal met (use cells I3 and I4 in the formula). You'll format the percentage later.

Tip If you need help completing this part of the mastery project, review the "Building a Worksheet with Titles, Headings, and Data" section in the chapter.

To make the worksheet easier to read, do the following:

Step 15. Add counting numbers in cells A9 through A14. To do so, first enter a 1 in cell A9. Then use the fill handle to highlight cells A9 through A14 and the Auto Fill Options tool to insert a series of counting numbers. Narrow column A, as shown in Figure 10-19.

Step 16. Use the Format Painter or the Auto Fill Options tool to format the cells as listed below. After you have added the formatting, adjust the widths of columns C through K to make sure all data is visible.

	Cell(s)	Formatting
1.	A1:K6	Accent 5 cell style
2.	A1	26 point
3.	A3:F5	14 point
4.	D7:K7	40% - Accent 5 cell style, Bold
5.	C9:C14	Phone Number
6.	E9:E14 G9:G14 I9:I14 K9:K14	Number format with two decimal places
7.	A17:B17	Accent 5 cell style
8.	C18:C20	Number format with two decimal places
9.	A15:K15	Total style and 40% - Accent 5 (This is two separate cell styles applied to this group of cells.)
10.	D15, F15, H15 and J15	Number format with zero decimal places
11.	E15, G15, I15, K15, and I3:I4	Currency with 2 decimal places
12.	I5	Percentage with zero decimal places

> **Hint** To select nonadjacent cells, hold down the **Ctrl** key as you click the cells.

Step 17. Select cells E7:E15. On the HOME ribbon, click the drop-down arrow beside the Borders button ⊞ and select **Right Border**. Do the same for cells G7:G15, I7:I15, and K7:K15. Save your work.

> **Tip** If you need help completing this part of the mastery project, review the "Printing a Worksheet" section in the chapter.

Here's how to print the worksheet:

Step 18. Go to the print preview window. Change the orientation to **Landscape**. Based on the preview, change the scaling option to ensure the worksheet prints on one page. If you have access to a printer, print the worksheet on a single page. Save your work and close the workbook.

Review Questions

Answer these questions to assess your skills and knowledge of the content covered in the chapter. Your instructor can provide you with the correct answers when you're ready to check your work.

1. By default, a blank workbook contains how many worksheets?

2. What is the file extension of an Excel 2013 workbook file?

3. By default, numbers in a cell are _____ aligned, and text in a cell is _____ aligned.

4. Accountants consider a number written in red on a worksheet to be a _____ number.

5. When you're entering a date into a cell, what two symbols can you use to separate the month, day, and year?

6. Which tool can be used to automatically insert counting numbers into a column?

7. What symbol does Excel display in a cell when the cell is too narrow to display a large number?

8. What symbol is always used to begin a formula in a cell?

9. When cell A5 is the active cell, what appears in the name box? What formula can you put in the cell to display today's date?

10. What command on the FORMULAS ribbon can be used to automatically insert a SUM function in a cell?

11. What method does an accountant use to indicate a value is the sum of a column of numbers? Which cell style uses this method?

12. The cell address $A$10 used in a formula doesn't change when the formula is copied to a new cell. What type of cell addressing is used?

13. Referring to question 12, how would you write the cell address if you wanted the address to change relative to its new location?

14. How many cells are summed in a cell that contains this formula: =SUM(A5:A7)?

15. Which button on the HOME ribbon is used to tilt column headings upward?

16. Which option under Delete on the HOME ribbon will delete an entire row of a worksheet?

17. By default, which cells in a worksheet does Excel print?

18. Cells A1:E7 are selected for print. What is this area called?

19. Answer the following questions about the Loan Schedule worksheet you created in the Mastery Project:
    a. What is the monthly payment?
    b. What is the total interest paid?
    c. If you make an extra optional payment of $25 per month, what is the total interest paid?

20. Answer the following questions about the Citrus Fruit Fundraiser worksheet you created in the Mastery Project:
    a. What is the formula in cell E9?
    b. What is the formula in cell G9?
    c. What is the formula in cell I9?
    d. What is the formula in cell J9? Does this formula use absolute referencing, relative referencing, or a combination of both?
    e. What is the formula in cell K9?
    f. What is the formula in cell D15?
    g. What is the formula in cell K15?
    h. What is the formula in cell I1?
    i. What is the formula in cell I4?
    j. What is the formula in cell I5?
    k. Which scaling option is used to print all data on one page?

Becoming an Independent Learner

Answer the following questions about becoming an independent learner:

1. To teach yourself to use Microsoft Excel, do you think it's best to rely on the chapter or on Excel Help when you need answers?

2. The most important skill learned in this chapter is how to teach yourself a computer skill. Rate yourself at Level A through E on how well you're doing with this skill. What is your level?
   - Level A: I was able to successfully complete the Chapter Mastery Project with the help of only a few of the On Your Own activities in the chapter.
   - Level B: I completed all the On Your Own activities and the Chapter Mastery Project without referring to any of the solutions in the Step-by-Step Solutions Appendix.

- Level C: I completed all the On Your Own activities and the Chapter Mastery Project by using just a few of the solutions in the Step-by-Step Solutions Appendix.
- Level D: I completed all the On Your Own activities and the Chapter Mastery Project by using many of the solutions in the Step-by-Step Solutions Appendix.
- Level E: I completed all the On Your Own activities and the Chapter Mastery Project and had to use all the solutions in the Step-by-Step Solutions Appendix.

To continue toward the goal of teaching yourself computer skills, if you're not at Level A, try to move up one level on how you learn in Chapter 11.

Projects to Help You

Now that you've mastered the material in this chapter, you're ready to tackle the three projects focused on your career, personal, or academic goals. Depending on your own interests, you might choose to complete any or all of these projects to help you achieve your goals.

Project 1: Beyond Office: Using the Google Drive Spreadsheet App

Google Project I understand that Google Drive has a free spreadsheet app. Can I use what I know about Excel to build worksheets on my Google Drive?

WATCH

CHAPTER 10
GOOGLE DRIVE
VIDEO

Google Drive offers a spreadsheet app that you can use to create workbooks that contain multiple worksheets. The worksheet you create in this project is shown in Figure 10-20. You first built the worksheet in the Chapter Mastery Project using Excel. Now you'll build it again using the free Google Drive spreadsheet app. A few details are changed because some features are not available in the Google spreadsheet app.

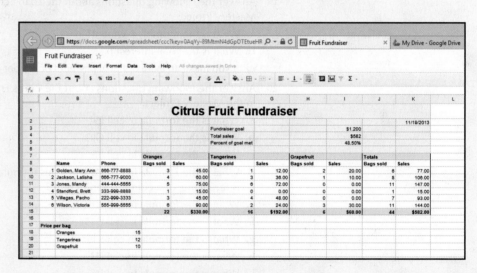

FIGURE 10-20   A worksheet built with the Google spreadsheet app.

Follow these steps to build the worksheet:

Step 1. Sign in to your Google account, go to your Google Drive, and create a new spreadsheet document. Name the document **FruitFundraiser**.

Step 2. Enter the titles and column headings at the top of the worksheet as follows:

Cell	Text
A1	Citrus Fruit Fundraiser
F3	Fundraiser goal
I3	1200
F4	Total sales
F5	Percent of goal met
D7	Oranges
F7	Tangerines
H7	Grapefruit
J7	Totals
B8	Name
C8	Phone
D8	Bags sold
E8	Sales

Step 3. The Google app doesn't allow text to flow into empty adjacent cells as does Excel. To allow text in cell A1 to be read, you must merge several cells into one. Select cells A1:K1 and click the **Merge cells** icon in the menu bar. In cell A1, center the text and format it as **24** point.

Step 4. Copy the text in cells D8 and E8 to cells F8 through K8, as shown in Figure 10-20.

Step 5. Make up six names and enter them into cells B9:B14. Make up phone numbers and enter them in to cells C9:C14. Google Drive currently doesn't offer a way to format phone numbers, so you must do that manually.

Step 6. Follow steps 10 through 12 in the Chapter Mastery Project to enter the Bags sold data, enter headings and values at the bottom of the worksheet, and enter formulas into the worksheet. Remember the formulas you need are listed above in step 12 in the Chapter Mastery Project. (After you enter a formula in one cell, you can copy it to adjacent cells in the same way you copy Excel formulas and data.)

Step 7. Use the **TODAY** function to insert today's date in cell K2.

Step 8. In cell I4, enter the formula **=K15** that puts the value of cell K15 in cell I4. In cell I5, enter the formula **=I4/I3** that calculates the percent of goal met. Format the cell as a percentage.

Step 9. Add counting numbers in cells A9 through A14. Narrow the width of column A, as shown in Figure 10-20.

Step 10. Format cells as follows:

	Cell(s)	Formatting
1.	A1:K6	Fill color is light yellow 3
2.	D7:K7	Bold, fill color is light green 3
3.	D15:K15	Bold, fill color is light green 3
4.	A17	Bold, fill color is light green 3
5.	B8:K8	Bold
6.	E9:E14 G9:G14 I9:I14 K9:K14	Number format with two decimal places
7.	I3, E15, G15, I15, and K15	Currency with two decimal places

Step 11. Select cells E7:E15. On the menu bar, use the Borders button to add a **Right border**. Do the same for cells G7:G15, I7:I15, and K7:K15. Compare your worksheet to Figure 10-20 and correct any errors you see.

Project 2: Using Excel in Your Personal Life

This project gives you some practice teaching yourself about Excel by expecting you to use some Excel skills not covered in the chapter. In this project, you enhance the CitrusFruitFundraiser worksheet you created in the Mastery Project. When this project is completed, the worksheet should look like that in Figure 10-21.

Personal Project I want to learn more about Excel, and I'm willing to explore and teach myself.

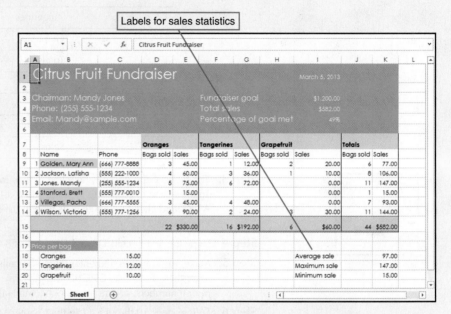

FIGURE 10-21 The fund-raiser worksheet has enhancements.

Do the following:

Step 1. Open the **CitrusFruitFundraiser** worksheet you created earlier in the Mastery Project.

Step 2. Increase the height of rows 7 through 15 so these rows stand out.

Step 3. Enter the labels for sales statistics in cells I18, I19, and I20.

Step 4. Enter formulas to calculate the average sale, maximum sale, and minimum sale in cells K18, K19, and K20.

Step 5. Suppose club members are expected to meet a minimum quota of $100 in sales. Use the Conditional Formatting feature of Excel to highlight in yellow the name of any club member who has not yet reached his or her quota.

Hint Select the cells to format (B9 through B14) and click **Conditional Formatting** on the HOME ribbon. Under Highlight Cells Rules, click **More Rules**. Click **Use a formula to determine which cells to format**. In the formula, use the less-than operator (<) and enter the following formula: **=K9<100**. After you enter the formula, click the **Format** button. In the Format Cells box, on the **Fill** tab, select a fill color for the cells that satisfy the criteria in the formula.

Step 6. Someone asks you to explain the formulas used in this worksheet. Change the display of the worksheet so the formulas display in cells rather than the calculated values.

Step 7. Save the document to your USB flash drive, hard drive, OneDrive, or other location given by your instructor. Name the document **CitrusFruitFundraiser-Enhanced**.

Academic Project My instructor has asked me to help her grade some worksheets. She specifically wants me to check for errors in the formulas.

Project 3: Using Excel in Your Academic Career

Your instructor has asked for your help in checking some worksheets created by other students. In the sample_files folder available at www.pearsonhighered.com/jump or in MyITLab, open the **Student01_Roster** workbook file. (In Chapter 2, you downloaded the sample_files folder to your USB flash drive.) Find and list the eight errors on this worksheet. Save the document to your USB flash drive, hard drive, OneDrive, or other location given by your instructor. Name the document **Student01_Roster Errors**.

> **Hint** To check the formulas used in the worksheet, you can point to each cell or use the **Show Formulas** command on the FORMULAS ribbon.

Project to Help Others

One of the best ways to learn is to teach someone else. And, in teaching someone else, you're making a contribution in that person's life. As part of each chapter's work, you're encouraged to teach someone a skill you have learned. In this chapter, help someone learn to use Excel.

Working with your apprentice, do the following:

Step 1. Show your apprentice the worksheets you created in this chapter. Explain the elements on the Excel window and how the worksheet is built.

Step 2. Show your apprentice the templates that Excel offers.

Step 3. Help your apprentice find a template that he finds useful. Show him how to enter data in the worksheet and save the workbook.

Step 4. If your apprentice is interested in building his own worksheet, help him design and create a worksheet of his choosing.

Step 5. Use Word to create a document file that contains answers about the tutoring session and send the file to your instructor. If you're using MyITLab, you can post the file in Dropbox in MyITLab. On the other hand, your instructor might prefer you post the file to your OneDrive or email the file as an attachment. Here are the questions:

1. Who is your apprentice?

2. What new skills using Excel did you help your apprentice learn?

3. Which template did your apprentice choose?

4. How do you think the tutoring session went? How would you like to improve it next time?

11 Organizing Data Using Excel

In This Chapter, You Will:

Use a Table to Manage Data

In this chapter, you'll learn how Excel can help you track, organize, and summarize large amounts of data. The worksheets you create in this chapter use Excel tables. An Excel table offers many shortcuts for managing data. Several tasks you learned to do manually in Chapter 10 are more automatic when using a table. In this chapter, you'll also learn to use several functions and to create charts that can visually summarize data.

As with all chapters in this book, you can choose which of the learning paths below best suits your needs. No matter which path you choose, as you work your way through the chapter, remember the most important computer skill is how to teach yourself a computer skill. Therefore, this chapter is designed to help you teach yourself how to organize data using Excel.

LEARNING PATHS

GUIDED LEARNING	EXPLORE AND DISCOVER	JUMP RIGHT IN
Read the Chapter *Watch the Objective Videos*	**On Your Own Projects** *Review Objective videos or use Step-by-Step Solutions*	**Mastery Project** *Use Objective videos & OYO projects for help*
On Your Own Projects *Review Objective videos or use Step-by-Step Solutions*		
Mastery Project *Use Objective videos & OYO projects for help*	**Mastery Project** *Use Objective videos & OYO projects for help*	**Explore Resources** *For help as needed*
Google Project (if applicable) *Watch Google video for help*	**Google Project (if applicable)** *Watch Google video for help*	**Google Project (if applicable)** *Watch Google video for help*
Helping You & Others Projects	**Helping You & Others Projects**	**Helping You & Others Projects**
MyITLab Assessment	**MyITLab Assessment**	**MyITLab Assessment**

Using a Table to Manage Data

In this chapter, we'll build a workbook for the Gently Used Consignment Shop. People bring furniture, books, clothing, and other items to the shop to sell, and the shop charges a commission for selling an item. Each month, the shopkeeper, Sarah Engels, writes a check to sellers for the money they're due for all items sold that month. The data for one month is managed using three worksheets shown in Figure 11-1.

Sales table tracks items and when they sell

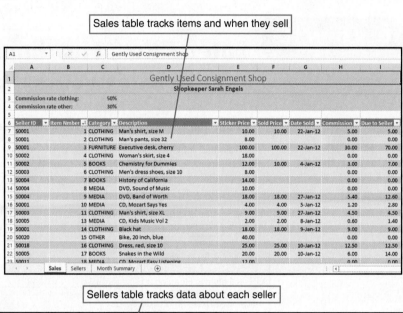

Sellers table tracks data about each seller

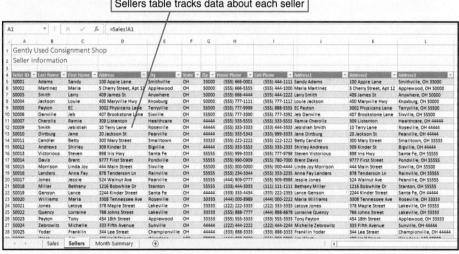

Month Summary table summarizes sales activity

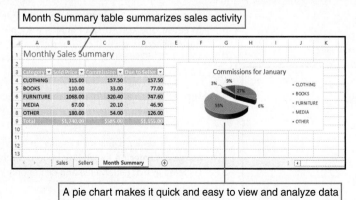

A pie chart makes it quick and easy to view and analyze data

FIGURE 11-1   The Sales and Sellers worksheets track the shop activity. The Month Summary worksheet summarizes that activity.

Objective 11.1: Use the Merge & Center and Freeze Panes Commands

The first worksheet, named the Sales worksheet, tracks items placed in the consignment shop by a seller as well as when the item sells. First, we'll enter the titles and column headings on the Sales worksheet, and then we'll add the data.

ON YOUR OWN 11.1

Enter Titles, Headings, and Data on the Sales Worksheet

Create the ConsignmentShop Workbook: Part 1 of 11

When this activity is completed, the Sales worksheet should look like that in Figure 11-2. The worksheet title and subtitle in cells A1 and A2 use the **Merge & Center** command to cause these titles to span several columns.

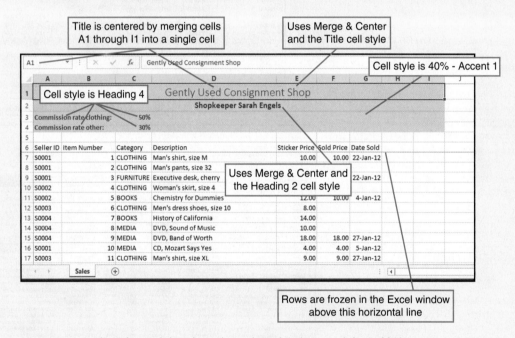

FIGURE 11-2 The Sales worksheet has titles, column headings, and data added.

> **Merge & Center**—A command on the HOME ribbon in the Alignment group that is used to cause one cell to span across multiple columns. Use it to center a title or column heading across several columns.

Do the following to enter and format the items in the first four rows of the worksheet:

Step 1. Open a new blank workbook. Enter the titles and labels in cells A1 through A4, as shown in Figure 11-2, and format the cells as indicated in the figure.

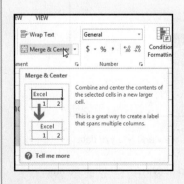

> **Hint** To center a title or heading in a range of cells, select the range of cells and click **Merge & Center** on the HOME ribbon. All the cells are merged into a single cell, and text is centered in that cell. Merge and center only one row at a time.

Step 2. The shop charges a higher commission rate for clothing than for other items. Enter **0.5** in cell C3 and **0.3** in cell C4. Format these cells using the Heading 4 cell style.

Step 3. Name this first worksheet **Sales**. Save the workbook file to your hard drive, USB flash drive, OneDrive, or another location given by your instructor. Name the file **ConsignmentShop**.

Do the following to enter column headings and data into the worksheet:

Step 4. Enter the column headings in row 6, as shown in Figure 11-2. Don't worry about the formatting or column width of the cells in this row. You'll handle both later.

Step 5. Format cells E7, F7, H7, and I7 as numbers with two decimal places.

Step 6. Format cell G7 as a date, using the **14-Mar-12** date format.

Step 7. Copy the formatting in row 7 down through row 72 or beyond.

Step 8. The data for the worksheet is stored in the Word document named **ConsignmentSalesTable** in the sample_files folder on the www.pearsonhighered.com/jump website and in MyITLab. Open the document in Word. Copy the data in the Word table into the Windows Clipboard. Paste the data into the worksheet beginning at cell **A7**. Use the Paste option that matches the destination formatting.

> **Not Working?** Be sure to copy all the rows in the ConsignmentSalesTable document except the first row that contains the column headings. If the data in your worksheet doesn't fill rows down to row 72, you probably didn't copy all the data rows. Go back and check your work.

> **Tip** When you use File Explorer in Windows 8 or Windows Explorer in Windows 7 to locate the ConsignmentSalesTable file in the sample_files folder, the Type column in Explorer reports the file to be a Microsoft Word Document file. When you double-click the file, it opens in a Word window.

Step 9. Adjust the column widths so all data and labels on the worksheet can be read.

To make the worksheet easier to use, the **Freeze Panes** command can freeze the title and column headings so they remain in view even when you scroll down through many rows of data.

> **Freeze Panes**—A feature in Excel that can freeze a few rows and/or columns on a worksheet so they stay put as you scroll down through a long worksheet.

Do the following:

Step 10. Make cell **A7** the active cell. On the VIEW ribbon, click **Freeze Panes**. Then click **Freeze Panes** in the drop-down menu. All the rows above row 7 are frozen on the window. A horizontal line appears on the worksheet to indicate which rows are frozen.

Step 11. To test the frozen rows, use your arrow keys to move down the rows. No matter how far you go down the worksheet, the first six rows stay in view.

Step 12. Save your work.

Solutions Appendix

For help: See *On Your Own 11.1* Step-by-Step Solution

Objective 11.2: Convert a Range of Data to an Excel Table and Add a Total Row

We're now ready to convert the data to a table. Here are some advantages to using an Excel table to manage your data:

> Rows in a table can easily be sorted.
> Rows can be filtered so that only rows that match a criterion display.
> A total row can quickly be added to the bottom of a table. This total row can contain various summary calculations for each column in the table. Excel uses the SUBTOTAL function to automatically produce these calculations.
> Each column in a table automatically receives a name, which is the same as the column heading. These names make it easy to build formulas using the table data.

In the following activities, you'll learn to use all these features of an Excel table.

ON YOUR OWN 11.2

Convert the Data to an Excel Table

Create the ConsignmentShop Workbook: Part 2 of 11

In this activity, you'll convert the data to a table. When the activity is completed, the worksheet should look like that in Figure 11-3.

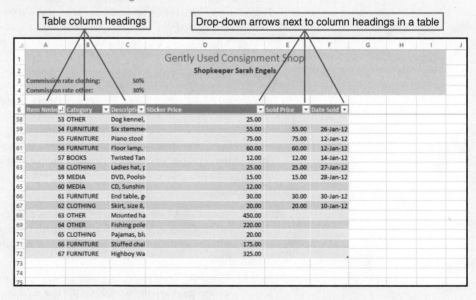

FIGURE 11-3   A table is used to manage the data in columns and rows.

Do the following to convert the data to a table:

Step 1. Click anywhere in the data. On the HOME ribbon, click **Format as Table**. In the list of table styles, select **Table Style Medium 9**. The Format As Table dialog box appears (see Figure 11-4).

Box with dotted lines defines column headings and data for the table

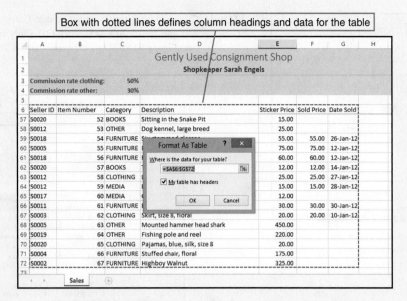

FIGURE 11-4   When creating a table, Excel automatically selects the area for the table and assigns column headings to the table.

Step 2.   Make sure **My table has headers** is checked and click **OK**. The table is created using the selected table style. This style uses alternating colors for each row (called banded rows), which makes it easier to read data across a long row.

Notice the drop-down arrows to the right of each column header. You can use these drop-down arrows to sort and filter the data. Do the following to find out how:

Step 3.   Click the drop-down arrow next to Seller ID. The drop-down list appears (see Figure 11-5). Click **Sort A to Z**. All the data in the table is sorted by Seller ID, and the Sort icon shows next to Seller ID. The advantage of using a table to sort data rather than selecting a range of rows and columns to sort is that you don't have to worry about making sure you have the correct range of cells selected.

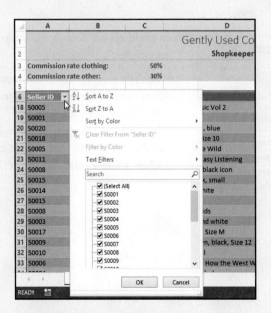

FIGURE 11-5   Excel can automatically sort or filter all data in a table.

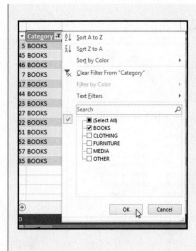

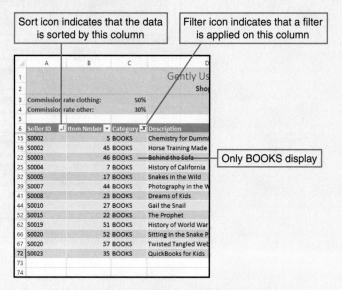

Step 4. Click the drop-down arrow next to Category. In the drop-down list, uncheck (**Select All**) and check **BOOKS**. Click **OK**. Only rows in the BOOKS category display (see Figure 11-6). The other rows are hidden, and the Filter icon shows next to Category.

FIGURE 11-6 A filter causes rows in a table to be hidden from view.

Step 5. To unhide the rows, click the drop-down arrow next to Category and check (**Select All**). Click **OK**. All the rows of data display.

Step 6. Sort the data by **Item Number** from smallest to largest.

Solutions
Appendix

For help: See *On Your Own 11.2* Step-by-Step Solution

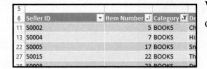

Tip If you don't want to use a table that you've created, click somewhere in the table and then click **Convert to Range** on the TABLE TOOLS DESIGN ribbon. The table formatting is retained, but Excel no longer recognizes the table.

When working with data in a table, you can tell whether the data has been filtered by using one of these methods:

> Look for missing row numbers on the left side of the Excel window. These missing row numbers indicate the rows are hidden. Excel displays adjacent row numbers in blue to indicate that hidden rows are nearby.

> Look for the Filter icon to the right of a column heading. The icon indicates a filter is applied to this column. To clear a filter, click the drop-down arrow next to the column heading, click **Clear Filter From**, and click **OK**.

ON YOUR OWN 11.3

Add New Rows to the Table

WATCH

OBJECTIVE 11.2
VIDEO

Create the ConsignmentShop Workbook: Part 3 of 11

When you add new rows for data, Excel automatically includes these new rows in the table. You can also add blank rows to the bottom of the table, insert rows and columns, and delete rows and columns.

Let's find out how:

> **Step 1.** Add the following row of data to the bottom of the table in row 73. Notice as you enter data into a cell, Excel automatically formats that data as part of the table.

Cell	Text or Number
A73	S0004
B73	68
C73	BOOKS
D73	War and Peace, hard bound
E73	12.50

Here are two tips that can help you prevent typo errors as you type new data:

- Right-click a blank cell in the Seller ID column or the Category column. In the shortcut menu, click **Pick From Drop-down List**. A drop-down list appears with entries already in this column. Click an entry to select it.

- Type the first few letters of the data. Excel completes the cell entry. Press **Enter** or **Tab** to accept the entry.

> **Step 2.** Next insert two new blank rows to the bottom of the table. Use the fill handle at the bottom right of the table—as you drag the fill handle, your pointer changes to a two-headed arrow. Save your work.

Solutions
Appendix

For help: See *On Your Own 11.3* Step-by-Step Solution

ON YOUR OWN 11.4

Add a Total Row to the Table

WATCH

OBJECTIVE 11.2
VIDEO

Create the ConsignmentShop Workbook: Part 4 of 11

Excel can quickly put formulas at the bottom of the table in a Total row. When this activity is completed, the Total row should look like that in Figure 11-7.

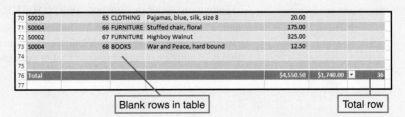

FIGURE 11-7   A Total row is easy to add to a table.

Do the following:

Step 1. Click anywhere in the table. The DESIGN tab appears under TABLE TOOLS whenever a table is active. On the DESIGN ribbon, check **Total Row**. A total row is created.

Step 2. Click the cell in column E of the total row. A drop-down arrow appears in the cell. Click the drop-down arrow to see a list of functions that Excel can use in the total row (see Figure 11-8).

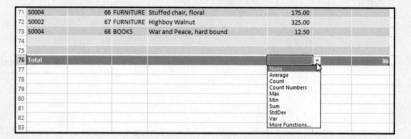

71	S0004	66	FURNITURE	Stuffed chair, floral	175.00	
72	S0002	67	FURNITURE	Highboy Walnut	325.00	
73	S0004	68	BOOKS	War and Peace, hard bound	12.50	
74						
75						
76	Total					36
77					None	
78					Average	
79					Count	
80					Count Numbers	
81					Max	
82					Min	
83					Sum	
					StdDev	
					Var	
					More Functions...	

FIGURE 11-8   Excel can insert a function in the Total row of a table.

Step 3. In the list, click **Sum**. The sum of the Sticker Price column is inserted. You don't need to select the range for the sum because Excel automatically uses the entire column E in the table.

Step 4. Insert a **Sum** in the total row for the Sold Price column. Also notice Excel automatically inserted a **Count** in the Date Sold column.

Step 5. Format cells E76 and F76 as **Currency** with **2** decimal places. Save your work.

Solutions
Appendix

For help: See *On Your Own 11.4* Step-by-Step Solution

WATCH

OBJECTIVE 11.3
VIDEO

Objective 11.3: Use the SUBTOTAL Function and Understand How It Handles Hidden Data

Click in cell E76 and notice the formula that Excel entered into this cell (see Figure 11-9). Excel could have used the SUM function that you learned about in Chapter 10, but it uses the SUBTOTAL function instead. The **SUBTOTAL function** is more versatile than the SUM function. It's really several functions in one, and you can set the function to include or ignore **hidden cells** . The actual function used depends on the function number. The 109 you see in Figure 11-9 says to sum the range and do not include hidden cells.

> **SUBTOTAL function**—An Excel function that is several functions in one, including an average, sum, count, maximum, and minimum. The function can be set to include or ignore hidden cells. To learn more about the function, look up **SUBTOTAL function** in Excel Help.
>
> **hidden cell**—A cell that is part of a hidden row or hidden column. Excel can hide or unhide a row or column using the Hide & Unhide command under the Format command on the HOME ribbon. In addition, filtering rows in a table can hide or unhide a row.

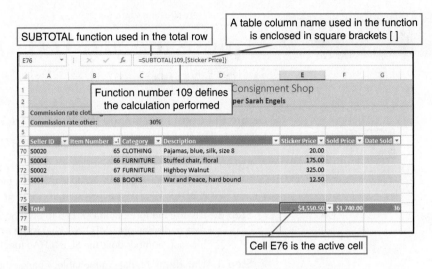

FIGURE 11-9   Excel uses the SUBTOTAL function to calculate the sum.

The SUBTOTAL function has two parts or **arguments** : the function number and a cell range. A few more examples of the SUBTOTAL function are listed in Table 11-1.

argument—In an Excel function, the parts of the function inside parentheses following the function name. Also called a *parameter*.

TABLE 11-1   The SUBTOTAL Function Number Determines the Calculation It Performs on a Range of Cells

Function Number	Description	Example
109	SUM function: Finds the sum and ignores hidden values	SUBTOTAL(109,A1:A10)
9	SUM function: Finds the sum and includes hidden values	SUBTOTAL(9,A1:A10)
101	AVERAGE function: Finds the average and ignores hidden values	SUBTOTAL(101,A1:A10)
1	AVERAGE function: Finds the average and includes hidden values	SUBTOTAL(1,A1:A10)
103	COUNTA function: Counts cells that are not empty and ignores hidden cells	SUBTOTAL(103,A1:A10)
3	COUNTA function: Counts cells that are not empty and includes hidden cells	SUBTOTAL(3,A1:A10)

Notice in Figure 11-9 the name [Sticker Price] is used for the cell range. Excel automatically named column E in the table as [Sticker Price]. When building formulas, you can use this name rather than defining a range of cells. Square brackets [ ] around a name indicate the name is a column heading name in a table.

ON YOUR OWN 11.5

Explore the SUBTOTAL Function in a Table

WATCH

OBJECTIVE 11.3
VIDEO

Create the ConsignmentShop Workbook: Part 5 of 11

Do the following to explore the power of the SUBTOTAL function:

Step 1. Note in Figure 11-7 the sum in cell E76 is $4,550.50. By default, the SUBTOTAL function sums only the cells that are not hidden. Filter the Category to display only **BOOKS**. What is the new sum in cell E76?

Step 2. Change the formula in cell E76 to find the **Average** rather than the sum. Filter the data to display only **MEDIA**. What is the average sticker price for Media? What function number does the SUBTOTAL function use in cell E76?

Step 3. Unhide all the data in the table. Change the formula in cell E76 to find the **Sum**. Save your work.

> **Tip** In a large worksheet, some rows might not display on the screen as you scroll through the data. These rows are still included in the SUBTOTAL calculations if they're not hidden rows.

Solutions Appendix

For help: See *On Your Own 11.5* Step-by-Step Solution

WATCH

OBJECTIVE 11.4
VIDEO

Objective 11.4: Apply Cell Names and Table Names in a Workbook

Names are easier to use in formulas than cell addresses. Excel automatically gives names to columns in a table. In addition, you can manually assign a name to a cell, range of cells, or an entire table:

> To name a cell or range of cells, select the cell or range of cells and type a name in the name box. Then press **Enter**. The name can be used in a formula in place of the absolute address of the cell or range of cells.

> Excel automatically assigns a name to a table. To change the default name, first click anywhere in the table. On the DESIGN ribbon, enter the new table name in the Table Name box.

If a cell has been assigned a name, its name appears in the name box when the cell is the active cell. To see a list of all names on the worksheet, click **Name Manager** on the FORMULAS ribbon. The Name Manager dialog box opens (see Figure 11-10). In this dialog box, you can delete, edit, or add a name.

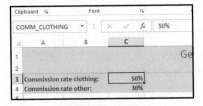

> **Tip** Excel names can include letters, numbers, periods, and underscores. The first character in the name can't be a period. The first character can be a backslash, but you can't use a backslash in the remaining characters.

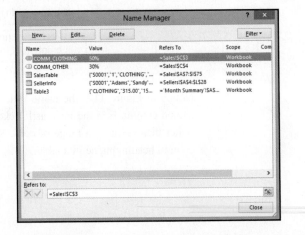

FIGURE 11-10 Use the Name Manager dialog box to view, delete, edit, and create new names. All the names you use in the ConsignmentShop workbook are listed in the box.

ON YOUR OWN 11.6

Name Cells and a Table

WATCH

OBJECTIVE 11.4
VIDEO

Create the ConsignmentShop Workbook: Part 6 of 11

Do the following to give names to cells C3 and C4:

Step 1. Assign the name **COMM_CLOTHING** to cell **C3**. You can now use this name in formulas rather than using $C$3.

Step 2. Name cell C4 as **COMM_OTHER**. Use this name in formulas rather than $C$4.

Step 3. Make cell C3 or C4 the active cell and notice the name of the cell appears in the name box.

> **Not Working?** Don't forget to press **Enter** after you type the cell name in the name box.

Step 4. What is the default name that Excel assigned to the table? Change the table name to **SalesTable**.

Solutions
Appendix

For help: See *On Your Own 11.6 Step-by-Step Solution*

WATCH

OBJECTIVE 11.5
VIDEO

Objective 11.5: Use the IF Function to Check a Condition

Our next step is to use the IF function to calculate the commission column. The **IF function** has three parts or arguments:

IF(*logical_test, value_if_true, value_if_false*)

> **IF function**—A function that checks if a condition is met and returns one value if true and another value if false.

The following IF function would not work in an Excel worksheet, but it does explain the concepts used by the function:

IF (Weather=raining, Umbrella, No umbrella)

> *Logical_test*: Weather = raining
> *Value_if_true*: Umbrella
> *Value_if_false*: No umbrella

So now let's use the IF function to calculate commission.

ON YOUR OWN 11.7

Add Two Calculated Columns to the Table

WATCH

OBJECTIVE 11.5
VIDEO

Create the ConsignmentShop Workbook: Part 7 of 11

Commission is a percentage of the sold price; the commission belongs to the consignment shop. The seller gets the sold price less the commission. Calculations for the commission and due to seller are in columns H and I on the Sales worksheet.

When you complete this activity, the Sales worksheet should look like that shown in Figure 11-11.

IF function is used to calculate commission

H64 f_x =IF([Category]="CLOTHING",[Sold Price]*COMM_CLOTHING,[Sold Price]*COMM_OTHER)

	A	B	C	D	E	F	G	H	I
1				Gently Used Consignment Shop					
2				Shopkeeper Sarah Engels					
3	Commission rate clothing:		50%						
4	Commission rate other:		30%						
5									
6	Seller ID	Item Nmber	Category	Description	Sticker Price	Sold Price	Date Sold	Commission	Due to Seller
62	S0020	57	BOOKS	Twisted Tangled Webs	12.00	12.00	14-Jan-12	3.60	8.40
63	S0012	58	CLOTHING	Ladies hat, purple	25.00	25.00	27-Jan-12	12.50	12.50
64	S0012	59	MEDIA	DVD, Poolside Fun	15.00	15.00	28-Jan-12	4.50	10.50
65	S0017	60	MEDIA	CD, Sunshine, Too	12.00			0.00	0.00
66	S0011	61	FURNITURE	End table, gold and glass	30.00	30.00	30-Jan-12	9.00	21.00
67	S0003	62	CLOTHING	Skirt, size 8, floral	20.00	20.00	10-Jan-12	10.00	10.00
68	S0005	63	OTHER	Mounted hammer head shark	450.00			0.00	0.00
69	S0019	64	OTHER	Fishing pole and reel	220.00			0.00	0.00
70	S0020	65	CLOTHING	Pajamas, blue, silk, size 8	20.00			0.00	0.00
71	S0004	66	FURNITURE	Stuffed chair, floral	175.00			0.00	0.00
72	S0002	67	FURNITURE	Highboy Walnut	325.00			0.00	0.00
73	S0004	68	BOOKS	War and Peace, hard bound	12.50			0.00	0.00
74								0.00	0.00
75								0.00	0.00
76	Total				$4,550.50	$1,740.00	36	$585.00	$1,155.00
77									
78									

Sales

FIGURE 11-11   The last two columns in the table on the Sales worksheet are calculated.

Let's get started:

Step 1. Add the following column headings. Notice that when you enter the text, Excel automatically includes columns H and I in the table.

Cell	Text
H6	Commission
I6	Due to Seller

The shop charges a higher commission for CLOTHING than for other categories. Therefore, the formula to calculate the commission for CLOTHING is different than it is for other categories. The IF function is used to decide which formula to use. The completed formula is shown in Figure 11-12.

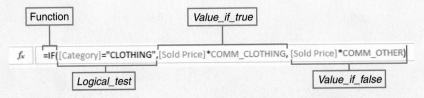

Function   Value_if_true

f_x =IF([Category]="CLOTHING",[Sold Price]*COMM_CLOTHING,[Sold Price]*COMM_OTHER)

Logical_test   Value_if_false

FIGURE 11-12   The IF function calculates commission after testing the Category.

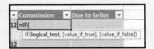

You could just type what you see in the figure, but let's take it one step at a time and see how Excel can help you build an IF function. Do the following:

Step 2. Go to cell **H7**. Type **=IF(**. When you type the **=**, Excel knows you're building a formula. When you type IF(, Excel knows you're using the IF function and responds by showing the three parts (or arguments) of the function. Each argument is separated by a comma.

Step 3. To complete the first argument, first click cell **C7**. When you do, [@Category] is added to the formula. (The @ symbol before Category indicates you inserted it using the clicking method rather than the typing method.) Type **="CLOTHING",** (don't forget the quotation marks and the comma) to complete the *logical_test* part of the IF function (see Figure 11-13).

> **Hint** When typing text in a formula, include double quotation marks around the text.

Excel shows the IF function as you build it.

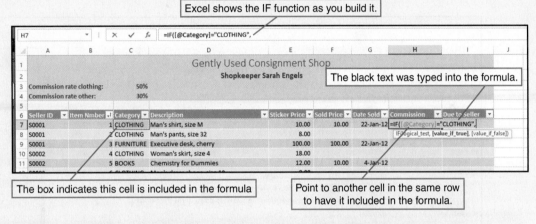

The box indicates this cell is included in the formula

The black text was typed into the formula.

Point to another cell in the same row to have it included in the formula.

FIGURE 11-13   As you build a formula in a cell, you can point to other cells you want included in the formula.

Step 4. To complete the second argument, click cell **F7**. When you do, [@[Sold Price]] is added to the formula. (Don't worry about the extra brackets and the @ symbol.) Type ***** (an asterisk) and then click cell **C3**. *COMM_CLOTHING is added to the formula. Next type **,** (a comma) to complete the *value_if_true* part of the IF function.

> **Tip** When you point to a cell as you're building a formula, notice that Excel assigns a color to the name. This color is also drawn around the cell.

Step 5. To complete the last argument, click cell **F7**, type ***** (an asterisk), and click cell **C4**. [@[Sold Price]]*COMM_OTHER is added to the formula to complete the *value_if_false* part of the IF function.

Step 6. Type **)** and press **Enter** to complete the formula. If other cells in the column are empty, Excel automatically copies the formula into the entire column.

> **Not Working?** If Excel reports an error in the formula, go back and check the formula, comparing it to Figure 11-12.

Do the following to complete the table:

Step 7. The Due to Seller column is the Sold Price less Commission. Enter the formula into this column.

Step 8. Enter the sums of the Commission column and the Due to Seller column in the total row at the bottom of the table. Format these totals as **Currency** with **2** decimal places.

Step 9. Adjust column widths as necessary and save your work.

Solutions Appendix

For help: See *On Your Own 11.7* Step-by-Step Solution

It's good to know more than one method when building a function in Excel. You already learned how to build an IF function by typing text in a cell and pointing to cells used by the function. Another way to build a function is to use the FORMULAS ribbon. Here's how it's done:

Step 1. Select the cell to contain the IF function and click **Insert Function** on the FORMULAS ribbon. The Insert Function dialog box appears. Move the dialog box on the screen so you can see the row that will contain the function and the formula bar on the Excel window.

Step 2. Under *Select a function*, click **IF** and click **OK**. The Function Arguments dialog box opens. Enter the three arguments for the **IF** function. You can type text and click cells you want in the function. As you fill in the Function Arguments dialog box, you can watch the function being built in the formula bar (see Figure 11-14). Click **OK** to enter the IF function in the cell.

> **Not Working?** If you don't see IF listed under *Select a function*, click Logical under *Or select a category*. IF will then appear in the list.

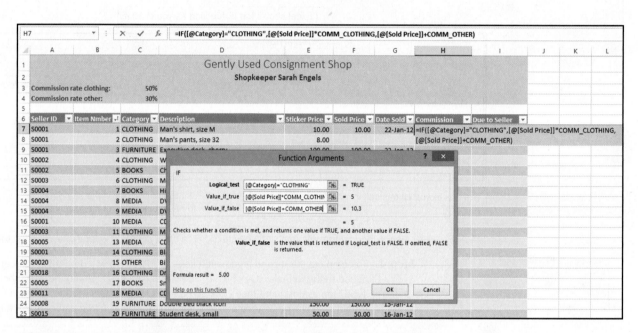

FIGURE 11-14 You can use the Function Arguments dialog box to build the IF function.

The Sales worksheet is completed. Because of the amount of data we're tracking, it's easier to organize the data if we put some of it on other worksheets.

Using Multiple Worksheets

Next let's explore how to manage multiple worksheets. As we do, you'll also learn to use two more functions: the CONCATENATE function and the SUMIF function.

Objective 11.6: Manage Multiple Worksheets in a Workbook

Notice on the Sales worksheet that the seller is identified by a Seller ID. We must track other information about the seller, including the seller name, address, and phone number. It's awkward to repeat that information in each row of the Sales worksheet. Seller information is kept on the Sellers worksheet, and we can use the Seller ID to find this seller information.

WATCH

OBJECTIVE 11.6 VIDEO

ON YOUR OWN 11.8

Build the Sellers Worksheet

WATCH

▶

OBJECTIVE 11.6
VIDEO

Create the ConsignmentShop Workbook: Part 8 of 11

When this activity is completed, the Sellers worksheet should look like that in Figure 11-15.

| Uses the Title cell style | The drop-down arrows indicate the data is formatted as a table | Two columns formatted as phone numbers |

| A1 | ▾ | × ✓ fx | =Sales!A1 |

	A	B	C	D	E	F	G	H	I	J	K	L	M
1	Gently Used Consignment Shop												
2	Seller Information												
3													
4	Seller ID	Last Name	First Name	Address	City	State	Zip	Home Phone	Cell Phone				
5	S0001	Adams	Sandy	100 Apple Lane	Smithville	OH	33000	(555) 666-0001	(555) 444-1111				
6	S0002	Martinez	Maria	5 Cherry Street, Apt 12	Applewood	OH	50000	(555) 666-5555	(555) 444-1000				
7	S0003	Smith	Larry	409 James St	Anywhere	OH	50000	(555) 666-4444	(555) 444-2222				
8	S0004	Jackson	Louie	400 Maryville Hwy	Knoxburg	OH	50000	(555) 777-1111	(555) 777-1112				
9	S0005	Payton	EC	3002 Physicans Lane	Terryville	OH	55500	(555) 777-9999	(555) 888-5555				
10	S0006	Danville	Jeb	407 Brookstone Lane	Sixville	OH	55500	(555) 777-3390	(555) 777-3392				
11	S0007	Cherolis	Ramie	309 Listenton	Healthcare	OH	44444	(555) 333-5555	(555) 333-5555				
12	S0009	Smith	Jebidiah	10 Terry Lane	Roseville	OH	44444	(555) 333-3333	(333) 444-3333				
13	S0010	Dirtburg	Jane	20 Jackson St	Pearville	OH	44444	(555) 333-5343	(333) 999-3333				
14	S0011	Candler	Betty	300 Mary Street	Smalltown	OH	33333	(555) 222-2222	(555) 222-1222				
15	S0012	Andrews	Shirley	309 Kinder St	Bigville	OH	44444	(555) 333-5553	(555) 333-2333				
16	S0013	Victorious	Steven	898 Iris Hwy	Santa Fe	OH	55555	(555) 999-3333	(555) 777-9798				

◄ ► Sales **Sellers** ⊕

FIGURE 11-15   The Sellers worksheet tracks information about each seller.

Do the following:

Step 1. Create a second worksheet and name it **Sellers**. To practice using a cell on one worksheet on a different worksheet, use cell A1 on the Sales worksheet to put the company name in cell A1 on the Sellers worksheet. Enter the subtitle in cell A2 and format the two titles, as indicated in Figure 11-15.

> **Hint** When you need to refer to a cell address on a different worksheet, enter the name of the worksheet followed by the exclamation symbol (!) and then the cell address, for example, **=Sales!A1**. You can also use the clicking method: Type = in a cell and then go to another worksheet, click the cell you want, and press **Enter**. Excel inserts the sheet name, exclamation point, and cell address or name in the formula.

Step 2. Open the Word document **SellerInfoTable** in the sample_files folder on the www.pearsonhighered.com/jump website and in MyITLab. Copy and paste the column headings and data in the Word table into the Sellers worksheet, beginning with cell A4. Use the Paste option that matches the destination formatting.

Step 3. Convert the seller information to a table using the **Table Style Medium 3**.

Step 4. Format columns H and I as phone numbers.

Step 5. Use **AutoFit Column Width** to adjust column widths as necessary.

Step 6. Name the table **SellerInfo**. Save your work.

Solutions Appendix

For help: See *On Your Own 11.8* Step-by-Step Solution

WATCH

OBJECTIVE 11.7
VIDEO

Objective 11.7: Use the CONCATENATE Function to Manage Text

The Sellers worksheet can be more useful if we create columns used for a mailing address. You can use the **CONCATENATE function** to build a three-line mailing address for each seller. The CONCATENATE function can have as many parts as you need. Each part is a cell that contains text or text enclosed in quotation marks. Figure 11-16 shows an example of the function.

> **CONCATENATE function**—A function that joins text together into one cell. The word "concatenate" means to connect items together in a chain.

FIGURE 11-16   Use the CONCATENATE function to join text together into a cell.

ON YOUR OWN 11.9

Add Mailing Address Columns to the Sellers Worksheet

WATCH

OBJECTIVE 11.7
VIDEO

Create the ConsignmentShop Workbook: Part 9 of 11

Let's add three new columns, Address1, Address2, and Address3, which can be used when the shop owner needs to mail something to a seller. When the activity is finished, the Sellers worksheet should look like that in Figure 11-17.

	A	B	C	D	E	F	G	H	I	J	K	L	M
1	Gently Used Consignment Shop												
2	Seller Information												
3													
4	Seller ID	Last Name	First Name	Address	City	State	Zip	Home Phone	Cell Phone	Address1	Address2	Address3	
5	S0001	Adams	Sandy	100 Apple Lane	Smithville	OH	33000	(555) 666-0001	(555) 444-1111	Sandy Adams	100 Apple Lane	Smithville, OH 33000	
6	S0002	Martinez	Maria	5 Cherry Street, Apt 12	Applewood	OH	50000	(555) 666-5555	(555) 444-1000	Maria Martinez	5 Cherry Street, Apt 12	Applewood, OH 50000	
7	S0003	Smith	Larry	409 James St	Anywhere	OH	50000	(555) 666-4444	(555) 444-2222	Larry Smith	409 James St	Anywhere, OH 50000	
8	S0004	Jackson	Louie	400 Maryville Hwy	Knoxburg	OH	50000	(555) 777-1111	(555) 777-1112	Louie Jackson	400 Maryville Hwy	Knoxburg, OH 50000	
9	S0005	Payton	EC	3002 Physicans Lane	Terryville	OH	55500	(555) 777-9999	(555) 888-5555	EC Payton	3002 Physicans Lane	Terryville, OH 55500	
10	S0006	Danville	Jeb	407 Brookstone Lane	Sixville	OH	55500	(555) 777-3390	(555) 777-3392	Jeb Danville	407 Brookstone Lane	Sixville, OH 55500	
11	S0007	Cherolis	Ramie	309 Listenton	Healthcare	OH	44444	(555) 333-5555	(555) 333-5555	Ramie Cherolis	309 Listenton	Healthcare, OH 44444	
12	S0008	Smith	Jehidiah	10 Terry Lane	Roseville	OH	44444	(555) 333-3333	(333) 444-3333	Jehidiah Smith	10 Terry Lane	Roseville, OH 44444	

FIGURE 11-17   The Address1 and Address 3 columns use the CONCATENATE function with data from other columns in the table.

To add the three new columns, do the following:

Step 1. On the Sellers worksheet, add three columns J, K, and L to the SellerInfo table. Make the column headings **Address1**, **Address2**, and **Address3**.

Step 2. In the Address1 column (column J), use the **CONCATENATE** function to join together the First Name column and the Last Name column to create the seller's full name. Don't forget the space between the first and last names.

Step 3. In the Address2 column (column K), use a formula to cause the same data in the **Address** column (column D) to display in column K. Don't copy the text from column D into column K; rather, use a formula so that changing a street address in column D automatically changes the same street address in column K.

Step 4. In the Address3 column (column L), use the **CONCATENATE** function to join together the **City** column, **State** column, and **Zip** column to create the city, state, and zip mailing address line. Don't forget the spaces and comma needed in the address line.

> **Not Working?** If you're having problems with typing the CONCATENATE function in a cell, try using the Insert Function command on the FUNCTION ribbon. In the Insert Function dialog box, don't forget to include the comma and spaces between city, state, and zip.

Step 5. Adjust column widths so all data can be read. Save your work. The Sellers sheet is finished.

Solutions Appendix

For help: See *On Your Own 11.9* Step-by-Step Solution

WATCH

OBJECTIVE 11.8
VIDEO

Objective 11.8: Use the SUMIF Function to Calculate Sums

The third worksheet is the Month Summary worksheet, which holds summary data for the month using data taken from the Sales worksheet. The Month Summary worksheet with summary information added is shown in Figure 11-18.

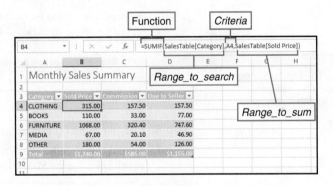

FIGURE 11-18 Summary information for the month is created using data from the Sales worksheet.

The summary calculations for each category are made using the SUMIF function. The **SUMIF function** has three arguments:

SUMIF (*range_to_search, criteria, range_to_sum*)

> **SUMIF function**—A function that searches a range of cells. If a cell meets the criteria given, a corresponding cell in the range to sum is added to the sum.

In Figure 11-18, the formula in cell B4 uses the SUMIF function to total the sold price for the "CLOTHING" category. The three arguments of the function are

> *Range-to-search:* The Category column of the SalesTable.
> *Criteria:* Cell A4 on the Month Summary worksheet. Cell A4 contains the text "CLOTHING." Therefore, the SUMIF function searches the Category column in the SalesTable for the text "CLOTHING."
> *Range_to_sum:* The Sold Price column in the SalesTable. If "CLOTHING" is found in the Category column, the value in the Sold Price column is added to the sum.

You're now ready to build the formulas for the monthly summary information.

Calculate Sales Totals for One Month

WATCH

OBJECTIVE 11.8
VIDEO

Use the Title cell style

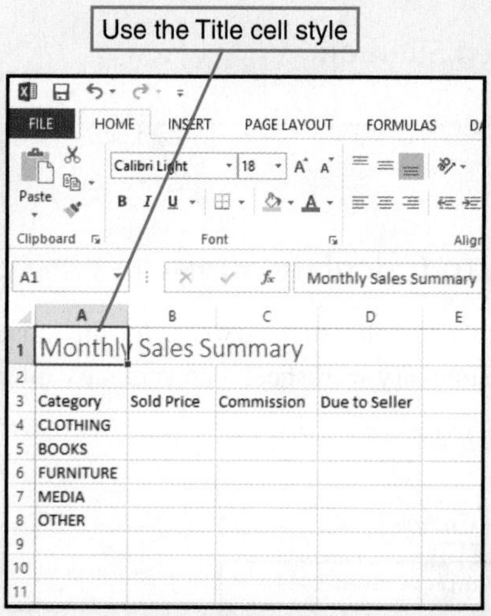

FIGURE 11-19 The Month Summary
worksheet has the title, column
headings, and first column entered.

Create the ConsignmentShop Workbook: Part 10 of 11

Do the following to start the Month Summary worksheet with titles and labels:

Step 1. Create a third worksheet named **Month Summary**. Enter the title in cell A1 and format it, as shown in Figure 11-19.

Step 2. Enter the column headings in row 3 and text in column A, as shown in Figure 11-19.

You're now ready to enter SUMIF functions in columns B, C, and D to sum the Sold Price, Commission, and Due to Seller amounts for each category.

Do the following to complete the worksheet:

Step 3. Go to cell B4 and enter the SUMIF function either by using the FORMULAS ribbon or by typing the formula directly in the cell. Use this information for the three arguments of the function:

Range to search:	SalesTable[Category]
Criteria:	A4
Range to sum:	SalesTable[Sold Price]

Step 4. Copy the formula down the column through cell B8.

Step 5. To sum Commission for each Category, use this information to create a formula in cell C4 using the SUMIF function:

Range to search:	SalesTable[Category]
Criteria:	A4
Range to sum:	SalesTable[Commission]

Step 6. Copy the formula in cell C4 down through cell C8.

Step 7. To sum Due to Seller for each Category, use this information to create a formula in cell D4 using the SUMIF function:

Range to search:	SalesTable[Category]
Criteria:	A4
Range to sum:	SalesTable[Due to Seller]

Step 8. Copy the formula in cell D4 down through cell D8.

Not Working? Values in columns C and D on your Month Summary worksheet depend on the calculations already entered in columns H and I on the Sales worksheet. If you see incorrect values on the Month Summary worksheet, go back to your Sales worksheet and check the calculations there. Then recheck your formulas on the Month Summary worksheet.

Step 9. Convert the data to a table using the **Table Style Medium 12**. Add a Total row at the bottom of the table. Add sums to the total row and format these cells, as shown earlier in Figure 11-18.

The summary calculations on the Month Summary worksheet should match up with totals and subtotals on the Sales worksheet. Do the following to spot-check the totals:

Step 10. Use filtering to find out the Sold Price for the OTHER category on the Sales worksheet. Does this value match the Sold Price for the OTHER category on the Month Summary worksheet? What is this value?

Step 11. Use filtering to find out the Due to Seller for the FURNITURE category on the Sales worksheet. Does this value match the Due to Seller for the FURNITURE category on the Month Summary worksheet? What is this value?

> **Tip** *Comparing values created by different calculations in a workbook is an excellent practice to help you know you haven't made mistakes in the formulas.*

Solutions Appendix

For help: See *On Your Own 11.10* Step-by-Step Solution

Enhancing Worksheets with Charts and Macros

Next let's look at how to add charts to a worksheet and explore the benefits of using Excel *macros*.

Objective 11.9: Insert and Format a Chart on a Worksheet

A chart is a quick and easy way to view data. Charts can help you make sense of data or analyze the data. Excel offers several types of charts, including a **pie chart**, **line chart**, and **column chart**.

> **pie chart**—A chart or graph that shows the parts of a whole.
>
> **line chart**—A chart or graph that shows trends over time.
>
> **column chart**—A chart or graph with vertical columns that is best used to compare values and can also show trends over time. Use it to quickly find the largest and smallest values.

The three types of charts are shown in Figure 11-20. The column chart or pie chart makes it easy to compare commissions for each category. A line chart is not as useful for this purpose.

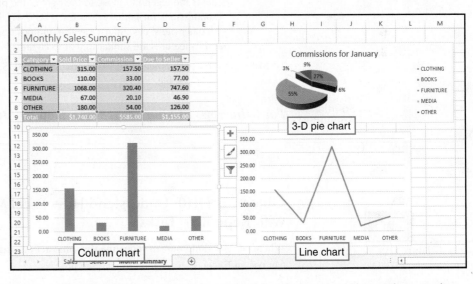

FIGURE 11-20 Excel offers a variety of chart types. Select the type that helps you best visualize the data.

To insert a chart in a worksheet, first select the data used to build the chart and then select a chart type on the INSERT ribbon. Excel automatically adds a chart title, labels, and a **legend** to the chart. You can then edit all these chart elements.

> **legend**—A list that tells you what each column or slice in a chart represents.

ON YOUR OWN 11.11

Insert a Chart in the Month Summary Worksheet

Create the ConsignmentShop Workbook: Part 11 of 11

When this activity is completed, the Month Summary worksheet should look like that in Figure 11-21.

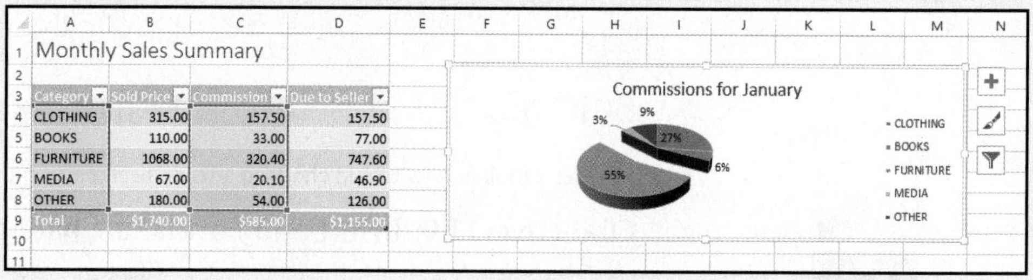

	A	B	C	D
1	Monthly Sales Summary			
2				
3	Category	Sold Price	Commission	Due to Seller
4	CLOTHING	315.00	157.50	157.50
5	BOOKS	110.00	33.00	77.00
6	FURNITURE	1068.00	320.40	747.60
7	MEDIA	67.00	20.10	46.90
8	OTHER	180.00	54.00	126.00
9	Total	$1,740.00	$585.00	$1,155.00

Commissions for January — CLOTHING, BOOKS, FURNITURE, MEDIA, OTHER (9%, 3%, 27%, 6%, 55%)

FIGURE 11-21 A pie chart shows the breakdown by category that accounts for January commissions.

Do the following:

Step 1. Go to the Month Summary worksheet and select the Category and Commission data. Insert a **3-D Pie** chart using that data. Move and resize the chart container box, as shown in Figure 11-21.

> **Hint** To select nonadjacent cells, hold down the **Ctrl** key as you press and drag.

Step 2. Using the **Quick Layout** button on the DESIGN ribbon, apply **Layout 6**, which causes the legend to move to the right of the pie chart. Change the chart title to **Commissions for January**. Move the FURNITURE slice outward to set it apart from the other pie slices. Adjust the size and position of the pie as necessary so your chart and its features are similar to that in Figure 11-21.

Step 3. The ConsignmentShop workbook is finished. Save your work and close the workbook file.

Solutions Appendix

For help: See *On Your Own 11.11* Step-by-Step Solution

Objective 11.10: Understand How Excel Macros Can Help with Repetitive Tasks

Whenever you find yourself repeating the same actions many times in a worksheet, know that you can use an Excel **macro** to automate the process.

> **macro**—A program embedded in a Word document, Excel workbook, or Access database that can perform instructions or steps that the programmer has previously recorded.

For example, look back at the Sellers worksheet in Figure 11-15. You used a formula to copy the company name from cell A1 on the Sales worksheet to cell A1 on the Sellers worksheet. If you needed to put the company name in many places on a workbook, you would find yourself repeating the same steps over and over. A macro can help.

ON YOUR OWN 11.12

Record and Use a Macro

WATCH

OBJECTIVE 11.10
VIDEO

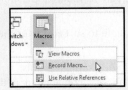

To create a macro to write titles or other text on a worksheet, do the following:

Step 1. Open a new blank workbook. On the VIEW ribbon, click the down arrow under Macros click **Use Relative References**. The macros you record now work anywhere on a worksheet. To start recording a macro, click the down arrow under Macros and then click **Record Macro**. Enter a name for the macro, assign the macro a shortcut key, and click **OK**.

Step 2. Use three cells to type your name and address on the worksheet. Then stop recording the macro.

> **Tip** To learn more about recording and using macros, search Excel Help using the search string **creating and running macros**. The link in Excel Help leads you to a video about macros that you can watch on the Office.microsoft.com website.

Step 3. Move to a new cell on the worksheet. Test your new macro using the Macros button on the VIEW ribbon and also using the shortcut key to the macro.

Solutions
Appendix

For help: See *On Your Own 11.12* Step-by-Step Solution

Unless you specify otherwise, Excel uses the Visual Basic programming language to record each step in a macro. You can edit or write a macro using **Visual Basic for Applications (VBA)** . To learn more about writing macros and using VBA, consider taking an advanced course about Excel.

> **Visual Basic for Applications (VBA)**—A programming language embedded within Office applications used to write short programs to enhance the application. VBA is a subset of the Visual Basic programming language. Visual Basic is a standalone language and more powerful than VBA.

Summary

Using a Table to Manage Data

> To cause a title, label, or heading to span multiple columns, use the Merge & Center command on the HOME ribbon. All cells in the range are merged into a single cell, and text is centered in that cell.

> Freezing rows or columns used for titles and headings can make it easier to identify the data on a large worksheet. These frozen rows and columns stay in view as you scroll through a large worksheet.

> An Excel table makes it easier to filter and sort data and to create formulas and summary information about the data.

> Use the drop-down menus in the column heading row of a table to sort and filter the data in the table.

> The Filter icon appears in the column heading cell when a filter is applied to this column. Rows that aren't included in the filter are hidden. The Sort icon appears in the column heading cell when this column is used for sorting the data in the table.

> You can insert a total row at the bottom of the table and then insert a summary function into that row.

> Functions available in the total row of a table include Sum, Count, Average, Max, and Min. These functions are produced using the versatile SUBTOTAL function. This function can ignore values in hidden cells.

> Excel automatically assigns column headings and column names to a table and a table name. You can manually assign a name to a cell or range of cells or change the default name of a table. Using names in formulas is easier than using absolute cell addresses.

> The IF function is used to check a condition. If the condition is met, one value is returned. If the condition is not met, another value is returned.

Using Multiple Worksheets

> Multiple worksheets are useful when organizing a large amount of data. Give each worksheet used a name that describes the purpose of the worksheet.

> When writing a formula on one worksheet, you can identify a cell on another worksheet by preceding the cell address with its worksheet name and an exclamation point, for example, Sheet2!C4.

> The CONCATENATE function joins text together into one cell. This text can be enclosed in quotation marks, or the function can refer to cells that contain text.

> The SUMIF function has three parts or arguments: a range to search, criteria, and a range to sum. The function searches the range of cells. If a cell meets the criteria given, a corresponding cell in a range to sum is added to the sum.

Enhancing Worksheets with Charts and Macros

> Excel offers several types of charts used to visually represent data, including the pie chart, line chart, and column chart. Use the type chart that best represents the way you want to interpret the data.

> A pie chart shows the parts of a whole. A line chart shows trends over time. A column chart compares values and can show trends over time.

> Use the INSERT ribbon to insert a chart on a worksheet. After the chart is inserted, you can edit items in the chart container box.

> An Excel macro is a program embedded in an Excel workbook that can perform instructions that the programmer has previously recorded.

> A macro is best used to perform a task that the developer or user of the workbook does repetitively.

CHAPTER MASTERY PROJECT

Now it's time to find out how well you've mastered the content in this chapter. If you can do all the steps in this Mastery Project without looking back at the chapter details and can answer all the Review Questions following this project, you've mastered this chapter. If you can complete the project by finding answers using the Excel Help window or the web, you've proven that you can teach yourself how to use Excel.

> **Hint** Several Excel functions are used in this mastery project or in the review questions. If you encounter a function you don't know about, such as SUMIF, enter the function name in the Excel Help search box.

If you find you need a lot of help doing the project and you have not yet read the chapter or done the activities, go back and start at the beginning of the chapter, watch the videos, review the step-by-step solutions as you work through the On Your Own activities, and then return to this project.

In this Mastery Project, you create the worksheets used by Adams Hardware to manage inventory purchases. The first worksheet is shown in Figure 11-22, and the second worksheet is shown in Figure 11-23.

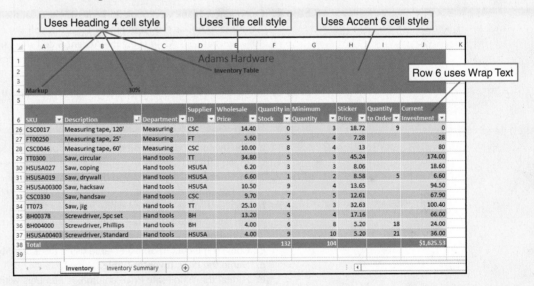

FIGURE 11-22   The Inventory worksheet tracks items in inventory and when it is time to order more items.

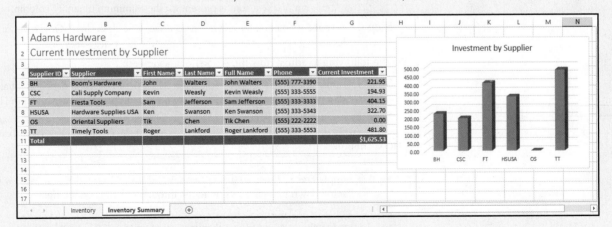

FIGURE 11-23   The Inventory Summary worksheet shows investments by supplier.

To make it easier for you to build the worksheets, here are the formulas you'll need, listed in no particular order:

=IF([Quantity in Stock]<[Minimum Quantity],[Minimum Quantity]*3-[Quantity in Stock]," ")

=Inventory!A1

=CONCATENATE(C5," ",D5)

=[Wholesale Price]*(MARKUP+100%)

=[Wholesale Price]*[Quantity in Stock]

=SUMIF(InventoryTable[Supplier ID],A5,InventoryTable[Current Investment])

> **Tip** If you need help completing this part of the mastery project, review the "Using a Table to Manage Data" section in the chapter.

On the Inventory worksheet for Adams Hardware shown in Figure 11-22, each type of stock item is assigned a SKU. Each supplier is assigned a Supplier ID.

> **Tip** SKU stands for stock-keeping unit. The SKU uniquely identifies a type of item in stock.

Do the following to enter titles, column headings, and data in the first worksheet:

Step 1. Open a new blank workbook and enter the text for the title, subtitle, and label in cells A1, A2, and A4, as shown in Figure 11-22. In cell B4, enter the markup value, which is 30%. Format cells A1:J4 using the **Accent 6** cell style and then format A1, A2, A4, and B4, as shown in the figure. Use the **Merge & Center** command to center the titles in the first two rows.

Step 2. Name this first worksheet **Inventory**. Cell B4 contains the percentage markup. Name the cell **MARKUP**.

Step 3. Follow these steps to create the InventoryTable:

   a. The inventory data is stored in a Word document named **HardwareInventoryTable** in the sample_files folder on the www.pearsonhighered.com/jump website and in MyITLab. (In Chapter 2, you downloaded the folder to your USB flash drive.) Locate and open the document.

   b. Copy and paste the entire table, including the data and column headings, from the file into the worksheet beginning with cell A6. When you paste the data into the worksheet, match the destination formatting.

   c. Convert the data to an Excel table using the **Table Style Medium 14**.

   d. Name the table **InventoryTable**.

   e. Format the Wholesale Price column as numbers with two decimal places.

   f. Add a total row to the table. In this row, add a sum for the Quantity in Stock column. Verify a sum is present for the Minimum Quantity column.

Step 4. Save the workbook file to your hard drive, USB flash drive, OneDrive, or another location given by your instructor. Name the file **HardwareStore**.

Do the following to adjust how the worksheet is viewed:

Step 5. Apply text wrap to row 6. Adjust the column widths so all data and labels on the worksheet can be viewed and text in row 6 wraps to two lines, as shown in Figure 11-22.

> **Hint** To wrap long text in a cell to multiple lines, select the cells and click **Wrap Text** on the HOME ribbon.

Step 6. Apply **Freeze Panes** so that column A and rows 1 through 6 stay in view when you scroll down through rows or across through columns on the right.

> **Hint** To freeze column A and rows 1 through 6, first go to cell B7 and then freeze panes.

Do the following to work with the table data:

Step 7. Add a new row to the table using this data:

Column	Data
SKU	HSUSA00403
Description	Screwdriver, Standard
Department	Hand tools
Supplier ID	HSUSA
Wholesale Price	4.00
Quantity in Stock	9
Minimum Quantity	10

Step 8. Sort the rows in the table alphabetically by the Description column. Filter the data so that only **Hand tools** display. Then remove the filter on the data so that all rows display.

Step 9. Do the following to add three new columns for calculations to the table:

a. Add column H to the table. Name the new column heading **Sticker Price**. Enter a formula in this column that calculates the sticker price. The calculated value is the **Wholesale Price** multiplied by the **MARKUP** plus **100%**. Be sure to use the column heading name Wholesale Price and the cell name MARKUP in the formula. Format the column as numbers with two decimal places.

> **Tip** When data is converted to an Excel table, the column headings of the table can be used in formulas to refer to that column.

b. Add column I to the table, which determines if new stock should be ordered. Name the column heading **Quantity to Order**. Use the IF function in the formula to calculate Quantity to Order. Use these three arguments for the IF function:

Logical_test:	Quantity in Stock is less than the Minimum Quantity.
Value_if_true:	Quantity to Order is three times the Minimum Quantity less the Quantity in Stock.
Value_if_false:	Enter a space in the cell.

c. Verify the formula is correct by checking row 37. Quantity in Stock is 9. Minimum Quantity is 10. Therefore, the Quantity to Order is 10*3−9=21. Cell I37 should display the value 21.

d. Add column J to the table, which calculates money invested in current stock. Name the column heading **Current Investment**. Enter the formula in the column for the calculation. The Current Investment is the **Wholesale Price** times the **Quantity in Stock**. Format the column using a number with two decimal places.

Step 10. Add a sum in the total row for Current Investment. Format this sum using **Currency**, 2 decimal places. Adjust column widths as needed so you can view the headings and data. Save your work.

> **Tip** If you need help completing this part of the mastery project, review the "Using Multiple Worksheets" section in the chapter.

The owner of Adams Hardware wants to know how much he has invested in inventory for each supplier. That information is shown in the Inventory Summary worksheet (see Figure 11-23).

Do the following to create the Inventory Summary worksheet:

Step 11. Create a second sheet and name it **Inventory Summary**. Put the company name in cell A1. To do so, enter a formula in cell A1 to copy cell **A1** on the Inventory worksheet to this worksheet. In cell A2, enter the subtitle, as shown in Figure 11-23. Format cells A1 and A2 using the Title cell style.

Step 12. Do the following to create the SuppliersTable on the worksheet:

    a. Open the Word document file **HardwareSuppliersTable** in the sample_files folder on the www.pearsonhighered.com/jump website, in MyITLab, or on your USB flash drive.

    b. Copy the entire table into the Inventory Summary worksheet beginning with cell A4. Be sure to match destination formatting.

    c. Format the data as a table using the **Table Style Medium 13**.

    d. Format the Phone column as phone numbers.

    e. In the Full Name column, enter a formula that uses the CONCATENATE function to string together the First Name and Last Name. Don't forget the space between the two names.

    f. Name the table **SuppliersTable**.

Step 13. Add a new column to the table, column G, naming the column heading **Current Investment**. Use the SUMIF function to enter a formula in the column to calculate the current investment. The SUMIF function has three arguments listed below. Format column G as numbers with two decimal places.

Range_to_search:	The Supplier ID column in the InventoryTable
Criteria:	Cell A5, which identifies the supplier
Range_to_sum:	The Current Investment column in the InventoryTable

Step 14. Add a total row to the table and format the total for column G as currency with two decimal places. Adjust column widths as necessary and don't forget to save your work.

> **Tip** If you need help completing this part of the mastery project, review the "Enhancing Worksheets with Charts and Macros" section in the chapter.

Do the following to insert a chart in the Inventory Summary worksheet:

Step 15. Select the data in column A and column G, not including the total row. Using that data, insert a column chart in the worksheet. Select an upright **3-D Clustered Column** chart, as shown earlier in Figure 11-23. Reposition and resize the chart container box as shown in the figure. Change the chart title to **Investment by Supplier**. Save your work.

Review Questions

Answer these questions to assess your skills and knowledge of the content covered in the chapter. Your instructor can provide you with the correct answers when you're ready to check your work.

1. What command on the HOME ribbon can you use to cause a heading to span two columns on a worksheet?

2. What command on the VIEW ribbon can you use to cause the first three rows of a worksheet to display as you scroll down through a long list of rows?

3. What are the four main advantages for using an Excel table to manage data?

4. Data in a table can be sorted or filtered using drop-down menus for the data. What button do you click to see one of these drop-down menus?

5. When entering data in a table, why would you select the data from a drop-down list of data items in the table rather than typing in the data?

6. What are two ways you can tell whether data in a table has been filtered or hidden?

7. How do you add a total row to a table?

8. What Excel function is used to insert a sum, average, count, or other summary information in a total row of a table?

9. What can you do to see a list of all names applied to cells or ranges of cells in a workbook?

10. Suppose cell A1 contains this formula: =IF(C3=D5,E10,F7). What value is displayed in cell A1 if cell C3 contains 25 and cell D5 contains 26?

11. When creating a formula on Sheet1, suppose you need to use cell A5 on Sheet3. How do you write this cell in the formula?

12. What is the main advantage of naming a cell?

13. When a cell in a table is selected, which ribbon can you use to view the name of the table?

14. Suppose cell A15 contains this formula: =CONCATENATE(E1,E2). Cell E1 contains "Fat." Cell E2 contains "Cat." What text displays in cell A15?

15. In question 14, what CONCATENATE formula is needed so that a space displays between the two words in cell A15?

16. Which type chart (pie, line, or column) is *not* appropriate to show your weight gain or loss over one month?

17. Would a line chart be useful to represent the data in column C when column C lists the parts of a whole? Explain your answer.

18. Which type chart is best to use to identify high and low values in a column of data?

19. What is the purpose of an Excel macro and why would you use one?

20. Which programming language does Excel use to build most macros?

Answer the following questions about the HardwareStore workbook you built in the Mastery Project:

21. With no filters applied (all rows in the table are visible), what is the total number Quantity in Stock? What is the total number of Hand tools in stock?

22. What is the formula that Excel inserted into the total row in cell G11 on the Inventory Summary worksheet to calculate the sum?

23. This formula contains the function argument 109. What is the purpose of the 109 function number? What would happen if the value 109 were changed to 9?

24. What is the grand total for current investments?

Becoming an Independent Learner

The most important skill learned in this chapter is how to teach yourself a computer skill. Rate yourself at Level A through E on how well you're doing with this skill. What is your level?

> Level A: I was able to successfully complete the Chapter Mastery Project with the help of only a few of the On Your Own activities in the chapter.

> Level B: I completed all the On Your Own activities and the Chapter Mastery Project without referring to any of the solutions in the Step-by-Step Solutions Appendix.

> Level C: I completed all the On Your Own activities and the Chapter Mastery Project by using just a few of the solutions in the Step-by-Step Solutions Appendix.

> Level D: I completed all the On Your Own activities and the Chapter Mastery Project by using many of the solutions in the Step-by-Step Solutions Appendix.

> Level E: I completed all the On Your Own activities and the Chapter Mastery Project and had to use all the solutions in the Step-by-Step Solutions Appendix.

To continue toward the goal of teaching yourself computer skills, if you're not at Level A, try to move up one level on how you learn in Chapter 12.

Projects to Help You

Now that you've mastered the material in this chapter, you're ready to tackle the three projects focused on your career, personal, or academic goals. Depending on your own interests, you might choose to complete any or all of these projects to help you achieve your goals.

Project 1: Using Excel in Your Professional Career

A great way to get an introduction to programming and to Visual Basic for Applications (VBA) is to record and use Excel macros. Do the following to find out about and create Excel macros:

Step 1. Open your browser and go to **office.com/training**. In the search box, enter **Excel macro**. A list of videos about Excel appears.

Step 2. Scroll down the list and click the link **Save time by creating and running macros in Excel 2010**.

Step 3. Creating and running macros in Excel 2013 works the same as in Excel 2010. Watch the four short videos about macros and answer the following questions:
 a. List the steps to display the DEVELOPER ribbon on the Excel window.
 b. Which button on the DEVELOPER ribbon do you click to record steps in a macro?
 c. What programming language does Excel use to record the steps in a macro?

Step 4. Using Excel, open a blank workbook. Create a macro to type **Gently Used Consignment Shop** in any cell on the worksheet and format the cell using the **Title** cell style. What is the name you assigned the macro? Run the macro to test it.

Step 5. Create a second macro to type and format the consignment shop name and shopkeeper name Sarah Engels on two rows of a worksheet. Name the macro **ShopOwner**. Run the macro to test it.

Step 6. View the list of macros. Select the **ShopOwner** macro and click **Edit** to see the code that Excel created for the macro. The code appears in a programming window where it can be edited. What is the name of the programming window?

Career Project I want to take my knowledge of Excel a step further and learn to record and use a macro. Can I create a macro without using a programming language? Will Excel write the program for me?

Project 2: Using Excel in Your Personal Life

Teaching yourself a computer skill requires exploring on your own and trying new things. Building on the skills you learned in the chapter and exploring on your own, do the following to enhance the HardwareStore workbook created in the Chapter Mastery Project:

Step 1. To dress up the Inventory worksheet, insert a photo on the worksheet appropriate for a hardware store. How did you insert the photo?

Step 2. On the Inventory worksheet, insert a Page Break after row 20, causing later rows to print on a new page. How did you insert the Page Break?

Step 3. Use buttons in the status bar to display the Inventory worksheet in **Page Layout** view and **Page Break Preview**. Then return to **Normal** view. How many pages will it take to print the worksheet? What must happen to frozen panes before you can use Page Layout View?

Personal Project I need to build an Excel worksheet that uses conditional formatting. I also want to dress up my worksheets with clip art, and I need to adjust print settings to make large worksheets easier to read when they're printed.

Academic Project My instructor has asked me to help her grade some worksheets. She specifically wants me to check for errors using tables and formulas in these tables. What types of errors do students typically make in these cases?

Project 3: Using Excel in Your Academic Career

Your instructor has asked for your help in checking some worksheets created by other students. Open the **Student01_ConsignmentShop** workbook file in the sample_files folder on the www.pearsonhighered.com/jump website and in MyITLab. Compare this student's work to the ConsignmentShop workbook you created in the chapter. The Sales worksheet has two errors; the Sellers worksheet has four errors, and the Month Summary worksheet has two errors.

Use these hints to help you find the errors:

1. Students often have problems with the Merge & Center command. Search for titles in the wrong columns or columns that are not merged.

2. A common mistake when using the IF function is to put the last two arguments for the function in the wrong order. To view the formulas on a worksheet so you can check for errors, click **Show Formulas** on the FORMULAS ribbon.

3. Make sure formulas are used rather than simply typing text or values into cells.

4. To verify that data is formatted as a table, look for the drop-down arrows in the column heading row of the table.

5. Search for missing columns in tables.

6. Check for errors with spaces when using the CONCATENATE function.

7. Check for misspelled words used in titles, labels, and column headings.

8. Check that currency, decimal places, and numbers are formatted correctly.

Project to Help Others

One of the best ways to learn is to teach someone else. And, in teaching someone else, you're making a contribution in that person's life. As part of each chapter's work, you're encouraged to teach someone a skill you've learned. In this chapter, help someone learn to use Excel.

Working with your apprentice, do the following:

Step 1. Show your apprentice the worksheets you created in this chapter. Explain how a table is created and used to track data. Also show her the formulas you used in the worksheet and how you inserted a chart in the worksheet.

Step 2. If your apprentice is interested in building her own worksheet, help her design and create a worksheet of her choosing.

Step 3. Use Word to create a file that contains your answers to the following questions about the tutoring session. Name the file **Chapter 11 Tutoring** and send the file to your instructor. If you're using MyITLab, you can post the file in a Dropbox assignment or email the file in MyITLab. On the other hand, your instructor might prefer you post the file to your OneDrive or email the file using your school email. Here are the questions:

1. Who is your apprentice?

2. What new skills using Excel did you help your apprentice learn?

3. Describe the topic, calculations, data, formatting, and other features your apprentice used when building her own workbook.

4. How do you think the tutoring session went? How would you like to improve it next time?

12 Connecting to the Internet and Securing a Computer

In This Chapter, You Will:

Connect a Computer to the Internet

12.1 Survey types of wired and wireless network connections to the Internet

12.2 Connect a computer to a wired or wireless network

12.3 Manage wired and wireless connection settings

Secure a Computer and Its Data

12.4 Secure a computer and its data using the three most important security practices

12.5 Back up important data

12.6 Set up a standard user account and manage passwords

Secure a Small Home Network

12.7 Secure a wireless network

12.8 Use a homegroup to share your data and printer

In previous chapters, you relied on a working computer that is already connected to the Internet. In this and the next two chapters of the book, you'll learn to take care of a computer and its Internet connection, fix a computer problem, and buy your own computer. In this chapter, you'll learn how to connect to the Internet and fix the connection when it stops working. You'll also learn how to secure your computer so your computer and its data stay safe.

As with all chapters in this book, you can choose which of the learning paths below best suits your needs. No matter which path you choose, as you work your way through the chapter, remember the most important computer skill is how to teach yourself a computer skill. Therefore, this chapter is designed to help you teach yourself how to make an Internet connection and secure your computer.

LEARNING PATHS

GUIDED LEARNING	EXPLORE AND DISCOVER	JUMP RIGHT IN
Read the Chapter *Watch the Objective Videos*	**On Your Own Projects** *Review Objective videos or use Step-by-Step Solutions*	**Mastery Project** *Use Objective videos & OYO projects for help*
On Your Own Projects *Review Objective videos or use Step-by-Step Solutions*	**Mastery Project** *Use Objective videos & OYO projects for help*	**Explore Resources** *For help as needed*
Mastery Project *Use Objective videos & OYO projects for help*		
Google Project (if applicable) *Watch Google video for help*	**Google Project (if applicable)** *Watch Google video for help*	**Google Project (if applicable)** *Watch Google video for help*
Helping You & Others Projects	**Helping You & Others Projects**	**Helping You & Others Projects**
MyITLab Assessment	**MyITLab Assessment**	**MyITLab Assessment**

Connecting a Computer to the Internet

Let's start by looking at the types of connections used to connect a computer to the Internet and how to make these connections.

WATCH

OBJECTIVE 12.1
VIDEO

Objective 12.1: Survey Types of Wired and Wireless Network Connections to the Internet

When a single computer connects to the Internet, it can connect directly to a **wide area network (WAN)** , or it can connect by way of a **local area network (LAN)** . Regardless of which is used, a computer always connects to the Internet by way of an **Internet service provider (ISP)** that stands between it and the Internet. Popular ISPs include AT&T, Comcast, Time Warner Cable, Verizon, and Charter. Figure 12-1 shows five types of technologies that can be used for a single computer to connect to an ISP over a WAN.

> **wide area network (WAN)**—A network that covers a large area. WANs are used to connect networks together, such as when several businesses or homes connect to the Internet.
> **local area network (LAN)**—A small network of computers and other connected devices covering a small area, such as a home, business, school, or airport.
> **Internet service provider (ISP)**—An organization that offers access to the Internet for a fee. Most often, an ISP offers email as part of the subscription service.

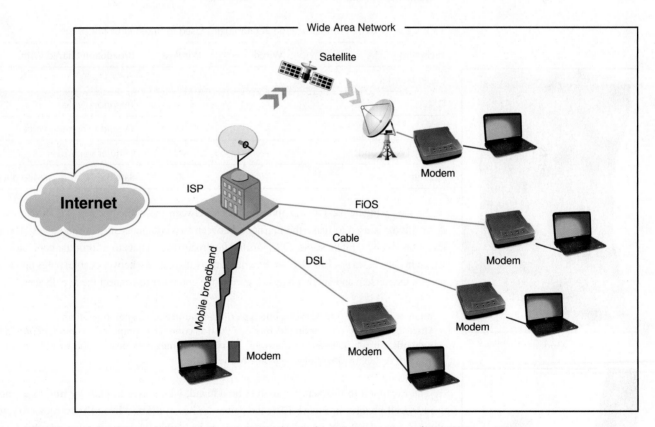

FIGURE 12-1   An ISP stands between the Internet and a single computer connected to a WAN.

Wired and Wireless WAN Connections to an ISP

As you can see from Figure 12-1, the five types of technologies used to connect to an ISP are **cable Internet**, **DSL**, **FiOS**, **mobile broadband**, and **satellite Internet**.

> **cable Internet**—A type of Internet access that uses TV cable lines and shares these lines with TV.
> **DSL (digital subscriber line)**—A type of Internet access that uses regular copper telephone lines and shares these lines with voice.
> **FiOS (fiber-optic service)**—A type of Internet access that uses fiber-optic cable all the way from an ISP to a home or business.
> **mobile broadband**—A type of Internet access that uses the same cellular network as do cell phones. Also called mobile Internet or cellular.
> **satellite Internet**—A type of Internet access that uses a satellite dish and satellite service. The technology is used in rural areas where the faster cable Internet, DSL, FiOS, or mobile broadband service is not available.

All these technologies are **broadband** technologies, and Table 12-1 lists the type of broadband shared with each technology. To use any of the transmission services provided by an ISP, you must subscribe to its service. For example, Comcast, Charter, and Time Warner Cable offer cable Internet, whereas AT&T, Comcast, Verizon, and Sprint offer mobile broadband.

> **broadband**—A technology where two types of transmissions share the same media. For example, cable Internet and TV share the same cable lines.

TABLE 12-1 WAN Communication Technologies Used for Internet Connections

Technology	Wired	Wireless	Broadband Shared With
Cable Internet	✓	—	TV cable
DSL	✓	—	Telephone voice
FiOS	✓	—	TV and telephone voice
Mobile broadband	—	✓	Cellular voice
Satellite Internet	—	✓	Satellite TV and satellite phone

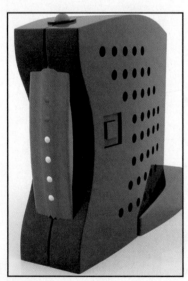

Modem

Notice in Figure 12-1 that a modem stands between the computer and the WAN connection. A **modem** is used to make the transition between two communication technologies. The modem translates satellite, FiOS, cable, DSL, or mobile broadband signals to a form the computer can use, which in most cases is **Ethernet**. An Ethernet cable (also called a network cable) plugs into a network port on the modem and another network port on the computer to connect the two devices.

> **modem**—A device that converts one type of communication signal to another.
> **Ethernet**—A wired networking technology used to connect a computer to a modem or to a local network. Currently, Ethernet transmits at 100 Mbps (megabits per second or million bits per second) or 1,000 Mbps (called gigabit Ethernet).

The exception to this setup is mobile broadband, which uses a **cellular network**, normally used by cell phones. In Figure 12-1, the computer has a **mobile broadband modem**, which is plugged into a USB port on the computer or is embedded in the computer. Later in the chapter, we discuss mobile broadband in more detail.

Mobile broadband modem

> **cellular network**—A wireless network made available by towers and first used by cell phones. Each tower covers the area around it, which is called a cell.
> **mobile broadband modem**—A device that connects a computer or local network to a cellular network. The modem might be portable or stationary. It might connect to a computer using USB, Bluetooth, or another type connection or be embedded in the computer. It goes by many names, including cell card, wireless Internet card, laptop connect card, USB broadband modem, and AirCard.

Wired and Wireless Connections in a LAN

Looking back at Figure 12-1, you see that only a single computer connects to a modem and on to the Internet. If several computers in a school, business, or home need to share an Internet connection, these computers are connected together in a LAN, and the LAN then connects to the Internet (see Figure 12-2).

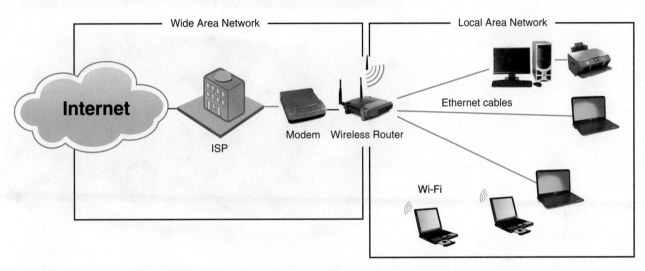

FIGURE 12-2   A local network is necessary to connect several computers to the Internet when using a single connection to an ISP.

Connections to the LAN can be wired (using network ports and Ethernet cables) or wireless (using **Wi-Fi**). Computers on the local network can share resources such as a printer, a scanner, or data. Looking at Figure 12-2, you can see a **router** is used to connect the LAN to the modem. (The modem can be a cable Internet, DSL, FiOS, or satellite Internet modem.) A wireless router that might be used in a small office or home is shown in Figure 12-3.

Wi-Fi—Wireless standards used for local networks. The latest Wi-Fi standard is called long-range Wi-Fi, wireless N, or 802.11n and has a range up to 1,400 feet and transmits at 300 Mbps. The previous standard is called 802.11g and has a range up to 300 feet and transmits at 54 Mbps.
router—A device used to connect one network to another. A small office or home router allows several wired or wireless computers to connect in a local network. It also connects this network to the Internet.

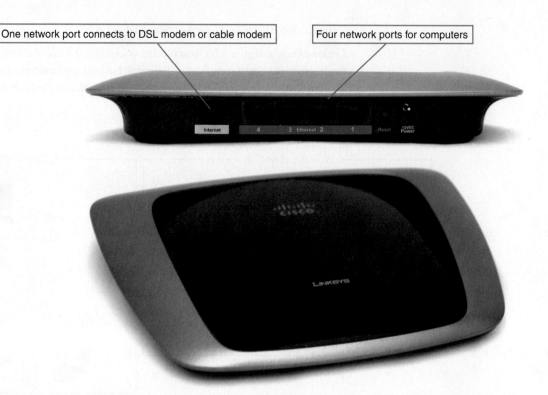

One network port connects to DSL modem or cable modem

Four network ports for computers

FIGURE 12-3   This wireless router designed for a home network connects wireless computers and up to four wired computers in a network.

For a small office or home, a router is a multifunction device that can

> Connect the local network to the ISP, which provides Internet access.
> Tie together the computers in the local network. Network ports on the router can be used to connect computers using network cables.
> Serve as a **wireless access point** to provide a **hot spot** for computers that use Wi-Fi to connect wirelessly to the LAN.

> **wireless access point**—A device that allows a wireless computer, printer, or other device to connect to a network.
> **hot spot**—An area within range of a Wi-Fi wireless access point that provides access to a local network. Hot spots can be used at home, in a park, in an office building, or in a restaurant.

> Serve as a **firewall** to protect the computers on the LAN.
> Include an embedded modem. Some routers are also a cable modem or DSL modem and can connect directly to the cable line or DSL phone line. A **modem router combo** is popular for home use when only two or three computers need to connect to the Internet.

> **firewall**—Software or hardware that blocks uninvited network traffic into a network or computer to keep the network or computer safe. A small office or home router can serve as a hardware firewall to protect the LAN, and Windows has a built-in software firewall to protect the computer.
> **modem router combo**—A multifunctional device that is a modem (converts cable Internet or DSL to Ethernet), a router (ties the local network to the WAN and the ISP), and a wireless access point (creates a Wi-Fi hot spot).

If wireless computers in your home connect to the Internet using Wi-Fi and you have only a single device providing the connection to cable Internet, DSL, FiOS, or satellite Internet, that device is a modem router combo, and you have a wireless LAN in your home. Some mobile broadband devices are also a modem router combo device. Let's explore the several possibilities.

Mobile Broadband Connections

For mobile broadband connections, your ISP is also your cell phone company, and it's possible to connect one or several computers to the Internet using mobile broadband. The data service provided over the cellular network might use the **3G**, **4G**, or **4G LTE** standard for data transfers.

> **3G**—An older set of standards (third generation) used for data transfers over a cellular network.
> **4G**—The latest set of standards used for data transfers over a cellular network. 4G networks have a range large enough to cover an entire city. 4G is expected to replace cable Internet and DSL as a way to wirelessly connect a computer or small network to the Internet.
> **4G LTE**—The latest 4G standard used by Verizon, AT&T, Sprint, and other carriers that is faster than regular 4G.

Some laptop computers come with the ability to access mobile broadband built in. If the technology isn't built into your laptop, you can use an external mobile broadband device. Figure 12-4 shows four external devices that can be used for mobile broadband connections. To use any of these devices, you must subscribe to a data plan with the cell phone company:

(a) Cell phone tethered to the computer

(c) Wi-Fi portable broadband modem

(b) Portable mobile broadband modem

(d) Stationary mobile broadband modem

FIGURE 12-4   These four external devices allow a computer to use mobile broadband.

> **Cell phone tethering.** If your cell phone can handle data and has a data port, you can connect it to your laptop (see Figure 12-4a). The phone is said to be tethered to the laptop and serves as the middleman between the cellular network and laptop. The connection uses a

USB cable. If your cell phone and computer both use **Bluetooth** , the cable isn't needed. Your cell phone company might require a separate data plan for Internet tethering, and you might need to install an app on your cell phone and/or software on your computer.

> **Bluetooth**—A wireless technology with a short range that is used to connect personal wireless devices to a computer, for example, to connect a cell phone, wireless keyboard, or wireless printer.

> **Portable mobile broadband modem.** Plug the mobile broadband modem into your computer to connect it to the cellular network (see Figure 12-4b). To use the device, you must subscribe to a data service with a carrier that supports the device.

> **Wi-Fi portable broadband modem.** The modem uses a battery and is small enough to hold in your hand (see Figure 12-4c). It connects to the cellular network and creates a portable hot spot (sometimes called pocket Wi-Fi) that can be used by several Wi-Fi computers. The modem serves as a modem router combo to create a small LAN where connected computers can share resources.

> **Stationary mobile broadband modem.** This type of modem plugs into an electrical outlet and is used to connect a local network to a cellular network (see Figure 12-4d). The computers on the LAN can connect using Wi-Fi or network cables. Mobile broadband used with this modem router combo device can replace cable Internet, DSL, or FiOS for a small office or home.

Now that you know a little about the technologies used, let's explore how to make the different types of connections.

Objective 12.2: Connect a Computer to a Wired or Wireless Network

WATCH

OBJECTIVE 12.2
VIDEO

When connecting to a wired network, connect the network cable to the network port on the computer and to the network device. Some computers have one or two lights near the network port to indicate network activity (see Figure 12-5). If the lights aren't on, check the cable connections at both ends. A steady light indicates connectivity. When Windows detects connectivity, it automatically sets up the wired connection. A blinking light indicates network activity.

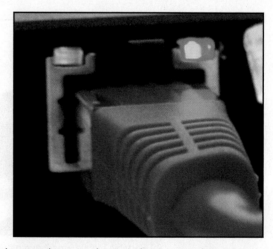

FIGURE 12-5   The lights near the network port indicate network activity.

To view your current network connections in Windows, open the Settings charm. Figure 12-6 shows the icons for wired and wireless networks.

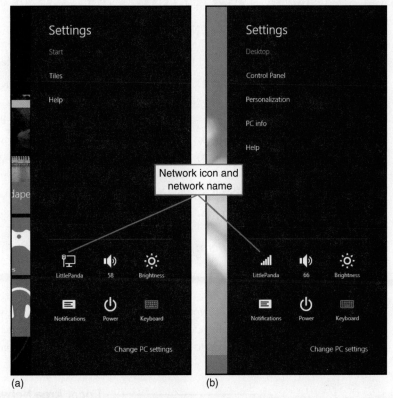

FIGURE 12-6   Network icons for a computer with (a) a wired connection and (b) a wireless connection.

Click the network icon, and the Networks pane appears. Figure 12-7 shows the Networks pane for a computer that has both wired and wireless connections. The device providing both connections is a wireless router named LittlePanda, and on this screen you can turn on or off Wi-Fi.

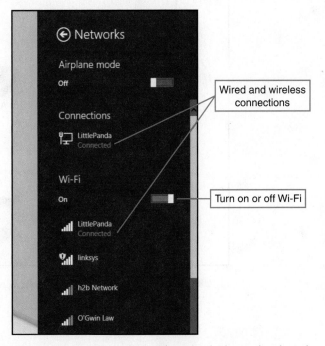

FIGURE 12-7   The Networks pane shows the computer has both wired and wireless connections.

ON YOUR OWN 12.1

Verify Your Wired Network Connection

WATCH

OBJECTIVE 12.2
VIDEO

You can do this activity if your computer is connected to a wired network. Do the following:

Step 1. If your computer has wireless capability, open the Networks pane and turn off Wi-Fi.

Step 2. Find the network port on your computer. Does the port have indicator lights nearby? If so, what is the status of these lights? If necessary, plug in the network cable.

Step 3. Open the Networks pane. Does Windows report a wired connection?

Step 4. Unplug the network cable. What is the status of the network indicator lights? What is the status of connections in the Networks pane?

Step 5. Plug in the network cable and verify that Internet access has been restored.

Step 6. If your computer has wireless capability, open the Networks pane and turn on Wi-Fi.

Solutions Appendix

For help: See On Your Own 12.1 Step-by-Step Solution

Suppose you want to use the free Wi-Fi service at your local coffee shop to connect your laptop to the Internet. The coffee shop uses a wireless access point to provide this hot spot. The access point connects to the coffee shop's local network and on to the Internet (see Figure 12-8).

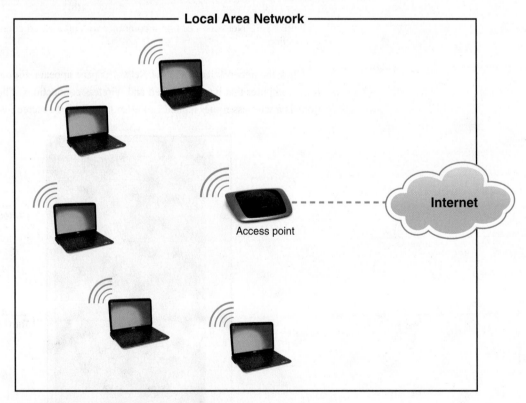

FIGURE 12-8   A coffee shop offers a public wireless hot spot.

ON YOUR OWN 12.2

WATCH

**OBJECTIVE 12.2
VIDEO**

Connect to a Wireless Hot Spot

You can do this activity if you have a wireless computer inside a wireless hot spot. Do the following to connect the wireless computer to a wireless network and on to the Internet:

Step 1. If the computer has a wireless switch, turn it on. Use the Settings charm to open the Networks pane and verify that Wi-Fi is turned on. Return to the Start screen.

Step 2. When wireless networks are available, the network icon in the Settings charm has a star and is labeled Available (see Figure 12-9a). Click the icon to see a list of available wireless networks (see Figure 12-9b). Click one of these networks to select it and then click **Connect**.

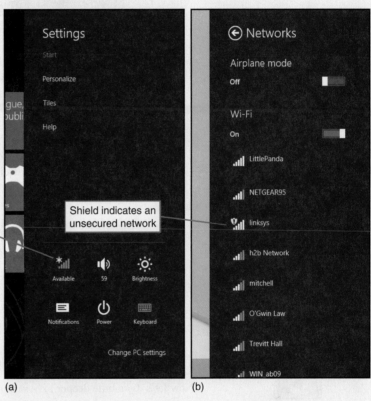

FIGURE 12-9   (a) Click the network icon to see available networks; (b) several wireless networks are available.

Step 3. If the wireless network is secured, you must enter a password, called the *network security key*, to use the network and then click **Next** (see Figure 12-10a). If the network is not secured, no password is required.

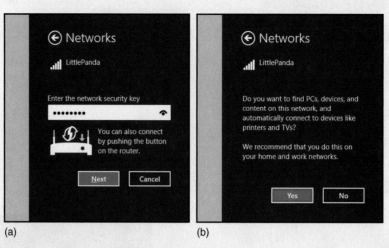

FIGURE 12-10   (a) When connecting to a secured wireless network, you must enter the security key or password. (b) For a public network, don't share your resources with others on the network.

Step 4.   When you first connect to a secured wireless network, the pane shown in Figure 12-10b appears, asking whether you want to share resources with other computers on the network. Click **Yes** if you're using a private network (for example, at home or work). Click **No** if you are using a public network (for example, at a coffee shop).

Step 5.   After you complete the connection, open **Internet Explorer** and try to surf the web. Some public hot spots require you to agree to the terms of use. If so, a web page appears when you first open Internet Explorer. You must agree to the terms before you can use the network.

> **Not Working?** If Internet Explorer can't display a web page, repeat steps 2 through 5. Other tips for solving a network problem are covered later in this chapter and the next.

Solutions Appendix

For help: See *On Your Own 12.2* Step-by-Step Solution

WATCH

OBJECTIVE 12.3
VIDEO

Objective 12.3: Manage Wired and Wireless Connection Settings

Now let's dig a little deeper in how to manage network connections and fix network problems.

Secure a Network Connection

Without using advanced sharing tools, Windows offers two basic choices for sharing resources on a network:

> **Share resources on a private network.** When you share your resources, other computers on the network can see you, and you can join a **homegroup** or a **Windows domain** . Use this setting when you want to share files or a printer with other computers in a small local network or when you're connected to a corporate or business network managed by a network administrator. A computer that has only a wired Ethernet connection automatically uses this setting.

> **homegroup**—A Windows feature that allows you to share data and other resources with other computers on a local network.
> **Windows domain**—A Windows feature used by large corporations to manage the computers, data, and other resources on the corporate network.

Tip *Computer technicians have many Windows advanced sharing tools available to them to precisely control which resources a computer may share on a network. These tools are not covered in this book.*

> **Don't share resources on a public network.** Other computers on the network can't see you because Windows sets up a strong firewall to protect you. You can't join a homegroup or Windows domain. Always use this setting when you're connected to any public network, for example, at a hotel or coffee shop.

If you're signed on to Windows using an administrator account and you're using a wireless computer, you can change the setting. Go to the Settings charm and click **Change PC settings**. On the PC settings screen, click **Network**. The Network screen appears (see Figure 12-11). Click a connection to see information about the connection and to change the sharing setting.

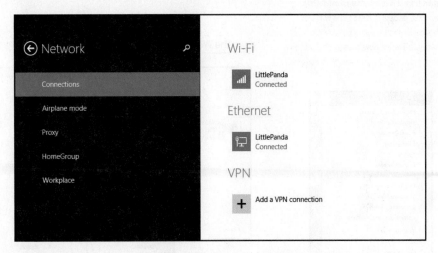

FIGURE 12-11   Use the Network screen to manage your network connections.

Not Working? *Windows remembers the last page you were on when you last left the PC settings screens and returns you to this page when you click **Change PC settings** on the Settings charm. You might need to press the back button to find the PC settings screen you need.*

For example, when you click the Wi-Fi connection, the screen in Figure 12-12 appears. *Find devices and content* is turned on in the figure. When you change the setting for either connection, it applies to both connections.

Not Working? *The Find devices and content setting will not be visible on a computer that is not wireless or when you are signed in to Windows using a standard user account.*

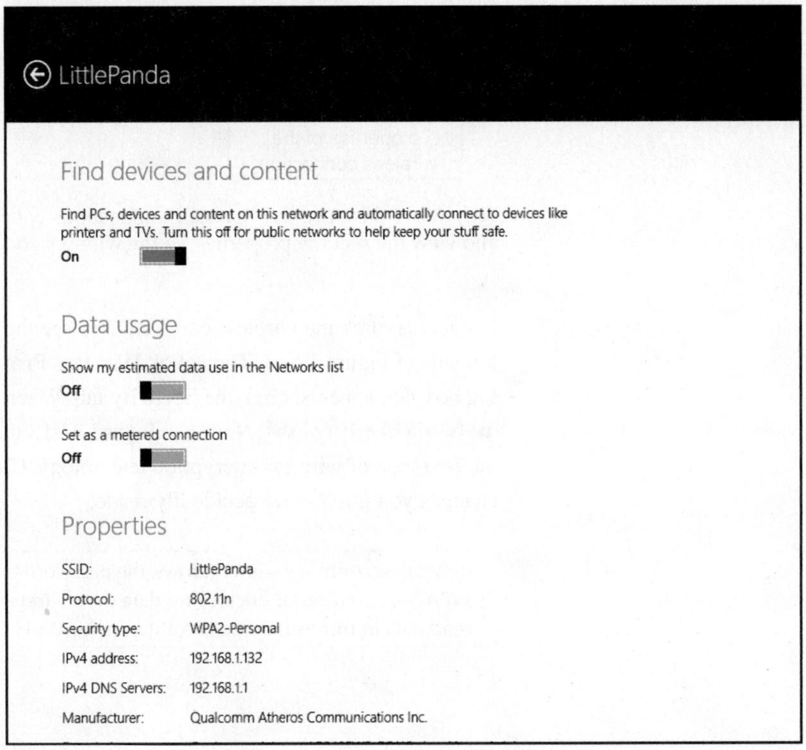

FIGURE 12-12   Decide whether you will share your computer's resources on the network.

View Wireless Security Settings

If a wireless network is secured, you must enter a password to the network the first time you connect. To find this password after a connection is made, press **Win+X** (hold down the Windows key and press X). The **Quick Link menu** appears. Click **Network Connections**. The Network Connections window opens (see the top of Figure 12-13).

> **Quick Link menu**—A menu that gives access to many Windows utilities and tools. To see the menu, press **Win+X**. Alternately, you can right-click the Start button on the Windows desktop.

Tip Never turn on sharing unless the wireless hot spot is secured with a password. Even if the hot spot is in your own home, if it's not secured with a password, people outside the walls of your house might be using it. Later in the chapter, you'll learn how to secure your own wireless network so a password is required.

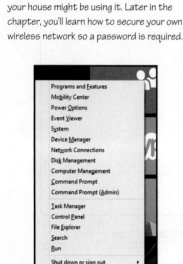

Quick Link menu

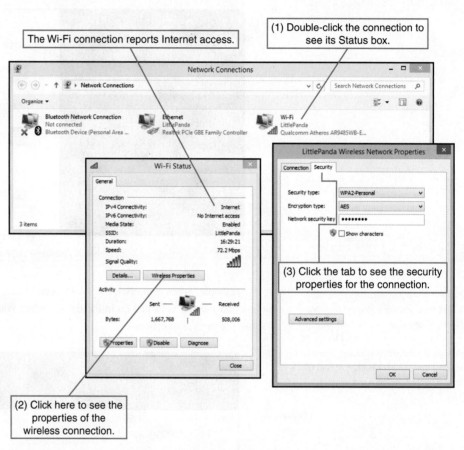

FIGURE 12-13   Use the Network Connections window to view the status of a network connection and view the security properties for the wireless connection.

Double-click the wireless connection to see the Wi-Fi Status dialog box shown on the bottom-left side of Figure 12-13. Then click **Wireless Properties**. In the Wireless Network Properties dialog box that appears, click the **Security** tab. When you check **Show characters**, you can read the network security key . Notice in Figure 12-13 that WPA2-Personal is used. WPA2 is currently the best type of wireless encryption technology. Click **Cancel** to close the box without saving any changes you might have accidently made.

> **network security key**—In Windows, the password to a wireless network. Also called the security key. **WPA2**—A method of encrypting data on a wireless network so that hackers can't intercept and read data in transmission. WPA2 stands for Wi-Fi Protected Access, Version 2.

Diagnose and Solve Problems with Network Connections

You can also use the Network Connections window to solve problems with a network connection. A problem is indicated by a red X, as shown in Figure 12-14. Click a connection to select it and then click **Diagnose this connection**. The Windows Network Diagnostics utility launches, as shown in the bottom window in Figure 12-14. If it cannot solve the problem, it makes suggestions as to what to try next.

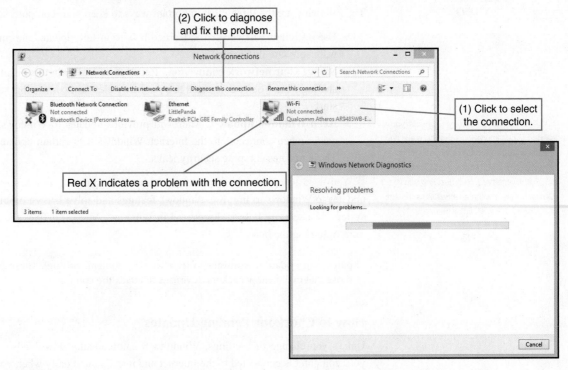

FIGURE 12-14   Use the Network Connections window to solve problems with network connections.

Examine Network Connections and Settings

WATCH

▶

OBJECTIVE 12.3 VIDEO

Let's take a look at your computer's network connections and settings and fix any problems you see:

Step 1. Use the network icon on the Settings charm to open the Networks pane. Does your computer have a wired or wireless connection or both types of connections?

Step 2. Open the **PC settings** screen and go to the Network screen. Click a network connection. Is the *Find devices and content* option visible? If so, is Windows set to share resources on the network?

Step 3. Open the Network Connections window. If the window reports a problem with a connection, troubleshoot the problem.

Step 4. If you are using a wireless network, open the Wireless Network Properties dialog box. Is the connection secured with a password? What type of security encryption is used?

Solutions Appendix

For help: See *On Your Own 12.3* Step-by-Step Solution

Securing a Computer and Its Data

Next let's explore how to use several methods to secure a computer and its data.

WATCH

OBJECTIVE 12.4
VIDEO

Objective 12.4: Secure a Computer and Its Data Using the Three Most Important Security Practices

As you learned in Chapter 2, the Internet is a dangerous place where viruses and thieves abound. The following are the three most important ways to keep your computer and its data safe:

> **Use antivirus software.** You learned how to install, update, and run antivirus and antispyware software in Chapter 2.
> **Secure your network connection.** Recall from earlier in this chapter that you can turn off sharing when you're connected to a public wireless network so that strangers cannot see your stuff.
> **Keep Windows updated.** Microsoft provides updates to Windows, which a computer receives when connected to the Internet. Windows tags certain updates as important updates. These updates can plug security leaks.

You need to make sure Windows updates are current on your computer. Microsoft releases updates to Windows to improve Windows features and solve known problems with the operating system. If a security hole is discovered in Windows, Microsoft fixes the problem and releases a **patch** to plug the hole.

Tip *Other ways to stay safe that you've learned about in previous chapters are to use strong passwords for all your online accounts, be careful to buy or download only from websites you trust, and use caution when opening an email attachment or clicking a link in an email message.*

> **patch**—An update to software to fix a known problem (or bug). These problems can include those that might allow hackers or viruses to attack the computer.

How to Check for Pending Updates

Unless you change the settings, Windows 8 automatically downloads important updates when your computer is connected to the Internet and installs them daily when you're not using the computer. (The default time of day to do this maintenance is 2:00 AM.) Sometimes an update requires the computer to restart.

To find out what's going on with these updates, open the Settings charm and click **Change PC settings**. On the PC settings page, click **Update and recovery**. On the Update and recovery page, click **Windows Update**. Figure 12-15 shows two situations. In Figure 12-15b, notice you can immediately install pending updates by restarting the computer.

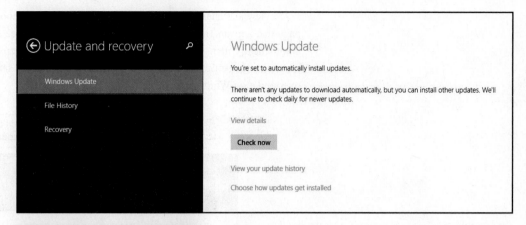

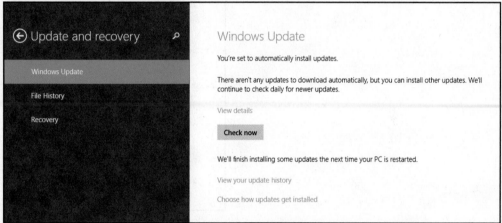

FIGURE 12-15   (a) You can check for new updates or (b) restart the computer to immediately install pending updates.

Click **View details** to see a list of optional updates. To install an optional update, check it and click **Install**, as shown in Figure 12-16.

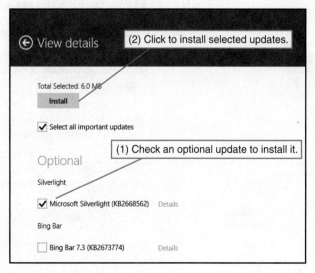

FIGURE 12-16   Select and install optional updates.

To view and change how updates get installed, click **Choose how updates get installed**. In the page that appears, make your changes and click **Apply** (see Figure 12-17). To allow Windows to automatically manage updates for Windows and other Microsoft products (such as Office 2013), make sure the settings are as shown in Figure 12-17. These settings give Windows the most control over updating Windows.

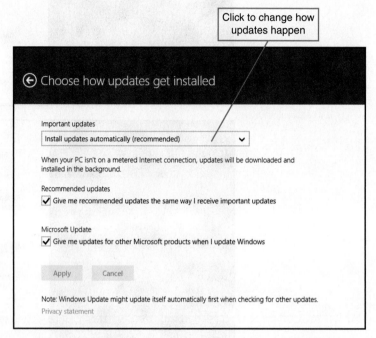

FIGURE 12-17   You can manage updates for Windows and other Microsoft products.

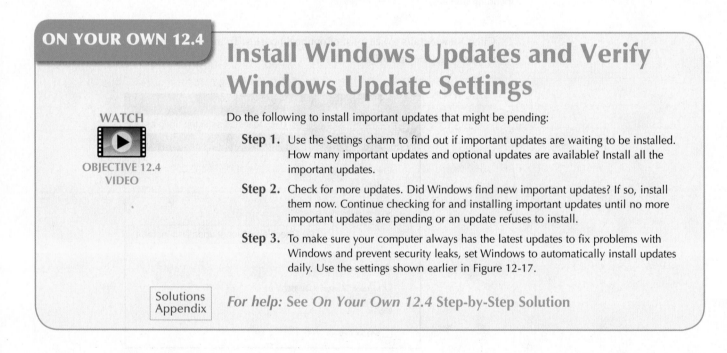

ON YOUR OWN 12.4

Install Windows Updates and Verify Windows Update Settings

WATCH

OBJECTIVE 12.4
VIDEO

Do the following to install important updates that might be pending:

Step 1. Use the Settings charm to find out if important updates are waiting to be installed. How many important updates and optional updates are available? Install all the important updates.

Step 2. Check for more updates. Did Windows find new important updates? If so, install them now. Continue checking for and installing important updates until no more important updates are pending or an update refuses to install.

Step 3. To make sure your computer always has the latest updates to fix problems with Windows and prevent security leaks, set Windows to automatically install updates daily. Use the settings shown earlier in Figure 12-17.

Solutions
Appendix

For help: See *On Your Own 12.4* Step-by-Step Solution

WATCH

OBJECTIVE 12.5
VIDEO

Objective 12.5: Back Up Important Data

Many of us keep important data on our computers, so it makes sense to be prepared in case the data is accidentally deleted or changed, the computer is lost or stolen, or the data get corrupted. One way of being prepared is to keep at least two copies of important data and to store this **backup** of your data on a different storage device than the original data.

> **backup**—An extra copy of a data file stored on a different storage device or in the cloud.

The following are four ways you can maintain a backup of your data:

> **Tip** When deciding what data you want to back up, think about what it would be like to lose those photos, videos, Internet Explorer favorites, email addresses, tax records, or other important documents stored on your computer. If you can't get along without it, back it up.

> **Use an online backup service.** When you use an online backup service, whenever you connect your computer to the Internet, the service automatically syncs your data files with copies it keeps in the cloud. You pay for the monthly or yearly subscription. Examples of websites that provide reliable online backup services are Mozy.com, Carbonite.com, and Idrive.com. An online backup service is the most reliable and most expensive backup method.

> **Keep your data in the cloud.** You can keep all your data on cloud-computing sites rather than on your local computer. Some sites that offer free storage are Dropbox.com, Google Drive at Google.com, and OneDrive at Live.com. These sites all keep good backups of data trusted to them.

> **Use Windows File History.** Windows **File History** is a Windows feature that backs up files on your hard drive to a different storage media (such as an external hard drive).

> **File History**—A Windows feature that can automatically make backups of files on your hard drive and store these backups on a different storage media. It can also keep multiple versions of a file.

> **Manually make copies of the data files on your computer.** This method requires you remember to copy the data to a second media (such as an external hard drive or USB flash drive) or to a cloud-computing site on a regular basis.

File History

File History backs up your Internet Explorer favorites and all the files on your desktop and in your libraries (Documents, Music, Pictures, and Videos). You can keep the backups on an external hard drive, a USB flash drive, or a drive on the local network.

For the most control over File History, open the File History window on the desktop. To do that, press **Win+X** and click **Control Panel**. The **Control Panel** window opens on the desktop (see Figure 12-18). The Control Panel gives you access to many Windows tools and settings.

> **Control Panel**—A window used to adjust computer settings. To open the window, press **Win+X** and click **Control Panel** in the Quick Link menu that appears.

Click to open the
File History window

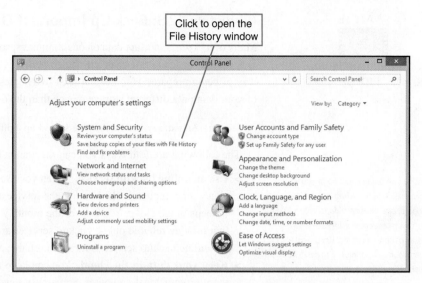

FIGURE 12-18   The Control Panel gives you access to many Windows utilities and allows you to change Windows settings.

Tip To limit the storage space needed for File History to keep its backups, consider not backing up your Videos and Music libraries. To exclude these libraries from the backup, click **Exclude folders** in the File History window.

To open the File History window, click **Save backup copies of your files with File History** in the System and Security group of Control Panel (refer to Figure 12-18). Figure 12-19 shows a File History window that recognizes a drive to hold the backups. When you click **Turn on**, Windows asks if you want to make the drive available to other computers in the homegroup. If you click **Yes**, those computers can use File History to back up to the drive connected to this computer.

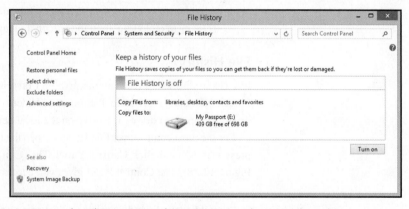

FIGURE 12-19   Use the File History window to turn on and manage the utility.

ON YOUR OWN 12.5

Use Windows File History

Not Working? During this activity, you must write to the hard drive. If your lab computer prevents you from writing to the hard drive, you can't do the activity.

WATCH

▶

OBJECTIVE 12.5 VIDEO

Let's set up File History and use it to restore a file:

Step 1.   Put a document file in your Documents library on the hard drive. For example, you can create a text file in the Documents library or copy the PeaceCorpsPaper document you created in Chapter 5 into the library.

Step 2.   Plug a USB flash drive into your computer. Open File History and turn it on to use the USB flash drive for backups. The backup happens every hour, and you can back up at any time by clicking **Run now** in the File History window. Run the backup now.

Step 3. Make a change to the document and run the backup again. Make a second change to the document and run the backup a third time. Then delete the document from the Documents library.

Step 4. Use the File History window to restore the last version of the file to the Documents folder. Now restore the original version of the file to the Documents folder.

Step 5. Use File Explorer to drill down into the backups of the Documents library on your USB flash drive. What is the name of the folder on your USB flash drive that holds all the backups made by File History? How many versions of the backed-up document are on your flash drive?

> **Tip** When you restore a file or folder using the File History window, the backup overwrites the original. To keep from losing the original, make a copy of it first before you restore it from backup. If the backup is not what you expected, you can return to the original.

Solutions Appendix   *For help: See On Your Own 12.5 Step-by-Step Solution*

WATCH

OBJECTIVE 12.6
VIDEO

Objective 12.6: Set Up a Standard User Account and Manage Passwords

Recall from Chapter 2 that an administrator user account in Windows has more rights than does a standard user account. When you're responsible for a computer, you need an administrator account to install or uninstall software, change Windows settings, and perform other administrative tasks.

If other people use your computer, you can set up a standard user account for each user. Each user then has his or her own libraries to hold data and can set all user preferences the way he or she likes. And the limited rights on the standard user account prevent other users from making changes to the computer that you don't know about or don't approve.

ON YOUR OWN 12.6

Create a Standard User Account

WATCH

OBJECTIVE 12.6
VIDEO

Use the PC settings page, which you access from the Settings charm, to create standard user accounts.

Let's get started:

Step 1. Make sure you're signed in to Windows using an administrator account.

Step 2. Using the Settings charm, set up a standard user account named **Mattie**. Make the account a local account and not a Microsoft account. Make the password to the account **Matt1E**.

Step 3. Sign in to Windows using the Mattie account. Verify you can view the contents of Mattie's Documents library. Find out whether the Mattie account can be used to create a user account. What link is missing on the Accounts page when you're signed in to Windows using the Mattie account?

Solutions Appendix   *For help: See On Your Own 12.6 Step-by-Step Solution*

ON YOUR OWN 12.7

Manage Windows Passwords

WATCH

OBJECTIVE 12.6
VIDEO

To keep other users from logging on using your account, be sure to assign a strong password to your administrator account. To be safe, you need to occasionally change this password. In addition, a user might forget her password. If this happens and you're responsible for the computer, you can reset her password.

You can change your own password from the PC settings page, but you must use tools in the Control Panel to reset another user's password. In Control Panel, click User Accounts and Family Safety to see the window shown in Figure 12-20.

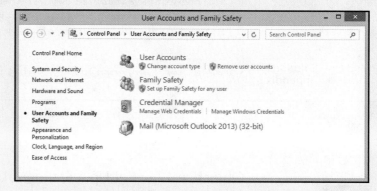

FIGURE 12-20   You can use tools in the Control Panel to manage user accounts other than your own.

Do the following:

Step 1. Sign in to your Windows account and change your password. Recall that a strong password contains upper- and lowercase letters and numbers.

Step 2. Suppose Mattie changed her password and you don't know it. She calls you to say she has forgotten her password. Reset the password to **changeme**. When you tell Mattie the new password, remind her to change it to a stronger password when she first signs in.

> Tip When working in a computer lab, your instructor might want you to delete the Mattie user account when you're done with it. If so, you can delete the account now. In Control Panel, click **User Accounts and Family Safety** and click **Remove user accounts**. Click the account to select it and click **Delete the account**. Then follow directions on screen.

Solutions
Appendix

For help: See *On Your Own 12.7* Step-by-Step Solution

Securing a Small Home Network

Next let's look at how to secure a wireless home network and share data and a printer with other computers in your home.

WATCH

OBJECTIVE 12.7
VIDEO

Objective 12.7: Secure a Wireless Network

If you have Internet access in your home, most likely you're using cable Internet or DSL to connect to the Internet. More than one wireless computer in your home might share this Internet connection.

> **Hint** How to buy the equipment and set up a home network are not covered in this chapter because there are so many situations and options to cover. Begin by subscribing to an Internet service (for example, cable Internet, DSL, or mobile broadband). When you subscribe to the service, the ISP sells you the right equipment and helps you set it up. After you have one computer connected to the Internet, it's time to set up your home network. You can begin the process by buying a wireless home router. Projects at the end of this chapter can help you get started with setting up your home network.

Tip Thieves might steal your data and use your unsecured network for illegal activities on the web. These activities can be traced back to you as the owner of the ISP account.

A wireless network needs to be secured because the wireless range extends past the walls of your home. The wireless range can be up to 1,400 feet, depending on the Wi-Fi standard used, the strength of the wireless device, and the interference around it. If you don't secure your network, computers in your neighborhood might be able to connect to your wireless network, use your Internet connection, and copy the data stored on your computers.

ON YOUR OWN 12.8

Secure a Wireless Network

WATCH

OBJECTIVE 12.7
VIDEO

You can do this activity if you have access to a wireless router in a small home network. Do the following to secure the wireless network:

Step 1. Look in the router's user guide or on the router manufacturer's website and find the following information needed to access the router setup program:

  a. The **IP address** of the router, for example, 192.168.1.1.
  b. The router password. You must have this password to view the router setup screens and make any changes.

> **IP address**—Four numbers separated by periods, such as 192.168.1.103. The address can be used to identify a computer or other device on a network.

Step 2. Use a computer that has a wired connection to the router. Go to the desktop and open **Internet Explorer**. Enter the IP address of the router in the IE address box. In the Windows Security box that appears, enter the password to the router. For most routers, you don't need to enter the User name. Click **OK**.

Step 3. The router setup main menu appears. If you have never changed the router's password, it might be the original password assigned by the router manufacturer, which is available online for this model of router. If you've never changed the router password, change it now. You don't want a hacker to hijack your router.

> **Tip** Write down the router password and the password to the wireless network. Keep both in a safe place. A good place to record the passwords is on the router documentation.

Step 4. Find the window that sets up the wireless security for the router, such as that shown in Figure 12-21. Yours might look different. Assign a password to the wireless network. If you have a choice for the security mode used, use WPA2 as it provides the best security. Save your changes and exit the router setup program.

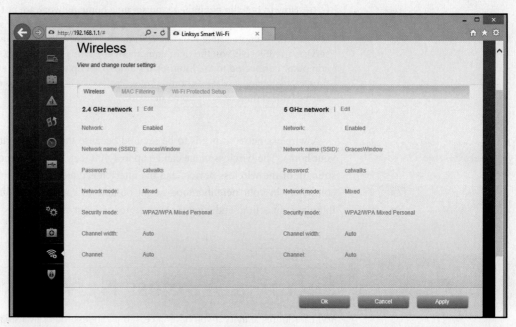

FIGURE 12-21   You can use this window (or one like it) provided by the router setup program to secure the wireless network.

Step 5.   Test your security by using a wireless computer to connect to the network. When you first attempt the connection, you must enter the password to the wireless network. Recall that Windows calls that password the security key or the network security key.

Solutions
Appendix

For help: See *On Your Own 12.8* Step-by-Step Solution

WATCH

OBJECTIVE 12.8
VIDEO

Tip Windows 8 and Windows 7 support a homegroup, but Windows Vista and Windows XP do not. If you have Vista or XP computers on your network, you must use more complex methods of sharing that aren't covered in this book.

Objective 12.8: Use a Homegroup to Share Your Data and Printer

Now that your home network is secure, you might want to share your data and perhaps a printer with other computers connected to your network. Windows offers several methods to share resources. A Windows homegroup is the easiest method to set up and to use.

The first computer that attempts to join a homegroup assigns the password to the homegroup. Windows 8 and Windows 7 computers on the network use this password to join the homegroup and then share specific libraries, folders, or files with the homegroup.

To manage a homegroup, open the Network screen and then click **HomeGroup** (see Figure 12-22). Using this window, you can change what you share with the homegroup, join or leave the homegroup, and view the homegroup password.

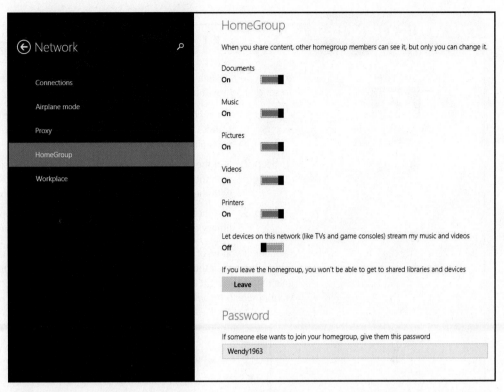

FIGURE 12-22 Use the HomeGroup window to view the homegroup password and to manage the homegroup.

Use File Explorer to access the shared resources of other computers in the homegroup. Look in the Homegroup area of File Explorer to see these resources (see Figure 12-23).

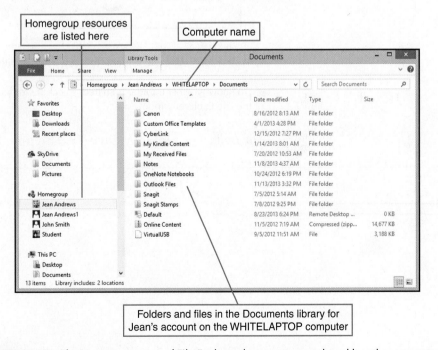

FIGURE 12-23 The Homegroup area of File Explorer shows resources shared by other computers on the network.

ON YOUR OWN 12.9

Use a Homegroup to Share Data

You can do this activity working with a partner using two computers connected to a network. To set up and use a homegroup, do the following:

Step 1. On each wireless computer, use the Network screen to verify that sharing resources on the network is turned on. (For computers with only wired connections, you can assume sharing is turned on.)

Step 2. Join the homegroup. Share the Documents, Music, Pictures, and Videos libraries with the homegroup. If your computer has a printer connected, share the printer with the homegroup. What is the password to your homegroup?

Step 3. Test the homegroup by using File Explorer to copy a file from the Documents library on one computer to the Documents library on the other computer.

Later, if you want to share other folders with the homegroup, use File Explorer to locate the folder. Right-click the folder and click **Share with** in the shortcut menu (see Figure 12-24). To give others the right to view and copy contents of the folder, click **Homegroup (view)**. If you want others to be able to change the contents of the folder, click **Homegroup (view and edit)**.

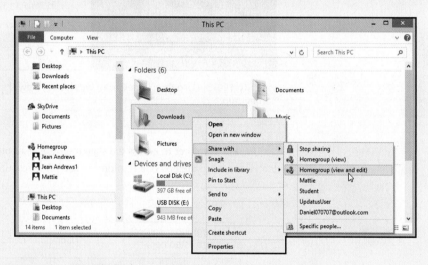

FIGURE 12-24   Use File Explorer to share a folder with the homegroup.

To know whether a folder is shared, select the folder. Its shared status appears at the bottom of the File Explorer window.

Solutions
Appendix

For help: See *On Your Own 12.9* Step-by-Step Solution

Summary

Connecting a Computer to the Internet

> A computer connects to the Internet by way of a local area network (LAN) or wide area network (WAN). The connection can be wired or wireless.

> Connections to the Internet are made through an Internet service provider (ISP). These WAN connections might use cable Internet, DSL, mobile broadband, FiOS, or satellite Internet, which are all broadband technologies.

> Using broadband, cable Internet shares TV cable lines with TV transmissions, DSL shares telephone lines with voice transmissions, mobile broadband shares a cellular network with voice transmissions, FiOS shares fiber optic with TV and telephone voice, and satellite Internet shares a satellite with satellite TV and satellite phone.

> Local wired networks use the Ethernet technology, and local wireless networks use Wi-Fi.

> Mobile broadband uses the same cellular network as do cell phones. Current technologies used for mobile broadband are 3G, 4G, and 4G LTE. Some laptops have mobile broadband built in. You can also buy a mobile broadband modem to connect a computer or small network wirelessly to the Internet using mobile broadband.

> Bluetooth is a technology used to wirelessly connect personal devices to a computer.

> A network port on a computer might have one or two lights near it to indicate network connectivity and activity.

> A wireless access point provides a Wi-Fi hot spot where a wireless computer can connect to the local network. If the access point has secured the network, you must enter a security key (password) to use the network. Use the network icon in the Settings charm to make the connection.

> Use the Network screen available from the Change PC settings page to view information about network connections. For wireless computers, you can use the screen to turn on or off sharing computer resources when you are signed in to Windows using an administrator account.

> Share resources on a network if you want to join a homegroup or a Windows domain. Don't share resources when using a public network.

> Data sent wirelessly should be encrypted while in transmission so it can't be stolen. The best wireless encryption technique is WPA2.

Securing a Computer and Its Data

> The three most important ways to protect a computer and its data are to use antivirus software, secure your network connections, and keep Windows updates current.

> Microsoft releases updates to Windows to fix known problems, which might include plugging up a security leak.

> Use the PC settings page available from the Settings charm to find out if updates are pending, install Windows updates, and manage when and how the updates are installed.

> To protect important data, always keep two copies of the data. Store the backup on a second storage device. To be extra safe, store your original data or your backups in the cloud.

> Four ways to maintain backups are to use an online backup service, keep your data on a website that maintains its own backups, use Windows File History or other backup software, and manually make copies of all your important data files. The safest and most reliable method is to use an online backup service.

> Set up a standard user account for each user of a computer. Protect the administrator account with a strong password.

> Use the Control Panel to change computer settings, including managing user accounts and user passwords other than your own.

Securing a Small Home Network

> A small home network that has Internet access is most likely to use cable Internet or DSL to connect to the Internet. A wireless router designed for home use connects wired and wireless computers to the network.

> Always secure a wireless network so that strangers can't hack into your network, use your Internet connection, and steal your data. Secure the network by using the setup program on the wireless access point device (such as a wireless router) to assign a password that must be used to access the network.

> Use your browser to access the setup program on a home router to configure the router. Enter the IP address of the router in the browser's address box.

> Windows 8 and Windows 7 support a homegroup, but Windows Vista and XP do not. The first computer to attempt to join a homegroup assigns the homegroup password. Other computers must use this password to join the homegroup.

> Use the Homegroup area of File Explorer to access resources shared by other computers in the homegroup. You can also use File Explorer to share folders with the homegroup or to remove the share status.

CHAPTER MASTERY PROJECT

Now it's time to find out how well you've mastered the content in this chapter. If you can do all the steps in this Mastery Project without looking back at the chapter details and can answer all the Review Questions following this project, you've mastered this chapter. If you can complete the project by finding answers using Windows Help and Support or searching the web, you've proven that you can teach yourself how to make Internet connections and secure a computer.

> **Hint** All the key terms in the chapter are used in this mastery project or in the review questions. If you encounter a key word you don't know, such as *homegroup*, enter **define:homegroup** in the Internet Explorer search box.

If you find you need a lot of help doing the project and you have not yet read the chapter or done the activities, go back and start at the beginning of the chapter, watch the videos, review the step-by-step solutions as you work through the On Your Own activities, and then return to this project.

> **Tip** If you need help completing this part of the mastery project, review the "Connecting a Computer to the Internet" section in the chapter.

Do the following to manage the network connections on your computer:

Step 1. Sign in to Windows using an administrator account. If your computer is not already connected, connect it to an Ethernet wired or Wi-Fi wireless network. For a wired network, check the status lights near the network port to verify connectivity and network activity. Use the network icon in the Settings charm to find out whether you have a wired or wireless connection or both connections.

Step 2. For a wireless computer, use the Settings charm to open the Network screen and find out whether content and devices are shared on the network. (You must be signed on to Windows using an administrator account to see this setting.)

Step 3. To verify you have connectivity, open your browser and navigate to a few websites.

Step 4. Using the Quick Link menu, open the Network Connections window. For a wireless computer, find the network security key to the wireless network and the type of wireless security used. To practice troubleshooting a failed connection, diagnose and repair the wired or wireless connection.

Tip If you need help completing this part of the mastery project, review the "Securing a Computer and Its Data" section in the chapter.

Do the following to investigate and install updates for Windows:

Step 5. Use the Settings charm to find out if updates are pending. Install any important updates. Verify there are not more important updates pending.

Step 6. Set Windows Update so that important and recommended updates are automatically installed every day. Allow other Microsoft software to receive updates.

You must have a USB flash drive and be able to write files to the hard drive to do this activity. Do the following to set up File History to back up files and favorites and restore a file from backup:

Step 7. Copy a photo from another location into the Pictures library. If you don't have a photo file, use a file in the sample_files folder available at www.pearsonhighered.com/jump or in MyITLab. (In Chapter 2, you stored the sample_files folder on your USB flash drive.)

Step 8. Plug in your USB flash drive and configure File History to back up to the flash drive. Then run the backup.

Step 9. Delete the photo from the Pictures library. Then use the File History window to restore the deleted photo to the Pictures library. Run the backup again.

Step 10. Drill down into the backed-up files on your USB flash drive and find the photo in the backup. Copy this photo to your Pictures library so you have two copies of the photo in the library.

Do the following to set up a standard account and manage passwords:

Step 11. Sign on to Windows using an administrator account. Use the Settings charm to create a standard account named **James**. Make the password for the account **JaMes5**.

Step 12. Sign on to Windows using the password-protected James account. Change the password to the account. View the Documents library for the account.

Step 13. Sign off Windows. Sign back on using an administrator account. Open the Manage Accounts window in Control Panel. Use the Windows Snipping Tool to take a snip of the window showing the James account. Create a Word document named **Chapter_12_Mastery_Project** and insert the snip into the document.

Step 14. Reset the password to the James account, making the new password **changeme**. Log on to the James account using the new password.

Step 15. Switch back to the administrator account. Delete the **James** account.

Tip If you need help completing this part of the mastery project, review the "Securing a Small Home Network" section in the chapter.

Work with a partner and two computers to set up and use a homegroup. Do the following:

Step 16. If the two computers are not already joined in a homegroup, join them.

Step 17. Share the Pictures library on both computers to the homegroup. Copy a photo from the Pictures library from one computer to the other.

Step 18. If the Documents library is shared with the homegroup, remove it from the homegroup. Verify one computer can't see the Documents library of the other computer. Use the Windows Snipping Tool to take a snip of your screen showing File Explorer with your partner's Pictures library listed in the Homegroup area of Explorer and the Documents library not listed. Insert the snip into the Chapter_12_Mastery_Project document you created in step 13.

Step 19. Enter your name and course information into the Chapter_12_Mastery_Project document containing the two snips and send the document to your instructor. If you're using MyITLab, you can post the file in a Dropbox assignment or email the file in MyITLab. On the other hand, your instructor might prefer you post the file to your OneDrive or email the file using your school email.

Review Questions

Answer these questions to assess your skills and knowledge of the content covered in the chapter. Your instructor can provide you with the correct answers when you're ready to check your work.

1. Which type of network covers a larger area: a LAN or a WAN?

2. List five technologies a single computer or local network might use to connect to the Internet. Which of these services are broadband?

3. Which broadband technology shares copper lines with telephone voice? Which broadband technology shares a cable with TV?

4. What are the two transmission speeds of Ethernet?

5. A Wi-Fi hot spot is provided by what type of device?

6. Suppose you have DSL and satellite Internet services in your area. Which one is the better choice? Why? What type of organization provides these services?

7. Why is mobile broadband considered to be a broadband technology?

8. When connecting to a wireless network, how can you tell that the wireless network is secured?

9. Suppose your wired network connection is not working and you see a blinking light near the network port. What does the blinking light indicate? What do you do next to fix the network problem?

10. What two choices does Windows offer for network security? Which choice creates the most secure firewall settings?

11. If your network connection is not sharing resources, can you join a Windows domain? Can you join a homegroup?

12. When you first make a network connection, how do you verify that you have Internet access?

13. What is the fastest technology currently used by mobile broadband on a cellular network?

14. A device plugged into a USB port on your computer to connect to the Internet using a cellular network is commonly called a cell card. What is its technical name?

15. Which technology is used to wirelessly connect two personal devices, such as a computer and a printer or a computer and a cell phone?

16. If your computer doesn't have built-in mobile broadband technology, what are four ways it can connect to a cellular network?

17. What are the three most important practices to secure a computer?

18. Which is more important to keep a computer safe: run antivirus software or use a strong password to your online banking service?

19. Which is more important to keep a computer safe: keep a backup of important data or keep important Windows updates current?

20. What is a single Windows update called to fix a known bug?

21. List four ways to back up important data on your computer. Which is the safest and most reliable method to use?

22. Why would you create a standard user account on a computer?

23. Why is it important to secure a wireless network in your home? How do you secure the network?

24. Why is it important to change the password to your home router as soon as you install it? What information do you need in order to access the router setup program?

25. What multifunction device can be used to network several computers together and connect that network to a DSL modem or cable modem?

26. How many numbers are there in an IP address, and what symbol is used to separate these numbers?

27. Which current wireless encryption standard offers the best security?

28. List the steps to find out the homegroup password.

29. List the steps to find the wireless password for the current wireless connection.

30. Why might the *Find devices and content* setting not be visible on a wireless computer when you view a network connection on the Network screen? Why might it not be visible when you are using a computer that has only an Ethernet connection?

Becoming an Independent Learner

Answer the following questions about becoming an independent learner:

1. To teach yourself to manage network connections and secure a computer, do you think it is best to rely on the chapter or on Window Help or the web when you need answers?

2. The most important skill learned in this chapter is how to teach yourself a computer skill. Rate yourself at Level A through E on how well you are doing with this skill. What is your level?

   - Level A: I was able to successfully complete the Chapter Mastery Project with the help of only a few of the On Your Own activities in the chapter.

   - Level B: I completed all the On Your Own activities and the Chapter Mastery Project without referring to any of the solutions in the Step-by-Step Solutions Appendix.

   - Level C: I completed all the On Your Own activities and the Chapter Mastery Project by using just a few of the solutions in the Step-by-Step Solutions Appendix.

   - Level D: I completed all the On Your Own activities and the Chapter Mastery Project by using many of the solutions in the Step-by-Step Solutions Appendix.

   - Level E: I completed all the On Your Own activities and the Chapter Mastery Project and had to use all of the solutions in the Step-by-Step Solutions Appendix.

   To continue toward the goal of teaching yourself computer skills, if you're not at Level A, try to move up one level on how you learn in Chapter 13.

Projects to Help You

Now that you've mastered the material in this chapter, you are ready to tackle the three projects focused on your career, personal, or academic goals. Depending on your own interests, you might choose to complete any or all of these projects to help you achieve your goals.

Project 1: Investigating Broadband Internet Services

Career Project I just started a new small business, and I need Internet service in the office. How do I get it? What equipment do I need to buy? Which is best: cable Internet, DSL, or FiOS?

Do the following to find out about broadband Internet services you might use yourself or recommend to others:

1. Search the Internet and find out if cable Internet, DSL, or FiOS is offered in your neighborhood. If you already have one of these three technologies, research the other two. If you don't yet have Internet broadband in your home, research the three services to decide which is best for you.

2. What company offers cable Internet, DSL, or FiOS in your neighborhood? How much does the service cost? Is there a setup fee? Does a technician come to your home to set up the service, or are you expected to set it up yourself? Is the modem included in the subscription, or must you purchase it?

3. Some neighborhoods have access to cable Internet, DSL, and FiOS. To choose between the three, consider the quality of service and cost. To find out how well the service performs in your neighborhood, ask your neighbors these questions: Are they satisfied with the service? Does it go down often or is it reliable? If a problem occurs, does the company provide good technical support?

4. Based on your research, which service would you recommend to a neighbor or might you choose for yourself? Why?

5. Write one or two paragraphs of your findings and conclusions and email these to your instructor.

Personal Project I just bought a laptop, and my roommate already has a desktop computer. We want a small home network where we can share files between the two computers and both computers can connect to the Internet. What equipment do I need to set up a home network to the Internet?

Project 2: Selecting a Router for a Home Network

Suppose you have cable Internet or DSL coming to your home and you want to set up a home network. You need a home router that connects wired and wireless computers to create the network. The router will also connect to your cable modem or DSL modem. Shop online for a home router and bookmark the URL of the web page showing the router you select. Also bookmark one online review of this router. Find a router that meets these requirements:

> The router serves as a wireless access point to provide a Wi-Fi hot spot. The router must allow you to secure the wireless network with a password and must support the WPA2 encryption standard.

> The router has a minimum of three network ports to connect three wired computers and another network port to connect to your modem. The ports must use the Ethernet 1000 Mbps standard.

> The router gets good online reviews that report it is easy to use, and technical support from the manufacturer is available.

As you shop for a router, you might encounter unfamiliar technical terms. Don't worry if you don't understand all the terms. Just make sure the router you select gets good online reviews and meets your requirements.

Send an email to your instructor containing the following information:

> The brand and model of the router

> A link showing the router for sale including its price

> A link of an online review of the router

Project 3: Sharing Files in a Homegroup

Working with a partner, do the following to learn how to manage the shared data in a homegroup:

> **Not Working?** You might not be able to do this project using computers in your school lab if lab computers are locked down so that sharing resources is not allowed.

Academic Project My study group meets every week in my home where I have cable modem service and a home router with Wi-Fi. We all bring our laptops. When we want to share files, we email them to each other. Is there an easier way to share these files? Is there a way each team member can see the files on the other computers?

Step 1. Work with a partner and set up a homegroup. Create two folders named Personal and Classwork in your Documents library. Put one document file in each folder.

Step 2. Share the Classwork folder with the homegroup so that others can manage files in the folder. List the steps to share the Classwork folder.

Step 3. You don't want to share the Personal folder. List the steps you would take if you needed to remove sharing from this folder.

Step 4. Verify you can access the file in the Classwork folder on your partner's computer, but you can't see the contents of your partner's Personal folder. Verify you can copy a file to your partner's Classwork folder.

Project to Help Others

One of the best ways to learn is to teach someone else. And, in teaching someone else, you are making a contribution into that person's life. In this chapter, help someone learn to connect to the Internet and secure his computer.

Does your apprentice use a computer that is connected to the Internet? If so, do the following:

Step 1. Show your apprentice how to use the Network Connection window to solve a connectivity problem. For a wireless computer, make sure the network security is set correctly to protect the computer from attack.

Step 2. Help your apprentice update Windows and make sure Windows is set to automatically download and install important updates.

Step 3. If your apprentice doesn't have an Internet connection in his home, step through Project 1 to help your apprentice understand the different technologies in the area and what they cost.

Step 4. Use Word to create a file that contains your answers to the following questions about the tutoring session. Name the file **Chapter12Tutoring** and send the file to your instructor. If you are using MyITLab, you can post the file in a Dropbox assignment or email the file in MyITLab. On the other hand, your instructor might prefer you post the file to your OneDrive or email the file using your school email. Here are the questions:

1. Who is your apprentice?

2. In step 1, which security setting for the network connection did your apprentice decide to use? Why?

3. In step 2, about how long did it take to completely update Windows?

4. How do you think the session went? How would you like to improve it next time?

13 Maintaining a Computer and Fixing Computer Problems

In This Chapter, You Will:

Keep a Computer Running Well

13.1 Perform preventive maintenance, including cleaning up the hard drive

13.2 Uninstall software you no longer need

13.3 Disable a program from launching when Windows starts

13.4 Protect computer hardware and manage power settings

Solve the Most Common Computer Problems

13.5 Common problems with quick fixes

13.6 The monitor screen is difficult to read

13.7 Internet Explorer can't find a requested web page

13.8 A document won't print

13.9 I think my computer has a virus

13.10 My computer is too slow

13.11 Windows gives strange errors

13.12 My computer won't start

Prepare to Talk with a Computer Repair Technician

13.13 Prepare to talk with a computer repair technician

If you are responsible for a computer, you need to know how to take care of it. A computer will run well for many years without giving problems if you take good care of it. In this chapter, you learn how to do just that.

As with all chapters in this book, you can choose which of the learning paths below best suits your needs. No matter which path you choose, as you work your way through the chapter, remember the most important computer skill is how to teach yourself a computer skill. Therefore, this chapter is designed to help you teach yourself how to maintain a computer and fix computer problems.

LEARNING PATHS

GUIDED LEARNING	EXPLORE AND DISCOVER	JUMP RIGHT IN
Read the Chapter *Watch the Objective Videos*	**On Your Own Projects** *Review Objective videos or use Step-by-Step Solutions*	**Mastery Project** *Use Objective videos & OYO projects for help*
On Your Own Projects *Review Objective videos or use Step-by-Step Solutions*	**Mastery Project** *Use Objective videos & OYO projects for help*	**Explore Resources** *For help as needed*
Mastery Project *Use Objective videos & OYO projects for help*		
Google Project (if applicable) *Watch Google video for help*	**Google Project (if applicable)** *Watch Google video for help*	**Google Project (if applicable)** *Watch Google video for help*
Helping You & Others Projects	**Helping You & Others Projects**	**Helping You & Others Projects**
MyITLab Assessment	**MyITLab Assessment**	**MyITLab Assessment**

Keeping a Computer Running Well

Let's start the chapter by learning about the tasks necessary to maintain a computer.

WATCH

OBJECTIVE 13.1 VIDEO

Objective 13.1: Perform Preventive Maintenance, Including Cleaning Up the Hard Drive

Most computer problems can be prevented through good **computer maintenance**. If you're responsible for a computer, you need to take the time to set it up so that it is securely protected. Then about every month, you need to do the routine maintenance needed to keep a computer running well.

> **computer maintenance**—Tasks that are done routinely or as needed to keep a computer protected and running well.

In Chapter 12, you learned to secure a computer. Recall the three most important tasks are to

> Set Windows Updates to automatically download and install updates
> Install and run antivirus software
> Secure the Windows network connection so the computer is protected from attacks coming from the local network or the Internet

Over time, a computer tends to run slower than it did when first purchased. Ongoing routine maintenance can prevent this from happening. One step in routine maintenance is to clean up your hard drive so your computer has the free space it needs to work.

> **Hint** Many of the activities in this chapter require you to know the password to an administrator account or to sign on to Windows using an administrator account. If you are responsible for a computer, you need access to this account. Recall that if you are signed on to Windows using a standard account and attempt to perform a task that only an administrator can do, the UAC box appears. Enter the administrator password to continue.

Not Working? Drive C: is the drive where Windows is installed. It might be shown as Local Disk (C:), OS (C:), or some other name that contains C: in the name. Look for it in the This PC group or Computer group in the left pane of File Explorer.

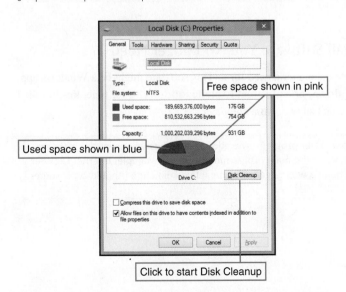

Clean Up the Hard Drive

Windows requires at least 15% of free space on the hard drive that it uses to do its work. Even more space is better. When a hard drive gets full, Windows runs slower and might report errors. Use the **Disk Cleanup** utility to free up some hard drive space.

> **Disk Cleanup**—A Windows utility used to delete temporary and optional files on the hard drive to free up hard drive space.

To clean up the hard drive, open File Explorer. Right click **Local Disk (C:)** and select **Properties** from the shortcut menu. The Local Disk (C:) Properties dialog box opens (see Figure 13-1). Click **Disk Cleanup** to start the cleanup process.

Notice on the Local Disk (C:) Properties dialog box you can compress the drive to save disk space. Compression is not considered a best practice and should be done only if you have no other way of freeing up hard drive space. A compressed drive runs slower than one that is not compressed.

FIGURE 13-1 The Properties dialog box of Local Disk (C:) shows free space on the drive that holds the Windows operating system.

ON YOUR OWN 13.1

Clean Up the Hard Drive

WATCH

OBJECTIVE 13.1
VIDEO

Do the following to clean up the hard drive:

Step 1. Recall the Recycle Bin is the place where Windows puts files and folders deleted from the hard drive. Empty the Recycle Bin to free up that space. Note that each user of a computer needs to empty his or her own Recycle Bin.

Step 2. Use Disk Cleanup on the Local Disk (C:) Properties dialog box to delete unneeded files on the hard drive (refer to Figure 13-1). Be sure to clean up **system files** as well as data files. To do so requires the administrator password.

> **system file**—A file that is part of the Windows operating system. Temporary system files can safely be deleted without causing a problem in Windows.

> **Not Working?** If you're working in a school computer lab that doesn't allow some of the activities in this chapter, you can still do the activities on your home computer.

Step 3. As you clean up the drive, you might see *Previous Windows installation(s)* listed in the Disk Cleanup for (C:) dialog box (see Figure 13-2). Deleting this item can free up space because it holds data from a version of Windows previously installed on this computer. If you see the item and know you no longer need anything from the old Windows installation, include it in the items to delete.

> **Hint** Be sure to delete Temporary files and Temporary Internet Files listed in the Disk Cleanup dialog box. These files can take up a lot of space and aren't needed.

FIGURE 13-2 This computer was upgraded from Windows 7 to Windows 8. The old Windows 7 data is no longer needed and can be deleted to free up 638 MB of disk space.

Step 4. Use the information on the Local Disk (C:) Properties dialog box to calculate the percentage of free space on the hard drive. If 15% is not free, consider moving some data folders to other devices, such as an external hard drive, or burn some data files or folders to CDs or DVDs.

Solutions
Appendix

For help: See *On Your Own 13.1* Step-by-Step Solution

WATCH

OBJECTIVE 13.2
VIDEO

Objective 13.2: Uninstall Software You No Longer Need

Most of us install software as we encounter a need for it. This software might be a Windows app, a desktop application, a device driver, or an Internet Explorer **add-on**. Over time, this installed software can fill up a hard drive and slow down a computer.

> **add-on**—A helper program to another program. The add-on launches whenever the main program launches to be available when the main program needs it. For example, Internet Explorer might use an add-on to help build a web page with interactive animation. An add-on is sometimes called a plug-in.

To free hard drive space and keep Windows running well, uninstall software you no longer want or need:

Step 1. To get a list of apps installed on your computer, go to the Apps screen. To uninstall apps obtained from the Windows store, right-click the app tile and click **Uninstall** at the bottom of the screen.

Step 2. To uninstall desktop applications, press **Win+X** to open the Quick Link menu and then click **Programs and Features**. The Programs and Features window appears listing all of the desktop applications and some of the add-ons installed on the computer (see Figure 13-3). Select a program and then click **Uninstall** to uninstall it.

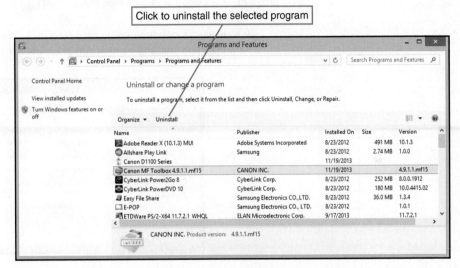

FIGURE 13-3   Use the Programs and Features window to uninstall desktop software or add-ons you no longer need.

ON YOUR OWN 13.2

Uninstall Software You No Longer Need

WATCH

OBJECTIVE 13.2
VIDEO

Do the following to investigate and uninstall software:

Step 1. Use the Programs and Features window to list the programs installed on your computer. Do you find programs listed you don't recognize? If so, copy the name of the program into a Google search box to search the web for information about the program. Even though you don't recognize it, it might be important to your computer. If you are not sure you need the software, keep it installed.

Step 2. Do you recognize a program that you installed but no longer need? If so, uninstall the program.

Step 3. Look around the Start screen for apps you don't want. If you find one, uninstall it.

Solutions
Appendix

For help: See On Your Own 13.2 Step-by-Step Solution

WATCH

OBJECTIVE 13.3
VIDEO

Objective 13.3: Disable a Program from Launching When Windows Starts

When software is first installed, it sometimes registers itself with Windows so it's launched each time Windows starts. When many programs launch at startup, Windows is slow to start and runs slowly because these programs running in the background are using up system resources. If you seldom use a program, you might want to disable it from launching at startup. You can still launch it manually at any time.

Use the **Task Manager** utility to control the programs that launch at startup. To open Task Manager, press **Win+X** to open the Quick Link menu and click **Task Manager**. If necessary, click **More details** to see the tabs at the top of the window. Click the **Startup** tab to view a list of programs that launch at startup (see Figure 13-4).

> **Task Manager**—A Windows utility used to manage startup programs, close open applications that aren't responding, and monitor computer and network performance.

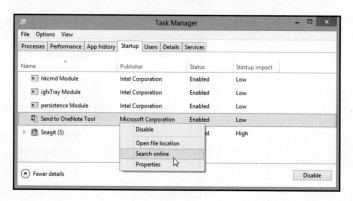

FIGURE 13-4   Using Task Manager, you can investigate a startup program and disable it from launching when Windows starts.

Tip Be careful to trust only reliable websites that give information about startup programs. Be especially careful to not download free software that claims to solve a problem with a startup program— the software might actually be malware. Two websites that can be trusted to give reliable information are www.processlibrary.com and www.liutilities.com.

To disable a program from launching, select it and click **Disable**. Then close Task Manager and restart your computer. Later, if you decide you need the program to launch every time Windows starts, return to Task Manager and enable the program.

You might need to investigate a startup program to decide whether you want to disable one. To do so, right-click the program and click **Search online**, as shown in Figure 13-4.

ON YOUR OWN 13.3

Limit Startup Programs Using Task Manager

WATCH

OBJECTIVE 13.3
VIDEO

Now let's use Task Manager:

Step 1.   Start **Task Manager** and investigate the list of programs that launch at startup. Are there any you don't recognize? If so, go online and investigate the purpose of the program.

Step 2.   Is there a program you decide you don't need launched each time Windows starts? If so, disable that program.

Step 3.   Restart your computer and verify that all is working as you expect. If you see a problem, return to Task Manager and enable the program that you disabled.

| Solutions Appendix |

For help: See *On Your Own 13.3* Step-by-Step Solution

WATCH

**OBJECTIVE 13.4
VIDEO**

Surge protector

Objective 13.4: Protect Computer Hardware and Manage Power Settings

Next you learn how to protect computer hardware and manage power settings.

Protect Computer Hardware

If hardware is cared for, a computer should last for many years. Here are a few tips for protecting computer hardware:

> **Use a surge protector.** To protect a computer against lightning or other power surges, use a **surge protector**. Plug the power cord from your computer into the surge protector and plug the surge protector into an electrical wall outlet. The surge protector doesn't allow electrical surges to pass through to your computer. A small, portable surge protector can be convenient when traveling with a laptop.

> **surge protector**—A device that allows you to plug in several electrical devices and protects these devices from power surges.

> **Keep computer vents clear and dust free.** If vents are obstructed, a computer can overheat. Never work with a laptop computer sitting on a fluffy pillow or blanket because there's not enough airflow for the vents on the bottom of the laptop. Make sure the vents of your desktop computer are not obstructed. If vents get filled with dust, you can use a can of compressed air to blow them clean.

> **Protect a desktop computer sitting under a desk.** Place the computer so you're not likely to accidentally kick it. Don't set it on thick carpet that doesn't allow good airflow. Don't move a desktop computer while it is working because doing so can damage the hard drive.

> **Protect a computer from high humidity and heat.** Heat and humidity are not good for a computer. Never leave your laptop in a hot car during the summer months. Keeping computers in a damp basement is also not a good idea.

Tip Heat, humidity, power surges, and static electricity can affect hardware over time. Even though you might not see immediate damage, components might not last as long after being exposed.

Here are some tips to keep hardware clean and working well:

> **Clean your keyboard.** Turn your keyboard upside down and shake it to dislodge crumbs. Use a vacuum to clean the keyboard or a can of compressed air to blow out the dust. Use a soft, slightly damp, lint-free cloth to clean the keyboard. For a really dirty keyboard, you can use cotton swabs dipped in alcohol to clean around each key.

> **Clean your mouse.** Clean the mouse with a damp cloth. For an optical mouse, clean the feet on the bottom of the mouse so it slides easily. Don't forget to clean the mouse pad. Built-up dirt on the pad can keep the mouse from sliding easily.

> **Clean your monitor screen.** Special electronic cleaning wipes work great to clean a monitor screen and other computer parts. If you don't have them, use a lint-free, soft, slightly damp cloth to clean the screen. Don't use alcohol or window cleaner on a monitor screen. And don't use paper towels that can scratch the surface.

> **Clean computer vents.** To keep a computer from overheating, you need to keep computer vents clean of dust and free from obstruction. Clean the vents with a can of compressed air. If you see a lot of dust built up around the vents of a desktop computer, ask a computer repair technician to show you how to safely open the computer case and clean the inside.

> **Don't unpack or turn on a computer that has just come in from the cold.** Cold air has a lot of **static electricity**, which is extremely dangerous to a computer. Wait for a computer to come to room temperature before unpacking it or turning it on.

> **static electricity**—The accumulation of an electrical charge that can cause sparks or a crackling sound. Even a small amount of static electricity that you can't see or hear can damage computer components.

> **Protect CDs and DVDs.** A scratched or dirty CD or DVD might not work. Heat and sunlight can also damage discs. Protect your optical discs from heat, direct sunlight, scratches, and dirt. If one gets scratched or dirty, use a soft, dry cloth or an optical disc cleaning kit to clean it. Wipe from the center of the disc out and not in a circle.

Manage Power Settings

You can use the power settings on a computer to extend a battery charge on a laptop or to save on electricity. For example, you can control how long a computer is inactive before it turns off the display or puts the computer to sleep. To manage power, press **Win+X** and click **Power Options**. Figure 13-5 shows the Power Options window for a laptop. The Power Options window for a desktop computer is missing two items, which are labeled in the figure.

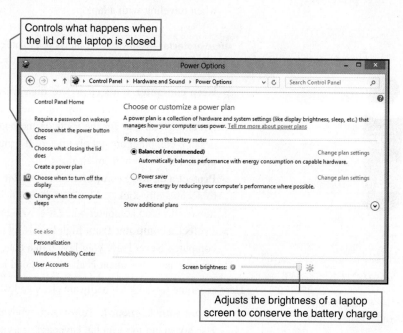

FIGURE 13-5   Windows offers power plans to conserve electricity.

You can extend the battery charge on a laptop or netbook by managing the power settings. Windows uses different power settings for a laptop or netbook depending on whether the computer is plugged into a power source or is using the battery. To see these settings, click **Choose what closing the lid does**. The System Settings window shown in Figure 13-6 appears.

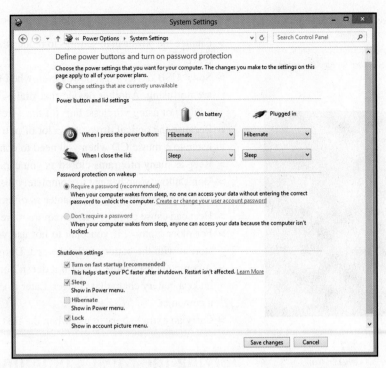

FIGURE 13-6   Power and lid settings can be different when a laptop is on battery or plugged in.

ON YOUR OWN 13.4

WATCH

▶

OBJECTIVE 13.4
VIDEO

Manage Power Settings

To investigate current power settings on your computer, do the following:

Step 1. Open the **Power Options** window and find answers to these questions:

1. How many minutes of inactivity pass before the computer turns off the display? Before the computer goes to sleep? (If you're using a laptop, find these answers when the laptop is plugged in.)
2. What happens when you press the power button on your computer?
3. When the computer wakes from sleep, is a password required to unlock the computer?

Step 2. If you're using a laptop or netbook, find answers to these questions:

1. What happens when you close the lid of the computer when the computer is on battery?
2. What happens when you close the lid of the computer when the computer is plugged in?

Step 3. Adjust your power settings as you like. If you made any changes in the power settings, save your changes. Close the window.

Solutions
Appendix

For help: See *On Your Own 13.4* Step-by-Step Solution

Tip To use Windows 8 to stop all wireless communication, open the **Settings** charm and click the network icon. In the Networks pane, turn on Airplane mode.

Tip Become an independent investigator. If you're faced with a computer problem and this chapter doesn't take you far enough to solve it, search the web for more information about the problem and what to do. Be sure to take advice only from reliable websites. If you still can't solve the problem, get professional help.

WATCH

OBJECTIVE 13.5
VIDEO

Here are some additional tips to make a laptop or netbook battery charge last longer:

> Change the power plan settings to reduce the screen brightness. A less bright screen uses less power.
> Some USB devices use power even when they are not active. Unplug all USB devices you are not using. Another device that drains a laptop of power is the wireless device. When you're not using wireless, turn off the wireless switch.
> Because the optical drive uses a lot of power when in use, don't watch a movie on DVD or listen to a music CD when you need to conserve power.
> Keep as many programs closed as you can.
> Don't allow your battery to completely discharge. Doing so can weaken the battery. When traveling, plug in your AC adapter as often as possible.
> Heat can cause components to require more electricity. Keep your laptop cool and vents free.
> For older laptops, if you plan to not use your laptop for a time (more than a week), don't store it with the battery fully charged. Doing so can weaken the battery.
> A computer uses more power if it doesn't have enough memory. Installing more memory can make a battery charge last longer. Later in the chapter, you learn about upgrading memory in a computer.
> Carry an extra battery to use when the first one is almost discharged.

Solving the Most Common Computer Problems

Most computer problems are easy to solve. In this part of the chapter, you learn how to solve the common ones.

Objective 13.5: Common Problems with Quick Fixes

Let's begin learning about solving computer problems by looking at easy-to-do quick fixes for three common problems.

A File Is Missing or Was Accidentally Deleted

If you accidentally deleted a file from the hard drive, look in the Recycle Bin to find the file and restore it. To open the Recycle Bin, double-click it on the desktop. To restore a file in the Recycle Bin, right-click the file and select **Restore** from the shortcut menu (see Figure 13-7).

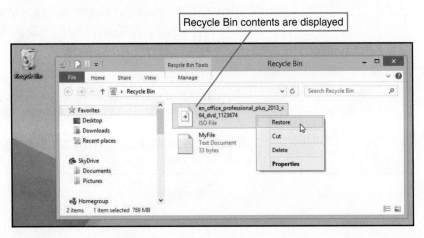

FIGURE 13-7   Look in the Recycle Bin for a deleted file.

In Chapter 12, you learned how to recover a file that was backed up using Windows File History. If you've been using File History or other backup methods, now's the time to go to the backup to recover the file.

A Device or Program Won't Install

Normally, when you plug in a new hardware device such as a USB flash drive or printer, Windows recognizes the device and automatically installs device drivers to support it. You see the progress of the installation reported at the bottom of your screen.

If a problem occurs when you're installing a device or software, the Windows **Action Center** can help. To open the Action Center, press **Win+X** and click **System**. In the System window, click **Action Center**. The Action Center window is shown in Figure 13-8.

See also

Action Center

Windows Update

> **Action Center**—A Windows utility that is a collection of several utilities and windows. Use it to solve problems with hardware and software installations and other Windows problems.

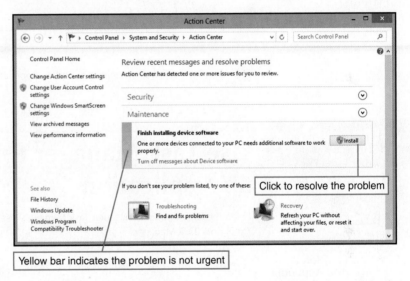

Click to resolve the problem

Yellow bar indicates the problem is not urgent

FIGURE 13-8   Use the Windows Action Center to solve problems with hardware and software.

Problems the computer is having are reported in the Action Center window with recommendations for solutions. To resolve a problem, click the button to the right of the problem message. Action Center steps you through the solution.

An Application Is Frozen and Won't Respond

When an application freezes, "Not responding" usually shows up in the title bar. You can try waiting for the application to respond, or you can force the application to close. If you force the application to close, you might lose any data not saved. To force it to close, open Task Manager. On the Processes tab, select the application and click **End task** (see Figure 13-9).

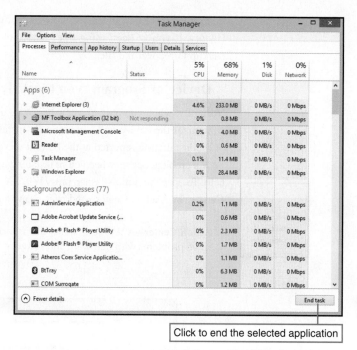

Click to end the selected application

FIGURE 13-9   Use Task Manager to end an application that's not responding.

ON YOUR OWN 13.5

WATCH

OBJECTIVE 13.5
VIDEO

Solutions
Appendix

Use Task Manager to Close an Application

Open the Paint application. Open Task Manager. Use Task Manager to close the Paint application. Then close Task Manager.

For help: See On Your Own 13.5 Step-by-Step Solution

WATCH

OBJECTIVE 13.6
VIDEO

Objective 13.6: The Monitor Screen Is Difficult to Read

To change monitor settings, you can use Windows settings or buttons on the front of the monitor. Sometimes you need to make changes in both places. Use the buttons on the front of the monitor to change the brightness and contrast of the screen and the position of the lighted area on the monitor screen. Laptops and netbooks might have buttons near the keyboard to control the display.

The **screen resolution** is changed using Windows display settings. Right-click somewhere on the desktop and select **Screen resolution** from the shortcut menu. The Screen Resolution window appears.

> **screen resolution**—The number of dots (called pixels) on a monitor screen used to create the screen, for example, 1680 × 1050. For best results, use the screen resolution recommended for your monitor, which is called the native resolution.

In the Resolution field, select the setting and click **Apply** (see Figure 13-10). The change is applied and a dialog box appears. If you like the new setting, click **Keep changes**. If you don't like what you see, click **Revert** to return to the previous setting. Then close the Screen Resolution window.

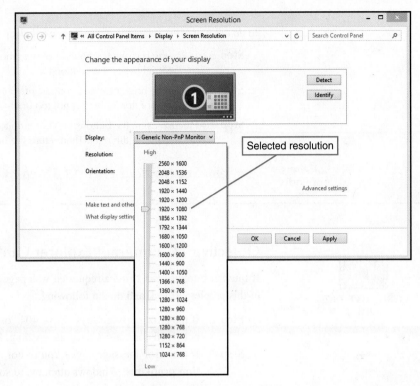

FIGURE 13-10   For best results, select the recommended or native resolution for your monitor.

Practice Changing Monitor Settings

WATCH

**OBJECTIVE 13.6
VIDEO**

When you're adjusting monitor settings, it's a good idea to first open a Word document so you can see black text against a white background. Adjust the monitor so the text is easy to read and the screen is not too bright. Do the following to practice changing the monitor settings:

Step 1. Open a Word document or a web page in your browser so you can see black text on a white background. Resize the window so you can view the window as well as the Windows desktop.

Step 2. Using Windows, find out your current screen resolution. Note this resolution so you can return to it later.

Step 3. Change the screen resolution of your monitor to 800 × 600. What problems do you see when viewing the screen at this resolution? Change the screen resolution to the highest setting. After you view the screen at this setting, return the setting to the original screen resolution.

Step 4. If the text on the screen is too small for you to read, you can enlarge it. What is the current setting for text size on your screen? Adjust the text size to Medium. After you view the screen at this setting, return the setting to the original text size.

Hint To change the text size, use the Display window in Control Panel.

To do this part of the activity, you need to use a desktop monitor and not a laptop. Do the following:

Step 5. Using the buttons on the front of your monitor, find out what is the current setting for the brightness of your monitor.

Step 6. Adjust the brightness and contrast of your monitor so that text on the screen is clear and the monitor lighting is not too bright.

Step 7. Practice using the buttons on your monitor to move the lighted part of the screen to the left and to the right. Then return the lighted screen to a center position.

| Solutions Appendix | *For help:* See *On Your Own 13.6* Step-by-Step Solution |

WATCH

OBJECTIVE 13.7
VIDEO

Objective 13.7: Internet Explorer Can't Find a Requested Web Page

If Internet Explorer can't find a requested web page, there are several possibilities for the source of this problem. Check and do the following:

Step 1. If the error message says "Error 404" or "Page not found," the URL might be bad or not typed correctly. Check the spelling. Does another URL work? Try **google.com**.

Step 2. If the error message says "You're not connected to a network," click **Fix connection problems**. Windows attempts to solve the problem and offers suggestions (see Figure 13-11). Follow through with the suggestion and click **Check to see if the problem is fixed**.

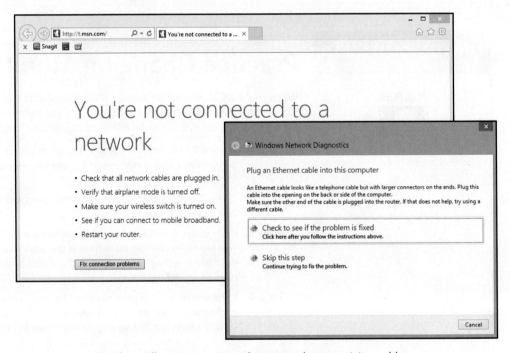

FIGURE 13-11 Windows offers a suggestion to fix a network connectivity problem.

If your problem is still not solved, do the following:

Step 1. The network connection might not be working. Open the Network Connections window, select the network connection, and click **Diagnose this connection**. Recall from Chapter 12 that a connection with a problem has a red X beside it in the Network Connections window.

Step 2. For a wired connection, check cable connections at both ends. Are the status indicator lights near the network port lit?

Step 3. For a wireless connection, check the signal strength. You might need to move the laptop to a stronger area of the wireless network.

Step 4. Are you at home and using a router and cable modem or DSL modem? If so, reset this equipment by following these steps:

    a. Turn off or unplug the cable modem or DSL modem. Turn off or unplug the router. Wait five minutes for the equipment at the Internet service provider (ISP) to reset.

    b. Plug in or turn on the cable modem or DSL modem and wait for the lights on the front of the device to settle. Then plug in the router.

    c. Watch on your computer taskbar as the network icon shows the connection being restored. If you still have no connection, report the problem to your ISP.

WATCH

OBJECTIVE 13.8
VIDEO

Objective 13.8: A Document Won't Print

Printer problems can be caused by the application used to print a document, Windows, connectivity to the printer, or the printer. The reason for a problem at the printer might be that the printer is not turned on or is not online, it is out of paper, the paper is jammed, the ink cartridge or toner cartridge is low, or power is not getting to the printer. When you're solving a printer problem, it helps to have a plan to sort out what works and doesn't work. Figure 13-12 can help.

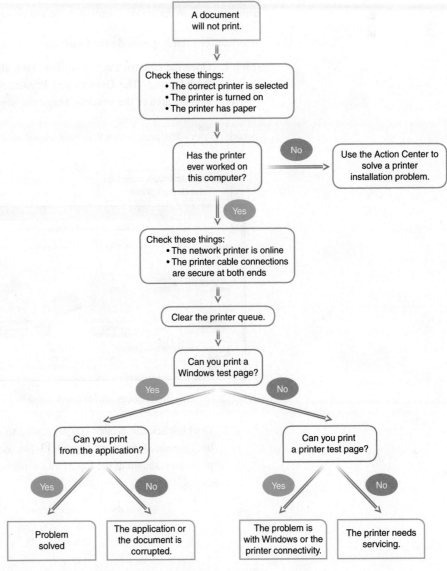

FIGURE 13-12   This plan can help solve a printer problem.

When you're solving a computer problem, check the most likely problems first. Do the following to solve a printer problem:

Step 1. Using the application, verify the correct printer is selected in the Print window.

Step 2. Look for a power light on the front of the printer. Is the printer turned on?

Step 3. Make sure the printer has paper.

Step 4. Check for a paper jam and clear it.

If the problem is still not solved, dig a little deeper and check the following:

Step 1. If the printer has never worked with this computer, perhaps the printer didn't install correctly. Check the Action Center to see whether a problem is reported. If you find the printer installation problem listed there, follow directions onscreen to solve the problem.

Step 2. For a network printer, check that the printer is online. A panel on the front of most network printers says *Ready* or displays a green light to indicate that the printer is online and connected to the network. Check that the network cable is connected at both ends.

Step 3. For a USB printer, check the USB cable connections at both ends.

Perhaps the problem is caused by a corrupted document that has blocked the **printer queue** .

printer queue—A list of documents that users have sent to the printer but have not yet printed.

To clear the printer queue, do the following:

Step 1. Open the Control Panel and click **View devices and printers** in the Hardware and Sound group. The Devices and Printers window opens (see Figure 13-13). In the Printers area of the window, notice the **default printer** has a green check mark.

default printer—The printer that Windows uses if another printer is not selected.

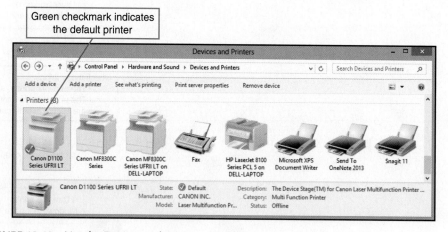

FIGURE 13-13   Use the Devices and Printers window to manage installed printers.

Step 2. Double-click the printer you are trying to reach. The printer window opens (see the background window of Figure 13-14). Any problems that Windows has with the printer are shown at the top of this window.

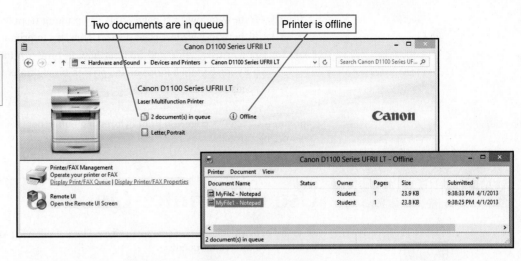

FIGURE 13-14   The printer window reports a problem with the printer.

Tip The options and commands on a printer window might be different for other printer manufacturers.

Not Working? You cannot cancel a document in a printer queue that was put there by another user unless you're logged on as an administrator.

Not Working? The method to use the printer window to print a test page might be different for your printer than the instructions given here.

Step 3. Double-click **document(s) in queue**. The printer queue window appears, listing documents in the queue (see the active window of Figure 13-14).

Step 4. To clear the print queue, click **Printer** and then click **Cancel All Documents**. Click **Yes**. Clearing the queue might take a few moments.

Step 5. Try to print from the application again.

If the problem is still not solved, it's time to find out whether Windows can reach the printer. To find out, you can print a **Windows test page**.

> **Windows test page**—A page that Windows prints to verify that it can communicate with a printer. If the page prints, the problem is with the application. If the page does not print, the problem is with Windows, the printer connectivity, or the printer.

Do the following to identify the source of the problem:

Step 1. If the printer queue is not empty, cancel all documents in the queue to empty the queue.

Step 2. Return to the Devices and Printers window. Right-click the printer and select **Printer properties** from the shortcut menu. In the printer's Properties window (see Figure 13-15), click **Print Test Page**.

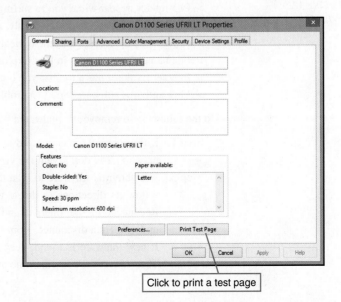

FIGURE 13-15   Print a Windows test page to verify that Windows can reach the printer.

Step 3.   If the Windows test page prints, try printing from the application again.

Step 4.   If the Windows test page doesn't print, try to print a **printer test page** . Look in the printer user guide and find out how to print a printer test page. You can do that by pressing certain buttons on the printer. If the printer test page doesn't print, the printer needs servicing.

> **printer test page**—A page you print by pressing buttons on the printer to verify that the printer is working correctly.

ON YOUR OWN 13.7

Use the Printer Queue

WATCH

OBJECTIVE 13.8
VIDEO

To do this activity, you need access to a printer. Do the following to practice solving printer problems by using the printer queue:

Step 1.   To set up the problem, turn off your printer. Open a Word document that you want to print. Command Word to print the document. Command Word to print the document a second time. Neither printout happens because the printer is turned off.

Step 2.   Open the printer window, which should show the printer is offline and two documents in queue. Open the queue so you can see the list of documents in the queue.

Step 3.   Delete one of these documents in the printer queue.

> **Hint**   To delete a single item in the printer queue, right-click it and select **Cancel** from the shortcut menu.

Step 4.   Turn on the printer. The one document should now print. Watch the printer queue as the document prints and the queue is empty. Then close all windows.

Solutions
Appendix

For help: See *On Your Own 13.7* Step-by-Step Solution

WATCH

OBJECTIVE 13.9
VIDEO

Objective 13.9: I Think My Computer Has a Virus

Symptoms that indicate the computer is infected with a virus or other malware include

> Pop-up ads appear when you're surfing the web.
> The system starts up and runs slowly, and programs take longer to launch.
> A hardware device, such as the optical drive or USB port, no longer works.
> File names and file sizes in File Explorer have changed.
> Internet Explorer has a toolbar you didn't ask for, or your home page has changed.
> Your antivirus software reports a problem.

Do the following to remove the malware:

Step 1.   If the computer is connected to a local network, immediately disconnect it from the network. You don't want the virus to spread to other computers on the network.

Step 2.   Use antivirus software to scan the entire hard drive for malware. If it finds malware, follow its directions to delete the malicious program. Then restart your computer. Reconnect to the Internet and command the antivirus program to download its updates. Then disconnect from the Internet and scan the hard drive again.

Step 3.   If new malware is found, keep repeating this process until a scan comes up clean. Then restart the computer one more time checking for errors.

Step 4. Connect to the Internet and make sure that all important Windows updates are installed. Also use the Network Connections window to verify that your network connection is secured to protect your computer.

Step 5. Open Internet Explorer on the Windows desktop, click the Tools icon, and then click **Internet options**. The Internet Options dialog box opens. If malware has changed your home page, use the **General** tab to correct the problem.

Step 6. To disable any add-ons you don't want in Internet Explorer, click the **Programs** tab and then click **Manage add-ons**. The Manage Add-ons window appears. Under *Show*, select **All add-ons** (see Figure 13-16). Select an add-on and click **Disable**.

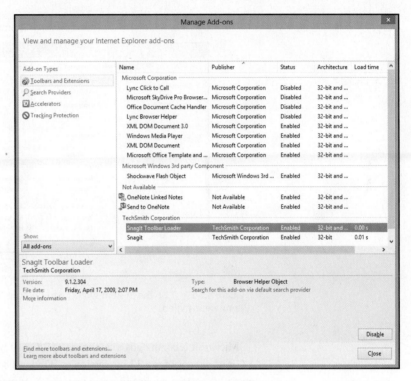

FIGURE 13-16   Disable Internet Explorer add-ons you don't need.

Step 7. Close all windows and then open Internet Explorer. Verify that all is working as it should.

If you're still having problems, know that an experienced technician can dig much deeper to clean up an infected system. It's time to ask for some expert help.

Objective 13.10: My Computer Is Too Slow

WATCH

OBJECTIVE 13.10
VIDEO

A computer might slow down over time if too many programs are running in the background or the hard drive is full. Other problems that cause a slow computer are not enough memory, a slow **processor** , or a slow Internet connection.

> **processor**—The component where all processing of data and instructions takes place. Processors for most personal computers are made by Intel (Intel.com) and AMD (AMD.com) and vary greatly in speed and other features. The processor is also called the central processing unit, or CPU.

Here's how to help solve the problem of a slow computer:

Step 1. Follow directions given earlier in the chapter to clean up the hard drive, uninstall software, and disable programs from launching at startup.

Step 2. Consider you might need more memory. Installing more memory (called upgrading memory) is not as expensive as other upgrades, such as upgrading your processor or hard drive. A memory upgrade might significantly improve computer performance.

Processor

To find out how much memory is installed on a computer, press **Win+X** and click **System**. The System window opens (see Figure 13-17). Information about the system, including the amount of installed memory (RAM), is reported on this window. In Figure 13-17, that amount is 4 GB. Also notice in the figure the system type is a **64-bit operating system**.

> **System window**—A window that displays the edition of Windows, processor, and amount of memory installed. It also shows other information about the system and provides you with access to several Windows tools.
>
> **64-bit operating system**—An operating system that processes 64 bits at a time.

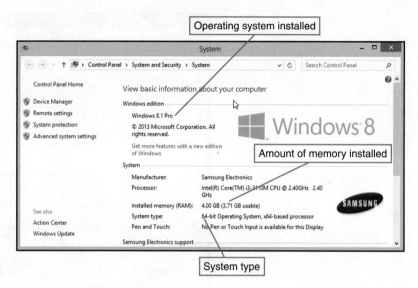

FIGURE 13-17   Use the System window to find out how much memory and which operating system are installed.

Microsoft recommends a minimum of 2 GB of memory for a 64-bit version of Windows 8 and 1 GB of memory for a 32-bit version of Windows 8. If you want to improve performance, a 64-bit operating system can benefit from up to 8 GB of memory. A **32-bit operating system** can benefit from up to 4 GB of memory.

> **32-bit operating system**—An operating system that processes 32 bits at a time. Each edition of Windows 8 comes in a 32-bit or a 64-bit version. The 64-bit versions are generally faster and require more memory than the 32-bit versions.

The amount of memory you need depends on how you use your computer. For example, the more applications you have open at the same time, the more memory you need. Task Manager can help you monitor memory use. Follow these steps:

Step 1.   Open **Task Manager** and click the **Performance** tab (see Figure 13-18). Then click **Memory**.

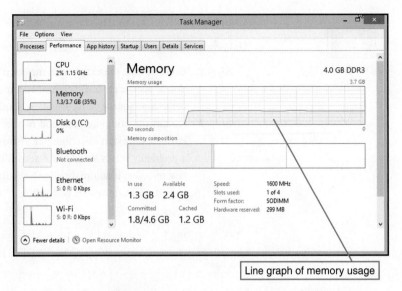

FIGURE 13-18 Use Task Manager to monitor how much of memory is being used.

Step 2. With the line graph displayed, use your computer as you normally would for an hour or so. Keep an eye on the line graph as you work. You know you can benefit from a memory upgrade if the line graph frequently shows no free memory.

If you decide to upgrade memory, be sure to purchase memory modules that are compatible with your computer and have an experienced technician install the modules.

ON YOUR OWN 13.8

WATCH

▶

OBJECTIVE 13.10
VIDEO

Decide Whether Your Computer Needs a Memory Upgrade

To decide whether your computer needs a memory upgrade, do the following:

Step 1. Investigate your system and then answer these questions:

1. What edition of Windows is installed on your computer?
2. Is your operating system a 32-bit or a 64-bit system?
3. How much memory is installed?

Step 2. Open the memory line graph in Task Manager. With the graph displayed, work at your computer for a few minutes and then answer these questions:

1. Did Task Manager report that the computer ran out of free memory as you worked?
2. Do you think your computer needs a memory upgrade? If so, what is the total amount of memory you need?

Solutions
Appendix

For help: See *On Your Own 13.8* Step-by-Step Solution

Objective 13.11: Windows Gives Strange Errors

Unknown Windows errors can be caused by a variety of problems. Here are some steps to try:

Step 1. Copy or type the exact error message in a Google search box and search for information about the error. Be careful because some websites can't be trusted. Microsoft.com is the best source of information about a Windows error.

Step 2. Restart the computer. A good rule of thumb when Windows or an application gives errors is to restart the computer. A fresh restart is sometimes all that's needed to solve a problem. When Windows 8 senses the computer has restarted a third time within a few minutes, it automatically starts diagnostic tools to attempt to solve problems. Try a third or fourth restart and watch as Windows heals itself.

> **Not Working?** If Windows is frozen so you can't restart from the Settings charm, press **Ctrl+Alt+Del**. The screen shown in Figure 13-19 appears. Click the icon in the lower-right corner and select **Restart**, as shown in the figure.

FIGURE 13-19 Use the recovery screen to manage Windows when Windows is frozen.

Step 3. If you find the error is caused by an application, consider the problem might be caused by a data file the application is using and not the application itself. Close the application. Open it again and try a different data file with the same application.

Step 4. If you're convinced the problem is a corrupted application, try updating and repairing the application. If that doesn't work, uninstall the application and then install it again.

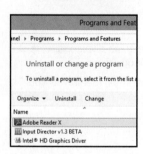

> **Hint** To find out if updates are available for a Windows interface app, first open the **Store** app and then open the **Settings** charm. On the Settings pane, click **App updates**. On the App updates screen, click **Check for updates**. To repair a desktop application, select it in the Programs and Features window and then click **Repair** or **Change** in the menu bar.

Step 5. Open the **Action Center** and check for reported errors. Sometimes one error can lead to another. Go ahead and follow the Action Center directions to resolve any errors.

Step 6. The problem might be caused by malware. Use antivirus software to scan the computer for malware.

Step 7. Windows updates can sometimes solve application or Windows problems. Make sure all important or recommended Windows updates are installed. You learned how to do that in Chapter 12.

Step 8. A healthy hard drive is essential to a healthy computer. A corrupted or failing hard drive often presents itself as a Windows or application error. Windows routinely checks the hard drive for errors and reports them in the Action Center. However, you can manually check the hard drive by following these steps:

   a. Use File Explorer to open the Local Disk (C:) Properties dialog box. Click the **Tools** tab (see Figure 13-20).

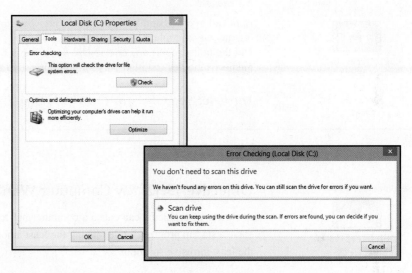

FIGURE 13-20   Check the hard drive for errors or corruption.

   b. Click **Check**. If you aren't signed in as an administrator, you must enter the administrator password in the UAC box. Then the Error Checking box appears, which is also shown in Figure 13-20. Click **Scan drive**.

   c. If the program reports the hard drive has errors, don't trust the drive with your important data and plan to replace the drive soon.

Step 9. Another essential hardware device is memory. A memory module might be going bad, which can cause random Windows errors. Windows routinely checks memory and reports errors in the Action Center. However, you can use the **Memory Diagnostic** utility to manually check memory.

> **Memory Diagnostic**—A Windows utility that tests for a failing memory module. Use the **mdsched** command to start the utility. The utility then restarts Windows and checks memory before Windows is loaded.

Do the following:

   a. Press **Win+X** and click **Run** in the Quick Link menu. In the Run box, type the command **mdsched** and click **OK**. If necessary, provide the administrator password in the UAC box. The Windows Memory Diagnostic dialog box appears (see Figure 13-21). Click **Restart now and check for problems (recommended)**.

   b. If the program reports a problem with memory, all the memory modules in the computer should be replaced.

FIGURE 13-21   The Windows Memory Diagnostic utility checks memory modules for problems.

Step 10. If Windows gives errors when it starts up, open **Task Manager** and go to the **Startup** tab. Disable all startup programs listed on this tab (refer to Figure 13-4 earlier in the chapter). If Windows starts without errors, you can then enable one startup program after another until you find the one causing the error.

Other problems that might give Windows errors include a failing hardware device, corrupted device driver, or corrupted Windows installation. These types of problems are best handled by an experienced computer repair technician.

ON YOUR OWN 13.9

WATCH

OBJECTIVE 13.11
VIDEO

Solutions
Appendix

Check Your Hard Drive and Memory for Errors

Application errors and Windows errors are sometimes caused by a failing hard drive or failing memory module. Use the hard drive Properties dialog box to scan the drive for errors. Did the utility report any errors? Use the Windows Memory Diagnostic utility to test the memory modules installed on your computer. Did the utility report any errors?

For help: See *On Your Own 13.9* Step-by-Step Solution

WATCH

OBJECTIVE 13.12
VIDEO

Objective 13.12: My Computer Won't Start

A variety of problems can cause a computer not to start. Here are the general steps to follow to solve a startup problem while making the least amount of changes to your system, which is called the least intrusive solution:

Step 1. Look for lights on the front of the computer and listen for the fan spinning. If you don't see lights or hear the fan, the computer might not be getting power. Is it plugged in and turned on? For a desktop computer, check the power switch on the back of the computer case. For a laptop, the battery might be low. Plug in the AC adapter.

Step 2. If the computer has power but the monitor is blank, check to see whether the monitor is plugged in and turned on. Look for a small light on the front of a monitor to indicate it's getting power.

Step 3. Before Windows starts, the processor goes through the steps of checking hardware and starting up essential hardware devices. During this stage of starting (also called booting), failures cause a message to display on a black screen (see Figure 13-22). Try a restart by turning off the computer and turning it back on. If you still see the same screen, it's best to get help from an experienced computer repair technician.

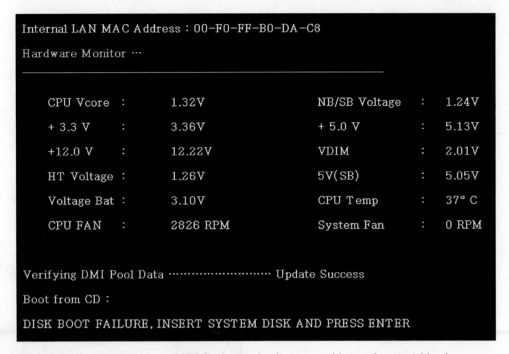

```
Internal LAN MAC Address : 00-F0-FF-B0-DA-C8

Hardware Monitor ···
_____


    CPU Vcore   :     1.32V           NB/SB Voltage  :   1.24V

    + 3.3 V     :     3.36V           + 5.0 V        :   5.13V

    +12.0 V     :     12.22V          VDIM           :   2.01V

    HT Voltage  :     1.26V           5V(SB)         :   5.05V

    Voltage Bat :     3.10V           CPU Temp       :   37° C

    CPU FAN     :     2826 RPM        System Fan     :   0 RPM


Verifying DMI Pool Data ····················· Update Success

Boot from CD :

DISK BOOT FAILURE, INSERT SYSTEM DISK AND PRESS ENTER
```

FIGURE 13-22   A message on a black background indicates a problem with essential hardware devices.

Step 4. If the problem happens when Windows is loading, you might be able to solve the problem yourself. Recall that Windows attempts to fix startup problems if it senses a third restart within a few minutes. Restart the system three or four times and watch to see how Windows handles the problem. Follow directions given by Windows as it presents solutions to you. For example, you might see the Windows Startup Menu in Figure 13-23.

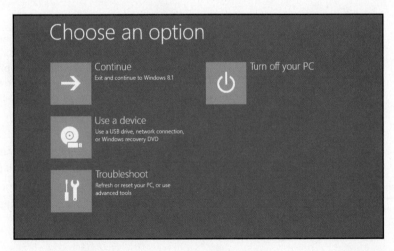

FIGURE 13-23   The Windows Startup Menu might appear if Windows can't start normally. Use the menu to troubleshoot the problem.

Step 5. If you want to attempt to fix the problem, click **Troubleshoot**. The menu in Figure 13-24 appears where you have three choices:

- *Refresh your PC.* When you refresh Windows , you can fix problems with the Windows installation. Your personal files and settings are not disturbed, but you'll lose all your applications except those you installed from the Windows Store. You'll need the Windows 8 setup DVD during the refresh process.

- *Reset your PC.* When you reset Windows , Windows is restored to its state when it was first installed. All your personal files and applications are lost. Use this option only if other troubleshooting steps have failed. You'll need the Windows 8 setup DVD during the reset process.

- *Advanced options* gives you access to less drastic troubleshooting tools. Try it before you try the first two.

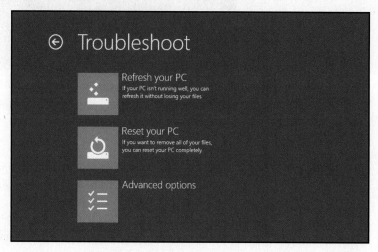

FIGURE 13-24   Windows offers options that allow you to refresh, reset, or troubleshoot Windows.

---

refresh Windows—A process that reinstalls Windows. Your personal files and settings and any apps installed from the Windows Store are backed up and then restored after Windows is reinstalled. You must then reinstall any desktop applications.

reset Windows—A process that returns Windows to its state when it was first installed or to the factory state for brand-name devices. All personal files and settings, Windows 8 apps, and desktop apps are lost.

Step 6. Click **Advanced options**. The Advanced options menu appears (see Figure 13-25). First try **Startup Repair**. Windows restores the files necessary to launch Windows. During the process, you must enter a password to an administrator account. The system will restart, and the problem might be solved.

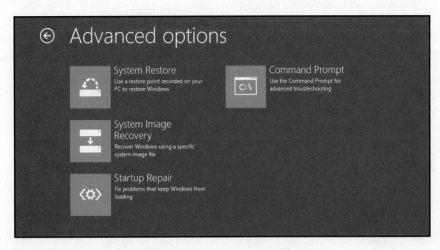

FIGURE 13-25   Windows offers several tools to fix startup problems.

Step 7. If the problem is not fixed, Windows will likely take you back to the Startup Menu in Figure 13-23. Click **Troubleshoot**. On the Troubleshoot screen (see Figure 13-24), click **Advanced options**. On the Advanced options screen (see Figure 13-25), click **System Restore**. **System Restore** returns Windows to a point in time when the system was healthy. On the following screens, select the most recent restore point so as to make the least amount of changes to your system (see Figure 13-26). Then click **Next** and follow directions on screen to apply the restore point. You'll be asked to restart the computer. If the problem is still not solved, return to the System Restore screen and select and apply an earlier restore point.

System Restore—A Windows process to restore the system to a point in time when a restore point or snapshot of Windows was taken. Restore points are automatically created just before major changes are made to the system, such as a critical Windows update being applied.

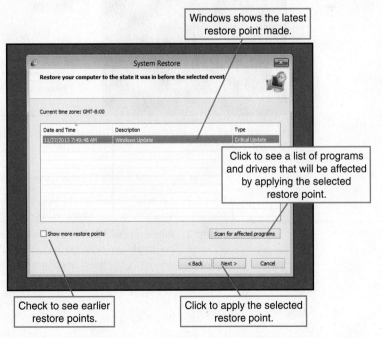

FIGURE 13-26   System Restore lists the most recent restore point so as to make the least changes to the system.

Step 8.   If System Restore still hasn't solved the problem, you can refresh or reset your computer using the Troubleshoot screen shown in Figure 13-24. However, first talk with an experienced computer repair technician. The technician can suggest or use more advanced tools to solve the problem so that a refresh or reset is not needed. If you have no other options, do a refresh. If that doesn't work, then try a reset.

ON YOUR OWN 13.10

View and Use Troubleshooting Tools

WATCH

OBJECTIVE 13.12 VIDEO

The Windows Startup Menu shown in Figure 13-23 will automatically launch when Windows cannot start, but you can manually launch it at any time. To do so, use the Settings charm to go to the PC settings screen and click **Update and recovery**. Then click **Recovery** (see Figure 13-27). Under Advanced startup, click **Restart now**. The computer restarts and displays the Windows Startup Menu.

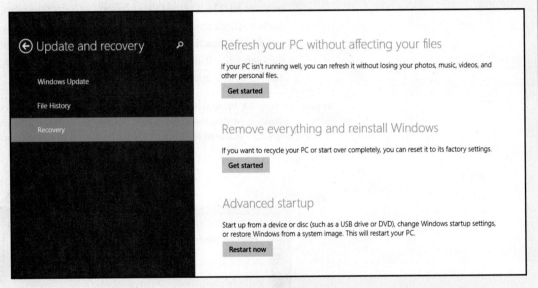

FIGURE 13-27   Use the Update and recovery screen to restart Windows and access tools to solve Windows problems.

Follow these steps to practice using some Windows troubleshooting tools:

Step 1.   Launch Windows to the Windows Startup Menu and perform **Startup Repair** available on the Advanced options menu. The system restarts.

Step 2.   Return to the **Advanced options** menu and click **System Restore**. How many restore points are available on the system? Which programs and devices will be affected if you apply the most recent restore point? Don't actually apply the restore point.

Step 3.   Restart Windows and return to the Start screen.

Solutions Appendix

For help: See *On Your Own 13.10* **Step-by-Step Solution**

Preparing to Talk with a Computer Repair Technician

You won't always be able to solve every computer problem. If this is the case, you need to turn to professional help.

Objective 13.13: Prepare to Talk with a Computer Repair Technician

Before you call for help, gather information about the problem and the computer. Do the following:

Step 1. Start at the beginning. Restart your computer and carefully check for error messages or the first time the problem presents itself. Note what works and what doesn't work. Write down the exact error message.

Step 2. Ask yourself, "When did the problem start? What had just happened when the problem started?" These are important first questions a technician asks when he or she begins the troubleshooting process.

Step 3. Is the computer under warranty? If so, have the purchase receipt and warranty available. You also need the model and serial number of the computer. For a laptop, look on the bottom of the computer. For a desktop, look on the back of the computer case.

Step 4. A technician needs to know the brand and model of a laptop, netbook, or brand-name computer. Do the following to find this information:

  a. If you can start the computer, press **Win+X** and click **Run**. In the Run box, enter **msinfo32** and click **OK**. The System Information window appears (see Figure 13-28). Useful information a technician might ask for is labeled in the figure.

> **System Information**—A Windows utility that reports technical information about a computer, hardware, and software. To launch the utility, use the msinfo32 command.

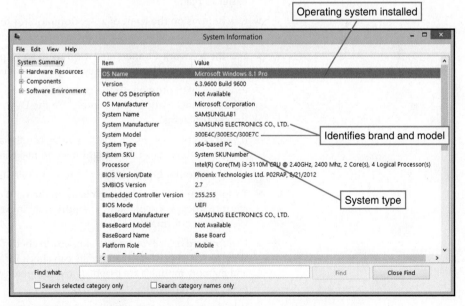

FIGURE 13-28 The System Information window gives useful information a technician can use for troubleshooting.

  b. If you can't start the computer, know that you can find the model and serial numbers on the bottom of a laptop or netbook. You also might find them in the documentation that came with your computer.

As you speak with the technician, state the problem as clearly as you can with as much detail as the technician needs.

Summary

Keeping a Computer Running Well

> Ongoing routine maintenance can keep a computer from slowing down over time.

> Routine maintenance includes keeping the hard drive from filling up, uninstalling software you no longer need, limiting unnecessary startup programs, and protecting hardware from damage caused by power surges, heat, and humidity.

> To clean up a hard drive, empty the Recycle Bin and use the drive Properties dialog box to clean up unneeded files.

> Use the Start screen to uninstall apps you no longer need and then use the Programs and Features window to uninstall desktop applications.

> Use Task Manager to control the programs that are launched when Windows starts. Too many startup programs can slow down Windows.

> Use a surge protector to protect a computer against surging electricity.

> To prevent a computer from overheating, keep vents clear of dust and unobstructed for good airflow. Don't leave a computer in a hot car or humid conditions. Protect a computer from static electricity.

> Use Windows power settings to conserve electricity and make a battery charge on a laptop last longer.

Solving the Most Common Computer Problems

> Look in the Recycle Bin to find a deleted file. Use the backups stored by File History to restore a file.

> Use Task Manager to end an application that is not responding.

> Use the Action Center to solve problems with Windows, software, and hardware, including problems installing software or hardware devices.

> Adjust screen resolution and text size using Windows display settings to make a screen easier to read.

> Use buttons on the front of a desktop monitor to adjust brightness, contrast, and position of the lighted area on the monitor screen.

> Use the Network Connections window to solve problems with network connectivity. For a network in your home, try recycling the modem and router.

> Problems with printing can be caused by the document, the application, Windows, printer connectivity, or the printer. Use the Devices and Printers window to help solve printer problems.

> If your computer is infected with a virus, run the antivirus software multiple times until the scan returns clean. You might need to make several scans to clean an infected system.

> Use the Internet Options dialog box to disable Internet Explorer add-ons.

> To speed up a slow computer, clean up the hard drive, uninstall software, and limit startup processes. Upgrading memory is an inexpensive option that can improve Windows performance.

> Use the hard drive Properties dialog box to check the hard drive for corruption. The Windows Memory Diagnostic utility can check for a failing memory module. The hard drive and memory modules are essential to a computer working well. If the device gives errors, it needs to be replaced.

> When a computer first starts, the hardware presents error messages on a black screen before Windows starts.

> Windows attempts to diagnose and solve startup problems after a third restart within a few minutes. Follow options presented by Windows to solve a startup problem.

> Tools for solving Windows startup problems, listed in the least intrusive order, include multiple restarts, Startup Repair, System Restore, refresh Windows, and reset Windows. Always try the least intrusive solution before you move on to one that will have more drastic effects on the system.

Preparing to Talk with a Computer Repair Technician

> Before talking with a computer repair technician, gather information about the problem and the system. The System Information window can help.

CHAPTER MASTERY PROJECT

Now it's time to find out how well you've mastered the content in this chapter. If you can do all the steps in this Mastery Project without looking back at the chapter details and can answer all the Review Questions following this project, you've mastered this chapter. If you can complete the project by finding answers using Windows Help and Support or on the web, you've proven that you can teach yourself how to fix the most common computer problems.

> **Hint** All the key terms in the chapter are used in this mastery project or in the review questions that follow. If you encounter a key word you don't know, such as *system files*, enter **define:system files** in the Internet Explorer search box.

If you find you need a lot of help doing the project and you have not yet read the chapter or done the activities, drop back and start at the beginning of the chapter, watch the videos, review the step-by-step solutions as you work through the On Your Own activities, and then return to this project.

> **Tip** If you need help completing this part of the mastery project, review the "Keeping a Computer Running Well" section in the chapter.

You need the Windows administrator password to do many of the activities in this project.

Step 1. Do the following computer maintenance to keep a computer in good running order:

1. Clean up the hard drive by emptying the Recycle Bin.

2. To continue cleaning up the hard drive, use Disk Cleanup to clean up data files and system files.

3. Use the Start screen to examine the list of apps installed on your computer. If you find a program listed that you did not know its purpose, research on the web and find out the purpose of the program. Uninstall any app for which you know the purpose and know that you no longer need.

4. Use the Programs and Features window to investigate applications and add-ons listed there. Uninstall any program for which you know the purpose and know that you no longer need.

5. Open Task Manager and select the **Startup** tab. If you find startup programs listed that you understand the purpose and know that you don't need them to launch at startup, disable the programs. Restart your computer and verify all is working as you expect. If you have a problem, go back and enable the program.

Do the following to adjust power settings on your computer:

Step 2. Using the Windows power settings, set your power plan to turn off the display after 10 minutes of inactivity and put the computer to sleep after 30 minutes. Require a password when the computer wakes up.

Step 3. Set the power button to shut down the computer. Test the power button function by pressing it. Does the computer perform an orderly shutdown?

> **Tip** If you need help completing this part of the mastery project, review the "Solving the Most Common Computer Problems" section in the chapter.

Do the following to practice the skills needed to solve computer problems:

Step 4. Create a file in the Documents library of your hard drive. Delete the file. Use the Recycle Bin to recover the deleted file.

Step 5. Open the Action Center. Does the Action Center report any problems to solve? If so, use the Action Center to resolve the problem.

Step 6. Open two instances of the Notepad program and open Task Manager. Use the Windows Snipping Tool to take a snip of your Task Manager window showing the two instances of Notepad running. Create a Word document named Chapter_13_Project and insert the snip into the document. Use Task Manager to close both Notepad windows.

Step 7. Note the current screen resolution for your system and then set it to the highest setting. Return the setting as you found it.

Step 8. Suppose your friend has poor eyesight and needs the text on the screen to be very large. Experiment with customizing the text size on the monitor screen. Set the text size at 200%. After you view the text at this size, return it to the default size.

Step 9. If you are using a desktop monitor, use the buttons on the front of the monitor to adjust the brightness and contrast to get the most contrast and the most brightness. This setting can help someone with poor eyesight. After you make the adjustments, return them to the settings you are comfortable using.

Step 10. If you have access to a printer, practice solving a printer problem by doing the following:

1. Note the printer that is your Windows default printer. Check the printer queue and clear any pending print jobs.

2. Print a Windows test page.

3. Print a printer test page.

Step 11. Use the Internet Options dialog box of Internet Explorer to look at the list of add-ons installed. Is there any add-on you no longer need? If so, disable it.

Step 12. Examine your system using the System window. Which Windows edition is installed? Do you have a 32-bit or a 64-bit operating system installed? How much memory do you have installed? Use the Windows Snipping Tool to take a snip of your screen showing the System window. Insert the snip into the Chapter_13_Project document you created in step 6.

Do the following to practice solving problems with a slow computer:

Step 13. Crucial.com sells reliable memory modules and offers a utility that can tell you how much memory you have installed and what memory modules you need to buy for an upgrade. Go to the Crucial.com site and run the Crucial System Scanner Tool on your computer. What memory modules did Crucial recommend you buy? Do not make the purchase and attempt to install the memory before first talking with an experienced computer technician.

Step 14. If you have not already done so, use the hard drive Properties dialog box to scan your hard drive for errors and corruption.

Step 15. If you have not already done so, use the Windows Memory Diagnostic utility to scan memory for a failing memory module.

Do the following to practice solving Windows startup problems:

Step 16. Restart Windows to the Windows Startup Menu and find out how many restore points are available if you were to perform a System Restore (don't actually do the System Restore). Then perform a Startup Repair and return Windows to the Start screen.

> **Tip** If you need help completing this part of the mastery project, review the "Preparing to Talk with a Computer Repair Technician" section in the chapter.

To find information useful for a computer repair technician, do the following:

Step 17. Open the System Information window. What is the reported System Model for your computer?

Step 18. Enter your name and course information into the Chapter_13_Project document containing the two snips and send the document to your instructor. If you are using MyITLab, you can post the file in a Dropbox assignment or email the file in MyITLab. On the other hand, your instructor might prefer you post the file to your OneDrive or email the file using your school email.

Review Questions

Answer these questions to assess your skills and knowledge of the content covered in the chapter. Your instructor can provide you with the correct answers when you are ready to check your work.

1. For a hard drive that holds a Windows installation, what minimum percentage of the drive should be free?

2. What are four external factors mentioned in the chapter that can cause hardware devices to not last as long as they should?

3. Suppose you leave a CD on the dashboard of your car in the summer. Why might it not last as long as a CD kept at your desk in your home?

4. What device can you use with your computer to protect the computer against lightning?

5. Why is it not a good idea to use your laptop while it is sitting on a pillow?

6. You accidentally left your laptop in your car on a freezing night and then brought it inside. Why is it important that you not turn it on immediately?

7. Why is it important to keep air vents on a computer unobstructed and free from dust? What inexpensive consumable product can you purchase to clean your computer vents and your keyboard?

8. Why is it important to put a desktop computer in a place where it will not get kicked?

9. Why is it important to not leave a laptop in a hot car? In a damp basement?

10. Why is it important to keep the mouse pad and the bottom of the mouse clean? What two chemicals are not good to use when cleaning the monitor screen?

11. List four types of hardware devices on a laptop that consume energy and whose use should be limited when you're trying to extend the battery charge.

12. What two items appear on the Power Options window of a laptop computer that don't appear on the Power Options window of a desktop?

13. You will be away from an electrical outlet all day, but your laptop battery lasts only four hours. What can you do to make sure you can use your laptop all day?

14. To conserve the battery charge, which two activities should you not do:
    a. Use your laptop to watch a movie on DVD
    b. Dim your monitor screen
    c. Watch a movie streamed over a public Wi-Fi network
    d. Watch a movie stored on the hard drive of your laptop

15. When you can't access a web page using Internet Explorer, which should you do first to fix the problem: use commands in Internet Explorer, use commands in the Network Connections window, or recycle a home router and modem?

16. What Windows utility do you use if you connect a USB scanner to your computer and the scanner does not install properly?

17. Your document will not print, so you decide to clear the printer queue. You notice another document first in the queue that belongs to another user. You are logged on to Windows with a standard user account. What can you do to clear the queue?

18. To demonstrate that the printer is working correctly, do you print a Windows test page or a printer test page?

19. In the Devices and Printers window, how can you identify which installed printer is the Windows default printer?

20. List six symptoms that indicate your computer might be infected with a virus.

21. Reorder the following task to remove malware:
    a. Use antivirus software to scan the system
    b. Remove unwanted add-ons and toolbars in Internet Explorer
    c. Install Windows updates
    d. Disconnect the computer from the local network

22. To improve computer performance, which is easier and less expensive to upgrade: the processor or memory?

23. If you get a Windows error message you do not understand, how can you get help to understand the message?

24. What is the optimum memory for a 32-bit installation of Windows 8? For a 64-bit installation of Windows 8?

25. Which Windows utility can you use to monitor how much memory Windows is currently using?

26. Suppose you have 2 GB of memory installed in a 32-bit Windows system and the Windows utility in question 25 reports less than 50% of memory is in use as you work normally at your computer. Will your system's performance improve with a memory upgrade?

27. What two essential hardware devices might be the source of random Windows error messages on-screen? What can you do to have Windows check these devices?

28. If an application gives an error when it opens a data file, what should you do before you repair or reinstall the app?

29. When Windows gives problems during or after startup, what is one of the first things you should do before you begin changing Windows or application settings or using Windows tools for troubleshooting?

30. When solving problems with Windows, which should you do first: scan for viruses, update Windows, or check the Action Center for reported errors?

31. Which color screen does hardware normally use when reporting a hardware error before Windows is started?

32. If your screen is blank when you first turn on a computer, what is the first thing you should check?

33. Which process will erase all your user data and settings: resetting Windows or refreshing Windows? Which of these processes should you use if you want to sell your computer and don't want any of your private data or information to get in the hands of the new owner?

34. List the following processes in the least intrusive order to be used when attempting to solve a Windows problem: reset Windows, refresh Windows, Startup Repair, and System Restore.

35. Before speaking with a computer repair technician, list four things you can do to prepare for the conversation.

Becoming an Independent Learner

Answer the following questions about becoming an independent learner:

1. To teach yourself to solve computer problems, do you think it is best to rely on the chapter or on the web and Windows Help when you need answers?

2. The most important skill learned in this chapter is how to teach yourself a computer skill. Rate yourself at Level A through E on how well you're doing with this skill. What is your level?

   - Level A: I was able to successfully complete the Chapter Mastery Project with the help of only a few of the On Your Own activities in the chapter.
   - Level B: I completed all the On Your Own activities and the Chapter Mastery Project without referring to any of the solutions in the Step-by-Step Solutions Appendix.
   - Level C: I completed all the On Your Own activities and the Chapter Mastery Project by using just a few of the solutions in the Step-by-Step Solutions Appendix.
   - Level D: I completed all the On Your Own activities and the Chapter Mastery Project by using many of the solutions in the Step-by-Step Solutions Appendix.
   - Level E: I completed all the On Your Own activities and the Chapter Mastery Project and had to use all of the solutions in the Step-by-Step Solutions Appendix.

To continue toward the goal of teaching yourself computer skills, if you're not at Level A, try to move up one level on how you learn in Chapter 14.

Career Project My boss has asked me to care for 10 computers in our office. I've decided that one day a month, I'll do all the required maintenance for each computer. I need a checklist to help me identify each computer and keep track of the maintenance I've done.

Personal Project My computer is only three years old and has started to run slowly. Is it getting old? Should I replace it, or can I do something to speed it up?

Academic Project I've been assigned a computer to use while in school, and I need to take good care of it. I want to make sure it stays protected and runs well. I also want to change some settings on the Windows desktop.

Projects to Help You

Now that you've mastered the material in this chapter, you're ready to tackle the three projects focused on your career, personal, or academic goals. Depending on your own interests, you might choose to complete any or all of these projects to help you achieve your goals.

Project 1: Computer Maintenance Form

Prepare a Word document that can be used as a maintenance form for an individual or business to track the routine maintenance done on a computer. Include on the form the information needed to identify the computer and the routine maintenance tasks you learned about in this chapter. Also include the date the maintenance was done and the name of the person who did the maintenance.

Send the file to your instructor. If you're using MyITLab, you can post the file in Dropbox in MyITLab. On the other hand, your instructor might prefer you post the file to your OneDrive.

Project 2: Maintaining a Personal Computer

A computer can slow down over time if it is not well maintained. Are you responsible for your own computer, or do you have a friend who needs help maintaining his or her computer? If so, do the following to make sure this computer is being well maintained:

Step 1. Following directions in the chapter, go through the steps to make sure the computer is secure, the hard drive is clean, and Windows is not bogged down with unnecessary startup processes.

Step 2. Check the hardware to make sure it is being protected from power surges, heat, and humidity. Clean the computer vents, keyboard, mouse, and monitor screen.

Step 3. Adjust the power settings as needed to conserve electricity. For a laptop, adjust the power settings as needed to conserve the battery charge.

Step 4. Display the window that shows what happens when you press the power button. Use the Windows Snipping Tool to take a snip of this System Settings window. Save the snip to a document file. Include in the file your name and course information and send the file to your instructor. If you're using MyITLab, you can post the file in Dropbox in MyITLab. On the other hand, your instructor might prefer you post the file to your OneDrive.

Project 3: Setting Up Windows Maintenance and the Windows Desktop

Suppose you have just received a computer to be used while you are working toward a degree. You need the computer to last for several years, and you want to set it up with your own preferences. To do that, you need the administrator password. Some tasks not covered in the chapter are included in this project. If you're not sure how to perform a task, check Windows Help and Support or search the web.

Do the following to make sure the computer is set up for good maintenance:

Step 1. Verify antivirus software is set to run in the background and automatically update itself.

Step 2. Verify Windows Update is set to install updates automatically. What is the name of the window where you can change how Windows installs updates?

Step 3. For a wireless computer, verify the wireless network connection is set to protect the computer from attacks.

Step 4. Open Task Manager. Leave the Performance tab displayed while you work at your computer. Does Task Manager show signs you don't have enough memory? Besides monitoring memory, what three other devices can Task Manager monitor on the Performance tab?

Do the following to customize the Windows desktop:

Step 5. You plan to use the Documents library to hold all your academic papers. Normally, Windows puts only the Recycle Bin on the desktop. Add an icon to the desktop that will open the Documents library in File Explorer when you double-click it. This icon on the desktop is called a shortcut icon. List the steps to create the shortcut. What is the name of the shortcut?

Step 6. Rename the shortcut icon to **My Academic Papers**. List the steps to rename the shortcut. To use the shortcut, double-click it.

Step 7. Change the desktop wallpaper to the **Lines and colors** theme. Which window did you use to make the change? After you view this theme when applied, change it to a different theme if you don't like this one.

Step 8. You plan to use Microsoft Word and Excel in your academic career. Normally, Windows puts only the Internet Explorer and File Explorer Quick Launch icons in the taskbar. To make Word and Excel easier to access, add these two program icons to the taskbar. List the steps to add the Word application as a Quick Launch icon in the taskbar.

Step 9. Sign off and then sign back on to Windows to verify all your preferences are applied when you first sign in.

After you complete this project, you might want to undo all the changes you made to the Windows desktop.

Project to Help Others

One of the best ways to learn is to teach someone else. In teaching someone else, you are making a contribution in that person's life. As part of each chapter's work, you are encouraged to teach someone else a skill you have learned. In this chapter, help someone learn to maintain a computer and fix a computer problem.

Working with your apprentice, do the following:

Step 1. People learn best when they want to learn and when they are ready to learn. Consider the computer skills your apprentice already knows. Based on these skills, list five tasks covered in this chapter that you believe your apprentice is ready to learn. Here are some suggestions, but you might have other ideas:

1. How to find a deleted file in the Recycle Bin
2. How to clean up the hard drive
3. How to change monitor settings
4. How to rid a system of a virus

Step 2. Ask your apprentice which of these skills she would like to learn and then help your apprentice learn these skills. Remember, a coach teaches from the sidelines. Watch as your apprentice explores and help her learn the art of teaching herself a computer skill.

Step 3. Use Notepad to create a text file that contains answers about the tutoring session and send the file to your instructor. If you're using MyITLab, you can post the file in Dropbox in MyITLab. On the other hand, your instructor might prefer you post the file to your OneDrive. Here are the questions:

1. Who is your apprentice?
2. In step 1, what topic did your apprentice choose to better understand?
3. In step 2, describe how successful your apprentice was at teaching herself. What resources did your apprentice use to learn this new skill?
4. Briefly describe how the apprentice evaluated the tutoring session.
5. How do you think the session went? How would you like to improve it next time?

14 Buying Your Own Personal Computer

In This Chapter, You Will:

Decide Between an Upgrade and a New Computer

14.1 Identify upgrades needed for your current computer

14.2 Decide whether it's cost effective to upgrade or buy a new computer

Decide on the Type of Computer

14.3 Decide between a PC (IBM-compatible computer) and a Mac (Apple computer)

14.4 Choose a desktop, all-in-one, or mobile computer

Shop for a Computer and Peripherals

14.5 Set a budget and research computer manufacturers and products

14.6 Select the processor and memory

14.7 Select the hard drive and the type and edition of Windows

14.8 Select the video components and other features

14.9 Know about the features to look for in a monitor or printer

In this chapter, you learn about all the different technologies used with today's computers so you can make the best upgrade and buying decisions. The computer market is constantly changing. The facts about the current computer market presented in this chapter are likely to be outdated quickly. Therefore, you must learn how to investigate hardware and software offerings on your own and make decisions based on your findings.

As with all chapters in this book, you can choose which of the learning paths below best suits your needs. No matter which path you choose, as you work your way through the chapter, remember the most important computer skill is how to teach yourself a computer skill. Therefore, this chapter is designed to help you teach yourself how to make computer upgrade and buying decisions.

LEARNING PATHS

GUIDED LEARNING	EXPLORE AND DISCOVER	JUMP RIGHT IN
Read the Chapter *Watch the Objective Videos*	**On Your Own Projects** *Review Objective videos or use Step-by-Step Solutions*	**Mastery Project** *Use Objective videos & OYO projects for help*
On Your Own Projects *Review Objective videos or use Step-by-Step Solutions*		
Mastery Project *Use Objective videos & OYO projects for help*	**Mastery Project** *Use Objective videos & OYO projects for help*	**Explore Resources** *For help as needed*
Google Project (if applicable) *Watch Google video for help*	**Google Project (if applicable)** *Watch Google video for help*	**Google Project (if applicable)** *Watch Google video for help*
Helping You & Others Projects	**Helping You & Others Projects**	**Helping You & Others Projects**
MyITLab Assessment	**MyITLab Assessment**	**MyITLab Assessment**

Deciding Between an Upgrade and a New Computer

You might be ready to buy your own computer or help someone else buy one. If you already have a computer, the first question to ask yourself is whether you need to upgrade your computer or buy a new computer.

WATCH

OBJECTIVE 14.1
VIDEO

Objective 14.1: Identify Upgrades Needed for Your Current Computer

Computers tend to need replacing about every four to six years. If you already have a computer that is less than five years old, consider upgrading it rather than replacing it. People usually replace a computer that isn't broken for two reasons: the computer doesn't have a device they want, or the computer is too slow.

Generally, the total cost of upgrades should not exceed the current value of your computer. The cost of each upgrade includes the cost of the component and the cost of labor to install it. Figure 14-1 can help you decide whether an upgrade can satisfy your needs.

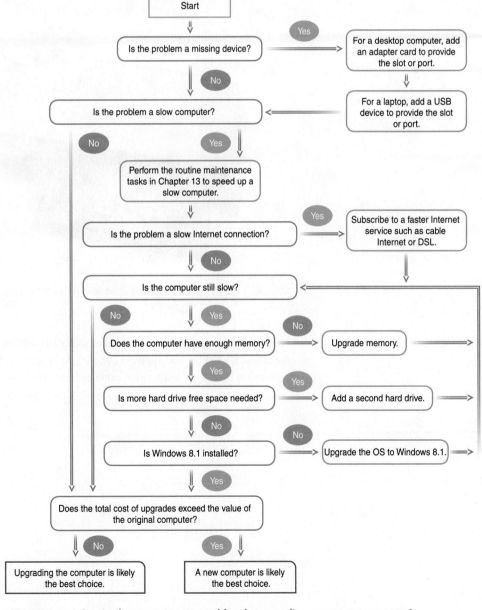

FIGURE 14-1   Can I solve my computer problem by upgrading my current computer?

Let's work our way through the diagram in Figure 14-1 to see whether an upgrade is your best option.

Is Your Computer Missing a Device?

You might be able to install a port, slot, or other hardware device that is missing. For example, suppose your new digital camera uses the latest **Secure Digital (SD) card** but your **memory card reader** in your three-year old laptop doesn't support the newer type of card. You can purchase a USB memory card reader that plugs into a USB port and provides the latest memory card slots (see Figure 14-2).

SD card

> **Secure Digital (SD) card**—A small storage card, commonly called an SD card, used in digital cameras, cell phones, tablets, and other mobile devices. Types of SD cards include the original SD card, MicroSD card, SDHC card, MicroSDHC card, SDXC card, and MicroSDXC card.
>
> **memory card reader**—A device that includes one or more slots to insert a memory card. The device can read and write to the card.

FIGURE 14-2   This USB memory card reader has three slots for three types of memory cards.

In another example, your desktop computer has a VGA video port, and your new monitor uses the newer DVI video port. In this case, you can use a small adapter (see Figure 14-3) to make the conversion between a VGA video cable and the DVI port on the monitor.

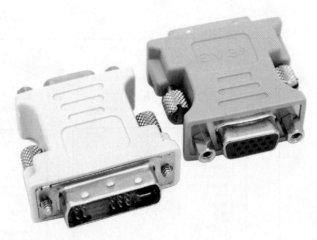

FIGURE 14-3   Use an adapter to connect a DVI port to a VGA cable.

Graphics card

Another option is to install a new graphics card in your computer. This type of adapter card provides a DVI port and a faster graphics experience. Another reason you might want to install a new graphics card is to provide an extra video port on your computer for a second monitor.

> **graphics card**—A type of adapter card that, for a desktop computer, provides one or more video ports for one or more monitors. A graphics card is also called a video card.
>
> **adapter card**—A circuit board that attaches to the motherboard inside the desktop computer case and provides ports that stick out the back of the case to connect a peripheral device.

Not all graphics cards or adapter cards fit every computer, so check with a computer technician to find out what types of cards your computer can handle.

Tip When upgrading memory, be sure to have an experienced technician select the memory modules that are compatible with your system and install the modules.

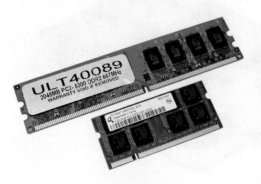

Is Your Computer Slow?

After you determine whether your computer is missing a device, the next question to ask is, "Is my computer slow?" A slow computer can be caused by a variety of problems:

> *Lack of routine maintenance.* See Chapter 13 to find out how to perform the routine maintenance needed to prevent a computer from slowing down over time.
> *Not enough memory.* Upgrading memory is the easiest and least expensive type of computer upgrade. Adding more memory can sometimes make a big difference in computer performance. See Chapter 13 to find out how much memory you have and how much your system needs.
> *Slow Internet or network connection.* If your cable Internet, DSL, dial-up, or mobile broadband connection to your house or office is slow, upgrading your computer won't solve the problem. You need to consider upgrading or replacing your Internet service subscription. On the other hand, you might speed up network performance by using a wired connection to the local network rather than a slower wireless connection. To find out the speed of your local network connection, open the Network Connections window and double-click the wired or wireless connection (see Figure 14-4).

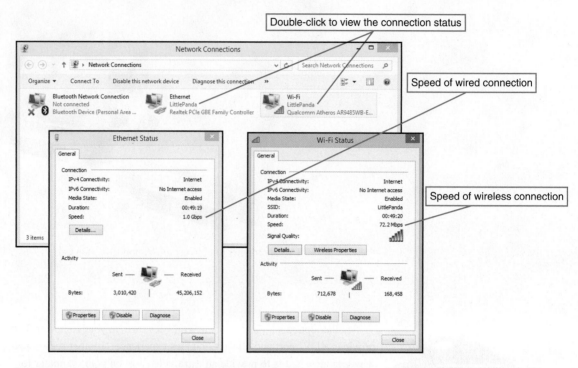

Double-click to view the connection status

Speed of wired connection

Speed of wireless connection

FIGURE 14-4 The connection status for the wired and wireless connections give the connection speed in Gbps or Mbps. The Ethernet connection is much faster than the Wi-Fi connection.

> *Not enough hard drive space.* In Chapter 13, you learned that Windows needs about 15% of free hard drive space to do its work. After you follow the directions in Chapter 13 to clean up your hard drive, you still might not have enough space. You can purchase a second hard drive and use it to hold your music, photos, movies, backups, and other data. Most desktop computers can accommodate a second hard drive installed inside the computer case. For desktops and laptops, you can also install an external hard drive (see Figure 14-5).

FIGURE 14-5 Use an external hard drive to add to the available hard drive space.

Most external drives plug into a USB port. The fastest USB ports are SuperSpeed USB ports. For best performance, make sure the USB port and the hard drive both use SuperSpeed USB. A SuperSpeed USB port is blue on the inside (see Figure 14-6). You can also use the System Information window to find out what types of USB ports are installed on your computer.

> **SuperSpeed USB**—USB standard 3.0 that's about 10 times faster than USB 2.0 (also called Hi-Speed USB) and 400 times faster than original USB.
>
> **Hi-Speed USB**—USB standard 2.0 that's about 40 times faster than original USB.

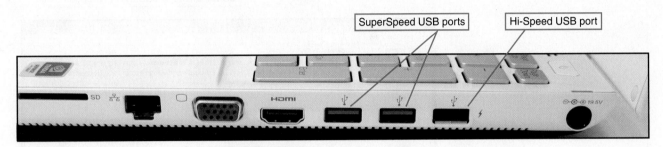

| SuperSpeed USB ports | Hi-Speed USB port |

FIGURE 14-6   This laptop has two SuperSpeed USB ports and one Hi-Speed USB port.

> *A slow operating system.* Windows 8.1 is the fastest operating system Microsoft has released so far. In addition, a 64-bit installation of Windows runs faster than a 32-bit installation. If your computer is using Windows 7, Windows XP, or Windows Vista, consider upgrading the operating system to Windows 8 and then installing the free Windows 8.1 update. First, make sure your computer can support Windows 8 and consider the cost of the upgrade. Here are the minimum hardware requirements for Windows 8 or Windows 8.1:
>   > At least 2 GB of memory (4 GB or more is better)
>   > A processor that runs at 1 GHz or faster
>   > About 30 GB of free hard drive space
> *The processor, hard drive, or video is too slow for the system.* One of these three key components might be a bottleneck slowing down the overall performance of your computer. An experienced computer technician can tell you which component might be affecting overall performance and whether your computer might benefit from upgrading this component.

ON YOUR OWN 14.1

Determine What Upgrades Would Improve Your Computer's Performance

WATCH

OBJECTIVE 14.1 VIDEO

To investigate your computer to find out which components might be slowing performance, follow these steps:

Step 1. Find out the speeds of your wired and/or wireless network connection. The highest speed for a wired connection is 1.0 Gbps. The highest speed for a Wi-Fi connection is 144 Mbps. What are your wired and/or wireless network connection speeds?

Step 2. Use the Speedtest.net website to find the speed of your Internet connection. Which is faster: your download speed or your upload speed?

Step 3. A slow USB port can slow down data transmissions with an external hard drive. To find out what type USB ports your computer has, open the System Information window and click **USB** in the Components group. For example, the computer in Figure 14-7 has one SuperSpeed USB port and two Hi-Speed USB ports. If your computer uses SuperSpeed USB, examine the USB ports and identify the SuperSpeed USB ports. When looking at a port, how can you tell if it's a SuperSpeed USB port?

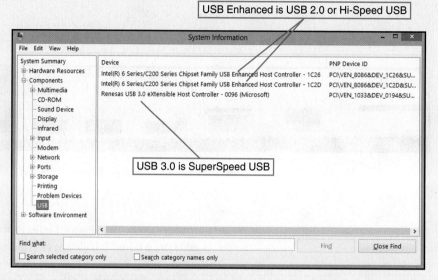

FIGURE 14-7   The System Information window reports the types of USB ports in a system.

Step 4. If you don't already have Windows 8 installed on your computer, use the Windows Upgrade Assistant at http://windows.microsoft.com/upgradeadvisor to find out if your system qualifies for Windows 8.1. What is the name of the program file that is executed?

Solutions Appendix

For help: See *On Your Own 14.1* Step-by-Step Solution

WATCH

OBJECTIVE 14.2
VIDEO

Objective 14.2: Decide Whether It's Cost Effective to Upgrade or Buy a New Computer

When deciding to upgrade your current computer or buy a new one, generally, upgrading is cost effective only if the total cost of upgrades doesn't exceed the value of the current computer. You therefore need to know your computer's current value, which is affected by these factors:

> Type of computer (desktop, laptop, netbook, or all-in-one).
> Brand and model unless the computer was assembled from parts.
> If the computer was assembled from parts, consider the brand, speed, and features of key components including the processor, **motherboard** , hard drive, and memory.

> **motherboard**—The main circuit board inside a computer case or laptop (see Figure 14-8). The board holds the processor, memory modules, and adapter cards and provides ports out the back of a desktop or on the back and sides of a laptop.

> Operating system installed.
> Applications installed.
> Age of the computer and remaining warranty period if any.

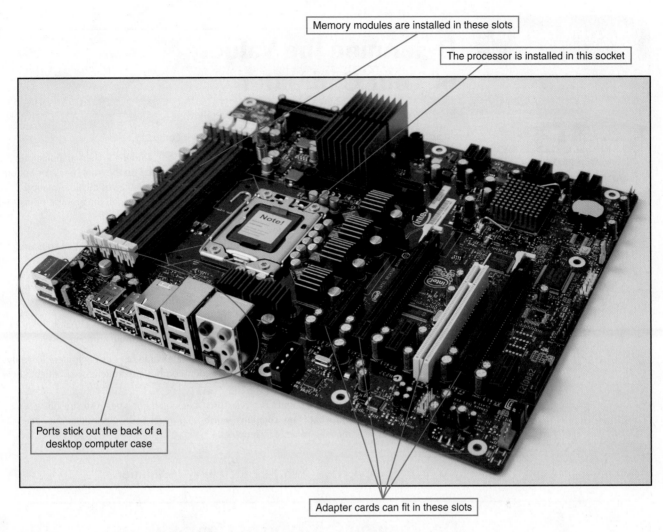

Memory modules are installed in these slots

The processor is installed in this socket

Ports stick out the back of a desktop computer case

Adapter cards can fit in these slots

FIGURE 14-8   A motherboard provides ports for external devices and slots for internal devices.

Tip If you want to move the applications installed on your old computer to your new computer, don't include the applications when determining the value of your old computer. Be sure to uninstall these applications before getting rid of the old computer. Remember, however, that an application designed for an older edition of Windows might not install on Windows 8.1.

With the information about your computer in hand, search the web for computers for sale that are comparable to yours. You can also talk with a used computer store for advice.

As a rule of thumb, a computer loses about 20% of its value immediately after you purchase it and another 20% each year. That means a computer older than four or five years is not worth much. Its low value probably doesn't justify expensive upgrades.

Determine the Value of Your Computer

WATCH

OBJECTIVE 14.2
VIDEO

To assign a current value to your computer, do the following:

Step 1. Collect the following information about your computer:

- For a brand-name desktop, laptop, or netbook, find the system manufacturer and system model. This information is often imprinted on the front, back, or bottom of a computer. The System Information window also gives this information.
- For a desktop built from parts, find the processor model, the amount of installed memory, and the size of the hard drive.
- The edition of Windows installed.
- A list of applications installed that were purchased as commercial software.
- The age of the computer and any warranty that might still apply.
- If available, the original price of the computer. If you know the computer's age and original price, use the 20%-reduction-per-year rule to calculate the computer's approximate value.

Step 2. Search the web for at least three comparable computers for sale. What is the price of each computer? What is the average price of all comparable computers?

Step 3. Based on your findings, what is the approximate value of your computer? To verify you have the right value, you can ask expert computer technicians you might know.

> **Hint** Both eBay.com and Craigslist.org offer used computers for sale. Also, try doing a Google.com search on **what is my computer worth**. You might find websites that offer free calculators to determine the value of a computer.

Solutions
Appendix

For help: See *On Your Own 14.2* Step-by-Step Solution

Deciding on the Type of Computer

If the total cost of the upgrades exceeds the value of your computer, it's time to consider buying a new computer. When you're deciding what type of computer you need, the first factors to consider are compatibility and mobility.

WATCH

OBJECTIVE 14.3
VIDEO

Objective 14.3: Decide Between a PC (IBM-Compatible Computer) and a Mac (Apple Computer)

Technically speaking, a PC is an **IBM-compatible computer** , which can be made by many different manufacturers, including Dell, IBM, HP, Asus, and Sony. All these computers are generally designed to use a Windows operating system by Microsoft or a **Linux** operating system. Most personal computers sold are IBM compatible and use the Windows operating system.

> **IBM-compatible computer**—Any computer that uses the Windows operating system or the Linux operating system and is not made by Apple. The term PC generally refers to an IBM-compatible personal computer because the first personal computers were made by IBM.
>
> **Linux**—A free or low-cost operating system developed by volunteer contributors. Linux is open source software, meaning that the code to write the software is openly available for anyone to see and edit. Linux is used on mainframe computers (large computers that support other computers), personal computers, and mobile devices.

The other computer design is produced solely by one manufacturer: Apple Inc. (www.apple.com). Apple makes desktop, all-in-one, notebook, netbook, and tablet computers. All Apple computers come with the Mac operating system preinstalled. The Mac operating system is also made by Apple, and an Apple computer is called a Mac.

> Mac operating system—The operating system used on all Apple desktop, notebook, and netbook computers. An Apple desktop or mobile personal computer is called a Mac.

Users of Macs generally like the intuitive user interface and beautiful graphics of the Mac operating system. Here are the important points to consider when you're thinking of purchasing a Mac:

> A good reason to buy a Mac is you're already familiar with the Mac OS and like the way it works.

> Another good reason to buy a Mac is your friends or coworkers use a Mac and you need to share data and work on the same projects as a team. If all team members are using Macs, compatibility is not a problem.

> All the applications you install on your Mac must be specifically written for the Mac OS. Applications in desktop publishing, graphics design, music, entertainment, and education abound for the Mac. If you are considering a career in one of these fields, knowing how to use a Mac can be a strong asset.

> All internal components you replace or add to your Mac must be Apple components or approved by Apple.

> Macs generally cost more than a comparable IBM-compatible computer.

Because IBM-compatible computers are so popular, this book focuses on these computers along with the Windows operating system they are most likely to use.

Objective 14.4: Choose a Desktop, All-in-One, or Mobile Computer

WATCH

OBJECTIVE 14.4
VIDEO

When choosing among a desktop computer, all-in-one, and mobile computer, keep these points in mind:

> A desktop computer offers you the most performance for your money. Desktop computers are easily upgraded and cost less than comparable laptops or all-in-one computers. Desktops vary widely in features and price.

> All-in-one computers cost more than a comparable desktop, but they take up less space. They're likely to include a touch screen and wireless keyboard and mouse.

> Laptops and high-end tablet PCs are mobile and cost more than desktops or all-in-ones with comparable performance. Types of mobile computers are shown in Figure 14-9.

Laptop or notebook is the best-performing mobile computer

Netbook is lightweight and has a small screen

Tablet PC lid can flip around to lie flat on the keyboard

A handheld tablet relies on a touch screen for input

Smart phone contains programs called apps

FIGURE 14-9 Types of mobile computers include a laptop, netbook, tablet PC, handheld tablet, and smart phone.

Here is a brief description of each type of mobile computer:

> **Laptop or notebook computer.** Laptops generally cost more than desktop computers with similar performance. You pay extra for the lighter-weight and longer-lasting battery, but you can get just as much performance in a laptop or **ultrabook** as you can a desktop if you are willing to pay for it.

ultrabook—A light and thin laptop that generally costs more than heavier and thicker laptops.

> **Netbook.** A netbook is a low-end laptop with a small screen and keyboard and slower performance. It's designed for low-budget general use, such as surfing the web and email. Netbooks can't support applications that require a lot of computing resources. On the other hand, netbooks are much lighter than laptops, and the battery can stay charged longer. Most netbooks don't have an optical drive.

> **Tablet PC.** The high-end tablet PC can perform just as well as a laptop or desktop. These tablet PCs are more expensive than either because the touch screen has the ability to flip around and lie flat on top of the keyboard. Tablet PCs are designed to receive and interpret handwriting and voice input in addition to touch pad and keyboard input.

> **Handheld tablet.** Various handheld tablet devices range from the more expensive iPad by Apple and PlayBook by BlackBerry to the less expensive **Android** -based tablets. Tablets use a virtual keyboard that appears on the screen when you need it. Some tablet devices are also smart phones.

> **Android**—An operating system used by smart phones, mobile computers, and desktop computers. The Android operating system is based on Linux.

> **Smart phones.** Most cell phones are also smart phones, which can hold a few applications that don't require much computing resources. A smart phone has Internet applications and personal management functions, such as a calendar, appointment book, address book, calculator, and notepad. You can use a smart phone to keep up on Facebook and Twitter, send and receive email, and access the web. A smart phone might have an embedded camera, MP3 player, or audio recorder. Some smart phones have touch screens; others have mini-keyboards.

The key factors to consider when selecting a mobile computer include

> **Manufacturer.** Choose a good manufacturer because almost all the future support for a computer comes from this manufacturer. Be sure to read some reviews about the manufacturer you are considering.

> **Screen size and size of the keyboard.** If you plan to do a lot of work at your mobile computer, a larger screen and keyboard are more comfortable.

> **Weight.** Realize the advertised weight of a mobile computer does not include the weight of the battery.

> **Expansion or upgrade.** Mobile computers are built with little room for expansion or upgrades. What you first buy is what you most likely will live with, except for, perhaps, a memory upgrade.

> **Battery charge.** Some netbooks and handheld tablets can keep a battery charge all day. Battery charge on a laptop or tablet PC might not last more than four or five hours. Batteries for mobile computers are rated by number of cells. Sometimes you can customize the battery for a laptop or netbook. The more cells the battery has, the longer the battery charge.
Some high-end laptops use two batteries. The regular battery is installed inside the case, and a second sheet battery fits on the bottom of the laptop (see Figure 14-10). The two batteries can yield up to 12 hours of continuous charge.

FIGURE 14-10   A sheet battery fits on the bottom of a laptop and enhances the charge from the main battery.

ON YOUR OWN 14.3

Compare Prices and Features for a Desktop and a Comparable Laptop

WATCH

OBJECTIVE 14.4
VIDEO

Desktop computers generally cost less than a laptop with comparable features and performance. To verify that, do the following:

Step 1. Shop online for a low-priced Windows 8.1 desktop computer that doesn't have many extra features. Collect information about the desktop in the second column of Table 14-1. You can find the table in the document file named CompareComputers-Table in the sample_files folder available at www.pearsonhighered.com/jump or in MyITLab.

TABLE 14-1   Comparison Chart Between a Desktop and Laptop Computer

Feature	Desktop	Laptop
Brand and model		
Price		
Processor brand and model		
Memory amount		
Size of hard drive		
Type of optical drive		
Windows edition		
Extra features		

Step 2. Now find a laptop computer that matches these specifications as closely as you can. How does the price of the laptop compare to the price of the desktop? Besides mobility and battery charge, what major features are different between the two computers?

Solutions Appendix

For help: See *On Your Own 14.3* Step-by-Step Solution

Shopping for a Computer and Peripherals

Now that you've decided what type of computer you want, it's time to start shopping. When shopping for a computer, you'll need to make choices about budget, computer manufacturers, retailers, components, accessories, and warranties. You also need to know what to look for when buying a monitor or printer. Let's get started.

WATCH

OBJECTIVE 14.5
VIDEO

Objective 14.5: Set a Budget and Research Computer Manufacturers and Products

Balancing performance, extra features, and mobility within your budget can be tricky. When considering how much to pay for a computer, keep these two points in mind:

> With computers, bigger is not always better. It's best to buy only what satisfies your current needs because computers rapidly decrease in value. You don't want to spend money on what you don't use and won't be worth much in a few short years. Computers are constantly improving. In just a few years, you can buy a much better computer than you can buy today for the same amount of money.

> The cost of buying a computer is not just the cost of the computer. You might also want an extended warranty, monitor, printer, applications software, carrying case for a laptop or netbook, or other products.

When you shop for a computer, you can

> Buy the computer directly from the website of the computer manufacturer, such as those listed in Table 14-2.

TABLE 14-2   Manufacturers of Brand-Name Computers

Manufacturer	Website	Types of Computers Made
Acer	Store.acer.com	Laptop, netbook, tablet, desktop, all-in-one, and handheld computers
Apple	Store.apple.com/us	Laptop, netbook, tablet, desktop, all-in-one, and handheld computers
Dell	Dell.com/computers	Laptop, netbook, tablet, desktop, all-in-one, and handheld computers
Hewlett Packard (HP)	Shopping.hp.com	Laptop, netbook, tablet, desktop, all-in-one, and handheld computers
Lenovo	Shop.lenovo.com	Desktop, all-in-one, laptop, netbook, and handheld computers that target the professional and corporate user
Sony	Store.sony.com	Laptop, netbook, tablet, desktop, all-in-one, and handheld computers
Toshiba	Toshiba.com	Laptop, netbook, tablet, and all-in-one computers

> Search retail sites that sell electronic equipment. Reputable retail sites include Amazon.com, Microcenter.com, Newegg.com, Tigerdirect.com, Bestbuy.com, and Computershopper.com.
> Walk into an electronics retail store and talk with an experienced sales technician.

Don't buy the first computer you find. Take your time, make comparisons, and read reviews. Expect to learn about computers as you shop. After you settle on the computer, search different retailers for the best price and decide how to customize the computer.

When shopping for a computer, be aware of "great deals" that might disappoint you later. Realize you will be tied to the manufacturer's customer support for your computer for several years to come. Select your brand and manufacturer carefully.

As you shop, research several brands of computers. As you do, keep in mind which manufacturer you prefer and factor that choice into your final selection.

Tip As you read a computer ad, you might encounter a term you don't understand. If so, open a new tab in Internet Explorer to do a Google search on the term. Then return to the Internet Explorer tab displaying the ad.

ON YOUR OWN 14.4

WATCH

OBJECTIVE 14.5
VIDEO

Investigate Computer Manufacturers

Each of the top computer manufacturers has a reputation in the computer industry. For example, Lenovo is known for its high-quality products and has a great reputation for customer service. Do the following to investigate computer manufacturers:

Step 1. Select three manufacturers listed in Table 14-2. Search the web and find one review or comment from a user about each of the three manufacturers. The review can be about a product the company sells, the customer service experience, or a warranty a company offers. Bookmark the review (add it to your Favorites), save the web page of the review, or print the review.

> **Hint** When searching for reviews about a manufacturer or product, search for reviews posted on sites other than the manufacturer's website. Some websites that offer excellent reviews and ratings you can count on are Toptenreviews.com, Reviews.cnet.com, PCmag.com, PCworld.com, and Computershopper.com.

Step 2. Based on your findings, rate the three manufacturers in order from the manufacturer you would most prefer to buy from to the least preferred.

Step 3. What other computer manufacturers came up during the research? Do you think one of these should have been included in Table 14-2? If so, explain why.

Solutions Appendix

For help: See *On Your Own 14.4* Step-by-Step Solution

WATCH

OBJECTIVE 14.6
VIDEO

Objective 14.6: Select the Processor and Memory

As you research computers available on a manufacturer website, you'll find lots of options for customizing a computer. Your most important selections for hardware are the processor and the amount of memory because these choices most affect the overall performance of your system. Let's learn how to evaluate each.

The Processor

The one component that most affects performance in a computer is the processor. Many computer manufacturers allow you a choice of processors. For example, in Figure 14-11, when customizing one HP laptop, you have four choices for a processor. A little explanation about processors might help you choose.

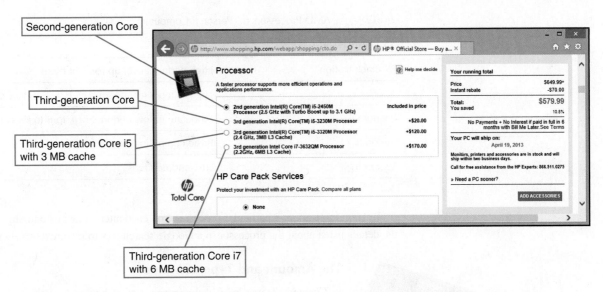

Second-generation Core

Third-generation Core

Third-generation Core i5
with 3 MB cache

Third-generation Core i7
with 6 MB cache

FIGURE 14-11   Four choices of processors are offered for this HP ENVY dv6t-7300 Select Edition laptop on the HP.com site.

Tip When deciding what computer manufacturer to buy from, ask an experienced computer technician—one who does not work for one of these manufacturers—for advice.

The performance of the processor is determined primarily by its speed (also called its frequency) measured in **MHz** or **GHz** , the number of **cores** the processor has, and the amount of **cache memory** in the processor housing. For processors made by Intel, you also need to consider the generation. Third-generation processors are designed for better performance than second-generation processors.

> **MHz**—A megahertz, which is 1 million hertz. A hertz (Hz) is one activity per second.
>
> **GHz**—A gigahertz, which is 1 billion activities per second.
>
> **core**—A component inside a processor that can process data. A processor with four cores can process data about twice as fast as one with two cores even though the speeds are rated the same.
>
> **cache memory**—A small amount of memory inside the processor housing used to speed up the overall processor performance. The more cache, the better.

Processors are made by Intel and AMD. Intel processors tend to perform better, are more popular than AMD, and generally cost slightly more than a comparable AMD processor. AMD processors are popular with hobbyists and gamers and are often used in low-end home computers. Table 14-3 lists some top Intel processors for personal computers, and Table 14-4 lists the top AMD processors for personal computers.

TABLE 14-3   Intel Processors for Personal Computers

Intel Processor	Description
Fourth-generation Core i7, Core i5, Core i3, or vPro	High-performing with added support for touch screens and extended battery charge. The vPro processor has enhanced security.
Third-generation Core i7, Core i5, or Core i3	High-performing processor, four cores
Second-generation Core i7, Core i5, or Core i3	Moderate to high performance, two to six cores
Previous-generation Core i7, Core i5, or Core i3	Low to moderate performance, two to six cores
Pentium or Celeron	Basic computing
Atom	Low-end performance, used in netbooks

TABLE 14-4   AMD Processors for Personal Computers

AMD Processor	Description
FX Black Edition	High performance, up to eight cores
A series	High to moderate performance, two to four cores
Phenom II	Moderate to low performance, four to six cores
Athlon II	Basic computing, one or two cores
Sempron	Low-end desktops

To learn more about a particular processor you encounter while customizing a computer, copy the details listed about the processor in a Google search box to read reviews about the processor.

The Amount and Type of Memory

In Chapter 13, you learned the importance of having enough memory for Windows and applications to work. The type of memory can also affect performance. Today's memory modules use a technology called DDR. The version of DDR used in most new computers today is **DDR3** .

> **DDR3**—A technology used by memory modules. When DDR3 modules are installed in pairs, they can work in tandem (called dual channels) to almost double the speed of single DDR3 modules. When DDR3 modules are installed in a group of three (called triple channels), they can almost triple the speed of single modules.

Tip For dual channeling to work, two matching memory modules must be installed side by side. For triple channeling to work, three matching memory modules must be installed side by side. These matching modules can then move data in and out of memory in sync at the same time.

When selecting a computer, pay attention to the amount and type of memory used. For example, Figure 14-12 shows memory choices for the HP Pavilion dv7t-7000 Quad Edition laptop. You can select 6, 8, 12, or 16 GB of DDR3 memory. A memory module is called a DIMM, and you can see in the ad that memory is stored on two DIMMs, which means the memory is using dual channels.

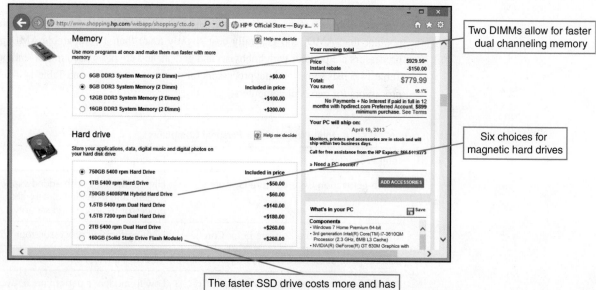

FIGURE 14-12   You can customize the amount of memory and the capacity and type of hard drive for the HP Pavilion dv7t-7000 Quad Edition laptop.

ON YOUR OWN 14.5

Investigate the Latest Intel Processors and the Cost of Memory

WATCH

OBJECTIVE 14.6
VIDEO

To search the web for information about processors and memory, do the following:

Step 1. Intel is constantly releasing new processors for desktop and laptop computers. By the time this book is in print, Table 14-3 might be out of date. Search the web and find out whether Intel has released a processor that is newer than the fourth-generation Core i7 or Core i5. If so, what is that processor?

Step 2. Go to Shopping.hp.com and find a desktop, laptop, or all-in-one computer for sale that offers choices for the amount of installed memory. Based on these choices, how much does each GB of memory cost?

Solutions
Appendix

For help: See *On Your Own 14.5* Step-by-Step Solution

WATCH

OBJECTIVE 14.7
VIDEO

Objective 14.7: Select the Hard Drive and the Type and Edition of Windows

The next two important selections you must make are the hard drive and the type and edition of the Windows operating system.

The Capacity, Speed, and Type of Hard Drive

When selecting a hard drive, you decide the drive's storage capacity, which can hold as many as 3 TB of data. In addition, the type of drive and its resulting speed can affect overall performance. Three types of hard drives are used in computers: magnetic hard drives, solid-state drives, and hybrid hard drives.

A **magnetic hard drive** has platters inside that spin at 5,400, 7,200, or 10,000 **RPM**. A **solid-state drive** (also called an **SSD**) is faster and more expensive than a magnetic drive. Figure 14-12 shows seven options for a hard drive when the buyer is customizing one HP laptop. Notice the SSD drive is more expensive and has a much smaller capacity compared to the magnetic hard drives. A compromise between speed, capacity, and price is the **hybrid hard drive**.

> **magnetic hard drive**—The most common hard drive technology where data is written as magnetic spots on spinning platters.
>
> **RPM**—Revolutions per minute.
>
> **solid-state drive or SSD**—Solid-state drive, also called a solid-state disk or SSD, is a hard drive with no moving parts. Data is stored on memory boards. SSDs are faster than magnetic drives and use less battery charge in mobile computers.
>
> **hybrid hard drive**—A magnetic hard drive that contains a small amount of memory to improve performance.

The Type and Edition of Windows

When you purchase a new computer, the operating system is already installed. Sometimes you have a choice as to which type or edition of Windows 8.1, 8, or 7 comes preinstalled on the computer. For example, Figure 14-13 shows choices for the operating system to be installed on one HP all-in-one computer.

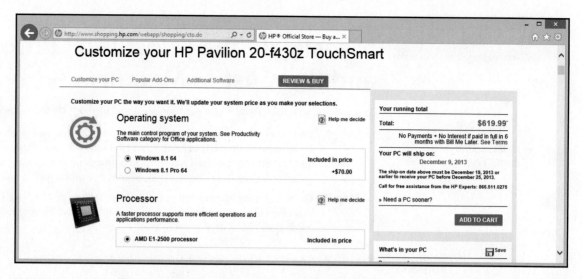

FIGURE 14-13   HP offers a choice of operating systems for this HP Pavilion all-in-one touch-screen computer.

Recall from Chapter 13 that Windows comes in either a 32-bit system or a 64-bit system. For best performance, choose a 64-bit version of Windows 8.1.

The edition you select affects the features of the OS and not its performance. Your choices of Windows editions might include

> **Windows 8.1, Windows 8,** or **Windows 7 Home** is for personal use at home, at school, when traveling, or in a small office.
> **Windows 8.1 Pro, Windows 8 Pro,** or **Windows 7 Professional** contains extra features used in a corporate or professional setting to connect to a corporate network (called a Windows domain) and to provide extra security for the system.

Microsoft has announced that it will continue to sell Windows 7 at least until the end of 2014.

ON YOUR OWN 14.6

WATCH

OBJECTIVE 14.7
VIDEO

Compare Prices for Hard Drives and Windows 8.1 Editions

To compare offerings for a hard drive and Windows 8.1 on a computer, follow these steps:

Step 1. Find a new computer for sale that can be customized with a magnetic or SSD hard drive. What is the storage capacity of the largest SSD drive? Of the largest magnetic drive? How much extra would you expect to pay if you request the SSD drive over the magnetic drive?

Step 2. Find a computer that can be customized with Windows 8.1 or Windows 8.1 Pro. How much extra would you pay for Windows 8.1 Pro over Windows 8.1?

Solutions Appendix

For help: See *On Your Own 14.6* Step-by-Step Solution

WATCH

OBJECTIVE 14.8
VIDEO

Objective 14.8: Select the Video Components and Other Features

The next component that can affect overall performance is the graphics card (also called the video card). Other components and features you need to consider are the video ports, optical drive, and extended warranty.

Integrated Video or a Graphics Card

The video subsystem can be **integrated video** or a dedicated graphics card. In most cases, integrated video is sufficient and is less expensive.

> **integrated video**—Video circuitry embedded on the motherboard, and the motherboard provides a video port. The quality of video is not as good as when a dedicated graphics card is used. Also called integrated graphics.

A desktop, laptop, or all-in-one computer can use a graphics card, which gives better video performance than integrated video. Figure 14-14 shows a graphics card used in a desktop. Graphics cards come in a wide variety of quality and price.

FIGURE 14-14   This high-end graphics card used in a desktop includes a fan to keep it cool.

For the best graphics experience in a gaming, entertainment, or multimedia computer, select your graphics card with care. For example, look at the three choices in Figure 14-15 for the video card in the Alienware M17x laptop by Dell. (Alienware is Dell's line of gaming computers.) The two major manufacturers of video cards (graphics cards) are AMD and NVIDIA, and Dell offers choices for each. To decide which graphic card you prefer, search for online reviews about each card and compare prices.

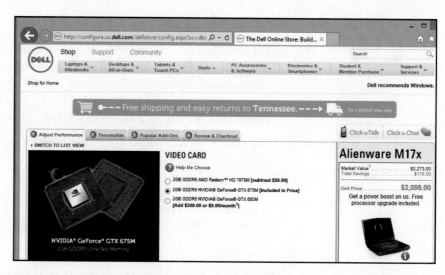

FIGURE 14-15   Dell offers three choices for the video card for an Alienware gaming laptop.

Video Ports

Four types of video ports used on today's computers are VGA, DVI, DisplayPort, and HDMI. **DisplayPort** and **HDMI** give better video than DVI, which is better than VGA. DisplayPort and HDMI can output audio as well as video.

DisplayPort

> **DisplayPort**—A type of video port that gives high-definition video to a computer monitor or can stream video and audio to a TV or home theater system. DisplayPort is expected to replace VGA and DVI video ports on computers. Some netbooks use a smaller version of the DisplayPort, called a Mini DisplayPort (mDP).
>
> **HDMI**—A type of video and audio port technology used to transmit video and audio to a monitor, high-definition TV (HDTV), or home theater system.

Be sure the video port on your computer matches your monitor or TV. Sometimes you can use an adapter or converter cable if the connectors don't match. Figure 14-16 shows a DVI to DisplayPort adapter, and Figure 14-17 shows a VGA to DisplayPort adapter.

HDMI

FIGURE 14-16   Use a DVI to DisplayPort adapter to connect a DVI monitor to a DisplayPort on a computer.

FIGURE 14-17   Use a VGA to DisplayPort adapter to connect a VGA monitor to a DisplayPort on a computer.

TIP   A CD can hold up to 700 MB of data. Depending on the number of layers used on the disc, a DVD can hold up to 15.9 GB and a BD can hold up to 50 GB.

Optical Drive

Netbooks and tablets don't have an optical drive, but other computers do. Most optical drives today support CDs and DVDs, and some also support Blu-ray Discs (BDs). A CD stores data on only one side of the disc, but a DVD or BD can use both sides in double layers. Make sure the optical drive supports the types of discs you plan to use.

Consider an Extended Warranty

One of the last steps in customizing your computer is to select a warranty. Most computers come with a complimentary warranty that covers parts and labor for one year. The manufacturer or retailer might offer an extended warranty. Pay attention to how long the warranty lasts (one to five years is common) and how much it costs. Figure 14-18 shows the screen when purchasing an Alienware laptop where you must select the number of years and level of support.

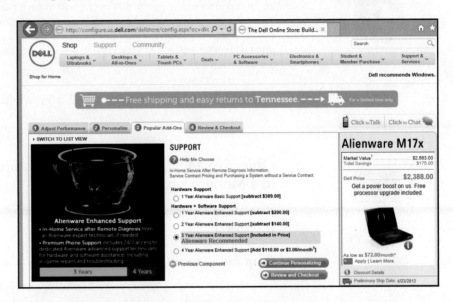

FIGURE 14-18   Dell offers basic and enhanced support that cover one to four years.

Find out what the warranty covers. Does it cover software problems or just hardware defects? Does the warranty include failing hardware or accidents such as spilling a soda across a laptop keyboard? You might have to read the fine print to find out.

Consider how the warranty works. Do you have to ship the computer back to the manufacturer? Do you get phone support? Is there a local computer service center where you can take the computer?

Summary of What You Can Customize

In summary, here's a list of the components and features you may be able to customize when buying a computer:

> *Processor.* The processor, made by Intel or AMD, varies in performance and price.
> *Memory.* You might see offered 2 GB to 16 GB of memory. The more the better.
> *Hard drive.* For magnetic hard drives, 7,200 RPM performs better than 5,400 RPM. Capacity is as high as 3 TB. An SSD drive is faster and more expensive than a magnetic drive.
> *Operating system.* Besides selecting the type and edition of Windows, sometimes you can buy recovery media on DVD in case the operating system gives trouble.
> *Video.* Look for integrated video or a graphics card. Also, for mobile computers, screen size matters.
> *Optical drive.* DVD and CD drives are standard for desktops and laptops. You pay extra for Blu-ray.
> *Warranty and support.* A complimentary warranty is included, and you can upgrade it for additional cost.

Tip After you buy your new computer, be sure to register it with the manufacturer so that you can get technical support and warranty service when you need it. Use a large envelope or folder to collect all the documentation that came with your computer, including the sales receipt, packing and shipping list, warranty information, and software documentation. Include in the envelope any CDs or DVDs that came with your computer. Label the envelope and keep it in a safe place. If later you have problems with your computer, you will need the sales receipt and warranty documentation to get help from the retail store's service center or the computer manufacturer.

WATCH

CHAPTER 14
DIVING DEEPER
VIDEO

ON YOUR OWN 14.7

Compare Prices for a Computer with a Blu-ray Burner

WATCH

OBJECTIVE 14.8
VIDEO

Just about all optical drives sold today can read and burn (write to) a CD or DVD. However, an optical drive that supports BDs might read but not burn a BD. Search the web for the least expensive new computer you can find that includes a Blu-ray burner (a drive that writes to Blu-ray discs). What are the website, brand, model, and price of the computer? Compare your price with other students in your class to see who can find the least expensive computer with a Blu-ray burner.

Solutions
Appendix

For help: See *On Your Own 14.7* Step-by-Step Solution

WATCH

OBJECTIVE 14.9
VIDEO

Objective 14.9: Know About the Features to Look For in a Monitor or Printer

Next let's look at the most important details you need to consider when shopping for a monitor or a printer.

Shop for a Monitor

For a desktop computer, you need a keyboard, mouse, and monitor. Laptop users sometimes appreciate a monitor connected to the laptop to provide extra screen space (called dual displays). Figure 14-19 shows an ad listing three 24-inch monitors.

FIGURE 14-19   This ad at Amazon.com lists key details for three monitors.

Here are important details to note when shopping for a monitor:

> **The size of the monitor viewing screen.** A monitor size is measured diagonally from one corner to the other. Typical sizes for desktop monitors are 18, 22, 24, and 26 inches, although you can buy larger ones.

> **The resolution.** Recall that the resolution is the number of horizontal and vertical dots or pixels on the monitor screen, for example, $1{,}920 \times 1{,}200$. The higher, the better.

> **The monitor speed.** Response time is the time it takes for the monitor to build one screen. The lower, the better. A response time of 1 ms (millisecond) is faster than a response time of 3 ms.

> **The connector types the monitor can use.** Choices are VGA, DVI, DisplayPort, and HDMI. HDMI is better than DVI, which is better than VGA. Make sure the connector type matches a video port on your computer. If, however, you buy a monitor with a connector type that doesn't match the port on your computer, you can use an adapter to convert one type connector to another (refer to Figures 14-3, 14-16, and 14-17).

> **Contrast ratio.** Contrast is measured as a contrast ratio, for example, 1,000:1, which is the contrast between true black and true white. The higher the number, the better.

> **Extra features.** Some monitors have touch screens, built-in speakers, an iPod port, and USB ports.

Shop for a Printer

Another purchase you might need to make is a printer. The least expensive type printer is an inkjet printer . Some inkjet printers are photo printers (see Figure 14-20a), meaning they are of high enough quality to print lab-quality photos on photographic paper. A laser printer (see Figure 14-20b) is more expensive, but the quality of the printout is much better.

> **inkjet printer**—A color printer that uses ink cartridges with small nozzles that jet the ink out onto the paper.
>
> **laser printer**—A black-and-white or color printer that creates an image on the page using a laser beam inside the printer and powdered ink called toner. The toner cartridge holds the toner.

a   b

FIGURE 14-20   Two types of printers: (a) an inkjet printer and (b) a laser printer.

When selecting a printer, consider these features:

> **Type of printer.** Inkjet printers are less expensive and produce lower-quality printouts over laser printers. A color laser printer costs more than a black-and-white laser printer. If you plan to print lots of color photos, use a color laser printer.

> **Connection types.** Printers connect to a computer by way of a USB cable or wirelessly (Wi-Fi or Bluetooth). A network printer connects directly to the network.

> **Cost of toner cartridges (for laser printers) and ink cartridges (for inkjet printers).** These cartridges can be quite expensive. Be aware that when you first buy a printer, the cartridges are only partially full, so you may need to buy new cartridges right away.
> **All-in-one device.** Some printers are also a scanner, copier, and fax machine rolled into one machine (called an all-in-one device).
> **The warranty and online support.** Check out the printer manufacturer's website. You should find support information for the printer and the option to download the device drivers and the user manual.

Before making a final buying decision, be sure to read reviews about the printer.

ON YOUR OWN 14.8

WATCH

▶

OBJECTIVE 14.9 VIDEO

Compare Two Monitors and Two Printers

Suppose you're ready to buy a new monitor to connect to your laptop to provide more screen space. You also need a new printer for your home office.

To compare features and prices for two monitors that are the same size and made by the same manufacturer follow these steps:

Step 1. Select a monitor manufacturer (for example, Acer, Asus, Dell, HP, Samsung, or ViewSonic). Find two 24-inch monitors made by this manufacturer that vary as widely in price as you can find. What are the brand, model, and price for each monitor?

Step 2. Identify differences in quality and features between the two monitors. List these qualities and features for each monitor.

> **Hint** A monitor manufacturer often allows you to filter its monitors by features. In addition, Amazon.com does a great job of allowing you to filter ads by manufacturer and product features.

To compare the difference in cost for a black-and-white all-in-one laser printer and a color all-in-one laser printer, follow these steps:

Step 3. Select a printer manufacturer (for example, HP, Canon, or Epson). Find an ad for an all-in-one black-and-white laser printer that is also a scanner and copier. Find a second ad for an all-in-one *color* laser printer that is also a scanner and copier, made by the same manufacturer. Answer the following questions:

1. What is the brand, model, and price of the black-and-white printer?
2. What is the brand, model, and price of the color printer?

Step 4. Find toner cartridges for each printer. For the black-and-white printer, only a black toner cartridge is needed. Most color laser printers need four cartridges: black, yellow, cyan, and magenta cartridges. Answer the following:

1. How much does the black toner cartridge cost for the black-and-white printer? How much does a set of toner cartridges cost for the color printer?
2. Based on your findings, what is the difference in cost between a color laser all-in-one printer and a black-and-white laser all-in-one printer, including the cost of replacement cartridges?

> **Hint** Many retail sites, such as Amazon.com, make it easy to match ink or toner cartridges with printers. Display the details of the printer and then click a link to drill down to matching cartridges for sale.

Solutions Appendix

For help: See *On Your Own 14.8* Step-by-Step Solution

Summary

Deciding Between an Upgrade and a New Computer

> You might want to replace or upgrade a computer if it is missing a device or is too slow.

> The total cost of upgrades should not exceed the current value of the computer. This cost includes parts and labor.

> Computer performance can be improved by routine maintenance, subscribing to a faster Internet connection, adding memory, adding an external hard drive, or upgrading the operating system, processor, hard drive, or graphics card.

> To find out how much your computer is worth, find comparable computers for sale.

Deciding on the Type of Computer

> Computers fall into two categories: IBM-compatible computers that use the Windows or Linux operating system and Macs, which are Apple computers that use the Mac operating system.

> When you are deciding what type of computer you need, the factors to consider are mobility, performance, compatibility, and budget. Mobile computers include laptops, netbooks, tablet PCs, handheld tablets, and smart phones.

Shopping for a Computer and Peripherals

> You can buy a new computer directly from the manufacturer or from retail websites or stores. Buy from reputable manufacturers because you might be dependent on them for future service of your computer.

> Components that most affect computer performance are the processor, amount of memory, hard drive, type of operating system, and video subsystem.

> Processor performance is rated by the speed of the processor and number of cores.

> The 64-bit Windows 8.1 operating system is currently the fastest OS by Microsoft.

> Hard drive performance is affected by the RPM rating of a magnetic hard drive. Solid-state disks (SSDs) are faster than magnetic drives but cost more.

> A graphics card in a computer provides better video than integrated video. Graphics cards vary widely in price and performance.

> Video ports on today's computers include VGA, DVI, DisplayPort, and HDMI.

> An extended warranty might cover manufacturer defects, failed hardware, accidents, and phone support.

> When selecting a monitor, consider size of the screen, resolution, speed, connectors, contrast ratio, and extra features.

> Two types of printers are inkjet printers and laser printers. Laser printers are a little more expensive and produce better quality than inkjets.

CHAPTER MASTERY PROJECT

Now it's time to find out how well you've mastered the content in this chapter. If you can do all the steps in this Mastery Project without looking back at the chapter details and can answer all the Review Questions following this project, you've mastered this chapter. If you can complete the project by finding answers using the web, you've proven that you can teach yourself how to make computer upgrade and buying decisions.

Hint All the key terms in the chapter are used in this mastery project or in the review questions. If you encounter a key word you don't know, such as *Android*, enter **define:Android** in the Internet Explorer search box.

If you find you need a lot of help doing the project and you have not yet read the chapter or done the activities, drop back and start at the beginning of the chapter, watch the videos, review the step-by-step solutions as you work through the On Your Own activities, and then return to this project.

> **Tip** If you need help completing this part of the mastery project, review the section "Deciding Between an Upgrade and a New Computer" in the chapter.

Do the following to investigate the performance and features of your computer:

Step 1. Find out the network connection speed for your wired and/or wireless connections.

Step 2. Find out what type of USB ports your computer has: regular USB, Hi-Speed USB, and/or SuperSpeed USB.

> **Tip** If you need help completing this part of the mastery project, review the section "Shopping for a Computer and Peripherals" in the chapter.

To shop for and customize a computer, follow these steps:

Step 3. Go to a computer manufacturer's website and select a computer for sale and step through the process of customizing the computer. As you do so, use the Windows Snipping Tool to take a snip of your window showing each of the following options available for customizing. Create a Word document named Chapter_14_Mastery_Project and insert snips into the document. Here are the options:

    a. *Type of computer.* Take a snip showing a photo of the computer that shows whether the computer is a desktop, all-in-one, or laptop. Include in the snip the brand and model of the computer.

    b. *Operating system.* Take a snip showing the choices for operating systems when customizing the computer. Make sure the snip shows the edition of OS (Windows 8 or 8.1 Pro, Windows 8 or 8.1, Windows 7 Professional, and/or Windows 7 Home Premium) and type of OS (64 bit and/or 32 bit).

    c. *Processor.* Make sure a snip shows the choices for processors. Verify the snip shows the speed (in MHz or GHz), cores, and cache memory for each processor.

    d. *Memory.* Make sure a snip shows the choices for the amount of memory installed.

    e. *Hard drive.* Make sure a snip shows choices for the hard drive. Verify the snip shows types of drive (magnetic hard drive, SSD, or hybrid hard drive), speed (for magnetic or hybrid drives), and capacity.

    f. *Graphics card or integrated video.* Make sure a snip shows choices for the graphics card or integrated video (sometimes called integrated graphics).

    g. *Warranty.* Make sure a snip shows the choices for extended warranties.

If the first computer you found doesn't offer choices for each option above, find another computer that does. It's okay to use snips from multiple computers to complete the list of options.

Step 4. Shop for a monitor. Take one or more snips of an ad for a monitor that shows the brand, model, price, and ratings of the monitor, including the monitor size, speed, resolution, contrast ratio, and connectors.

Step 5. Shop for a printer. Take one or more snips of an ad for a printer that shows the brand, model, price, and ratings of the printer, including the type of printer (laser or inkjet) and features (color, black and white, and connection types), and all-in-one features (scanner, copier, or FAX machine built in).

Step 6. Shop for the ink or toner cartridges for the printer. Take one or more snips of an ad that shows the type of cartridge and its price.

Step 7. Enter your name and course information into the Chapter_14_Mastery_Projects document containing your snips and send the document to your instructor. If you are using MyITLab, you can post the file in a Dropbox assignment or email the file in MyITLab. On the other hand, your instructor might prefer you post the file to your OneDrive or email the file using your school email.

Review Questions

Answer these questions to assess your skills and knowledge of the content covered in the chapter. Your instructor can provide you with the correct answers when you are ready to check your work.

1. What is the first thing you should do to speed up a slow computer before you consider an upgrade?

2. What is the least expensive hardware upgrade that can improve a computer's performance?

3. Suppose your old desktop computer has a DVD reader rather than a DVD burner but you want to burn some DVDs. What are two ways you can upgrade your computer?

4. Suppose your memory card reader in your laptop only uses xD-Picture cards and not SD cards. What device can you purchase to read SD cards? What port on your laptop is this device likely to use?

5. What type of adapter card can be installed in a desktop so the desktop has an extra video port?

6. Which type of USB port is the fastest and recommended to be used for external hard drives? Suppose your computer has two USB ports; the inside of one port is blue, and the other is black. Which port is faster?

7. Which performs better: a 32-bit installation of Windows 8.1 Professional or a 64-bit installation of Windows 8.1?

8. If your desktop computer has only one video port but you want to use two monitors, what can you do to upgrade your computer?

9. When a desktop computer is assembled from parts, what four components inside the computer can be used to determine the value of the computer?

10. Pick two questions that best can be used to determine the value of a computer:
    a. How old is the computer?
    b. What is the size of the hard drive?
    c. What are the values of other comparable computers?
    d. How much memory is installed?

11. How rapidly does a computer reduce in value each year?

12. If your old computer is six years old and the total cost of upgrades is about $400, why is it better to buy a new computer than upgrade this one?

13. Suppose your hard drive can hold 120 GB, and 40 GB is free space. Will your computer's performance improve if you upgrade the drive to a 500 GB drive that uses the same technology and speed as your old drive?

14. Suppose your Windows XP computer has 1 GB of memory, 40 GB of free hard drive space, and a 1.7 GHz processor. What hardware upgrade is needed before you can install Windows 8.1?

15. Why is it not always a good idea to buy the best computer you can afford?

16. Which type of computer has the longer battery charge: a tablet PC or a handheld tablet, such as an iPad?

17. Which memory configuration gives better performance: one DDR3 module installed as a single module or two DDR3 modules installed in dual channeling?

18. What two companies manufacture processors for personal computers?

19. Which is a better-performing processor, the Intel Core i5 or the Intel Pentium?

20. Which is faster: a magnetic hard drive running at 5,400 RPM or an SSD? Capacity being the same, which costs more: a magnetic hard drive or an SSD?

21. Which costs more: Windows 8.1 or Windows 8.1 Professional? Which OS has better security features?

22. All Apple computers use what operating system?

23. What are two reasons you might buy a Mac over an IBM-compatible computer?

24. Which two operating systems might be used by IBM-compatible computers?

25. Which operating system that is based on Linux is used on smart phones and handheld tablets?

26. Which edition of Windows 7 should someone use if he or she needs to connect a computer to a corporate network that uses a Windows domain? Which edition of Windows 8.1 is required?

27. What are two disadvantages of a laptop over a desktop computer?

28. Which two types of video ports can output audio as well as video?

29. Which can hold more data: CD, DVD, or Blu-ray discs? Which costs more: a DVD optical drive or a Blu-ray optical drive?

30. Which yields better video: integrated video or a graphics card?

31. Which monitor is faster: one with a rating of 3 ms or one with a rating of 5 ms?

32. When you buy a new computer, why is it important to gather up documentations, discs, and receipts and save them in an envelope?

Becoming an Independent Learner

Answer the following questions about becoming an independent learner:

1. To teach yourself about computer upgrade and buying decisions, do you think it is best to rely on the chapter or on the web when you need answers?

2. The most important skill learned in this chapter is how to teach yourself a computer skill. Rate yourself at Level A through E on how well you're doing with this skill. What is your level?

   - Level A: I was able to successfully complete the Chapter Mastery Project with the help of only a few of the On Your Own activities in the chapter.
   - Level B: I completed all the On Your Own activities and the Chapter Mastery Project without referring to any of the solutions in the Step-by-Step Solutions Appendix.
   - Level C: I completed all the On Your Own activities and the Chapter Mastery Project by using just a few of the solutions in the Step-by-Step Solutions Appendix.
   - Level D: I completed all the On Your Own activities and the Chapter Mastery Project by using many of the solutions in the Step-by-Step Solutions Appendix.
   - Level E: I completed all the On Your Own activities and the Chapter Mastery Project and had to use all of the solutions in the Step-by-Step Solutions Appendix.

To continue toward the goal of teaching yourself computer skills, if you're not at Level A, try to move up one level on how you learn in Chapter 15.

Projects to Help You

Now that you've mastered the material in this chapter, you're ready to tackle the three projects focused on your career, personal, or academic goals. Depending on your own interests, you might choose to complete any or all of these projects to help you achieve your goals.

Project 1: Recycling an Old Computer

After you've purchased a new computer, it's better to donate or recycle an old computer rather than throw it in the trash. Do the following:

Step 1. Search the web and find an organization in your area that will receive a computer as a donation. The PC repair instructor at your school might take an old computer so that his or her class can fix it up and donate it. List at least one organization or individual in your area willing to receive an old computer as a donation.

Step 2. Find an organization in your area that will recycle a computer. For example, try doing a Google search on **where to recycle computers in Cleveland**. What organization or business in your area will receive a computer for recycling? Email your findings to your instructor.

Career Project As a responsible professional and citizen, I want to do my part to donate or recycle old computers I or my company no longer need. How do I do that in my area?

> **Tip** If you were really donating or recycling a computer, before it goes out the door, you should uninstall any applications that you intend to use on your new computer, copy any personal data on the hard drive to another storage device or to your new computer, and delete any personal data from the hard drive (or remove and destroy the old hard drive).

Personal Project I want to buy a super-responsive gaming computer with realistic graphics. What makes a gaming computer perform better than any machine out there? What can I do to beef it up?

Project 2: Customizing a Gaming Computer

Pretend that money is no object when buying a gaming computer. Compete with others in your class to see who can design the most expensive gaming computer. Do the following:

Step 1. Dell offers some extreme (and expensive) gaming computers that you can customize. Go to Dell.com and pump up Dell's best gaming computer with all the extras Dell offers. Take a screen snip of the web page showing the details of the system and its price and email the snip file to your instructor.

Step 2. Compare prices with others in your class to see who designed the most expensive gaming computer.

Project 3: Using a Comparison Table to Select a Computer

Suppose you have decided to buy a laptop to use during your academic career. Because you are a good researcher, you decided to use a comparison table to help make up your mind. Table 14-5 can help you compare features. You can find the table in the document file named CompareComputersTable in the sample_files folder available at www.pearsonhighered.com/jump or in MyITLab.

Research a laptop computer. Find three computers that you like and enter the information in the table. Based on your comparisons, which computer would you consider buying? Why? Email the completed document to your instructor.

Academic Project I've decided to buy a computer to use during my academic career. I want to research and find the best buy for my money with all the features I need. It must last me for four years, so I don't want to make a mistake.

TABLE 14-5   Comparison Chart When Buying a Laptop

Feature	Laptop 1	Laptop 2	Laptop 3
Brand and model			
Processor speed and number of cores			
Memory amount and type			
Hard drive size and type			
Weight			
Screen size			
Time battery charge lasts			
Optical drive			
Windows edition and type			
Video (integrated or graphics card)			
Bluetooth	Yes/No	Yes/No	Yes/No
Other extra features			
Warranty			
Price			

Project to Help Others

One of the best ways to learn is to teach someone else. And, in teaching someone else, you are making a contribution in that person's life. As part of each chapter's work, you are encouraged to teach someone else a skill you have learned. In this chapter, help someone learn about upgrading or buying a computer.

Working with your apprentice, do the following:

Step 1. Ask your apprentice to assume he is in the market for a new computer or to upgrade his old computer.

Step 2. If your apprentice has a computer, help him determine what upgrades he might want and how much the upgrades will cost. Try to determine the value of his computer to decide if an upgrade is appropriate.

Step 3. If your apprentice wants to shop for a new computer, help him go shopping online. Help him choose the type of computer, key components, and extra features that will best meet his needs.

Step 4. Ask your apprentice to tell you how he thinks the tutoring session went and what he learned as you worked together.

Step 5. Use Notepad to create a text file that contains answers about the tutoring session and send the file to your instructor. If you're using MyITLab, you can post the file in Dropbox in MyITLab. On the other hand, your instructor might prefer you post the file to your OneDrive. Here are the questions:

1. Who is your apprentice?

2. In steps 2 and 3, was your apprentice interesting in upgrading his existing computer or buying a new computer?

3. In step 3, if your apprentice shopped for a new computer, describe the success of the experience. If your apprentice decided to upgrade an old computer, what type of upgrades did he decide was needed? What questions did your apprentice have during the process?

4. Briefly describe how the apprentice evaluated the tutoring session.

5. How do you think the session went? How would you like to improve it next time?

15 Creating and Using Databases with Microsoft Access

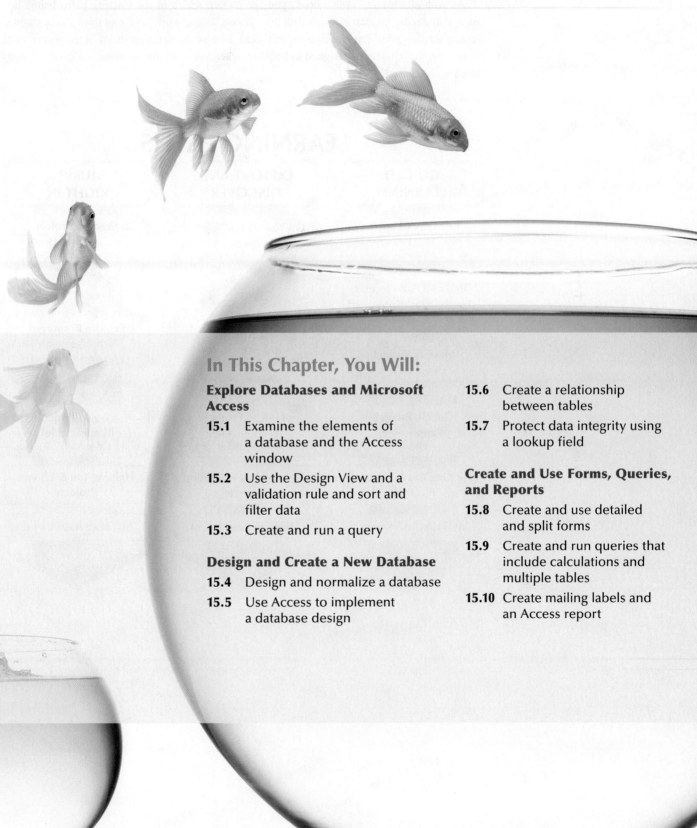

In This Chapter, You Will:

Explore Databases and Microsoft Access

15.1 Examine the elements of a database and the Access window

15.2 Use the Design View and a validation rule and sort and filter data

15.3 Create and run a query

Design and Create a New Database

15.4 Design and normalize a database

15.5 Use Access to implement a database design

15.6 Create a relationship between tables

15.7 Protect data integrity using a lookup field

Create and Use Forms, Queries, and Reports

15.8 Create and use detailed and split forms

15.9 Create and run queries that include calculations and multiple tables

15.10 Create mailing labels and an Access report

In this chapter, you learn about databases and the way databases work. You learn to use Microsoft Access to create a new database and to create the forms, queries, and reports used to manage the data in the database.

As with all chapters in this book, you can choose which of the learning paths below best suits your needs. No matter which path you choose, as you work your way through the chapter, remember the most important computer skill is how to teach yourself a computer skill. Therefore, this chapter is designed to help you teach yourself how to manage a database using Microsoft Access.

LEARNING PATHS

GUIDED LEARNING	EXPLORE AND DISCOVER	JUMP RIGHT IN
Read the Chapter *Watch the Objective Videos*	**On Your Own Projects** *Review Objective videos or use Step-by-Step Solutions*	**Mastery Project** *Use Objective videos & OYO projects for help*
On Your Own Projects *Review Objective videos or use Step-by-Step Solutions*		**Explore Resources** *For help as needed*
Mastery Project *Use Objective videos & OYO projects for help*	**Mastery Project** *Use Objective videos & OYO projects for help*	
Google Project (if applicable) *Watch Google video for help*	**Google Project (if applicable)** *Watch Google video for help*	**Google Project (if applicable)** *Watch Google video for help*
Helping You & Others Projects	**Helping You & Others Projects**	**Helping You & Others Projects**
MyITLab Assessment	**MyITLab Assessment**	**MyITLab Assessment**

Exploring Databases and Microsoft Access

In Chapters 10 and 11, you learned to use Excel, which is useful when managing lists, calculations, and tables. If the amount of data becomes too much to view and manage easily on one or more worksheets, a database and Microsoft Access can help. Let's explore both.

WATCH

OBJECTIVE 15.1
VIDEO

Objective 15.1: Examine the Elements of a Database and the Access Window

Microsoft Access is an application that stores and maintains data in a **database** . Access is an example of a **database management system (DBMS)** used to manage a small database on a personal computer.

> **Microsoft Access**—One of the applications included in Microsoft Office and used to manage a database. Use it to create and edit database tables and to build queries, forms, and reports that use the tables.
>
> **database**—A collection of data about a topic that is organized so the data can be searched and retrieved quickly. Using Access, a database is stored in a file with a .accdb file extension.
>
> **database management system (DBMS)**—Software that stores and updates data in a database. A small-scale DBMS manages a database on a personal computer, and a large-scale DBMS manages a database on a mainframe computer with many personal computers updating that data. Access is an example of a small-scale DBMS. SQL Server by Microsoft and Oracle by Oracle Corporation are examples of a large-scale DBMS.

A database keeps data in one or more tables. A table is made up of records (rows) and fields (columns). Each field has a field name (column heading). Figure 15-1 shows the Access window displaying the AnimalShelter database that has one table. A database with only one table is sometimes called a flat-file database.

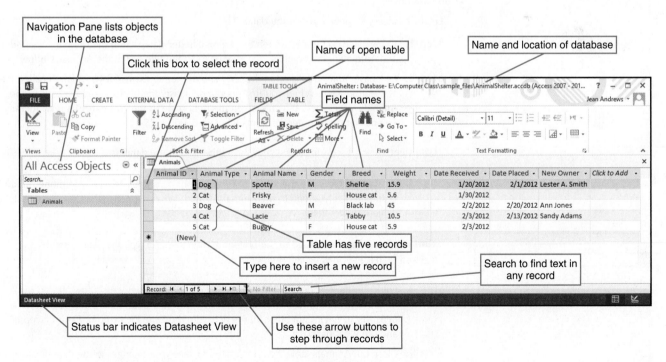

FIGURE 15-1   A table in a database is made up of records (rows) and fields (columns).

Tip In Figure 15-1, the title bar shows Access 2007–2013 file format. Access 2013 uses the .accdb file extension and format for a database that was first introduced with Access 2007. The title bar reminds us of this fact.

Normally, Access keeps only **raw data** in a database. Calculations using the raw data are created and displayed by a **query**, **form**, or **report**.

> **raw data**—Data recorded by a user. The data is not created by a calculation.
> **query**—In Access, a view of the data in a database that has selected fields and records and can include calculations. You can view and edit the data in a query and use a query to decide what data goes into a report.
> **form**—In Access, a screen that is used to view and edit the data in a database. The form controls what you can see and do with the data and helps to protect the integrity of the data.
> **report**—In Access, data, calculations about the data, charts, and other information presented in a visually pleasing way appropriate for printing.

Access and databases are more complex to learn, create, and use than Excel workbooks. The main reasons you would use Access over Excel are

> Large quantities of data are easier to manage in a database than in a workbook.
> Access is better at protecting the integrity of the data than is Excel.
> Access works well when you need to make complex queries into the data or produce complex reports of the data.

ON YOUR OWN 15.1

Explore the AnimalShelter Database and the Access Window

WATCH

OBJECTIVE 15.1 VIDEO

Use the AnimalShelter Database: Part 1 of 3

The AnimalShelter database is located in the sample_files folder on the pearsonhighered.com/jump website and in MyITLab. Recall that in Chapter 2, you downloaded the sample_files folder to your USB flash drive.

Let's use Access to view and edit the database:

Step 1. Using Microsoft Access, open the **AnimalShelter** database in the sample_files folder. The AnimalShelter database name appears in the title bar of the Access window.

Step 2. Database tables are listed in the left pane of the Access window, which is called the Navigation Pane. When you first open a database, the tables are closed. Open the **Animals** table. The table appears in the right pane in the **Datasheet View**. Identify on your own computer the items labeled in Figure 15-1.

> **Datasheet View**—A view in Access that shows the data in the database.

Step 3. Add a new record to the table making up your own data. Notice a counting number is automatically added to the Animal ID field. What happens when you try to enter a value into this field?

> **Hint** To add a new record, go to the bottom of the table and type the data in the blank record, which is indicated by an asterisk (*).

Step 4. Entries in the Gender field must match a criteria before Access allows it into the field. Try to enter a letter other than M or F into the Gender field and see what happens. Try to enter data other than a date into the Date Received or Date Placed field and see what happens.

Step 5. Close the Animals table. You don't need to save your changes to the data because Access automatically does that for you.

Solutions Appendix

For help: See On Your Own 15.1 Step-by-Step Solution

WATCH

OBJECTIVE 15.2
VIDEO

Objective 15.2: Use the Design View and a Validation Rule and Sort and Filter Data

Each field in a table is assigned a **data type** . You can see the data type for each field when you view the table in **Design View** . You can also use the Design View to set a **validation rule** .

> **data type**—A property of a field that determines what kind of data the field can store, for example, text, date, or currency. Also called field type.
>
> **Design View**—A view in Access that allows you to change the design of a table, for example, to add a new field to a table.
>
> **validation rule**—A criteria that must be met before Access allows data to be entered into a table.

ON YOUR OWN 15.2

Edit a Validation Rule and Sort and Filter Data in the Animals Table

WATCH

OBJECTIVE 15.2
VIDEO

Use the AnimalShelter Database: Part 2 of 3

Before you can create or edit a validation rule, you must view the table in Design View. Do the following:

Step 1. Using the AnimalShelter database, open the **Animals** table and go to **Design View** (see Figure 15-2).

Hint To go to Design View, right-click the table name in the table tab and click **Design View**.

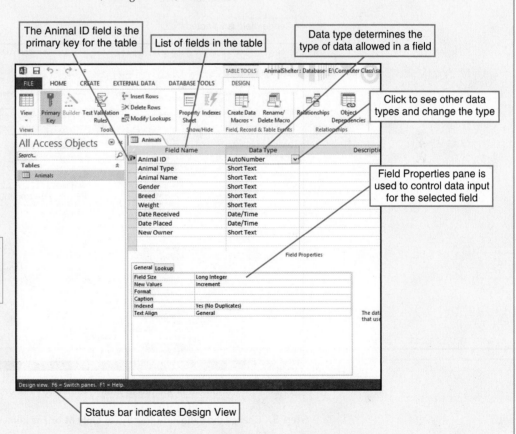

FIGURE 15-2 The Design View shows information about the table design.

Step 2. The Data Type column shows the type for each field. Click in a Data Type box and then click the drop-down arrow to the right of the data type to see a list of types. In this chapter, we use only the AutoNumber, Short Text, Date/Time, Number, and Currency types.

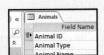

Step 3. Notice in Figure 15-2 the following about the design of this table:

- The Animal ID field uses the AutoNumber data type. This data type automatically inserts a sequential counting number in the field for each new record.
- The Weight field uses the Short Text data type. Unless a field is used for calculations, use the Short Text data type even if the field contains only numeric values.
- The Date Received and Date Placed fields use the Date/Time data type, which allows only dates into these fields.
- Each table has a **primary key**. The key icon beside Animal ID identifies this field as the primary key.

> **primary key**—One or more fields in a table that uniquely identify each record in the table. Access doesn't allow you to enter duplicate primary key values in a table.

You're now ready to edit the validation rule that protects the integrity of data in the Gender field. Here's how:

Step 4. Click on the **Gender** field. The Field Properties pane displays the properties for this field (see Figure 15-3). Note the following:

- The Field Size is set to 1, which prevents a user entering more than one character into the field.
- The Validation Rule is set to "M" or "F", which limits data input to one of these characters.
- The Validation Text will display whenever a user enters data that doesn't fit the Validation Rule.

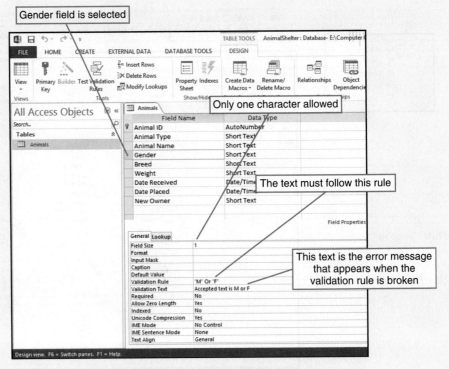

FIGURE 15-3   Use the field properties to protect the integrity of data in the field.

Step 5. Change the Validation Text to say **Only M or F is allowed.**

Step 6. Access automatically saves changes made to the data in a database table, but you must tell Access to save changes you make to the table design. To save your changes to the table design, right-click the **Animals** tab at the top of the Design View and click **Save** in the shortcut menu.

> **Tip** To save your changes as you work on a table design or other design, you can also click the Save icon in the Quick Access Toolbar.

Step 7. Return to the **Datasheet View**. Enter a new record or edit an existing record. What displays when you enter a character other than M or F in the Gender field?

You can sort and filter data using the Sort & Filter group on the HOME ribbon. You can also sort and filter a table just as you learned to do with Excel in Chapter 11. Do the following to find out how:

Step 8. In Datasheet View, click the drop-down arrow to the right of the Gender field name. Sort the data by Gender.

Step 9. Sort the data by Animal ID.

Step 10. Filter the data so that only cats are displayed. What field did you use for the filter?

Step 11. Remove the filter so that all records appear. Delete one record in the table and save your changes to the design of the Animals table.

> **Hint** To delete a record, click the selection box to the left of the record to select it. Then click **Delete** on the HOME ribbon. You can also delete a record by right-clicking the selection box and selecting **Delete Record** from the shortcut menu.

Solutions Appendix

For help: See *On Your Own 15.2* Step-by-Step Solution

WATCH

OBJECTIVE 15.3
VIDEO

Objective 15.3: Create and Run a Query

A query allows you to select what part of the data you want to see on-screen or in a report. You can create a query when you find you need to occasionally view only part of the data. When you run a query, only the data that satisfies the criteria for the query appears on screen. You can edit the data in the query, and these edits are applied to the underlying tables that hold the data.

ON YOUR OWN 15.3

WATCH

OBJECTIVE 15.3
VIDEO

Create and Run a Query

Use the AnimalShelter Database: Part 3 of 3

Using the AnimalShelter database, create a query to display only those animals that have been placed with new owners. The query results are shown in Figure 15-4. The Design View of the finished query is shown in Figure 15-5.

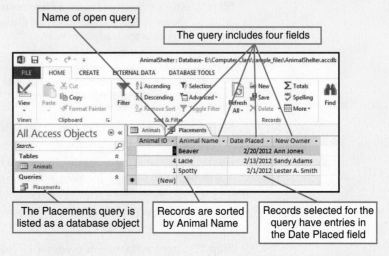

FIGURE 15-4   A query shows selected fields and lists only records that match the given criteria.

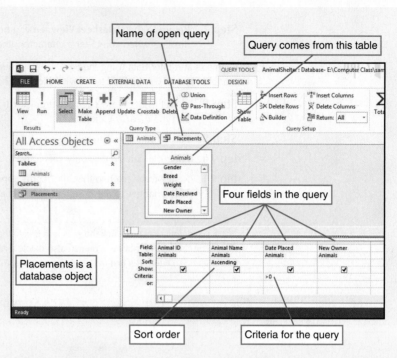

FIGURE 15-5   The query design shows selected fields, sort order, and criteria used to select the records for the query.

Do the following to create and run the query:

Step 1. Use the **Query Design** command on the CREATE ribbon to create a new query. Add the **Animals** table to the query.

Step 2. Add **Animal ID**, **Animal Name**, **Date Placed**, and **New Owner** to the query. To add a field to the query, double-click the field.

Step 3. You use the lower pane of the query design to specify which records to include in the query and how you want the data to appear. Use the lower pane to specify that the records should be sorted by Animal Name in **Ascending** order.

Step 4. Set the criteria for the query so that Date Placed is greater than zero.

> **Hint** The criteria for a query are used to determine which records will appear in the query results. The criteria are applied to a field and can use the =, >, and < operators. The criterion for the Date Placed field is >**0**.

Step 5. Save the query and name it **Placements**. The Design View of the finished query is shown in Figure 15-5. Notice the Placements query is now listed as a **database object** in the Navigation Pane.

> **database object**—A table, form, query, report, or macro that holds or manages the data in a database. Access stores all database objects in the .accdb file and lists these objects in the Navigation Pane of the Access window.

Step 6. To run the query, click **Run** on the DESIGN ribbon, or you can return the query to Datasheet View.

When you use Access to create queries, forms, and reports, Access stores the designs for these objects in the .accdb database file along with the database tables. Each time you run a form, query, or report, Access fills or populates the object with data from the tables.

Do the following to practice opening and closing a query, table, database, and the Access application:

Step 7. Close the **Placements** query, saving your changes.

Step 8. Close the **Animals** table, saving your changes.

Step 9. Open the **Animals** table and the **Placements** query. Practice moving between a view of all the data and a view of only the query's data.

Step 10. Use the FILE tab to close the **AnimalShelter** database, saving any changes. Notice that Access still remains open, but no database is in view. Close the Access window.

Solutions Appendix   *For help:* See *On Your Own 15.3* Step-by-Step Solution

Designing and Creating a New Database

Now that you've explored a database and created a query, let's see how to create a new database.

WATCH

OBJECTIVE 15.4
VIDEO

Objective 15.4: Design and Normalize a Database

When creating a database from scratch, follow these steps:

Step 1. *Decide on the output.* Begin by deciding what you want the database to do for you. What information do you want the database to provide? What queries and reports do you need, and what information goes on each? (Recall that a query presents data on screen and that a report is appropriate for printing.)

Step 2. *Identify the data items.* Make a list of all the data items you must keep to produce these queries and reports.

Step 3. *Group the data into tables.* Group the data items into one or more tables so as to avoid repetition of data. Identify the primary key for each table and how the tables will relate to each other.

Step 4. *Use Access to implement your design.* Create the tables, relationships between tables, forms, queries, and reports.

The first three steps produce a design for your database, and in step 4 you use Access to implement your design. When implementing the design in Access, you begin by creating each table and the relationships between tables. Let's follow these steps to create a database to track the entries in classes for a dog show.

Decide on the Output from the Database

To design the database, you need to first decide on the output. This database requires one query and two reports for the dog show:

> A query displayed on screen that shows total entry fees received for all classes.
> A report listing the dogs and their owners in each class. This report goes to the ringmaster for each class in the show. The report is shown in Figure 15-6. Notice the show has three classes: Agility, Showmanship, and Working.
> Mailing labels for all dog owners. These labels will be used to mail advertisements about future shows. Mailing labels ready to print are shown in Figure 15-7.

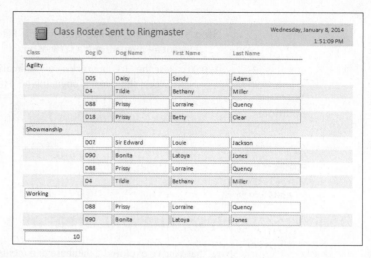

FIGURE 15-6   Begin your database design by deciding what reports you need from the database. This roster report for all classes is used by the ringmaster.

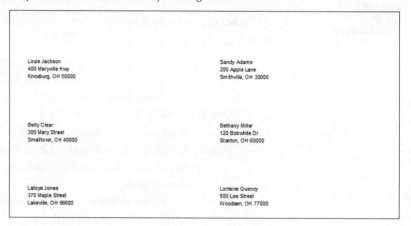

FIGURE 15-7   Mailing labels are used to send advertisements about future shows.

Identify the Data Items in the Database

Use the query and reports to come up with a list of data items the database must track. Figure 15-8 shows a table containing the list of data items and sample data. Notice some of the data is repeated because a dog can enter more than one class. Each time a dog is entered into a class, the dog name and owner name and address are repeated. You can avoid repetition of data, called **data redundancy**, by using more than one table for the data.

> **data redundancy**—Entering the same data more than once. Use enough tables in your database so as to avoid redundancy.

Dogs Entered into Classes

Class	Dog ID	Entry Fee	Dog Name	First Name	Last Name	Street	City	State	Zip
Showmanship	D90	18	Bonita	Latoya	Jones	378 Maple Street	Lakeville	OH	66600
Working	D90	15	Bonita	Latoya	Jones	378 Maple Street	Lakeville	OH	66600
Agility	D05	15	Daisy	Sandy	Adams	200 Apple Lane	Smithville	OH	30000
Agility	D18	15	Prissy	Betty	Clear	300 Mary Street	Smalltown	OH	40000
Agility	D88	15	Prissy	Lorraine	Quency	500 Lee Street	Woodsen	OH	77000
Showmanship	D88	18	Prissy	Lorraine	Quency	500 Lee Street	Woodsen	OH	77000
Working	D88	15	Prissy	Lorraine	Quency	500 Lee Street	Woodsen	OH	77000
Showmanship	D07	18	Sir Edward	Louie	Jackson	400 Maryville Hwy	Knoxburg	OH	50000
Agility	D4	15	Tildie	Bethany	Miller	120 Bobwhite Dr	Stanton	OH	60000
Showmanship	D4	18	Tildie	Bethany	Miller	120 Bobwhite Dr	Stanton	OH	60000

FIGURE 15-8   When all the data is contained in a single table, some data is repeated.

Group the Data into Tables

The next step is to group the data into tables. The idea is to use as many tables as necessary to avoid redundancy. The process is called **normalizing** the database. In Figure 15-8, you can see that the dog name and owner name and address are repeated multiple times in the table. This data redundancy can be eliminated by breaking the data into two tables, as shown in Figure 15-9.

> **normalizing**—The process of grouping data into more than one database table so that data redundancy is avoided.

Dogs

Dog ID	Dog Name	First Name	Last Name	Street	City	State	Zip
D05	Daisy	Sandy	Adams	200 Apple Lane	Smithville	OH	30000
D07	Sir Edward	Louie	Jackson	400 Maryville Hwy	Knoxburg	OH	50000
D18	Prissy	Betty	Clear	300 Mary Street	Smalltown	OH	40000
D4	Tildie	Bethany	Miller	120 Bobwhite Dr	Stanton	OH	60000
D88	Prissy	Lorraine	Quency	500 Lee Street	Woodsen	OH	77000
D90	Bonita	Latoya	Jones	378 Maple Street	Lakeville	OH	66600

Entries

Class	Dog ID	Entry Fee
Agility	D05	15
Agility	D18	15
Agility	D4	15
Agility	D88	15
Showmanship	D07	18
Showmanship	D4	18
Showmanship	D88	18
Showmanship	D90	18
Working	D88	15
Working	D90	15

FIGURE 15-9   When the data is contained in two tables, data redundancy is avoided.

Information about a dog is kept in the Dogs table, and the Dog ID identifies each dog. The Entries table contains one line of data for each time a dog is entered into a class. The Dog ID identifies the dog in the Entries table. By using two tables, you don't need to type the dog name or owner name and address each time a dog is entered into a class.

Next, we identify the primary key for each table. Recall that the primary key is one or more fields in a table that uniquely identify a record. Here are the primary keys for each table:

> **The primary key for the Dogs table is Dog ID.** Each record in the table represents one dog. Two dogs might have the same name, but they don't have the same Dog ID.

> **The primary key for the Entries table is Dog ID and Class.** The Dog ID might be listed multiple times if the dog enters more than one class. A Class is listed multiple times, once for each entry. However, the combination of Dog ID and Class is never repeated because a dog cannot enter the same class more than one time.

Objective 15.5: Use Access to Implement a Database Design

Now that you have a database design, it's time to use Access to create the database. First, we create each database table and enter sample data into the table. The sample data can help you visualize how queries, forms, and reports will look.

WATCH

OBJECTIVE 15.5
VIDEO

Create a Database

WATCH

**OBJECTIVE 15.5
VIDEO**

Create the DogShow Database: Part 1 of 8

When this activity is completed, the DogShow database should look like that in Figure 15-10 with the Datasheet View of the Dogs table showing.

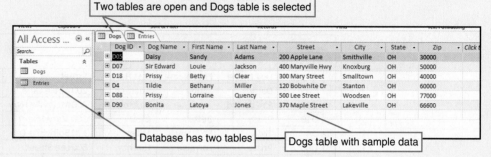

Two tables are open and Dogs table is selected

Database has two tables

Dogs table with sample data

FIGURE 15-10   The DogShow database contains the Dogs table and Entries table.

Let's create the two tables in the database:

Tip   Access does not allow you to save a database file to OneDrive unless you are signed onto Windows 8 using a Microsoft account.

Step 1.   Open Access, create a new blank database named **DogShow** and save it to your USB flash drive, hard drive, OneDrive, or another location given by your instructor. What file extension does Access assign to the database file?

Step 2.   When you create a new database, Access automatically creates one table named Table1 that has one field named ID. Rename the table as the **Dogs** table and rename the ID field as the **Dog ID** field. Set the Data Type to Short Text.

Step 3.   Add seven more fields to the Dogs table. Allow only two characters in the State field and five characters in the Zip field. Here is the complete list of fields:

  a. Dog ID, data type Short Text
  b. Dog Name, data type Short Text
  c. First Name, data type Short Text
  d. Last Name, data type Short Text
  e. Street, data type Short Text
  f. City, data type Short Text
  g. State, data type Short Text, two characters only
  h. Zip, data type Short Text, five characters only

Step 4.   By default, the first field listed in a table is identified as the primary key. Verify the Dog ID field is the primary key for the Dogs table. Save the table design.

Step 5.   Create the Entries table, which contains these fields:

  a. Class, data type Short Text
  b. Dog ID, data type Short Text
  c. Entry Fee, data type Currency

Hint   To create a new table in a database, click **Table** on the CREATE ribbon.

Step 6.   Make the Dog ID and Class fields the primary key for the Entries table.

Step 7.   Enter sample data shown in Figure 15-9 into the Dogs table and Entries table or make up your own sample data for each table. Be sure that a Dog ID listed in the Entries table has a match in the Dogs table. Figure 15-11 shows data in the Entries table.

Tip Regardless of the order that you enter records into a table, when you close and open the table, Access automatically sorts the records by the first field.

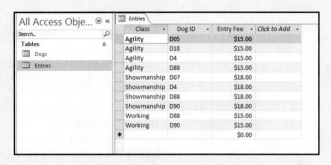

FIGURE 15-11 The Entries table is shown in Datasheet View.

Step 8. Access protects the integrity of data by not allowing duplicate values for the primary key into a table. Try to enter two records in the Dogs table that have the same Dog ID and describe what happens.

Step 9. Try to enter two records in the Entries table that have the same Dog ID and Class and describe what happens.

Step 10. Close both tables and save the database.

Solutions Appendix

For help: See On Your Own 15.4 Step-by-Step Solution

WATCH

OBJECTIVE 15.6
VIDEO

Objective 15.6: Create a Relationship Between Tables

An important feature of Access is the ability to connect or relate tables in a database. A relationship between tables is created by a field they have in common. After you create the relationship, you can display related data from both tables in a seamless query or report. A database that has tables related in this way is called a **relational database** .

> **relational database**—A database that links two or more tables together using fields they have in common.

The most common type of relationship between tables is a **one-to-many relationship** . When tables use this type of relationship, a **field value** occurs one time in the first table (called the parent table) and multiple times in the second table (called the child table). For the DogShow database, a value for the Dog ID occurs one time in the Dogs table and multiple times in the Entries table.

> **one-to-many relationship**—A relationship between database tables where a field value occurs one time in the first table and multiple times in the second table.
> **field value**—The value (text, number, or date) in a field.

ON YOUR OWN 15.5

WATCH

OBJECTIVE 15.6
VIDEO

Relate Two Database Tables

Create the DogShow Database: Part 2 of 8

Using the DogShow database, create a relationship between the Dogs table and Entries table using the Dog ID field they have in common:

Step 1. If necessary, open the **DogShow** database. Make sure the Dogs table and Entries table are closed. A table is closed when you don't see the table tab in the right pane of the Access window.

Step 2. Use the **Relationships** command on the DATABASE TOOLS ribbon to create a one-to-many relationship between the Dogs table and the Entries table.

> **Hint** To create a one-to-many relationship between the Dogs and Entries tables, first add the Dogs table to the relationship and then add the Entries table.

Step 3. To create the relationship, press and drag the **Dog ID** field in the Dogs table to the **Dog ID** field in the Entries table. Be sure you drag from the Dogs table to the Entries table, not the other direction. When you press and drag the Dog ID field from one table to the next, the Edit Relationships dialog box appears (see Figure 15-12). Verify that the field selected in both tables is Dog ID and that Access recognizes the relationship as a one-to-many relationship.

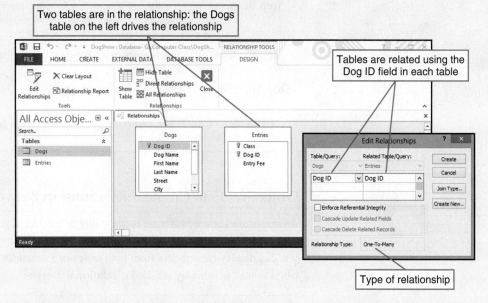

FIGURE 15-12 Build a one-to-many relationship between the Dogs table and Entries table using the Dog ID field.

Step 4. Check **Enforce Referential Integrity** and click **Create**. When you enforce **referential integrity**, a value for Dog ID is allowed in the Entries table only if there is a matching value in the Dogs table.

> **referential integrity**—In a one-to-many relationship, a field value in the child table must match the corresponding field value in the parent table before the entry is allowed in the child table. The parent table is the table driving the relationship, and the child table is the table driven by the relationship.

> **Not Working?** When you choose Enforce Referential Integrity, Access verifies that the Entries table conforms to this enforcement. If it finds a Dog ID in the Entries table that doesn't have a match in the Dogs table, an error occurs, and you cannot complete the relationship. Go back to the Entries table and correct the data. Then try to build the relationship again.

Step 5. Figure 15-13 shows the relationship created. Notice the 1 and the infinity symbol (∞) on the relationship line that indicate the one-to-many relationship. Save and close the relationship.

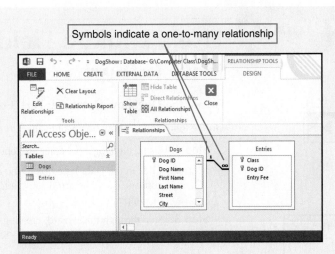

FIGURE 15-13   A one-to-many relationship is built between the Dogs and Entries tables.

> **Not Working?** If the relationship is not working and you want to start over, click on the line between the tables and press the **Delete** key to delete the relationship between the tables. Then build the relationship again.

Step 6. To see how the relationship works, open the **Dogs** table and notice the + to the left of each record. When you click the +, the related records in the Entries table appear. For example, when you click the + beside D4, two records in the Entries table appear (see Figure 15-14). Close the **Dogs** table.

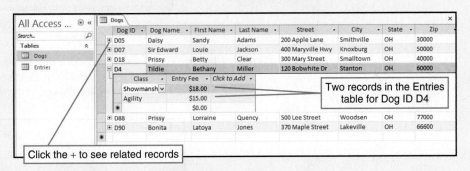

FIGURE 15-14   Related records in the Entries table appear under a record in the Dogs table.

Step 7. Open the **Entries** table. Try to enter a new record in the table that uses a Dog ID that is not found in the Dogs table. An error message appears, and the invalid entry is not allowed. Close the **Entries** table.

> Solutions Appendix

For help: See On Your Own 15.5 Step-by-Step Solution

WATCH

OBJECTIVE 15.7
VIDEO

Objective 15.7: Protect Data Integrity Using a Lookup Field

So far, you've seen how data integrity can be protected using a field's properties, using primary keys, and enforcing the one-to-many relationship between tables. Another useful tool to protect the data from errors is a **lookup field** . Let's use a lookup field to make sure the Class field always has valid entries.

> **lookup field**—A list of values allowed in a field. You can type the list, or you can specify a field in a table from which the list can be taken.

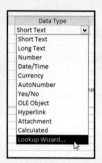

ON YOUR OWN 15.6

WATCH

OBJECTIVE 15.7
VIDEO

Use a Lookup Field to Protect Data Integrity

Create the DogShow Database: Part 3 of 8

Do the following to allow only valid values in the Class field of the Entries table:

Step 1. Using the DogShow database, open the **Entries** table and go to **Design View**.

Step 2. Click in the Data Type box to the right of the Class field name. A drop-down arrow appears. Click the arrow and then click **Lookup Wizard**. The Lookup Wizard dialog box appears.

Step 3. Step through this wizard, creating a list of values that are allowed into the Class field, as shown in Figure 15-15. Save your work and return to the **Datasheet View**.

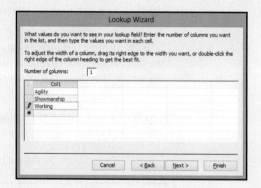

FIGURE 15-15   Enter the values that you want to allow into the Class field.

Step 4. When you click in the Class field, a drop-down arrow appears. Use the drop-down arrow to see the lookup list (see Figure 15-16). You can click your selection or type it. Only values from the list are allowed in the field. Close the **Entries** table.

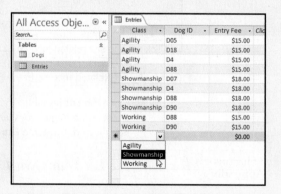

FIGURE 15-16   Only values in the list are allowed into the Class field.

Solutions
Appendix

For help: See *On Your Own 15.6* Step-by-Step Solution

Creating and Using Forms, Queries, and Reports

Now that you've learned how to create a database and protect the integrity of the data, let's see how forms, queries, and reports can help you manage the database.

WATCH

OBJECTIVE 15.8
VIDEO

Objective 15.8: Create and Use Detailed and Split Forms

An Access **detailed form** displays one record at a time and is used to edit this record. You can select which fields appear on the form. Two other types of forms are the **multiple items form** and the **split form** .

> **detailed form**—A form that displays one record at a time. To create the form, begin by clicking **Form** on the CREATE ribbon.
> **multiple items form**—A form that displays more than one record at a time. The form is similar to the Datasheet View but gives more control over what the user can see and do. To create the form, click **More Forms** on the CREATE ribbon and then click **Multiple Items**.
> **split form**—A form that is split on the screen. The top half displays one record, and the bottom half lists several more records. To create the form, click **More Forms** on the CREATE ribbon and click **Split Form**.

When you first create a form, Access displays it in **Layout View** . You must switch to **Form View** before you can use the form to edit data.

> **Layout View**—A view in Access where you can make design changes to a form or report. Live data displays in the form to help you with design changes, but you cannot edit the data.
> **Form View**—A view in Access where a form can be used to edit data.

ON YOUR OWN 15.7

Create and Use Detailed and Split Forms

WATCH

OBJECTIVE 15.8
VIDEO

Create the DogShow Database: Part 4 of 8

In this activity, you create a detailed form to edit the Dogs table and a split form to edit the Entries table. When the activity is completed, the detailed form for the Dogs table should look like that in Figure 15-17.

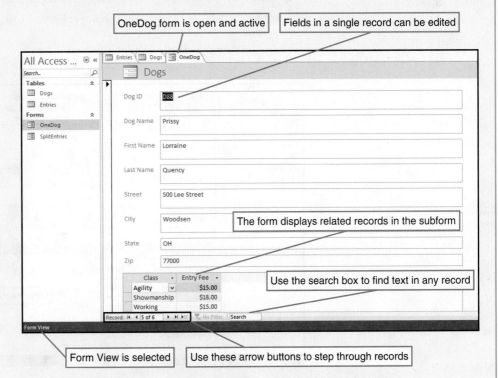

FIGURE 15-17   Use the OneDog form to edit a single record in the Dogs table.

Do the following to create and use a detailed form to edit the Dogs table:

Step 1. Open the **Dogs** table in the DogShow database. Use the **Form** command on the CREATE ribbon to create a detailed form named **OneDog**. The form is listed as an object in the Navigation Pane.

> **Not Working?** Objects in a database (tables, queries, forms, reports, and macros) are listed in the left pane of the Access window. If you don't see an object, right-click in the pane and select **Navigation Options** from the shortcut menu. In the Navigation Options dialog box, select **Object Type**, and make sure all object types are selected.

Step 2. Switch the form from Layout View to **Form View** so you can use it to edit data. Then use the left and right arrows at the bottom of the form to step through the Dogs records. Go to the first and last records in the table. As you step through the Dogs records, notice the related records in the Entries table appear at the bottom of the Dogs form. This **subform** is automatically created when the main form uses a table that has a related table.

> **subform**—A form under the main form that contains data from a table related to the parent table used in the main form.

Step 3. Enter a new record in the table, making up your own data.

Step 4. Use the search box at the bottom of the form to search for text you know to be in the data. Does the record with the data appear?

> **Not Working?** The OneDog form provides two sets of arrow buttons used to step through records. One set applies to the Entries table, and the other set applies to the Dogs table. Use the set at the very bottom of the form that applies to the Dogs table.

Step 5. Close the **OneDog** form, saving your changes.

Step 6. Open the **Dogs** table and verify the new record appears. Close the Dogs table.

> **Not Working?** If you don't see the record, the Datasheet View might need refreshing. To refresh a view of the data, click **Refresh All** on the HOME ribbon. You can also press the **F5** key to refresh the view.

The split form to edit the Entries table is shown in Figure 15-18. Do the following to create and use the form:

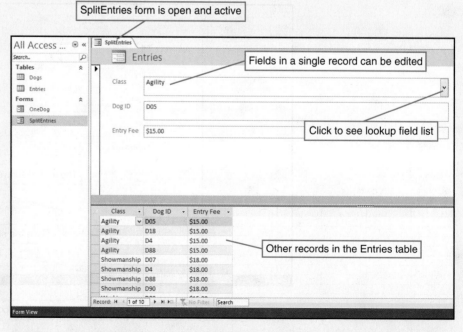

FIGURE 15-18   Use the SplitEntries form to edit a single record in the Entries table and view multiple records in the table.

Step 7. Create a split form using the Entries table. Name the form **SplitEntries**.

Step 8. Using the Forms View, step through the records. Go to the first and last records, add a new record, and search for text in the Entries table.

Step 9. Close the **SplitEntries** form, saving your changes. Then open the Entries table and verify the new record is displayed.

Solutions Appendix

For help: See *On Your Own 15.7* Step-by-Step Solution

WATCH

OBJECTIVE 15.9 VIDEO

Objective 15.9: Create and Run Queries That Include Calculations and Multiple Tables

Earlier in the chapter, you learned to create a query using a single table in the AnimalShelter database. Now let's see how you can add a calculation to a query and build another query that uses two tables.

ON YOUR OWN 15.8

Create a Query That Includes a Calculation

WATCH

OBJECTIVE 15.9 VIDEO

Create the DogShow Database: Part 5 of 8

In this activity, you create the Fees query that calculates the sum of total fees paid. The completed query is shown in Figure 15-19.

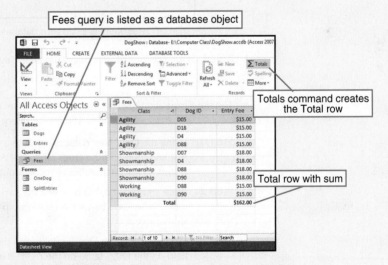

FIGURE 15-19   The Fees query includes the sum of total fees paid.

Let's create the query:

Step 1. Create a query that uses the **Entries** table and add all three fields in the table to the query. Name the query **Fees**. Sort the records by Class.

Step 2. Add a Total row to the query. In the Total row, sum the Entry Fee column.

> **Hint** To add a Total row to a query, switch to Datasheet View and click **Totals** on the HOME ribbon. In the Total row, add a sum in the appropriate column.

Step 3. Compare your query to that shown in Figure 15-19. Your data might be different. Verify the Entry Fee column is summed in the Total row. Correct any problems you see. Save and close the query.

Solutions Appendix

For help: See On Your Own 15.8 Step-by-Step Solution

ON YOUR OWN 15.9

Create a Query That Uses Two Tables

WATCH

OBJECTIVE 15.9 VIDEO

Create the DogShow Database: Part 6 of 8

In this activity, you create the ClassRoster query that uses the Dogs and Entries tables. The completed query is shown in Figure 15-20. This query lists each entry sorted by Class and shows information from both tables. Later in the chapter, you use this query to create the Class Roster report that goes to the show ringmaster.

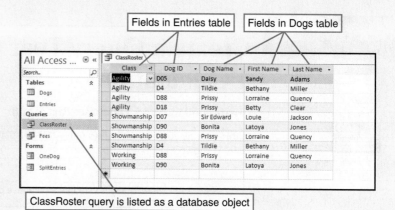

Fields in Entries table   Fields in Dogs table

ClassRoster query is listed as a database object

FIGURE 15-20 The ClassRoster query uses the Dogs and Entries tables and lists entries in each class.

The order you add tables to a query is important because the first table added to a query drives the number of records displayed by the query. Do the following to create the query:

Step 1. Using the **DogShow** database, create a new query. Add the **Entries** table to the query first and then add the **Dogs** table to the query. (Because the Entries table is added first, it drives the number of records displayed by the query.)

Step 2. Break the relationship between the two tables by deleting the line or lines between them. When you break the relationship, the query is free to establish a new relationship as needed.

Step 3. Press and drag the Dog ID field from the Entries table on the left to the Dog ID field on the Dogs table on the right. A line is drawn. Notice the line is not defined as a one-to-many relationship using the 1 and ∞ symbol. In fact, the relationship between Entries and Dogs is a **many-to-one relationship**.

> **many-to-one relationship**—A relationship between database tables where a field value occurs many times in the first table and only one time in the second table.

Step 4. We want the query to show all records in the Entries table. To make this the rule, right-click the line and select **Join Properties** from the shortcut menu.

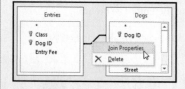

> **Not Working?** If Join Properties doesn't show in the shortcut menu, you probably missed the line. Try right-clicking the line again.

Step 5. The Join Properties dialog box appears. Verify the Entries table is the Left Table Name and the Dogs table is the Right Table Name. Select **2: Include ALL records from 'Entries' and only those records from 'Dogs' where the joined fields are equal**, as shown in Figure 15-21. Click **OK** to close the box. Notice the line between the tables is now an arrow pointing from Entries to Dogs.

FIGURE 15-21   The Join Properties dialog box shows how records will be selected for a query.

Step 6. Add the following fields to the query in this order:

    a. Class in the Entries table
    b. Dog ID in the Entries table
    c. Dog Name in the Dogs table
    d. First Name in the Dogs table
    e. Last Name in the Dogs table

Step 7. Sort the record list in the query by **Class** in **Ascending** order.

Step 8. Save the query, naming it **ClassRoster**.

Step 9. Return to Datasheet View and view the results of the query. Check your work against Figure 15-20 and correct any problems you see. Your data might be different from that shown. Verify that the number of rows displayed in the query is the same as the number of records in the Entries table. How can you tell how many records appear in the query without counting them?

> **Not Working?** If the number of records in the query is not correct, perhaps the problem is with the relationship between tables in the query. To verify this relationship, go to Design View and display the Join Properties dialog box. The Join Properties box should look like that shown in Figure 15-21.

Step 10. Close all open objects in the database.

WATCH

CHAPTER 15
DIVING DEEPER
VIDEO

Solutions
Appendix

For help: See *On Your Own 15.9* Step-by-Step Solution

WATCH

OBJECTIVE 15.10
VIDEO

Objective 15.10: Create Mailing Labels and an Access Report

An Access report can be used to present the data, charts, calculations, and other information about the data in a format appropriate for printing. You can use a database table to create a simple report or mailing labels. If the report uses data from multiple tables, it's easier to create a query first and then generate the report from the query.

ON YOUR OWN 15.10

Create Mailing Labels from a Single Table

WATCH

OBJECTIVE 15.10
VIDEO

Create the DogShow Database: Part 7 of 8

In this activity, you create mailing labels that are printed two across, 14 labels to a page. Peel-off labels using this standard are shown in Figure 15-22. The finished mailing labels are shown in Figure 15-23.

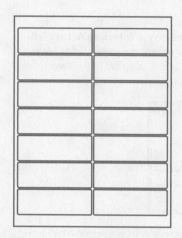

FIGURE 15-22 These mailing labels are 4" × 1.33" and print two across and 14 to a page.

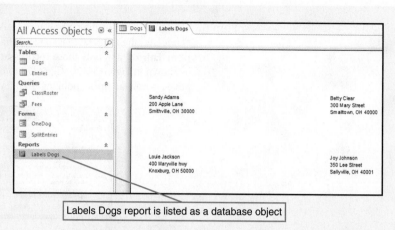

Labels Dogs report is listed as a database object

FIGURE 15-23 Mailing labels will print two across and are sorted by last name and first name.

To create the mailing labels from the Dogs table, do the following:

Step 1. Open the **Dogs** table in the DogShow database. Make sure the Dogs tab is selected in the right pane. Use the **Labels** command on the CREATE ribbon to create mailing labels using data in the Dogs table. Here are the details you'll need to create the labels:

- The labels use the **Avery USA 5162** standard.
- Use the default choices for font and color of text.
- The fields that go on the labels are First Name, Last Name, Street, City, State, and Zip. Format this data as a mailing address.
- Sort the labels by Last Name, First Name.

Step 2. Save the labels, naming them **Labels Dogs**. Notice the labels are listed in the left pane as one of the database objects in the Reports group. Close the Labels Dogs report.

Solutions Appendix

For help: See *On Your Own 15.10* Step-by-Step Solution

You can use the Report Wizard to create a report from multiple database tables. To start the Report Wizard, click **Report Wizard** on the CREATE ribbon. Another way to create a report from multiple tables is to start with a query that contains the data from multiple tables. The advantage of using an existing query for the report is that you already have part of the work done.

ON YOUR OWN 15.11

Create a Report from a Query

WATCH

OBJECTIVE 15.10 VIDEO

Create the DogShow Database: Part 8 of 8

In this activity, you create the ClassRosterReport that will be printed and sent to the ringmaster during the show. The ringmaster is responsible for making sure only dogs on the roster are allowed in the show ring. The completed report is shown in Figure 15-24.

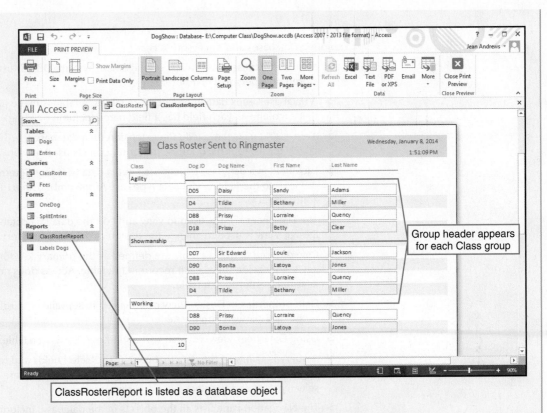

FIGURE 15-24   The Class Roster report lists dog entries sorted and grouped by Class.

Do the following to create the report:

Step 1. Using the DogShow database, open the **ClassRoster** query you created earlier in On Your Own 15-9. Use the **Report** command on the CREATE ribbon to create a report from the query. Name the report **ClassRosterReport**.

Step 2. The title at the top of the report is ClassRoster. Change the title to **Class Roster Sent to Ringmaster**.

Step 3. Narrow the field widths so the fields don't spill off the page. To adjust a field width, select the field box and press and drag the edge of the box to resize it.

Step 4. Position the page number box at the bottom of the report so it doesn't spill off the page.

Step 5. Sort the report by Class and add a group header for each Class. To add a group header at the beginning of each group of classes, use the **Group & Sort** command on the DESIGN ribbon. Add a group to the report, grouping by Class.

Step 6. Change to **Report View** to view the report with its data. Then change to **Print Preview** view to see how the report will look on the printed page.

Step 7. Save the report and close it.

Solutions Appendix

For help: See *On Your Own 15.11* Step-by-Step Solution

Summary

Exploring Databases and Microsoft Access

> Microsoft Access is a database management system (DBMS) used to manage databases stored on a personal computer.

> A database keeps data in one or more tables. A table is made up of records (rows) and fields (columns). Each field has a field name (column heading).

> Access 2013 uses the .accdb file extension for a database file. The file contains the data tables, forms, reports, queries, and other objects used to store and manage the data.

> Each field in a database table is assigned a data type that determines what type of data can go into the field. Some data types are AutoNumber, Short Text, Number, Date/Time, and Currency.

> The Datasheet View is used to view and edit the data in a database table or query. The Design View is used to change the design of the table or query.

> One or more fields in a table are defined as the primary key for the table. The primary key uniquely identifies each record in the table. Access does not allow duplicate primary keys to be entered in a table.

> Field properties in Design View can be used to set validation rules to protect the integrity of the data allowed into the table.

> Using Datasheet View, you can sort and filter records in a table.

> A query is a view of the data that contains selected fields and records that match the criteria for the query and can include calculations. Queries are used to display and edit selected data and to select data for a report.

> The Navigation Pane lists all the objects in the database, including tables, queries, forms, and reports. Open objects display in the right pane of the Access window.

Designing and Creating a New Database

> To design a database, first consider how you will use the information in the database and determine what queries and reports you need. Then decide what data items you must keep to produce these queries and reports.

> The next step to design a database is to decide how many tables you need in the database so as to avoid data redundancy. Start with sample data in a single table and then break out the data into two or more tables so that data is not duplicated.

> Breaking a table into two or more tables so as to avoid data redundancy is called normalizing the database.

> Two tables can be linked together using a field the tables have in common. The link is called a relationship. A relationship can be a one-to-many relationship or a many-to-one relationship.

> To create a new database in Access, first name the database file and save it to a storage device. Then create each table in the database, assigning field names and data types to each field in a table. Entering sample data in the tables can help you visualize how queries, forms, and reports will look as you design these objects.

> After you have created the database tables with sample data, the next step is to create relationships between the tables.

> When you choose to enforce referential integrity in a database relationship, data is not allowed into a table unless it has a matching reference in the other table.

> A lookup field provides a list of values that are allowed into the field. You can set up a lookup field using the Design View for a database table.

Creating and Using Forms, Queries, and Reports

> A form is used to view and edit data and provides more opportunities to protect the integrity of data than when editing data directly in a table.

> Three types of forms are a detailed form, multiple items form, and split form.

> You use the Form View to edit data and the Layout View to change the design of the form.

> A query displays records that match the given criteria. The query can include a Total row and calculations, and records might be sorted. A query can use multiple tables in the database.

> Relationships between tables in a query apply only to the query. The Join Properties dialog box for the relationship is used to specify how the relationship will work.

> Mailing labels can be created as one type of Access report. The Label Wizard is used to design the labels.

> A report can be created using the Report Wizard or using an existing query.

> The Report View is used to display data in a report. The Layout View is used to change the design of the report. The Print Preview shows the report as it will look when printed.

> The Group & Sort command on the DESIGN ribbon can be used to add groups to a report. First, sort the records in the report on a field and then group the report by this field. A group can have a group header that identifies the group.

CHAPTER MASTERY PROJECT

Now it's time to find out how well you've mastered the content in this chapter. If you can do all the steps in this mastery project without looking back at the chapter details and can answer all the review questions following this project, you've mastered this chapter. If you can complete the project by finding answers using the web, you've proven that you can teach yourself how to create and manage a database using Access.

Hint All the key terms in the chapter are used in this mastery project or in the review questions. If you encounter a key word you don't know, such as *primary key*, enter **define:primary key** in the Internet Explorer address box or in the Access Help search box.

If you find you need a lot of help doing the project and you have not yet read the chapter or done the activities, drop back and start at the beginning of the chapter, watch the videos, review the step-by-step solutions as you work through the On Your Own activities, and then return to this project.

Tip If you need help completing this part of the mastery project, review the "Designing and Creating a New Database" section in the chapter.

Figure 15-25 shows two tables used by Adams Hardware Store to manage its inventory. The Suppliers table has one row for each supplier. Each supplier is identified by a Supplier ID. The Inventory table has one row for each inventory item, which is identified by a SKU. (SKU stands for stock-keeping unit.)

Suppliers

Supplier ID	Supplier	Street	City	State	Zip
BH	Boom's Hardware	1827 South Oak St	Topeka	KS	66607
CSC	Cali Supply Company	1291 North 18th St	Akron	OH	44305
FT	Fiesta Tools	382 Hill St	Cimarron	NM	87714
HSUSA	Hardware Supplies USA	839 Lakeview Blvd	Dallas	TX	75201
OS	Oriental Suppliers	300 Industrial Way	Northcutt	FL	30049
TT	Timely Tools	283 Parkway St	Alexandria	VA	22307

Inventory

SKU	Description	Department	Supplier ID	Wholesale Price	In Stock
FT002	Drill, corded	Power tools	FT	22.00	3
BH0020	Blades, copping saw	Hand tools	BH	3.88	6
BH0025	Blades, hacksaw	Hand tools	BH	2.06	2
FT0010	Axe, single headed	Hand tools	FT	18.88	0
CSC0011	Axe, wedge	Hand tools	CSC	17.67	2
BH0015	Axe head repair kit	Hand tools	BH	3.21	1
CSC0017	Measuring tape, 120'	Measuring	CSC	14.40	0
CSC0045	Blades, circular saw	Hand tools	CSC	4.44	2
CSC0046	Measuring tape, 60'	Measuring	CSC	10.00	8
CSC0050	Clamps, quick release	Hand tools	CSC	7.63	5
CSC0330	Saw, handsaw	Hand tools	CSC	9.70	7
FT00001	Axe, double headed	Hand tools	FT	22.38	2
BH00002	Axe, fiberglass	Hand tools	BH	31.26	3
FT00040	Blades, jigsaw	Hand tools	FT	2.61	1

FIGURE 15-25   Two tables are used to manage inventory for a hardware store.

The HardwareStore database has seven objects (two tables, one query, two forms, and two reports). First use Microsoft Access to create the two tables:

> **Tip** Access doesn't allow you to save a database file to OneDrive unless you are signed on to Windows 8 using a Microsoft account.

Step 1. Create the HardwareStore database on your USB flash drive, hard drive, OneDrive, or another location given by your instructor.

Step 2. Create the Suppliers table, which has these fields:

  a. Supplier ID, primary key, data type Short Text

  b. Supplier, data type Short Text

  c. Street, data type Short Text

  d. City, data type Short Text

  e. State, data type Short Text, two characters only

  f. Zip, data type Short Text, five characters only

Step 3. Create the Inventory table, which has these fields:

  a. SKU, primary key, data type Short Text

  b. Description, data type Short Text

     c. Department, data type Short Text

     d. Supplier ID, data type Short Text

     e. Wholesale Price, data type Currency

     f. In Stock, data type Number

Step 4. Save the table designs and create a relationship between the tables. Link the Suppliers table to the Inventory table using a one-to-many relationship. Enforce referential integrity so that a user cannot enter a field value for the Supplier ID in the Inventory table that doesn't have a match in the Suppliers table.

Step 5. Enter sample data into the Suppliers table. You can use the data shown in Figure 15-25 or make up your own data. Sort the data by Supplier ID.

Step 6. Enter sample data into the Inventory table. You can use the data shown in Figure 15-25 or make up your own data. (You don't need to enter all the data shown in Figure 15-25.) Be sure to use only these field values in the Department field:

- Hand tools
- Measuring
- Power tools

Step 7. Verify that when you attempt to enter a value in the Supplier ID field in the Inventory table that doesn't have a match in the Suppliers table, an error message appears and you're not allowed to continue to a new record until you enter a valid value. Practice filtering the data to display only Hand tools, Measuring, or Power tools. Then remove all filters.

Step 8. View the Suppliers table in Datasheet View. Verify that when you click the + beside a record, you can view related records in the Inventory table.

Step 9. View the Inventory table in Design View. Create a lookup field for the Department field. The possible values for the Department field are **Hand tools**, **Measuring**, and **Power tools**. Require that only these three values be allowed into the field.

Step 10. Save your changes and return to the Datasheet View. What happens when you attempt to enter a value other than values in the lookup list in the Department field?

> **Tip** If you need help completing this part of the mastery project, review the "Creating and Using Forms, Queries, and Reports" section in the chapter.

Step 11. Do the following to create the two forms in the database:

     a. Create a detailed form using the Suppliers table. Name the form **OneSupplier**. Go from Layout View to Form View and use the form to step through records in the Suppliers table and add a new record to the Suppliers table. Notice Access also created a subform that contains records in the Inventory table.

     b. Open the Suppliers table in Datasheet View. Verify you can see the new record. If you don't see the record, press F5 to refresh the data.

     c. Create a split form to edit the Inventory table. Save the form, naming it **SplitInventory**. Go to the Form View and use the form to step through records in the Inventory table.

     d. Close all open tables and forms, saving your changes.

The database has one query taken from the Inventory and Suppliers tables. The query (see Figure 15-26) includes a calculated column named Investment. The value in this column is the money invested in an item, which is Wholesale Price multiplied by In Stock. The column is summed in a Total row at the bottom of the query.

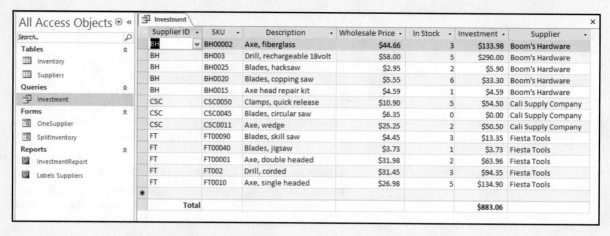

FIGURE 15-26   The Investment query has a calculated column and Total row.

Step 12. Do the following to create the query:

a. Use the Inventory table to create the query, and add the Supplier ID, SKU, Description, Wholesale Price, and In Stock fields to the query. Name the query **Investment**.

b. Using the Design View, create a sixth column named Investment, which has a calculation in it. To create this sixth column, right-click the Field row and select **Zoom** from the shortcut menu. In the Zoom dialog box, type the following and click **OK**:

> Investment:[Wholesale Price]*[In Stock]

c. The calculated column is added to the query. Save the query and run it. The Investment column shows the product of Wholesale Price and In Stock for each inventory item.

d. Add a Total row to the query and put in it the sum of the Investment column. Save your changes.

e. Add the Suppliers table to the query. Break the link between the two tables.

f. Create a new link from Inventory to Suppliers using the Supplier ID field. Open the Join Properties dialog box and select **2: Include ALL records from 'Inventory' and only those records from 'Suppliers' where the joined fields are equal**.

g. Add to the query the Supplier field from the Suppliers table. Sort the query by the Supplier field.

h. The query Design View should look like that in Figure 15-27. Save your changes and run the query. Results should be similar to that shown in Figure 15-26. Your data might be different from that in the figure.

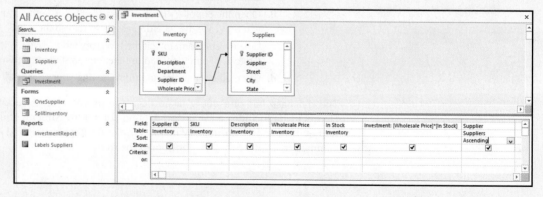

FIGURE 15-27   The Design View of the query shows one calculated column and two tables used for the query.

Step 13. Using the Suppliers table, create mailing labels for all suppliers. Use the **Avery USA 5160** standard, which is 1″ × 2 5/8″ and three across the page. Include on the mailing labels the Supplier, Street, City, State, and Zip. Don't forget the comma and spaces between City, State, and Zip. Sort the labels by Supplier. The Print Preview of the mailing labels is shown in Figure 15-28. Your data might be different.

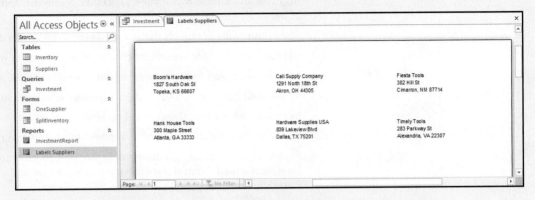

FIGURE 15-28 Mailing labels to suppliers print three across the page.

Step 14. Create a report using the Investment query. Save the report, naming it **InvestmentReport**. Change the title of the report to **Investments by Supplier**.

Step 15. Adjust field widths so the report doesn't spill off the page on the right side. Sort records by Suppliers and group the data by Suppliers. Display a Print Preview of the report, which should look like that in Figure 15-29. Your data might be different.

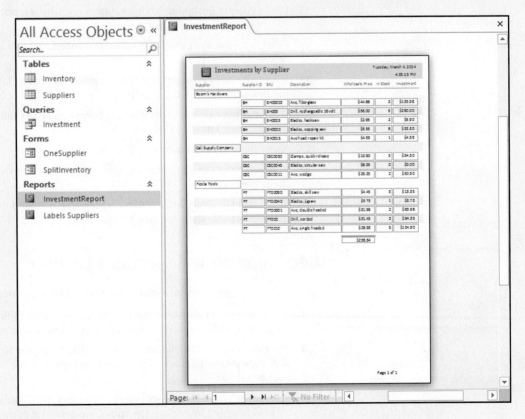

FIGURE 15-29 The Investment query is used to create the Investments by Supplier report.

Step 16. Close any open objects (tables, query, forms, or reports). Verify seven objects are listed in the Navigation Pane of the Access window. Save your changes and close the HardwareStore database.

Review Questions

Answer these questions to find out if you have learned the skills and concepts covered in the chapter. Your instructor can provide you with the correct answers when you are ready to check your work.

1. Access is an example of a small-scale DBMS. Name two applications that are examples of a large-scale DBMS.

2. Name four types of objects that Access keeps in an .accdb database file.

3. List three reasons why you might choose to use Access to manage data rather than Excel.

4. What is data called that is entered by a user and is not calculated?

5. Which data type is best to use when zip codes are stored in a field?

6. By default, which field does Access make the primary key in a table?

7. Can you edit the data displayed in a query? In a form? In a report?

8. Suppose you are creating a query to display only those records that have a value in the Date Placed field. What is the criterion you must type in the Criteria row for the Date Placed field?

9. What type of rule is required so that the entries in a Gender field are limited to "M" or "F"?

10. List the four steps to design and create a database.

11. Suppose you are designing a database and have split the data items into two tables. When examining the sample data in the second table, you discover data is repeated in many records. What do you do next?

12. What is the database design process called of splitting tables into multiple tables so as to avoid data redundancy?

13. When you are designing a table listing dogs, why is it not a good idea to make the name of a dog the primary key for the table?

14. What is a database called that has tables linked together using a field they have in common?

15. If Table A has one record that links to many records in Table B, what type relationship is the link from Table A to Table B?

16. If Table A has many records that link to one record in Table B, what type relationship is the link from Table A to Table B?

17. Name three types of forms used in Access.

18. Why is it more convenient to create a report from an existing query rather than using the Report Wizard?

19. When two tables are included in a query, which table determines the number of records that will appear when you run the query?

Becoming an Independent Learner

Answer the following questions about becoming an independent learner:

1. To teach yourself about databases and Access, do you think it's best to rely on the chapter or on the web or Access Help when you need answers?

2. The most important skill learned in this chapter is how to teach yourself a computer skill. Rate yourself at Level A through E on how well you're doing with this skill. What is your level?

   - Level A: I was able to successfully complete the Chapter Mastery Project with the help of only a few of the On Your Own activities in the chapter.
   - Level B: I completed all the On Your Own activities and the Chapter Mastery Project without referring to any of the solutions in the Step-by-Step Solutions Appendix.
   - Level C: I completed all the On Your Own activities and the Chapter Mastery Project by using just a few of the solutions in the Step-by-Step Solutions Appendix.

- Level D: I completed all the On Your Own activities and the Chapter Mastery Project by using many of the solutions in the Step-by-Step Solutions Appendix.
- Level E: I completed all the On Your Own activities and the Chapter Mastery Project and had to use all of the solutions in the Step-by-Step Solutions Appendix.

To continue toward the goal of teaching yourself computer skills, if you're not at Level A, try to move up one level on how you learn in Chapter 16.

Projects to Help You

Now that you've mastered the material in this chapter, you're ready to tackle the three projects focused on your career, personal, or academic goals. Depending on your own interests, you might choose to complete any or all of these projects to help you achieve your goals.

Project 1: Importing Data from Word into Access

Knowing how to move data from one application to another, such as from a Word table into an Access database, can be a valuable skill in a business environment. Do the following to learn how:

Step 1. Research and find out how to import data from Word into Access. You can search Access Help or the web, or you can explore and try commands on the EXTERNAL DATA ribbon in Access.

Step 2. Test your skills by using the HardwareSuppliersTable.docx file in the sample_files folder on the www.pearsonhighered.com/jump website and in MyITLab that you downloaded to your USB flash drive. Open the document in Word.

Step 3. To convert the data in this table to a comma-delimited text file, select the table and then click **Convert to Text** on the LAYOUT ribbon. In the Convert Table to Text dialog box, select Commas to be used to separate text. Each row of data in the table will be written on a single line with commas separating items. Then save the document as a plain text file, which has a .txt file extension. Name the document HardwareSuppliersTableText.

> **Hint** Text can be imported from a plain text file into an Access database. The fields in the text file are separated using a comma, and the file is called a comma-delimited text file. The LAYOUT ribbon in Word can be used to create a comma-delimited text file. First, select the table and then click **Convert to Text** on the LAYOUT ribbon.

Step 4. Using Access, create a new blank desktop database. Name the database **Import**. On the EXTERNAL DATA ribbon, in the Import & Link group, click **Text File** and follow directions onscreen. Import the comma-delimited text file into a new table in the Access database. When you import, make sure the Phone field is using the Short Text format. Send the **Import** database to your instructor.

Project 2: Comparing Access and Excel

In Chapter 11, you learned how the Gently Used Consignment Shop uses worksheets to track inventory, sellers, commissions, and monthly reports to sellers. Design a database to track the same information. Decide what tables the database should have and what fields should go in each table. Identify and design each query and report needed for the database. Use Access to create the database tables and enter sample data into the tables.

Answer the following questions:

1. List 15 data items the database must keep.
2. How many tables are in your database?
3. What is the primary key of each table?
4. List two queries the database must include.

Career Project My manager has stored a lot of data in Word tables, and now she wants to move that data into an Access database. She has asked me to help her figure it out. How do I begin?

Personal Project I've kept records for a small business using Excel, and I want to convert this data to an Access database. How do I design and set up the database using my worksheets to guide me?

Academic Project I need some extra practice managing a database using Access.

Project 3: Access in Your Academic Career

Do the following to further explore the AnimalShelter database you used in the chapter:

Step 1. Using Microsoft Access, open the AnimalShelter database in the sample_files folder on the www.pearsonhighered.com/jump website and in MyITLab that you downloaded to your USB flash drive. Open the Animals table. Add a new record to the table, making up your own data.

Step 2. Change the Field Properties for the Gender field so that a value is required in this field. Which Field Property did you change?

Step 3. Create a new field in the Animals table and name the field Phone Number. In the Field Properties, add an Input Mask to allow only 10-digit numbers in the field, storing the placeholder characters in the field. What is the input mask that Access created?

Step 4. Filter the records so that only Dogs are listed. Which field did you filter? Remove the filter.

Step 5. Create a query using the Animals table. Save the query, naming the query **Cats**. Include in the query **Animal ID**, **Animal Type**, **Animal Name**, **Gender**, and **Date Received**.

Step 6. Add criteria to the query that displays only cats. Which field received the criteria? What is the criteria you put in the Criteria row?

Step 7. Sort the records in the query by Animal Name. Which row in the query received your entry to require sorting?

Step 8. Save the query. Go to Datasheet view and verify only records for cats are listed and the records are sorted by Animal Name.

Step 9. Close the AnimalShelter database, saving your changes.

Project to Help Others

One of the best ways to learn is to teach someone else. And, in teaching someone else, you are making a contribution into that person's life. In this chapter, help someone learn to use Access. Working with your apprentice, do the following:

Step 1. Explain to your apprentice a little about Access and how it works to manage data in a database using tables, forms, queries, and reports. Use the database examples in this chapter to demonstrate how to use a table, form, query, and report.

Step 2. Review with your apprentice how data can also be managed using Excel worksheets. Discuss with her when it might be appropriate to use Excel and when it might be appropriate to use Access to manage data.

Step 3. What conclusions did you and your apprentice reach about which tool to use in different situations?

Step 4. Use Word to create a document file that contains answers about the tutoring session and send the file to your instructor. If you're using MyITLab, you can post the file in Dropbox. On the other hand, your instructor might prefer you post the file to your OneDrive. Here are the questions:

1. Who is your apprentice?

2. Briefly describe the conclusions you and your apprentice reached in step 3 regarding when to use Access and when to use Excel.

3. How do you think the tutoring session went? How would you like to improve it next time?

16 Authoring Your Own Website

In This Chapter, You Will:

Create a Website from Beginning to End

16.1 Create a web page using a text editor and publish the website

16.2 Use HTML tags in a web page

Enhance a Website Using HTML Structure and Other Tools

16.3 Use HTML structure and formatting tags

16.4 Use subfolders to organize files on a website

16.5 Use hyperlinks to connect to other pages and websites

Survey Web Authoring Software

16.6 Explore and use web authoring software

In this chapter, you build your own website from the ground up. You start by creating a simple web page and publishing it to a web hosting site. Then you learn how to add photos, links, and multiple pages to your website. Note that in this chapter, you use a text editor to create the web pages. If you want to move on to build more complex websites, you can use better web authoring tools that are introduced at the end of the chapter.

As with all chapters in this book, you can choose which of the learning paths below best suits your needs. If you already know how to build a website, consider jumping straight to the mastery project. No matter which path you choose, as you work your way through the chapter, remember the most important computer skill is how to teach yourself a computer skill. Therefore, this chapter is designed to help you teach yourself how to author a website.

LEARNING PATHS

GUIDED LEARNING	EXPLORE AND DISCOVER	JUMP RIGHT IN
Read the Chapter *Watch the Objective Videos*	**On Your Own Projects** *Review Objective videos or use Step-by-Step Solutions*	**Mastery Project** *Use Objective videos & OYO projects for help*
On Your Own Projects *Review Objective videos or use Step-by-Step Solutions*	**Mastery Project** *Use Objective videos & OYO projects for help*	**Explore Resources** *For help as needed*
Mastery Project *Use Objective videos & OYO projects for help*		
Google Project (if applicable) *Watch Google video for help*	**Google Project (if applicable)** *Watch Google video for help*	**Google Project (if applicable)** *Watch Google video for help*
Helping You & Others Projects	**Helping You & Others Projects**	**Helping You & Others Projects**
MyITLab Assessment	**MyITLab Assessment**	**MyITLab Assessment**

Creating a Website from Beginning to End

We begin the chapter by showing just how simple creating a website can be.

WATCH

OBJECTIVE 16.1
VIDEO

Objective 16.1: Create a Web Page Using a Text Editor and Publish the Website

A website is a collection of web pages and related files that a web server can present to a browser. Recall that web pages are documents constructed using HTML . Each website has one page called the home page or default page. This page is presented to the browser if no particular page is requested.

> **HTML**—Text used as commands in a text file to format fonts, colors, graphics, and hyperlinks. A browser is used to interpret the commands and display the document as a web page. HTML stands for Hypertext Markup Language.

The four steps to create a website are

Step 1. Create the website pages. Each page is stored in its own file. You can use a **text editor** to manually create the pages or use **web authoring software** that automatically does a lot of the work for you.

Step 2. Test the website by displaying it in your browser.

Step 3. Publish the website by uploading the files to the web server.

Step 4. Test the website using the URL to the site.

> **text editor**—An application such as Notepad or WordPad used to create and edit text files. Text in a text file contains no formatting and can be read by all word processing programs and many other programs.
>
> **web authoring software**—An application used to create web pages that automatically generates the HTML text in the document.

Tip As you build a website, be sure to put all the files that you use into one folder on your computer. Later, you can copy the contents of this folder to the computer hosting the website.

Create a Web Page Using Notepad

In this chapter, we build a website about a family vacation. Our first step is to create a simple home page. Later in the chapter, we enhance this page and add a second web page to our website. We use the Notepad text editor that comes with Windows to create the pages so that you can learn how to write the HTML text without software doing it for you.

ON YOUR OWN 16.1

Create a Web Page

WATCH

OBJECTIVE 16.1
VIDEO

Build a Website: Part 1 of 8

To see just how simple creating a web page can be, let's first create a web page that has only a single sentence. At the end of this activity, our very simple web page should look like that in Figure 16-1.

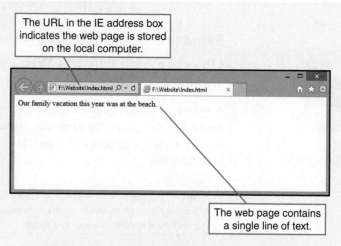

The URL in the IE address box indicates the web page is stored on the local computer.

The web page contains a single line of text.

FIGURE 16-1   A simple web page is created containing a single line of text.

Do the following to create the web page:

Step 1. Create a folder on your USB flash drive, hard drive, or another location given by your instructor. Name the folder **Website**. All the files and subfolders for your website will be kept in this folder.

Step 2. Use **Notepad** to create a file that contains this one sentence. Be sure to press **Enter** at the end of the sentence.

> Our family vacation this year was at the beach.

Step 3. Save the file and name it **Index.html**. Don't allow Notepad to add the .txt file extension to the file. File Explorer (Windows Explorer in Windows 7) should recognize the file as an HTML Document File. You can now close the Notepad window.

> **Index.html**—The default file name and extension of the home page on a website. Most web servers also allow the file name Index.htm or Default.html. Files with an .html or .htm file extension are HTML document files.

Step 4. Test the web page by viewing it in your browser. To do so, use File Explorer (for Windows 7, use Windows Explorer) to locate the file and double-click it. The file opens in Internet Explorer.

> Tip Some web servers require you be consistent with upper- and lowercase letters in file names, whereas others don't care. To avoid a problem when publishing a website, always be consistent with the case used in your file names.

Solutions Appendix   *For help:* See *On Your Own 16.1* Step-by-Step Solution

Publish Your Web Page

Now it's time to publish the web page. Many websites offer storage space and services to host multiple websites, called   shared web hosting . Some offer limited storage space and services for free.

> **shared web hosting**—A single web server makes available multiple websites to publish to the web.

To find a good free web hosting site, do a Google search on **free web hosting**. Be sure to read reviews about a hosting site before you use it. When using a web hosting site, generally you must follow these steps:

Step 1.   Set up an account on the web hosting site, which requires your name, mailing address, and email address. The site also requires you decide on a password to your account.

Step 2.   Respond to an email sent to your email address. This response validates the email address. You can then log on to your web hosting account.

Step 3.   When you first log on, you need to explore the hosting site to find the page that provides the tools you need to set up your website. Look for how to set up your **subdomain name** and how to upload files to your website. If you're having trouble navigating the site, look for a Help feature where you can find tutorials or videos on how to get started.

> **subdomain name**—A domain name that includes the domain name of the web hosting site and is unique for your site. For example, if the hosting site is awardspace.com, your subdomain name might be mywebsite.awardspace.com.

Not Working? *Use a different subdomain name than myvacation .atwebpages.com. That one is taken.*

Step 4.   Set up your subdomain name for your website. Figure 16-2 shows the window when setting up the subdomain name *myvacation.atwebpages.com*. The name myvacation was provided by the user, and the name atwebpages.com was provided by the hosting site. When you set up a subdomain name, the hosting site creates a subfolder on the web server computer by this name.

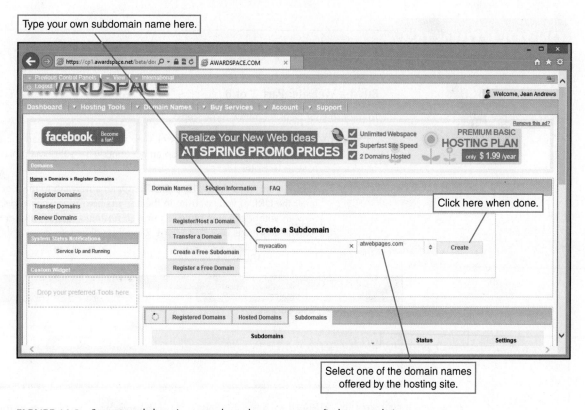

FIGURE 16-2   Set up a subdomain name that others can use to find your website.

Step 5.   Post your web pages and related files to this subfolder. For our hosting site, you click **File Manager**. Then you select your subdomain name and then the folder by that name. Finally, you see the window shown in Figure 16-3. To upload a file, click **Upload** and follow directions on screen. Notice you can also create folders, delete files and folders, and download files using this window. Your hosting site might work differently.

Click to upload a file to the site.

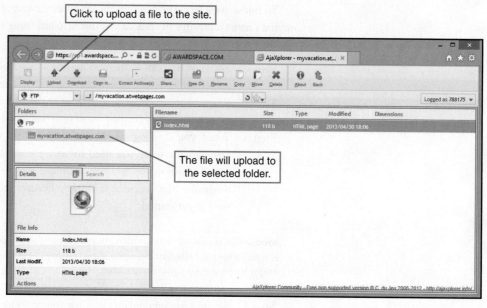

The file will upload to the selected folder.

FIGURE 16-3   For this sample website, upload files to the folder named myvacation.atwebpages.com.

Be sure one of the files you put in the subfolder is named Index.html or Index.htm. The web server sends out this web page when a user enters the URL myvacation.atwebpages.com in his or her Internet Explorer address box.

ON YOUR OWN 16.2

WATCH

OBJECTIVE 16.1
VIDEO

Publish Your Web Page

Build a Website: Part 2 of 8

To publish your website, follow these steps:

Step 1. Use Google.com to search for free web hosting sites and read some reviews about the sites. Select a site and set up an account. What subdomain name did you assign to your website?

Step 2. Publish your Index.html file to the site. Open a new tab in Internet Explorer and enter the URL of your website in the address box. Your website displays. You are now an author of a website! For our web hosting site, the browser window looks like that in Figure 16-4, but your URL will be different.

URL to the website

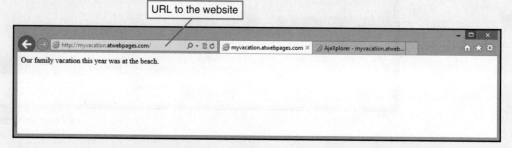

Our family vacation this year was at the beach.

FIGURE 16-4   The web page is published by the web server and displays in the browser window.

Tip   Although some hosting sites encourage you to purchase your own domain name, know this is not necessary when setting up a website on a hosting site. With shared hosting, you can use the domain name of the hosting site.

Solutions
Appendix

For help: See On Your Own 16.2 Step-by-Step Solution

You now know the bare-bones basics of authoring and publishing your own website. Let's build on that knowledge by learning to use HTML tags.

WATCH

OBJECTIVE 16.2
VIDEO

Objective 16.2: Use HTML Tags in a Web Page

Browsers use HTML tags in a web page document to format text and to add graphics and hyperlinks to the page.

> **HTML tag**—Text in a web page document that a browser recognizes as a command rather than text to display. A tag is almost always enclosed in angle brackets < >.

Let's first learn to use one simple HTML tag, the line break tag <br>. A line break causes the text following the <br> tag to print on the next line. We begin by editing the Index.html file and inserting the <br> tag into the text.

ON YOUR OWN 16.3

Add a Line Break Tag to the Page

WATCH

OBJECTIVE 16.2
VIDEO

Build a Website: Part 3 of 8

Do the following to learn how an HTML tag works:

Step 1. Open **Notepad**. Using the Notepad **File** menu, open the **Index.html** file stored on your local computer. Add a new line of text so that your screen looks like that in Figure 16-5. Press **Enter** at the end of the line.

> **Hint** To edit the Index.html file, you need to first open it using Notepad. To open the Index.html file in Notepad, know that you cannot double-click the Index file name because that action opens the file using Internet Explorer. Instead, you have to first open Notepad and then use the File menu in Notepad to locate and open the file.

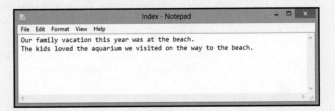

FIGURE 16-5 The Index.html file now has two lines of text.

> **Tip** When you make changes to the Index.html file, don't use Microsoft Word to edit the file because Word automatically inserts many HTML tags into an HTML document. In this chapter, we use Notepad because it's a simple text editor that inserts into the file only the text we type.

Step 2. Save the file and view it in Internet Explorer. Notice all the text appears on one line. The problem is the browser doesn't recognize the hard return that Notepad entered into the file. A browser recognizes only text and HTML tags and not hard returns or other formatting commands.

Step 3. Type the line break tag <br> at the end of the first line. Save the file and view it in Internet Explorer. The text appears on two lines (see Figure 16-6).

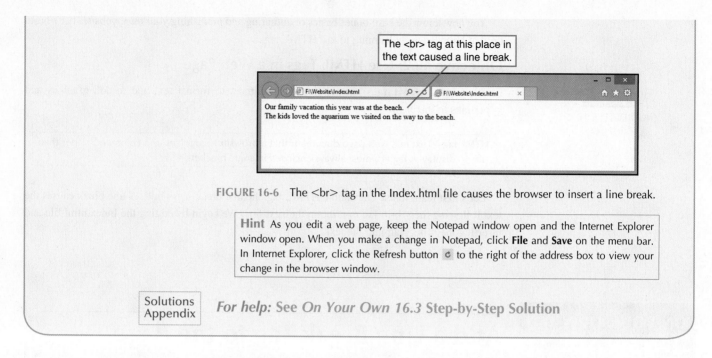

> The <br> tag at this place in the text caused a line break.

FIGURE 16-6   The <br> tag in the Index.html file causes the browser to insert a line break.

> **Hint** As you edit a web page, keep the Notepad window open and the Internet Explorer window open. When you make a change in Notepad, click **File** and **Save** on the menu bar. In Internet Explorer, click the Refresh button ⟳ to the right of the address box to view your change in the browser window.

Solutions Appendix

For help: See *On Your Own 16.3* Step-by-Step Solution

Enhancing a Website Using HTML Structure and Other Tools

Let's take the Index.html file a step further by adding an HTML structure that is common to all HTML documents. Then you'll learn to use other HTML tools to build your website.

Objective 16.3: Use HTML Structure and Formatting Tags

WATCH

OBJECTIVE 16.3 VIDEO

An HTML document is divided into two areas: the **header** area and the **body** area.

> **header**—In an HTML document, the header gives information about the document that's not always displayed by the browser. It contains the title of the web page displayed in the page tab of Internet Explorer. The header can give key words that help a search engine, such as Google, find the page.
>
> **body**—In an HTML document, the body contains the text and tags that are used to build the web page displayed in a browser window.

The <html> and </html> tags are used at the beginning and end of an HTML document. The <head> and </head> tags mark the header area. The <body> and </body> tags mark the body area. Figure 16-7 shows the Index.html file open in Notepad with these tags added.

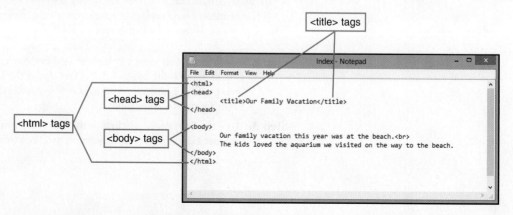

FIGURE 16-7   The Index.html file with <html>, <head>, <title>, and <body> tags added.

Tip When HTML tags are used in pairs, the second tag always includes a slash /. For example, consider the <title> and </title> tags.

The <title> tag places a title for the web page in the Internet Explorer tab for the page (see Figure 16-8).

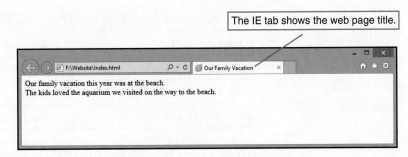

The IE tab shows the web page title.

FIGURE 16-8   The <title> tag puts a title on the IE tab displaying the page.

Tip HTML tags are not case sensitive, which means it doesn't matter whether you use upper- or lowercase letters when typing a tag.

When writing HTML, be sure to use hard returns, indentations, and double spacing to help people read the tags. But know that the browser ignores this formatting when displaying the web page. Table 16-1 lists some common HTML tags. We use several of them in this chapter.

TABLE 16-1   Some Common HTML Tags

Tag	Description
<html> </html>	Marks the beginning and end of an HTML document.
<head> </head>	Marks the beginning and end of the header in an HTML document.
<title> </title>	Used in the header to mark the title of the web page. The title appears in the page tab of the browser window.
<meta name="KEYWORDS">	Used in the header after the <title> tag to give words that a search engine finds to include the page in search results. Table 16-2 shows an example.
<body> </body>	Marks the beginning and end of the body in an HTML document.
 	Inserts a line break.
<p> </p>	Marks the beginning and end of a paragraph. A double space is inserted before and after the paragraph.
<h1> </h1> <h2> </h2> <h3> </h3> <h4> </h4> <h5> </h5> <h6> </h6>	Provides six levels of headings or styles. Use headings to format titles on the page.
<b> </b>	Begins and ends boldface.
<i> </i>	Begins and ends italics.
<hr>	Inserts a horizontal line across the entire page.
<img src=filename>	Inserts an image or graphic on the page. Replace filename with the location and name of the file, including the file extension. If no location is given, the web server looks for the file in the same location as the web page.

As you can see from Table 16-1, some HTML tags work in pairs with a beginning and ending tag. When tags work in pairs, the last tag always includes a slash. Table 16-2 shows a few examples of how HTML tags look when they are used.

TABLE 16-2   Some Examples of How HTML Tags Are Used

Example of Tag	Results or Description of Results
<h1>This Is My Title</h1>	The text between the tags is formatted as a heading.
This is a great day!	Results: This is a **great** day!
This is a <i>great</i> day!	Results: This is a *great* day!
<meta name="KEYWORDS" contents="beach aquarium vacation">	The three words increase the likelihood the site will be included in search results when any of these words is used in a search.
<img src=MyPhoto.png>	The photo displays on the web page in place of the <img> tag.

Let's continue to build the Index.html web page by adding the HTML structure, some more text, and tags for formatting.

ON YOUR OWN 16.4

Use HTML Structure and Formatting Tags

WATCH

OBJECTIVE 16.3
VIDEO

Build a Website: Part 4 of 8

When this activity is completed, the Index.html web page should look like Figure 16-9 when displayed by the browser before the page is published. The browser also displays the HTML tags used to generate the page.

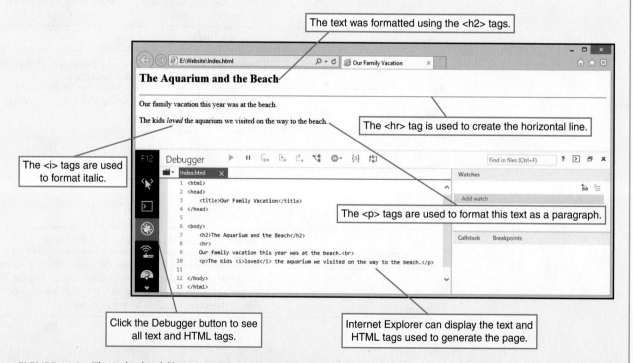

FIGURE 16-9   The Index.html file uses HTML structure and tags to format the text.

Do the following to add text and HTML tags to the file:

Step 1. Use Notepad to open the **Index.html** file. Add the <**html**>, <**head**>, and <**body**> tags to define the structure of the HTML document. Include in the header the title for the web page. Refer back to Figure 16-7.

Step 2. Save the file and display it using Internet Explorer. What changes do you see in the browser window after you add the <title> tags?

Step 3. Add the additional tags and text to complete the web page as shown in Figure 16-9. You'll use the <h2>, <hr>, <p>, and <i> tags on the page to add the page heading and horizontal line and to format the text. Save and view the page using Internet Explorer.

> **Not Working?** If Internet Explorer doesn't display the page correctly, check the file displayed in the Notepad window and look for errors using the tags. Make sure the pairs of tags are used as shown in Table 16-1. Are you missing an ending tag, or is the ending tag in the wrong place?

> **Hint** This book assumes you are using Windows 8.1 and Internet Explorer version 11. If you are using an earlier version of IE, click **Script** in the developer pane to see all text and HTML tags.

Step 4. Internet Explorer allows you to view the source code for a web page it displays. To see the web page as text and HTML tags, click the Tools button ⚙ in the upper-right corner of the Internet Explorer window and click **F12 Developer Tools**. (Alternatively, you can press **F12**.) The text and HTML tags appear in the developer pane at the bottom of the IE window. Click the Debugger button on the left to see all the text and tags (see Figure 16-9). Notice how Internet Explorer color-codes the tags.

Solutions
Appendix

For help: See *On Your Own 16.4* Step-by-Step Solution

Most websites use clip art, background patterns, drawings, and photos. Each of these graphic elements is stored in a graphics file, and these files must be stored on the web server. When a browser receives a web page, it scans the page for references to other files and then requests these files from the web server.

WATCH

**CHAPTER 16
DIVING DEEPER
VIDEO**

Pay close attention to the size of files used on your websites. Large files take a long time to download and can make a web page slow to load in a browser window. The most popular types of graphics files used on websites are PNG files and **GIF files** . Both types are compressed to reduce the file size.

> **GIF file**—A file type typically used for clip art or animated clip art and sometimes for photos. Photos stored in GIF files might not retain the most accurate color.

ON YOUR OWN 16.5

Add a Photo to the Web Page

WATCH

**OBJECTIVE 16.3
VIDEO**

Build a Website: Part 5 of 8

Add a photo to the Index.html page. When this activity is completed, the web page should look like Figure 16-10 when displayed by the browser.

>

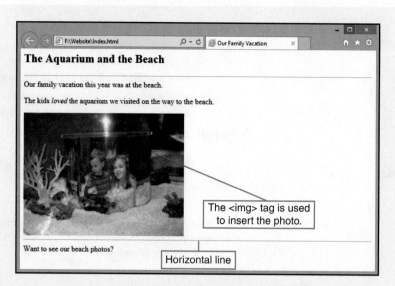

FIGURE 16-10   A photo is added to a web page using the <img> tag.

Do the following to add the photo, a second horizontal line, and more text:

Step 1. Use File Explorer (or Windows Explorer in Windows 7) to copy the **Aquarium.png** file from the sample_files folder on the www.pearsonhigher.com/jump website or in MyITLab to the **Website** folder on your local computer. Recall you downloaded the sample_files folder to your USB flash drive in Chapter 2.

Step 2. Use Notepad to edit the Index.html file. Insert the <img> tag that points to the **Aquarium.png** file. Position the <img> tag so the image is located as shown in Figure 16-10.

Step 3. Below the photo, insert a horizontal line and the additional text, as shown in the figure.

Step 4. Save the Index.html file and display it in your browser. Verify you can see the page and photo correctly and correct any errors you see.

Solutions Appendix   *For help:* See *On Your Own 16.5* Step-by-Step Solution

WATCH

OBJECTIVE 16.4 VIDEO

Objective 16.4: Use Subfolders to Organize Files on a Website

A website might have many web pages and related files. It's a good idea to organize all these files in subfolders. For a small website, you might consider putting all the images in a subfolder of the main website folder.

When an image is in a subfolder of the website folder, you must specify that subfolder in the <img> tag so the browser or web server can find the file. The browser and server assume the subfolder is in the main website folder. Therefore, you do not need to give the entire path to a file.

ON YOUR OWN 16.6

Use a Subfolder to Organize Files on Your Website

WATCH

OBJECTIVE 16.4
VIDEO

Build a Website: Part 6 of 8

Do the following to put the Aquarium.png file in a subfolder on your local computer. Later in the chapter, you'll add the same folder to your web hosting site.

Step 1. Use File Explorer (Windows Explorer in Windows 7) to create a subfolder on your local storage device. Put the folder under the Website folder and name it **Images**. Move (not copy) the Aquarium.png file to this subfolder. Verify the file is no longer in the Website folder and is in the Website/Images folder.

Step 2. Use Notepad to edit the Index.html file. Include the location in the <img> tag:

> **<img src=Images/Aquarium.png>**

Step 3. Save the Index.html file and view it in Internet Explorer. Correct any errors you see.

Solutions
Appendix

For help: See *On Your Own 16.6* Step-by-Step Solution

WATCH

OBJECTIVE 16.5
VIDEO

Objective 16.5: Use Hyperlinks to Connect to Other Pages and Websites

Next let's put some links on your web page. A hyperlink (or link) can be used to link your web page to other pages on your website or to pages on other websites. A hyperlink can also be used to link to a different location on the same web page. An anchor tag is used to create a hyperlink. The tag always begins with <a> and ends with </a>. The tag has many variations, the most common of which are listed in Table 16-3.

TABLE 16-3   Common HTML Anchor Tags

Tag	Description
<a href=*filename*> </a>	An anchor tag that inserts a hyperlink to another page on the same website. Replace *filename* with the location and name of the HTML file. If no location is given, the web server looks for the file in the same location as the web page. The text between the beginning and ending tags becomes the hyperlink and is colored blue and underlined.
<a href=*link*> </a>	An anchor tag that inserts a hyperlink to another web page. Replace *link* with the URL to the other web page. Begin the URL with http://.
<a href=#*section-name*> </a>	An anchor tag that inserts a hyperlink to another location in the same document. Replace *section-name* with the name that has been assigned to the other location.
<a name=*section-name*> </a>	An anchor tag that assigns a section name to a location in a document.

Here's one example of using anchor tags, which are colored in red:

> **To read about my family history, <a href=Family.html>click here</a>.**

In this example, the text **click here** becomes a link to the web page Family.html. When displayed by the browser, this text is blue and underlined to indicate it's a hyperlink. Because no location for the Family.html file is given, the browser and web server assume it is in the same folder as the current web page.

ON YOUR OWN 16.7

Add a Link to a Second Web Page on Your Site

WATCH

▶

OBJECTIVE 16.5
VIDEO

Build a Website: Part 7 of 8

In this activity, you add a second web page to your site and link the first page to it. The second web page is shown in Figure 16-11 as displayed by Internet Explorer. When the user clicks "beach photos" on the Index.html page, the second page appears.

The <h2> tags are used to format this text.

Use two <br> tags at the end of this line.

Zack.png

Shark.png

Use <hr> tags to create these lines.

FIGURE 16-11   The second web page contains two photos.

Do the following to create the second web page:

Step 1. Copy two photos, **Zack.png** and **Shark.png**, from the sample_files folder on the www.pearsonhighered.com/jump website or in MyITlab to the **Website/Images** folder you created earlier on your local computer. (Recall you downloaded the sample_files folder to your USB flash drive in Chapter 2.)

Step 2. Use Notepad to create a file named **Beach.html**. Save the file in the **Website** folder on your local computer.

Step 3. Enter the HTML tags and text to build the page, as shown in Figure 16-11.

Step 4. Save the Beach.html file and view it in Internet Explorer. Correct any errors you see.

Hint   To save time, you can copy and paste the HTML tags and text from one web page to a new page and then edit the new page.

The first anchor tag listed in Table 16-3 is used to link one page to another page on the same site. Do the following to add a hyperlink to the Index.html page:

Step 5. Use Notepad to edit the **Index.html** file. Create an anchor tag using the existing text **beach photos** for the link. Insert the beginning anchor tag before this text and the ending anchor tag after the text.

Step 6. Save the Index.html file and view it in Internet Explorer. When you click the link on the page, the second web page displays. Correct any errors you see.

Solutions Appendix   *For help:* See *On Your Own 16.7* Step-by-Step Solution

---

ON YOUR OWN 16.8

Add a Link to Another Website and Publish Your Website

WATCH

OBJECTIVE 16.5 VIDEO

Build a Website: Part 8 of 8

In this activity, you make the aquarium photo on your website home page a hyperlink to the Ripley's Aquarium website. When you hover over a photo that is a hyperlink, a hand icon appears, and the URL to the link displays (see Figure 16-12).

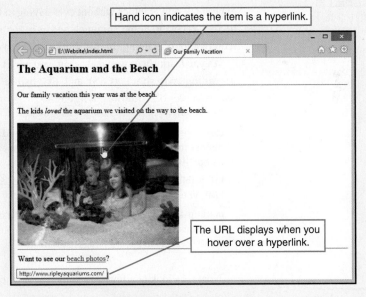

FIGURE 16-12   The photo is a hyperlink to another website.

A link to another website uses the second anchor tag listed in Table 16-3. Do the following:

Step 1. Use Notepad to edit the Index.html file. Surround the <img> tag in the document with the beginning and ending anchor tags. The anchor tag points to the URL **http://www.ripleyaquariums.com**.

Step 2. Save the Index.html file and view it in Internet Explorer. When you click the link on the page, the Ripley's Aquarium site displays. Correct any errors you see.

Your website is finished, and it's time to publish it. Follow these steps:

Step 3. If you're not already logged on to your web hosting site, open a new tab in Internet Explorer and log on to the site.

Step 4. Create a subfolder named **Images** under the subdomain folder. For the web hosting site shown earlier in Figure 16-3, you would click the **New Dir** button at the top of the page to create a folder. Your web hosting site might work differently.

Step 5. Upload the **Index.html** and **Beach.html** files to the subdomain folder. Upload the **Aquarium.png**, **Zack.png**, and **Shark.png** files to the **Images** subfolder.

Step 6. Open a new tab in Internet Explorer and enter the URL of your website. Your home page appears. Click the link to view the second page. On the second page, click the link to the Ripley Aquarium website. If errors appear, fix the problem.

Solutions Appendix

For help: See *On Your Own 16.8* Step-by-Step Solution

Surveying Web Authoring Software

By now, you must be thinking that building a website is a time-consuming and tedious task. If you had to type every HTML tag in a text editor, it certainly would be. Fortunately, web authoring tools are available that generate the HTML tags for you.

WATCH

OBJECTIVE 16.6 VIDEO

Objective 16.6: Explore and Use Web Authoring Software

A web authoring application, also called an HTML editor, allows you to enter and format text, hyperlinks, and graphics without ever having to type one HTML tag. Web authoring programs can be free or costly. Some are quick and easy to use, and others are complex professional tools that require a lot of training. In this section, we survey a few well-known programs.

As you learn about web authoring, you are likely to encounter two languages other than HTML: **cascading style sheets (CSS)** and **Extensible Markup Language (XML)** . XML and HTML are two examples of a **markup language** .

> **cascading style sheets (CSS)**—A language used to create a style sheet, which is a document that defines the styles used when formatting web pages. The styles help give consistency to formatted text on the website.
>
> **Extensible Markup Language (XML)**—A language used to write a new markup language. Using XML, you can create your own HTML tags.
>
> **markup language**—A language that inserts commands in a file that also contains text. You distinguish the commands from the text by enclosing them in special characters. HTML uses angle brackets to separate tags from text.

Now let's look at a few web authoring applications.

Easy and Complex Web Authoring Applications

Web authoring applications range from the simple to the complex. An application might step you through building a website with lots of help designed for beginners, or it might assume you already know HTML and how to build complex sites. When selecting a web authoring application, be sure to read reviews about the application to decide whether it's right for you.

Two web authoring applications that work for beginners are

> **WebEasy Professional** by Avanquest Software (www.avanquest.com). The application is easy to learn and use. The website includes articles on how to get started as well as how to build comprehensive websites.

> **CoffeeCup Free HTML Editor** by CoffeeCup Software (www.coffeecup.com). The free software is a good HTML text editor that works in coding mode to help you write HTML tags. You can purchase the full version, which works in **WYSIWYG** mode. Using this WYSIWYG editor, you can visually build the website, and the software generates the tags for you. CoffeeCup also offers Visual Site Designer, which makes it easy to use themes and graphics on a site.

> **WYSIWYG**—Stands for "What You See Is What You Get" and is pronounced "Whiz-E-Wig." A WYSIWYG program allows you to visually build a web page or other document by placing text, graphics, and other objects on the program's window. The program generates the underlying code for you.

Tip To find out more about the best web authoring applications, use Google to search on **top 10 web authoring software**. Click links to read reviews about the software.

Microsoft Word Generates HTML Tags

Microsoft Word can be used as a web authoring application to build simple websites. Using Word, you can save a document as a web page. When you do that, Word creates the HTML tags in the document and assigns to the file the .htm file extension. It also creates a subfolder and puts in the folder any graphics files needed to build the web page. Also, Word can be used to insert hyperlinks into a normal Word document.

ON YOUR OWN 16.9

Use Word to Create a Web Page

WATCH

OBJECTIVE 16.6 VIDEO

In this activity, you create a Word document named Default.docx that includes the Aquarium.png photo (see Figure 16-13). Then you insert a hyperlink in the document to the Beach.html page, as shown in Figure 16-13. Finally, you convert the document to a web page.

> **Hint** To insert a horizontal line in a Word document, type the underscore (_) three times and press **Enter**.

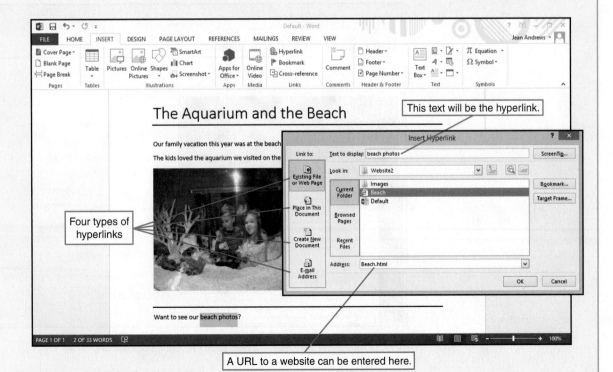

FIGURE 16-13   You can insert four types of hyperlinks into a Word document.

Let's get started:

Step 1. Create a folder named **Website2** where you will store the files you create in this activity. Copy (don't move) the **Beach.html** file to this folder. Also, copy (don't move) the **Images** folder you created earlier to the Website2 folder. Recall the Images folder contains three images.

Step 2. Use Word to create the document shown in Figure 16-13 that contains text and the **Aquarium.png** photo. Store the document in the **Website2** folder, naming the document **Default**. Word automatically assigns a .docx file extension to the document file.

Step 3. Insert a hyperlink in the document to the **Beach.html** web page. First select the text or graphic that will be the hyperlink. In Figure 16-13, that text is *beach photos*. Next use the **Hyperlink** command on the INSERT ribbon to create the hyperlink. The Insert Hyperlink dialog box opens. Notice in the figure the four options that the link can point to:

- An existing file or web page (use the dialog box to locate the file or enter a URL in the Address box)
- A place in this document
- A new document not yet created
- An email address

Step 4. Point to the **Beach.html** file in the Website2 folder. Click **OK** to create the hyperlink.

Step 5. Test the hyperlink. To use a hyperlink in a Word document, press **Ctrl** and click the link. If the link is to a web page stored locally or a URL on the web, the browser opens to display the requested web page.

Step 6. Save the Word document and then save it again as a web page. When you save as a web page, the Default.htm file is created along with the subfolder containing the one image needed to build the page.

Step 7. Close Word. Display the Default web page in Internet Explorer along with the HTML tags created by Word (see Figure 16-14). Word put a lot of tags in the file! You can search through these tags and find the tags that you used in this chapter to create your own version of this web page.

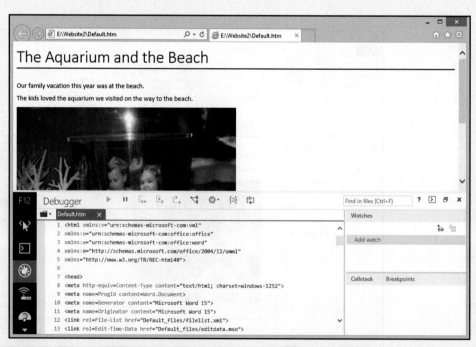

FIGURE 16-14   Word created a web page that contains extensive HTML tags.

Solutions Appendix

For help: See On Your Own 16.9 Step-by-Step Solution

Summary

Creating a Website from Beginning to End

> A website is a collection of web pages and related files. The pages are built using HTML tags. A web server makes the pages available to the web. You can use a text editor to create a web page, but web authoring software is more automatic and faster after you learn to use it.

> The four steps to create a website are to create the web pages, test the pages in your browser, publish the pages to a web server, and test the website using its URL.

> Notepad can be used to create a simple web page because it doesn't automatically add HTML tags to the page. Microsoft Word, on the other hand, automatically embeds many tags in a web page.

> The home page on a website is named Index.html, Index.htm, or Default.html. File names are case sensitive for some web servers, whereas other servers don't pay attention to case. A file with an .html or .htm file extension is an HTML document.

> A good way to learn to build a website is to use a shared web hosting site. Many of these sites offer limited free services, and you can use a subdomain name for your website.

> HTML tags can be used to format text on the page. Most HTML tags are enclosed in angle brackets to distinguish them from text in the document.

Enhancing a Website Using HTML Structure and Other Tools

> Every HTML document has two sections: the header and body. HTML tags are used to mark these sections.

> Photos and other graphics are included on a website by posting the graphics files to the site. Keep file sizes small so the page is not slow to download. Common file types used for websites are PNG and GIF files. These file types are compressed to reduce size.

> Organize your files on a website in subfolders.

> Heading tags such as <h1> and <h2> are used to format text as headings on the page.

> The <img> tag is used to embed an image in a web page. The <a> anchor tags are used to create hyperlinks on the page.

Surveying Web Authoring Software

> HTML is a markup language, meaning the HTML tags are included in the same file with text. Two other programming languages used to build websites are CSS (cascading style sheets) and XML (Extensible Markup Language). CSS is used to define and apply styles to text in web pages, and XML is used to write customized HTML tags.

> Web authoring software can range from the simple, designed for beginners, to the complex, designed for web masters. Before deciding on a product, read reviews about it.

> Word can be used to create web pages from Word documents. It assigns to the web page document the .htm file extension and also creates a folder that contains images used by the web page.

CHAPTER MASTERY PROJECT

Now it's time to find out how well you've mastered the content in this chapter. If you can do all the steps in this mastery project without looking back at the chapter details and can answer all the review questions following this project, you've mastered this chapter. If you can complete the project by finding answers using the web, you've proven that you can teach yourself how to build and publish a website.

> **Hint** All the key terms in the chapter are used in this mastery project or in the review questions. If you encounter a key word you don't know, such as *cascading style sheets*, enter **define:cascading style sheets** in the Internet Explorer search box.

If you find you need a lot of help doing the project and you have not yet read the chapter or done the activities, drop back and start at the beginning of the chapter and then return to this project.

For this project, you are creating a website about a visit to an aquarium. The home page for the site is shown in Figure 16-15.

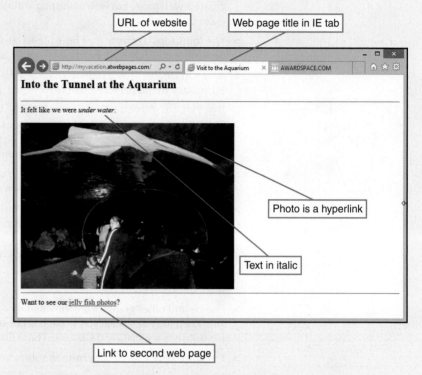

FIGURE 16-15   A website about a visit to an aquarium includes this home page.

Do the following to create the website:

Step 1.   Create a folder named **Website3** on your USB flash drive, hard drive, or other location given by your instructor. Create a subfolder named **Images** in the Website3 folder.

Step 2.   Copy the **Tunnel.png**, **JellyFish1.png**, and **JellyFish2.png** files from the sample_files folder on the www.pearsonhigher.com/jump website or in MyITLab to the Website3\Images folder on your local computer. Recall you downloaded the sample_files folder to your USB flash drive in Chapter 2.

Step 3.   Open the text editor Notepad. Use it to create the HTML file named Index.html. Save the file to the Website3 folder on your local storage device.

Step 4.   Enter the HTML tags and text used to create the web page shown in Figure 16-15. The page includes the following HTML tags:

  a. The <html>, <head>, and <body> tags are used to build the HTML structure for the document, including the header and body areas.

  b. The title to the web page that appears on the Internet Explorer page tab is **Visit to the Aquarium** and uses the <title> tag.

  c. The <h2>, <hr>, <i>, and <p> tags are used to format the text on the page.

  d. The <img> tag is used to put the photo on the page. The photo file is **Tunnel.png** stored in the Website3\Images folder.

  e. The <a href> anchor tag is used to make the photo a hyperlink to the Ripley's Aquarium website at **http://www.ripleyaquariums.com**.

  f. The <a href> anchor tag is used to make the text "jelly fish photos" a hyperlink to the second page on the website, named **JellyFish.html**.

Step 5.   Save the **Index.html** file to the Website3 folder and view the file in Internet Explorer. Correct any errors you see. (The link to the second page will not work until you create the second page.)

The second web page is shown in Figure 16-16. To create this second web page, do the following:

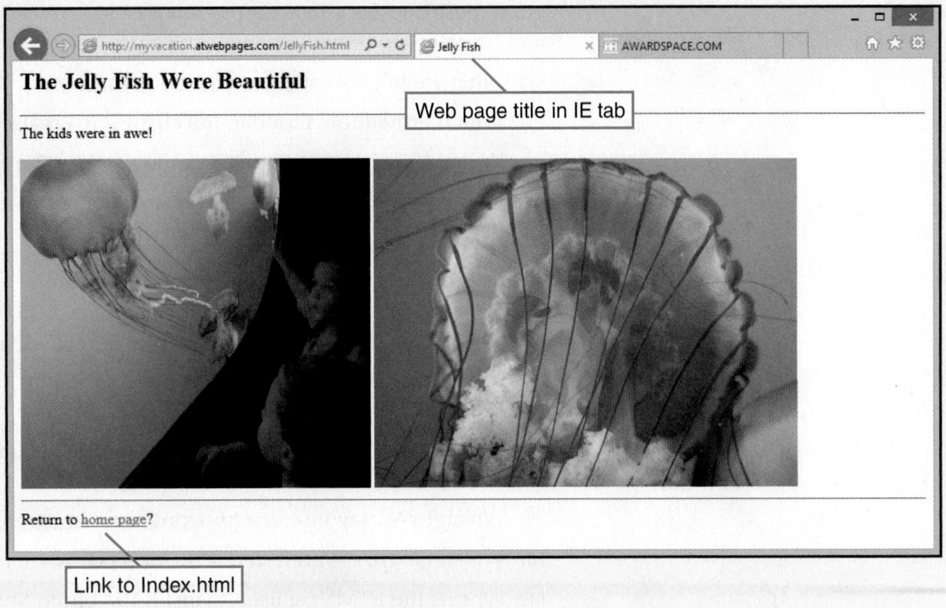

FIGURE 16-16   The second web page has two photos and a link back to the home page.

Step 6. Using Notepad, create the HTML file named **JellyFish.html** and save it to the **Website3** folder you created earlier.

Step 7. Enter the HTML tags and text used to create the web page shown in Figure 16-16. The page includes the following HTML tags:

    a. The <html>, <head>, and <body> tags are used to build the HTML structure for the document.

    b. The title to the web page that uses the <title> tag is **Jelly Fish**.

    c. The <h2>, <hr>, and <br> tags are used to format the text on the page.

    d. Two <img> tags are used to put the photos on the page. The photo files are **JellyFish1.png** and **JellyFish2.png** stored in the Website3\Images folder.

    e. An <a href> tag is used to create a link back to the Index.html page when the user clicks "home page."

Step 8. Save the JellyFish.html file and view it in Internet Explorer. Test the link on the Index.html page to the Jelly Fish page.

If you have already set up an account on a web hosting site, you can skip these next two steps. Do the following to set up a shared web hosting account:

Step 9. Do a Google search on **free web hosting**. Read some reviews about the sites and select one.

Step 10. Go to the web hosting site and set up your user account on the site. After you log on to the site, set up your subdomain name for your website. What is the URL to your website?

Do the following to publish the web pages to your web hosting site:

Step 11. If you have not already done so, create a subfolder named **Images** on the web hosting site.

Step 12. Copy the Index.html and JellyFish.html files to the subdomain folder. Copy the three PNG files to the Images subfolder under the subdomain folder.

Step 13. Open a new tab in Internet Explorer and enter the URL of your subdomain name. Check the links on both web pages to make sure they work. Correct any errors you see and email the URL to your instructor.

Review Questions

Answer these questions to assess your skills and knowledge of the content covered in the chapter. Your instructor can provide you with the correct answers when you are ready to check your work.

1. What are the four steps to create a website?

2. Which text editor is used in the chapter to create web pages?

3. What is the most common filename used for the home page on a website?

4. You can purchase your own domain name, or a web hosting site can provide a domain name for you. What is the domain name called that is provided by a web hosting site?

5. What is the HTML tag to insert a line break in a page?

6. Which two HTML tags are used to mark the beginning and end of the header section in an HTML document?

7. Which two HTML tags are used to mark the title that appears in the page tab of Internet Explorer?

8. Which two HTML tags are used to mark the beginning and end of italics applied to text on the page?

9. Which HTML tag inserts a horizontal line in a web page?

10. Which file type is preferred (PNG or JPEG) when posting a photo to a website? Why?

11. What is the HTML tag used to insert the photo MyPhoto.png on a web page? The photo is in the same folder as the web page.

12. What is the HTML tag used to insert a link to the www.facebook.com website on a web page?

13. When viewing a web page in Internet Explorer, what key do you press to use the developer tools to see the underlying HTML tags?

14. Which programming language is used to create styles in a style sheet that is used to format text on a website?

15. What are the two modes that web authoring software can work in?

16. Why would you use subfolders on the web hosting site when building a website?

17. Which file type would you use on your website so that the file size is minimal: JPG or GIF? Why are small file sizes important for a website?

18. Which language is a markup language: CSS or XML? Which language is used to create consistent text formatting on a website?

19. Which authoring mode, WYSIWYG or coding mode, does not require you to enter HTML tags in an HTML document?

20. When using Microsoft Word to build a web page, how can you view the HTML tags that Word creates?

Becoming an Independent Learner

The most important skill learned in this book is how to teach yourself a computer skill. For each chapter, you have been rating yourself on how well you are doing with this skill. What is your overall rating for the entire book?

> Level A: I was able to successfully complete the Chapter Mastery Projects with the help of only a few of the On Your Own activities in the chapter. **I have proven that I can teach myself a computer skill without directions given by others.**

> Level B: I completed all the On Your Own activities and the Chapter Mastery Projects without referring to any of the solutions in the Step-by-Step Solutions Appendix. **I have proven that I can teach myself a computer skill without directions given by others.**

> Level C: I completed all the On Your Own activities and the Chapter Mastery Projects by using just a few of the solutions in the Step-by-Step Solutions Appendix. **I need some help, but for the most part I can teach myself computer skills.**

> Level D: I completed all the On Your Own activities and the Chapter Mastery Projects by using many of the solutions in the Step-by-Step Solutions Appendix. **I still need some help when learning a new computer skill.**

> Level E: I completed all the On Your Own activities and the Chapter Mastery Projects and had to use all of the solutions in the Step-by-Step Solutions Appendix. **I learn new computer skills by following directions given by others.**

Projects to Help You

Now that you've mastered the material in this chapter, you're ready to tackle the three projects focused on your career, personal, or academic goals. Depending on your own interests, you might choose to complete any or all of these projects to help you achieve your goals.

Career Project I work for a small company, and my boss asked me to build a company website. I need to know what software to use and how to get started.

Project 1: Using Web Authoring Software and an FTP Client

Now that you know a little about HTML tags and how to publish a website, you are ready to get started using more advanced software. Do the following:

Step 1. Go to www.coffeecup.com and download the free version of the web authoring software called THE FREE HTML EDITOR by CoffeeCup Software. Install the program on your computer and use it to create one of the web pages in this chapter.

Step 2. Take a snip of the CoffeeCup window and insert the snip in a Word document.

Websites might require hundreds of files. In these situations, better tools are needed to upload the files rather than the simple ones offered by a free web hosting service. FTP is a file transfer protocol and software that can be used to upload files to a website. Do the following:

Step 3. CuteFTP by GlobalSCAPE is reliable and easy-to-use file transfer software. Go to www.globalscape.com/cuteftp and read about the software. Download the free version of the software and install it on your computer. Use it to upload files from your local computer to your web hosting site.

Step 4. Take a snip of your screen showing the CuteFTP window and insert the snip in your Word document. Email the document with the two snips to your instructor.

Personal Project I want to build my own personal website with links to other sites. I want to include a history of my family and family photos. What do I need to know to get started?

Project 2: Building Your Personal Website

Now that you know how to build a simple website, create your own personal site. Collect a few of your favorite photos and include them on the site. If you don't have photos, use any you find in the sample_files folder. Include in your website the following:

> At least two web pages. The first page links to the second.

> A hyperlink to another website of your choosing.

> One or more photos.

> Formatted text that uses the heading tags or paragraph tags listed in Table 16-1.

Publish the website and email your instructor the URL to the site.

Academic Project My club built a website and has assigned me the job of testing the site before it goes live. I displayed it in my browser, and it looks fine. Is there anything more I need to do?

Project 3: Testing a Website

Expect your website will be viewed by people using a variety of browsers, screen resolutions, and devices. Web developers test their sites for these situations:

> Different browsers, including Internet Explorer, Mozilla Firefox, Google Chrome, and Apple Safari and different versions of these browsers

> Different screen resolutions, such as 1,024 × 768 or 1,280 × 800

> Different devices, such as a personal computer, smartphone, or tablet

Do the following to test a website you've created for this chapter:

Step 1. Set your screen resolution to one of the lowest values your monitor offers and use your browser to display the pages on your website. Also test at a higher resolution and a midrange resolution. Which two screen resolutions did you use?

Step 2. If you have access to a different browser other than Internet Explorer, test your website using this browser. Which browser did you use?

Step 3. If you have access to a smart phone or tablet, use this device to open your browser and view your website. Which device(s) did you use?

Step 4. Based on your tests, what changes do you need to make in the website so it works well in many situations? Email your instructor the answers to the questions in steps 1, 2, and 3 and any changes you see needed in the website you tested.

Project to Help Others

One of the best ways to learn is to teach someone else. And, in teaching someone else, you are making a contribution in that person's life. As part of each chapter's work, you are encouraged to teach someone else a skill you have learned. In this chapter, help someone learn how to build a website.

Working with your apprentice, do the following:

Step 1. Show your apprentice one of the websites you built in this chapter. Explain how the web pages were created using HTML tags. Explain the purpose of each tag.

Step 2. Help your apprentice build his own website using photos and links. Use Notepad to build the web pages. If your apprentice wants to publish his website, help him set up an account on a web hosting site and publish the website.

Step 3. Use Word to create a file that contains your answers to the following questions about the tutoring session. Name the file **Chapter_16_Tutoring** and send the file to your instructor. If you're using MyITLab, you can post the file in a Dropbox assignment or email the file in MyITLab. On the other hand, your instructor might prefer you post the file to your OneDrive or email the file using your school or personal email. Here are the questions:

1. Who is your apprentice?
2. In step 2, what part of building the website was the most difficult for your apprentice?
3. In step 2, what is the URL to your apprentice's website?
4. How do you think the session went?
5. Describe what you have learned by tutoring others in this course.

Solutions Appendix

CHAPTER 1 STEP-BY-STEP SOLUTIONS
Using Windows 8 to Manage Applications and Data

The solutions in this appendix are for you to use if you get stuck when doing an On Your Own activity in the chapter. To learn how to teach yourself a computer skill, always try the On Your Own activity first before turning to these solutions.

On Your Own 1.1 Step-by-Step Solution How to Start a Windows Session

Follow these steps to turn on your computer and start Windows:

Step 1. If your computer isn't already turned on, press the power button on your computer to turn it on.

Step 2. Windows might provide a sign-on screen like the one shown in Chapter 1 in Figure 1-10. If the user name isn't correct, click the left arrow button to see more accounts. A list of other user accounts set up on this computer appears. Click your user account.

> **Not Working?** If you don't see your user account, press any key. If you still don't see your user account, use both hands to press three keys at the same time: **Ctrl**, **Alt**, and **Delete** (commonly written as **Ctrl+Alt+Delete**). You might need to enter your user account in the box that appears. When you're using a lab computer, ask your instructor for specific directions for signing on.

Step 3. Enter the password and press the **Enter** key. The Start screen appears.

Step 4. When you move the pointer to the upper-right corner of the screen, the charms bar appears. The charms bar also appears when you move the pointer to the lower-right corner of the screen. Each time you press the Windows key, you return to the Start screen or the Windows desktop.

> **Not Working?** This book uses Windows 8 with the Windows 8.1 update installed. If you have another operating system installed, your screens might not look the same as the ones shown in this book, and the steps to use the operating system might be different.

On Your Own 1.2 Step-by-Step Solution How to Manage Apps in the Windows 8 Interface

Follow these steps to use apps in the Windows 8 interface:

Step 1. Go to the Start screen. Click the **Maps** tile. The Maps page appears.

Step 2. Move your pointer to the top of the screen until it changes to a hand. Press and drag the hand down a bit and then all the way to the right side of the screen. The page snaps to the right side.

Step 3. Press the **Windows** key to return to the Start screen. Click the **Weather** tile. The Weather page appears.

Step 4. To change the sizes of the pages, press and drag the bar between the two pages to the left or the right.

Step 5. Press the **Windows** key to return to the Start screen. Click the **Photos** tile. The Pictures library page appears as a square on your screen (see Figure S1-1). Click the left or right side of the square to make the page snap to the left or right side of your screen.

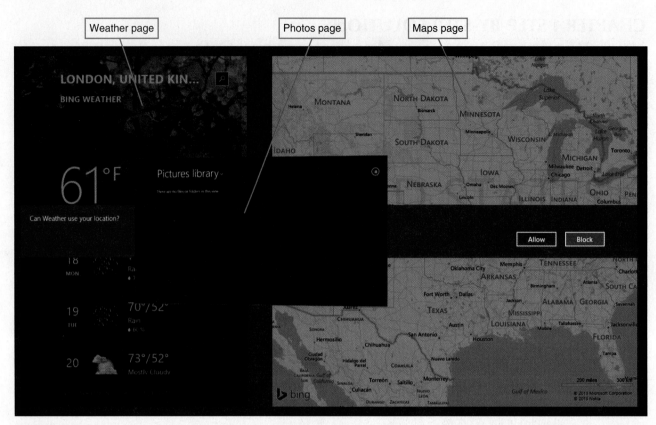

FIGURE S1-1
The last app opened is waiting for you to decide which side of the screen the page will snap to.

Step 6. To switch to the page that isn't visible, move your pointer to the upper-left corner of the screen, move the pointer down the screen, and click the thumbnail of the page that appears.

Step 7. To close an app, move your pointer to the top of the screen until the pointer becomes a hand. Press and drag the hand to the bottom of the screen. The app and its page close. Close all open apps.

On Your Own 1.3 Step-by-Step Solution   How to Start a Program That Uses the Desktop

Follow these steps at your computer to start the Paint program:

Step 1. Go to the **Start screen** and type **paint**. The text appears in the search box of the Search charm, and a list of apps and other content appears on the right.

Step 2. In the list, click **Paint**. The Windows desktop and the Paint window appear.

On Your Own 1.4 Step-by-Step Solution   How to Move a Window

Follow these steps to learn how to manage a window:

Step 1. Open the Paint program if it is not already open.

Step 2. Position your pointer in the title bar at the top of the Paint window. Press and drag the title bar over the screen to move the window.

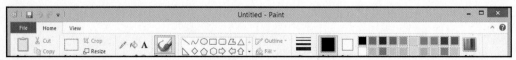

Top of Paint window

Step 3. Press and drag the title bar to the top of your screen until your pointer reaches the top. Then release the left mouse button. This action causes the window to maximize, filling the entire screen. You can also use the maximize button to do the same thing.

Maximize paint window

Step 4. Press and drag the title bar of the Paint window downward from the top of the screen (not too far). The window returns to its previous size. It is now said to be resized.

Step 5. Press and drag the title bar to the right until your pointer touches the right side of the monitor screen. The window snaps to the right side.

Step 6. Press and drag the title bar to the left until your pointer touches the left side of the monitor screen. The window snaps to the left side.

Step 7. Click the **minimize** button in the title bar of the Paint window. The Paint window minimizes. Notice that the Paint icon is still in the taskbar. When you see the Paint icon, you know the application is still open, but the window is not visible.

Minimize paint window

Step 8. Click the **Paint icon** in the taskbar. The Paint window restores.

On Your Own 1.5 Step-by-Step Solution   How to Resize and Close a Window

Follow these steps to resize the Paint window and then close the Paint program:

Step 1. You can make a window any size you like. To do so, move your pointer to one edge of the window. With the double arrows showing, press and drag the edge of the window to resize the window. Practice resizing on all four edges of the Paint window.

Step 2. Press and drag the bottom of the window to shorten the height of the window. When the window height is short enough, a scrollbar appears on the right side of the window.

Step 3. You can resize both the width and the height of a window at the same time by grabbing a corner of a window. Move your pointer to a corner of the Paint window. The pointer changes to double diagonal arrows. With the double diagonal arrows showing, press and drag the corner to resize the window.

Resize double arrow

Step 4. To close the Paint window, click the red **X** 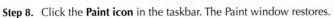 in the upper-right corner of the window. If you have drawn on the window, Paint asks whether you want to save your work. Click **Don't Save**. The Paint window closes.

On Your Own 1.6 Step-by-Step Solution   How to Manage Multiple Windows

Follow these steps to manage two windows:

Step 1. Go to the **Start screen** and open the **Paint** app. The desktop and the Paint window appear.

Step 2. In the taskbar at the bottom of the desktop, click the **File Explorer** Quick Launch icon ▤. File Explorer opens; this program allows you to manage files and folders on your computer. You now have two windows open.

> **Not Working?** If the File Explorer icon isn't showing in the taskbar, to open File Explorer, go to the **Start screen**. Then type **file** and click **File Explorer** in the list of apps. File Explorer appears on the desktop.

Step 3. Press and drag the title bar of the File Explorer window so that the two windows overlap on the monitor screen. Your screen should look similar to that in Figure S1-2.

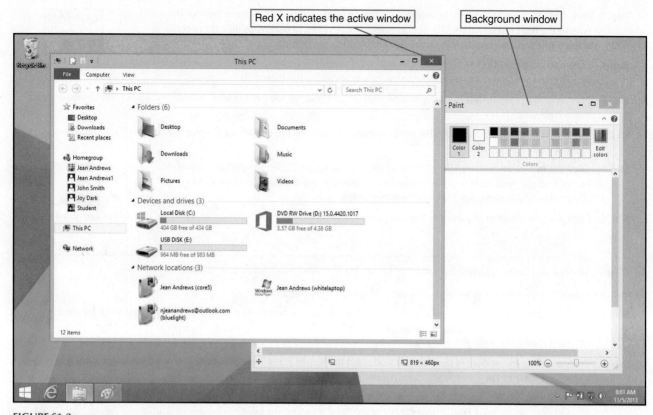

FIGURE S1-2
Two application windows overlap. The File Explorer window is the active window. The active window has a red close button.

Step 4. Click anywhere in the **Paint** window. Notice that the Paint window comes to the foreground. The window in the foreground is called the active window, the window you are currently using. To use another window, you can click on it to make it the active window. You can easily tell which window is the active window because the close button is red ![X] .

> **Not Working?** If Windows isn't using default display settings, the active window might not have the red X. Also, some applications, such as Microsoft Office apps, don't use the red color for the X close button.

Step 5. Another way to make a window the active window is to use the program icon in the taskbar. Click the **File Explorer icon** in the taskbar to make it the active window.

Step 6. Close both windows by clicking the close button on each window.

On Your Own 1.7 Step-by-Step Solution   How to Explore Files, Folders, and Libraries on the Hard Drive

Follow these directions to explore the folders and files on the hard drive:

Step 1. Click the **File Explorer icon** in the taskbar. File Explorer opens (see Figure S1-3). The window is divided into two parts called panes. You use the left pane, called the navigation pane, to navigate through devices and folders. You use the right pane to view the contents of a device, folder, or library. A scrollbar might be provided to scroll through the contents in a pane if the window is too small to show all the contents. The four libraries provided by Windows are Documents, Music, Pictures, and Videos.

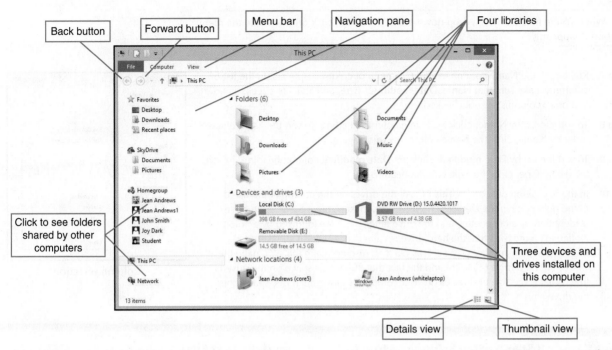

FIGURE S1-3
Using File Explorer, you can manage libraries, folders, and files on your computer and get to other resources on the network.

Step 2. In the navigation pane on the left side of the window, click **Desktop**. The four commands that display in the menu bar are File, Home, Share, and View.

Step 3. In the right pane, double-click **Libraries**. Then double-click **Documents**. The contents of the Documents library appear in the right pane. It is said that you have drilled down to the Documents library. As you drill down into libraries, folders, and subfolders, you might find that you are denied access. Some folders are secured to protect their contents.

Step 4. Click the **back arrow button** ⊖ near the top of the File Explorer window to move back up one level in the folder tree.

Step 5. To drill down to drive C:, first click **This PC** in the navigation pane. In the right pane, double-click drive C: in the Devices and drives group. For example, in Figure S1-3, you would double-click **Local Disk (C:)**. The many files and folders in the root, or top level, of the hard drive display in the right pane.

Step 6. Click the **Details** icon in the lower-right corner of the File Explorer window. The Details view displays (see Figure S1-4). To change the view, you can also click **Details** on the View ribbon, as shown in Figure S1-4.

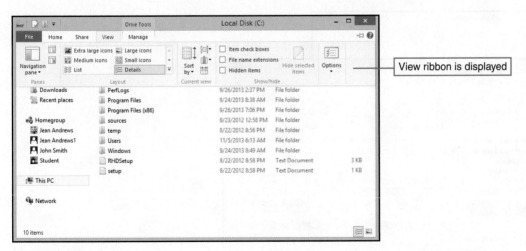

FIGURE S1-4
Folders and files in the root of Local Disk (C:) are displayed using the Details view.

> **Hint** When you're finished with a drop-down menu or ribbon, click off it to make the menu or ribbon disappear.

Step 7. Right-click the **Name** column heading. A menu of columns appears. In the list of columns, make sure that **Name**, **Date modified**, **Type**, and **Size** are checked and that other columns are not checked.

Step 8. To sort the list by Name, click the **Name** column heading. To sort the list in reverse order by Name, click the **Name** column heading again.

Step 9. To sort the list by Date modified, click the **Date modified** column heading. To sort the list by Type, click the **Type** column heading.

Step 10. In the navigation pane, click **This PC**. All the drives on the computer are listed in the right pane in the Devices and drives group (see Figure S1-3). Each drive is identified by a drive letter, and the drive letter is always followed by a colon. Notice in Figure S1-3 that the hard drive is called Local Disk (C:). Your drive C: might be written another way, such as OS (C:). Also notice in the right pane the size of the hard drive (434 GB) and the fact that 398 GB of space on the drive is free. What is the size of drive C: on your computer? How much free space does the drive have?

Column selection

On Your Own 1.8 Step-by-Step Solution   How to Create and Edit Text Files Using Notepad

Follow these directions to create a text file and save it to your USB flash drive:

Step 1. Plug in your USB flash drive in a USB port. If the AutoPlay dialog box appears, ignore it and it will disappear.

Step 2. To open Notepad, go to the Start screen and start typing **notepad**. Click the **Notepad** tile. The Notepad window opens on the Windows desktop.

Step 3. Notice a blinking bar in the white area of your Notepad window, which indicates your insertion point. When you type in the window, you're typing at this insertion point. In the window, type your name and press **Enter**. If you make a mistake as you type, use the Backspace key to correct it.

Step 4. Type the name of this class and press **Enter**.

Step 5. On the menu bar at the top of the window, click **File** and then click **Save As**. The Save As dialog box appears.

Step 6. If necessary, click the white arrow to the left of This PC in the left pane to open the This PC group. Click the USB flash drive. (The drive might be listed as USB, Removable Disk, Lexar Media, or another brand name.) The files and folders in the root of the USB flash drive appear in the right pane. Figure S1-5 shows one USB flash drive, but yours might look different.

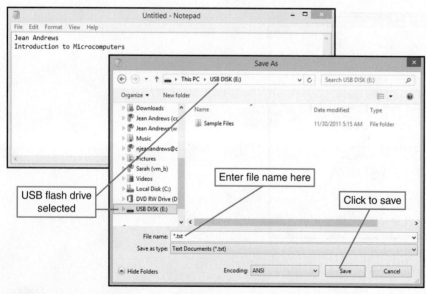

FIGURE S1-5
Select the storage device where you want to save the file.

Step 7. In the File name box, replace the text with **MyText1**, which is the file name. Don't leave the .txt file extension in this box because doing so can cause the file to have two file extensions.

Step 8. Verify that the Save As type box shows **Text Documents (*.txt)**. This selection causes Notepad to automatically add a .txt file extension to the file.

Step 9. Click **Save** to save the file. Notice that *MyText1 – Notepad* is showing in the title bar at the top of the Notepad window.

Step 10. Close the Notepad window.

Step 11. Open File Explorer. In the This PC group in the navigation pane, select your USB flash drive. In the right pane, you should see the MyText1 file.

Follow these steps to open the file you just created, edit it, and save it under a new name:

Step 1. In the This PC group of the navigation pane of File Explorer, select your USB flash drive. In the right pane, you should see the MyText1 file. Double-click the file. The file opens in a Notepad window.

Step 2. Click on the blank line below the class name.

> **Not Working?** If you can't click on this third line, you might not have pressed Enter at the end of the second line. Go to the end of the second line and press **Enter**.

Step 3. On the third line, type today's date and press **Enter**.

Step 4. Click **File** and click **Save As**. The Save As dialog box opens. You should see MyText1 listed in the right pane.

Step 5. Change the File name to **MyText2**. Make sure Text Documents (*.txt) is listed as the Save As type. Click **Save** to save the file.

Step 6. Close the Notepad window.

Step 7. Return to File Explorer. You should see the two files in the right pane.

> **Not Working?** If you don't see the two files in the right pane, make sure the USB flash drive is selected in the navigation pane.

Step 8. To view the properties of the **MyText2** file, right-click the file. In the shortcut menu, click **Properties**. The Properties dialog box displays. The Type of file includes the file extension, which is .txt. Close the dialog box.

On Your Own 1.9 Step-by-Step Solution   How to Manage Folders and Files on a USB Flash Drive

This solution has several parts:

▶ How to create a folder on a USB flash drive

▶ How to delete a folder

▶ How to rename a folder using a shortcut menu

▶ How to copy files from one folder to another

▶ How to move a file from one folder to another

▶ How to rename and delete a file

How to Create a Folder on a USB Flash Drive

Follow these steps to create a folder named Computer Class on your USB flash drive:

Step 1. If necessary, plug your USB flash drive into a USB port. If Windows displays the AutoPlay dialog box, ignore the box.

Step 2. If necessary, open File Explorer.

Step 3. In the This PC group in the navigation pane, select the USB flash drive. The right pane now shows the contents of your USB flash drive. You should see listed the two files, MyText1 and MyText2, that you created in the previous activity.

Step 4. Click **Home** in the menu bar of File Explorer. On the Home ribbon, click **New folder**. A new folder appears on your flash drive. The name of the folder is New folder, and that name is highlighted so that you can change the name. Type **Computer Class** as the name of the new folder and press **Enter**.

Step 5. Double-click **Computer Class**. The right pane shows the folder is empty (see Figure S1-6). Notice the Computer Class folder is listed in the address bar and title bar at the top of File Explorer.

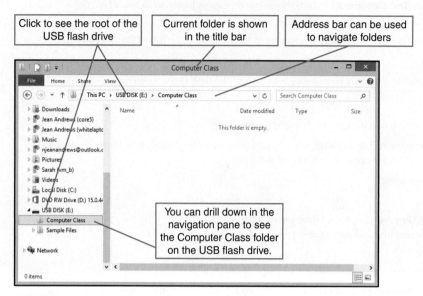

FIGURE S1-6
The Computer Class folder is empty.

How to Delete a Folder

Now let's practice creating and deleting a folder. Follow these steps:

Step 1. Click **Home** and click **New folder** on the Home ribbon. Enter **Data** for the name of the new folder. The Data folder is now a subfolder of the Computer Class folder.

Step 2. If necessary, click the **Data** folder to select it.

Step 3. To delete the folder, press the **Delete** key. The Delete Folder dialog box appears (see Figure S1-7). Click **Yes**. The Data folder is deleted.

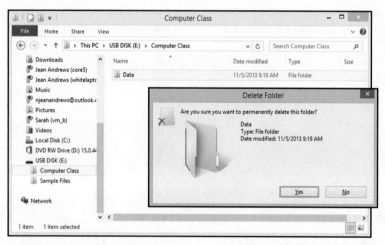

FIGURE S1-7
Click Yes to delete the Data folder.

How to Rename a Folder Using a Shortcut Menu

Follow these steps to create a subfolder and rename it. In this solution, we use shortcut menus to create and rename a folder:

Step 1. In the navigation pane of File Explorer, click your USB drive. The files and folders in the root of the USB flash drive appear in the right pane. The Computer Class folder is included in this list.

Step 2. Right-click anywhere in the white space of the right pane. A shortcut menu appears similar to the left menu in Figure S1-8.

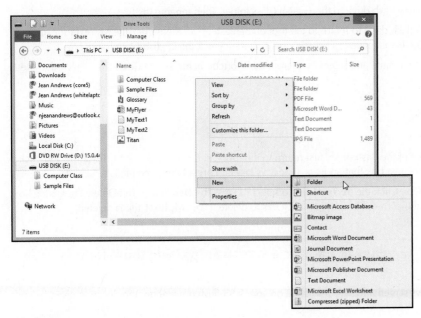

FIGURE S1-8
Create a new folder using the shortcut menu in the right pane.

> **Not Working?** When you right-click an item and the wrong menu appears, try right-clicking again. Most likely, your pointer was not in the correct position.

Step 3. Using your pointer, point to **New**, as shown in the figure. A second menu appears showing all the items that you can create. Click **Folder**. A new folder is created. Name the folder **History Class**.

Step 4. Click anywhere in the white space in the right pane so that the History Class folder is not selected. You now have at least two folders at the top level of your USB flash drive: Computer Class and History Class.

Step 5. To rename the History Class folder, right-click it and select **Rename** from the shortcut menu. Name the folder **English Class**.

How to Copy Files from One Folder to Another

Follow these steps to copy a file from the root of the USB flash drive to the Computer Class folder:

Step 1. Click the USB flash drive in the navigation pane of File Explorer. The files and folders in the root of the drive appear in the right pane. No files or folders are selected.

Step 2. Right-click the **MyText1** file and select **Copy** from the shortcut menu. The file is copied into the Windows Clipboard.

Step 3. Double-click the **Computer Class** folder to see its contents in the right pane. Right-click in the white area of the right pane and select **Paste** from the shortcut menu. The MyText1 file is copied into the Computer Class folder.

A quicker way to copy a file is to use the drag and drop operation. Let's use that method:

Step 1. Click the USB flash drive in the address bar of File Explorer. (Or you can click the USB flash drive in the navigation pane.) The contents of the root of the flash drive appear in the right pane. No folders or files are selected in the right pane.

Step 2. Hold down your **Ctrl** key as you press and drag the **MyText2** file and drop it on the Computer Class folder. You can still see the file in the root of the flash drive.

Step 3. To verify that the folder copied without errors, in the right window, double-click the **Computer Class** folder. The two files are listed in the folder contents.

How to Move a File from One Folder to Another

Follow these steps to move a file from the root of the flash drive to the English Class folder. Then rename the file:

Step 1. In the navigation pane, click the USB flash drive to return to the root of the flash drive. Right-click the **MyText1** file and select **Cut** from the shortcut menu. The file is moved to the Clipboard. Double-click the **English Class** folder.

Step 2. Right-click in the white space of the right pane and select **Paste** from the shortcut menu. The MyText1 file is moved to the English Class folder.

How to Rename and Delete a File

Follow these steps to rename and delete a file:

Step 1. To rename the **MyText2** file in the root of the flash drive, first return to the root. Then right-click the **MyText2** file and click **Rename** from the shortcut menu. In the text box that appears, type **MyClass** and press **Enter**. The file is renamed.

Step 2. Double-click the **Computer Class** folder. Click the **MyText1** file to select it. Press the **Delete** key. The Delete File dialog box appears. Verify that you are deleting the correct file and then click **Yes** to delete it. The MyText1 file is deleted.

On Your Own 1.10 Step-by-Step Solution   How to Capture a Screen Snip Using the Windows Snipping Tool

Follow these steps to take a snip of your Windows screen and save it to a file on your USB flash drive or another location given by your instructor:

Step 1. If necessary, insert your USB flash drive in the USB port. If the AutoPlay dialog box opens, ignore it. Open File Explorer and select your USB flash drive so that the contents of the root appear in the right pane.

Step 2. Go to the Start screen and type **snip**. Then click **Snipping Tool**. The desktop with the Snipping Tool dialog box appears.

Step 3. Click the arrow to the right of New to see a list of types of snips you can capture (see Figure S1-9). Click one.

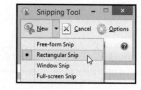

FIGURE S1-9
Select the type of snip.

Step 4. If you selected a free-form snip or rectangular snip, your pointer changes to a crosshair ✛. Press and drag to select the area of your screen you want to capture.

Step 5. If you selected a window snip, click the window on your desktop you want to snip.

Step 6. The Snipping Tool window opens showing your snip. Click **File**, **Save As**. The Save As dialog box opens (see Figure S1-10).

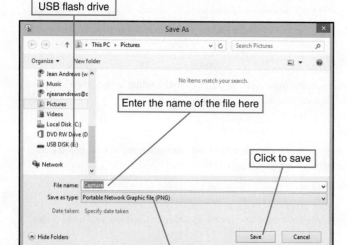

FIGURE S1-10
Tell Windows where to save the file and what to name it.

Step 7. In the left pane, click your USB flash drive.

Step 8. Under *File name*, replace the text with **MySnip1**. Notice that the *Save as type* is PNG. The file will be saved as a PNG file.

Step 9. Click **Save**. The file is saved to your USB flash drive. Close all open windows.

On Your Own 1.11 Step-by-Step Solution   How to End a Windows Session

This solution has three parts:

▶ How to sign off a computer

▶ How to put your computer to sleep

▶ How to shut down a computer

How to Sign Off a Computer

Follow these steps to sign off:

Step 1. Go to the Start screen and click your user name in the upper right corner of the screen. Then click **Sign out** (see Figure S1-11a).

Step 2. To sign back on to Windows, press any key. The sign-on screen appears, and you can sign back on.

(a)   (b)

FIGURE S1-11
Options to end a Windows session: (a) Sign out and (b) Sleep, Hibernate, Shut down, and Restart.

How to Put Your Computer to Sleep

To put a computer to sleep, follow these steps:

Step 1. Move the pointer to the upper-right corner of the screen to display the charms bar. Click the **Settings** charm.

Step 2. In the Settings pane, click **Power**. Then click **Sleep** in the menu that appears (see Figure S1-11b). Windows puts the computer to sleep.

Step 3. To wake up the computer, press any key or move the mouse or touch pad.

How to Shut Down a Computer

To shut down a computer using the Windows desktop, follow these steps:

Step 1. Close any open windows or pages.

Step 2. Go to the Windows desktop. Right-click the **Start** button. Point to **Shut down or sign out**. Click **Shut down** in the submenu that appears. Windows closes, and the computer is powered down.

Step 3. To power the computer back up, press the power button.

CHAPTER 2 STEP-BY-STEP SOLUTIONS
Finding and Using Information on the Web

The solutions in this appendix are for you to use if you get stuck when doing an On Your Own activity in the chapter. To learn how to teach yourself a computer skill, always try the On Your Own activity first before turning to these step-by-step solutions.

> **Not Working?** Websites change from time to time. The step-by-step instructions were accurate when we wrote them, but be aware that you might have to adjust them to account for later website changes.

On Your Own 2.1 Step-by-Step Solution   How to Use Internet Explorer

This solution has two parts:

► How to use Internet Explorer in the Windows 8 interface

► How to use Internet Explorer from the desktop

How to Use Internet Explorer in the Windows 8 Interface

Follow these steps to open and use Internet Explorer from the Start screen:

Step 1. Go to the Windows 8 Start screen.

Step 2. Click the **Internet Explorer** tile. The Internet Explorer page opens, and a web page displays inside the IE page (see Figure S2-1). Look in the address box of your browser for the text beginning with http://. This text is the address of your home page. Windows automatically makes the home page http://www.msn.com or http://t.msn.com, but your home page might have been changed to some other page.

FIGURE S2-1
Internet Explorer using the Windows 8 interface displays a web page.

Step 3. Move your pointer over the web page. When the shape of your pointer changes from an arrow ⬚ to a hand ⬚ , you have located a link.

Step 4. Click a link, and another web page displays. When you click a link and a new web page displays, notice the address in the address box changes. The address showing is the address of the new web page.

Step 5. To return to the previous web page, click the Back button, which is the left arrow ⬅ in the bottom-left corner of the screen. If you don't see the black pane with the arrow, right-click anywhere on the page.

Besides clicking links to find new web pages, you can also enter the address in the address box. Follow these steps:

Step 1. Press and drag your pointer over all the text in the address box so that all the text is selected. Selected text is highlighted in blue.

Step 2. Let's get some CNN news. Type **www.cnn.com**, which replaces the high-lighted text. Press **Enter**. The CNN web page appears. Notice that when you enter www.cnn.com in the address box, Internet Explorer automatically adds http:// to the beginning of the address.

Highlighted text in IE address bar

> **Not Working?** Make sure all the old address is deleted. Only one address at a time can be in the address box. You can use your Backspace key to delete an old address.

Step 3. Click a link on the www.cnn.com page to display another page. Then click a link on this new page.

Step 4. Click the left arrow ⬅ in the address bar. Your browser goes to the last previously visited page, returning you to the www.cnn.com page.

Step 5. Click the Forward button, which is the right arrow ➡ in the address bar, to go forward to the web page you just left. By using the left and right arrows, you can revisit web pages you have seen since the browser was opened.

How to Use Internet Explorer from the Desktop

Follow these steps to open and use Internet Explorer from the desktop:

Step 1. Go to the Windows desktop. Recall you can do that by pressing the **Windows** key (also called the **Win** key) or by clicking the **Desktop** tile on the Start screen.

Step 2. Click the **Internet Explorer** icon in the taskbar. Internet Explorer opens, and a web page displays inside the IE window (see Figure S2-2). Look in the address box of your browser for the text beginning with http://. This text is the address of your home page.

FIGURE S2-2
The Internet Explorer window opened from the desktop.

Step 3. Click a link, and another web page displays. The address now showing is the address of the new web page. Also notice the name of the web page appears in the tab above the page.

Step 4. You can return to your home page at any time. To return, click the **Home** button , which is labeled in Figure S2-2.

Follow these steps to use the address box:

Step 1. Press and drag your pointer over all the text in the address bar so that all the text is selected. Selected text is highlighted in blue.

Step 2. Let's get some CNN news. Type **www.cnn.com**, which replaces the highlighted text. Press **Enter**. The CNN web page appears.

> **Not Working?** Make sure all the old address is deleted. Only one address at a time can be in the address box. You can use your Backspace key to delete an old address.

Highlighted text in IE address box

Step 3. Click a link on the www.cnn.com page to display another page. Then click a link on this new page.

Step 4. Click the Back button, which is the left arrow ← in the title bar. Your browser goes to the last previously visited page, returning you to the www.cnn.com page.

Step 5. Click the Forward button, which is the right arrow → in the title bar. The browser goes forward to the web page you just left.

> **Not Working?** If the right arrow is not available, the website might have disabled it to try to force you to click a link on the current page.

On Your Own 2.2 Step-by-Step Solution   How to Manage Multiple Web Pages Using IE Tabs

This solution has two parts:

▶ How to manage multiple web pages using IE in the Windows 8 interface

▶ How to manage multiple web pages using IE from the desktop

How to Manage Multiple Web Pages Using IE in the Windows 8 Interface

Follow these steps to visit four websites:

Step 1. If **Internet Explorer** isn't already open, open it by using the Start screen.

Step 2. Type **cnn.com** in the address box and press **Enter**. The CNN page appears.

> **Not Working?** If a web page doesn't immediately appear after you press Enter, try pressing the refresh button ◉ to the right of the address box. If it still doesn't appear, the website might be having problems.

Step 3. To open a new tab, right-click anywhere on the page. In the black pane at the bottom of the page, click the **New Tab** button ⊕ in the upper-right area of the black pane. A new blank page appears. The lower part of the page is shown in Figure S2-3.

New tab IE page

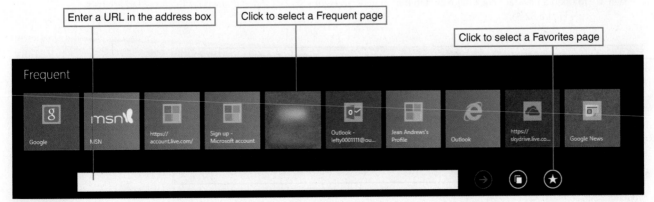

FIGURE S2-3
A new blank page displays with suggestions for frequently visited web pages.

Step 4. In the address box, type **news.yahoo.com** and press **Enter**. The Yahoo! News web page appears.

Step 5. Open a third tab. Type **news.google.com** in the address box and press **Enter**. The Google News web page appears.

> **Not Working?** If you get an error, make sure you've deleted all the text in the address box before you enter a new address.

Step 6. Open a fourth tab and head to **foxnews.com**.

Step 7. You now have four tabs open. To view any of the four pages, right-click on the screen and then select the page from the thumbnails that appear at the bottom of the screen. Click the **Google News** thumbnail to return to that page.

Step 8. To close a tab, click the gray X on the thumbnail of that page. To close the Google News tab, right-click to see the thumbnails, as shown in Figure S2-4. Then click the gray X on the **Google News** thumbnail.

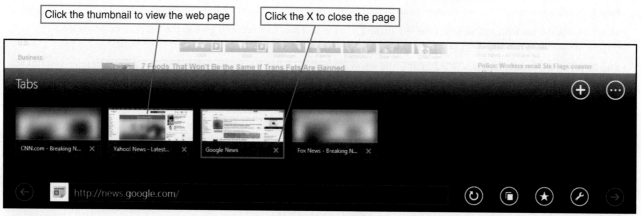

FIGURE S2-4
Internet Explorer has four tabs open, and you can click a thumbnail to return to that open tab.

How to Manage Multiple Web Pages Using IE from the Desktop

Follow these steps to visit four websites using IE from the desktop:

Step 1. If Internet Explorer isn't already open, open it by going to the Windows desktop and clicking the Internet Explorer icon in the taskbar.

Step 2. Type **cnn.com** in the address box and press **Enter**. The CNN page appears.

> **Not Working?** If a web page doesn't immediately appear after you press Enter, try pressing the refresh button ↻ to the right of the address box. If it still doesn't appear, the website might be having problems.

Step 3. To open a new tab, click the **New Tab** button (refer to Figure S2-2) to open a new tab. The New Tab appears (see Figure S2-5).

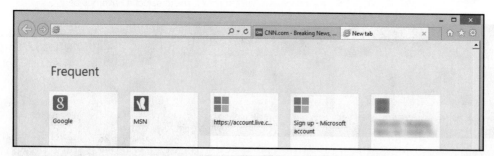

FIGURE S2-5
A new tab allows you to view a new page without losing the previous page.

Step 4. In the address box, type **news.yahoo.com** and press **Enter**. The Yahoo! News web page appears.

Step 5. Open a third tab. Type **news.google.com** in the address box and press **Enter**. The Google News web page appears.

Step 6. Open a fourth tab and visit the web page **foxnews.com**. The four tabs are showing in Figure S2-6.

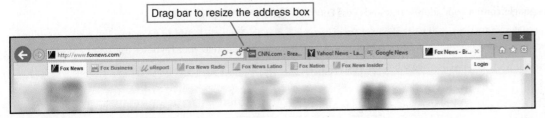

Drag bar to resize the address box

FIGURE S2-6
Press and drag the bar to the right of the address box to adjust the space used for the address box and tabs.

Step 7. You now have four tabs open. You can view any of the four pages by clicking its tab button. Click the **Google News** tab to return to that page.

Step 8. To close a tab, first select it. The selected tab has a gray X on the right side of the tab. Select the **Google News** tab. Click the gray **X** to close this tab.

Gray X on selected tab

On Your Own 2.3 Step-by-Step Solution   **How to Save a Favorite and Change Your IE Home Page**

This solution has three parts:

▶ How to save a web page to your Favorites using IE in the Windows 8 interface

▶ How to save a web page to your Favorites using IE from the desktop

▶ How to change your IE home page

How to Save a Web Page to Your Favorites Using IE in the Windows 8 Interface

Follow these steps to save a web page to your favorites:

Step 1. If Internet Explorer isn't already open, open it using the Start screen.

Step 2. Type **news.google.com** in your address box and press **Enter**. The Google News page appears.

Step 3. Right-click on the page to see the black pane at the bottom of the screen. In the pane, click the Favorites button and then click the Add to favorites button. Click **Add**. The Google News site is added to your Favorites list.

Step 4. Later when you want to revisit the site, right-click the current page so that the black pane appears at the bottom of the screen. Click the Favorites button. In the list of Favorites tiles, click **Google News**.

IE Favorites button

How to Save a Web Page to Your Favorites Using IE from the Desktop

Follow these steps to save a web page to your favorites:

Step 1. If Internet Explorer isn't already open, open it by going to the Windows desktop and then clicking the **Internet Explorer** icon in the taskbar.

Step 2. Type **news.google.com** in your address box and press **Enter**. The Google News page appears.

Step 3. To the right of the address bar and tabs, click the **Favorites** star ⭐ icon. Then click **Add to favorites**. The Add a Favorite dialog box appears (see Figure S2-7). Click **Add**. The Google News site is added to your Favorites list.

Step 4. Later when you want to revisit the site, click the **Favorites** star ⭐ and then click the site in the list of Favorites that appears.

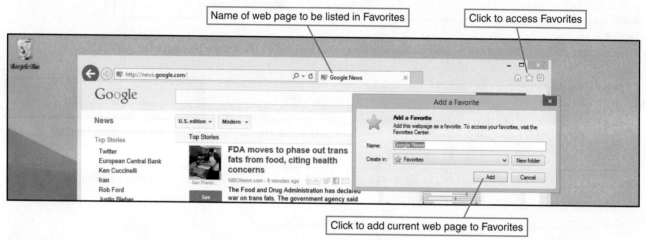

FIGURE S2-7
Add a website address to your Favorites list so you can easily return to it.

How to Change Your IE Home Page

Tools drop-down menu shows Internet Options

Follow these steps to change your home page to **espn.go.com**:

Step 1. If Internet Explorer isn't open on the Windows desktop, go to the desktop and open it.

Step 2. In the upper-right corner of the window, click the **Tools** icon ⚙. In the drop-down menu, click **Internet options**. The Internet Options dialog box appears (see Figure S2-8).

FIGURE S2-8
The Internet Options dialog box allows you to change your Internet Explorer settings.

Step 3. Each tab on the dialog box contains IE settings. If necessary, click the **General** tab so that tab is the active tab.

Step 4. In the Home page area, highlight the address currently showing and type **espn.go.com** to replace the highlighted text. You don't need to include http://.

Step 5. Click **Apply**. Notice IE added http:// to the home page string. Click **OK** to close the dialog box.

Step 6. Close Internet Explorer.

Step 7. Open Internet Explorer from the desktop or the Start screen. Either way, the espn.go.com page appears as your home page.

> **Not Working?** If espn.go.com doesn't appear as your home page, open the Internet Options dialog box again and check your spelling. Perhaps you misspelled the address.

On Your Own 2.4 Step-by-step Solution   How to Use a Search Engine

Follow these steps to learn to use Google to find information on the web:

Step 1. If Internet Explorer isn't already open, open it from either the Start screen or the desktop.

Step 2. To go to the Google site, type **google.com** in the address box and press **Enter**. The Google web page appears.

Step 3. Enter **seattle weather** in the search box. As you type, notice the autosuggest feature of Google offers suggestions for the completion of your search string (see Figure S2-9).

FIGURE S2-9
Google autosuggest offers suggestions to complete your search string.

Step 4. Also notice the instant search feature of Google gives search results as you type. Before you finish typing *seattle weather*, the weather forecast for Seattle, Washington, displays. To use a suggestion, click it. Click **seattle weather** in the drop-down list of suggestions. (If you don't want to use a suggestion, finish typing your search string and press **Enter** or click the **Search** icon.)

Step 5. The list of hits Google found about your search appears. The number of hits shows at the top of the list. Mouse over the first line in a hit (the line that is blue and underlined). Your pointer changes to a hand . Click this first line to drill down to the link.

> **Not Working?** The step-by-step instructions given here were accurate when we wrote them, but be aware that you might have to adjust them to account for later website changes.

Follow this step to practice using the Internet Explorer address box as a search box:

Step 1. In the Internet Explorer address box, type **how to change the oil in my car** and press **Enter**. The page showing the results includes the name of the search engine used. Bing is used unless the default setting for the IE search has been changed.

Search text typed in IE address box

On Your Own 2.5 Step-by-Step Solution   How to Perform Google Advanced Searches

Google.com options button

Follow these steps to get information on how a search engine works searching only the wikipedia.org website:

Step 1. If Internet Explorer isn't already open, open it. In the address box, type **google.com** and press **Enter**. The Google search page opens.

Step 2. Type **site:wikipedia.org how a search engine works** and press **Enter**. The list of hits appears. Notice all the hits come from the wikipedia.org site.

> **Tip** *Google can build an advanced search for you. To find out how, click the options button on the right side of a screen that shows search results. Then click* **Advanced search** *in the drop-down menu that appears.*

Follow these steps to limit the preceding search to content updated in the past 24 hours and then remove the limitation:

Step 1. Under the Google search box, click **Search tools**. The hit count disappears and a list of advanced tools appears.

Step 2. Click the down arrow beside **Any time** and then click **Past 24 hours** (see Figure S2-10). The hit count is greatly reduced.

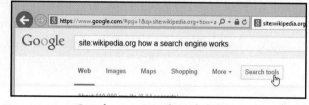

Google.com Search tools button

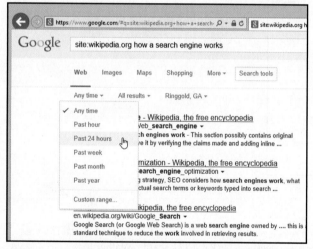

FIGURE S2-10
Limit the search to a time limit since a web page was last updated.

Step 3. To undo the time limitation placed on the search, click **Clear**.

Follow these steps to limit the search to exact words and to exclude a word from the search:

Step 1. To search for exact wording, put quotation marks around the phrase. In the Google search box, type **"who invented google earth"** and press **Enter**. Be sure to include the quotation marks as you type. Only sites that use this exact phrase are listed.

Step 2. Use a hyphen before a word to exclude it from search results. To search for an apartment near Emory University but eliminate luxury apartments from your search, type **rent apartment near emory university-luxury** in the Google search box and press **Enter**.

> **Not Working?** Don't type a space following the hyphen.

On Your Own 2.6 Step-by-Step Solution   **How to Find Images, Videos, Directions, and Translations**

This solution has three parts:

▶ How to find images and videos

▶ How to find driving directions

▶ How to find translations

How to Find Images and Videos

Follow these steps to find images and videos:

Step 1. If Internet Explorer isn't already open, open it. Go to the **google.com** search page.

Step 2. Enter **hurricane sandy** in the Google search box and press **Enter**.

Step 3. Click **Images** in the menu at the top of the Google page. Images of the hurricane appear.

Step 4. To have Google search for videos, click **More** in the menu bar and then click **Videos** from the drop-down menu. Notice the Google page shows Videos selected in the list below the search box.

Google menu below search box

Step 5. Enter **how to make a homemade pizza** in the Google search box and press **Enter**. Links to videos appear.

How to Find Driving Directions

Follow these steps to find driving directions from Baltimore, Maryland, to Newark, New Jersey:

Step 1. Go to **maps.google.com**. The Google maps page appears.

Step 2. Click **Get directions** to see the page shown in Figure S2-11.

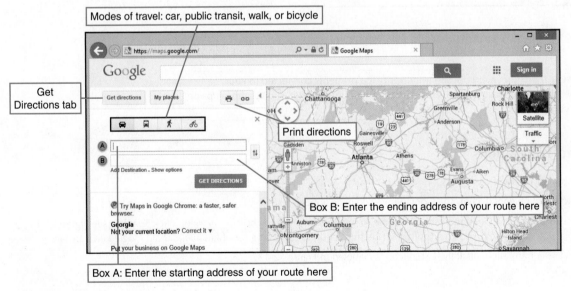

FIGURE S2-11
Use Google Maps to find driving, transit, walking, and bicycling directions.

Step 3.   In box A, enter **baltimore, md**.

Step 4.   In box B, enter **newark, nj**.

Step 5.   Make sure the car icon above the boxes is selected, indicating that your search will give you driving directions. Click the **GET DIRECTIONS** button below the destination boxes. Driving directions appear. The trip is 180 miles. You can also enter full addresses including street address, city, and state in boxes A and B to get driving directions to a specific address.

Step 6.   You might need printed directions that you can take with you as you drive. To print the directions, click the **Printer** icon 🖨 near the top of the window to the left of the map. A new tab opens showing directions designed for printing.

Step 7.   Click **Print** in the upper-right corner of the window. On the Print dialog box (see Figure S2-12), select your printer and click **Print**. The document prints.

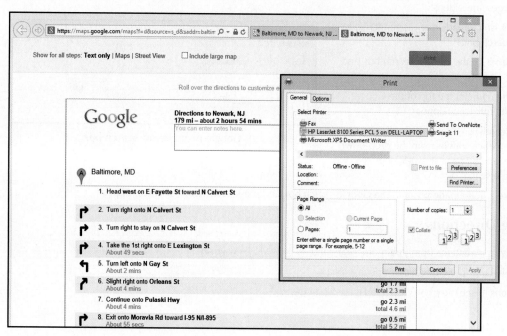

FIGURE S2-12
The Print dialog box allows you to select a printer and then print.

> **Not Working?**   If the document doesn't print, verify the printer is connected to your computer. Does the printer have paper? Is the printer turned on? Chapter 13 gives more tips on solving a printer problem.

How to Find Translations

Follow these steps to translate text:

Step 1.   Go to **translate.google.com**. The Google Translate page appears.

Step 2.   In the text box, type **Good morning. Welcome to my home.** Above the box on the right, click **Spanish** (see Figure S2-13). Notice you can click the down arrow above the translation to see a long list of languages that Google can translate.

Step 3.   To hear the translation, click the Listen icon, as labeled in Figure S2-13.

FIGURE S2-13
Translate text from English to Spanish and listen to the translation.

Not Working? To hear the translation, the volume on your computer must be turned up high enough. To turn up the volume, use the volume icon ◀ in the Settings charm or in the taskbar on the Windows desktop.

On Your Own 2.7 Step-by-Step Solution   How to Download Files from the Web

To use Internet Explorer on the desktop to download the sample_files folder from the companion website, follow these steps:

Step 1. If necessary, open Internet Explorer from the Windows desktop. Go to **www.pearsonhighered.com/jump**. Then click **Companion Website** on the right side of the page.

Step 2. On the next page, click **Sample Files**. The Internet Explorer dialog box appears, asking what you want to do with the folder (see Figure S2-14). Click **Save as**. The Save As dialog box appears.

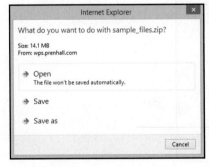

FIGURE S2-14
Internet Explorer wants to know what to
do with the file to download.

Step 3. Point to your USB flash drive and click **Save**. The file downloads to your flash drive.

Step 4. Open File Explorer and select your USB flash drive. Note that as the sample_files compressed folder downloads, the Type appears as Partial Download. When the download is complete, the Type is listed as Compressed (zipped) Folder.

Step 5. Using File Explorer to uncompress the folder, double-click it to drill down into the folder. In the compressed folder, you'll find a regular folder, also named sample_files.

Step 6. Right-click the regular **sample_files** folder and select **Copy** from the shortcut menu.

Step 7. Return to the root of the USB flash drive. Right-click in the white space and select **Paste** from the shortcut menu. The regular sample_files folder is copied to the root of your USB flash drive. You should now see two new folders in the root: the sample_files compressed folder and the sample_files regular folder. If you like, you can delete the sample_files compressed folder.

Step 8. To see files in the sample_files regular folder, drill down into it as you would any regular folder.

On Your Own 2.8 Step-by-Step Solution   How to Set Up and Use a OneDrive

This solution has four parts:

- ► How to set up a Microsoft account and OneDrive
- ► How to upload a file to a OneDrive folder
- ► How to share a OneDrive folder
- ► How to sign out of your OneDrive

Not Working?   The live.com website changes often, so the instructions given below might need adjusting.

How to Set Up a Microsoft Account and OneDrive

If you already have an outlook.com, hotmail.com, or live.com email address, you already have a OneDrive and you can skip this section and move on to "How to Upload a File to a OneDrive Folder."

If you don't yet have a Microsoft account with a OneDrive and you want to get one, follow these steps:

Step 1.   If Internet Explorer isn't open, open it. Go to **signup.live.com** (see Figure S2-15).

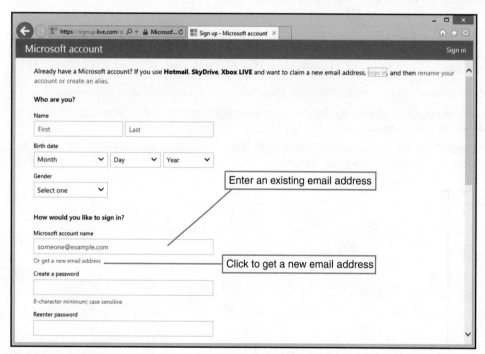

FIGURE S2-15
Sign up for a Microsoft account using an existing email address or by creating a new email address.

Step 2.   Enter your First Name, Last Name, Birth date, and Gender.

Step 3.   If you want to use your existing email address—for example, janedoe@sample.edu—enter it in the Microsoft account name box.

Step 4.   If you want to get a new email address, click **Or get a new email address**. To create an outlook.com, hotmail.com, or live.com email address, enter your name or some other group of characters in the Microsoft account name box. Notice that @outlook.com will be added to the characters to complete your email address. You can use the down arrow to the right of outlook.com to change the ending to hotmail.com or live.com.

New email domain choices

Step 5.   Enter the password to your account twice.

Step 6. Continue to fill in all boxes on the page, including your Phone number, Alternate email address (or select a Security question), Country/region, and ZIP code. Type the characters you see in the box at the bottom of the screen. When you're finished, click **I accept**.

Step 7. Check the page for any errors and fix any problems. If the email address you're trying to create is taken, try a different address. Click **I accept** to try your entries again.

Step 8. Be sure to write down or record your new email address and your password to your Microsoft account in a safe place so you won't forget it.

Step 9. To sign out of your account, click your name in the upper-right corner of the page and then **Sign out**. To sign back into your account, enter **live.com** in the address box of your browser and then enter your Microsoft account and password. Click **Sign in**. A video about Outlook email might appear. If you see it, click **Continue to inbox**. The Outlook page appears where you can manage your Microsoft account email (see Figure S2-16).

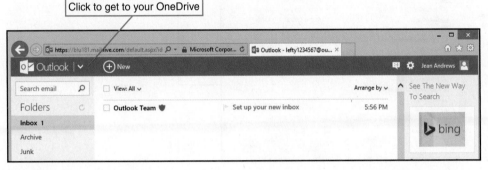

FIGURE S2-16
Sign up for a Microsoft account using an existing email address or by creating a new email address.

Outlook dropdown arrow

Step 10. In the upper-left corner of the page, click the down arrow beside Outlook. In the black bar that appears, click **OneDrive**. Folders in your OneDrive appear. Currently, the three folders created by Microsoft for your OneDrive are Documents, Pictures, and Public. The OneDrive has 7 GB of available storage.

How to Upload a File to a OneDrive Folder

> **Not Working?** The live.com website changes often, so the instructions given below might need adjusting.

Follow these steps to sign in to your Microsoft account and upload a document file to your OneDrive:

Step 1. If necessary, plug your USB flash drive into a USB port. Use the flash drive that contains the sample_files folder you downloaded in On Your Own 2.7. If you haven't yet downloaded the folder to your flash drive, do so now.

Step 2. If Internet Explorer is not already open, open it. If you're not already signed into your Microsoft account, go to **live.com** and sign in. The Outlook page appears.

Step 3. In the upper-left corner of the page, click the down arrow beside Outlook and click **OneDrive**. The OneDrive page appears. Click the **Documents** folder to open it.

> **Not Working?** At the time we wrote this book, Windows Live assigned the Documents, Pictures, and Public folders to any new OneDrive. Your OneDrive might contain different folders. Add your files to whatever folder the OneDrive offers.

Step 4. To upload a file to your Documents folder, click **Upload** in the menu bar. The Choose File to Upload dialog box appears.

Step 5. To locate the LettertoDave file, click **This PC** in the navigation pane and then click the USB flash drive in the Devices and drives group in the right pane. Drill down into the sample_files folder. Click the **LettertoDave** file to select it (see Figure S2-17). Click **Open**. The file uploads to the Documents folder on your OneDrive.

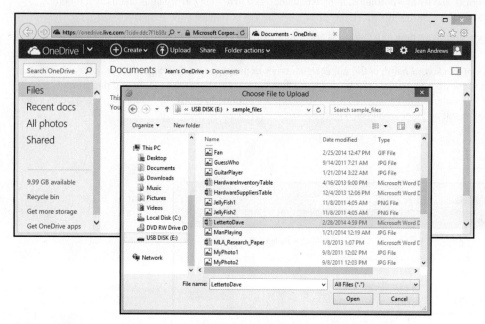

FIGURE S2-17
Add a file to the Documents folder on your OneDrive.

Not Working? If you put the wrong file in a OneDrive folder, you can delete the file. To delete a file, right-click the file and click **Delete** in the shortcut menu that appears. You might need to scroll down the shortcut menu to find the Delete command (see Figure S2-18).

FIGURE S2-18
Delete a file in a OneDrive folder.

Step 6. To return to the top level of your OneDrive, click the OneDrive link as labeled in Figure S2-18. The **OneDrive** page shows the folders in the root of your OneDrive.

How to Share a OneDrive Folder

If your instructor wants you to store your homework files in the Documents folder and give him or her access to this folder, follow these steps to give access:

Step 1. If Internet Explorer isn't open, open it. Go to the **live.com** site. Enter your Microsoft account email address and password and click **Sign in**.

Step 2. Your account name should appear in the upper-right corner of the screen. If OneDrive is not showing in the upper-left corner, click the down arrow and click **OneDrive**. Your OneDrive folders appear.

Step 3. Click the **Documents** folder to open it and view its contents. You should see the LettertoDave document file in the folder.

Step 4. On the menu bar, click **Share**. When the message, "Are you sure you want to share this folder?" appears, click **Share this folder**. The Share page appears (see Figure S2-19).

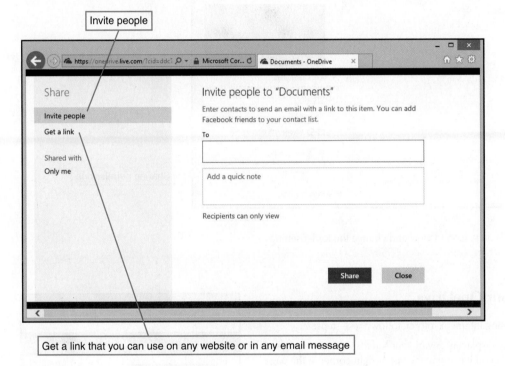

FIGURE S2-19
Decide how you want to notify someone that you're sharing a folder.

> **Tip** If you want to get a link to any folder or file on your OneDrive, in the Share page (refer to Figure S2-19), click Get a link. You can then get a link for viewing only or for viewing and editing. If the link is too long, you can also shorten the length of the link.

Step 5. In the To box, enter the email address of your instructor. You can also enter text that will go into the email message. To allow your instructor to edit what's in the folder, click **Recipients can only view** and then click **Recipients can edit**. Click **Share** to send the email. Then click **Close**. Your instructor is sent an email message with links to the files in your Documents folder. He or she can click the links to find each file you place in the Documents folder of your OneDrive. In later chapters, you learn how to save documents to the Documents folder using Office applications.

> **Not Working?** Before you can proceed with sharing, you might be asked to do a security check. If you are asked to provide a security check, follow directions on screen to enter characters in a box.

Step 6. If you need to see a list of those you have given permission to access a OneDrive folder, first open the folder. Then click the **Show or hide the details pane** icon ▣ on the right side of the folder window. The details pane appears (see Figure S2-20). If necessary, click **Sharing** to see the list of people with whom you have shared the folder. Using this list, you can remove someone from the Sharing list or change the edit or view status for someone. To change sharing permissions, click the email address and then make your changes in the page that appears.

Show or hide the details pane for the open folder

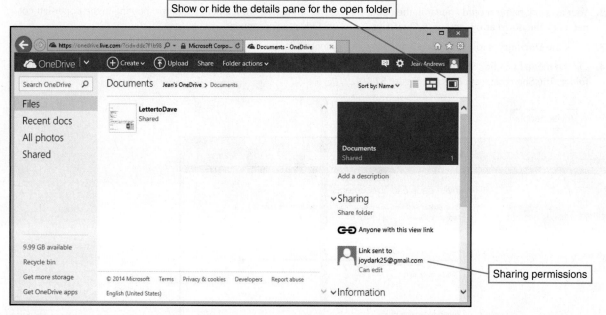

FIGURE S2-20
Click the Show or hide the details pane icon to view and change the folder settings.

How to Sign Out of Your OneDrive

To sign out of OneDrive when using Internet Explorer, follow these steps:

Step 1. With Internet Explorer displaying any of your Microsoft account pages, click your Microsoft account name in the upper-right corner of the page.

Step 2. In the menu that appears, click **Sign out**.

> **Tip** When you sign out of OneDrive using Internet Explorer, you might still be signed in to your Microsoft account in Windows 8 or in Microsoft Office applications that you will learn to use later in this book.

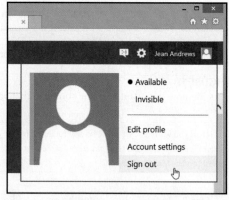

Sign out of OneDrive

On Your Own 2.9 Step-by-Step Solution   How to Print and Save a Web Page

This solution has two parts:

▶ How to print a web page

▶ How to save a web page to a data file

How to Print a Web Page

Follow these steps to print a web page:

Step 1. If Internet Explorer isn't already open, open it. Go to the web page **paypal.com**.

Step 2. To print the page, click the **Tools** icon 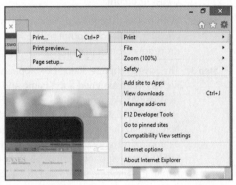 in the upper-right corner of the IE window. Point to **Print** and then click **Print preview** in the drop-down menu that appears. A new window opens containing a preview of how the printout will appear (see Figure S2-21). It might be a messy view of the page with some graphics missing, but important text on the page is present.

Tools > Print > Print preview

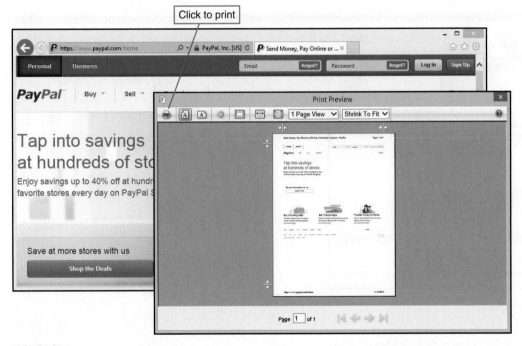

FIGURE S2-21

A printed web page is sometimes needed for important transactions and records.

Step 3. To print the page, click the printer icon in the menu bar of the Print Preview window. The Print dialog box appears.

Step 4. Click your printer to select it and click **Print**. The page prints.

Printer icon

How to Save a Web Page to a Data File

Follow these steps to save a web page and verify it is saved correctly:

Step 1. If Internet Explorer isn't already open, open it. Go to the web page **wellsfargo.com**.

Step 2. With the wellsfargo.com web page displayed in your browser window, click the **Tools** icon, point to **File**, and then click **Save as** from the drop-down menu that appears.

Step 3. The Save Webpage dialog box appears (see Figure S2-22). Notice the file has been assigned a file name and an .mht or .html file extension. (A possible file name is Wells Fargo - Personal & Business Banking - Student, Auto & Home Loans - Investing & Insurance_com-.mht.) Navigate to the device and folder where you want to save the file. For example, in Figure S2-22, to save to the USB flash drive, click **USB DISK** in the left pane. (Your USB flash drive might have a different name and different drive letter.) Click **Save**. The file saves.

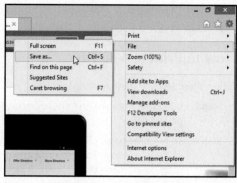

Tools > File > Save as

Not Working? Sometimes Windows cannot save all the graphics on the page and an error message appears. Most likely the page is still saved with most parts included.

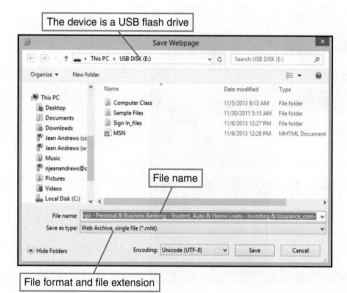

FIGURE S2-22
Save the web page in the .mht file format to the USB flash drive.

Tip Some web pages are saved as .html files rather than .mht files. When a page is saved as an .html file, a folder is also saved that contains additional files needed to build the page.

Step 4. To verify the file saved correctly, first close the Internet Explorer window.

Step 5. Open File Explorer and locate the file, for example, the **Wells Fargo - Personal & Business Banking - Student, Auto & Home Loans - Investing & Insurance_com-.mht** file, on the storage device where you saved it.

Step 6. Double-click the file to open it. Internet Explorer opens and the file displays. Notice the location and name of the file displays in the address box of Internet Explorer.

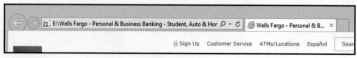

MHT file saved on USB DISK

On Your Own 2.10 Step-by-Step Solution   How to Check Windows Defender Settings

Follow these steps to check Windows Defender settings:

Step 1. Go to the **Start screen**. Type **defender**. In the list of apps that appears, click **Windows Defender**. Windows Defender opens in a window on the desktop.

Step 2. In the Home tab, make sure **Real-time protection** is On. If it's not on, click the **Settings** tab and check **Turn on real-time protection (recommended)**.

Step 3. If you made a change, click **Save changes**.

Step 4. Close the Windows Defender window.

On Your Own 2.11 Step-by-Step Solution   How to Install and Use an App from the Windows Store

Follow these steps to install an app in Windows 8:

Step 1. Go to the Start screen and click the **Store** tile. The Store app opens.

Step 2. You might like to scroll through all the apps in the store looking for a free app. A quicker way to find a specific app is to search for it. To search, type the name of the app in the search box on the page.

Step 3. The app page appears. Click **Install**. If you did not sign on to Windows 8 with a Microsoft account, the Switch to a Microsoft account on this PC screen appears (see Figure S2-23). Click **Sign into each app separately instead (not recommended)**.

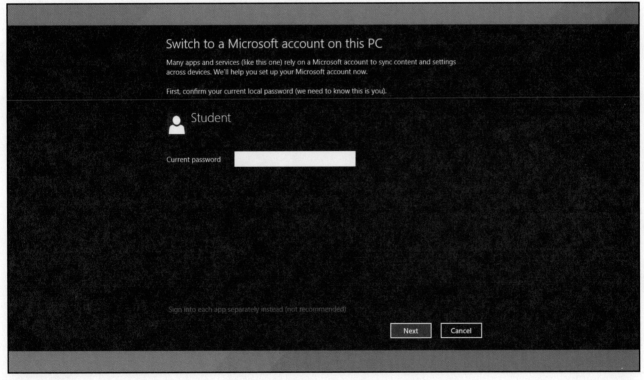

FIGURE S2-23
Windows wants you to switch Windows sign on to a Microsoft account

Step 4. On the next screen, enter your Microsoft account and password and click **Save**. The free app installs.

Step 5. If a message appears asking for payment information, click **Ask me later**. Close the Store app page.

Follow these steps to use an app:

Step 1. On the Start screen, find the app tile. You might need to scroll the Start screen to the right to find the tile. If you still don't see the app, click the down arrow to see the Apps screen with more apps. Click the app tile to open the app. The app opens for you to use it.

Step 2. To close an app, press and drag the top of the app page to the bottom of the screen.

On Your Own 2.12 Step-by-Step Solution   How to Switch Windows 8 Sign On to Your Microsoft Account and Use Your OneDrive

This solution has two parts:

▶ How to switch Windows 8 to a Microsoft account

▶ How to use a OneDrive with the SkyDrive app and File Explorer

How to Switch Windows 8 to a Microsoft Account

Follow these steps to switch Windows 8 from a local account to your Microsoft account:

Step 1. You should be signed on to Windows using a local user account. From the Start screen, open the charms bar. Click **Settings** and then click **Change PC settings**. On the PC settings page, click **Accounts**. If necessary, click **Your account** to select it. In the right pane, click **Connect to a Microsoft account**.

Step 2. On the next screen, enter the password to your local account. (This is the account you're currently signed on with.) Click **Next**.

Step 3. On the next screen, enter the email address to your Microsoft account. If you didn't already have a Microsoft account, recall that you created one in On Your Own 2.8. Click **Next**.

Step 4. On the next screen, you are given the opportunity to designate the computer as a trusted device by receiving a code. To skip this step, click **I can't do this right now**.

Step 5. On next screen, you are asks if you want to turn off access to your OneDrive. To keep access to your OneDrive, click **Next**.

Step 6. On the next screen, click **Switch**.

Step 7. On the PC settings page, notice your email address is now listed under your account name. Close the **PC settings** page.

Follow these steps to sign off and sign back on to Windows 8:

Step 1. On the Start screen, notice your name is listed as the name kept by the live.com website that is associated with your Microsoft account. To sign off of Windows, click your name and then click **Sign out** in the drop-down menu.

Step 2. Click anywhere on the Windows opening screen. If necessary, click your user name to select it. Notice your email address associated with your Microsoft account is listed under your account name. Enter the password to your Microsoft account and press **Enter**. The Start screen appears.

How to Use a OneDrive with the SkyDrive App and File Explorer

Recall that OneDrive used to be called SkyDrive and Windows 8 still uses the SkyDrive name. Follow these steps to sign in to your Microsoft account and use the SkyDrive app and File Explorer to view your OneDrive:

Step 1. If you're not signed in to Windows 8 using your Microsoft account, do so now.

Step 2. Go to the Start screen and click the **SkyDrive** tile. The folders in your OneDrive appear. Right-click the page to see the menu bar at the bottom of the screen (see Figure S2-24).

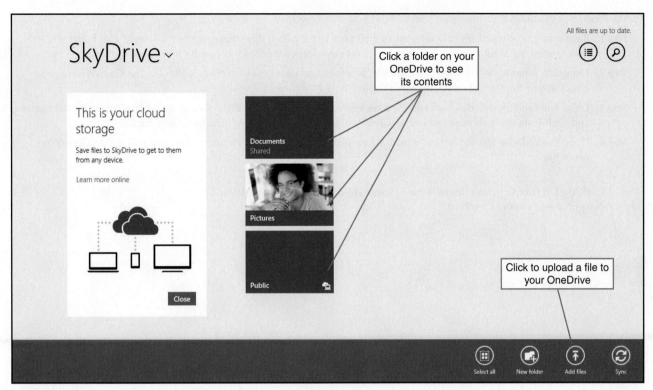

FIGURE S2-24
Access your OneDrive using the SkyDrive app in Windows 8.

Step 3. To see the LettertoDave file, click the **Documents** folder to open it.

Step 4. Return to the Start screen. Click the **Desktop** tile to open the Windows desktop.

Step 5. On the desktop, open **File Explorer**. To open your OneDrive, click **SkyDrive** in the navigation pane. The folders on your OneDrive appear in the right pane (see Figure S2-25).

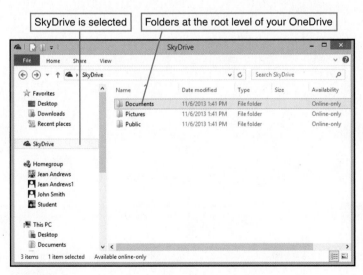

FIGURE S2-25
Access your OneDrive by using the SkyDrive group in File Explorer.

Follow these steps to upload a file from your USB flash drive to your OneDrive:

Step 1. If necessary, plug your USB flash drive into a USB port. Use the flash drive that contains the sample_files folder you downloaded in On Your Own 2.7. If you haven't yet downloaded the folder to your flash drive, do so now.

Step 2. Using File Explorer, drill down into the **sample_files** folder on your USB flash drive. Right-click the **GuessWho** file and click **Copy** in the shortcut menu. The file is copied to your Windows Clipboard.

Step 3. Using File Explorer, drill down into the **Pictures** folder on your OneDrive. Right-click in the white space in the right pane and click **Paste** in the shortcut menu. The GuessWho file is copied to the Pictures folder on your OneDrive.

Step 4. Open the **SkyDrive** app on the Start screen. When you drill down into the **Pictures** folder, you will see the GuessWho photo file.

Not Working? If your OneDrive doesn't have a Pictures folder, upload the GuessWho file to the Documents folder of your OneDrive.

CHAPTER 3 STEP-BY-STEP SOLUTIONS
Creating Documents with Microsoft Word

The solutions in this appendix are for you to use if you get stuck when doing an On Your Own activity in the chapter. To learn how to teach yourself a computer skill, always try the On Your Own activity first before turning to these solutions.

On Your Own 3.1 Step-by-Step Solution   How to Create a Blank Document and Use the Word Window

Create the Checklist Document: Part 1 of 8

In this On Your Own, you are creating part of the Checklist document shown in Figure 3-1 in the chapter. Follow these steps to open Word and examine the Word window:

Step 1. If you're using Windows 8, click the **Word 2013** tile on the Start screen. (If you don't see the tile, type Word and then click Word 2013 in the list that appears.) The desktop opens along with the Microsoft Word window. If you're using Windows 7, click **Start**, click **All Programs**, click **Microsoft Office**, and click **Microsoft Word 2013**. The Microsoft Word window opens.

Step 2. To open a blank document, click the **Blank document** icon. A blank document opens. If the Word window is not maximized, maximize it.

Word 2013 tile

Blank document icon selected

Step 3. Study Figure 3-1 shown earlier in the chapter and compare it to your open window.

Step 4. If you don't see the horizontal or vertical rulers, click the **VIEW** tab. Then check **Ruler** on the VIEW ribbon. The rulers appear.

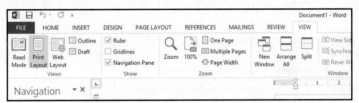

Ruler check box on the VIEW ribbon

Step 5. If the ribbon does not stay put on the window, click the **HOME** tab. The HOME ribbon appears. Click the **Pin the ribbon** icon 📌 to keep the ribbon pinned to the window.

> Tip When the ribbon is pinned, the Pin the ribbon icon becomes an arrow-up icon, which you can use to unpin the ribbon.

Pin the ribbon icon on HOME ribbon

Step 6. If the Print Layout button ▣ is not selected, click it to make it the selected layout.

Step 7. Find your insertion point |, which is in the upper-left area of the document inside the document margins.

Print layout button

Step 8. To open the Word Help window, click the **Help** button ? in the upper-right area of the Word window. The button is shaped like a question mark.

Step 9. In the Search box of the Word Help window, type **skydrive** and press **Enter**.

Step 10. Click **Getting Started with Office and OneDrive**. (Recall that OneDrive used to be called SkyDrive.) Your browser opens and displays a video about the topic. Notice that the website that holds the video is office.microsoft.com.

Step 11. Close the **Word Help** window.

> Tip As you work, if you accidently attempt to close the Word window, Word displays a dialog box asking whether you want to save your work. Click **Cancel**. The Word window stays open.

Create the Checklist Document: Part 2 of 8

In this On Your Own, you enter text in the Word document you started in On Your Own 3.1. Using the document you created in On Your Own 3.1, do the following:

Zoom bar

Step 1. Move the Zoom slider in the status bar to 100% or higher. Type the following text. Press **Enter** after each line. Check your work for errors.

> Overnight Trip to Piedmont Falls State Park
> Dear Parent or Guardian:

Step 2. To move your insertion point to the end of the document, press **Ctrl+End.** (As you hold down the **Ctrl** key, press the **End** key.) The insertion point is now on a blank line. Type the following paragraph. Do not press **Enter** until you finish typing all the text. Then press **Enter**.

> The team will take an overnight trip to Piedmont Falls State Park on June 3, and return on June 4. Please have your child at the ballpark at 4:00PM on Friday, June 3, ready to go. Plan to pick up your child at the ballpark between 3:30 and 4:00PM on Saturday, June 4. Please do not be late when picking up your child.

> **Not Working?** If your insertion point is at the end of the last line after you press Ctrl+End, press **Enter** to advance to a new line.

Step 3. Your document should now look like that in Figure S3-1. Check your document and correct any mistakes you find.

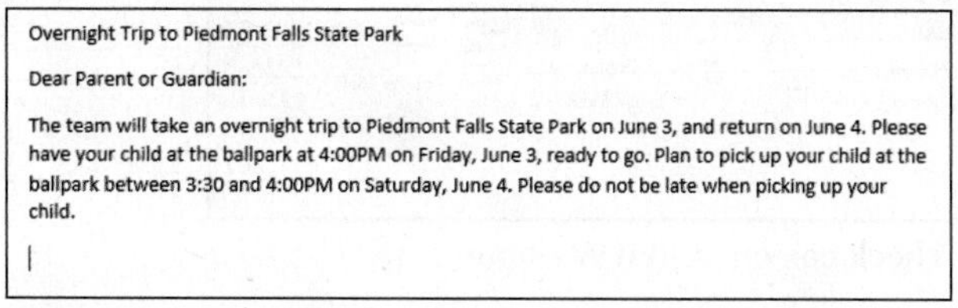

> Overnight Trip to Piedmont Falls State Park
>
> Dear Parent or Guardian:
>
> The team will take an overnight trip to Piedmont Falls State Park on June 3, and return on June 4. Please have your child at the ballpark at 4:00PM on Friday, June 3, ready to go. Plan to pick up your child at the ballpark between 3:30 and 4:00PM on Saturday, June 4. Please do not be late when picking up your child.

FIGURE S3-1
The first lines of text have been added to the document.

Create the Checklist Document: Part 3 of 8

This solution has four sections:

▶ How to save the document to your hard drive

▶ How to save the document to your USB flash drive

▶ How to save the document to your OneDrive

▶ How to resave, close, and reopen your document

How to Save a Document to Your Hard Drive

Follow these steps to save a document to your hard drive:

Step 1. With the document still open, click the **FILE** tab 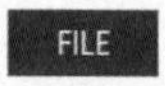 FILE and click **Save**. Because this is the first time you have saved the document, the Save As window appears.

Step 2. To save the document to your hard drive, make sure **Computer** is selected, which is the default option.

Step 3. Click **Documents** to save the document to your Documents library on your hard drive. Click **Desktop** to save the document to your desktop on your hard drive. To save the document to another location on your hard drive, click **Browse**.

Step 4. The Save As window appears (see Figure S3-2). If you chose **Documents** or **Desktop**, that location is already selected. Using this window, follow the four steps labeled in the figure to save the document:

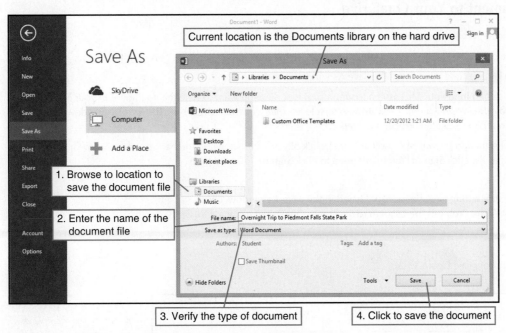

FIGURE S3-2
The Save As window allows you to enter the name, location, and file type for the document you are saving.

1. If you want to change the save location, use the left pane of the Save As window to find and select a new location.

2. In the *File name* box, type **Checklist** as the file name.

3. Verify the document type. Word Document is correct.

4. Click **Save**. The file is saved to the location you have selected.

Not Working? If you try to save a document to the hard drive and get an error such as "You don't have permission to save to this location," most likely you are trying to save to a protected area of the hard drive. Try saving to a different folder or library, or you can save to your USB flash drive instead.

How to Save a Document to a USB Flash Drive

Follow these steps to save a document to a USB flash drive:

Step 1. Insert a USB flash drive into a USB slot on your computer.

Step 2. Click the **FILE** tab FILE and click **Save**. If this is the first time you have saved the document, the Save As window appears.

Tip If you want to save a document to a different location than the first time you saved it, click the **FILE** tab and then click **Save As**. You can then save to a new location.

Step 3. Make sure Computer is selected and click **Browse**. The Save As window appears (refer to Figure S3-2).

Step 4. On the left pane, make sure the Computer group is open and items are listed under it. Scroll down until you find your USB flash drive. It might be named Removable Disk, Removable, or some other name. Click the drive. The folders and files on the USB flash drive appear in the right pane.

Step 5. If you are using the same USB flash drive that you used in Chapter 1, you see the folder Computer Class. If so, double-click **Computer Class** to save the file to that folder. If the folder is not there, save the file to the root of the USB drive.

Step 6. In the File name box, type **Checklist** as the file name.

Step 7. Click **Save**. The file is now saved on your flash drive.

How to Save a Document to Your OneDrive

Follow these steps to save a document to your OneDrive:

Step 1. Make sure you are connected to the Internet. You must have an Internet connection to access your OneDrive.

Step 2. Click the **FILE** tab FILE and click **Save**. The Save As window appears.

Step 3. If you are already signed in to your Microsoft account, Word assumes you want to save the document to your SkyDrive (OneDrive) and has already selected it. Click **Browse** to select a folder on your OneDrive. The Save As window appears with the Documents folder selected. Proceed to Step 8.

Step 4. If you have not yet signed in to your Microsoft account, click **SkyDrive** as shown in the background window in Figure S3-3. In the SkyDrive window, click **Sign In**. You might need to click **Sign In** a second time.

> **Not Working?** If you see the wrong SkyDrive account listed in the Save As window, click **Add a place** and then click **SkyDrive**. You can then sign in to SkyDrive (OneDrive) using a different Microsoft account.

Step 5. The Sign in box appears (see Figure S3-3).

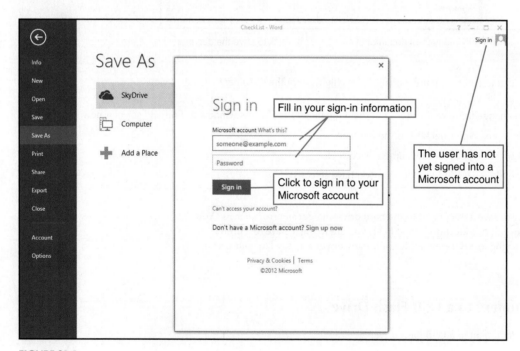

> **Tip** Look in the upper-right corner of the Word window to see the user name of the Microsoft account signed in.

FIGURE S3-3
Sign in to OneDrive (or SkyDrive) with your Microsoft account.

Step 6. Enter your Microsoft account email address and password and then click **Sign in**. Recall that you set up your Microsoft account in Chapter 2. After signing in, your Microsoft account name appears on the Save As window, and the Documents folder on your OneDrive is selected.

Step 7. Click **Browse**. The Save As window appears with the Documents folder selected.

Step 8. Change the file name to **Checklist** and click **Save**. The file Checklist.docx is saved to the Documents folder on your OneDrive. After the save is complete, Word returns to the documents window. Your Microsoft account appears in the upper-right corner of the Word window.

How to Save, Close, and Reopen Your Document

To practice saving your document after it has been saved the first time, follow these steps:

Step 1. Click the **FILE** tab. Notice the location and name of the document displays at the top of the Info page (see Figure S3-4). This document is saved to a USB flash drive.

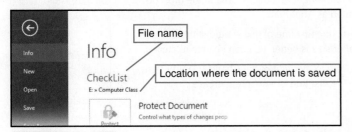

FIGURE S3-4
The document location is the Computer Class folder on the USB flash drive.

> **Hint** If the location displayed is not the correct location, click **Save As** and save the document to a new location.

Step 2. Click **Save**. Any changes you have made to the document since the last save are now saved to the drive.

Step 3. To practice a shortcut method of saving, hold down your **Ctrl** key while you press **S**.

Step 4. To demonstrate a third method to save, click the **Save** button 🖫 in the Quick Access Toolbar. The document saves again.

Quick Access Toolbar

> **Tip** When you use any of these methods to save, if the document has not been saved the first time, Word displays the Save As window.

To close and reopen your document, follow these steps:

Step 1. Close the Word window.

Step 2. Open Word. The FILE tab is automatically selected, and recent documents are listed in the left pane.

Step 3. In the list of Recent documents, click the **Checklist.docx** document. If the document is saved to your OneDrive, you might be asked to sign in by entering your Microsoft account email address and password.

> **Not Working?** If you don't see the document in the Recent documents list, click either **SkyDrive** or **Computer** and drill down to the document. You might be asked to sign in to your Microsoft account to access your OneDrive.

Another method of opening a document is to use **File Explorer** in Windows 8. (Note that File Explorer is called Windows Explorer in Windows 7.) Locate the document and double-click the document file name. The document opens.

On Your Own 3.4 Step-by-Step Solution   How to Format Text Using the Font Tools

Create the Checklist Document: Part 4 of 8

Follow these steps to format all the text in your Checklist document and then format the first line of text:

Step 1. To select all the text in the document, hold down your **Ctrl** key and press **A**. All the text is highlighted.

Step 2. If necessary, click the **HOME** tab to select the HOME ribbon.

Step 3. Click the down arrow to the right of the Font box. The drop-down list of fonts appears. Use the scrollbar on the right side of the list to scroll down.

Step 4. Locate and click the **Tahoma** font.

Select font

Step 5. Click the down arrow to the right of the Font Size box. The list of font sizes appears. As you move your pointer over the list of sizes, notice that each size is highlighted and that the size of the text changes so you can see the effect of the change. Click **12**.

Step 6. To select the first line of text, press and drag your pointer across the text so that all the text in the line is selected (highlighted).

Step 7. With the text still highlighted, click the down arrow to the right of the Font box. In the drop-down list of fonts, click **Arial Black**. The title is now formatted as Arial Black.

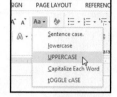

Select case

Step 8. Click the down arrow to the right of the Font Size box (the first line of text should still be highlighted). Click **14**. If you decide a larger or smaller size is better, you can change it later.

Step 9. With the first line still highlighted, click the down arrow to the right of the Change Case button and select **UPPERCASE** from the drop-down menu. The first line is now in uppercase.

Follow these steps to format text using underline and bold:

Step 1. Press and drag your pointer over the text **4:00PM on Friday, June 3**. Be sure not to include the comma following the text.

Highlight time and date

Step 2. Click the **Underline** button in the Font group.

Step 3. Press and drag your pointer over the text **3:30 and 4:00PM on Saturday, June 4**. Be sure not to include the period following the text.

Step 4. Click the **Underline** button in the Font group.

Step 5. Press and drag your pointer over the text **Please do not be late when picking up your child.** Be sure to include the period as part of the selected text.

Step 6. Click the **Italic** button in the Font group.

Step 7. Check the document for errors and save it.

On Your Own 3.5 Step-by-Step Solution   **How to Create a Bulleted List and Use the Format Painter**

Create the Checklist Document: Part 5 of 8

Follow these steps to center text and add more text in your Checklist document:

Step 1. Click anywhere in the title line. The line does not need to be highlighted, but your insertion point should be inside the line.

Step 2. In the Paragraph group, click **Center**.

Step 3. Press **Ctrl+End** to move your insertion point to the bottom of the document.

Center text

Step 4. Type the following text, pressing **Enter** after each line:

> Items your child should bring:
> Rain gear
> Sleeping bag
> Flashlight
> Change of clothes
> Extra pair of shoes

Hint Don't forget to press **Enter** after the last line.

Follow these steps to use the Format Painter to format text:

Step 1. Click anywhere on the first line of the document, *Overnight Trip to Piedmont Falls State Park*. Click the **Format Painter**. Your pointer changes to a paintbrush.

Step 2. Press and drag the paintbrush over the six lines of text at the bottom of the document. The text is formatted the same as the first line, which is Arial Black, 14 point, Centered.

Format painter with tip

Step 3. Click anywhere on the second line of the document, *Dear Parent or Guardian:*. Click the **Format Painter**. Your pointer changes to a paintbrush. Press and drag the paintbrush over the six lines of text at the bottom of the document. The text is formatted the same as the second line, which is Tahoma, 12 point.

Step 4. Select the last five lines of text. Click the **Bullet** button :≡ ▾ in the Paragraph group. The five lines become a bulleted list.

Step 5. To complete the text in the document, move your insertion point to the bottom of the document and press **Enter** twice. Type the following line and press **Enter**:

Signature of parent or guardian: _____

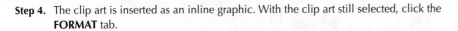

Follow these steps to copy the title from the top of the document to the bottom of the document:

Step 1. Select the first line in the document, the title line. On the HOME ribbon, click **Copy**. The text is copied into the Windows Clipboard.

Step 2. Press **Ctrl+End** to move to the bottom of the document. Press **Enter** to drop down to a new line. On the HOME ribbon, click **Paste**. The title is copied to the new line. The formatting should be the same as the first line. Make sure the title on the last line is centered.

Step 3. The text in the document is now finished. Save the document.

On Your Own 3.6 Step-by-Step Solution   How to Insert Clip Art into a Document

Create the Checklist Document: Part 6 of 8

Do the following to insert clip art of a camp counselor into your Checklist document:

Step 1. Position your insertion point at the end of the line **Items your child should bring**.

Step 2. Click the **INSERT** tab. On the INSERT ribbon, click **Online Pictures**. The Insert Pictures box opens. In the Office.com Clip Art box, type **camp** and press **Enter**.

Step 3. In the list of clip art that appears, click the clip art of the camp counselor. Click **Insert**.

> **Not Working?** Microsoft websites change often. If you can't find the clip art used here, substitute another appropriate online picture.

Search for camp clip art

Step 4. The clip art is inserted as an inline graphic. With the clip art still selected, click the **FORMAT** tab.

> **Hint** To know if an object is selected, look for sizing handles around the object.

Step 5. Click the **Wrap Text** button on the FORMAT ribbon. In the drop-down box of positions, select **Square**. The graphic can now be moved into position.

Step 6. With the graphic still selected, position your pointer inside the graphic. Your pointer changes to a four-directional arrow ⊹. Press and drag the graphic. Position the graphic to the right of the bulleted list.

Step 7. You might want to resize the graphic. To do so, grab a resizing handle on a corner of the graphic and drag the handle. To keep the graphic proportions from changing, hold down the **Shift** key as you resize it. The exact size of the graphic is not important.

Step 8. Save the document.

**Select Square
Wrap Text**

On Your Own 3.7 Step-by-Step Solution   How to Change Document Properties

Create the Checklist Document: Part 7 of 8

Follow these steps to view and change the properties of a document:

Step 1. Click the **FILE** tab to show the Info group. The document properties are shown in the right pane.

Step 2. If you need to change the author, right-click the author and select **Edit Property** from the shortcut menu that appears. The Edit person dialog box appears.

Step 3. Replace the name with your name and click **OK**. You might also want to change the name listed for Last Modified By.

Step 4. Save the document.

Create the Checklist Document: Part 8 of 8

Before printing a document, you should verify that the number of pages makes sense. Do the following:

Step 1. With your Checklist document open, if the **HOME** ribbon is not selected, select it.

Step 2. Look in the bottom-left corner of the window for the page count. It should be displayed as PAGE 1 of 1.

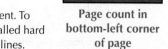

Page count in
bottom-left corner
of page

Step 3. If the document has more than one page, look for extra lines at the bottom of the document. To do that, click the **Show/Hide** button ¶ in the Paragraph group. Paragraph marks (also called hard returns) appear. Delete any unnecessary paragraph marks, which delete the unnecessary lines.

Step 4. Save the document.

Step 5. Click the **FILE** tab. Click **Print**. The Print window appears. See Figure 3-11 shown earlier in the chapter.

Step 6. Verify that the printer listed is the one that you want to use. To change printers, click the down arrow to the right of the printer name and select a printer from those listed.

Step 7. Click **Print**. 🖨 The document prints.

Step 8. You are finished with the Checklist document. Close the document.

Create the JazzConcert Document: Part 1 of 5

In this On Your Own, you are creating the *Jazz in the Park* document shown in Figure S3-5.

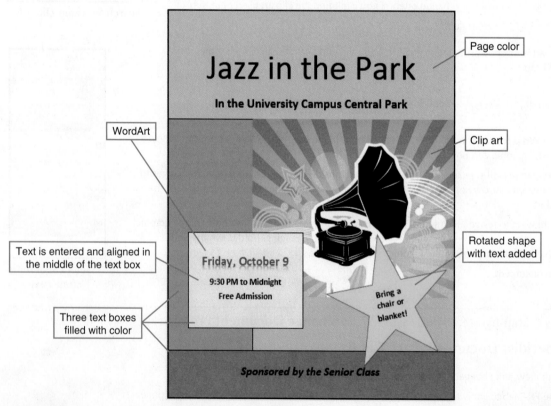

FIGURE S3-5
This "Jazz in the Park" document uses three text boxes, page color, WordArt, clip art, and a shape.

Follow these steps to create the document and add page color and the first two lines of text:

Step 1. Do one of the following to create a new blank document:

- If Word is not already open, open Word 2013. The Recent list appears. To create a new document, click **Blank document**. The document window opens.

- If Word is already open, click the **FILE** tab and click **New**. Then click **Blank document**. The document window opens.

Step 2. Click the **DESIGN** tab. Then click **Page Color** in the Page Background group on the ribbon. A group of Theme Colors appears. As you mouse over a color, the document color changes. Select a medium orange. **Orange, Accent 2, Lighter 40%** works well.

Step 3. Type the following two lines of text and press **Enter** after each line:

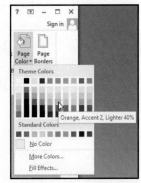

Dropdown of page color with one selected.

> Jazz in the Park
> In the University Campus Central Park

Step 4. Select the first line of text. Format it to **Calibri (Body) font, 72 point**.

Step 5. Select the second line of text. Format the text to **Calibri (Body), 26 point**, and **Bold**.

Step 6. Select both lines of text and **Center** the text on the page.

Step 7. Save the document to your USB flash drive, hard drive, OneDrive, or other location given by your instructor. Name the document **JazzConcert**. If you need help, see directions given earlier in On Your Own 3.3 Step-by-Step Solution for saving a document.

Step 8. Click somewhere off the text so it is no longer selected.

Do the following to create the text box on the left side of the page:

Step 1. If you want to position large text boxes, it helps to see the entire page on the screen. To view the entire page, click the percent to the right of the Zoom slider. In the Zoom dialog box, click **Whole page** and click **OK**. You can now view the entire page.

> **Tip** To zoom in and out on a page, click the plus + or minus — to the right or left of the Zoom slider.

Step 2. Click the **INSERT** tab. On the INSERT ribbon, click **Text Box**. A drop-down list appears. Click **Draw Text Box**. Your pointer changes to a crosshair +. Press and drag to draw the text box. Don't worry about its exact size or position. You can change that in step 4.

Step 3. The next step is to move the text box. To move a text box, position your pointer on the edge of the selected text box until your pointer is shaped like four directional arrows. Then press and drag to move the box. Move the box to the edge of the left side of the page and just below the second line of text.

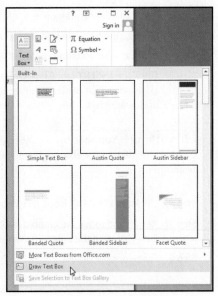

Select Draw Text Box

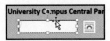

Move the text box

Step 4. Use the bottom-right corner sizing handle to re-size the text box so that it is tall and goes down the left side of the page. The size and position of the text box should now be about the same as the one in Figure S3-6.

Step 5. With the text box still selected, click the **FORMAT** tab. On the FORMAT ribbon, click **Shape Fill**. A list of colors appears. Select a dark orange. **Orange, Accent 2** works well.

Step 6. Save the document. Click somewhere off the text box so it is no longer selected.

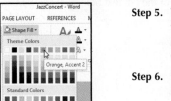

Select color for Shape Fill

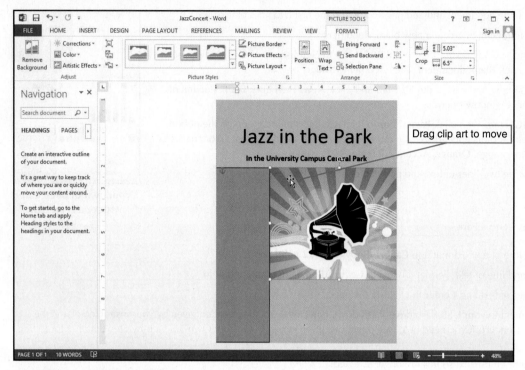

FIGURE S3-6
Position the clip art graphic along the top and left side of the tall text box.

On Your Own 3.10 Step-by-Step Solution   How to Insert Clip Art and a Text Box
into a Document

Create the JazzConcert Document: Part 2 of 5

Do the following to add the gramophone clip art to your *Jazz in the Park* document:

Step 1.   Change the page view so that you can see the entire page in your Word window.

Step 2.   Position your insertion point outside the text boxes and after the two lines of text at the top of the document.

Step 3.   Click the **INSERT** tab. Click **Online Pictures**. In the Office.com Clip Art box, enter **gramophone** and press **Enter**. Scroll down in the list of clip art to locate the gramophone clip art and click it. Click **Insert**. The clip art appears in the document and is selected.

> **Not Working?** You need to be connected to the Internet when using the Online Pictures tool. Also, the Microsoft websites change often. If you can't find the clip art used here, substitute another.

Step 4.   Click the **FORMAT** tab. Click **Wrap Text** and click **Square**. The graphic is now a floating graphic.

Step 5.   Resize and move the graphic into position, aligning the top of the graphic with the top of the tall text box (see Figure S3-6). Don't worry if the enlarged graphic spills off the page on the right side.

Step 6.   Save your document.

Follow these steps to add the second text box:

Step 1. Insert a second text box that will fit at the bottom of the page. Move and resize the text box so that it fits along both sides and across the bottom of the page, as shown in Figure S3-5. Fill the text box with the color **Red**.

Step 2. Zoom in from the whole page view so that you can view the page at 100%.

Step 3. Click in the red text box. An insertion point appears inside the box. Type **Sponsored by the Senior Class.**

Step 4. Select the text you just typed. Make the text **Italic**. Change its size to **24 point**. **Bold** and **Center** the text.

Step 5. Click the **FORMAT** tab. Click **Align Text**. Then click **Middle**. The text is now positioned in the middle of the text box.

Step 6. Save the document.

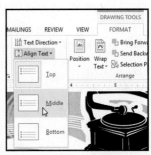

Align Text, Middle

Create the JazzConcert Document: Part 3 of 5

Follow these directions to insert a star and format it, adding text inside the star:

Step 1. Using the *Jazz in the Park* document, click the **INSERT** tab. Click **Shapes** and then click the **5-Point Star**.

Step 2. A cross insertion point + appears. Press and drag to create the star. (If you hold the Shift key down as you press and drag, the star stays in proportion.) Make the star large enough to hold text. The exact size and position can be changed later. The star is created with a blue fill color.

Step 3. With the star still selected, press and drag the white rotation handle to the left to rotate the star. Point the star toward the upper-left corner of the document.

Step 4. Right-click the star and click **Add Text** from the shortcut menu that appears. An insertion point blinks inside the star.

Step 5. Type the following text inside the star. You might need to use the Zoom slider to enlarge the page so that you can better see what you are typing:

Select Shape, 5-Point Star

Bring a chair or blanket!

Step 6. Select the text and change the text color to **Black** and **Bold** the text. Change the size of the text to **18 point**. Click somewhere off the star so that the text inside the star is no longer selected.

Step 7. Select the star. If you need to resize it so that all the text appears, do so now. On the **FORMAT** ribbon, click **Shape Fill**. Select **Yellow** for the star.

Step 8. Save the document.

Create the JazzConcert Document: Part 4 of 5

Follow these directions to add a text box with WordArt to your *Jazz in the Park* document:

Step 1. Insert a text box into the document. Position the box as shown earlier in Figure S3-5.

Step 2. Use the Shape Fill tool on the FORMAT ribbon to fill the text box with a light orange. **Orange Accent 2, Lighter 80%** works well.

Step 3. Enter the following text in the text box. You might want to use the Zoom slider to enlarge the documents so that you can better see what you type:

> **Not Working?** The FORMAT tab appears when text in a text box is selected.

Friday, October 9
9:30 PM to Midnight
Free Admission

Step 4. Select the first line of text. On the FORMAT ribbon, click the drop-down arrow beside the WordArt **Text Fill** button in the WordArt Styles group. Click **Gold, Accent 4, Darker 50%**.

Step 5. Click the drop-down arrow beside the WordArt **Text Effects** in the WordArt Styles group. Point to **Reflection** and select a reflection in the Reflection Variations group.

Step 6. Click the **HOME** ribbon and click **Bold**.

Step 7. Format the text size to **26 point**.

Step 8. Format the last two lines of text in **Calibri (Body), 18 point, bold**.

Step 9. Center all the text in the text box. Align the text in the middle of the text box.

Step 10. Take a moment to look back at Figure S3-5. Correct any problems you see with your work and save the document.

WordArt text fill, color selected

WordArt text effects, reflection selected

On Your Own 3.13 Step-by-Step Solution   **How to Save a Document as a PDF File**

Create the JazzConcert Document: Part 5 of 5

This solution has two sections:

▶ How to Save a Document as a PDF to Your Computer

▶ How to Save a Document as a PDF to Your OneDrive

How to Save a Document as a PDF to Your Computer

Follow these steps to save a document as a PDF file to your hard drive, USB flash drive, or another local storage device:

Step 1. Save the document as usual.

Step 2. Click the **FILE** tab. Click **Save As**. The Save As window appears. Choose your location to save the document. A second Save As window appears.

Step 3. In the Save As window, in the field labeled *Save as type*, select **PDF** (see Figure S3-7). Save the file in the same location where you saved the Word document file.

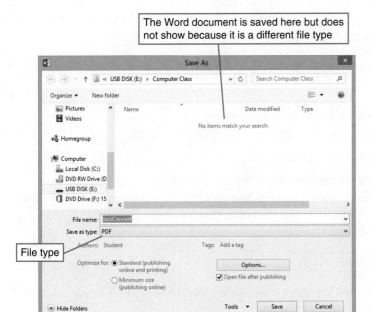

FIGURE S3-7
The PDF file is saved to the USB flash drive where the Word document file was previously saved.

Step 4. Click **Save**. A PDF file is created. Close the Word window.

Step 5. If you are using Windows 8, open **File Explorer**. If you are using Windows 7, open **Windows Explorer**. Verify that you have saved two files: the JazzConcert.docx file and the JazzConcert.pdf file. Double-click the PDF file. The PDF file opens and can be viewed. You will not be able to edit the PDF file unless you have PDF editing software installed.

How to Save a Document as a PDF to Your OneDrive

Recall that OneDrive is also called SkyDrive in several places in Office applications and in Windows. Follow these steps to save a document as a PDF file to your OneDrive:

Step 1. Save the Word document as usual.

Step 2. Click the **FILE** tab. Click **Save As**. Select your SkyDrive (or OneDrive) and then click the **Documents** folder on your OneDrive. (Windows might ask you to sign on to your Microsoft account.) The Save As window appears.

Step 3. In the field labeled *Save as type*, select **PDF**. Click **Save**. The PDF file is saved to your OneDrive.

Step 4. The SkyDrive app in Windows 8 is still called SkyDrive even though it uses OneDrive. If you are using Windows 8, open the **SkyDrive** app on your Start screen and verify that the file is saved to your OneDrive Documents folder. If you are using Windows 7, open **Internet Explorer**, go to the **live.com** site, and verify that the files are saved to your OneDrive Documents folder. If you need help navigating the live.com site, see the On Your Own 2.8 Step-by-Step Solution.

On Your Own 3.14 Step-by-Step Solution   **How to Use a Thank You Note Template**

Create the ThankYou Document

Word finds templates online, so make sure you are connected to the Internet. Then follow these steps to find and use the template:

Step 1. Open Microsoft Word. On the FILE tab, click **New**. A list of templates appears (see Figure 3-16 in the chapter). Click **Cards** in the menu below the search box. In the Category pane on the right, click **Business**. Scroll down to and click **Administrative professional thank you card (quarter-fold)**. Select the template shown in Figure 3-17 in the chapter.

Search box with menu below

> **Not Working?** If you don't see Cards in a menu under the search box when opening a new document, you are not connected to the Internet. If the template you're looking for has already been downloaded to your computer, you might see it listed on the screen and you can select it. If not, you must connect to the Internet to continue. Close Word, make sure you have an Internet connection, and then open Word again.

> **Not Working?** Microsoft websites change often. If you don't find the template used here, select another one for a thank you card.

Step 2. With the template selected, click **Create**. A new document is created.

Step 3. If necessary, zoom in on the document so that you can read and edit the text.

Step 4. The text you need to edit appears upside down on the screen. To edit the text, click in it. The text box turns right side up so you can see your edits. Replace the text on the left with the text on the right:

Text in Template	Replace With
With appreciation	To Sheila, with appreciation

Step 5. The text should now look like that in Figure S3-8. Click anywhere off the text box. The text should again appear upside down. (Remember, if you make a mistake, click Undo to undo your change.)

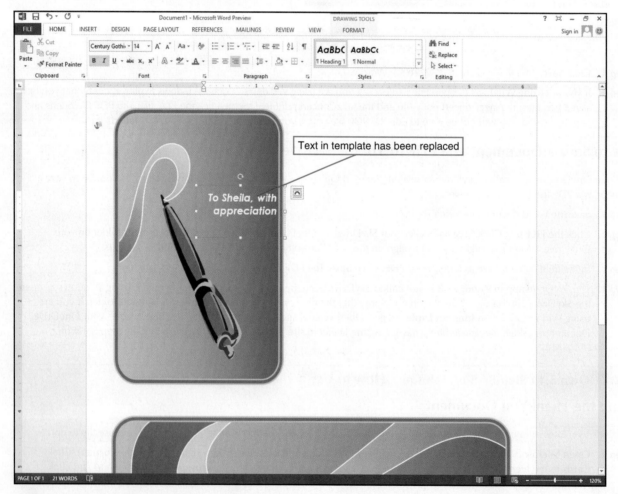

FIGURE S3-8
Select and replace text in the document to suit your own needs.

Step 6. Check the document properties and verify that the author of the document is your name. Save the document to your USB flash drive, hard drive, OneDrive, or other location given by your instructor. Name the document **ThankYou**.

Step 7. Print the document. Fold the printed page in half and then in quarters so that the document looks like a quarter-fold card.

CHAPTER 4 STEP-BY-STEP SOLUTIONS
Using OneNote to Research Online

The solutions in this appendix are for you to use if you get stuck when doing an On Your Own activity in the chapter. To learn how to teach yourself a computer skill, always try the On Your Own activity first before turning to these solutions.

> **Not Working?** Websites change from time to time. The step-by-step instructions were accurate when we wrote them, but be aware that you might have to adjust them to account for later website changes.

On Your Own 4.1 Step-by-Step Solution   How to Create and Set Up a New Notebook in OneNote

Collect the Peace Corps Research in OneNote: Part 1 of 9

This solution has two parts:

▶ How to create a new notebook

▶ How to set up the notebook for research

How to Create a New Notebook

Follow these steps to open OneNote:

Step 1. If you are using Windows 8, go to the **Start screen** and click the **OneNote 2013** tile. You may have to scroll to the right to find it, or you can type **OneNote** to search for the app. If a box appears asking you to sign in to OneDrive or SkyDrive, you can sign in or just close the box.

Step 2. If you are using Windows 7, click **Start**, click **All Programs**, click **Microsoft Office 2013**, and click **OneNote 2013**.

Step 3. When OneNote is started, it opens any notebooks already identified on your computer. Compare your OneNote window to Figure S4-1. The name of the open notebook is shown near the top left corner of the OneNote window. Your window might show no notebooks open or another notebook open.

> **Tip** When OneNote 2013 is started for the first time on your computer, a dialog box might appear asking if you would like to use OneNote as the default program for OneNote hyperlinks. If you see the box, you can click **Yes** and then click **Save**.

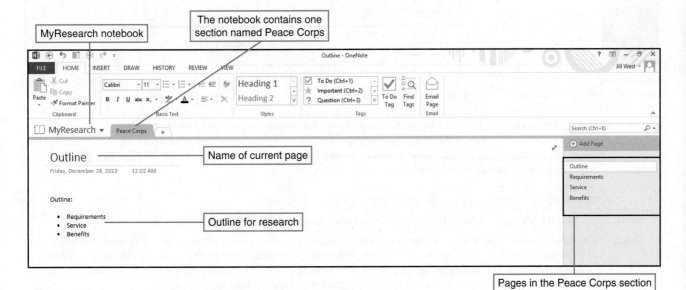

FIGURE S4-1
The OneNote window is used to manage notebooks, sections, pages, and notes.

Step 4. The ribbon at the top of the OneNote window should be displayed as shown in Figure S4-1. If you can't see the ribbon, click the **HOME** tab. The HOME ribbon appears. Click the **Pin the ribbon** icon ↠ to keep the ribbon pinned to the window.

Pin the ribbon

Create a new notebook and save it to your USB flash drive, hard drive, OneDrive, or another location given by your instructor. Follow these steps to create a new notebook on your USB flash drive or hard drive:

Step 1. If you are saving your notebook to your USB flash drive, insert the drive.

Step 2. Click the **FILE** tab and click **New**. The New Notebook window appears.

Step 3. Click **Computer**.

Step 4. Enter **MyResearch** as the Notebook Name.

Step 5. Click **Create in a different folder**. The Create New Notebook dialog box appears.

Step 6. To save the notebook to your USB flash drive, click it in the left pane. If you want to save the notebook in a folder on the USB flash drive, double-click the folder in the right pane to drill down into it. For example, Figure S4-2 shows the MyResearch notebook about to be saved to the Computer Class folder on the USB flash drive. Click **Create** to create the new blank notebook.

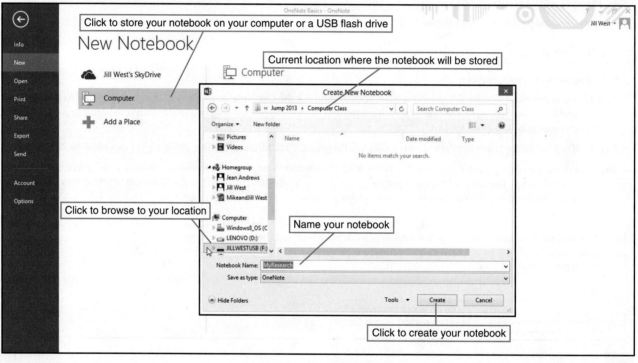

FIGURE S4-2
The new notebook will be created in the Computer Class folder on the USB flash drive.

Step 7. To save the notebook to your hard drive, know that Windows has already created the OneNote Notebooks folder in the Documents library. This folder is the default location for saving notebooks on your hard drive. In the left pane of the Create New Notebook dialog box, click **Documents** in the Libraries group. Double-click the **OneNote Notebooks** folder to open that folder. Click **Create** to create the new blank notebook.

To save the notebook to the OneDrive you created in Chapter 2, follow these steps:

Step 1. Click the **FILE** tab and click **New**. The New Notebook window appears.

Step 2. Make sure OneDrive is selected. If you are not already signed in to your Microsoft account, including your OneDrive, you can do so now. To sign in, click **Sign in** in the upper-right corner of the screen and enter your email address and password to your Microsoft account. Figure S4-3 shows the New Notebook screen after Jean Andrews is signed in. If the account name you see displayed on your screen is not the correct account, do the following:

   1. Click **Account**. On the Account window, click **Remove** and click **Yes**.

   2. Click **New** to return to the New Notebook window. Click **Sign In** and sign in to your Microsoft account using your email address and password. Your OneDrive should now be listed on the New Notebook window.

FIGURE S4-3
When signed in to your Microsoft account, you can save a notebook to your OneDrive.

Step 3. Enter **MyResearch** as the Notebook Name. Click **Create Notebook**. A dialog box appears asking if you would like to share the notebook. To continue without sharing, click **Not now**. By default, the notebook is saved in the Documents folder on your OneDrive.

> **Tip** If you have already shared the Documents folder with your instructor, he or she has access to the notebook saved in this folder.

Do the following to verify where your OneNote notebooks are stored:

Step 1. Click the **FILE** tab.

Step 2. Click **Info**. All open notebooks are listed along with their locations. In Figure S4-4, notice the first notebook is saved to the USB flash drive, the second is saved to the hard drive, and the third is saved to OneDrive. Your locations might be different.

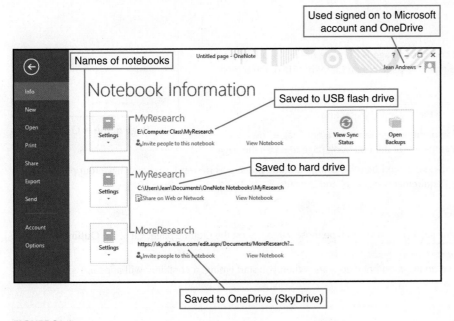

FIGURE S4-4
The Info window displays the names and locations of open notebooks.

> **Tip** If you want to close a notebook, click **Settings** in the Info window shown in Figure S4-4 and then click **Close** in the drop-down menu. To open a notebook, click the **FILE** tab and click **Open**.

How to Set Up OneNote for Research

Follow these steps to rename the existing section and page:

Step 1. Click the **HOME** tab. Verify that the MyResearch notebook is the current notebook.

> **Not Working?** If MyResearch is not the current notebook, click the down arrow ▼ to the right of the current notebook and click **MyResearch** in the list of notebooks.

Step 2. After a notebook is created, OneNote shows the blank notebook. Notice that the notebook has only one section titled *New Section 1* and only one page called *Untitled page*.

Step 3. Right-click the **New Section 1** tab. In the shortcut menu that appears (see Figure S4-5), click **Rename**. Type **Peace Corps** and press **Enter**. The section is now named Peace Corps.

FIGURE S4-5
Rename the section.

Drop down menu to select notebook

Step 4. The text field in the upper-left corner of a page is the page name. Click in the text field and type **Outline**. As you type, the page tab on the right side of the screen changes names.

Page name is Outline

Follow these steps to add three new pages to the Peace Corps section:

Step 1. Click **Add Page** on the right side of the screen to create a new page. Then type **Requirements** in the text field at the top of the notebook page to name the page.

Step 2. Create a page titled **Service** and a page titled **Benefits** using the same process as in step 1. You now have four pages to hold your research named Outline, Requirements, Service, and Benefits.

Follow these steps to add the outline to the Outline page:

Step 1. Because you already know some subtopics, you can type those subtopics on the Outline page. Click the **Outline** page tab to return to that page.

Step 2. Click anywhere on the page and an insertion point appears. When you start typing, a container will appear. Type the following:

> Outline:
> Requirements
> Service
> Benefits

Step 3. To make the three subtopics a bulleted list, highlight them. On the HOME ribbon, click **Bullets** (see Figure S4-6).

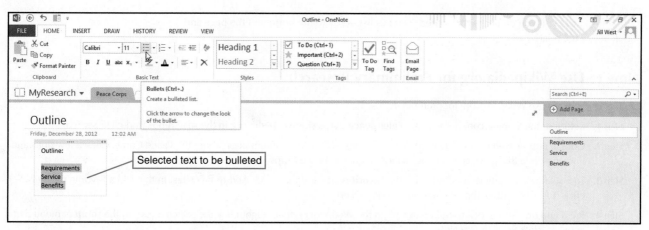

FIGURE S4-6
Create and format the outline on the Outline page to help you plan and organize your research.

Tip As you work with OneNote, notice how the commands are similar to the Word ribbons and commands. All Office applications have many common commands and elements.

Step 4. OneNote automatically saves the changes you've made to your notebook. Click the [✕] in the top-right corner of your screen to close OneNote.

On Your Own 4.2 Step-by-Step Solution   **How to Find Preliminary Research and Subtopics about Your Topic**

Collect the Peace Corps Research in OneNote: Part 2 of 9

This solution has three parts:

▶ How to use Google.com for preliminary research

▶ How to use Wikipedia.org for preliminary research

▶ How to use a clustering search engine

How to Use Google.com for Preliminary Research

Do the following to use Google.com for preliminary research:

Step 1. Open OneNote 2013. To open or select your MyResearch notebook, click the **FILE** tab. If you see your notebook listed under Notebook Information, click **View Notebook**. Your notebook appears. If you don't see your MyResearch notebook listed, click **Open**. If you saved your notebook on your OneDrive, click the **MyResearch** notebook under Open from OneDrive at the top of the screen.

Step 2. If you saved the notebook to a USB flash drive or hard drive, click **Computer** under Open from other locations in the bottom-left pane of the window. Under Computer in the bottom-right pane of the window, click the name of the folder where your notebook is located. The Open Notebook window appears. Click the **MyResearch** folder to select it, then click **Open** and click **Open** again. Your notebook appears.

Step 3. Using Internet Explorer, go to **google.com** and enter **peace corps** in the search box. As you type, Google autosuggest completes the search string. These suggestions might give you ideas for subtopics. Choose two subtopics and add those subtopics as pages in your OneNote notebook.

Google [peace corps]
　　　　peace corps
　　　　peace corps **jobs**
　　　　peace corps **wiki**
　　　　peace corps **application**

Google autosuggest

Step 4. In the Google results window, look for a list titled *Searches related*, *Something different*, or a similar title. In the list, Google gives suggestions for other topics that are similar. Look through these topics to see whether anything interests you. These topics may be useful if you need to broaden your topic. For example, a broader topic than the Peace Corps might be *volunteer service organizations*. Choose one broader topic and add that topic as a new page in your OneNote notebook.

Searches related to **peace corps**
peace corps **requirements**　　peace corps **jobs**
peace corps **alternatives**　　peace corps **blogs**
americorps　　　　　　　　peace corps **wiki**
peace corps **history**　　　　peace corps **headquarters**

Google related searches

> **Not Working?** If you don't see the related searches list, scroll to the bottom of the page and look below the related ads.

How to Use Wikipedia.org for Preliminary Research

Do the following to use Wikipedia.org for preliminary research:

Step 1. Return to the **Google.com** home page. Enter **peace corps site:wikipedia.org** in the search box and click **Search**.

Step 2. Google returns web pages only from Wikipedia.org, and all have information about the Peace Corps. Click a few links and find an article that gives general information about the Peace Corps.

Step 3. To bookmark the article you find, click the **Favorites** star and then click **Add to favorites**. In the Add a Favorite dialog box, click **Add**. The URL of the article is now bookmarked.

Step 4. Press and drag to select a useful paragraph in the Wikipedia article. Right-click the selected text. In the shortcut menu that appears, click **Send to OneNote**.

> **Not Working?** If you don't see Send to OneNote in the shortcut menu that appears, close OneNote and reopen it. This might be the first time OneNote is opened on your computer, and the link in the shortcut menu is added to the menu the first time you close OneNote.

Step 5. The Select Location in OneNote dialog box appears so that you can select the notebook, section, and page in OneNote that will receive the text (see Figure S4-7). If you don't see the Outline page, click the + sign to the left of MyResearch. Drill down to the **Peace Corps** section and click the **Outline** page. Click **OK**. The selected text is copied into OneNote.

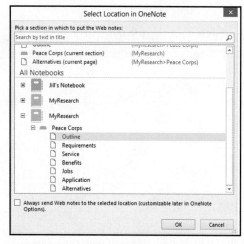

FIGURE S4-7
Select the notebook, section, and page to
receive the text.

Step 6. Go to the OneNote window and the Outline page to find the paragraph. The URL is listed below the paragraph as a link to the page where the paragraph was taken. If needed later, you can return to the page in your browser by clicking this link.

Step 7. Press and drag to select one sentence in the paragraph that you find important. With the text selected, click the **HOME** tab. On the HOME ribbon, select a color from the highlighting tool (see Figure S4-8). The sentence is now highlighted. Click anywhere on the page outside the text container.

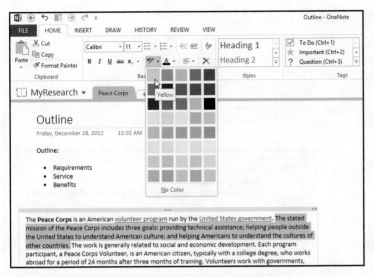

FIGURE S4-8
Highlight selected text in OneNote to mark important information for
your research.

Not Working? If you don't see the ribbons in the OneNote window, click the **HOME** tab
then click the **Pin the ribbon** icon ➥ to keep the ribbon pinned to the window.

Do the following to explore subtopics of the Peace Corps topic and insert text in OneNote:

Step 1. Make the **Internet Explorer** window the active window. The Wikipedia.org article is still
showing.

Step 2. Scroll down the page until you find the Contents section, which serves as an outline to a
Wikipedia.org article. Two topics you might consider for subtopics are the history of the
Peace Corps and laws concerning the Peace Corps. Add these subtopics as new pages in your
notebook.

How to Use a Clustering Search Engine

Do the following to use the carrot2.org search engine:

Step 1. Using Internet Explorer, go to **carrot2.org**. Enter **peace corps** in the search box and click
Search. A list of subtopics appears in the left pane, and hits appear in the right pane. To see a
circle visual of subtopics, click the **Circles** tab (see Figure S4-9). Click or double-click an item
in the circle to see more hits and subtopics.

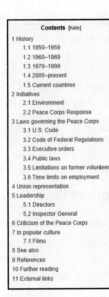

Wikipedia.org outline

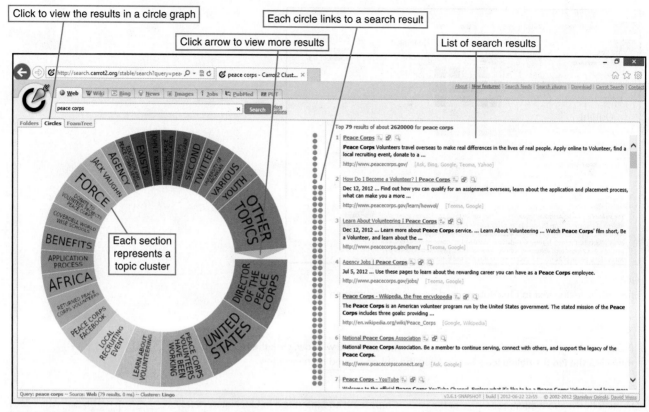

FIGURE S4-9
Carrot2.org gives a visualization of subtopics.

Step 2. To see a different type of visual for subtopics, click the **FoamTree** tab. Subtopics appear in a foam tree. Click an item to see hits about this subtopic.

Step 3. Choose one more subtopic to add to your notebook.

On·Your Own 4.3 Step-by-Step Solution   How to Use the OneNote Screen Clipping Tool

Collect the Peace Corps Research in OneNote: Part 3 of 9

Do the following to view Google Images and copy them into OneNote using the Screen Clipping tool:

Step 1. Using Internet Explorer, go to **www.google.com**. Type **peace corps** in the search field and press **Enter**. Click **Images** at the top of the screen. Images related to the Peace Corps appear.

Step 2. Return to the OneNote window and click the **INSERT** tab. Then click **Screen Clipping**. The OneNote window disappears, and a crosshair **+** appears for your pointer. Press and drag the pointer to select one or more images from the Google window. The Select Location in OneNote dialog box appears.

Step 3. Under Recent Picks, select **Outline** and click **Send to Selected Location**. The images are copied onto the Outline page of OneNote.

Step 4. If you don't like the location of the container boxes on the page, press and drag them to move them on the page.

> **Tip** OneNote keeps the Send to OneNote Tool icon in the Windows taskbar for easy access. To use the tool, click the **Send to OneNote Tool** icon in the taskbar and then click **Screen Clipping** in the box that appears (see Figure S4-10).

FIGURE S4-10
The Screen Clipping tool allows you to easily insert graphics into OneNote.

On Your Own 4.4 Step-by-Step Solution   How to Find Online Newspaper Articles and Blogs

Collect the Peace Corps Research in OneNote: Part 4 of 9

Follow these steps to find a newspaper article about the Peace Corps and save the information to OneNote:

Step 1. Using Internet Explorer, go to the Google News site at **news.google.com**.

Step 2. Enter this search string: **peace corps volunteers make a difference.**

Step 3. Find one article describing the difference a Peace Corps volunteer has made in a foreign country. Highlight text in the article and then right-click the text. In the shortcut menu that appears, click **Send to OneNote** (see Figure S4-11). Select the **Service** page of OneNote and click **OK**. The text goes to OneNote and OneNote becomes your active window; verify that your research text got copied to OneNote.

Google search string

FIGURE S4-11
Send the highlighted text to OneNote.

Step 4.   Using the Highlighter tool in OneNote, highlight text in the paragraph that you think is most useful.

Step 5.   Include on the page in OneNote all the information you will need to cite the newspaper article later in your Works Cited list. This information includes

- ▶ Author of the article (might not be available)
- ▶ Article title
- ▶ Newspaper title (for example, *Taunton Gazette*)
- ▶ Date published (month, day, year)
- ▶ URL (for example, www.tauntongazette.com)
- ▶ Date you accessed the web page

Figure S4-12 shows the content and citation information for one article. Yours might be different.

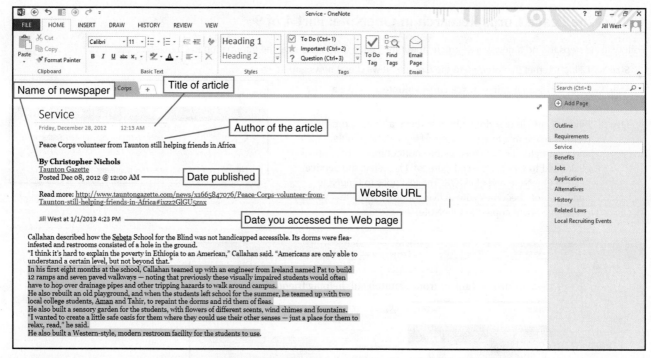

FIGURE S4-12
An online newspaper article requires you cite the author, title of the article, newspaper, date published, and the date you accessed the article online.

Follow these steps to find a recent blog written by a Peace Corps volunteer:

Step 1.   Using Internet Explorer, go to **google.com**.

Step 2.   The two most popular blogging sites are wordpress.com and blogspot.com. Use one of these search strings in the Google search box:

   peace corps blog site:blogspot.com

   peace corps blog site:wordpress.com

Step 3.   Just above the search results, click **Search tools**. Click the **Any time** drop-down menu and select **Past year**.

Step 4.   Click links and find a blog entry that describes what it's like to serve in the Peace Corps. Highlight and then right-click the text. In the shortcut menu that appears, click **Send to OneNote**. Select the Service page or the Benefits page of OneNote and click **OK**. The text goes to OneNote, and OneNote becomes your active window; verify that your research text got copied to OneNote.

Step 5.   Using the Highlighter tool in OneNote, highlight text that you think is most useful.

Step 6. Use either the text selection method or the Screen Clipping method to copy the citation information into OneNote. Include this information:

▶ Author of the blog (if available)

▶ Title of the blog

▶ Date of the blog entry

▶ URL

▶ Date you accessed the site

Figure S4-13 shows one blog entry and citation information in OneNote, but yours might look different.

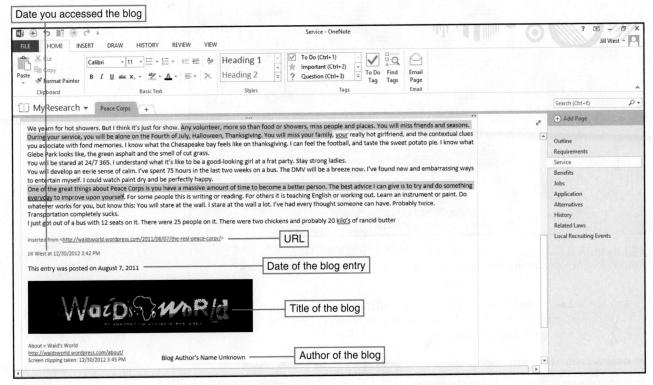

FIGURE S4-13
A blog entry requires you cite the author, title of the blog, date of the blog entry, URL, and date you accessed the site.

On Your Own 4.5 Step-by-Step Solution   How to Use Wikipedia.org to Locate and Collect Authoritative Content

Collect the Peace Corps Research in OneNote: Part 5 of 9

Wikipedia.org is not an authoritative source, but it can lead you to these sources. Do the following to use Wikipedia.org to locate authoritative content:

Step 1. Using Internet Explorer, click the **Favorites** star. In the list of Favorites, click the Peace Corps Wikipedia article you bookmarked earlier. The article appears in your browser window.

Step 2. Scroll down the article to find a section labeled **References** and another section labeled **Further reading**. Links in these sections can lead you to authoritative content.

Step 3. Scroll down toward the bottom of the article to find **External links**. This list is likely to include a link to the official Peace Corps website at www.peacecorps.gov. Click that link.

> **Not Working?** Wikipedia.org articles change often. The article you found might not have a link to the www.peacecorps.gov website. If this is the case, go directly to the **www.peacecorps.gov** site.

Step 4. Bookmark the **www.peacecorps.gov** site. Because the site has a .gov top-level domain name, you can conclude that the Peace Corps is an agency of the government.

Step 5. Find information on the site about who can be a volunteer. Highlight and then right-click the text. In the shortcut menu that appears, click **Send to OneNote**. Select the **Requirements** page of OneNote and click **OK**. The text goes to OneNote, and OneNote becomes your active window; verify that your research text got copied to OneNote. Figure S4-14 shows text on the Peace Corps site that answers this question along with several others in this activity. However, remember that websites might change, so the text you find on the site might be different.

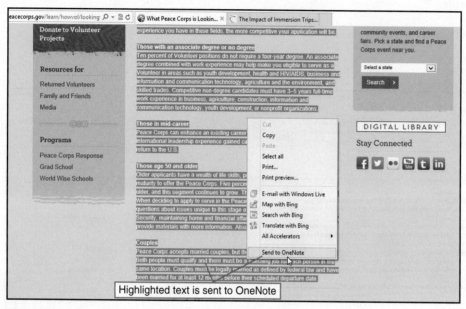

FIGURE S4-14
Text on the www.peacecorps.gov site's FAQs page answers several research questions.

Step 6. Go back to the Internet Explorer window, find text describing the application process and send the text to the Requirements page of OneNote, and then verify that the text was sent to OneNote successfully. Figure S4-15 shows this text, but the text you find might be different.

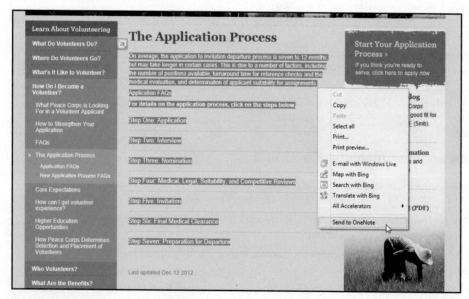

FIGURE S4-15
Text on the application process to be copied into OneNote.

Step 7. Return to the Peace Corps website and find text on how long is the commitment a volunteer makes to the Peace Corps. If you have not already sent the text to the Requirements page in OneNote, do so now and verify that the text was sent.

Step 8. Return to the Peace Corps website and find text describing the training. If you have not already sent the text to the Requirements page in OneNote, do so now and verify that the text was sent.

Step 9. Return to the Peace Corps website and find text on the types of jobs a volunteer might do. If you have not already sent the text to OneNote, do so now and verify that the text was sent.

Step 10. Use the highlighting tool you learned to use earlier in the chapter to highlight important text in all segments just copied.

In our example, we stored all the answers to our research questions in five segments of text copied from the www.peacecorps.gov site onto the Requirements page of OneNote.

Follow these steps to include citation information in OneNote:

Step 1. Citation information for a website includes the title of the website. The title of this site showing on its home page is Peace Corps. Copy the text **Peace Corps** from the web page to OneNote or type the text in OneNote on the Requirements page.

> **Not Working?** If the title of a web page is a link or a graphic, you might have trouble copying the text. In this case, type the web page title into OneNote or use the Screen Clipping tool to copy the title into OneNote.

Step 2. To insert the date you accessed the site, right-click on the OneNote page where you want the date to appear. A shortcut menu appears. Click the date (see Figure S4-16). The date is inserted on the page.

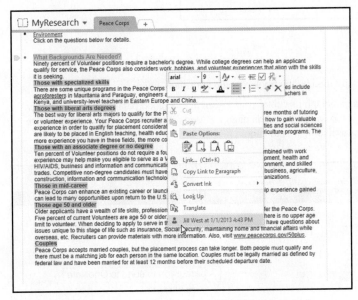

FIGURE S4-16
Insert the date a website was accessed.

On Your Own 4.6 Step-by-Step Solution   How to Find Books Using Wikipedia.org, Google Books, and Worldcat.org

Collect the Peace Corps Research in OneNote: Part 6 of 9

Do the following to use Wikipedia.org, Google Books, and Amazon.com to find a book and its text online:

Step 1. Using Internet Explorer Favorites, return to the Wikipedia.org article about the Peace Corps that you bookmarked earlier.

Step 2. Look in the **Further reading** section and find a book about serving in the Peace Corps. One book found in the chapter is *So, You Want to Join the Peace Corps: What to Know Before You Go,* by Banerjee Dillon, but you might find a different book.

Step 3. Go to **google.com** and enter **peace corps** in the search box and press **Enter**. Click **More** and click **Books**. A list of books appears. Figure S4-17 shows the list where we found a similar book by Dillon, *The Insider's Guide to the Peace Corps: What to Know Before You Go*.

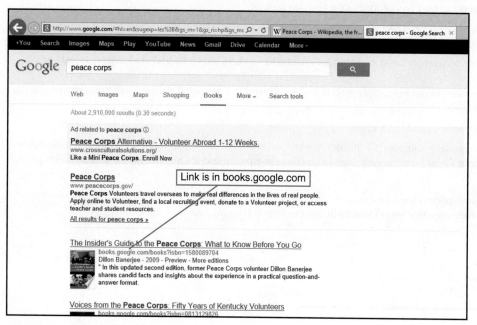

FIGURE S4-17
Google Books provides books online.

Step 4. Click a book in the hit list. Be sure to select a link provided by the books.google.com site.

Step 5. Scroll down through the pages of the book to find a paragraph useful for your research. One good paragraph in *The Insider's Guide to the Peace Corps: What to Know Before You Go* can be found on page 115 (see Figure S4-18). In the figure, notice the search box in the left pane that you can use to search for text in the book.

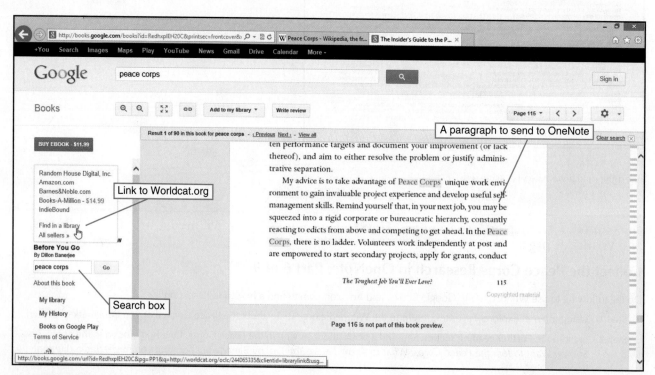

FIGURE S4-18
Google Books presents some of the pages in a book.

Not Working? If pages in the book are not available at books.google.com, try looking for the book on Amazon.com.

Step 6. You can't select text on the book pages for copying into OneNote, but you can do a Screen Clipping of the paragraph. Go to the OneNote window.

Step 7. In the Peace Corps section of OneNote, select the **Service** page. Click somewhere on the page where you want the clipping to go. Click the **INSERT** tab and click **Screen Clipping**. Select the paragraph on the Google Books page. The selection is copied into OneNote.

Step 8. If the page number where you found the paragraph in the book is not showing in the OneNote clipping, type the page number on the OneNote page for future reference.

Do the following to put the citation information into OneNote:

Step 1. Return to the Google Books page and find the citation information. You need the title and author of the book, the publisher, city of publication, and year of copyright. You can likely find all of this information on the page following the front cover.

Step 2. With the citation information displayed, return to OneNote. On the INSERT ribbon, click **Screen Clipping**. Use the Screen Clipping tool to copy the information into OneNote (see Figure S4-19).

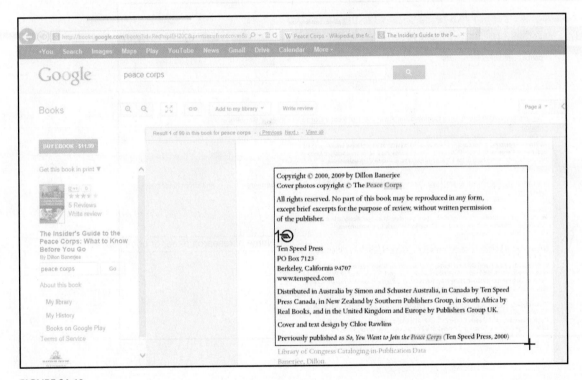

FIGURE S4-19
Look for publication information about a book on the first page of the book.

If you cannot find a book online or the pages in the book are not available online, use Worldcat.org to find a library that holds the book. Follow these steps:

Step 1. With the book displayed in Google Books, click **Find in a library** in the left pane (see Figure S4-18). The link takes you to the Worldcat.org site, which shows libraries near you that hold the book.

Find in a library

> **Not Working?** If the link to the Worldcat.org site doesn't take you directly to the book, enter the title of the book in the search box on the Worldcat.org web page.

Step 2. To get more accurate results, enter your ZIP Code in the *Enter your location* box on the Worldcat.org page. (You might need to scroll down the page to find the link.) Then click **Find libraries**. Which is the closest library to you that holds the book?

On Your Own 4.7 Step-by-Step Solution **How to Use Google Scholar to Find a Journal Article**

Collect the Peace Corps Research in OneNote: Part 7 of 9

Do the following to use Google Scholar to find a journal article:

Step 1. Using Internet Explorer, go to **scholar.google.com**. Enter **peace corps volunteer benefits** in the search box and click **Enter**. A list of scholarly articles and books appears.

Step 2. Notice on the left of the page you can limit the search to recent years to find current sources (see Figure S4-20). Limit your search to articles written since 2008.

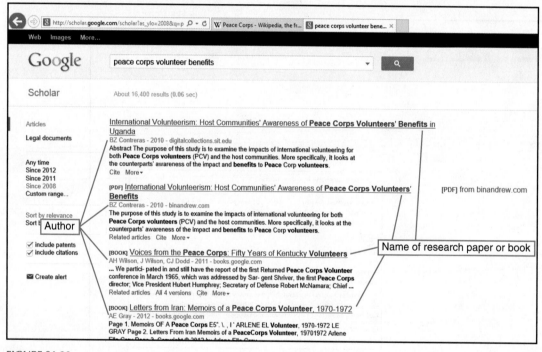

FIGURE S4-20
Google Scholar returns journals and books.

Step 3. Click some links and find an article that you think is useful. For example, one article is shown in Figure S4-21, but you might find a different article.

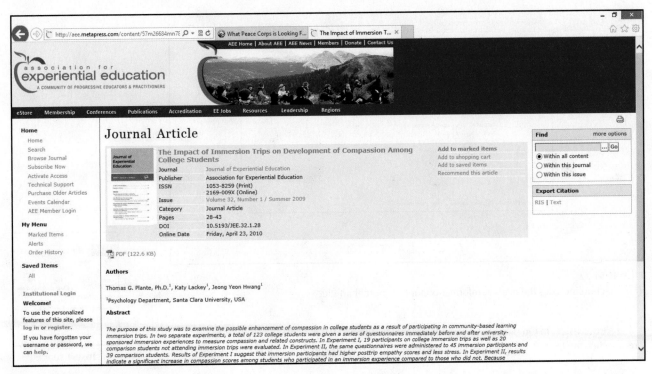

FIGURE S4-21

This web page shows an article abstract taken from the Journal of Experiential Education.

Step 4. Select and copy the abstract of the article onto the Benefits page of OneNote. In OneNote, highlight any text that you think is important.

Step 5. Copy into OneNote all the information you need to cite the article. For a journal article, you need

- ▶ Author name
- ▶ Title of the article
- ▶ Journal title
- ▶ Volume number
- ▶ Issue number (if applicable)
- ▶ Date published
- ▶ Pages the article spans or first page if the article jumps pages

Select the text or use the Screen Clipping tool to copy the citation information for your article into OneNote. Figure S4-22 shows the information to be copied into OneNote for the article shown earlier in Figure S4-21, but your citation information might be different.

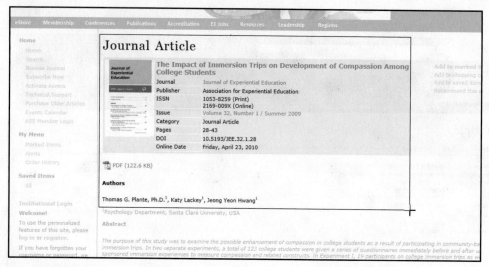

FIGURE S4-22
The selection includes the citation information for this journal article.

Insert space

> **Not Working?** In OneNote, if you need to move containers down on a page to make more room, click the **INSERT** tab and then click **Insert Space**. Then press and drag to make more room.

Step 6. Many websites display the abstract but not the full article. To view the full text of the article, click a link on the page. For example, in Figure S4-22, you would click **PDF (122.6 KB)** to view the full PDF of the article. However, when this link is clicked, a message appears saying that the PDF of the article is available only to members of a specific organization. Some websites make their articles available to the public, but you must pay a fee. Your school pays for subscriptions to many journals. Rather than pay for the article yourself, see if you can use your school library website to locate and view the article for free.

On Your Own 4.8 Step-by-Step Solution   **How to Explore Your School Library's Website**

Collect the Peace Corps Research in OneNote: Part 8 of 9

Do the following to use your school library website:

Step 1. Determine the URL of your school's website. If you are not sure, ask your instructor.

Step 2. Using Internet Explorer, access that website. Look on the home page to find a link to sign on to the site.

Step 3. Log on to the site using your user ID and password assigned by your school. If you don't know your user ID and password, ask your instructor to whom you should go to find out. You might have to retrieve the information through your school's website.

> **Not Working?** Some school library websites provide a list of organization-wide passwords for each database rather than requiring you to sign in as an individual user. If there's nowhere to sign in on your library's website, look for an online library resources list or something similar to find these passwords. You may have to sign in to a different part of your school's website to access these passwords.

Step 4. Go to the online library and explore the online databases that your library provides.

Step 5. Try to find the journal article you found using Google Scholar earlier in the chapter. For example, for one school library website, this article can be found on the library site and is shown in Figure S4-23. Can you find your article?

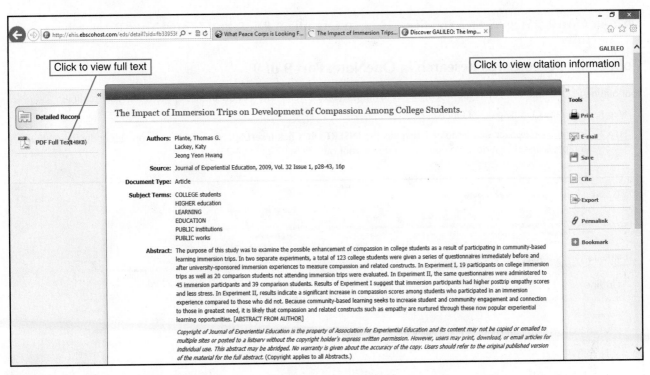

FIGURE S4-23
The full text of a journal article is available by way of a school library's website.

Step 6. Try to view the full article. For example, in Figure S4-23, to view the full article, you would click **PDF Full Text**. Can you view the full text of your article?

Step 7. Is there a link on your web page to view the citation information? For example, in Figure S4-23, to view the citation information for this article, click **Cite**. The citation information is shown in Figure S4-24. Copy the text under **Works Cited** into OneNote. This text is formatted exactly as it should appear in a Works Cited list. Can you find citation information already prepared for a Works Cited list?

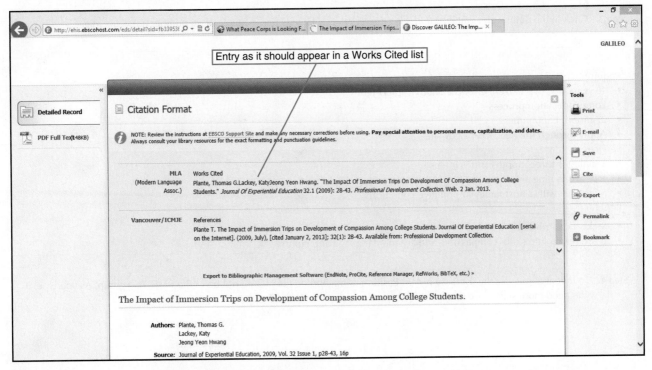

FIGURE S4-24
The web page provides citation information already arranged and formatted for a Works Cited list.

Collect the Peace Corps Research in OneNote: Part 9 of 9

Your outline in OneNote will guide you when you are writing your research paper. Follow these steps to refine your outline:

Step 1.   Go to the Outline page of OneNote.

Step 2.   To open some space under the outline, click the **INSERT** tab. Click **Insert Space**. Position your pointer under the outline and press and drag it down to open space under your outline (see Figure S4-25).

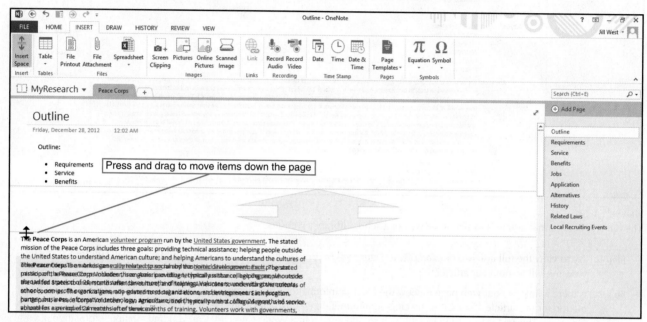

FIGURE S4-25
Insert space under the outline to make room for more text.

Step 3.   Click in the outline and edit it so that it is more complete. Here is one example of an outline, but yours might be different:

Outline:
- Requirements
  - 18 years old, U.S. citizen, physical health is important
  - Long application process
  - 27-month commitment
  - Apply through the peacecorps.gov site
- Service
  - Training is three months and is intense
  - Jobs are in nine areas
  - Might live with a host family in primitive conditions
- Benefits
  - Make a contribution to others
  - Learn leadership skills, compassion, and another language and culture

Step 4.   To indent a line, use the **Increase Indent Position** command on the HOME ribbon in the Basic Text group. As you type, if you need more space, use the **Insert Space** command on the **INSERT** ribbon.

To practice copying a note container from one page to another page in OneNote, follow these steps:

Step 1. Go to the Requirements page. Right-click the title bar of any container on the page. The container is selected and a short-cut menu appears. Click **Copy** on the shortcut menu.

Step 2. Click the **Service** tab to go to that page. Scroll down to the bottom of the page and right-click white space below the last entry on the page. In the shortcut menu, click the leftmost **Paste** icon. The container is copied to the page.

> **Hint** If you want to move a container from one page to another rather than copy the container, use **Cut** and **Paste** rather than Copy and Paste on the shortcut menus.

Step 3. To delete the new entry you just made on the Service page, right-click in the title bar of the container and click **Delete** from the shortcut menu.

To delete unused pages in your notebook, do the following:

Step 1. Click the Outline page. Notice there is content on this page, so leave it be.

Step 2. Click the Requirements page. Again, there is content on this page, so leave it in place.

Step 3. Continue checking each page. When you get to a page with no content, right-click the page name in the pages list on the right side of the screen and click **Delete**.

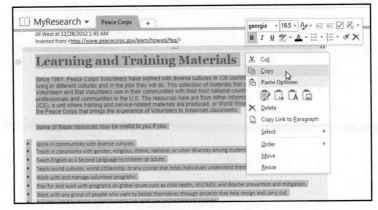
Copy container

If you have access to a printer, follow these steps to print the entire Peace Corps section of your OneNote notebook:

Step 1. Click the **FILE** tab. Click **Print**. Click **Print Preview**. The Print Preview and Settings dialog box appears. In the drop-down list under **Print range**, select **Current Section**, (see Figure S4-26).

Paste container

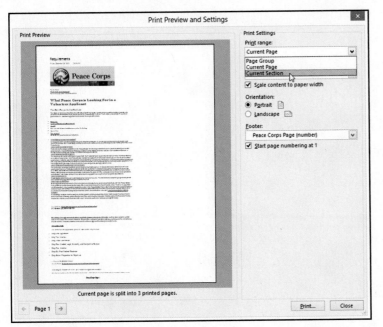

FIGURE S4-26
Print all the pages in the current section of your OneNote notebook.

Step 2. Click **Print**. The Print dialog box appears. Select your printer and click **Print**. All the pages in the section print.

Follow these steps to create an .mht file that contains all the research notes in the Peace Corps section of your notebook:

Step 1. Click the **FILE** tab. Click **Export**. In the Export Current area, click **Section**. In the Select Format area, click **Single File Web Page (*.mht)**. Click **Export**. The Save As dialog box appears.

Step 2. Point to the location to save the file and click **Save**. The Peace Corps file is created.

Step 3. To view the file, open **File Explorer** in Windows 8 or **Windows Explorer** in Windows 7. Locate the **Peace Corps** file and double-click it. The file displays in Internet Explorer.

CHAPTER 5 STEP-BY-STEP SOLUTIONS
Writing Research Papers Using Word Templates and Tools

The solutions in this appendix are for you to use if you get stuck when doing an On Your Own activity in the chapter. To learn how to teach yourself a computer skill, always try the On Your Own activity first before turning to these solutions.

On Your Own 5.1 Step-by-Step Solution   How to Create a Document Using an MLA Template

Create the Peace Corps Paper: Part 1 of 9

This solution has three parts:

▶ How to download and use an MLA template to create a document

▶ What to do if you can't find the template

▶ How to examine and save the document

How to Download and Use an MLA Template to Create a Document

Do the following to download an MLA template and create a document using this template:

Step 1. If Microsoft Word is already open, click the **FILE** tab and click **New**. If Microsoft Word is not already open, open it. Either way, a list of templates appears.

Step 2. In the search box, enter **MLA style research paper** and press **Enter**. Click **MLA style research paper** to select it. Then click **Create**. The new document is created.

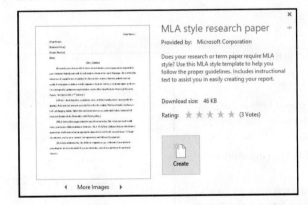

What to Do If You Can't Find the Template

Office.com occasionally changes the templates it makes available. If you can't find the MLA style research paper template, know that we have provided in the sample_files folder the MLA_Research_Paper document that was created using the template. Do the following to use the document:

Step 1. Locate the sample_files folder, which is stored on the www.pearsonhigher.com/jump website and in MyITLab. Recall that you downloaded the sample_files folder to your USB flash drive in Chapter 2. If you need more help finding the folder, see On Your Own Step-by-Step Solution 2.7 in this appendix.

Step 2. Open File Explorer (called Windows Explorer in Windows 7). Drill down to the **sample_files** folder.

Step 3. Double-click the **MLA_Research_Paper** document. The document opens in Word.

How to Examine and Save the Document

Do the following to examine the document that was created using the MLA template:

Step 1. To display paragraph marks, click the **Show/Hide** button on the **HOME** ribbon. Identify on your screen the items labeled in Figure S5-1.

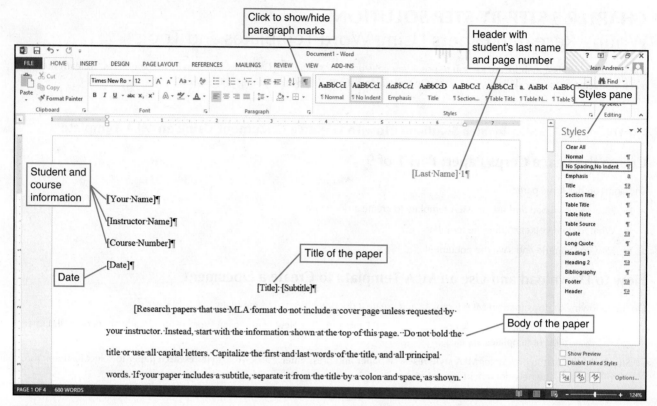

FIGURE S5-1

A document is created using an MLA template for a research paper.

Step 2. If you don't see the Styles pane on the right side of the window, on the HOME ribbon, click the down arrow ⬇ in the bottom-right corner of the Styles group. The Styles pane appears.

Step 3. To determine what style is applied to the first paragraph, click somewhere in the paragraph. The style that is applied to the text is selected in the Styles pane. The selected style is the **Normal** style.

Step 4. In the Styles pane, right-click the **Normal** style and select **Modify** from the shortcut menu. The Modify Style dialog box appears.

Step 5. In the lower-left corner of the box, click **Format** and select **Paragraph** from the menu. The Paragraph dialog box appears. You can view all the paragraph formatting required by MLA for the style (see Figure S5-2). If necessary, you can make changes to the style using this box.

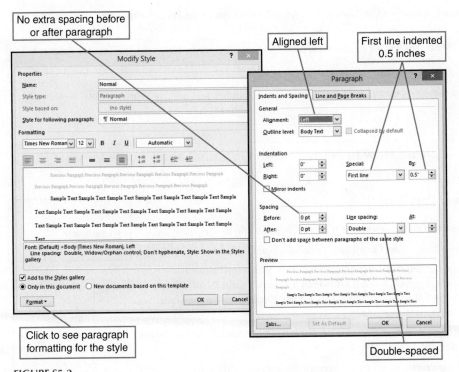

FIGURE S5-2
The formatting for a style can be viewed and modified.

Step 6. Click **Cancel** twice to close both dialog boxes. (If you had made changes to the style, you would click **OK** to save these changes.)

Step 7. To save the document, click the **FILE** tab and click **Save As**. Save the document to your USB flash drive, hard drive, OneDrive, or other location given by your instructor. Name the document **PeaceCorpsPaper**.

On Your Own 5.2 Step-by-Step Solution   How to Open the OneNote Notebook to View Research Notes and Text for the Paper

Create the Peace Corps Paper: Part 2 of 9

Follow these steps to open the notebook:

Step 1. Open **File Explorer** (called Windows Explorer in Windows 7).

Step 2. Locate the sample_files folder, which is stored on the www.pearsonhighered.com/jump website and in MyITLab. Recall that you downloaded the sample_files folder to your USB flash drive in Chapter 2. If you need more help finding the folder, see On Your Own Step-by-Step Solution 2.7 in this appendix.

Step 3. Drill down into the **sample_files** folder. In that folder, drill down into the **Ch05_MyResearch** subfolder (see Figure S5-3). There you find the Peace Corps file. Double-click the **Peace Corps** OneNote file. You might be asked to log on to your Microsoft account.

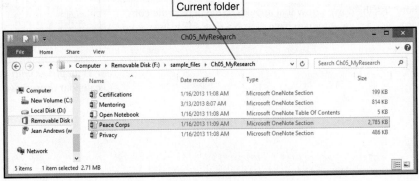

FIGURE S5-3
Find the Peace Corps file in the Ch05_MyResearch folder.

Step 4. The Ch05_MyResearch notebook opens in a OneNote window. Click each page in the Peace Corps section to view the research.

Step 5. To save you typing time, we created the text for the research paper for you. To view the text, click the **Text for Research Paper** page tab.

Leave the OneNote window open so you can copy research and text from the OneNote window into the Word window as you build the paper.

On Your Own 5.3 Step-by-Step Solution   How to Enter a Header, Student and Course Information, a Date, and a Paper Title

Create the Peace Corps Paper: Part 3 of 9

Do the following to enter a header, student and course information, a date, and the title to your paper:

Step 1. Return to your Word window with the PeaceCorpsPaper document open.

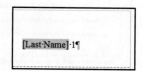

Step 2. Double-click somewhere in the header of the document to select it. When the header is selected, the body of the document is grayed. Click **[Last Name]** to select it and type **Witt**. Notice that one space is between the last name and the page number. Double-click somewhere in the body of the document to return to this area.

Step 3. Click **[Your Name]** to select it. Type **Jos**. Then click the **INSERT** tab. Click **Symbol** and click **More Symbols**. The Symbol dialog box appears.

Step 4. Under Subset, click **Latin-1 Supplement**. Scroll down through the symbols and click **é** (see Figure S5-4).

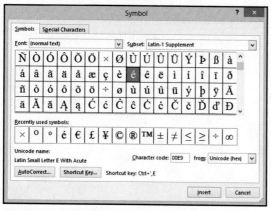

> **Not Working?** If you don't see *Latin-1 Supplement* under Subset, make sure that *(normal text)* is selected under Font.

FIGURE S5-4
Symbols can be inserted into a Word document.

Step 5. Click **Insert**. Close the Symbol dialog box. Type a space followed by **Witt**.

Step 6. Click **[Instructor's Name]** and change it to **Professor Chen**.

Step 7. Click **[Course Number]** and change it to **English Composition 101**.

Step 8. Click the **[Date]** Content Control. Then click the down arrow that appears to the right of the control. A calendar appears where you can pick a date. After you have picked a date, click away from the date to deselect it.

Date picker with calendar drop-down

Step 9. The paper does not have a subtitle. Click **[Subtitle]** and press **Delete** to delete it. Also delete the space and colon next to it.

Step 10. Click **[Title]** and change it to **So You Want to Know About the Peace Corps**.

Step 11. Press and drag to select all the text in the paper following the title down through the end of the paper including the Works Cited page. Press **Delete** to delete it.

Step 12. Save the document.

On Your Own 5.4 Step-by-Step Solution   How to Enter the First Two Paragraphs and Create Citations

Create the Peace Corps Paper: Part 4 of 9

Follow these steps to copy the text for the introductory paragraph from OneNote into your document and format the paragraph:

Step 1. To select the OneNote window, click the **OneNote** icon in the taskbar. The Peace Corps section of your notebook should still be selected.

Step 2. In OneNote, select the **Text for Research Paper** page. Press and drag your pointer to select the first paragraph on that page (see Figure S5-5). Do not include in your selection the title above the paragraph.

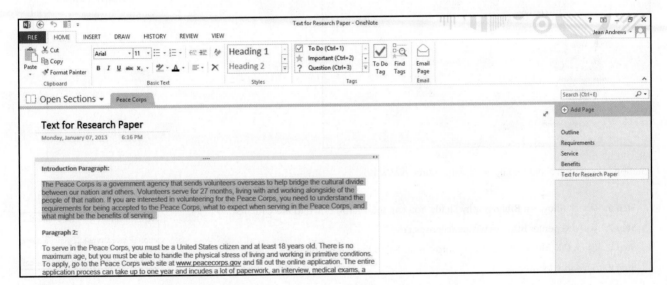

FIGURE S5-5
Select the first paragraph on the Text for Research Paper page of OneNote.

Step 3. On the HOME ribbon, click **Copy**. Alternately, you can right-click the selected text and click **Copy** on the shortcut menu. The text is copied into the Windows Clipboard.

Step 4. To return to the Word window, click the **Word** icon in the taskbar.

Step 5. To position the insertion point below the title of the paper, first position your insertion point at the end of the title line and then press **Enter**.

Step 6. On the HOME ribbon, click **Paste**. The paragraph is inserted in the Word document.

Step 7. Click somewhere in the paragraph. In the Style pane, click the **Normal** style. The style is applied to the paragraph.

Follow these steps to insert a citation:

Step 1. Position the insertion point before the period at the end of the second sentence in the paragraph.

Insertion point before period

Step 2. Click the **REFERENCES** tab. In the Citations & Bibliography section, click **MLA Seventh Edition** if it is not already selected under Style.

Step 3. On the REFERENCES ribbon, click **Insert Citation**. In the drop-down menu, click **Add New Source**. The Create Source dialog box opens.

Step 4. For the Type of Source, select **Web site** from the drop-down list. The fields in the Create Source dialog box change to fit those needed to cite a website.

Step 5. Use the following information to create the source as shown in Figure S5-6:

- For Name of Web Page, enter **Peace Corps**.

- For Year Accessed, enter **2013**.

- For Month Accessed, enter **Jan.** (include the period).

- For Day Accessed, enter **1**.

- For Medium, enter **Web**.

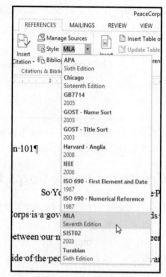

Drop-down menu with MLA Seventh Edition

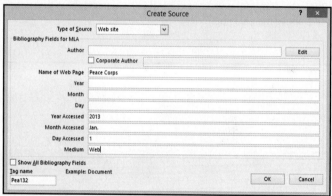

FIGURE S5-6
Citation information is entered in the Create Source dialog box.

Step 6. Check **Show All Bibliography Fields**. You can then scroll down to the URL field.

Step 7. For URL, enter **http://www.peacecorps.gov.**

Step 8. Click **OK**. The citation (Peace Corps) is added to the paragraph.

Step 9. Save the document.

Do the following to add the second paragraph to the paper:

Step 1. Go to the OneNote window and the **Text for Research Paper** page. Select the text under the title **Paragraph 2**. Do not include the title. On the HOME ribbon, click **Copy** to copy the text into the Windows Clipboard.

Step 2. Return to your Word document. Position the insertion point below the first paragraph.

Step 3. On the HOME ribbon, click **Paste**. The paragraph is pasted at the end of the document.

Step 4. Apply the **Normal** style to the paragraph.

Step 5. The URL, www.peacecorps.gov, in the text is not formatted correctly. In the paragraph, right-click the link **www.peacecorps.gov** and se**lect Remove Hyperlink** from the shortcut menu.

Step 6. Press and drag your pointer over **www.peacecorps.gov** to highlight this text. Click the **Normal** style in the Styles pane. The text is now formatted correctly.

Follow these steps to add a citation at the end of the second paragraph:

Step 1. Position the insertion point before the period at the end of the last sentence of the paragraph.

Step 2. On the REFERENCES ribbon, click **Insert Citation**. Because the Peace Corps source has already been used, it's listed in the drop-down menu. Click **Peace Corps**. The citation is inserted in the text.

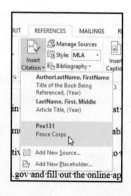

Step 3. Save the document.

On Your Own 5.5 Step-by-Step Solution   How to Enter More Text, a Blog Citation, and a Footnote

Create the Peace Corps Paper: Part 5 of 9

Follow these steps to insert the third paragraph into the document:

Step 1. Go to the **OneNote** window and the **Text for Research Paper** page. Select the text under the title **Paragraph 3**. Copy the selection to the Windows Clipboard.

Step 2. Return to your Word document.

Step 3. Position the insertion point below the last paragraph in the document and paste the text into the document.

Step 4. Apply the **Normal** style to the paragraph.

Step 5. To have Word ignore the problem with "kilo's" in the direct quotation, right-click the text and click **Ignore**. (When words are misspelled in a direct quotation, leave them that way.)

Follow these steps to insert a citation for a blog:

Step 1. Position the insertion point at the end of the direct quote before the period.

Step 2. On the REFERENCES ribbon, click **Insert Citation**. Click **Add New Source**. The Create Source dialog box appears. Beside Type of Source, select **Web site** from the drop-down list. The fields in the box change to accommodate entries for a website. The information for the citation can be found on the Service page of OneNote and is shown in Figure S5-7.

with·12·seats·on·it.·There·were

f·rancid·butter To·find·out·mo

Insertion point following quote and before period

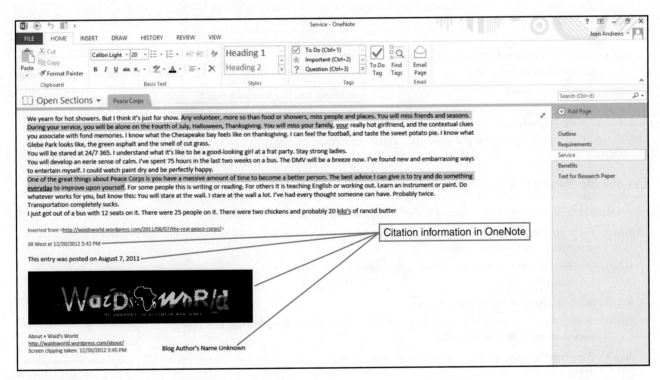

FIGURE S5-7
Entry and citation information are shown for the Waid's World blog.

Step 3. Use the following information to create the source. Note the author is unknown:

Type of Source	Web site
Name of Web Page	Waid's World
Date	7 Aug. 2011
Date accessed	30 Dec. 2012
Medium	Web
URL	http://waidsworld.wordpress.com

Step 4. Click **OK** to close the Create Source dialog box and create the citation in the document.

> Tip   When citing a website, it's not necessary to enter the complete URL. You need only the domain name preceded by http://.

Follow these steps to add a footnote:

Step 1. Position the insertion point at the end of the paragraph, following the last period.

Step 2. On the REFERENCES ribbon, click **Insert Footnote**. The footnote area appears at the bottom of the page.

Step 3. Type this text in the footnote area:

> To find blogs written by Peace Corps volunteers, use Google.com and the following search string: Peace Corps volunteer blogs.

Step 4. To apply the Normal style to the footnote, click **Normal** in the Styles pane.

Step 5. Save the document.

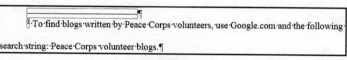

Footnote

On Your Own 5.6 Step-by-Step Solution   **How to Enter More Text, a Long Quotation, and a Book Citation**

Create the Peace Corps Paper: Part 6 of 9

Follow these steps to insert the fourth paragraph and format the long quotation in this paragraph:

Step 1. Go to the **OneNote** window and the **Text for Research Paper** page. Select the text under the title **Paragraph 4**. Copy the selection to the Windows Clipboard.

Step 2. Return to your Word document. Position the insertion point below the last paragraph in the document. Paste the text into the document.

Step 3. Apply the **Normal** style to the paragraph.

Step 4. Position the insertion point following the colon in the text **Dillon Banerjee had this advice regarding this unique opportunity:**

Step 5. Press **Enter** to insert a hard return. The text following the insertion point moves down into a new paragraph.

Step 6. Click somewhere in this last paragraph to select it and then click **Quote** in the Styles pane. The Quote style is applied, which causes the paragraph to be indented one inch.

> **Not Working?** Don't use the Long Quote style that this template provides because this style uses a first-line indent, which MLA guidelines require for long quotations of two or more paragraphs.

Follow these steps to add the citation to this quotation:

Step 1. Position the insertion point following the period at the end of the long quotation.

Step 2. On the REFERENCES ribbon, click **Insert Citation**. Click **Add New Source**. The Create Source dialog box appears. The information to go into the Create Source box is taken from the Service page of OneNote as shown in Figure S5-8.

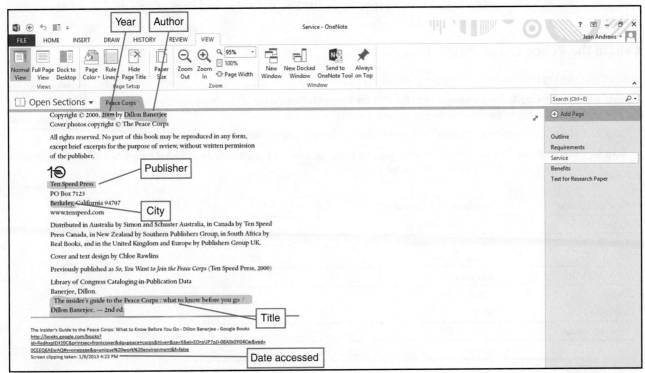

FIGURE S5-8
Citation information for the book in the OneNote research notes.

Step 3. Here is all the information for the book citation:

Type of Source	Book
Author	Banerjee, Dillon
Title	The Insider's Guide to the Peace Corps: What to Know Before You Go
Year	2009
City	Berkeley
Publisher	Ten Speed Press
Medium	Web
Year Accessed	2013
Month Accessed	Jan.
Day Accessed	6

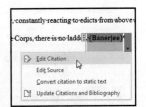

Step 4. Click **OK** to close the Create Source box and create the citation in the document.

Follow these steps to insert the page number in the citation:

Step 1. Click the citation to select it. A box appears around the citation. Click the down arrow on the right side of the box. Select **Edit Citation** from the drop-down menu.

Step 2. The Edit Citation box appears. Under Pages, enter **115**. Click **OK**.

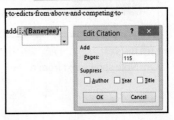

Step 3. The citation now shows the page number. When you click away from the citation, it is no longer selected.

Step 4. Save the document.

On Your Own 5.7 Step-by-Step Solution   **How to Enter the Conclusion Paragraph and Two More Citations**

Create the Peace Corps Paper: Part 7 of 9

Follow these steps to insert the conclusion paragraph and a citation:

Step 1. Copy the **Conclusion Paragraph** from the **Text for Research Paper** page in OneNote into the Word document. Apply the **Normal** style to the paragraph.

Step 2. Position the insertion point after the third sentence in the paragraph, before the period.

Step 3. Insert a citation. The citation information is taken from the *Taunton Gazette* article recorded on the Service page of One-Note (see Figure S5-9). Use this citation information:

Type of Source	Article in a Periodical
Author	Nichols, Christopher
Title	Peace Corps volunteer from Taunton still helping friends in Africa
Periodical Title	Taunton Gazette
Date	8 Dec. 2012
Medium	Web
Year Accessed	2013
Month Accessed	Jan.
Day Accessed	1

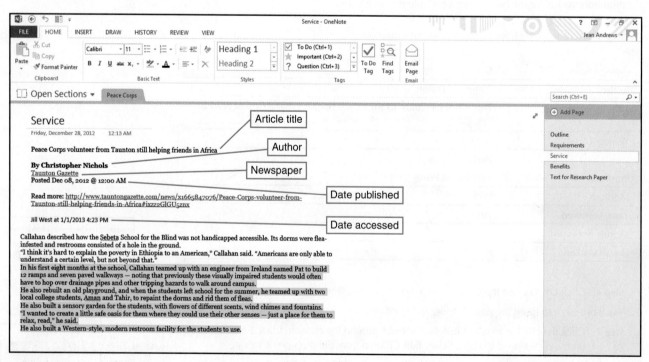

FIGURE S5-9
OneNote shows text from a newspaper article including citation information.

Step 4. To see all the fields you need to use, click **Show All Bibliography Fields**. When finished, click **OK** to close the Create Source box and create the citation in the document.

Follow these steps to insert a citation for a journal article:

Step 1. Position the insertion point at the end of the fifth sentence in the paragraph and before the period. This sentence is "Expect to grow in compassion, courage, and leadership skills."

Step 2. On the **REFERENCES** ribbon, click **Insert Citation**. Click **Add New Source**. The Create Source dialog box appears.

Step 3. Use this information to create the source:

Type of Source	Journal Article
Author	Plante, Thomas G., Katy Lackey, and Hwang Jeong Yeon
Title	The Impact of Immersion Trips on Development of Compassion Among College Students
Journal Name	Journal of Experiential Education
Year	2009
Pages	28–43
Volume	32
Issue	1
Medium	Web
Year Accessed	2013
Month Accessed	Jan.
Day Accessed	6

Step 4. When finished, click **OK** to close the Create Source box. The citation is inserted in the document.

Step 5. Edit the citation, adding the page numbers **28–43**.

Step 6. Save the document.

On Your Own 5.8 Step-by-Step Solution   **How to Create a Works Cited Page**

Create the Peace Corps Paper: Part 8 of 9

Before you create the Works Cited page, it's a good idea to check each source for errors. You also need to delete the two sample sources that were in the template. Do the following:

Step 1. On the REFERENCES ribbon, click **Manage Sources**. The Source Manager dialog box appears (see Figure S5-10). You should see seven sources listed in the Current List on the right. Two of these sources are the example sources that need to be deleted. To delete these two sources, follow these steps:

    1. Click the **AuthorLastName** source and click **Delete**.

    2. Click the **LastName** source and click **Delete**.

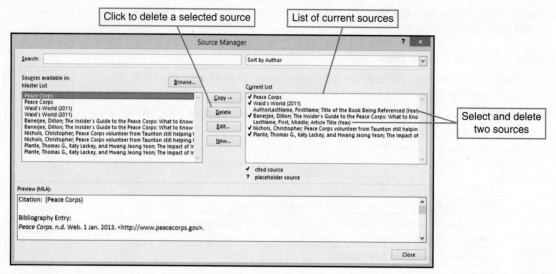

FIGURE S5-10

Use the Source Manager dialog box to edit and delete sources.

Step 2. The five remaining sources under Current List are the Peace Corps, Waid's World, Banerjee, Nichols, and Plante sources. If you want to edit a source, click it to select it and then click **Edit**.

Step 3. When you're finished editing sources, click **Close** to close the Source Manager box.

Do the following to create a Works Cited page:

Step 1. Position the insertion point at the end of the last paragraph in the document. On the INSERT ribbon, click **Page Break**. A new page is created, and your insertion point should be on this new page.

Step 2. On the REFERENCES ribbon, click **Bibliography**. Click **Works Cited** in the drop-down list. The list is inserted in the document.

> **Hint** If you find a mistake in the source information used to generate the Works Cited list, return to the Source Manager box and correct the error. Then generate a new Works Cited page. Any manual edits you made to the Works Cited page are lost and must be made again.

Step 3. To center the page title, select it and click the **Center** command on the HOME ribbon.

Step 4. Position the insertion point before the text "Web. 6 Jan. 2013." in the Banerjee entry and add the name of the online database as follows:

Google Books. Web. 6 Jan. 2013.

Step 5. Select **Google Books** and apply **Italic**.

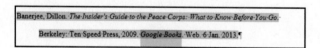

Step 6. Position the insertion point before "Web. 6 Jan. 2013." in the Plante, Thomas G. entry and add the name of the online database as follows:

Professional Development Collection. Web. 6 Jan. 2013.

Step 7. Select the **Professional Development Collection** database name and apply **Italic**.

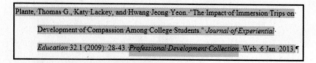

Step 8. Save the document.

Create the Peace Corps Paper: Part 9 of 9

To practice revising and proofing a paper, do the following:

Step 1. In the third sentence of the paper, select the word **interested** and click **Thesaurus** on the REVIEW ribbon. The Thesaurus pane appears. To use a word in the Thesaurus pane, right-click the word and select **Insert** from the shortcut menu. To undo any change, click **Undo** in the Quick Access Toolbar.

Step 2. To search for the text **Peace Corps**, click **Find** on the HOME ribbon. In the search box on the Navigation pane, enter **peace corps**. Instances of the text are highlighted in the paper. Click the up and down arrows in the Navigation pane to step through instances of the text.

Step 3. To view the word count, look in the left corner of the status bar at the bottom of the Word window.

Step 4. To display paragraph marks, click the Show/Hide button on the HOME ribbon. The button toggles between hiding and showing the paragraph marks, also called hard returns.

Step 5. To change the font used for the entire paper, do the following:

1. Press **Ctrl+A** to select all text in the paper except the headers and footers. On the HOME ribbon, select the **Arial** font.

2. Double-click in the header area to access the header. With your insertion point in the header, select all the text in the header. On the HOME ribbon, select the **Arial** font. Double-click anywhere in the body of the text to deselect the header.

3. Press and drag to select all the text in the footnote. On the HOME ribbon, select the **Arial** font.

4. Now it's time to undo your changes to the font. To undo your changes, click the Undo button three times to return all the text in the paper to Times New Roman.

Step 6. Misspell a word in the first sentence of the paper. To use the Spelling pane to check the paper for spelling errors, click **Spelling & Grammar** on the REVIEW ribbon. Save your work.

CHAPTER 6 STEP-BY-STEP SOLUTIONS
Communicating with Others Using the Internet

The solutions in this appendix are for you to use if you get stuck when doing an On Your Own activity in the chapter. To learn how to teach yourself a computer skill, always try the On Your Own activity first before turning to these solutions.

> **Not Working?** Websites change from time to time. The step-by-step instructions here were accurate when we wrote them, but be aware that you might have to adjust them to account for later website changes.

On Your Own 6.1 Step-by-Step Solution **How to Manage Email Using a Website**

Follow these steps to use a website to view and print email messages:

Step 1. Open Internet Explorer and go to the website of your email provider. For example, if your email address is andrewsjean7@gmail.com, enter **gmail.com** in your browser address box. Sign in to your email account using your email address and password. In this solution, we're using the gmail.com website. Your website might work differently, but the functions should be the same.

Most websites show your inbox when you first log on. How many messages are in your inbox? For gmail.com, the number of messages in the inbox shows up in the upper-right corner of the window.

Step 2. To read a message, you might need to click it or double-click it. For gmail.com, when you click a message, it opens so you can read it. For example, in Figure 6-3 shown in the chapter, when I click the first message in the inbox, the message from Joy Dark appears. If you have a message in your inbox, open it now.

Step 3. To print a message you're viewing, look for a Print button on the screen. For gmail.com, click the **Print all** icon (looks like a printer) on the right side of the window. The print preview of the open message appears. The Print dialog box also appears (see Figure S6-1). Select your printer and click **Print**.

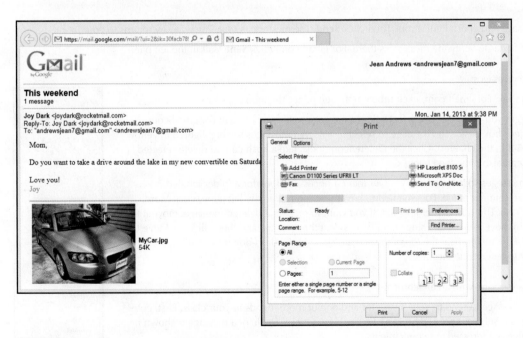

FIGURE S6-1
To print a message, select the printer and click **Print**.

Follow these steps to compose and send a new message:

Step 1. To start the process, look for a button on the screen such as New or Compose. For gmail.com, click **COMPOSE** in the left pane. A blank message area appears where you can type your message.

Step 2. Enter the email address of each recipient, subject line, and body of the message. Figure S6-2 shows the message after these items have been entered. To format text in the message, you must first click the **Formatting options** button at the bottom of the window. The formatting tools bar appears, which is used to format the text.

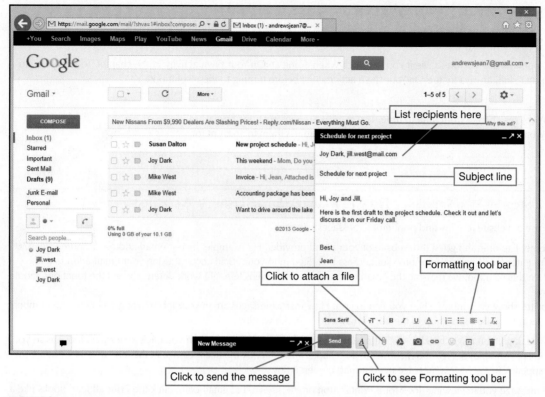

FIGURE S6-2
A new email message needs the receiver's email address, the subject line, and the body of the message.

Step 3. Reread the message and check it for errors. Then click **Send**. The message is sent. The window returns to your inbox.

Step 4. Open your Sent folder to verify the message is there. For gmail.com, click **Sent Mail** in the left pane.

Follow these steps to delete messages:

Step 1. Return to your inbox. For gmail.com, click **Inbox** in the left pane. The inbox appears.

Step 2. To delete messages you no longer need, first select a message and then delete it. For gmail.com, you click the check box beside the message to select it. Selected messages are highlighted in yellow (refer to Figure 6-2 in the chapter). Click the **Delete** icon (looks like a trash can) to delete selected messages. (You can also press the Delete key.)

Step 3. To see deleted messages so that you can recover them if necessary, look for a folder labeled Trash, Deleted Items, or a similar name. For gmail.com, hover your pointer in the left pane, click **More**, and then click **Trash**. The Trash folder appears. If you want to recover a deleted message, move it to another folder. To move a message using gmail.com, select the message and then click the **Move to** icon (looks like a file folder) near the top of the screen. Then, in the drop-down list that appears, select the folder to receive the message.

Follow these steps to send a message with an attachment:

Step 1. Write a second message to send to your instructor and one or more friends in your class. First, enter the email addresses, subject line, and body of the message. One example of a message is shown in Figure S6-2, which is addressed to two recipients.

Not Working? For some email websites, you must separate each recipient's email address with a comma or semicolon.

Step 2. Look on your screen for a way to attach a file. For example, in Figure S6-2, click the **Attach files** icon (looks like a paper clip). The Choose File to Upload box appears. Drill down on your computer storage device to find the file and then click **Open**. Figure S6-3 shows the box when the **MyPhoto1** file in the sample_files folder on a USB flash drive is selected.

FIGURE S6-3
Find and select the file to attach to the email message.

> **Hint** Recall that you downloaded the sample_files folder to your USB flash drive in Chapter 2. If you need more help finding the folder, see On Your Own 2.7 Step-by-Step Solution in this appendix.

Step 3. The file is attached. You should see the file name somewhere in the new message area. Click **Send** to send the message.

When you open an email message with an attached file, the file doesn't immediately open. Follow these steps to open and save the attachment:

Step 1. Messages with attachments have a paper clip icon or some other way to identify the attachment. For example, the message from Joy Dark shown in the chapter in Figure 6-2 has an attached file. In Figure 6-3 in the chapter, you can see the file name at the bottom of the open email message and the photo displays. Click **View** to open the file in a new window. (Note that your screen might work differently.)

Step 2. To download the file to your computer so you can save it, click **Download**. In the bar that appears at the bottom of the IE window, click the down arrow to the right of Save. In the drop-down menu that appears, click **Save as**. The Save As box appears. Navigate to your USB flash drive or other location to save the attachment. Then click **Save** (see Figure S6-4).

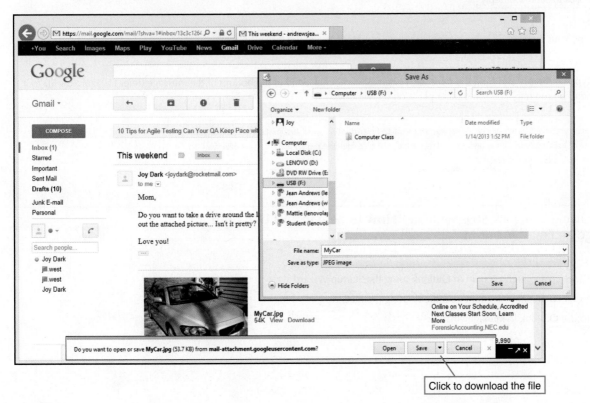

Click to download the file

FIGURE S6-4
Save the email attachment to a local storage device.

Look back at Figure 6-3 in the chapter and note that you can click Reply to reply to the sender or click Forward to send the message to a third person. Follow these steps to reply to the sender:

Step 1. To reply to the message, look for a Reply button. For gmail.com, click **Reply** at the bottom of the message. A new message is created so that you can reply to the sender (see Figure S6-5). Your reply is automatically inserted above the original message even though that's not obvious by looking at the screen.

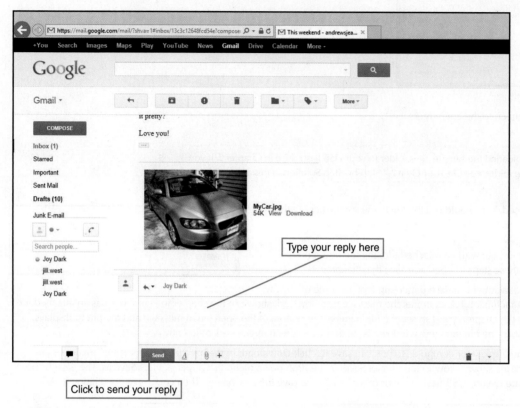

FIGURE S6-5
Reply by typing your message. The latest reply is always put at the top of the thread of replies.

Step 2. Type your reply and send the message. For gmail.com, click **Send** at the bottom of the message (refer to Figure S6-5). Your Send button might be some other place on the window.

> Tip Sometimes you might be working on a message and want to finish it later. Gmail automatically saves unsent messages in the Drafts folder. To find unsent drafts, click the Drafts folder. All websites offer a similar way to save drafts of messages not yet finished.

On Your Own 6.2 Step-by-Step Solution   How to Set Up and Use Outlook to Manage an Email Account

This solution has three parts:

▶ How to set up an email account in Outlook using the Startup Wizard

▶ How to set up an email account in Outlook using the FILE tab

▶ How to use Outlook to manage email

How to Set Up an Email Account in Outlook Using the Startup Wizard

Follow these steps to open Outlook for the first time and use the Startup Wizard to set up an email account:

Step 1. When using Windows 8 to open Outlook 2013, go to the Start screen and click the **Outlook 2013** tile. When using Windows 7 to open Outlook 2013, click **Start**, **All Programs**, **Microsoft Office 2013**, and then **Outlook 2013**. If this is the first time the program has been opened, the Welcome to Microsoft Outlook 2013 window appears. Click **Next**.

Step 2. Follow directions on screen to enter your name, email address, and password. A connection is made to the server, and your email is downloaded to Outlook. Click **Finish**. The Outlook window appears.

How to Set Up an Email Account in Outlook Using the FILE Tab

After Outlook has been launched the first time, the Startup Wizard will not appear. In this situation, you must set up a new account in Outlook using the FILE tab. Follow these steps:

Step 1. When using Windows 8 to open Outlook 2013, go to the Start screen and click the **Outlook 2013** tile. When using Windows 7 to open Outlook 2013, click **Start**, **All Programs**, **Microsoft Office 2013**, and then **Outlook 2013**. The Outlook window appears.

Step 2. Click the **FILE** tab and click **Add Account**. The Add Account dialog box opens.

Step 3. Enter your name, email account, and password (see Figure S6-6). Click **Next**.

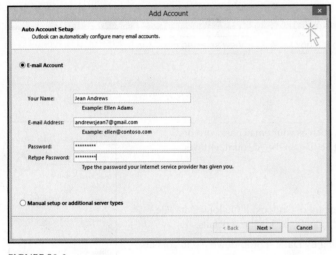

FIGURE S6-6
Enter email account information.

Step 4. The connection is made to your mail server. A test email message is sent, and email messages on the server are downloaded to Outlook. Click **Finish**. The Outlook window appears.

How to Use Outlook to Manage Email

Follow these steps to use Outlook to view and print your email messages:

Step 1. If Outlook isn't already open, open it.

Step 2. Look for your email address listed in the Folder pane. If necessary, click the right arrow above All Folders to open the Folder pane.

Step 3. To view a list of folders under your email account, if necessary, click the white triangle in the left pane beside your account. The triangle is now black because the view is expanded.

Step 4. Click **Inbox** under the email address to view messages in the inbox (see Figure S6-7). The items in your inbox appear in the middle pane.

Details of the Outlook Data File folder are hidden

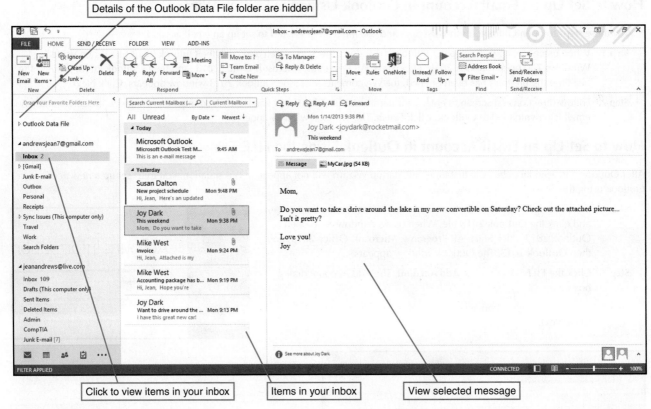

Click to view items in your inbox   Items in your inbox   View selected message

FIGURE S6-7
Outlook is set up to manage a single email account.

> **Not Working?** If you want to change email account settings, such as your email password or email name, on the **FILE** tab, click **Account Settings**, then **Account Setting**. In the Account Settings box, select the email account and click **Change**.

Step 5. In this book, we're not using the Outlook Data Files feature of Outlook. If Outlook Data File details are showing in the Folder pane, click the black triangle to hide these details.

Step 6. To reorder the items by sender, click the column heading **By Date**. A drop-down menu appears. Click **From**.

Step 7. To read a message, click it to select it. A selected message appears in blue. The contents of the message appear in the right pane.

Step 8. To print a message or messages, first select the messages. To select multiple messages, hold down the **Ctrl** key as you click messages. Click the **FILE** tab and then click **Print**. Print previews appear (see Figure S6-8). If you have multiple messages selected, you must click Preview to generate the Print previews. Select your printer and click **Print**.

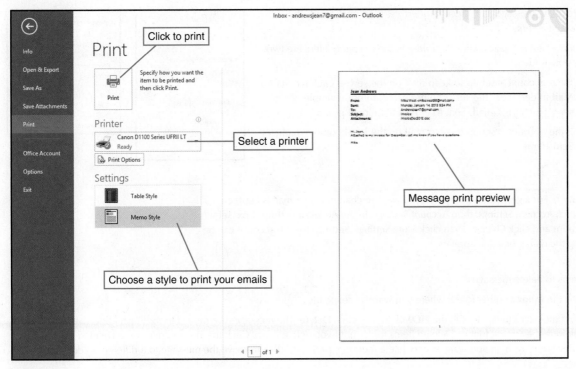

FIGURE S6-8
Selected message is ready to print.

Follow these steps to compose and send a new message:

Step 1.   On the **HOME** ribbon, click **New Email**. A new Message window opens.

Step 2.   Enter the email address of the receiver (a friend in your class), subject line, and body of the message. Figure S6-9 shows the message after these items have been entered. Notice that when the body of the message is selected, all the formatting tools on the MESSAGE tab are available for you to format the text.

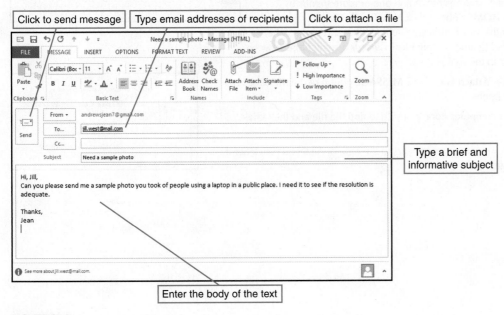

FIGURE S6-9
A new email message needs the receiver's email address, subject line, and body of the message.

Step 3. Reread the message and check it for errors. Then click **Send**. The message is sent.

Step 4. To view sent messages, click the folder in the left pane. Here are two possible folders:

- If the account is set up to keep mail on the server, click the **Sent Mail** folder under the server folder name. In our example, the server folder is **Gmail**. Sent Mail is in the Gmail group.

- If the account is set up to keep mail on the local computer, click **Sent Items**.

> **Not Working?** For a gmail.com account, if you want to change where mail is kept, on the **FILE** tab, click **Account Settings**, then **Account Settings**. In the Account Settings box, select the email account and click **Change**. Then click **More Settings**. Settings for the account can be changed using the dialog box that appears.

Follow these steps to delete messages:

Step 1. Click the **Inbox** or other folder where you want to delete files.

Step 2. Select messages to delete. On the **HOME** ribbon, click **Delete**. The messages are moved to the Trash folder. Messages remain in the Trash folder or Deleted Items folder until you delete them. Click the **Trash** folder or the **Deleted Items** folder to view your trash. (If you want to undelete a message, press and drag to move the message to a different folder.)

Follow these steps to use the Windows Snipping Tool to take a screen capture and then send the capture file to your instructor as an email attachment:

Step 1. With the Outlook window in view, open the Windows Snipping Tool and take a snip of the Outlook window or the full screen. Save the snip to a .png file stored on your USB flash drive, hard drive, OneDrive, or another location given by your instructor. If you need help using the Windows Snipping Tool, follow instructions given in Step-by-Step Solution 1.10 in Chapter 1. Make sure you note the location where you saved the file.

Step 2. Create a new email to your instructor and one or more friends in your class. On the **HOME** ribbon, click **New Email**. The Message box appears. Enter the email addresses, subject line, and body of the message. Notice that Outlook automatically inserts a semicolon between each email address in the To field.

Step 3. To attach a file, click **Attach File** on the **MESSAGE** ribbon of the Message box. The Insert File box opens.

Step 4. Drill down on your computer storage device to find the file and then click **Insert**.

Step 5. The file is attached. The file name appears to the right of Attached. Click **Send** to send the message.

Follow these steps to open and save an attachment:

Step 1. When you view an email message in the right pane of Outlook, the file names of attached files show up in the bar above the body of the message. Refer to Figure 6-4 in the chapter. To view the file, click the file name. The file appears in the right pane (see Figure S6-10).

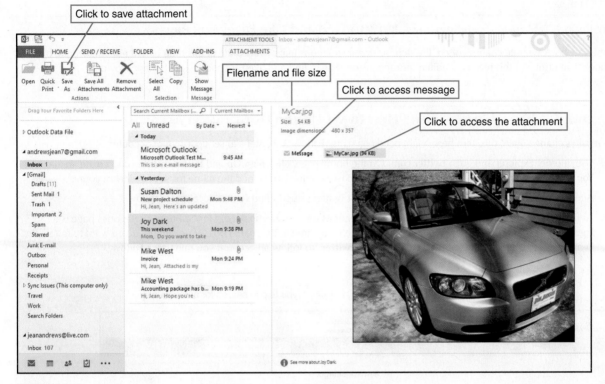

FIGURE S6-10
Outlook displays a photo file that was attached to an incoming email message.

Step 2. To save the file to a new location, on the **ATTACHMENTS** ribbon, click **Save As**. The Save Attachment box opens. Navigate to the location to save the file and click **Save**.

Step 3. To return to the message, click **Message** next to the file name. The message appears in the right pane.

To respond to the selected message, use the Reply, Reply All, or Forward buttons on the HOME ribbon. Follow these steps to reply to the message:

Step 1. With the message selected, click the **HOME** tab and click **Reply**. The Message window opens.

Step 2. Type your reply and click **Send**.

On Your Own 6.3 Step-by-Step Solution   How to Sign Up for Facebook and Build Your Profile

Because the Facebook website changes often, the step-by-step instructions that are accurate at this time would not be accurate by the time the book is in print. For this reason, detailed instructions are not provided.

On Your Own 6.4 Step-by-Step Solution   How to Find Friends on Facebook

Because the Facebook website changes often, the step-by-step instructions that are accurate at this time would not be accurate by the time the book is in print. For this reason, detailed instructions are not provided.

On Your Own 6.5 Step-by-Step Solution **How to Explore Facebook in More Depth**

Because the Facebook website changes often, the step-by-step instructions that are accurate at this time would not be accurate by the time the book is in print. For this reason, detailed instructions are not provided.

On Your Own 6.6 Step-by-Step Solution **How to Find and Like Facebook Pages**

Because the Facebook website changes often, the step-by-step instructions that are accurate at this time would not be accurate by the time the book is in print. For this reason, detailed instructions on how to find and like Facebook pages are not provided.

On Your Own 6.7 Step-by-Step Solution **How to Set Up and Use a Twitter Account**

Because websites change often, the steps here might need changing. Follow these steps to set up a Twitter account:

Step 1. Use Internet Explorer and go to **twitter.com**. On the home page, click **Sign Up** and follow directions to create an account. You must enter your name, a valid email address, a password for Twitter, and the name for your Twitter account.

Step 2. After you create an account, you are taken through a Twitter setup to find Twitter accounts to follow.

Step 3. To find Twitter accounts to follow, click **Browse categories** on your Home page. On the Browse categories page (see Figure S6-11), you can drill down into categories or type a name in the search box. For example, if you want to follow the White House, enter **White House** and click **Search Twitter**. To follow an account you find, click **Follow**.

FIGURE S6-11
Search or drill for Twitter accounts to follow.

Step 4. To get the full benefits of Twitter, you must confirm your email account. Look in your email inbox for a message from Twitter and click the link in the message.

Step 5. Whenever you go to twitter.com and sign in, the Tweets of those you follow appear on the right pane of your Home page (refer to Figure 6-17 in the chapter). Using this window, you can write a Tweet to those following you and set up your profile to make it easier for others to find you on Twitter.

Not Working? To return to your Home page from any Twitter.com page, click **Home** in the menu bar.

Step 6. If you're searching for a friend to follow on Twitter, try clicking **Find friends** on your Home page. In the window that appears, enter the email address of a friend. Your friend is sent an email invitation asking whether you can follow him or her on Twitter.

Step 7. If you want others to be able to find you by email in the same way, make sure your Twitter settings allow your email address to be used in this way. To change your settings, click the **Tools** icon in the menu bar and then click **Settings**. After you've made your changes, click **Save changes** at the bottom of the page.

On Your Own 6.8 Step-by-Step Solution   How to Create a Blog and Post to It

To create a blog, go to the home page of a blogging site such as blogspot.com or wordpress.com and sign up for a blog account. Then follow directions onscreen to create your blog. Because websites change often, the steps here might need changing. Follow these steps to create a blog on the wordpress.com site:

Step 1. Go to **wordpress.com** and click **Get Started**. On the sign-up window, enter your email address, user name, password for WordPress, and a name for your blog. Click **Create Blog**.

Step 2. WordPress sends an email message to you. You must click the link in the email message to activate your account.

Step 3. Using your browser, enter the URL to your blog to see what the world sees. My blog is named lifewithjean, so the URL is lifewithjean.wordpress.com. Yours will be different. Figure S6-12 shows my blog before I added anything.

FIGURE S6-12
Here's my blog before I posted anything.

Not Working? The instructions here were correct when we wrote them, but websites change from time to time. You might have to adjust them to account for website changes.

Step 4. Open a new tab in Internet Explorer and go to **wordpress.com** and log on using your blog name and password. Then click **My Blogs** in the menu bar. On the My Blog page, click **Blog Admin**. The Dashboard page is the place where you manage your blog (see Figure S6-13). As you make changes to your blog from the Dashboard, you can switch back to the first tab in Internet Explorer to see the results. Don't forget to refresh the page when you return to the first tab.

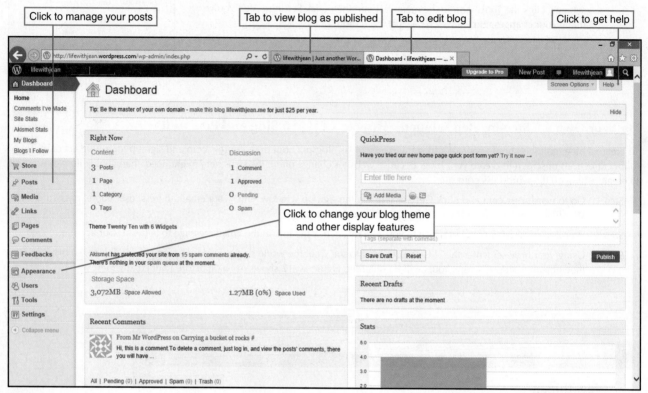

FIGURE S6-13
Use the Dashboard to manage your blog.

> **Hint** To refresh a page in Internet Explorer, press **F5** or click the Refresh icon ⟳ on the right side of the address box.

Step 5. When you're first learning new software, what should you always do first? Find out how to get help. You can find links on the Dashboard for getting started and to other documentation pages. Take a few minutes to check them out so you know where to go when you have questions.

Step 6. In the left pane, click **Appearance**. The Manage Themes page appears. You can choose from these WordPress themes for your blog design. Let's go with the default theme. After you learn the basics of blogging, you might want to go back and pick a different theme.

Step 7. To return to the Dashboard, click **Dashboard** in the left pane.

Follow these steps to make your first post:

Step 1. Your blog does not yet have any posts. Let's add one. Using the Dashboard page, in the left pane, click **Posts** then **Add New**. The Add New Post page appears. Enter a title for the post. Write your own post (see Figure S6-14).

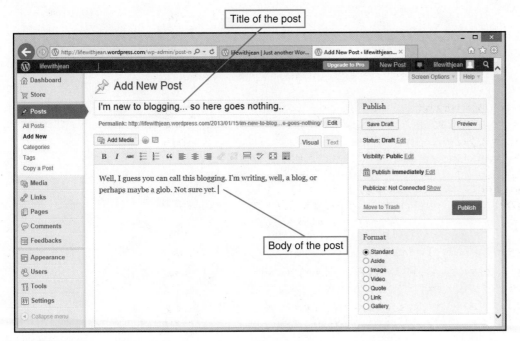

FIGURE S6-14
Create your first blog post.

> **Step 2.** Click **Publish**.
>
> **Step 3.** Return to the first tab in Internet Explorer and refresh the page. Your post appears. My first post is showing in Figure S6-15 as a user would see it.

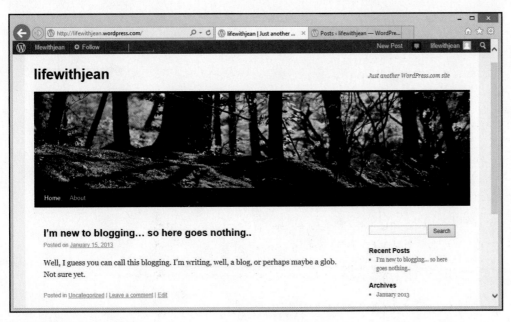

FIGURE S6-15
My blog as the world sees it.

To email a link to your blog to your instructor, follow these steps:

> **Step 1.** With your blog showing in the first tab, highlight the URL in the address box. Right-click and click **Copy** on the shortcut menu. The URL is copied to the Windows Clipboard.
>
> **Step 2.** Access your email account. Compose a new email message to your instructor. When you're ready for the URL, right-click somewhere in the body of the message and click **Paste** on the shortcut menu. The URL is copied into the email message.

CHAPTER 7 STEP-BY-STEP SOLUTIONS
Finding a Job Using the Web, a Résumé, and a Business Letter

The solutions in this appendix are for you to use if you get stuck when doing an On Your Own activity in the chapter. To learn how to teach yourself a computer skill, always try the On Your Own activity first before turning to these solutions.

On Your Own 7.1 Step-by-Step Solution   How to Create a Contacts Document Including Tables

Follow these steps to create one table ready for contact information:

Step 1. Create a new blank document in Word.

Step 2. Type **My Contacts** and apply the **Heading 1** style to the title. Press **Enter** twice.

Step 3. On the INSERT ribbon, click **Table**. In the drop-down box that appears, click the third row, second column. A table with two columns and three rows appears in the document.

Step 4. Click the insertion point in the first cell of the table. Enter the following text in the table. Press **Tab** to move from column to column or to create a new row. If you need to go back to a column or row, click a new insertion point.

Company	
Name	
Title	
Phone	
Email	
Address	
Actions	

Step 5. Save the document to your USB flash drive, hard drive, OneDrive, or another location given by your instructor. Name the document **MyContacts**.

> **Not Working?** If you try to save a document to the hard drive and get an error such as "Path Not Found," most likely you don't have permission to save to the hard drive. Try saving to a USB flash drive instead.

You can change a column width in a table by dragging a column pointer on the horizontal ruler above the document. First, you must select the table. One way to select a table is to use a grabber handle (also called the table selector) that appears when you mouse over a table. Follow these steps:

> **Not Working?** If you don't see the rulers at the top and on the right side of the document, go to the VIEW ribbon and check **Ruler**.

Step 1. Mouse over the table, which causes a box, called a grabber handle (table selector), to appear above the upper-left corner of the table. Click the grabber handle to select the entire table. The entire table is highlighted.

> **Hint** When a table is first created or selected, the TABLE TOOLS DESIGN tab and LAYOUT tab show up. Use the LAYOUT ribbon to insert or delete rows and columns in the table and to format the table.

Step 2. With the table highlighted, press and drag the second column pointer in the ruler. Drag the pointer to the left to narrow the column width so that it is about 1.5 inches wide (see Figure S7-1).

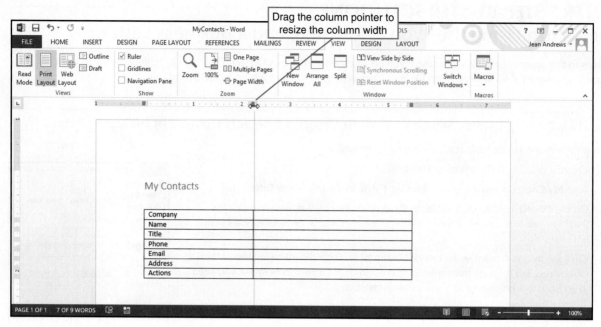

FIGURE S7-1

With the table selected, drag a column pointer on the ruler to resize a column width.

> **Step 3.** Widen the second column width so that it is about five inches wide.

Follow these steps to make two copies of the table and add data:

> **Step 1.** Press **Ctrl+End** to move the insertion point to the end of the document. Press **Enter** to create a blank line under the table.
>
> **Step 2.** Select the table again. On the HOME ribbon, click **Copy**. (Alternately, you can select the table and then right-click on the table and select Copy from the shortcut menu.)
>
> **Step 3.** Press **Ctrl+End**. The insertion point is placed at the end of the document. On the HOME ribbon, click **Paste**. A copy of the table is inserted in the document.
>
> **Step 4.** Place one more copy of the table in the document with a blank line between each table.

> **Hint** If two tables in the document join together as one and you want to split them, click in the row below where you want to split the table and click **Split Table** on the LAYOUT ribbon.

> **Step 5.** Go back to the first table and enter the contact information for Andy Knight. The contact information can be found in the On Your Own 7.1 activity in the chapter.
>
> **Step 6.** The text in the second column to the right of Actions needs to be formatted as a bulleted list. Select this text in the second column and click the Bullets icon ⁝☰ ▾ on the HOME ribbon. The text becomes a bulleted list, as shown in Figure S7-2.

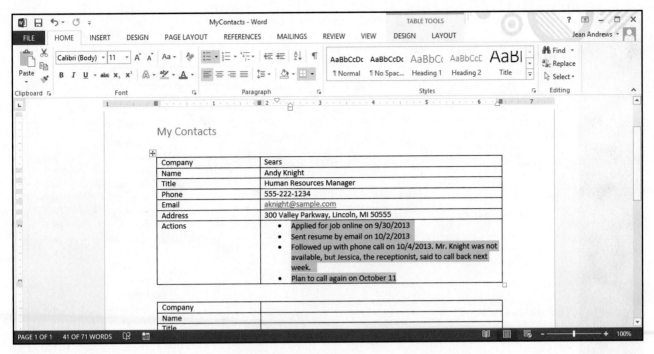

FIGURE S7-2
Format the list of actions as a bulleted list.

Step 7. Enter and format the contact information for **Sarah Smith** in the second table. The contact information can be found in On Your Own 7.1 activity in the chapter.

Step 8. Make sure the document properties show you as the author of the document. Save and close the document.

On Your Own 7.2 Step-by-Step Solution   **How to Create a Résumé Using a Résumé Template**

This solution has two parts:

▶ How to create the résumé

▶ How to export a Word document as a PDF file

How to Create the Résumé

The finished résumé for Andrea Champion is shown in Figure 7-5 in the chapter. Follow these steps to create the résumé:

Step 1. In Word, click the **FILE** tab, select **New**, and then click **Resume** under the search box. In the group of résumés, click **Basic resume** (see Figure S7-3). Click **Create**. The document is created.

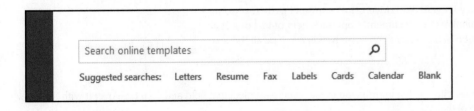

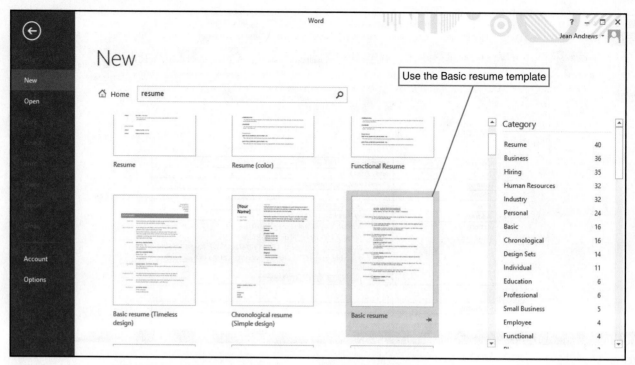

FIGURE S7-3
Create a document using the Basic resume template.

Not Working? If you don't see "Resume" in a menu under the search box when opening a new document in Word, you're not connected to the Internet. If the Basic resume template has already been downloaded to your computer, you might see it listed on the screen and you can select it. If not, you must connect to the Internet to continue. Close Word, make sure you have an Internet connection, and then open Word again.

Tip When searching for a résumé template to meet your specific needs, notice you can filter résumés using the list on the right side of the résumés shown.

Step 2. Save the document using the filename **AndreaChampionResume**.

Step 3. Press and drag to select the name at the top of the résumé and replace it with **Andrea Champion**.

Hint To save you typing time, you can open the AndreaInformation document in the sample_files folder available at www.pearsonhighered.com/jump or in MyITLab. (In Chapter 2, you downloaded the sample_files folder to your USB flash drive.) Then copy and paste text from this document into the AndreaChampionResume document. Copy each item of text one at a time and paste it into the proper location in the résumé. Alternately, you can type all the text into the résumé.

Step 4. Referring to the following table, click on the information in the résumé to select that field and then type over it with the information on the right side of the table.

Template	Replace With
[Street Address, City State ZIP Code]	138 Walnut Avenue, Grand Rapids, MI 49503
[Email]	achampion@sample.com
[Telephone]	616-555-7760

> **Not Working?** When pasting text from the AndreaInformation document into the résumé document, to retain formatting in the résumé document, click the down arrow under the **Paste** button on the HOME ribbon. Then click the first Paste icon (Use Destination Theme).

Step 5. In the OBJECTIVE section, using the following table, replace the text on the left with the text on the right:

Template	Replace With
Check out the few quick tips below to help you get started. To replace any tip text with your own, just click it and start typing.	Retail employment fulfilling multi-faceted roles (e.g., cashiering, customer service desk, and floor sales) during summers and holidays off from college.

Step 6. In the SKILLS & ABILITIES section, using the following table, replace the text on the left with the text on the right:

Template	Replace With
On the Design tab of the ribbon, check out the Themes, Colors, and Fonts galleries to get a custom look with just a click. Need another experience, education, or reference entry? You got it. Just click in the sample entries below and then click the plus sign that appears.	Experienced in customer service, cash handling, retail sales, inventory, display design, and gift wrapping. Offer excellent customer service skills, a "can-do" approach to all tasks, and a consistently high level of productivity. Technical skills include POS systems, computerized cash registers, inventory control systems, and MS Office (Word, OneNote, and Outlook).

Step 7. In the EXPERIENCE section, using the following table, replace the text on the left with the text on the right:

Template	Replace With
[JOB TITLE]	Summer Seasonal Associate
[COMPANY NAME]	Sears, Roebuck and Co., Holland, MI
[DATES FROM – TO]	May to August, 2013
This is the place for a brief summary of your key responsibilities and most stellar accomplishments.	• Demonstrated fast learning capacity, flexibility, and versatile skill-set. Worked on the sale floor (Major Appliances), in the customer service desk, and as a front-end cashier. Responsible for inventory records for department. • Recognized by store management team for customer service excellence and outstanding job performance through the "Rising Star" award in July, 2012.
[JOB TITLE]	Department Retailer
[COMPANY NAME]	JC Penney Company, Inc., Holland, MI
[DATES FROM – TO]	October to December, 2012
This is the place for a brief summary of your key responsibilities and most stellar accomplishments.	• Worked during the Fall and Winter breaks designing seasonal displays and in the Gift Wrapping department. Thrived during the fast-paced holiday seasons providing exceptional and expedient customer service. • Worked in the Customer Service department after the holiday season. Assisted with returns and exchanges until the end of Winter break.

> Tip If it were needed, notice you could click the plus sign on the far right side of the EXPERIENCE field to add a new row for a third company.

Step 8. In the EDUCATION section, using the following table, replace the text on the left with the text on the right:

Template	Replace With
[SCHOOL NAME]	University of Michigan
[LOCATION]	Grand Rapids, MI
[Degree]	Pursuing BS in Psychology, Minor in Music
You might want to include your GPA here and a brief summary of relevant coursework, awards, and honors.	August, 2011 to Present (Current GPA: 3.2)

Step 9. In the LEADERSHIP section, using the following table, replace the text on the left with the text on the right:

Template	Replace With
Are you president of your fraternity, head of the condo board, or a team lead for your favorite charity? You're a natural leader—tell it like it is!	Captain of the Freshman Cheerleading team, Fall, 2011.

Step 10. In the REFERENCES section, using the following table, replace the text on the left with the text on the right:

Template	Replace With
[REFERENCE NAME]	Jack Taylor
[TITLE]	Retail Manager
[COMPANY]	Sears, Roebuck and Co.
[Contact Information]	jtaylor@sample.com or 555-666-1234

Step 11. To remove the hyperlink that Word places on an email address, right-click **jtaylor@sample.com** and click **Remove Hyperlink** on the shortcut menu.

Andrea has nothing to include in the COMMUNICATION section, so it needs to be deleted. The résumé is built using a table. Do the following to view the borders of the table, delete the COMMUNICATION row, and then hide the borders:

Step 1. To view the borders of the table, click the grabber handle (table selector) in the upper left corner of the document. The entire table is selected.

Step 2. On the HOME ribbon, click the down arrow to the right of the Borders button and then click **All Borders** in the drop-down menu (see Figure S7-4). All borders in the table appear.

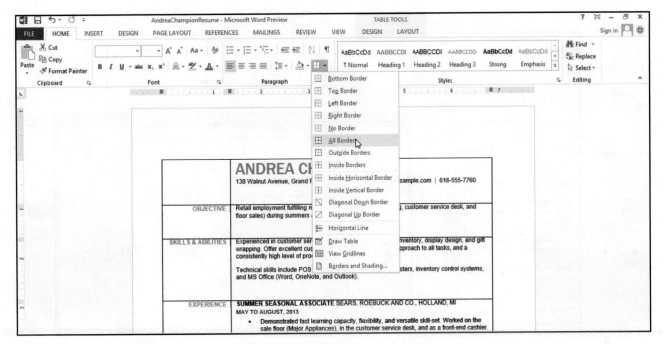

FIGURE S7-4
Show all borders for all cells in the table used to build the résumé.

Step 3. Click anywhere in the COMMUNICATION row so that it is the current row. On the LAYOUT ribbon, click **Delete**. In the drop-down menu, click **Delete Rows**. The COMMUNICATION row is deleted.

Step 4. To hide the table borders, click the grabber handle (table selector) at the top left corner of the table. The entire table is selected. On the HOME ribbon, click the down arrow beside the Borders button and then click **No Border** in the drop-down menu. All borders in the table disappear.

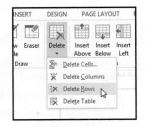

How to Export a Word Document as a PDF File

The résumé document is finished. Do the following to save the document and then save it again as a PDF file:

Step 1. Save the Word document.

Step 2. To save the document again, this time as a PDF file, click the **FILE** tab and then click **Export**. Click **Create PDF/XPS**.

Step 3. In the Publish as PDF or XPS dialog box, make sure **PDF** is selected in the Save as type box. Make sure **AndreaChampion-Resume** shows in the File name box. Click **Publish** to save the PDF file in the same location as the Word document.

On Your Own 7.3 Step-by-Step Solution   How to Email a Résumé PDF

Follow these steps to send an email message with the résumé PDF attached and request a read receipt using Outlook:

Step 1. Open Outlook. Create a new email message. Type **Interested in Holiday Employment** in the subject line.

Step 2. Type the body of the email message. You can find the message in the On Your Own 7.3 activity in the chapter.

Step 3. Double-check the message for errors.

Step 4. On the MESSAGE ribbon, click **Attach File**. The Insert File dialog box opens. Locate the **AndreaChampionResume.pdf** file (see Figure S7-5).

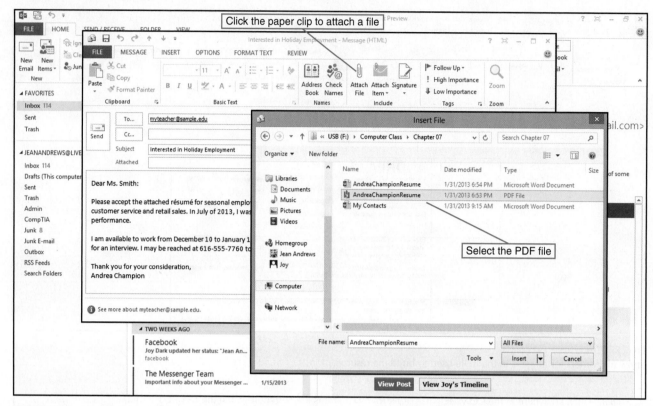

FIGURE S7-5
Be sure to attach the PDF file and not the Word document file to the email message.

Step 5. Click **Insert**. The file is listed in the Attached field.

Step 6. Click the **OPTIONS** tab and select **Request a Read Receipt**. The receipt is emailed to you when the receiver opens the message and agrees to send the read receipt.

Step 7. Type your instructor's email address in the To field. Click **Send** to send the message.

> **Tip** Leave the To field blank until you have double-checked your message for errors. That way, even if you accidently click **Send** before it's perfect, the email won't go to the potential employer.

On Your Own 7.4 Step-by-Step Solution   How to Create a Personal Letterhead for Business Letters

Follow these steps to create a personal letterhead document:

Step 1. In Word, click the **FILE** tab and click **New**. Under the search box, click **Letters**. In the Category pane on the right, click **Stationery**. Click **Cover letter (blue)**. (Or select another template you like better.) Click **Create**. A new document opens.

Step 2. Word tries to help you by putting your name at the top of the letter. Replace your name with Andrea's name and replace the other information at the top of the letter with Andrea's information. Using the following table, replace the text on the left with the text on the right:

Template	Replace With
Your or another name	Andrea Champion
[Address, City, ST ZIP Code]	138 Walnut Avenue, Grand Rapids, MI 49503
[Telephone]	616-555-7760
[Email]	achampion@sample.com

Step 3. Word might format the email address as a hyperlink. If it does that, remove the hyperlink. Right-click the address and click **Remove Hyperlink** in the shortcut menu.

Step 4. Save the document, naming it **AndreaChampionLetterhead**. If you see a message saying the document will be upgraded to the newest file format, click **OK**.

On Your Own 7.5 Step-by-Step Solution   How to Create an Interview Follow-Up Letter

Create and Email the SarahSmith Letter: Part 1 of 3

Not all letterhead templates work the same way. The template we're using provides a structure for you to enter the details of a business letter, and useful styles are also provided. Do the following to use the letterhead to create an interview follow-up letter:

Step 1. If necessary, open the **AndreaChampionLetterhead** document.

Step 2. Click the **FILE** tab and then click **Save As**. Name the new document file **SarahSmith**. Save the document to your USB flash drive, hard drive, OneDrive, or other location given by your instructor.

Step 3. Click **[Date]** and then click the down arrow to the right and select today's date.

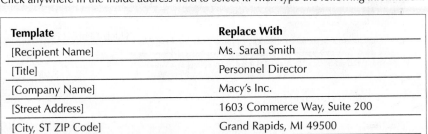

Step 4. Click anywhere in the inside address field to select it. Then type the following information:

Template	Replace With
[Recipient Name]	Ms. Sarah Smith
[Title]	Personnel Director
[Company Name]	Macy's Inc.
[Street Address]	1603 Commerce Way, Suite 200
[City, ST ZIP Code]	Grand Rapids, MI 49500

Step 5. In the salutation, replace [Recipient] with **Ms. Smith**.

Step 6. Select the four paragraphs in the body of the letter (see Figure S7-6) and delete the selected text. Save the document.

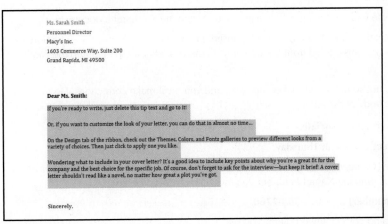

FIGURE S7-6
Select and delete the body of the letter.

Not Working? Templates at office.com change from time to time. If you can't find one used here, use another that fits your need.

Step 7. Without closing the SarahSmith document, click the **FILE** tab and then click **New**. In the search box, type **thank you for interview** and press **Enter**. Click the **Thank you for interview** template that appears. Click **Create**. The document is created. (If you can't find the thank you for interview template, try searching for a template named **Interview thank you letter**.)

Thank you for interview template

Step 8. Select the two paragraphs in the body of the letter (see Figure S7-7). Notice that these paragraphs contain six fields. On the HOME ribbon, click **Copy**. The text is copied to the Windows Clipboard.

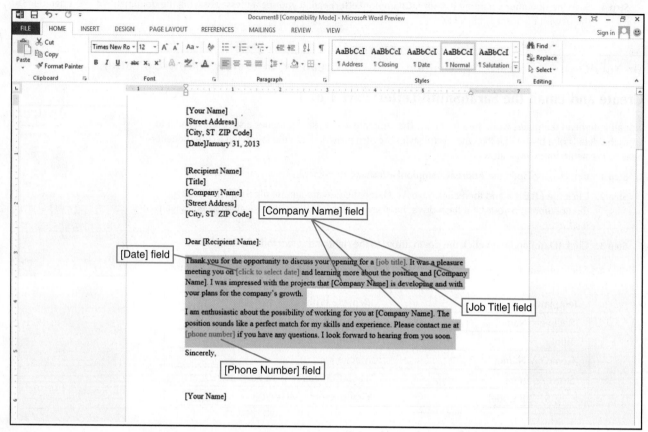

FIGURE S7-7
A letter template can help you write the body of a business letter.

Step 9. Close the new document that was just create without saving it. You're then returned to the SarahSmith document.

Step 10. Position your insertion point below the salutation line. You might need to insert a new blank line below the salutation. On the HOME ribbon, click **Paste**. The two paragraphs copied from the interview thank you letter are pasted into the Sarah-Smith document.

Word attempts to replace a field with the correct text, but sometimes it makes mistakes, and you must make corrections. Do the following to put the correct text in the six fields in the body of the letter:

Step 1. In the first paragraph, replace **[job title]** with **sales associate**.

Step 2. In the first paragraph, replace **[click to select date]** with **Thursday**.

Step 3. In the first and second paragraphs, replace **[Company Name]** with **Macy's** for all three occurrences. (Word might have already put Andrea's email address in the [Company Name] field, but you must correct this problem.)

Step 4. In the second paragraph, replace **[phone number]** with **616-555-7760**.

Step 5. Double-check the spelling and formatting and correct any problems you see.

Step 6. Save the document.

On Your Own 7.6 Step-by-Step Solution   How to Add an Envelope to the SarahSmith Letter

Create and Email the SarahSmith Letter: Part 2 of 3

Follow these steps to add an envelope to a letter:

Step 1. If necessary, open the follow-up letter you wrote for Andrea Champion to Ms. Smith named **SarahSmith**.

Step 2. Click the **MAILINGS** tab, and then click **Envelopes**. The Envelopes and Labels dialog box appears, as shown in Figure 7-9 in the chapter.

Step 3. Enter Sarah Smith's address as the Delivery address:

Ms. Sarah Smith
Personnel Director
Macy's Inc.
1603 Commerce Way, Suite 200
Grand Rapids, MI 49500

Step 4. Enter Andrea Champion's address as the Return address:

Andrea Champion
138 Walnut Avenue
Grand Rapids, MI 49503

Step 5. Click **Add to Document**. A dialog box appears asking whether you want to save the new return address as the default return address. Click **No**.

Step 6. The envelope appears as the first page of the document. Save the document.

Step 7. If you have access to a printer and an envelope, insert the envelope in the printer. Orient the envelope according to the instructions in your printer manual. Print the document. The envelope prints first, followed by the letter.

On Your Own 7.7 Step-by-Step Solution   **How to Email the Follow-Up Letter**

Create and Email the SarahSmith Letter: Part 3 of 3

Follow these steps to email the follow-up letter:

Step 1. In Word, open the follow-up letter you wrote for Andrea Champion named **SarahSmith**.

Step 2. Press and drag to select the text beginning with *Dear Ms. Smith* through the name *Andrea Champion* (see Figure S7-8). On the HOME ribbon, click **Copy.** The text copies to the Windows Clipboard.

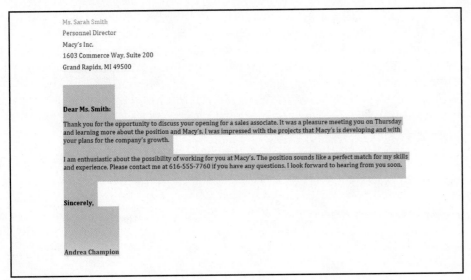

FIGURE S7-8
Select the portion of the follow-up letter to be inserted in an email message.

> **Hint** Besides using the HOME ribbon, you can right-click and use a shortcut menu to copy. Another way to copy is to select text and press **Ctrl+C**.

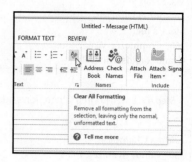

Step 3. In Outlook, create a new email message. Position your insertion point in the body of the message. Then click **Paste** on the MESSAGE ribbon. The text is copied into the message.

Step 4. To remove the text formatting, press **Ctrl+A** to select all the text in the message. Then click the **Clear All Formatting** button on the MESSAGE ribbon.

Step 5. If necessary, insert a double space following the salutation and each of the two paragraphs.

Step 6. Insert Andrea's cell phone number below her name at the bottom of the message: **Cell: 616-555-7760**.

Step 7. Type **Sales Associate Position** in the subject line of the email.

Step 8. Double-check the spelling and formatting and correct any problems you see.

Step 9. Type your instructor's email address in the **To:** field and send the email to your instructor.

CHAPTER 8 STEP-BY-STEP SOLUTIONS
Using PowerPoint to Give a Presentation

The solutions in this appendix are for you to use if you get stuck when doing an On Your Own activity in the chapter. To learn how to teach yourself a computer skill, always try the On Your Own activity first before turning to these solutions.

On Your Own 8.1 Step-by-Step Solution   **How to Explore the PowerPoint Window**

Follow these steps to learn about the PowerPoint window:

Step 1. If you're using Windows 8 to open PowerPoint, click the **PowerPoint 2013** tile on the Start screen or start typing PowerPoint to search for the application. If you're using Windows 7 to open PowerPoint, click **Start**, click **All Programs**, click **Microsoft Office 2013**, and click **PowerPoint 2013**.

Step 2. In the PowerPoint window, click **Blank Presentation**. A blank presentation is created. Maximize the PowerPoint window.

Step 3. To see a ribbon, click the tab for that ribbon.

Step 4. To add a second slide that uses the Comparison layout, on the HOME ribbon, click the down arrow next to New Slide. In the drop-down gallery of slide types that appears, click **Comparison**. The Comparison slide layout has five text boxes.

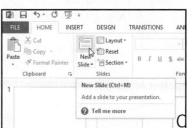

Step 5. To add a new slide that's the same as the previous slide, on the HOME ribbon, click the new slide icon above **New Slide**.

Step 6. To open PowerPoint Help, click the Help icon **?** in the upper-right corner of the window.

Step 7. To find out how to apply a theme, type **apply a theme** in the Help search box and press **Enter**. In the list that appears, click **Apply color and design to my slides (theme)**.

Step 8. To find out how to add slide numbers to a presentation, type **slide numbers** in the Help search box and press **Enter**. In the list that appears, click **Insert or change the page numbers on your slides**.

Step 9. To close the presentation without saving your changes, click the **FILE** tab. Click **Close**. In the dialog box that appears, click **Don't Save**.

On Your Own 8.2 Step-by-Step Solution   **How to Choose a Theme**

Create and Present the Motivation Presentation: Part 1 of 7

Follow these steps to open a blank presentation:

Step 1. If PowerPoint is not open, open it. Create a blank presentation. If PowerPoint is already open and you need to create a blank presentation, click the **FILE** tab. Click **New** and then click **Blank Presentation**. A blank presentation is created.

Step 2. Maximize the window.

Follow these steps to apply a theme to the presentation:

Step 1. Click the **DESIGN** tab. Click the More arrow to the right of the themes to see more themes. In the drop-down gallery of themes, click the **Slice** theme to apply it to all slides.

> **Hint** The name of a theme appears when you move your mouse pointer over a theme.

Step 2. To view the color schemes of the Slice theme, on the DESIGN ribbon, click the **More** arrow to the right of Variants and point to **Colors**. Mouse over the colors and watch how the colors change on the title slide. Click off the menu so it disappears.

Step 3. Besides Colors, other options under Variants are Fonts, Effects, and Background Styles. To explore these options, click the **More** arrow and mouse over each option. Click off the menu so it disappears.

Step 4. Click the **FILE** tab and, if necessary, change the author to your name.

> **Hint** If you need help changing the author to your name, refer to On Your Own 3.7 Step-by-Step Solution.

Step 5. Save the PowerPoint file to your hard drive, USB flash drive, OneDrive, or other location.

> **Hint** Saving a file in PowerPoint works the same as it does in Word. If you need help, see the instructions in On Your Own 3.3 Step-by-Step Solution.

On Your Own 8.3 Step-by-Step Solution   **How to Create the Title Slide**

Create and Present the Motivation Presentation: Part 2 of 7

Follow these steps to create the title slide, which is shown in the chapter in Figure 8-6:

Step 1. Click in the title text box on the slide and type **What Motivates Us**.

Step 2. Press and drag to select the text. With the text selected, click the **HOME** tab. Click the **Increase Font Size** button ᴀ˙ to increase the font size. Keep clicking until the title fills the text box without spilling over to a new line.

> **Hint** If the font size is too big, click the **Decrease Font Size** button. ᴀ˙.

Step 3. Click in the subtitle text box and type **By Jawana Washington**.

Step 4. Select the subtitle text. In the Font Size box on the HOME ribbon, select **40** points. Click the **Bold** button ʙ to bold the text.

Follow these steps to add a text box and the Einstein quote:

Step 1. Click the **INSERT** tab and click **Text Box**. Press and drag to create a text box near the top of the slide. In the text box, type the following text, pressing **Enter** at the end of each line:

> "Try not to become a person of success, but rather a person of value."
> Albert Einstein

Step 2. Select all the text in the text box. Set the font size to **32** points. If necessary, resize and move the text box so all the text fits on the slide and the line breaks right after the comma.

Step 3. Click somewhere in the name **Albert Einstein**. Click the **Align Right** button ≡ on the HOME ribbon.

Step 4. Select the text **Albert Einstein**. Click the **Italic** button ɪ on the HOME ribbon.

Step 5. Compare the slide to that shown in Figure 8-6 in the chapter and correct any problems you see. You might need to move the third text box so the quote is in the right position.

> **Hint** To move a text box, click on the box to select it. Mouse over the edge of the box until your pointer changes to a cross and arrow ✛. Press and drag to move the box.

Follow these steps to finish the slide:

Step 1. Speaker notes are typed in the notes pane at the bottom of the slide labeled *Click to add notes*. To increase the height of this pane, press and drag the top of the pane upward. Type the following in the pane:

> Motivated people tend to be happier and produce more than others.
> We all need to know our strongest motivators.

Step 2. To view the slide as it appears in a slide show, click the **SLIDE SHOW** tab. Click **From Current Slide**. Press **Escape** to return to Normal view.

Step 3. To change views in the Slide/Outline pane on the left, first click the **VIEW** tab. To see the Outline view, click **Outline View** on the VIEW ribbon. To see the thumbnails of slides in the left pane, click **Normal** on the VIEW ribbon.

Normal view

> **Not Working?** If you don't see the Slide/Outline pane on your window, click **Normal** on the VIEW ribbon.

Step 4. To save your work, click the **Save** button in the Quick Access Toolbar of the PowerPoint window.

On Your Own 8.4 Step-by-Step Solution   **How to Add a Slide with a Bulleted List and Graphics**

Create and Present the Motivation Presentation: Part 3 of 7

Do the following to create the second slide:

Step 1. On the HOME ribbon, click the arrow to the right of the New Slide button and click the **Title and Content** slide. A new slide is added to the presentation.

Step 2. Click inside the second text box near the bottom of the slide and type **Others Motivate Us**. Select the text and click the **Increase Font Size** button ⌃ on the HOME ribbon. Keep clicking until the title fills the text box.

Step 3. Click in the first text box near the top of the slide and type the following text:

> Incentives
> Reward
> Punishment

Step 4. Click an insertion point before **Incentives** and press the **Backspace** key to delete the bullet.

Step 5. Select all three lines of text and set the font size to **32** points and **Bold**.

Follow these steps to insert a photo about rewards:

Step 1. On the INSERT ribbon, click **Online Pictures**. The Insert Pictures dialog box appears. In the Bing Image Search search box, enter **punishment** and press **Enter**.

> **Not Working?** The photo you find will be different than the one used in the chapter.

Step 2. Select a photo and click **Insert**. The photo then appears on the slide. Press and drag a corner sizing handle to resize the photo and to keep proportions the same. Make the size about the same as that in Figure S8-1.

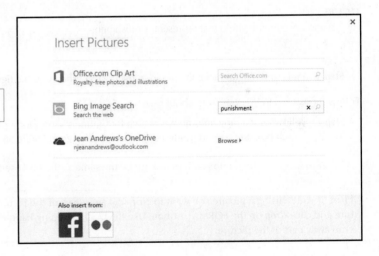

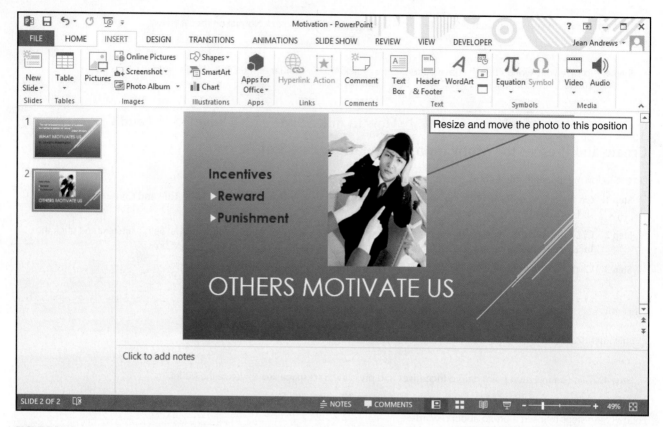

FIGURE S8-1
Resize and position the photo that represents punishment.

Step 3. Press and drag to move the photo to the position shown in the figure. Align the top of the photo with the top of the slide.

Follow these steps to insert a photo about reward:

Step 1. Following the directions above, search for Online Pictures for a photo on reward. Enter **reward** in the Bing Image Search search box. Resize and position the photo, as shown in Figure S8-2. Align the photo along the top of the slide.

Not Working? The photo you find will not be the same as the one used here.

Hint If you're using a picture you want to crop (cut away part of the picture), select the picture and click **Crop** on the FORMAT ribbon. Use the black cropping handles that appear to crop away part of the picture.

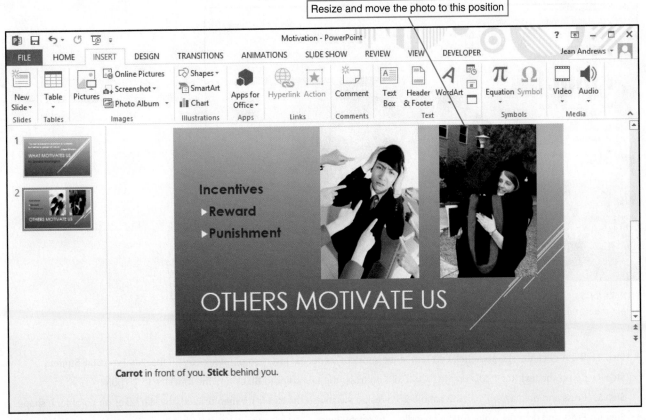

FIGURE S8-2
A second photo is added to the slide.

To insert and format the star shape, follow these steps:

Step 1. On the INSERT ribbon, click **Shapes**. In the drop-down list, click **24-Point Star**. Your pointer changes to a crosshair **+**. Press and drag to draw the star on the slide.

Move the star into position so that it overlaps the photo about rewards.

Step 2. If necessary, click the star to select it. With the star selected, click the **FORMAT** tab. On the FORMAT ribbon, click the down arrow to the right of Shape Fill and click **Orange** (see Figure S8-3).

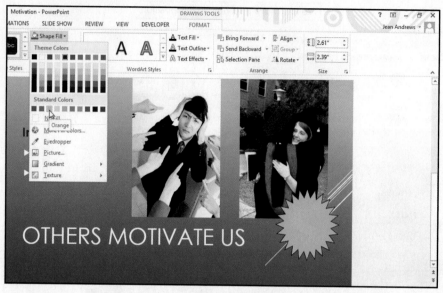

FIGURE S8-3
Select the star and set the Shape Fill color to orange.

Step 3. Right-click the star and click **Edit Text** in the shortcut menu. An insertion point appears in the star. Type **Star Student**.

Step 4. Select the text. Use tools on the HOME ribbon to set the text color to **Black** and the font size to **28** points.

Step 5. Press and drag a corner sizing handle ↗ to resize the star so the text fits. When resized, the star takes on an oblong shape.

Step 6. Press and drag the white rotating handle ⟳ to rotate the star. If necessary, move it so that it overlaps the photo and doesn't cover the title.

Step 7. Compare your slide to that in Figure 8-7 in the chapter and correct any problems you see.

Step 8. To view the slide as it will appear in a slide show, click the **SLIDE SHOW** tab and click **From Current Slide**. Press **Escape** to return to Normal view.

Follow these steps to finish the slide:

Step 1. In the notes pane below the slide, enter the following speaker notes:

Carrot in front of you. Stick behind you.

Step 2. Select the word **Carrot** and bold it. Select the word **Stick** and bold it.

Step 3. Save your work.

On Your Own 8.5 Step-by-Step Solution   How to Add a Slide with SmartArt

Create and Present the Motivation Presentation: Part 4 of 7

Follow these steps to add a slide with SmartArt:

Step 1. Click the **New Slide** button on the HOME ribbon. A new slide is added.

Step 2. Type **We Motivate Ourselves** in the title text box at the bottom of the slide. Select the text and increase the font size to fill the space.

Step 3. Click in the content text box at the top of the slide. Click the **INSERT** tab and click **SmartArt**. The Choose a SmartArt Graphic dialog box appears.

Step 4. Scroll down a bit and click **Vertical Curved List** (see Figure S8-4). Click **OK** to insert the SmartArt.

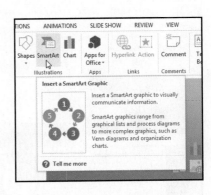

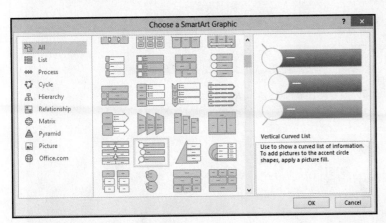

FIGURE S8-4
Choose the SmartArt graphic.

Step 5. When the SmartArt is selected, you can see the SmartArt container box, as shown in Figure S8-5. In the figure, you can also see the SmartArt text pane where you can type, view, and format the text in the SmartArt graphic. You can also type directly in the text boxes inside the SmartArt container box. Type **Mastery** for the first bullet in the text pane.

Not Working? If you accidentally close the SmartArt text pane, first select the SmartArt so the SmartArt container box appears. Then click the arrow on the left side of the SmartArt container box. The text pane appears.

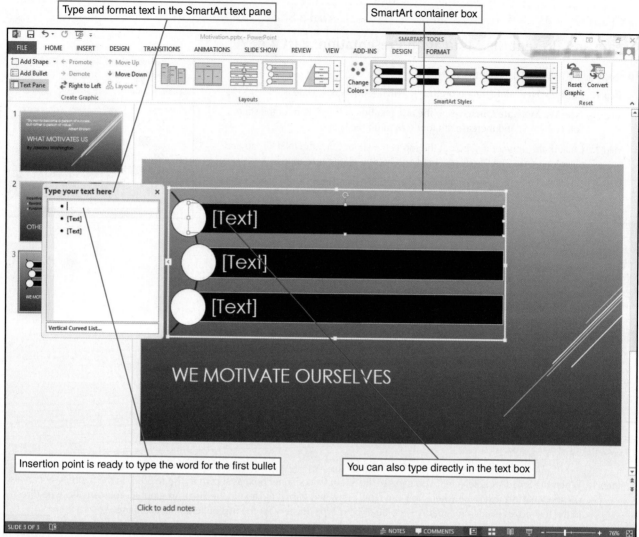

FIGURE S8-5
SmartArt provides a text pane you use to type, view, and format the text in the SmartArt graphic.

Step 6. Click in the next text area and type **Independence**.

Step 7. Click in the third text area and type **Contribution**.

Step 8. Using the SmartArt text pane, press and drag to select the three lines of text. (Alternately, you can select the SmartArt container box itself.) Then use the HOME ribbon to set the font size. A size of **44** points works well. Center the text.

Step 9. With the SmartArt text or container box still selected, click the **DESIGN** tab under SMART-ART TOOLS. Click **Change Colors**. Click **Colorful - Accent Colors**, as shown in Figure S8-6.

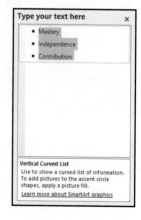

Not Working? The PowerPoint window offers two DESIGN tabs. Be sure to click the DESIGN tab under SMARTART TOOLS.

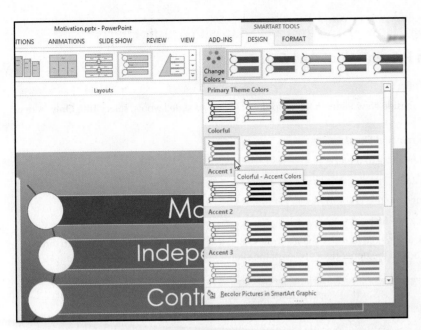

FIGURE S8-6
Change the colors of the SmartArt elements.

Step 10. Compare the slide to that shown in Figure 8-8 in the chapter and correct any problems you see. View the slide as it will appear in a slide show and correct any problems.

Follow these steps to enter speaker notes for this slide:

Step 1. Increase the height of the notes pane below the slide.

Step 2. Type the following text into the notes pane:

Mastery
Opportunity to do something very well
Independence
Right to make our own decisions
Decide what, when, how, and with whom we work
Contribution
Make a difference for others
This is the most powerful motivator

Step 3. In the speaker notes pane, select **Mastery** and bold it. Also bold **Independence** and **Contribution**.

Step 4. Click on the second line and then click the **Increase List Level** button on the HOME ribbon to indent the line. Do the same for other lines in the notes that need indenting.

Step 5. Save your work.

Create and Present the Motivation Presentation: Part 5 of 7

Follow these steps to insert the slide and add the title:

Step 1. On the HOME ribbon, click the arrow beside **New Slide**. In the drop-down gallery of slide layouts, select **Title Only**. A new slide is added.

Step 2. In the text box, type the title **How Do You Find Flow?**

Step 3. Using the HOME ribbon, apply this formatting to the title:

    a. Select the word **Flow** and set it to italic.

    b. Select all the text in the title. Change the text color to black.

    c. Right-justify the text. Set the font size to **66** points.

Step 4. Press and drag the lower-left corner sizing handle to resize the text box so that text wrap causes the text to flow to three lines (see Figure S8-7). Move the text box to the upper-right corner of the slide.

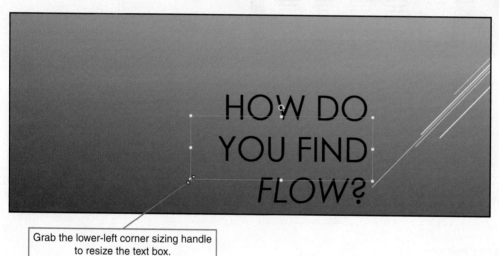

Grab the lower-left corner sizing handle to resize the text box.

FIGURE S8-7
Resize the text box to make the title wrap to three lines.

Follow these steps to insert an Online Pictures photo and format the photo:

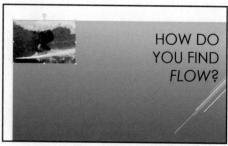

Step 1. Insert an Online Pictures photo of a surfer on a wave. The words **riding a wave** can be used in the Bing Image Search search box. The photo is inserted in the center of the slide.

Not Working? The photo you find will not be the same as the one used here.

Step 2. Press and drag the photo to the upper-left corner of the slide.

Step 3. Press and drag the lower-right corner sizing handle to resize the photo so that it fills the entire slide, covering even the title. Make sure the photo covers the entire slide. As you do so, the photo might spill off the bottom or right side of the slide.

Hint You don't need to cut off (crop) the part of the photo that spills off the slide. However, if you want to crop a photo, first select the photo. Then click **Crop** on the FORMAT ribbon.

Step 4. Right-click the photo. In the shortcut menu, click **Send to Back**. The title appears on top of the photo.

Step 5. With the photo still selected, click the **FORMAT** tab. Click **Artistic Effects**. In the drop-down gallery of effects, click **Glow Diffused** (see Figure S8-8).

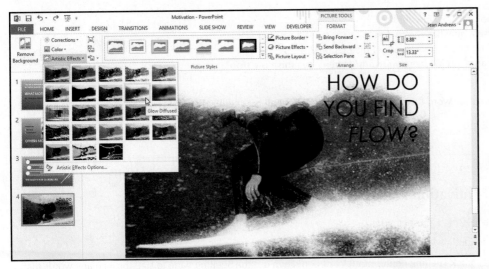

FIGURE S8-8
Artistic effects can make a photo more interesting and appealing.

Step 6. With the photo still selected, click the **FORMAT** tab and click **Color**. Then click **Light Turquoise, Text color 2 Dark** (see Figure S8-9). Save your work.

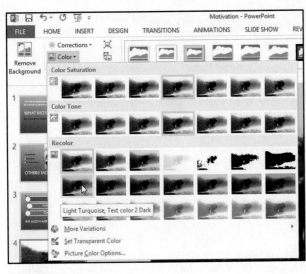

FIGURE S8-9
Apply color to a photo.

Step 7. Compare the slide to that shown in Figure 8-10 in the chapter and correct any problems you see. View the slide as it will appear in a slide show and correct any problems.

Follow these steps to complete the slide and add speaker notes:

Step 1. The last slide invites the audience to apply the presentation to their own lives. You can ask questions to encourage thought and discussion. Enter the following notes in the notes pane for this slide:

> To know what motivates you, look for flow in your life.
>   Flow is when you "lose yourself" in what you're doing.
>   When do you lose track of time and are not aware of distractions?
>   What are you doing? Where are you? Who are you with? When does this flow stop?

Step 2. To format the notes, bold the word **flow** in the first line and indent all but the first line of text.

Step 3. Save your work.

On Your Own 8.7 Step-by-Step Solution   **How to Review and Revise the Presentation**

Create and Present the Motivation Presentation: Part 6 of 7

Follow these directions to practice revising a presentation:

Step 1. Click a slide in the Slide/Outline pane to move to it.

Step 2. To use the spell checker, click **Spelling** on the REVIEW ribbon. Then use the Spelling pane to step through any words that PowerPoint thinks are misspelled. Close the Spelling pane when you're done.

Step 3. Use the Slide/Outline pane to move a slide. Press and drag the slide up or down to a new position. Then return it to its original location.

Step 4. On the VIEW ribbon, click **Slide Sorter** or click the Slide Sorter button ⊞ in the status bar. Press and drag to move a slide. Then return it to its original location.

Step 5. To insert a new slide following the first slide, right-click the first slide in the Slide/Outline pane. Then click **New Slide** in the shortcut menu.

Step 6. To delete a slide, right-click it in the Slide/Outline pane. Then click **Delete Slide** in the shortcut menu.

Step 7. To view slides in the Notes Page view, click the **VIEW** tab and then click **Notes Page**. Click **Normal** to return to Normal view.

Step 8. To view your presentation as a slide show, click the Slide Show button ▤ in the status bar. Use the up- and down-arrow keys or left- and right-arrow keys to step through all the slides.

On Your Own 8.8 Step-by-Step Solution   **How to Print the Presentation and Save as a PowerPoint Show**

Create and Present the Motivation Presentation: Part 7 of 7

Follow these steps to find out about printing a presentation and to print:

Step 1. Click the **FILE** tab. Click **Print**. Slides appear on the screen in print preview. If you don't see Color in the drop-down menu at the bottom of the Print window, click the down arrow next to Grayscale or Pure Black and White and then click **Color**.

Step 2. To see how you can print handouts, click the down arrow next to **Full Page Slides**. Print Layout options appear (see Figure S8-10).

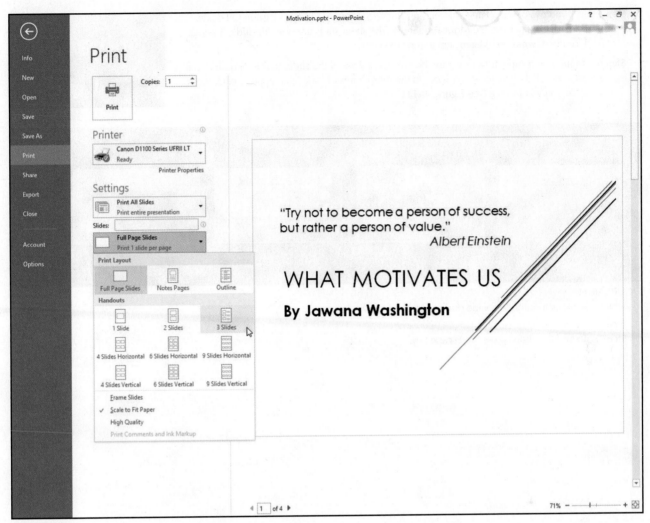

FIGURE S8-10
Select a method to use for printing the slides.

Step 3. Under Handouts, click **3 Slides**. The write-on lines next to the slide are for your audience to take notes during the presentation. To print the handouts, make sure your printer is selected and click **Print**.

Step 4. Click **3 Slides**. In the list of Print Layout options, click **Notes Pages**. The preview shows that one slide prints to a page with speaker notes printed under the slide. To print the notes, click **Print**.

Follow these steps to create and use a PowerPoint show:

Step 1. If necessary, click the **FILE** tab. Click **Save As**. Navigate to the location to save the show.

Step 2. The Save As window appears. Click the down arrow next to *Save as type* and click **PowerPoint Show (*.ppsx)**.

Step 3. In the File name box, type **MotivationShow**. Click **Save**. The presentation is saved as a slide show, and the file extension is .ppsx.

Step 4. Close the PowerPoint window.

Step 5. In Windows 8, open File Explorer. (In Windows 7, open Windows Explorer.) Locate and double-click the file **MotivationShow**. The show starts and the title slide appears. Use the down-arrow key to step to the next slide.

Step 6. To jump to a slide, hover over the bottom-left corner of the slide. In the menu bar that appears, click the slide sorter icon. In the thumbnails of slides that appear, click the slide you want to see (see Figure S8-11).

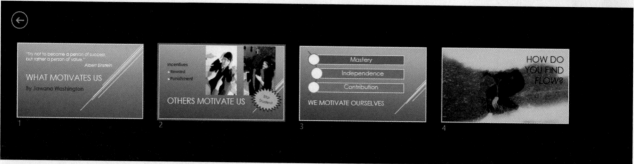

FIGURE S8-11
Use the thumbnails to jump to a slide during the slide show.

Step 7. To end the show, press the **Escape** key.

CHAPTER 9 STEP-BY-STEP SOLUTIONS
Adding Action and Sound to a PowerPoint Presentation

The step-by-step solutions in this appendix are for you to use if you get stuck when doing an On Your Own activity in the chapter. To learn how to teach yourself a computer skill, always try the On Your Own activity first before turning to these solutions.

On Your Own 9.1 Step-by-Step Solution   How to Edit the Slide Master

Create the GarageBand Presentation: Part 1 of 7

Follow these steps to add shapes to the slide master:

Step 1. Open a new blank presentation in PowerPoint and maximize your window.

Step 2. Click the **VIEW** tab and click **Slide Master**. The Slide Master view opens. Click the first thumbnail in the left pane, which is the slide master. (You might need to scroll to the top of the thumbnails to see it.)

Step 3. On the INSERT ribbon, click **Shapes** and click the **Freeform** shape in the Lines group. Your pointer changes to a crosshair ＋.

Step 4. Press and drag to draw a jagged long shape on the left side of the master slide. First, draw down and then draw up. When the end of the line overlaps the beginning of the line, the form fills in. Release the mouse button to stop the drawing. The shape is created and is selected.

Step 5. With the shape still selected, on the FORMAT ribbon, click **Shape Fill** and select **Dark Red** from the drop-down gallery of colors that appears.

Step 6. With the shape still selected, on the FORMAT ribbon, click **Shape Outline** and click **No Outline** in the drop-down gallery.

Step 7. To add the second shape on the right side of the slide master, you can copy the first shape and paste it on the right, or you can draw a new shape and format the color and line.

Slide master

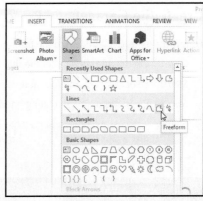
Freeform shape

> **Hint** To copy an object, select it and click the **Copy** icon ⌨ on the HOME ribbon. To paste it, click the slide and then click **Paste** on the HOME ribbon. Then drag the new object to its correct position.

Follow these steps to format the background and text on the slide master:

Step 1. On the SLIDE MASTER ribbon, click **Background Styles** and click **Style 4** (see Figure S9-1). The background is now black.

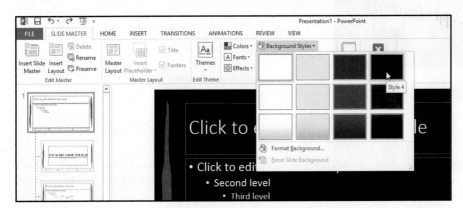

FIGURE S9-1
Change the background style to black.

Step 2. Select the text in the title text box. Click the **HOME** tab. Change the font to **Trebuchet MS** and the font size to **44** points.

Step 3. Click in the footer text box. The text disappears, but don't worry—you're still changing the formatting in this box. On the HOME ribbon, format the footer text box using the **Chiller** font, **Dark Red**, and **32** points. When you click the text box border or click outside the box, you can see the footer text is formatted.

Step 4. Click the **SLIDE MASTER** tab and click **Close Master View**.

Step 5. Click the **HOME** tab. Click the down arrow next to the New Slide button. Slide layouts appear. Each layout should have the red shapes and a black background.

> **Not Working?** If the design isn't applied to all layouts, most likely you made changes to a slide master layout and not to the slide master. Return to Slide Master view, scroll up in the left pane, and click the first thumbnail. All your work should be done on this slide.

Step 6. Save the presentation to your hard drive, USB flash drive, OneDrive, or another location, naming the file **GarageBand**. A PowerPoint presentation file is saved the same way as a Word document file. If you need help saving the file, see On Your Own 3.3 Step-by-Step Solution.

On Your Own 9.2 Step-by-Step Solution **How to Add Video to the Title Slide**

Create the GarageBand Presentation: Part 2 of 7

Follow these steps to add text to the title slide:

Step 1. On the title slide, enter the title **Out of the Garage Onto the Road**.

Step 2. Select the text and format it using the **Chiller** font, **80** point, **Dark Red**.

Step 3. Press and drag the rotating handle to rotate the text box to the left so the box tilts downward to the left.

Step 4. If necessary, press and drag the lower-right corner sizing handle to shorten the width of the text box. When you do that, the text wraps to two lines, as shown in Figure S9-2.

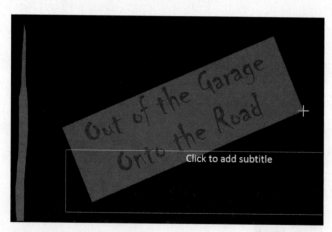

FIGURE S9-2
Resize the text box using the bottom-right corner sizing handle.

Step 5. Move the text box to the top-left area of the slide. It's okay if the corners of the text box flow off the slide—just make sure the text is positioned where you want it.

Step 6. Enter the subtitle **By Aimee Peters**. To select the text box, click the text box border. Then increase the font size to **32** point. Click the **Align Text** button ⊞ on the HOME ribbon and choose **Middle**. Move the text box down and left to make room for the video box below the text box.

Follow these steps to add a video clip to the slide:

Step 1. Use File Explorer (in Windows 7, use Windows Explorer) to locate the RockBand video file in the sample_files folder on your USB flash drive. Recall that in Chapter 2, you downloaded the sample_files folder to your USB flash drive from www.pearsonhighered.com/jump or from MyITLab.

Step 2. On the INSERT ribbon, click **Video**. Then select **Video on My PC** from the drop-down menu. The Insert Video box appears. Locate the **RockBand** video file in the sample_files folder. Click **Insert**. The video box appears on the slide.

Step 3. To add a red border to the video, make sure the video box is selected. On the VIDEO TOOLS FORMAT tab, click **Video Border** and then click **Dark Red**.

Step 4. Position the video box, as shown in the chapter in Figure 9-6.

Step 5. To test the video, click the video box. The controls at the bottom of the box appear. Click the **Play** button. The video plays.

Step 6. To test the slide, click the **Slide Show** button ▦ at the bottom of the PowerPoint window. Click anywhere inside the red video box and play the video. Press **Escape** to close the slide show.

Step 7. Save your work.

On Your Own 9.3 Step-by-Step Solution   **How to Create the Second Slide with Audio and Animation**

Create the GarageBand Presentation: Part 3 of 7

Follow these steps to add the second slide with a title, footer, and bulleted list:

Step 1. On the HOME ribbon, click the down arrow next to New Slide and select the **Two Content** slide layout.

Step 2. Enter the slide title: **Start with the Press Kit**. Center the title in the text box.

Step 3. To add the footer, on the INSERT ribbon, click **Header & Footer**. The Header and Footer dialog box opens.

Step 4. Check **Footer** and add the text **Out of the Garage onto the Road**. Check **Don't show on title slide**, as shown in Figure S9-3.

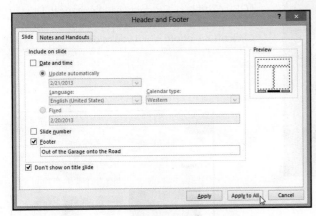

FIGURE S9-3
Type the footer to go on every slide except the title slide.

Step 5. To apply the footer to all slides except the title slide, click **Apply to All**.

Step 6. Notice the footer is using text wrap and fills two lines. To fix this problem, you have to correct it on the Slide Master. On the VIEW ribbon, click **Slide Master**. In the Slides/outline pane on the left, scroll up and select the slide master—the thumbnail at the top of the list. Select the footer text box and press and drag each side of the text box so that it's wide enough for the footer to fit on one line and the footer text box is centered on the slide (see Figure S9-4). Close the Slide Master view.

FIGURE S9-4
Widen the footer text box and center it on the slide.

Step 7. On the second slide, click in the text box on the right side of the slide and enter the following text to create a bulleted list:

- Band bio & photo
- Past & future gigs
- Song & equipment list
- Website & Facebook
- Business cards
- Who to contact

Step 8. Select the text and change the font size to **40** points.

Follow these steps to add clip art:

Step 1. On the INSERT ribbon, click **Online Pictures**. In the Bing Image Search search box, enter **garage door**. Press **Enter**.

Step 2. In the list of photos, click a garage door photo and click **Insert**. The photo is inserted.

Step 3. Move and resize the photo so that it fits under the title and above the footer (see Figure S9-5). Use a corner sizing handle to resize so the photo proportions don't change.

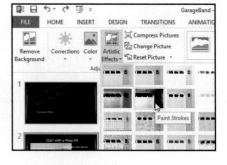

FIGURE S9-5
The photo is in position and is behind the text.

Step 4. With the photo selected, click the **FORMAT** tab. Click **Artistic Effects** and click **Paint Strokes**.

Step 5. On the FORMAT ribbon, click **Color** and in the Color Saturation group, click **Saturation 0%**.

Step 6. Save your work.

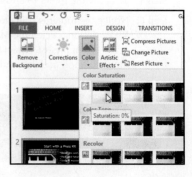

Follow these steps to add an audio clip to the slide:

Step 1. On the INSERT ribbon, click **Audio**, then **Online Audio**. The Insert Audio dialog box opens. In the Office.com Clip Art search box, enter **revving car engine** and press **Enter**.

Step 2. In the list of audio clips, click **Revving car engine** and click **Insert**. The audio clip icon is added to the slide. Move the audio clip icon to the lower-right corner of the slide (see Figure S9-6). To hear the audio, click the **Play** button.

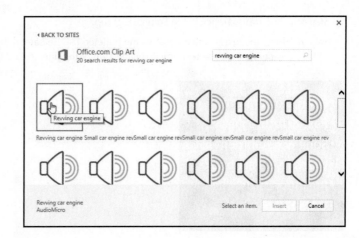

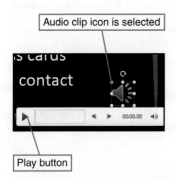

FIGURE S9-6
Position the audio clip icon in the lower-right area of the slide.

Step 3. Click the **Slide Show** button 🖳 to view the slide as a slide show and play the audio. Press **Escape** to return to Normal view. Correct any errors you see.

Step 4. Save your work.

Follow these steps to add animation to the objects on the slide:

Step 1. Select the audio icon. Click the **ANIMATIONS** tab and click **Play**.

Step 2. Run the slide show again. When you click anywhere on the slide, the sound plays. Return to Normal view.

Step 3. Select the photo. On the ANIMATIONS ribbon, click the **More** arrow to the right of the animations.

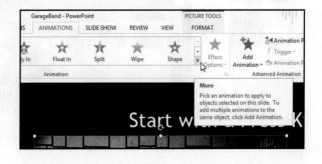

Step 4. Click **Transparency** in the Emphasis group.

Step 5. Select the text box that contains the bulleted list. Be careful to select the box and not the text inside the box. The text box is selected when the line around the box is solid and not dashed.

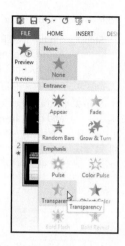

Step 6. On the ANIMATIONS ribbon, click **Grow & Turn** in the Entrance group. Watch as each bulleted item grows and turns onto the slide.

Step 7. View the slide as a slide show. As you click, the sound, photo, and text animations happen. Keep clicking the slide until all the bulleted items display. Then return to Normal view.

Step 8. PowerPoint displays on the slide the order that animation happens. The correct order is shown in Figure S9-7, which is first the sound, then the photo, and then each item in the bulleted list. If the order on your slide is not correct, click the **ANIMATIONS** tab and click **Animation Pane**. The Animation Pane appears as shown in Figure S9-7. You can press and drag an item in this pane to change the animation order.

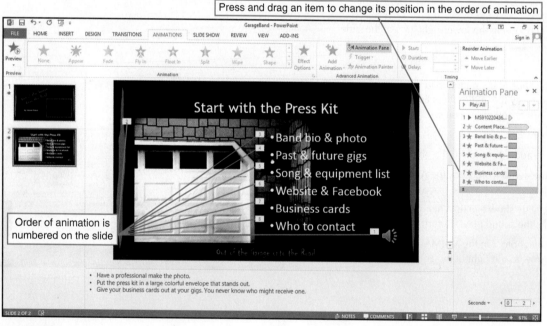

FIGURE S9-7
Animations 1 through 8 are identified on the slide.

Hint If all the animated items are not listed in the Animation Pane, click the down arrow in the pane to see hidden items.

Follow these steps to add speaker notes for this slide:

Step 1. Enter this text for the speaker notes in the Notes pane (see Figure S9-7):

Have a professional make the photo.
Put the press kit in a large colorful envelope that stands out.
Give your business cards out at your gigs. You never know who might receive one.

Expand Animation Pane

Step 2. Format the notes as a bulleted list.

Step 3. Save your work.

> **Not Working?** If you don't see the Notes pane in your window, click NOTES in the status bar at the bottom of the window.

On Your Own 9.4 Step-by-Step Solution   How to Create the Third Slide with WordArt

Create the GarageBand Presentation: Part 4 of 7

When this activity is completed, the third slide should look like that in Figure S9-8.

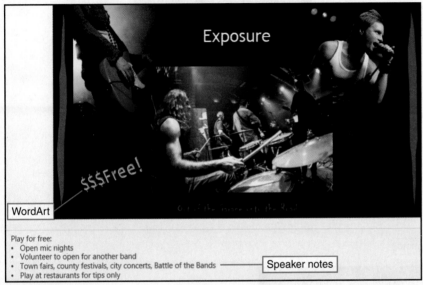

FIGURE S9-8
The third slide has three photos and WordArt.

Follow these steps to create the third slide with photos:

Step 1. Add a new slide using the **Title Only** layout. Enter the slide title **Exposure**. Center the title.

Step 2. On the INSERT ribbon, click **Online Pictures**. Enter **electric guitar** in the Office.com Clip Art search box and press **Enter**. Click a photo and click **Insert**. The photo appears on the slide.

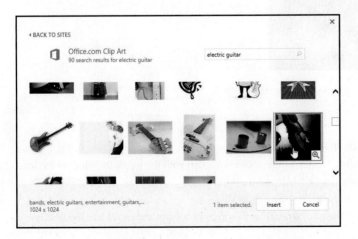

> **Not Working?** Microsoft websites change often. If you can't find the picture used here, substitute another. To search the web for a picture, click **Online Pictures** and enter the search text in the Bing Image Search search box.

Step 3. The photo we're using needs cropping on both sides. If you need to crop your photo, first select the photo. With the photo selected, click the **FORMAT** tab and click **Crop**. Cropping handles appear on the corners and sides of the photo. Hover over the crop handle on the right side of the photo until your pointer changes to a crop shape ⊩.

Step 4. Press and drag to the left to crop the right side of the photo. When you're cropping a photo, your pointer changes to a crosshair.

Grab a cropping handle

Use a crosshair to crop

Not Working? If your pointer is not a crosshair as you press and drag, you are resizing or moving the object and not cropping it. Click **Undo** and try again.

Step 5. For our photo, we also need to crop the left side as shown in Figure S9-9. If you're using a different photo than the one shown, crop your photo as appropriate for the slide.

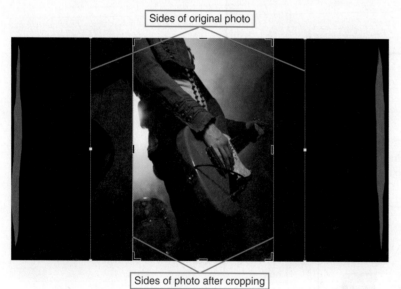

Sides of original photo

Sides of photo after cropping

FIGURE S9-9
The photo has been cropped on both sides.

Step 6. Click off the photo to remove the cropping handles from the photo.

Step 7. Resize and position the photo, as shown in Figure S9-8. The top of the photo is aligned with the top of the slide on the left.

Step 8. Use Online Pictures to search for an online photo of a **singer**. After you insert the photo, crop and resize the photo as appropriate, and align the photo with the top of the slide on the right.

Step 9. Search for an online photo of a **band**. After you insert the photo, resize and crop as necessary and move it to the bottom and center of the slide.

Not Working? Microsoft websites change often. If you can't find a picture used here, substitute another. Try searching the web for an appropriate picture by using the Bing Image Search search box in the Insert Pictures dialog box

Follow these steps to insert WordArt and speaker notes:

Step 1. Click the **INSERT** tab and click **WordArt**. In the list of WordArt fill styles, click **Fill – Gold, Accent 4, Soft Bevel**. The WordArt text box appears on the slide.

Step 2. Select the text in the WordArt text box and replace it with **$$$Free!**

Step 3. Select the WordArt text. On the FORMAT ribbon, click **Shape Effects**. Point to **3-D Rotation**. Click **Perspective Heroic Extreme Left**.

Step 4. Press and drag the WordArt text box to position it in the lower-left area of the slide (see Figure S9-8). Rotate the text box counterclockwise.

Step 5. View the slide as a slide show and check your work.

Step 6. Enter these speaker notes, making the last four lines a bulleted list:

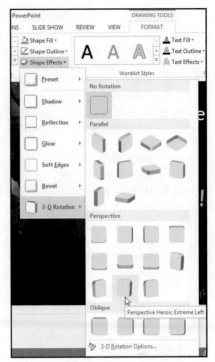

Shape Effects

> Play for free:
> - Open mic nights
> - Volunteer to open for another band
> - Town fairs, county festivals, city concerts, Battle of the Bands
> - Play at restaurants for tips only

Step 7. Save your work.

On Your Own 9.5 Step-by-Step Solution   How to Add Animated Graphics and a Screen Clipping to a Slide

Create the GarageBand Presentation: Part 5 of 7

Follow these steps to add a screen clipping to a slide:

Step 1. Add a new slide, using the **Title Only** layout. Enter the slide title: **Not Enough Fans?** Center the title.

Step 2. To find the photo, open Internet Explorer and go to **lifewithjean.wordpress.com**. Scroll down the page to find the photo of fans at a concert. Make sure the full photo is displayed in your browser window.

Step 3. When using Windows 8, go to the Start screen and start typing **Snipping Tool**. Click **Snipping Tool**. You automatically return to the screen you left open on your desktop, and the Snipping Tool dialog box opens.

Step 4. When using Windows 7, click **Start**, **All Programs**, **Accessories**, and **Snipping Tool**. The screen dims, the Snipping Tool dialog box appears, and your pointer changes to a crosshair.

> **Not Working?** Windows 7 Starter installed on a netbook does not include the Snipping Tool. In this case, you can't complete this part of the activity.

Step 5. In the Snipping Tool dialog box, click the down arrow next to New and click **Rectangular Snip**. The screen dims, and your pointer changes to a crosshair. (You can move the Snipping Tool dialog box out of your way, but even if it's over the area you're snipping, it won't show in the snip.)

Step 6. Press and drag to select the photo. Your snip appears in the Snipping Tool dialog box and is copied to the Windows Clipboard.

Step 7. Return to PowerPoint. On the HOME ribbon, click **Paste** and click the first Paste icon. The screen clipping appears on the slide.

Step 8. Resize the photo to fill most of the slide, as shown in Figure 9-10 in the chapter.

Follow these steps to add animated clip art to the slide:

Step 1. Using Internet Explorer, browse to **office.microsoft .com.** In the search box, type **fan** and press **Enter.** Under Image results, click **More.** To narrow the results to just animated graphics, under MEDIA TYPES, click **Animation**.

Step 2. Click the graphic of a fan. Then click the green **Copy** button to copy the animated graphic to the Windows Clipboard. Return to the PowerPoint window and the fourth slide. On the HOME ribbon, click **Paste.** The fan appears on the slide.

Step 3. With the graphic selected, click **Copy** on the HOME ribbon.

Step 4. On the HOME ribbon, click **Paste** multiple times to add many fans to the slide. If you don't see multiple fans appear, don't worry. The images are stacked on top of each other. Press and drag each fan so the fans are scattered over the slide.

Not Working? If you can't find the animated fan used here, select another animated fan.

Step 5. View the slide as a slide show. The fans should turn. Then return to Normal view.

Not Working? If the fans don't turn during the slide show, most likely you selected a graphic in clip art that isn't animated. Go back and make sure only **Animation** is selected under MEDIA TYPES on the office.microsoft.com site.

Step 6. Add the following speaker notes to the slide:

If you're not getting the opportunities you want, change what you're doing until you find what works for you.

Step 7. Save your work.

On Your Own 9.6 Step-by-Step Solution   **How to Embed a Link in a Slide**

Create the GarageBand Presentation: Part 6 of 7

Follow these steps to embed a link in a slide:

Step 1. Select the third slide titled Exposure. Select the upper-right photo of a singer on the slide.

Step 2. Click the **INSERT** tab and click **Hyperlink.** The Insert Hyperlink dialog box appears. Click **Existing File or Web Page.** In the Address box, type **http://www.battleofthebands.com.** Click **OK** to close the dialog box.

Step 3. To run the slide show, on the SLIDE SHOW ribbon, click **From Beginning.** Click through until you get to the third slide and then click the photo of the singer. Internet Explorer opens and finds the requested link.

Step 4. When you close or minimize the Internet Explorer window, you return to the slide show. Press **Escape** to return to Normal view. Save your work.

On Your Own 9.7 Step-by-Step Solution   **How to Add Transitions to the Presentation**

Create the GarageBand Presentation: Part 7 of 7

Follow these steps to add the same transition to all slides in the presentation:

Step 1. Select the first slide. On the TRANSITIONS ribbon, click a transition to select it.

Step 2. On the TRANSITIONS ribbon, click **Apply To All.** Save your work. Run the slide show and make sure the transition is applied to all slides.

CHAPTER 10 STEP-BY-STEP SOLUTIONS
Managing Numbers and Text Using Excel

The solutions in this appendix are for you to use if you get stuck when doing an On Your Own activity in the chapter. To learn how to teach yourself a computer skill, always try the On Your Own activity first before turning to these solutions.

On Your Own 10.1 Step-by-Step Solution   **How to Create a Worksheet and Use a Template and the Excel Window**

This solution has two parts:

▶ How to examine the Excel window and tools

▶ How to use a template

How to Examine the Excel Window and Tools

Follow these steps to examine the Excel window and tools:

Step 1. When using Windows 8 to open Excel, click the **Excel 2013** tile on the Start screen or start typing Excel to search for the application. Click **Blank workbook** to open a new workbook. Maximize the window. When using Windows 7 to open Excel, click **Start**, **All Programs**, **Microsoft Office**, and **Excel 2013**. Click **Blank workbook** to open a new workbook. Maximize the window.

Step 2. The Excel window is shown in Figure S10-1. Click each ribbon tab (**FILE**, **HOME**, **INSERT**, **PAGE LAYOUT**, **FORMULAS**, **DATA**, **REVIEW**, and **VIEW**). Take a look at the items on each ribbon. Some of these items work as they do in Microsoft Word and PowerPoint.

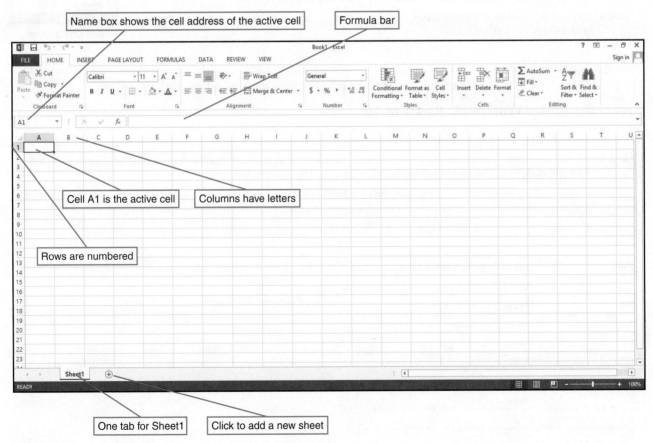

FIGURE S10-1
The Excel spreadsheet program opens a blank workbook with one worksheet.

Step 3. By default, the active cell is A1. Click a different cell and notice that the name box changes to identify the active cell. Enter text in this cell and press **Enter**. The text is left-aligned in the cell, and if the text is long enough, it spills over to the next cell when the next cell is empty.

Step 4. Click another cell and enter a number in the cell. The number is right-aligned in the cell.

How to Use a Template

Follow these steps to use an Excel template to manage a family monthly budget:

Step 1. Click the **FILE** tab. Click **New**. Below the search box, click **Budget**. Scroll down to and click **Family monthly budget planner**. The Family monthly budget planner box appears with a description of the template. Click **Create**. A workbook is created using this template.

Step 2. Click on cell **E18**, type **6000**, and press **Enter**. Notice the Variance in cell F18 changes, and the color code in the cell is now green.

Step 3. Click on cell **E18** again, type **100**, and press **Enter**. Notice the Variance in cell F18 is now a negative number, and the color code in the cell is now red. Also notice the bars in the chart at the top of the worksheet changed.

> **Hint** Data must be entered into the cell before calculations using the cell are updated. To enter the data, you must make another cell the active cell or press **Enter**.

Step 4. To add a new sheet to the workbook, click the plus sign ⊕ in the gray bar near the bottom of the Excel window. A new sheet is created named Sheet1. To rename the sheet, right-click **Sheet1** and select **Rename** from the shortcut menu. Name the sheet **Budget Notes**.

Step 5. To find out more about creating and renaming sheets, click the Help button **?** in the upper-right corner of the Excel window. In the Excel Help search box, enter **rename a worksheet** and browse through the search results. Close the Excel Help window when you're done.

Step 6. To close this workbook without saving it, click the **FILE** tab and click **Close**. In the dialog box that appears, click **Don't Save**.

Rename a sheet

Create the Roster Workbook: Part 1 of 10

Follow these steps to enter titles and headings:

Step 1. If Excel is not open, open it. Create a new blank workbook. If Excel is already open and no worksheet is open, click the **FILE** tab, click **New**, and click **Blank workbook**. A new workbook is created.

Step 2. Verify cell A1 is the active cell. Type **2014 Girls Softball Season** in the cell. As you type, the text appears in the formula bar. It also appears in cell A1 and spills across the row of empty cells.

Step 3. Continue by entering the following text in the indicated cells:

Cell	Text to Enter in Selected Cell
A3	Coach Chris Stevens
A4	Phone: 251-555-2574
A5	Email: chris.stevens@sample.com
C7	Player
D7	DOB
E7	Parents
F7	Phone
G7	Email
H7	Fees Paid
I7	Fees Due

When you're finished, your worksheet will look like Figure 10-4 in the chapter.

Step 4. Click the **FILE** tab. The **Info** page appears. If you're not the author of the file, right-click the author's name and click **Edit Property** in the shortcut menu that appears. In the Edit person dialog box, enter your name and click **OK**.

Step 5. Save the workbook file, naming the file **Roster**. If you need help saving the file to the hard drive, USB flash drive, OneDrive, or other location, see the instructions in On Your Own 3.3 Step-by-Step Solution.

On Your Own 10.3 Step-by-Step Solution   How to Format Using Styles and Themes

Create the Roster Workbook: Part 2 of 10

Follow these steps to format using styles and themes:

Step 1. Open the **Roster** workbook if you don't have it open already.

Step 2. Press and drag over cells **A1** through **I6**. A selection box appears over these cells. On the **HOME** ribbon in the Styles group, click **Cell Styles**. A gallery of available styles appears (see Figure S10-2). Click **Accent 5**. The style colors are applied.

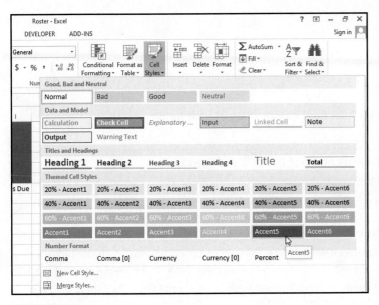

FIGURE S10-2
The Cell Styles offers options for applying styles to cells.

Step 3. Click in cell **A1**. On the **HOME** ribbon in the Font group, click the down arrow in the Font size box. In the drop-down list of font sizes, click **26**.

Step 4. Click in cell **A3**. Change the font size to **14**.

Step 5. Press and drag to select cells **A4** and **A5**. Change the font size to **12**.

Step 6. Press and drag to select cells **C7** through **I7**. On the **HOME** ribbon in the Alignment group, click the Orientation button ✧. In the drop-down menu, click **Angle Counterclockwise**. The text in the cells is now tilted upward.

Step 7. To see the themes, click the **PAGE LAYOUT** tab and click **Themes**. As you hover over a theme, the worksheet formatting changes (see Figure S10-3). Click **Mesh** to select this theme. The font and color changes appear in the worksheet.

Angle counterclockwise

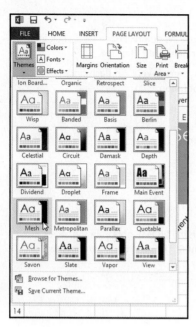

FIGURE S10-3
Themes in Excel apply professional formatting to a worksheet.

> **Step 8.** To save the workbook file, click the Save icon ⊟ in the Excel window's Quick Access Toolbar.

On Your Own 10.4 Step-by-Step Solution   How to Format Rows for Team Data and Add One Team Member

Create the Roster Workbook: Part 3 of 10

Follow these steps to format the cells in row 8 and enter data in the row:

> **Step 1.** Using the Roster workbook, click on cell **D8**. On the HOME ribbon in the Cells group, click **Format**. In the drop-down menu, click **Format Cells**. The Format Cells box appears. Under Category, click **Date**. Click the **14-Mar-12** format. Click **OK**.

> **Step 2.** Click on cell **F8**. On the HOME ribbon, click **Format**. In the drop-down menu, click **Format Cells**. The Format Cells box appears. Under Category, click **Special**. Click **Phone Number**. Click **OK**.

> **Step 3.** Select cells **H8** and **I8**. On the HOME ribbon, click **Format**. In the drop-down menu, click **Format Cells**. The Format Cells box appears. Under Category, click **Number**. Under Decimal places, verify that **2** is selected. Click **OK**.

> **Step 4.** Enter the following data in the indicated cells:

Cell	Data to Enter in Selected Cell
C8	West, Jessica
D8	5/14/2000
E8	Mike and Jill West
F8	2515558549
G8	mjwest@sample.com
H8	33

> **Step 5.** Select cells **C7** through **I8**. Click **Format** on the HOME ribbon and click **AutoFit Column Width** on the drop-down menu.

> **Step 6.** To remove the hyperlink from the email address, right-click cell **G8** and click **Remove Hyperlinks** in the shortcut menu.

> **Step 7.** To use the Auto Fill Options tool to copy formatting, press and drag to select cells **C8** through **I8**. In the lower-right corner of the selection box, press and drag the fill handle down through row **18**. Click the **Auto Fill Options** button that appears. In the drop-down menu that appears, click **Fill Formatting Only**. The copied data disappears, and the formatting is copied to the new selection. After you complete this activity, don't forget to save your work.

On Your Own 10.5 Step-by-Step Solution   How to Copy Team Data from a Word Table and Edit the Data

Create the Roster Workbook: Part 4 of 10

Follow these steps to copy team data from a Word table and edit data:

Step 1. For Windows 8, open File Explorer (for Windows 7, open Windows Explorer) and locate the **sample_files** folder on your USB flash drive. (Recall that you downloaded the folder from the www.pearsonhigher.com/jump website in Chapter 2.) If you need more help finding the folder, see On Your Own 2.7 Step-by-Step Solution.

Step 2. Locate the **RosterTable** file in the **sample_files** folder. Double-click the file to open it in Word.

Step 3. Press and drag to select all columns and rows in the table except the column headings.

Step 4. Right-click the selection and click **Copy** in the shortcut menu (see Figure S10-4). The selection is copied into the Windows Clipboard.

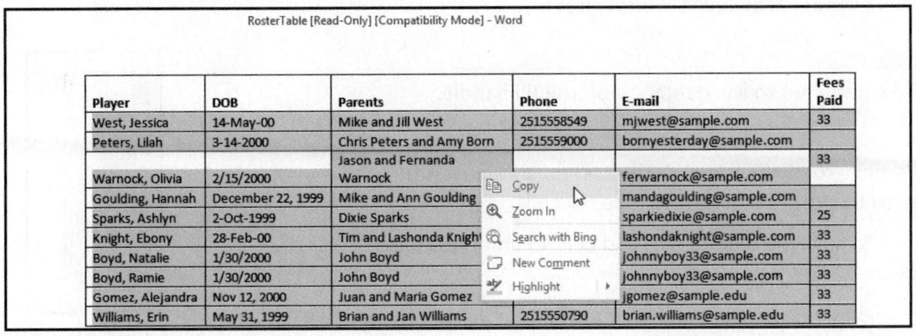

RosterTable [Read-Only] [Compatibility Mode] - Word

Player	DOB	Parents	Phone	E-mail	Fees Paid
West, Jessica	14-May-00	Mike and Jill West	2515558549	mjwest@sample.com	33
Peters, Lilah	3-14-2000	Chris Peters and Amy Born	2515559000	bornyesterday@sample.com	
Warnock, Olivia	2/15/2000	Jason and Fernanda Warnock		ferwarnock@sample.com	33
Goulding, Hannah	December 22, 1999	Mike and Ann Goulding		mandagoulding@sample.com	
Sparks, Ashlyn	2-Oct-1999	Dixie Sparks		sparkiedixie@sample.com	25
Knight, Ebony	28-Feb-00	Tim and Lashonda Knight		lashondaknight@sample.com	33
Boyd, Natalie	1/30/2000	John Boyd		johnnyboy33@sample.com	33
Boyd, Ramie	1/30/2000	John Boyd		johnnyboy33@sample.com	33
Gomez, Alejandra	Nov 12, 2000	Juan and Maria Gomez		jgomez@sample.edu	33
Williams, Erin	May 31, 1999	Brian and Jan Williams	2515550790	brian.williams@sample.edu	33

(shortcut menu: Copy, Zoom In, Search with Bing, New Comment, Highlight)

FIGURE S10-4
Copy the roster table in the Word document.

Step 5. If the **Roster** workbook is not already open in Excel, open it.

Step 6. Using the Roster workbook, click in cell **C9**. On the HOME ribbon in the Clipboard group, click the drop-down arrow next to **Paste**. In the shortcut menu that appears, click the second **Paste Options** icon, as shown in Figure S10-5. This icon is the Match Destination Formatting icon. The data is pasted in the worksheet, and formatting in the worksheet cells is applied.

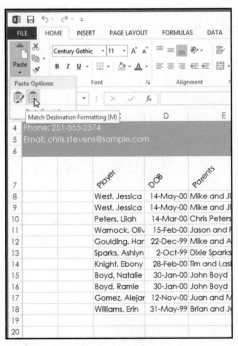

FIGURE S10-5
Paste the data into the worksheet and use the destination formatting.

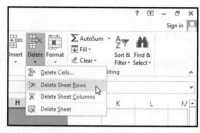

Step 7. Because you typed a row for Jessica West and her data was also in the Word table, you have a duplicate row for this team member. Click somewhere in a row that contains the Jessica West data. On the HOME ribbon in the Cells group, click the down arrow under the **Delete** button and click **Delete Sheet Rows**. Team data for the 10 team members is now in rows 8 through 17.

Step 8. Select the block of cells **C7** through **I17**. On the HOME ribbon, click **Format** and click **AutoFit Column Width**.

Step 9. Save your work.

Delete sheet rows

On Your Own 10.6 Step-by-Step Solution   **How to Sort Data and Add Row Numbers**

Create the Roster Workbook: Part 5 of 10

Follow these steps to sort team members and add row numbers:

Step 1. Using the Roster workbook, select the block of cells **C8** through **H17**.

> **Hint** When selecting a block of cells, be careful not to accidentally grab the fill handle.

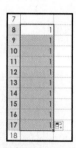

Step 2. On the HOME ribbon in the Editing group, click **Sort & Filter**. Then click **Sort A to Z** in the drop-down menu. The data is sorted by the first column in the range of cells.

Step 3. To enter row numbers in column A, first type the number **1** in cell **A8** and press **Enter**. Then click on cell A8. The selection box appears ▣.

Step 4. Move your pointer to the lower-right corner of cell A8 until you see your pointer shaped like a black cross ✚ and then press and drag the fill handle down through cell A17.

Select A8:A17

Step 5. Click the **Auto Fill Options** button that appears ▦. In the drop-down menu, click **Fill Series**. Counting numbers fill the selected area.

Step 6. To change the width of column A, locate the vertical bar to the right of column A above the worksheet area. Press and drag this vertical bar to adjust the column width to approximately 22 pixels. Change the width of column B using the same method.

Width Column A

Step 7. Save your work.

On Your Own 10.7 Step-by-Step Solution   **How to Enter Labels and Values for the Calculations**

Create the Roster Workbook: Part 6 of 10

Follow these steps to enter and format the labels:

Step 1. Enter the text as follows:

Cell	Text to Enter in Selected Cell
A19	Total
A21	Operating expenses
C21	Uniform fee
C22	Party fee
A24	Total fee per child
A26	Percentage paid

Step 2. To format the cells, start by clicking cell **A5**.

Step 3. Double-click the Format Painter ✎ on the HOME ribbon.

Step 4. Click cells **A19**, **B19**, **A21**, **B21**, **A24**, **B24**, **A26**, and **B26**. All these cells are formatted the same as cell A5.

Step 5. Click the Format Painter icon again to stop the Format Painter.

Step 6. Select cells **C19** through **I19**. On the HOME ribbon, click **Cell Styles**. In the list of cell styles under Titles and Headings, click **Total**.

Step 7. Increase the width of column A so that all of the text is visible. (The column width should be about 180 pixels.)

Follow these steps to enter and format the values for fees:

Step 1. In cell **D21**, enter **25**. In cell **D22**, enter **8**.

Step 2. Format cells D21 and D22 as **Number** format with **2** decimal places. If you need help, see On Your Own 10.4 Step-by-Step Solution.

Step 3. Save your work.

On Your Own 10.8 Step-by-Step Solution **How to Enter Two Sums in the Worksheet**

Create the Roster Workbook: Part 7 of 10

Recall that when you enter a formula or number into a cell and the cell is too narrow to display the number, the cell is filled with the hash symbol, also called the pound sign (#####). To fix the problem, make the cell wide enough to display the number.

Follow these steps to calculate the total fee per child:

Step 1. In cell **D24**, enter the formula =**D21**+**D22** and press **Enter**.

> **Not Working?** If the correct value of 33.00 doesn't display in the cell, click the cell again and then click the formula bar. You can then edit the existing formula here. When you're finished, press **Enter**.

Step 2. Click cell **C19** to select it. Click the Format Painter tool on the HOME ribbon. Press and drag to select **C24** and **D24**. The Total cell style is applied.

Step 3. Format cell **D24** using **Currency**, **2** decimal places.

> **Hint** You can also format the number in a cell using the Number Format tool on the HOME ribbon in the Number group. Click the down arrow next to the General selection and select **Currency**. Use the Increase Decimal or Decrease Decimal tools to adjust the number of decimal places.

Step 4. To sum the values in column H, go to cell **H19**. On the FORMULAS ribbon, click **AutoSum**. The formula, =SUM(H14:H18), appears in the cell, and a selection box appears above the cell. Grab an upper corner of the selection box and drag it up to include cell **H8**. The formula changes to =SUM(H8:H18). Press **Enter** to enter the formula in cell H19.

Step 5. Format cell H19 using **Currency** with **2** decimal places. Adjust column widths as necessary so you can see all the cell contents. After you complete this activity, remember to save your work.

On Your Own 10.9 Step-by-Step Solution **How to Calculate Fees Due**

Create the Roster Workbook: Part 8 of 10

Follow these steps to calculate the fees due:

Step 1. Go to cell **I8**. Enter the following formula and press **Enter**.

```
=$D$24-H8
```

Step 2. The value displayed in the cell should be zero. If it isn't, click in the cell and then use the formula bar to correct your work. Also make sure the formula and displayed value in cell D24 is correct.

Step 3. Go to cell **I8**. Click the Copy button on the HOME ribbon. A blinking box appears around the cell.

Step 4. Select cells **I9** through **I17**. On the HOME ribbon, click the **Paste** button. The formula in cell I8 is copied to the new cells. To terminate the copy and paste operation, press the Escape key. The blinking box around cell I8 disappears.

Step 5. To verify the formula copied correctly, click cell **I9**. The formula in cell I9 that appears in the formula bar should be =$D$24-H9. If this isn't the case, go back to step 1 and carefully do the steps again.

> **Hint** As you work, if a blinking box appears around cells and you want to start over, click the **Escape** key to remove the blinking box. Then start again.

Follow these steps to sum the Fees Due column:

Step 1. Go to cell **I19**.

Step 2. On the FORMULAS ribbon, click **AutoSum**. A SUM function is entered into the cell. The selection box for the range to sum appears around cells I8 through I18. If this isn't the case, press and drag the selection box for AutoSum to include cells **I8** through **I18**. Press **Enter** to enter the formula into cell I19.

Step 3. Use the Format Painter to copy the formatting in cell **H19** to cell **I19**.

On Your Own 10.10 Step-by-Step Solution   **How to Calculate the Percentage Paid**

Create the Roster Workbook: Part 9 of 10

Follow these steps to calculate the percentage paid:

Step 1. Go to cell **D26**, enter the following formula, and press **Enter**.

=H19/(H19+I19)

> **Tip** Just as in math, when Excel makes a calculation using a formula, it always calculates what is inside parentheses first.

Step 2. The value displayed in the cell is $0.78. The formatting is currency because Excel used the same formatting in cell D26 that it found in cells H19 and I19. If this value doesn't display, return to cell D26, click in the formula bar, and correct your work. If D26 isn't formatted as currency, go back and format cells H19 and I19 as currency with two decimal places.

Step 3. Format cells **C26** and **D26** using the **Total** cell style.

Step 4. Make cell **D26** the active cell. On the HOME ribbon, click **Format** and click **Format Cells**. In the Format Cells dialog box, click **Percentage**. Change the decimal places to **0**. Click **OK**. The value in the cell displays as 78%.

Step 5. Save your work.

> **Not Working?** Calculations in a cell depend on values and formulas stored in other cells on the worksheet. If your calculations aren't correct, the problem might be with values and formulas in other cells. Carefully go back and check your work for the entire worksheet. Compare each value displayed to those shown in Figure 10-3 in the chapter.

On Your Own 10.11 Step-by-Step Solution   **How to Print the Worksheet**

Create the Roster Workbook: Part 10 of 10

Follow these steps to print the worksheet:

Step 1. Click the **FILE** tab and click **Print**.

Step 2. Click the down arrow to the right of Portrait Orientation and click **Landscape Orientation**.

Step 3. Click the down arrow to the right of **No Scaling** and click **Fit Sheet on One Page**.

Step 4. Make sure your printer is selected and click **Print**. The worksheet prints on a single page.

CHAPTER 11 STEP-BY-STEP SOLUTIONS
Organizing Data Using Excel

The solutions in this appendix are for you to use if you get stuck when doing an On Your Own activity in the chapter. To learn how to teach yourself a computer skill, always try the On Your Own activity first before turning to these solutions.

> **Hint** Several formulas used in the worksheets you build in this chapter depend on other formulas already entered in the worksheets. A mistake in a formula or a missing formula can have a snowball effect through the worksheets. As you work your way through these solutions, work carefully so that a mistake doesn't affect later calculations.

On Your Own 11.1 Step-by-Step Solution **How to Enter Titles, Headings, and Data on the Sales Worksheet**

Create the ConsignmentShop Workbook: Part 1 of 11

When this activity is completed, the worksheet should look like that in Figure S11-1.

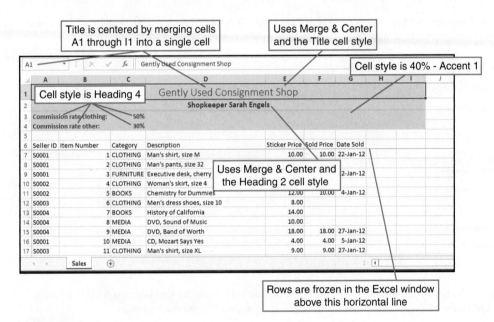

FIGURE S11-1
The Sales worksheet has titles, column headings, and data added.

Follow these steps to enter and format the text in the first four rows:

Step 1. Open Excel and open a **Blank workbook**. Enter the following text or number in the indicated cells:

Cell	Text or Number
A1	Gently Used Consignment Shop
A2	Shopkeeper Sarah Engels
A3	Commission rate clothing:
C3	0.5
A4	Commission rate other:
C4	0.3

Step 2. Format cells A1 through I4 using the **40% - Accent1** cell style.

Step 3. Select cells A1 through I1. Click **Merge & Center** on the HOME ribbon.

Step 4. Select cells A2 through I2. Click **Merge & Center** on the HOME ribbon.

Step 5. Format cell A1 using the **Title** cell style. Format cell A2 using the **Heading 2** cell style. Format cells A3 through C4 using the **Heading 4** cell style.

Step 6. Select cells C3 through C4. On the HOME ribbon, click **Format** and click **Format Cells**. In the Format Cells dialog box, click **Percentage** and change the Decimal places to **0**. Click **OK**.

Step 7. Widen column A or B so the labels in rows 3 and 4 can be read. You can also use the Merge & Center command to merge cells A3 and B3 and also merge cells A4 and B4.

> **Hint** To merge cells that are left-aligned, select the cells and then click the down arrow to the right of the Merge & Center command. In the dropdown menu, click **Merge Across**. Cells are merged and are still left-aligned.

Follow these steps to name the worksheet and save the workbook file:

Step 1. Right-click the sheet tab at the bottom of the Excel window and click **Rename** in the shortcut menu. Type **Sales** on the sheet tab and press **Enter**.

Step 2. Save the workbook file as **ConsignmentShop**. If you need help saving the file to the hard drive, USB flash drive, OneDrive, or other location, see the instructions in On Your Own 3.3 Step-by-Step Solution.

Follow these steps to enter column headings and format data cells:

Step 1. Enter the following column headings:

Cell	Text
A6	Seller ID
B6	Item Number
C6	Category
D6	Description
E6	Sticker Price
F6	Sold Price
G6	Date Sold

Step 2. Select cells **E7**, **F7**, **H7**, and **I7**. Recall that to select nonadjacent cells, you hold down the **Ctrl** key as you click the cells. Use the **Format** command on the HOME ribbon to format the cells as numbers with two decimal places.

Step 3. Format cell G7 as a date, using the **14-Mar-12** date format.

Step 4. To use AutoFill to copy formatting, first select cells **A7** through **I7**. Then press and drag the fill handle in the lower-right corner of the selection box down through row 72 or beyond.

Follow these steps to copy the data from the ConsignmentSalesTable document into the worksheet:

Step 1. Open File Explorer in Windows 8 (for Windows 7, open Windows Explorer) and use it to locate the **sample_files** folder on your USB flash drive. (Recall you downloaded the folder from the www.pearsonhighered.com/jump website to your USB flash drive in Chapter 2.) If you need more help locating the folder, see the instructions in On Your Own 2.7 Step-by-Step Solution.

Step 2. Locate the **ConsignmentSalesTable** file in the **sample_files** folder. Double-click the file. The file opens in a Word window.

Step 3. Select all the data in the table except the first row, which contains column headings. The table uses two pages, as shown in Figure S11-2. Be sure to select all the data as shown in the figure.

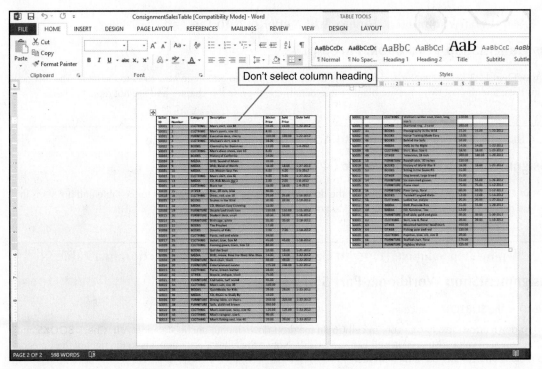

FIGURE S11-2
Select all the data in the table except the column heading row.

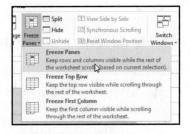

Step 4. Click **Copy** on the HOME ribbon.

Step 5. Return to the Excel window. Click cell **A7**. On the HOME ribbon, click the down arrow under Paste. In the drop-down menu, click the second Paste icon, which is labeled **Match Destination Formatting**. The data is pasted into the worksheet.

Step 6. Select cells A6 through I72. On the HOME ribbon, click **Format** and click **AutoFit Column Width**. Column widths are adjusted. If necessary, adjust columns A or B so labels in rows 3 and 4 can be seen.

Follow these steps to freeze panes:

Step 1. Click cell **A7** to make it the active cell. On the VIEW ribbon, click **Freeze Panes**. Then click **Freeze Panes** in the drop-down menu. All the rows above row 7 are frozen on the window.

Step 2. To test the frozen rows, use your arrow keys to move down the rows. No matter how far you go down the worksheet, the first six rows stay put.

Step 3. Compare your worksheet to that shown in Figure S11-1 and correct any problems you see.

Step 4. To save your work, click the **Save** button in the title bar of the Excel window.

On Your Own 11.2 Step-by-Step Solution   **How to Convert the Data to an Excel Table**

Create the ConsignmentShop Workbook: Part 2 of 11

Step 1. Go to On Your Own 11.2 in the chapter and follow the details given there to convert the data to an Excel table and sort and filter the data in a table. These details are given in the chapter and are not repeated here.

Create the ConsignmentShop Workbook: Part 3 of 11

Step 1. Go to On Your Own 11.3 in the chapter and follow the details given there to add three new rows to the table. The first new row contains data, and the last two rows are blank. These details are given in the chapter and are not repeated here.

Create the ConsignmentShop Workbook: Part 4 of 11

Step 1. Go to On Your Own 11.4 in the chapter and follow the details given there to add a Total row to the table and put sums in that row. These details are given in the chapter and are not repeated here.

Create the ConsignmentShop Workbook: Part 5 of 11

Follow these steps to explore the SUBTOTAL function:

Step 1. Click the drop-down arrow next to Category in cell C6. In the drop-down menu, uncheck **(Select All)**. Check **BOOKS** and click **OK**. The new sum value displayed in cell E76 is $193.50. Notice the Filter icon ▾ appears to the right of the Category heading to indicate the column has a filter applied.

> **Not Working?** If your value in cell E76 is $181.00, most likely you have not yet entered the new data in row 73 in On Your Own 11.3.

Step 2. Click cell E76 in the total row. Click the drop-down arrow that appears to the right of the selected cell. Click **Average**.

Step 3. Click the drop-down arrow next to Category in cell C6. In the drop-down menu, uncheck **BOOKS**. Check **MEDIA** and click **OK**. The average sticker price for MEDIA appears in cell E76, which is $11.10. The SUBTOTAL function in cell E76 uses the function number 101, which calculates an average and ignores hidden cells.

Step 4. To unhide all the data in the table, click the drop-down arrow next to Category in cell C6. In the drop-down menu, check **(Select All)**. Click **OK**.

Step 5. Change the formula in cell E76 to find the **Sum**. Save your work.

Create the ConsignmentShop Workbook: Part 6 of 11

Follow these steps to name cells C3 and C4:

Step 1. Go to cell **C3**. You should now see C3 in the name box and 50% in the Formula bar. (To expand the length of the name box, you can press and drag the bar between the name box and the Formula bar.) In the name box, type **COMM_CLOTHING** and press **Enter**. The name appears in the name box.

Step 2. Name cell C4 as **COMM_OTHER**.

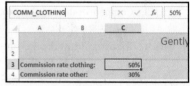

Name cell C3

> **Not Working?** Don't forget to press **Enter** after you type the cell name in the name box.

To name the table, follow these steps:

Step 1. Click anywhere in the table so the DESIGN tab under TABLE TOOLS displays. Click the **DESIGN** tab. On the DESIGN ribbon, notice the Table Name is Table1.

Step 2. In the Table Name field, type **SalesTable** and press **Enter**.

Create the ConsignmentShop Workbook: Part 7 of 11

Follow these steps to build the Commission and Due to Seller columns:

Step 1. Go to cell H6, type **Commission** and press **Enter**.

Step 2. Go to cell I6, type **Due to Seller** and press **Enter**.

Step 3. To adjust the widths of columns H and I, first select cells H6 and I6. On the HOME ribbon, click **Format** and then click **AutoFit Column Width**.

Step 4. Go to cell H7, enter the following formula, and press **Enter**:

```
=IF([Category]="CLOTHING", [Sold Price]*COMM_CLOTHING, [Sold Price]*COMM_OTHER)
```

Not Working? If Excel doesn't automatically copy the formula into the entire column, the cells in the column aren't empty. In this situation, you can manually copy the formula into the entire column.

Step 5. Enter this formula in cell I7 and press **Enter**:

```
=[Sold Price]-[Commission]
```

Step 6. The Total row is row 76. Click cell **H76**. Click the drop-down arrow next to the cell. Click **Sum** and press **Enter**. Click cell **I76**. Click the drop-down arrow next to the cell. Click **Sum** and press **Enter**. Format these totals as Currency with two decimal places.

Step 7. Compare your Sales worksheet with that shown in Figure 11-11 in the chapter and correct any problems you see. Save your work.

Create the ConsignmentShop Workbook: Part 8 of 11

To build the Sellers worksheet, follow these steps:

Step 1. Using the ConsignmentShop workbook, add a second worksheet and name it **Sellers**.

Step 2. In cell A1, enter **=Sales!A1**. In cell A2, enter **Seller Information**. Format both cells using the **Title** cell style.

Step 3. Use File Explorer in Windows 8 (in Windows 7, use Windows Explorer) to locate the **sample_files** folder on your USB flash drive. (Recall you downloaded the folder to your USB flash drive from the www.pearsonhighered.com/jump website in Chapter 2.) In the sample_files folder, double-click the **SellerInfoTable** document file. The file opens in a Word window.

Step 4. To select the entire table, first click anywhere in the table. Then click the selection icon in the upper-left corner of the table.

Step 5. On the HOME ribbon, click **Copy** (see Figure S11-3). The table is copied into the Windows Clipboard.

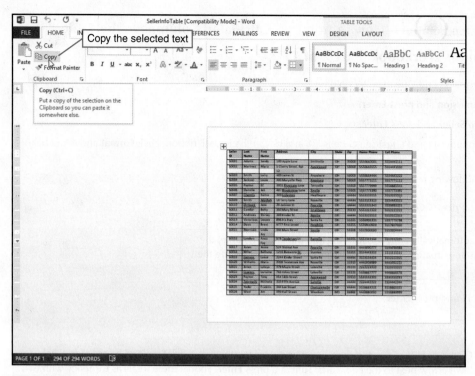

FIGURE S11-3
Copy the entire Word table into the Windows Clipboard.

Step 6. Return to the Excel window. Click cell **A4**. On the HOME ribbon, click the down arrow under Paste. In the drop-down menu, click the second Paste icon, which is labeled **Match Destination Formatting**. The column headings and data are pasted into the worksheet.

Step 7. Click anywhere in the data. On the HOME ribbon, click **Format as Table**. In the list of table styles, select **Table Style Medium 3**. Click **OK**. The table is created.

Step 8. To format the last two columns in the table as phone numbers, first select cells **H5** through **I29**. Click **Format** on the HOME ribbon. Click **Format Cells**. Click **Special**. Click **Phone Number** and click **OK**.

Step 9. Select the entire table. Use **AutoFit Column Width** to adjust the column widths.

Step 10. To name the table, first click anywhere in the table. Click the **DESIGN** tab under TABLE TOOLS. Type **SellerInfo** in the Table Name box and press **Enter**.

Step 11. Save your work.

On Your Own 11.9 Step-by-Step Solution   How to Add Mailing Address Columns
to the Sellers Worksheet

Create the ConsignmentShop Workbook: Part 9 of 11

Follow these steps to add the mailing address columns to the SellerInfo table:

Step 1. On the Sellers worksheet, go to cell J4, enter **Address1**, and press **Enter**. In cell K4, enter **Address2**. In cell L4, enter **Address3**. Three columns are added to the table.

Step 2. Select J4 through L4 and AutoFit the column widths.

Step 3. Enter the following formula in cell J5. The formula is automatically copied down the entire Address1 column (column J) of the table. Be sure to include a space between the quote marks.

=CONCATENATE([First Name]," ",[Last Name])

Alternately, you can use the FUNCTIONS ribbon to create the formula:

1. Go to cell **J5** and click **Insert Function** on the FORMULAS ribbon. In the Insert Function dialog box, select the **CONCATENATE** function and click **OK**.

2. Click in the Text1 box and then click cell **C5**. [@[First Name]] is inserted in the Text1 box.

3. Click in the Text2 box and type a space.

4. Click in the Text3 box and then click cell **B5**. [@[Last Name]] is inserted in the Text3 box (see Figure S11-4).

5. Click **OK** to insert the formula in the Address1 column.

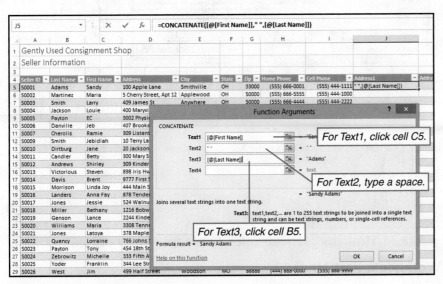

FIGURE S11-4
Use the Function Arguments dialog box to build a CONCATENATE function for the Address1 column.

Step 4. To build the Address2 column, go to cell **K5**. Type = and click cell **D5**. The formula that appears in the formula bar is =[@ Address]. Press **Enter**. The formula is automatically copied down column K of the table.

Step 5. To build the Address3 column, go to cell **L5** and enter the following formula. The formula is automatically copied down the entire column L of the table. Be sure to include a space and a comma between the first set of quote marks and a space between the second set of quote marks as shown.

=CONCATENATE([City],", ",[State]," ",[Zip])

Alternately, you can use the FORMULAS ribbon to build the formula:

1. Go to cell **L5** and click **Insert Function** on the FORMULAS ribbon. In the Insert Function dialog box, select the **CONCATENATE** function and click **OK**.

2. Enter text or click a cell to build the function. Directions for each entry are shown in Figure S11-5. Click **OK** to insert the formula in the Address3 column.

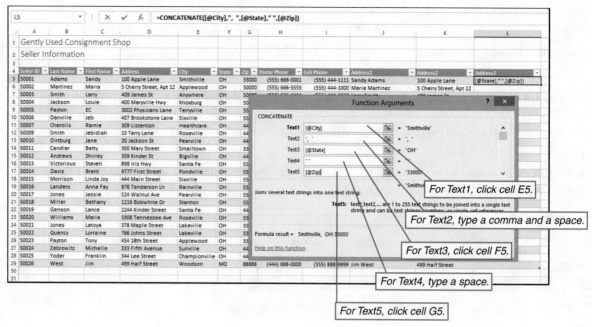

FIGURE S11-5

Use the Function Arguments dialog box to build a CONCATENATE function for the Address3 column.

Step 6. Select cells J4 through L29 and AutoFit the column widths.

Step 7. Save your work.

On Your Own 11.10 Step-by-Step Solution   **How to Calculate Sales Totals for One Month**

Create the ConsignmentShop Workbook: Part 10 of 11

Follow these steps to create the Month Summary worksheet and put labels on it:

Step 1. Using the ConsignmentShop workbook, add a third worksheet and name it **Month Summary**.

Step 2. Enter the worksheet title **Monthly Sales Summary** in cell A1 and format the cell using the **Title** cell style.

Step 3. Enter the following text:

Cell	Text
A3	Category
B3	Sold Price
C3	Commission
D3	Due to Seller
A4	CLOTHING
A5	BOOKS
A6	FURNITURE
A7	MEDIA
A8	OTHER

Step 4. Select cells A3 through D8 and AutoFit the column widths.

Step 5. Use one of the following methods to create the SUMIF function in cell B4:

To use the FORMULAS ribbon, follow these steps:

1. Go to cell **B4** and click **Insert Function** on the FORMULAS ribbon. The Insert Function dialog box appears.

2. In the *Search for a function* field, enter **SUMIF** and click **Go**. In the list of functions, click **SUMIF** and click **OK**. The Function Arguments dialog box appears (see Figure S11-6).

3. In the Range box, type **SalesTable[Category]**.

4. In the Criteria box, type **A4**.

5. In the Sum_range box, type **SalesTable[Sold Price]**. Click **OK** to enter the function into cell B4. You should see the calculation 315 appear in cell B4.

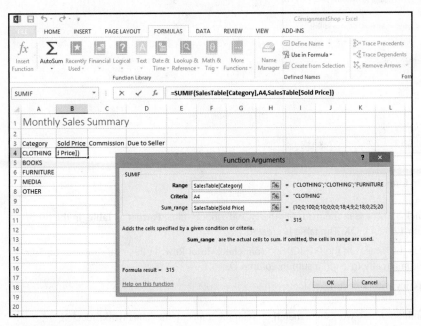

FIGURE S11-6
The SUMIF function has three arguments.

Not Working? It's easiest to type the entries you see in Figure S11-6 into the Function Arguments dialog box. However, if you want to use the click method, for the Range, go to the Sales sheet and press and drag to select all the data in the Category column (rows 7 through 75). For the Sum_range entry, press and drag to select all the data in the Sold Price column (rows 7 through 75).

To type the SUMIF function in cell **B4**, follow these steps:

1. Go to cell B4.

2. Type the following formula and press **Enter**:

=SUMIF(SalesTable[Category],A4,SalesTable[Sold Price])

Follow these steps to complete the calculations:

Step 1. To copy the formula to other cells in column B, go to cell B4. Press and drag the fill handle in the lower-right corner of the selection box down through row 8.

Step 2. Enter the following formula in cell C4 and copy the formula down through row 8:

=SUMIF(SalesTable[Category],A4,SalesTable[Commission])

Step 3. Enter the following formula in cell D4 and copy the formula down through row 8:

=SUMIF(SalesTable[Category],A4,SalesTable[Due to Seller])

Step 4. Calculations in your table should look like that in Figure S11-7. Format cells B4 through D8 using **Number** with **2** decimal places.

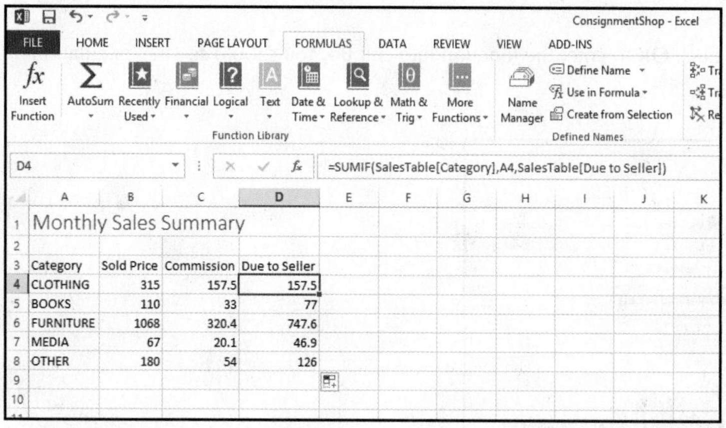

FIGURE S11-7
Check your calculations and correct any errors in formulas

Step 5. To convert the data to a table, first click anywhere in the data. On the HOME ribbon, click **Format as Table**. In the list of table styles, select **Table Style Medium 12**. Click **OK**. The table is created.

Step 6. To enter a Total row, click anywhere in the table. On the DESIGN ribbon, check **Total Row**. In the total row, insert a **Sum** in column B and in column C. Excel automatically inserted a sum in column D.

Step 7. Format the sums in row 9 using **Currency** with **2** decimal places.

Follow these steps to verify the totals on the Month Summary worksheet match up with the totals on the Sales worksheet:

Step 1. On the Sales worksheet, click the down arrow next to Category. Uncheck **(Select All)** and check **OTHER**. Click **OK**. The total Sold Price is $180.00. This total matches the value in cell B8 on the Month Summary worksheet.

Step 2. On the Sales worksheet, click the down arrow next to Category. Uncheck **OTHER** and check **FURNITURE**. Click **OK**. The total Due to Seller is $747.60. This total matches the value in cell D6 on the Month Summary worksheet.

Step 3. On the Sales worksheet, clear the filter from Category.

On Your Own 11.11 Step-by-Step Solution   How to Insert a Chart in the Month Summary Worksheet

Create the ConsignmentShop Workbook: Part 11 of 11

Follow these steps to insert a chart using the Category and Commission data:

Step 1. Using the ConsignmentShop workbook, select the **Month Summary** worksheet. Press and drag to select cells A4 through A8. Hold down the **Ctrl** key and press and drag over cells C4 through C8. Both columns of data are selected.

Step 2. On the INSERT ribbon, click the drop-down arrow next to the Insert Pie or Doughnut Chart icon. Click **3-D Pie**, as shown in Figure S11-8.

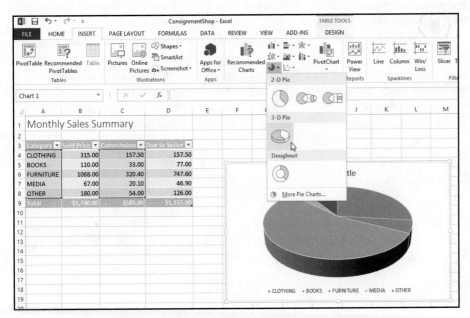

FIGURE S11-8
Select data in two columns and then insert a chart that is built using the selected data.

Step 3. Press and drag an edge of the chart container box to move it to the right of the data. To resize the box, press and drag a corner of the box.

Step 4. With the container box still selected, click the **DESIGN** tab under TABLE TOOLS. On the DESIGN ribbon, click **Quick Layout** and click **Layout 6**. Percentages are added and the legend is moved to the side of the pie.

Step 5. To change the chart title, click anywhere on the text Chart Title. The Chart Title text box appears. Select all the text in this text box and change the text to **Commissions for January**. Click off the text box to deselect it.

Step 6. Click on the pie and notice all slices are selected. Click the **FURNITURE slice** to select only it. Press and drag it outward away from the other slices.

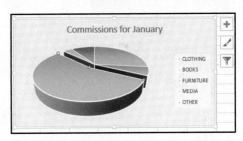

Step 7. To resize the pie, click near the pie to select the pie box. Press and drag the corners of the box to move and resize it.

Step 8. Save your work. The ConsignmentShop workbook is finished.

On Your Own 11.12 Step-by-Step Solution   How to Record and Use a Macro

Follow these steps to record and use a macro:

Step 1. Open a new blank workbook. Note that the current or active cell is A1.

Step 2. On the VIEW ribbon, click the down arrow under **Macros** and click **Use Relative References**. The macros you record now work anywhere on the worksheet.

Step 3. To start recording a macro, on the VIEW ribbon, click the down arrow under **Macros** and click **Record Macro**. The Record Macro dialog box appears. Enter a name for the macro in the Macro name box.

Step 4. In the Shortcut key box, type **K**. The shortcut for your macro is now Ctrl+**K**. Click **OK**.

> **Not Working?** If for some reason the Ctrl+**K** shortcut key is not available, Excel assigns a different shortcut key. Take note of any changes it makes for the shortcut key. You can use the key it suggests or try a different letter other than **K**.

Step 5. Type your name in cell A1 and press **Enter**. Type your street address in cell A2 and press **Enter**. Type your city, state, and zip in cell A3 and press **Enter**. Your name and address are now in three cells of the worksheet.

Step 6. To stop recording the macro, on the VIEW ribbon, click the down arrow under **Macros** and click **Stop Recording**. Excel creates the macro.

Step 7. Move to a new cell on the worksheet. To run the macro, click the **Macros** button or click the down arrow under Macros and click **View Macros**. Either way, the Macro dialog box appears. Select the macro and click **Run**. Your name and address are put in the new location.

Step 8. To test the shortcut key, go to a new location on the worksheet and press **Ctrl+K**. Your name and address appear at the new location.

CHAPTER 12 STEP-BY-STEP SOLUTIONS
Connecting to the Internet and Securing a Computer

The solutions in this appendix are for you to use if you get stuck when doing an On Your Own activity in the chapter. To learn how to teach yourself a computer skill, always try the On Your Own activity first before turning to these solutions.

On Your Own 12.1 Step-by-Step Solution   How to Verify Your Wired Network Connection

You can do this activity if your computer is connected to a wired network. Follow these steps:

Step 1. To turn off Wi-Fi, open the charms bar and click the **Settings** charm. Click the network icon. Under Wi-Fi, if the setting is on, click the bar to turn Wi-Fi off.

Step 2. Does your network port have status indicator lights? If so, check the status of these lights. Are the lights lit or blinking?

Step 3. If the indicator lights are not lit, make sure the network cable is solidly connected at both ends.

Step 4. On the charms bar, click the **Settings** charm and click the Network icon. In the Networks pane, Windows should report a wired connection.

Step 5. Unplug the network cable. The network indicator lights on the network port are not lit. No network connections appear in the Networks pane.

Step 6. To fix the problem, plug in the network cable. Wired connectivity is restored and is reported in the Networks pane.

Step 7. To verify that Internet access is restored, open Internet Explorer and try to surf the web.

Wired connection and Wi-Fi off

Step 8. If you turned off Wi-Fi earlier, turn it back on. Go to the charms bar, click the **Settings** charm and click the network icon. In the Networks pane, turn on Wi-Fi.

On Your Own 12.2 Step-by-Step Solution   How to Connect to a Wireless Hot Spot

Follow these steps to connect to a wireless hot spot:

Step 1. If the computer has a wireless switch, turn it on. Open the Settings charm and click the network icon. If Wi-Fi is not on, turn it on. Press the **Win** key to return to the Start screen.

Step 2. Click the **Settings** charm and then click the network icon. Click one of the Wi-Fi networks listed. Then click **Connect**.

Step 3. If the wireless network is secured and your computer doesn't already know the network security key, Windows requests the key. Enter the key and click **Connect**. The network connection is made.

Connect to wireless

Step 4. If this is the first time to connect to a secured wireless network, you're asked whether you want to share resources. If you see this pane, click **No**.

Step 5. To verify you have connectivity, open Internet Explorer and try to surf the web. Some public hot spots require you to agree to the terms of use. If so, a web page appears when you first open Internet Explorer. You must agree to the terms before you can use the network.

On Your Own 12.3 Step-by-Step Solution   How to Examine Network Connections and Settings

Follow these steps to examine your network connections and settings:

Step 1. Open the Settings charm and click the network icon. Look at the connections, which indicate a wired or wireless connection or both connections. You'll have one or two connections.

Step 2. To find out if resources are shared on the network, open the **Settings** charm and click **Change PC settings**. On the PC settings page, click **Network**. The Network screen appears. Click one of the connections in the right pane. If resources are shared, *Find devices and content* is turned on.

> **Not Working?** Windows remembers the last page you were on when you last left the PC settings screens and returns you to this page when you click Change PC settings on the Settings charm. You might need to press the back button to find the PC settings screen you need.

Step 3. To open the Network Connections window, press **Win+X** and click **Network Connections** in the menu that appears. The Network Connections window appears. A problem with a connection is reported as a red X. To fix a problem, first click a connection to select it and then click **Diagnose this connection** in the menu bar near the top of the window. The Windows Network Diagnostics window opens, and the utility starts up. Close the window when the utility stops.

Step 4. You must have a Wi-Fi wireless connection to do this step. To find out the security settings for a wireless network, double-click the Wi-Fi connection. The Wi-Fi Status dialog box opens. Click **Wireless Properties**. On the Wireless Network Properties dialog box, click the **Security** tab. The type of security encryption used is listed to the right of *Security type*. Refer to Figure 12-13 in the chapter. Also on the Security tab, to see the password to the wireless network, check **Show characters**.

On Your Own 12.4 Step-by-Step Solution   How to Install Windows Updates and Verify Windows Update Settings

Follow these steps to find out whether updates are pending and install important updates:

Step 1. Open the charms bar and click **Settings**. Click **Change PC settings**.

Step 2. On the PC settings page, click **Update and recovery**. If necessary, click **Windows Update**. The right pane reports whether updates are pending, no updates have been found, or a restart is needed to complete the update installation. If a restart is requested, restart the computer and then return to the Windows Update page.

Step 3. To view optional updates, click **View details**. If Windows reports it has important updates pending, click **Install** to install them (see Figure S12-1).

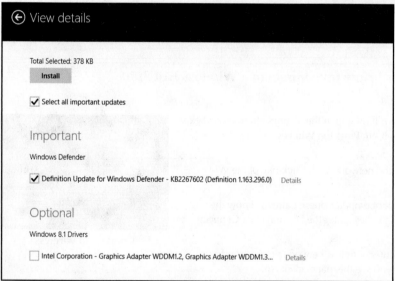

FIGURE S12-1
Windows reports the status of pending updates.

Step 4. Click the back button to return to the Windows Update page. To check for more updates, click **Check now**. Windows searches for updates. Click **View details** to find out if more important updates are ready to install. If so, install them.

Step 5. Continue checking for and installing updates until no more important updates are found.

Follow these steps to verify Windows Update settings:

Step 1. To verify Windows Update settings, on the Windows Update page, click **Choose how updates get installed**. The *Choose how updates get installed* page appears (see Figure 12-17 in the chapter).

Step 2. Verify these settings:

- Under Important updates, select **Install updates automatically (recommended)**.
- Check **Give me recommended updates the same way I receive important updates**.
- Check **Give me updates for other Microsoft products when I update Windows**.

On Your Own 12.5 Step-by-Step Solution   How to Use Windows File History

Follow these steps to set up File History and use it to back up and restore a file:

Step 1. To create a file in the Documents library, open File Explorer. In the left pane, if necessary, expand the This PC group. In the This PC group, click **Documents**. The contents of the Documents library appear in the right pane. Right-click in the white space in the right pane. In the shortcut menu, point to **New** and click **Text Document** (see Figure S12-2). A new text file is created. Name the new file **MyFile**. Double-click the new file to open it. Type some text in the file and save and close the file. Leave the File Explorer window open.

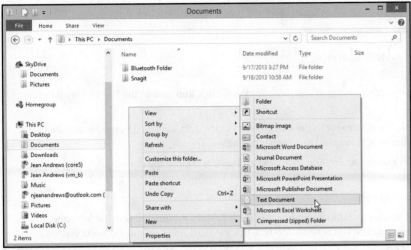

FIGURE S12-2
Create a new text file in the Documents library.

Step 2. Plug a USB flash drive into your computer.

Step 3. Press **Win+X**. In the Quick Link menu, click **Control Panel**. In the Control Panel window, under System and Security, click **Save backup copies of your files with File History**. The File History window opens.

Step 4. What you see in the File History window depends on current settings. If the USB flash drive is not shown in the *Copy files to:* area, click **Select drive** in the left pane. In the Select Drive window, select the flash drive and then click **OK**. If File History has been set to use a different drive, a dialog box appears asking if you want to move files to the flash drive (see Figure S12-3). If you see this dialog box, click **No**.

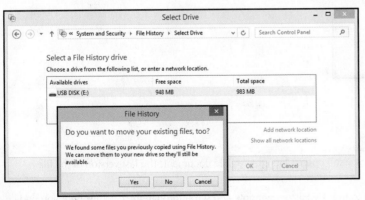

FIGURE S12-3
Select the drive to receive the backups and decide how to handle previous backups.

Step 5. In the File History window, if File History is not turned on, click **Turn on**. File History is now set to back up favorites and files to the flash drive and starts backing up your files immediately. When the backup completes, your File History window should look similar to that in Figure S12-4.

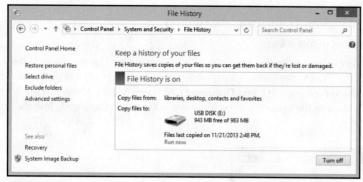

FIGURE S12-4
File History is set to back up favorites and files to the USB flash drive.

Step 6. The backup happens every hour, and you can back up at any time. To do so, click **Run now** in the File History window. Leave the File History window open.

Step 7. Return to File Explorer and open the MyFile document in the Documents library. Add some text to the file and then save and close the file. Return to the File History window and run the backup again.

Step 8. Use File Explorer to open the MyFile document again. Add more text and save and close the document. Using the File History window, run the backup again.

Step 9. Use File Explorer to delete the MyFile document.

Step 10. To restore the file from backup, return to the File History window and click **Restore personal files** in the left pane. In the Home – File History window, drill down into the Documents library. Click the right arrow to find the latest version of MyFile. To restore it, select the file and then click the green circle at the bottom of the window (see Figure S12-5).

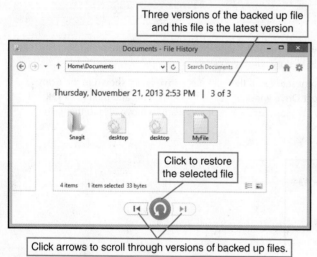

FIGURE S12-5
Select files and folders to restore from backup.

Step 11. Return to File Explorer with the Documents library still open. Open the MyFile document. The last version of the file is restored.

Step 12. To restore the original version of the file, return to the File History window and scroll through the backups until you find the first occurrence of MyFile. Select it and click the green button. In the box that appears, click **Replace the file in the destination**. In File Explorer, open MyFile and verify the original file is restored.

Follow these steps to see all the versions of backed up files kept on the USB flash drive:

Step 1. Use File Explorer to drill down into the USB flash drive into the FileHistory folder all the way down into the Documents library. Here is the path you will use:

FileHistory*username**computername*\\Data\\C\\Users*username*\\Documents

Step 2. There you will find all three versions of MyFile that were created the three times you ran the backup (see Figure S12-6).

Step 3. Close all open windows.

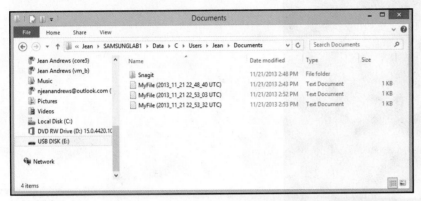

FIGURE S12-6
Find backups in the FileHistory folder on your backup storage device.

On Your Own 12.6 Step-by-Step Solution   How to Create a Standard User Account

You need an administrator account and password to do this activity. Follow these steps to create a standard account and explore how the account works:

Step 1. Sign in to Windows with an administrator account.

Step 2. Open the charms bar and click **Settings**. Click **Change PC settings**. On the PC settings page, click **Accounts**. Click **Other accounts** (see Figure S12-7).

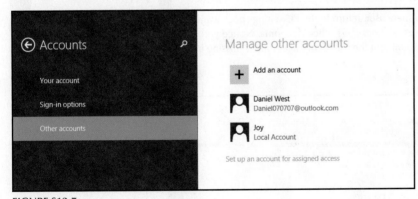

FIGURE S12-7
Manage user accounts and create new accounts.

Step 3. Click **Add an account**. The *How will this person sign in?* page appears. Click **Sign in without a Microsoft account (not recommended)**. On the next page, click **Local account**. On the next page, enter the user name **Mattie**, the password **Matt1E**, and a password hint (see Figure S12-8). Click **Next**. On the next page, click **Finish**.

FIGURE S12-8
Enter information to set up a new local user account.

Step 4. To sign in to Windows using the Mattie account, return to the Start screen. Click the user name icon in the top-right corner of the Start screen and select **Mattie**. On the sign-on screen, enter the password to the Mattie account. The first time a user logs in, Windows prepares the Start screen, desktop, and user folders and libraries.

Step 5. Go to the desktop and open File Explorer. Drill down into the Documents library. You might see folders placed there by apps installed on the computer, but you should not see files because no personal files have yet been created.

Step 6. To see if the Mattie account can add a new user, return to the PC settings page available from the **Settings** charm. On the PC settings page, click **Accounts**. Notice you can change settings for the Mattie account, but the link *Other accounts* is missing in the left pane (see Figure S12-9).

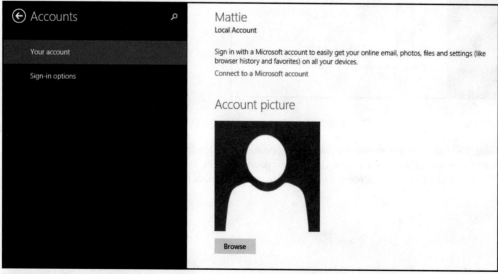

FIGURE S12-9
A standard account has limited control of Windows and cannot create user accounts.

On Your Own 12.7 Step-by-Step Solution   How to Manage Windows Passwords

Follow these steps to change your password:

Step 1. Sign in to your Windows administrator account. Open the Settings charm and click **Change PC settings**. On the PC settings page, click **Accounts**. Click **Sign-in options**. Under Password, click **Change** (see Figure S12-10). (If your account doesn't have a password, click **Add**.)

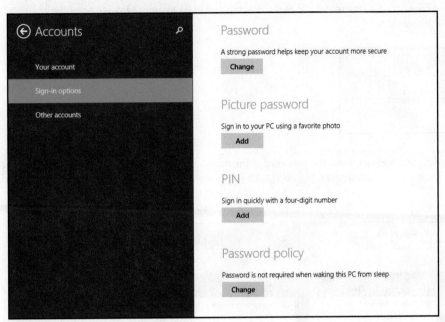

FIGURE S12-10
Change the password for your user account.

Step 2. On the next page, type your old password and click **Next**. On the next screen, type your new password two times. Type a Password hint. Click **Next**. On the next page, click **Finish**. Close the Accounts page.

Using an administrator account, follow these steps to reset a password for another user:

Step 1. To open the Control Panel window, press **Win+X** and click **Control Panel**. Under *User Accounts and Family Safety*, click **Change account type**. Click the **Mattie** account. The Change an Account window appears for the Mattie account (see Figure S12-11).

FIGURE S12-11
Make changes to or delete a user account other than your own.

Step 2. Click **Change the password**. Type the password **changeme** twice. Type a Password hint and click **Change password**. Close the window.

On Your Own 12.8 Step-by-Step Solution   How to Secure a Wireless Network

You can do this activity if you have access to a wireless router in a small home network. Follow these steps to access the router setup program and change the router password:

Step 1. Look in the user guide of the wireless router to find the IP address of the router and the router password assigned by the router manufacturer. Know that this original password might have been changed. It is likely the IP address is 192.168.1.1.

Step 2. Use a computer that has a wired connection to the router. Go to the desktop and open Internet Explorer. Enter the IP address of the router in the IE address box.

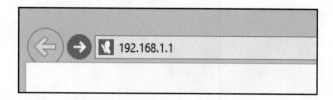

Step 3. In the Windows Security dialog box that appears, enter the password to the router and click **OK**. (The User Name is most likely not required.) The router setup main menu appears. Figure S12-12 shows the main menu window for one router, but yours might look different.

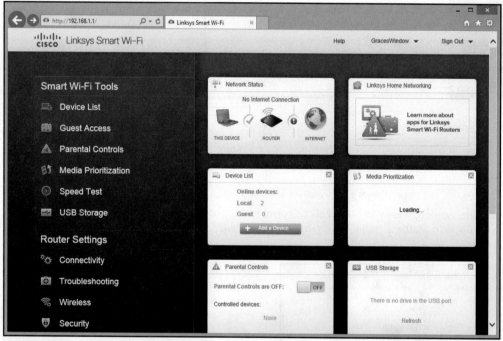

FIGURE S12-12
This main menu window is provided by the wireless router setup program.

Step 4. To change the router password for the Linksys router used in this solution, click **Connectivity**. The Connectivity page appears (see Figure S12-13). In the Router Password area, click **Edit** and enter the new password. Your router setup software might work differently.

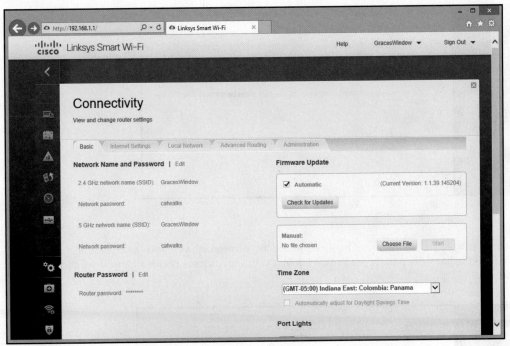

FIGURE S12-13
Change the password used to access the router setup software.

Follow these steps to secure the wireless network:

Step 1. Find the window that sets up the wireless security for the router, such as that shown in the chapter in Figure 12-21. To access this window on this particular router, click **Wireless** on the main screen, shown in Figure S12-12. If you have options for the Security Mode, select **WPA2**, as shown in Figure 12-21 in the chapter. Enter a strong password to the wireless network. Be sure to write down the password. A good place to write it is in the router user guide.

Step 2. Save your changes and exit the router setup program. Close Internet Explorer.

Step 3. Using a wireless computer, connect to the wireless network. You must enter the wireless network password when you make the connection. If you need help, refer to On Your Own 12.2 Step-by-Step Solution.

On Your Own 12.9 Step-by-Step Solution   **How to Use a Homegroup to Share Data**

Follow these steps on each computer to set up a homegroup:

Step 1. Open the Settings charm and click **Change PC settings**. On the PC settings page, click **Network**. The Network screen appears. Click one of the network connections in the right pane. Make sure *Find device and content* is turned on.

Step 2. Click the back arrow to return to the Network screen. On the Network screen, click **HomeGroup**. Here are two possibilities for what you'll see on screen:

- If no homegroup is available, you'll see a screen similar to Figure S12-14. Click **Create** to create the homegroup. Windows assigns a password to the homegroup, and a screen appears where you can decide what to share with the homegroup. Turn on **Documents**, **Music**, **Pictures**, and **Videos**. If a printer is connected to the computer, turn on **Printers**. Make note of the password so that you can give it to someone using another computer that wants to join the homegroup.

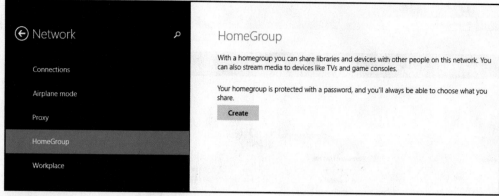

FIGURE S12-14
Windows did not find a homegroup on the network.

- If a homegroup is available and the computer has never joined this homegroup, you'll see a screen similar to Figure S12-15. Enter the homegroup password and click **Join**. On the next screen, decide what you want to share with the homegroup.

FIGURE S12-15
The homegroup password is required to join the homegroup.

> **Tip** If you leave a homegroup, Windows remembers the homegroup password, and you can join the homegroup again without having to reenter the password.

To complete this part of the activity, you need to be able to write files to the hard drive. Follow these steps to copy a file from one computer to the other:

Step 1. Open File Explorer. In the left pane, drill down into the Homegroup group to see users in the homegroup that are currently signed in and have shared libraries and folders on their computers. Drill down into your partner's computer. Double-click the **Documents** library on that computer.

Step 2. In the right pane of File Explorer, right-click a file in the Documents library of the other computer (see Figure S12-16). Click **Copy** on the shortcut menu. The file is copied to the Windows Clipboard.

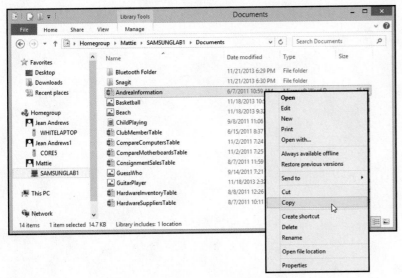

FIGURE S12-16
Drill into the users listed in the Homegroup group to find shared data.

Step 3. In the left pane of File Explorer, if necessary, expand **This PC**. In the This PC group, click **Documents**. In the right pane, right-click anywhere in the white space. Click **Paste** on the shortcut menu. The file is copied from the other computer to your Documents library of your computer.

> Tip   In a computer lab, your instructor might want you to leave the homegroup before you sign out of Windows. If so, use the Settings charm to return to the Network screen, click **HomeGroup**, and click **Leave**. The computer no longer belongs to the homegroup.

CHAPTER 13 STEP-BY-STEP SOLUTIONS
Maintaining a Computer and Fixing Computer Problems

The solutions in this appendix are for you to use if you get stuck when doing an On Your Own activity in the chapter. To learn how to teach yourself a computer skill, always try the On Your Own activity first before turning to these solutions.

On Your Own 13.1 Step-by-Step Solution   How to Clean Up the Hard Drive

Follow these steps to clean up the hard drive:

Step 1. Go to the Windows desktop and right-click the **Recycle Bin**. In the shortcut menu, click **Empty Recycle Bin**. Click **Yes** in the dialog box that appears.

Step 2. Open **File Explorer** and open the **This PC** group. Right-click **Local Disk (C:)** in the left pane and click **Properties** in the shortcut menu. In the Properties dialog box, click **Disk Cleanup**. Disk Cleanup calculates how much space can be cleared.

Step 3. To include system files in the list, click **Clean up system files**. If you are not logged on as an administrator, you must enter the administrator password to continue. Disk Cleanup recalculates how much space can be cleared, and the list of files to delete now includes temporary system files.

Step 4. In the Disk Cleanup for (C:) dialog box, check the items that you want to delete under *Files to delete*. Click **OK**. Then click **Delete Files**.

Follow these steps to calculate the percentage of free space on the hard drive:

Step 1. In the drive's Properties dialog box, note the Capacity and Free space. For example, in Figure 13-1 in the chapter, the Capacity of the drive is 931 GB. The Free space is 754 GB.

Step 2. Divide the amount of free space by the capacity of the drive. Then convert the fraction to a percentage. In our example, the calculation is $754 \div 931 = 0.809$. This fraction rounds up to 81%.

On Your Own 13.2 Step-by-Step Solution   How to Uninstall Software You No Longer Need

Follow these steps to uninstall software:

Step 1. Press **Win+X** and click **Programs and Features**. The Programs and Features window appears.

Step 2. To uninstall a program, select it and then click **Uninstall** in the menu bar. Follow directions on-screen to uninstall the program.

Step 3. To uninstall an app on the Start screen, right-click the app you want to uninstall. Then click **Uninstall** in the status bar at the bottom of the screen.

On Your Own 13.3 Step-by-Step Solution   How to Limit Startup Programs Using Task Manager

Follow these steps to use Task Manager:

Step 1. Press **Win+X** and click **Task Manager**. The Task Manager window opens. If details are not showing, click **More details**.

Step 2. Click the **Startup** tab. A list of programs that launch at startup appears. To go online to learn about a startup item, right-click it and select **Search online** in the drop-down menu. Internet Explorer opens and searches for information about the item.

Step 3. To keep a program from launching each time Windows starts, select the program and click **Disable**.

Step 4. If you made any changes, restart your computer for the change to take effect.

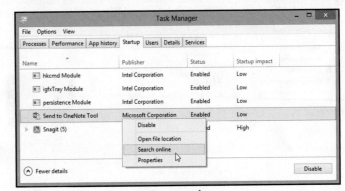

Startup tab

On Your Own 13.4 Step-by-Step Solution   How to Manage Power Settings

Follow these steps to manage power settings:

Step 1. Press **Win+X** and click **Power Options**. The Power Options window opens.

Step 2. Note which power plan is selected. To find the power settings for this plan, click **Change plan settings** to the right of the selected plan. If you made changes, click **Save changes** to return to the Power Options window or **Cancel** to return without saving changes.

Step 3. To find out what the power button does, click **Choose what the power button does**. To find out about a password required at wake-up, look in the area labeled *Password protection on wakeup*. If you made changes, click **Save changes** to return to the Power Options window or **Cancel** to return without saving changes.

Step 4. Using a laptop or netbook, to find out what happens when you close the lid, click **Choose what closing the lid does**. If you made changes, click **Save changes** to return to the Power Options window or **Cancel** to return without saving changes.

On Your Own 13.5 Step-by-Step Solution   How to Use Task Manager to Close an Application

Follow these steps to use Task Manager:

Step 1. To open the Paint application, go to the **Start screen** and type **Paint**. Click **Paint** in the list of Apps.

Step 2. To open Task Manager, press **Win+X** and click **Task Manager**.

Step 3. To close the Paint program, first make sure the **Processes** tab of Task Manager is selected. Then select the **Paint** program in the Apps group and click **End task**. The Paint program closes. Any changes you might have made in the Paint window are not saved.

Step 4. Close Task Manager.

On Your Own 13.6 Step-by-Step Solution   How to Practice Changing Monitor Settings

Follow these steps to practice changing the monitor settings:

Step 1. Working from the Windows desktop, open a Word document or a web page in your browser so you can see black text on a white background. Resize the window so you can view the window as well as the Windows desktop.

Step 2. To adjust the screen resolution, right-click somewhere on the desktop and select **Screen resolution** from the shortcut menu. Click the down arrow next to Resolution. In the drop-down menu, use the sliding scale to select your resolution. Click off the menu and then click **Apply**. In the box that appears, click **Keep changes** to save your changes or **Revert** to return to the previous setting. Click **OK** to close the window.

Step 3. To adjust text size, right-click on the desktop and select **Personalize** from the shortcut menu. Click **Display** in the left pane of the Personalization window. The Display window appears. Check **Let me choose one scaling level for all my displays**. Then select **Medium – 125%** (see Figure S13-1). Click **Apply** and follow directions on-screen to make the change. You must sign off Windows and sign back on for your changes to take effect.

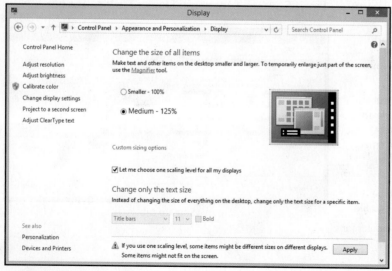

FIGURE S13-1
Adjust display setting to enlarge text so it is easier to read.

> **Tip** Another way to get to the Display window is to open the **Control Panel** and click **Appearance and Personalization** and then click **Display**.

To adjust the settings on a desktop monitor, do the following:

Step 1. Not all monitor buttons work the same way. In general, press the **Menu** button to open a menu on the monitor screen and then use other buttons to work your way through this menu.

Step 2. Know that most monitors have an Auto or Reset option that you can use to return the monitor to default settings if you have a problem.

On Your Own 13.7 Step-by-Step Solution   How to Use the Printer Queue

Follow these steps to use the printer queue:

Step 1. Turn off your printer. Open a Word document that you want to print or create a short one-sentence Word document. Command Word to print the document. Command Word to print the document a second time. How to print a Word document was covered in Chapter 2. Neither printout happens because the printer is turned off.

Step 2. To open the printer window, press **Win+X** and click **Control Panel** in the Quick Link menu. In Control Panel, click **View devices and printers** in the Hardware and Sound group. In the Devices and Printers window, double-click the printer icon. The printer window opens.

Step 3. To see the items in the printer queue, click **document(s) in queue**. The printer queue opens. To delete one of the items, right-click it and click **Cancel** on the shortcut menu. Click **Yes**. The item is deleted from the queue.

> **Not Working?** The options and commands on the printer window might vary for some printer manufacturers.

Step 4. Turn on the printer. The one document should now print. Watch the printer queue as the document prints and the queue is empty. Close all windows.

On Your Own 13.8 Step-by-Step Solution   How to Decide Whether Your Computer Needs a Memory Upgrade

Follow these steps to decide whether your computer needs a memory upgrade:

Step 1. To open the System window, press **Win+X** and click **System**. In the System window, find the edition of Windows (for example, Windows 8 or Windows 8.1 Pro), system type (for example, 32-bit operating system or 64-bit operating system), and amount of memory installed (for example, 2 GB, 4 GB, or 8 GB).

> **Hint** If you want to keep Task Manager always on top of other windows, click **Options** and click **Always on top**.

Step 2. Open **Task Manager**. In the Task Manager window, click the **Performance** tab. Then click **Memory** in the left pane.

Step 3. Open Microsoft Word. Leave the Word window open. Open Internet Explorer and surf the web.

Step 4. As you work, watch the Task Manager line graph. Did the line graph show all memory is used?

Follow these guidelines to decide whether you need an upgrade:

▶ A 32-bit operating system benefits from 4 GB of memory. If you don't have 4 GB of memory, you might improve performance with an upgrade.

▶ A 64-bit operating system benefits from 8 GB of memory. If you don't have 8 GB of memory, you might improve performance with an upgrade.

On Your Own 13.9 Step-by-Step Solution   How to Check Your Hard Drive and Memory for Errors

Detailed directions for scanning the hard drive for errors and using the Windows Memory Diagnostic utility are listed in the chapter in the section "Windows Gives Strange Errors" and are not repeated here.

13

Follow these steps to use some troubleshooting tools:

Step 1. Click **Settings** on the charms bar. Click **Change PC settings**. On the PC settings page, click **Update and recovery** and then click **Recovery**. In the right pane, click **Restart now** under *Advanced startup*. The system restarts and displays the Windows Startup Menu (refer to Figure 13-23 in the chapter). The screen is titled Choose an option.

Step 2. Click **Troubleshoot**. On the Troubleshoot screen, click **Advanced options**. On the Advanced options screen, click **Startup Repair**. Follow directions on-screen, and the system restarts.

Step 3. Use the **Settings** charm to restart the system and return to the Windows Startup Menu. Click **Troubleshoot**. On the Troubleshoot screen, click **Advanced options**. On the Advanced options screen, click **System Restore**. The System Restore screen appears. To continue, click an administrator account. Then enter the password to the account and press **Enter**.

Step 4. On the System Restore window, click **Next**. To find out how many restore points are available, check **Show more restore points**.

Step 5. Select the first restore point in the list. Then click **Scan for affected programs**. In the box that appears, you can see which programs and drivers might be deleted or restored if the restore point is applied. Click **Close**.

Step 6. On the System Restore window, click **Cancel**. You are returned to the Choose an option screen. Click **Continue** to exit and continue to Windows. Sign in to Windows to return to the Start screen.

CHAPTER 14 STEP-BY-STEP SOLUTIONS
Buying Your Own Personal Computer

The solutions in this appendix are for you to use if you get stuck when doing an On Your Own activity in the chapter. To learn how to teach yourself a computer skill, always try the On Your Own activity first before turning to these solutions.

On Your Own 14.1 Step-by-Step Solution   How to Determine What Upgrades Would Improve Your Computer's Performance

This solution has four parts:

► How to find out a network connection speed

► How to find out the Internet connection speed

► How to find out the type of USB ports installed

► How to find out if your computer qualifies for Windows 8.1

How to Find Out a Network Connection Speed

For Windows 8, follow these steps to find out the speeds of your network connections:

Step 1.   Press **Win+X** and click **Network Connections** in the Quick Link menu. The Network Connections window opens.

Step 2.   For a wired connection, double-click **Ethernet**. For a wireless connection, double-click **Wi-Fi**. The network status dialog box opens. The Speed displays in this box.

For Windows 7, follow these steps to find out the speed of your network connection:

Step 1.   On the Windows desktop, right-click the network icon in the taskbar. Click **Open Network and Sharing Center**.

Step 2.   In the Connections group, for a wired connection, click **Local Area Connection**. For a wireless connection, click **Wireless Network Connection**. The network status dialog box opens. The Speed displays in this box.

How to Find Out the Internet Connection Speed

Follow these steps to find out the speed of your Internet connection:

Step 1.   Open Internet Explorer and go to **Speedtest.net**.

Step 2.   Click **BEGIN TEST**. The meters display upload speed and download speed. The download speed is faster than the upload speed. The best indication of your Internet connection speed is the download speed.

How to Find Out the Type of USB Ports Installed

Follow these steps to find out what types of USB ports are installed:

Step 1.   In Windows 8, press **Win+X** and click **Run**. In the Run box, type **msinfo32** and press **Enter**. In Windows 7, click **Start,** type **msinfo32** in the search box, and click **OK**. The System Information window appears.

Step 2.   In the left pane of the System Information window, click the plus sign (+) to the left of Components. Click **USB**. The list of USB devices appears.

Step 3.   You can widen the Device column in the right pane to see more information. In the list, USB Enhanced is Hi-Speed USB (also known as USB 2.0). USB 3.0 is SuperSpeed USB.

Step 4.   To identify a SuperSpeed USB port, look into the port. The SuperSpeed USB ports are blue.

How to Find Out If Your Computer Qualifies for Windows 8.1

Follow these steps to find out if a computer that does not have Windows 8.1 installed qualifies for Windows 8.1:

Step 1.   Open Internet Explorer and go to **windows.microsoft.com/upgradeadvisor**. When you start the process of upgrading your operating system to Windows 8.1, the Upgrade Advisor is run. In these directions, you will only run the Upgrade Advisor and will stop the process before you actually buy and install the upgrade. Click **Upgrade now**. (If you are using Windows 7, you must then click the down arrow next to Save and then click **Save As**.)

Not Working?   If Windows 8.1 is already installed on your computer, you won't see the *Upgrade now* link on the Microsoft page that appears and you cannot continue with this activity.

Step 2. In the Save As dialog box that appears, save the WindowsUpgradeAssistant.exe file to your Windows desktop. To do that, click **Desktop** in the left pane and then click **Save**. The file saves to the desktop.

Step 3. Double-click the file on your desktop. In the Security Warning dialog box that appears, click **Run** (see Figure S14-1). Then respond to the UAC box.

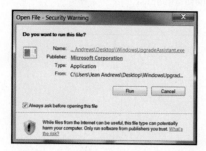

FIGURE S14-1

Run the Windows 8.1 Upgrade Assistant to find out whether a computer qualifies for Windows 8.1.

Step 4. The Windows 8.1 Upgrade Assistant dialog box appears, and the program scans hardware and applications to see whether they will work with Windows 8.1. When the scan completes, results appear (see Figure S14-2). To see an itemized report, click **See compatibility details**. A report of apps and hardware that are not compatible with Windows 8.1 appears. You'll need to investigate each item that is not compatible to find out if you can upgrade the app or device before you continue with the Windows 8.1 installation.

Click to see a detailed report

FIGURE S14-2

The Windows 8.1 Upgrade Assistant reports items you need to review before you install Windows 8.1.

Step 5. To see which edition of Windows 8.1 is recommended for your system, click **Next** in the Windows 8.1 Upgrade Assistant dialog box. In the next box, make sure **Windows settings, personal files, and apps** is selected and click **Next**. The next box shows the editions of Windows 8.1 and the prices. Click **Close** to close the program.

> **Not Working?** When using Windows 7, the Upgrade Assistant offers you the option to save only **Personal files**. Windows settings and apps are lost when you upgrade from Windows 7 to Windows 8.1.

On Your Own 14.2 Step-by-Step Solution   How to Determine the Value of Your Computer

Follow these steps to collect the information you need to determine the value of your computer:

Step 1. For Windows 8, press **Win+X** and click **Run**. In the Run box, type **msinfo32** and press **Enter**. The System Information window opens.

For Windows 7, click **Start**, type **msinfo32** in the *Search programs and files* box, and press **Enter**. The System Information window opens.

Step 2. On the System Information window, locate the System Manufacturer and System Model. If your computer is not a brand-name desktop but a desktop that was built from parts, this information applies to the motherboard. Otherwise, it applies to the computer itself.

Step 3. On this window, locate the Processor information and the amount of memory installed.

Step 4. For Windows 8, open **File Explorer**. Select **This PC** in the left pane. In the right pane, look in the Devices and drives group to find the size of the hard drive. (For Windows 7, open **Windows Explorer** and double-click **Computer** in the left pane.)

Step 5. For Windows 8, press **Win+X** and click **System**. (For Windows 7, click **Start**, right-click **Computer**, and click **Properties** in the shortcut menu.) The System window opens. On this window, locate the Windows edition installed.

Step 6. If you are including the applications installed with the computer, use one of these methods to open the Programs and Features window:

- For Windows 8, press **Win+X** and click **Programs and Features**.
- For Windows 7, click **Start**, **Control Panel**, and **Uninstall a program**.

Step 7. Make a list of the installed applications that you know were purchased. You don't need to include add-ons, free apps, or drivers in your list.

You now have the information you need to determine the value. For example, suppose this is the information for your computer:

▶ It is a two-year-old Sony VAIO laptop, model SVS151190X.

▶ The processor is a Core i7 2.10 GHz, 12 GB of memory is installed, and the hard drive is 500 GB.

▶ Windows 7 Professional is installed.

▶ The warranty has expired.

Follow these steps to find the value of this Sony VAIO laptop:

Step 1. Open Internet Explorer and go to eBay.com. Search for a laptop for sale. The eBay site allows you to refine your search for a laptop by offering options on the left side of the search window. Check the options to refine your search.

Step 2. You also can try to enter a description of the computer in the search box on eBay. For example, search on "Sony VAIO laptop SVS151190X."

Step 3. Go to Craigslist.org and search for a comparable computer.

Step 4. Calculate the average price of all the comparable computers you found to determine the value of your computer. In our example, the calculations are reported in Table S14-1 that were current prices at the time we wrote this chapter. Your calculations might be different.

TABLE S14-1   Average Price of Comparable Computers

Computer	Price
Sony VAIO SVS151190X laptop	$928.00
Sony VAIO SVS151190X laptop	$829.98
Sony VAIO SVS13A1CGXB	$1,047.84
Average price	$935.00

On Your Own 14.3 Step-by-Step Solution   **How to Compare Prices and Features for a Desktop and a Comparable Laptop**

Follow these steps to find online a low-priced desktop without extra features:

Step 1. Open Internet Explorer and go to **Tigerdirect.com**. Search for a new (not refurbished) low-priced desktop computer. One search turned up the HP Pro 3500 D8D40UT desktop shown in Figure S14-3. Your search results might be different.

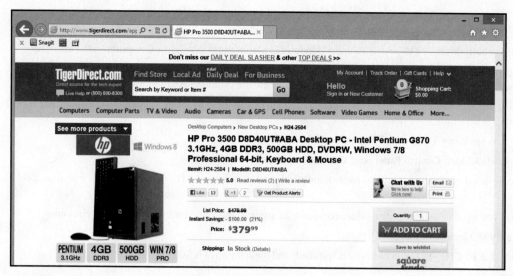

FIGURE S14-3
This HP desktop sells for $379.99.

Step 2. Find in the ad the specifications for the desktop, which are recorded in Table S14-2 for the HP Pro 3500 D8D40UT.

TABLE S14-2   Comparison Chart Between a Desktop and Laptop Computer

Feature	Desktop	Laptop
Brand and model	HP Pro 3500 D8D40UT	HP 650 C6Z72UT
Price	$379.99	$449.99
Processor brand and model	Pentium G870 3.1 GHz by Intel	Pentium Dual-Core B980 2.4 GHz by Intel
Memory amount	4 GB	4 GB
Size of hard drive	500 GB	320 GB
Type of optical drive	DVD with read/write	DVD with read/write
Windows edition	Windows 8 or 7 Professional 64-bit	Windows 8 64-bit
Extra features		

Step 3. Search the Tigerdirect.com site for a laptop using the same or similar processor, memory, hard drive, optical drive, and operating system. If you can't find an exact match, try to match at least the brand, processor, and operating system. For example, one search on the Tigerdirect.com site turned up the laptop shown in Figure S14-4. The information about the laptop is recorded in the third column of Table S14-2. Your results might be different.

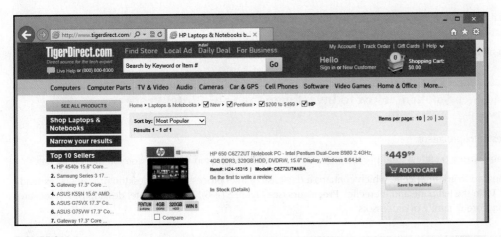

FIGURE S14-4
This HP laptop sells for $449.99.

The price of the laptop is $70 more than the desktop. However, when considering the total cost of the system, don't forget you might need to buy a monitor to use with the desktop. The major features that are different between the two computers are the capacity of the hard drive and the edition of Windows 8. Your results might be different.

On Your Own 14.4 Step-by-Step Solution   How to Investigate Computer Manufacturers

Here are some general tips to help you find a review about a product, customer service, or warranty from each of the computer manufacturers listed in Table 14-2 in the chapter:

▶ Go to one or more of the websites mentioned in the chapter to find reliable reviews of computer manufacturers or reviews about a computer made by the manufacturer. These sites are Microcenter.com, Newegg.com, Tigerdirect.com, Bestbuy.com, Computershopper.com, and Amazon.com. For example, go to **Amazon.com** and find a computer made by Acer, such as the one shown in Figure S14-5, and click **customer reviews**. Take one sentence from one of these reviews.

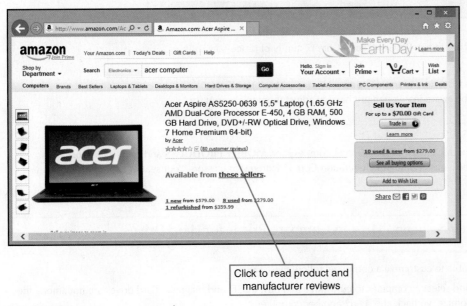

Click to read product and manufacturer reviews

FIGURE S14-5
Amazon.com publishes customer reviews about its products.

▶ Do a Google.com search on a product review. For example, the MacBook Pro is a laptop made by Apple. Use Google.com to search on **review of the Apple MacBook Pro**. Find a review and take one sentence from the review.

▶ To find a review about Dell's customer service, do a Google search on **dell customer service reviews**.

▶ To find a review about the warranty offered by a company, do a Google search on key words such as **review for warranty with Hewlett Packard**.

▶ Use Google.com to search on **laptop reviews 2014**. The search results should turn up reviews for the top-selling laptops for this year. Most of the manufacturers in Table 14-2 are likely to appear in the reviews.

▶ Do a Google.com search on **best desktops reviews 2014**. Any manufacturers you have not yet found are likely to be in this list.

On Your Own 14.5 Step-by-Step Solution   How to Investigate the Latest Intel Processors and the Cost of Memory

Do the following to find the latest Intel processor:

Step 1.   Go to Google.com and search on **latest Intel processor for desktops or laptops**. Find the processor you think is the latest.

Step 2.   To verify your findings, go to **ark.intel.com**, which contains a database of Intel processors. For desktop processors, expand **DESKTOP PRODUCTS** in the left pane and then click **Processors** (see Figure S14-6). The latest Intel desktop processors are in the 4th Generation Core i7 family of processors.

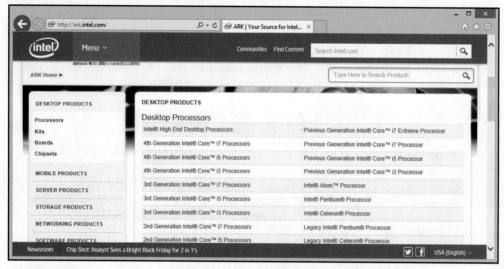

FIGURE S14-6
The latest desktop processors by Intel are in the 4th Generation Core i7 family of processors.

> **Not Working?**   Websites change from time to time. The step-by-step instructions were accurate when we wrote them, but be aware that you might have to adjust them to account for later website changes.

Step 3.   To see a list of the latest mobile processors at ark.intel.com, expand **MOBILE PRODUCTS** and then click **Processors**. The latest mobile Intel processors are the 4th Generation Core i7 Extreme processors. Your search might turn up a newer processor family.

On Your Own 14.6 Step-by-Step Solution   How to Compare Prices for Hard Drives and Windows 8.1 Editions

To compare hard drives that are available to customize a computer, follow these steps:

Step 1.   Go to Shopping.hp.com and select a computer to customize and buy. If SSD and magnetic hard drives are not among the components you can customize, go back and select another computer.

> **Hint**   In a computer ad, if the RPM is listed for a hard drive, you know the drive is a magnetic hard drive.

Step 2.   Figure S14-7 shows the choices for one HP laptop. The choices you find might be different. The answers to the questions about the choices for hard drives shown in the figure are

- The capacity of the largest SSD drive is 160 GB.
- The SSD drive costs $210 more than the largest magnetic hard drive when you exclude the hybrid hard drive from the choices.

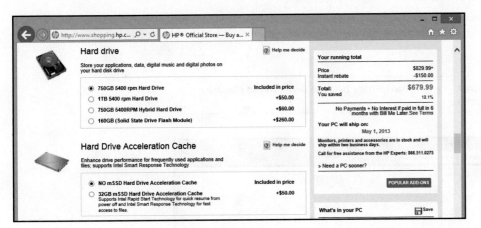

FIGURE S14-7
HP offers a choice of hard drives for one laptop.

To compare the difference in price between Windows 8.1 and Windows 8.1 Pro, follow this step:

Step 1. Go to Shopping.hp.com and select a computer to customize and buy. If Windows 8.1 and Windows 8.1 Pro are not among the operating systems you can customize, go back and select another computer. Figure S14-8 shows the choices for one HP all-in-one. In the figure, you can see the difference in price between Windows 8.1 and Windows 8.1 Pro is $70. The difference you see in price might be different.

Hint Look in the HP line of business computers for computers that can be customized with choices for Windows 8.1 and Windows 8.1 Pro.

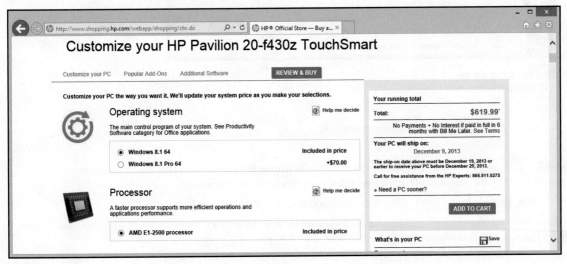

FIGURE S14-8
HP offers a choice of operating systems for this HP Pavilion all-in-one touch-screen computer.

On Your Own 14.7 Step-by-Step Solution   How to Compare Prices for a Computer with a Blu-ray Burner

Follow these steps to find an inexpensive new computer with a Blu-ray burner:

Step 1.   Because desktops are usually less expensive than laptops, let's search for a desktop computer. Go to Google.com and enter **desktop with blu-ray** in the search box and click **Shopping** in the menu bar. A list of products and prices appear (see Figure S14-9).

> **Hint** Don't include the word "burner" in your search string because doing so can eliminate from the hit list computers that really do have a burner.

FIGURE S14-9
Refine your search for a desktop computer with a Blu-ray burner.

Step 2.   The search results might include stand-alone optical drives. To narrow the search to desktop computers, look for that category in the left pane. For example, click **Desktop Computers** to narrow the search.

Step 3.   Use the Sort by field on the right side of the window to sort results by **Price: low to high**.

Step 4.   Drill down to each computer until you find the least expensive computer with a Blu-ray burner. A computer might appear in the list that has a DVD burner and a Blu-ray player or reader, so you need to verify the details.

Step 5.   A computer built from parts might be the least expensive and is available only from the source where you found it. However, if you find a brand-name computer, you might want to do a Google search on the brand and model to find the best buy.

On Your Own 14.8 Step-by-Step Solution   How to Compare Two Monitors and Two Printers

Follow these steps to find two monitors by the same manufacturer for comparison of features:

Step 1. Go to Dell.com and search on **Monitors**. In the pane on the left, narrow your search to the least expensive Dell monitor you can find (see Figure S14-10). To find details about the monitor, you can click **More details**, **Tech Specs**, or a similar link.

FIGURE S14-10
Use the left pane to narrow your search for a low-end or high-end monitor.

Step 2. Open a new tab in Internet Explorer and do another search to find the most expensive Dell monitor.

Step 3. Collect this information about each monitor:

- Model of Dell monitor (for example, Dell E Series E2013H)

- Price (for example, $139.99)

- Screen size (for example, 20")

- Native resolution (for example, 1,600 × 900)

- Pixel pitch (for example, 0.284 mm)

- Contrast ratio (for example, 1000:1)

- Response time (for example, 5 ms)

- Input connectors (for example, DVD-D and VGA)

- Display type (for example, LED-backlit LCD monitor/TFT active matrix)

Follow these steps to find two multifunction laser printers by the same manufacturer for price comparison between an all-in-one black-and-white laser printer and an all-in-one color laser printer, including the cost of toner:

Step 1. Go to **www.usa.canon.com** and drill down in the Home Office group to **Printers & Multifunction**. In the left pane, click **Black & White Laser Multifunction**. Select a printer in the list, for example, the ImageCLASS MF5950dw printer. Click **Features** and make sure the selected printer is also a scanner and copier. The price for our selected printer is $399.00.

Step 2. Click **Supplies & Accessories**. Find the cost of a black toner cartridge. For our selected printer, the price is $92.00.

Step 3. In the left pane, click **Color Laser Multifunction**. Select a printer in the list, for example, the Color imageCLASS MF8280Cw. Click **Features** and make sure the selected printer is also a scanner and copier. The price for our selected printer is $449.00.

Step 4. Click **Supplies & Accessories**. Find the price of the black, cyan, magenta, and yellow toner cartridges. For our selected printer, the price is $69.00 for the black cartridge, $85.00 for the cyan cartridge, $85.00 for the magenta cartridge, and $85.00 for the yellow cartridge.

Step 5. Calculate the total price of each printer, including its toner cartridges:

- For the black-and-white printer, our total price is $399.00 + $92.00 = $491.00.

- For the color printer, our total price is $449.00 + $69.00 + $85.00 + $85.00 + $85.00 = $773.00.

Your results might be different.

CHAPTER 15 STEP-BY-STEP SOLUTIONS
Creating and Using Databases with Microsoft Access

The solutions in this appendix are for you to use if you get stuck when doing an On Your Own activity in the chapter. To learn how to teach yourself a computer skill, always try the On Your Own activity first before turning to these solutions.

On Your Own 15.1 Step-by-Step Solution   How to Explore the AnimalShelter Database and the Access Window

Use the AnimalShelter Database: Part 1 of 3

Follow these steps to open the database:

Step 1. Open **File Explorer** in Windows 8 and 8.1 (for Windows 7, open **Windows Explorer**) and locate the sample_files folder on your USB flash drive. (Recall that you downloaded the sample_files folder to your USB flash drive from the www .pearsonhighered.com/jump website in Chapter 2.) If you need more help locating the folder, see the instructions in On Your Own 2.7 Step-by-Step Solution.

Step 2. Locate the **AnimalShelter** file in the **sample_files** folder. Double-click the file. The file opens in an Access window. The file name and extension appear in the title bar as AnimalShelter.accdb.

> **Not Working?** If the Access window doesn't open when you double-click the AnimalShelter database, your Windows settings might be wrong. Ask an experienced technician to help you configure Windows to associate a .accdb file with Microsoft Access for your computer.

Step 3. If the yellow SECURITY WARNING bar appears below the Access HOME ribbon, click **Enable Content** to close this security bar.

Follow these steps to explore and edit the database:

Step 1. To open the Animals table, double-click **Animals** in the left pane (the Navigation Pane). Records in the table appear in the right pane in the Datasheet View, and the Animals tab appears above the data (see Figure S15-1).

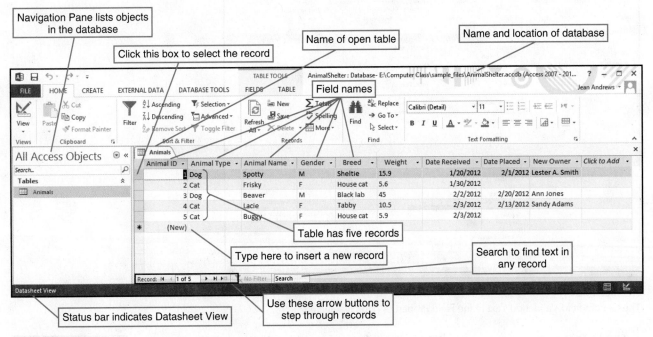

FIGURE S15-1
A table in a database is made up of records (rows) and fields (columns).

Step 2. To add a new record to the table, click the Animal Type field in the last record of the table, which has an asterisk (*) on the left. Enter **Dog** or **Cat** in the Animal Type field. Press **Tab** to move to the next field on the right. A new counting number is automatically inserted in the Animal ID field. You cannot enter a value into this field.

Step 3. Enter values for the Animal Name, Gender, Breed, Weight, and Date Received fields. Here is what happens if you enter invalid data:

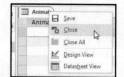

- If you try to enter a letter other than M or F into the Gender field, an error message appears in a dialog box. Click **OK** and type **M** or **F** into the Gender field.

- If you try to enter a value other than a date into the Date Received or Date Placed field, an error message appears. To correct the problem, click **Enter new value** and enter a valid date.

Step 4. To close the Animals table, right-click the **Animals** tab and click **Close** in the shortcut menu.

On Your Own 15.2 Step-by-Step Solution   **How to Edit a Validation Rule and Sort and Filter Data in the Animals Table**

Use the AnimalShelter Database: Part 2 of 3

Follow these steps to view the Animals table in Design view:

Step 1. Using the AnimalShelter database, double-click the **Animals** table in the left pane to open it. Right-click the **Animals** tab in the right pane and select **Design View** from the shortcut menu. The Design View appears. Design view is listed in the status bar at the bottom of the Access window.

Step 2. In the Field Name column, click the **Gender** field. The Field Properties pane for this field displays at the bottom of the Access window.

Step 3. Select the text **Accepted text is M or F** (see Figure S15-2). Replace this text with **Only M or F is allowed**.

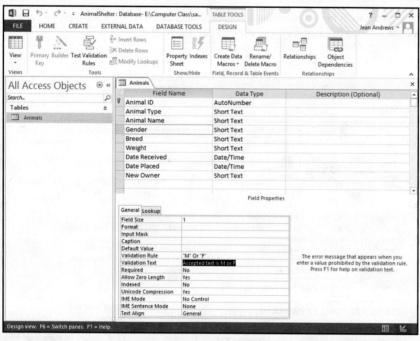

FIGURE S15-2
The Gender field Validation Text in the Field Properties pane is selected.

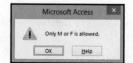

Step 4. To save your design changes, right-click the **Animals** tab and select **Save** from the shortcut menu. (Alternately, you can click the Save icon in the Quick Access Toolbar.)

Step 5. To return to Datasheet View, right-click the **Animals** tab and select **Datasheet View**.

Step 6. Enter a new record or edit an existing record. If you enter text other than M or F in the Gender field, a dialog box appears showing *Only M or F is allowed.* Click **OK** and correct the problem.

Follow these steps to sort and filter the records in the Animals table:

Step 1. Look in the status bar to verify the Animals table is showing in the Datasheet View. Click the drop-down arrow to the right of the Gender field name. Click **Sort A to Z**. The data is sorted by Gender.

Step 2. Click the drop-down arrow to the right of the Animal ID field. Click **Sort Smallest to Largest**.

Step 3. Click the drop-down arrow to the right of the Animal Type field. Uncheck **(Select All)** and check **Cat**. Click **OK**. Only cats are listed.

Step 4. To remove the filter, click the drop-down arrow to the right of Animal Type. Check **(Select All)** and click **OK**. All records are listed.

Step 5. To delete a record, use one of these methods:

- Right-click the box to the left of the record and click **Delete Record** in the shortcut menu. A dialog box appears. Click **Yes** to delete the record.

- To select the record, click the box to the left of the record. The entire record is selected. On the HOME ribbon, click **Delete**. A dialog box appears. Click **Yes** to delete the record.

Step 6. Right-click the **Animals** tab and click **Save** on the shortcut menu.

On Your Own 15.3 Step-by-Step Solution   How to Create and Run a Query

Use the AnimalShelter Database: Part 3 of 3

Follow these steps to create and run a query that displays only animals that have been placed with new owners:

Step 1. If the Animals table in the AnimalShelter database is not open, open it. Records in the Animals table should be listed in the right pane, and Datasheet View appears in the status bar.

Step 2. On the CREATE ribbon, click **Query Design**. The Show Table dialog box appears (see Figure S15-3). Verify the **Animals** table is selected. Click **Add**. The Animals table is added to the query. Click **Close** to close the dialog box.

FIGURE S15-3
Use the Show Table dialog box to select tables to use in the query.

> **Not Working?** If the Show Table dialog box doesn't appear, click **Show Table** on the DESIGN ribbon.

Step 3. Double-click the **Animal ID** field in the list of fields for the Animals table. The Animal ID field is added to the field list at the bottom of the query design pane. Double-click **Animal Name**, **Date Placed**, and **New Owner** to add these fields to the query. Four fields are now listed in the query design.

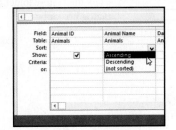

Step 4. In the lower pane of the query design, click in the box in the Animal Name column and in the Sort row. A drop-down arrow appears in the box. Click the drop-down arrow. In the drop-down list that appears, click **Ascending**.

Step 5. Click in the box in the Date Placed column in the Criteria row. Type **>0** in the box.

Step 6. To save the query, right-click the **Query1** tab and click **Save**. The Save As dialog box appears. Type **Placements** and click **OK**. The Placements query is listed in the Navigation Pane of the Access window. The query tab is named Placements and is currently selected.

Step 7. To run the query, right-click the **Placements** tab in the right pane and click **Datasheet View**. Only records that have values in the Date Placed field are listed. Only the four fields selected for the query are listed. Records are listed sorted by Animal Name.

Follow these steps to practice opening and closing a query, table, database, and the Access application:

Step 1. To close the Placements query, right-click the **Placements** tab and select **Close** from the shortcut menu. The Placements tab disappears.

Step 2. To close the Animals table, right-click the **Animals** tab and select **Close**. If you have made changes to the table design since you last saved it, a dialog box appears asking whether you want to save your changes. If so, click **Yes**. The Animals tab disappears from the right pane.

Step 3. To open the Animals table, double-click it in the left pane.

Step 4. To open the Placements query, double-click it in the left pane. To move between the open table and open query, click the appropriate tab above the data.

Step 5. To close the database, click the **FILE** tab. Click **Close**. Your changes are saved and the database is closed.

Step 6. Close the Access window.

On Your Own 15.4 Step-by-Step Solution   How to Create a Database

Create the DogShow Database: Part 1 of 8

Follow these steps to create the tables in the DogShow database:

Step 1. To open Access in Windows 8, on the Start screen, click **Access 2013**. To open Access in Windows 7, click **Start**, **All Programs**, **Microsoft Office 2013**, and **Access 2013**. The Access window opens (see Figure S15-4).

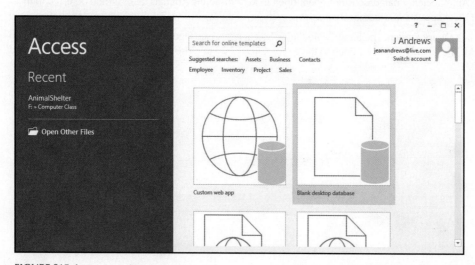

FIGURE S15-4
Create a new blank desktop database.

Step 2. Click **Blank desktop database**. The Blank desktop database dialog box appears. In the File Name box, enter **DogShow**. Click the yellow folder icon to browse for a location to put your database (see Figure S15-5). The File New Database dialog box appears.

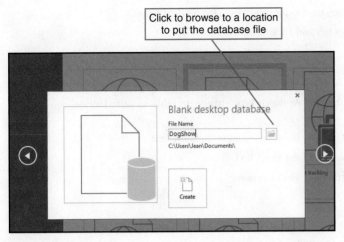

FIGURE S15-5
Name the database file and point to the location to store the file.

Step 3. Navigate to your USB flash drive, hard drive, or another location given by your instructor and select the folder where you want the database to be stored. Click **OK** to close the dialog box.

Step 4. Verify the file name and location are correct and click **Create**. The database file is created and Access assigns the file extension of .accdb to the file. The new database looks like that in Figure S15-6. To give yourself plenty of screen space to work, maximize your window.

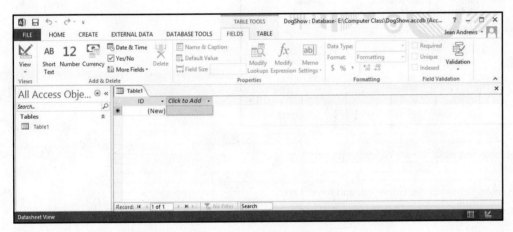

FIGURE S15-6
A new database has one table, which has one field.

Follow these steps to change the names of the table and the field and add seven more fields to the Dogs table:

Step 1. Right-click the **Table1** tab and click **Design View** in the shortcut menu. The Save As dialog box appears. Change the name of the table to **Dogs** and click **OK**.

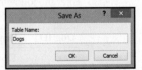

Step 2. Change the name of the ID field to **Dog ID**. Change the Data Type of the field from AutoNumber to **Short Text**.

Step 3. Tab to the next Field Name and enter **Dog Name**. Set the Data Type to **Short Text**.

Step 4. Tab to the next Field Name and enter **First Name**. Set the Data Type to **Short Text**.

Step 5. Tab to the next Field Name and enter **Last Name**. Set the Data Type to **Short Text**.

Step 6. Tab to the next Field Name and enter **Street**. Set the Data Type to **Short Text**.

Step 7. Tab to the next Field Name and enter **City**. Set the Data Type to **Short Text**.

Step 8. Tab to the next Field Name and enter **State**. Set the Data Type to **Short Text**.

Step 9. Tab to the next Field Name and enter **Zip**. Set the Data Type to **Short Text**.

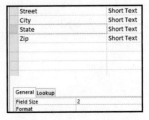

Step 10. Click in the **State** field name to select that field. In the Field Properties pane at the bottom of the window, change the Field Size from 255 to **2**.

Step 11. Select the **Zip** field and change the Field Size from 255 to **5**.

Step 12. To Verify the Dog ID is the primary key, look for the key icon to the left of the Dog ID field name.

Step 13. To save your changes to the table, right-click the **Dogs** tab and click **Save**.

Follow these steps to create the Entries table:

Step 1. Click the **CREATE** tab. On the CREATE ribbon, click **Table**. A new table is created.

Step 2. Right-click the **Table1** tab and click **Design View**. In the Save As dialog box, change the table name to **Entries** and click **OK**.

Step 3. Change the ID field name to **Class** and change the Data Type from AutoNumber to **Short Text**.

Step 4. Add a new field named **Dog ID**. In the Data Type column, select **Short Text**.

Step 5. Add a new field named **Entry Fee**. In the Data Type column, select **Currency**.

To set the primary key for the Entries table, follow these steps:

Step 1. Click the selection box to the left of the Class field. This row is selected. Hold down your **Shift** key and click the selection box to the left of the Dog ID field. Both rows are now selected.

Step 2. On the DESIGN ribbon, click **Primary Key**. A key icon appears beside both fields indicating the two fields are now the primary key for the table (see Figure S15-7).

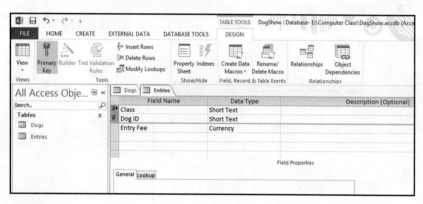

FIGURE S15-7
Select two fields in the Entries table and make the two fields the primary key.

Step 3. To save the Entries table, right-click the **Entries** tab and select **Save**.

Step 4. Right-click the **Entries** tab and click **Close** on the shortcut menu.

Follow these steps to enter sample data into the Dogs table:

Step 1. If necessary, open the **Dogs** table. Right-click the **Dogs** tab and click **Datasheet View**.

Step 2. Enter the following sample data into the Dogs table or make up your own data:

Dog ID	Dog Name	First Name	Last Name	Street	City	State	Zip
D05	Daisy	Sandy	Adams	200 Apple Lane	Smithville	OH	30000
D07	Sir Edward	Louie	Jackson	400 Maryville Hwy	Knoxburg	OH	50000
D18	Prissy	Betty	Clear	300 Mary Street	Smalltown	OH	40000
D4	Tildie	Bethany	Miller	120 Bobwhite Dr	Stanton	OH	60000
D88	Prissy	Lorraine	Quency	500 Lee Street	Woodsen	OH	77000
D90	Bonita	Latoya	Jones	370 Maple Street	Lakeville	OH	66600

Step 3. Try to enter two records in the Dogs table that have the same Dog ID. Note that an error occurs and you must correct the problem. Because the Dog ID is the primary key for the Dogs table, duplicate entries are not allowed.

Step 4. To save the Dogs table, right-click the **Dogs** tab and click **Save**. To close the **Dogs** table, right-click the **Dogs** tab and click **Close**.

Follow these steps to enter sample data in the Entries table:

Step 1. Double-click the **Entries** table in the left pane. The Entries table opens in Datasheet view.

Step 2. Enter the following sample data into the Entries table or make up your own data:

Class	Dog ID	Entry Fee
Agility	D05	15
Agility	D18	15
Agility	D4	15
Agility	D88	15
Showmanship	D07	18
Showmanship	D4	18
Showmanship	D88	18
Showmanship	D90	18
Working	D88	15
Working	D90	15

Step 3. Try to enter two records in the table that have the same Class and Dog ID. Note that an error occurs and you must correct the problem. Because the Class and Dog ID make up the primary key for the Entries table, duplicate entries for Class and Dog ID are not allowed.

Step 4. Right-click the **Entries** tab and click **Save** on the shortcut menu. Right-click the **Entries** tab again and click **Close** on the shortcut menu.

On Your Own 15.5 Step-by-Step Solution   **How to Relate Two Database Tables**

Create the DogShow Database: Part 2 of 8

Follow these steps to create a relationship between the Dogs table and Entries table:

Step 1. If necessary, open the **DogShow** database. If you see the **Dogs** tab in the right pane, right-click it and click **Close**. If you see the **Entries** tab in the right pane, right-click it and click **Close**.

Step 2. On the DATABASE TOOLS ribbon, click **Relationships**. The Relationships tab opens, and the Show Table dialog box appears.

Step 3. Select the **Dogs** table and click **Add**. Select the **Entries** table and click **Add**. Both tables are added to the relationship. Close the Show Table dialog box.

Step 4. To create the relationship, press and drag the **Dog ID** field in the Dogs table to the **Dog ID** field in the Entries table. Be sure you drag from the Dogs table to the Entries table, not the other direction. When you press and drag the Dog ID field from one table to the next, the Edit Relationships dialog box appears (see Figure S15-8).

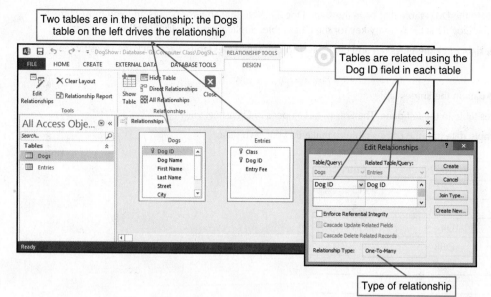

Two tables are in the relationship: the Dogs table on the left drives the relationship

Tables are related using the Dog ID field in each table

Type of relationship

FIGURE S15-8
Build a one-to-many relationship between the Dogs table and Entries table using the Dog ID field.

Step 5. Verify the field selected in both tables is Dog ID. Notice that Access recognizes the type of relationship as a one-to-many relationship.

> **Not Working?** If Dog ID is not listed for both tables in the Edit Relationships dialog box, click the field listed and select **Dog ID** from the drop-down list.

Step 6. Check **Enforce Referential Integrity** and click **Create**.

> **Not Working?** When you choose Enforce Referential Integrity, Access verifies the Entries table conforms to this enforcement. If it finds a Dog ID in the Entries table that doesn't have a match in the Dogs table, an error occurs, and you cannot complete the relationship. Go back to the Entries table and correct the data. Then try to build the relationship again.

Step 7. On the relationship line between the two tables, verify the 1 is on the left and the infinity symbol (∞) is on the right to indicate a one-to-many relationship, as shown in Figure 15-13 in the chapter. Correct any problems you see. To save the relationship, right-click the **Relationships** tab and select **Save** from the shortcut menu. To close the Relationship, right-click the **Relationships** tab and select **Close** from the shortcut menu.

> **Not Working?** If you make a mistake building the relationship and want to start over, click on the line between the tables and press the **Delete** key to delete the relationship between the tables.

Step 8. Double-click the **Dogs** table to open it. Notice the + to the left of each record. When you click the +, the related records in the Entries table appear, as shown in Figure 15-14 in the chapter. Close the **Dogs** table.

Step 9. Open the **Entries** table. Try to enter a new record in the table that uses a Dog ID that is not found in the Dogs table. An error message appears, and the invalid entry is not allowed. Close the **Entries** table.

On Your Own 15.6 Step-by-Step Solution   How to Use a Lookup Field to Protect Data Integrity

Create the DogShow Database: Part 3 of 8

Do the following to allow only valid values in the Class field of the Entries table:

Step 1. Using the DogShow database, open the **Entries** table and go to **Design View**.

Step 2. Click in the Data Type box to the right of the Class field name. A drop-down arrow appears. Click the arrow and then click **Lookup Wizard**. The Lookup Wizard dialog box appears.

Step 3. Select **I will type in the values that I want**. Click **Next**.

Step 4. In the next box, type the three classes in Col1. In the first row, enter **Agility**. In the second row, enter **Showmanship**. In the third row, enter **Working**. Click **Next**.

Step 5. In the next box, check **Limit To List** and click **Finish**.

Step 6. Right-click the **Entries** tab and click **Save**. Right-click the **Entries** tab and click **Datasheet View**.

Step 7. When you click in the Class field, a drop-down arrow appears. Click the drop-down arrow. The three classes appear.

Step 8. To close the table, right-click the **Entries** tab and click **Close**.

On Your Own 15.7 Step-by-Step Solution   How to Create and Use Detailed and Split Forms

Create the DogShow Database: Part 4 of 8

This solution has two parts:

▶ How to create a detailed form

▶ How to create a split form

How to Create a Detailed Form

Follow these steps to create and use the OneDog detailed form:

Step 1. Using the DogShow database, click the **Dogs** table in the left pane so it's selected. It's not necessary to open the table.

Step 2. Click **Form** on the CREATE ribbon. The Dogs form is created. Layout View appears in the status bar at the bottom of the Access window.

Step 3. Right-click the **Dogs** form tab and click **Save** in the drop-down menu. In the Save As dialog box, name the form **OneDog** and click **OK**. The form is saved, and you can see it listed as an object in the left pane under Forms.

Step 4. Right-click the **OneDog** tab and click **Form View** in the shortcut menu. You can now edit the data.

Step 5. Notice the two groups of arrows at the bottom of the form. The group at the very bottom is used to navigate the Dogs records. The group of arrows above the bottom group is used to navigate through the Entries records that relate to the current Dog record. Click the left and right arrows at the very bottom of the form to step through records in the Dogs table. Click the **First record** arrow to go to the first record. Click the **Last record** arrow to go to the last record.

Not Working? The OneDog form provides two sets of arrow buttons used to step through records. One set applies to the Entries table, and the other set applies to the Dogs table. Use the set at the very bottom of the form that applies to the Dogs table.

Step 6. To enter a new record in the Dogs table, click the **New (blank) record** arrow at the very bottom of the form. Enter data for a new record.

Step 7. To search for text, first click in the search box at the bottom of the form. For example, suppose the name Betty is in the data. Enter **Betty** in the box, and the record appears with Betty highlighted.

Step 8. To save the form, right-click the **OneDog** tab and click **Save** in the shortcut menu. Right-click the **OneDog** tab again and click **Close**.

Step 9. Double-click the **Dogs** table in the left pane. The Dogs table opens in Datasheet view. If you don't see your new record, press **F5** to refresh the data. Close the Dogs table.

How to Create a Split Form

Do the following to create a split form to edit the Entries table:

Step 1. In the left pane, click the **Entries** table to select it. It's not necessary to open the table.

Step 2. On the CREATE ribbon, click **More Forms** and click **Split Form**. The split form is created and is named **Entries**.

Step 3. Right-click the **Entries** form tab and click **Save**. In the Save As dialog box, name the form **SplitEntries** and click **OK**. The SplitEntries form is listed under Forms in the left pane.

Step 4. To switch to Form View, right-click the **SplitEntries** form and click **Form View** in the shortcut menu.

Step 5. Using the arrows at the bottom of the form, step through the records and go to the first and last records.

Step 6. Add a new record to the Entries table.

Step 7. Use the Search box at the bottom of the form to search for text. Enter **Working**. The first record that contains Working appears. Press **Enter** to step through other records that contain this text.

Step 8. To save the form, right-click the **SplitEntries** tab and click **Save** in the shortcut menu. Right-click the **SplitEntries** tab again and click **Close**.

Step 9. Double-click the **Entries** table in the left pane. The Entries table opens. If necessary, press **F5** to refresh the data. Close the table.

On Your Own 15.8 Step-by-Step Solution   **How to Create a Query That Includes a Calculation**

Create the DogShow Database: Part 5 of 8

Follow these steps to create the Fees query:

Step 1. Using the DogShow database, click **Query Design** on the CREATE ribbon. The Show Table dialog box appears. (If it doesn't appear, click **Show Table** on the DESIGN ribbon.)

Step 2. In the Show Table dialog box, click **Entries** and click **Add**. Click **Close** to close the Show Table box.

Step 3. In the Entries box, double-click **Class**. Class is added as the first column in the query. Double-click **Dog ID** to add it as the second column. Double-click **Entry Fee** to add it as the third column in the query.

Step 4. To save the query, right-click the **Query1** tab and click **Save** in the drop-down menu. In the Save As dialog box, name the query **Fees** and click **OK**.

Step 5. To sort rows in the query, click the box in the Class column and Sort row. A drop-down arrow appears. Click the drop-down arrow and click **Ascending**.

Step 6. Return to Datasheet View to see the data, which is sorted by Class.

Step 7. While still in Datasheet View, click **Totals** in the Records group on the HOME ribbon. A Total row is added to the query.

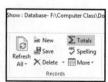

Step 8. Click in the Entry Fee column of the Total row. Then click the down arrow that appears. In the drop-down list, click **Sum**. A sum is added to the Total row.

Step 9. Compare your query to that shown in Figure 15-19 in the chapter. Your data might be different. Verify the Entry Fee column is summed in the Total row. Correct any problems you see. Save and close the query.

On Your Own 15.9 Step-by-Step Solution   How to Create a Query That Uses Two Tables

Create the DogShow Database: Part 6 of 8

Follow these steps to create the ClassRoster query:

Step 1. Using the DogShow database, click **Query Design** on the CREATE ribbon. The Show Table dialog box appears. Add the **Entries** table to the query. Add the **Dogs** table to the query. Close the Show Table dialog box.

Step 2. To break the relationship between the two tables, click on the line connecting the tables and press **Delete**. The line disappears.

Step 3. Press and drag the Dog ID field from the Entries table to the Dog ID field on the Dogs table. A line is drawn. Be sure to drag from the Entries table to the Dogs table and not in the other direction.

Step 4. Right-click the line joining the two tables and select **Join Properties** from the shortcut menu. The Join Properties dialog box appears (see Figure S15-9).

FIGURE S15-9
The Join Properties box shows how records will be selected for a query.

> **Not Working?** If you don't see Join Properties in the shortcut menu when you right-click the line, try moving your pointer more toward the center of the line and then right-click again.

Step 5. Verify the Entries table is on the left and the Dogs table is on the right. Select **2: Include ALL records from 'Entries' and only those records from 'Dogs' where the joined fields are equal**. Click **OK** to close the box.

Step 6. Double-click the following fields to add them to the query:

   a. Class in the Entries table

   b. Dog ID in the Entries table

   c. Dog Name in the Dogs table

   d. First Name in the Dogs table

   e. Last Name in the Dogs table

Step 7. At the bottom of the query design pane, click the box in the Class column and the Sort row. Select **Ascending** from the drop-down list. Records in the query will be sorted by Class in ascending order.

Step 8. Right-click the **Query1** tab and click **Save**. Name the query **ClassRoster**.

Step 9. Return to Datasheet View and view the results of the query. The query should list all the records in the Entries table and related data in the Dogs table.

Step 10. Check your work against Figure 15-20 in the chapter. Your data might be different from that shown, but the column headings should be the same. The number of records in the query appears at the bottom of the query. Compare this number to the number of records listed at the bottom of the Entries table. The numbers should be the same.

Step 11. If you have made any changes since you last saved the query, save the query again.

Step 12. To close all open objects in the database, look for tabs in the right pane. If you see any, right-click it and select **Close**. Save any changes as you close an object.

On Your Own 15.10 Step-by-Step Solution   How to Create Mailing Labels from a Single Table

Create the DogShow Database: Part 7 of 8

Do the following to create mailing labels from the Dogs table:

Step 1.   Open the **Dogs** table in the DogShow database. Make sure the Dogs tab is selected.

Step 2.   On the CREATE ribbon in the Reports group, click **Labels**. The Label Wizard dialog box opens (see Figure S15-10).

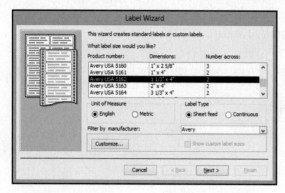

FIGURE S15-10
The Label Wizard requires you to select how labels will print on the page.

Step 3.   For the size of the labels, select the **Avery USA 5162** standard and click **Next**.

Step 4.   On the next box, no changes are required for the font and color of text. Click **Next**.

Step 5.   On the next box, you select the fields to go on each label (see Figure S15-11). Under Available fields, double-click **First Name** to place it on the label. The field is placed in the Prototype label box and is enclosed in braces { }. In the Prototype label box, type a space to insert a space following the first name. Double-click **Last Name** to insert this field. Press **Enter** to advance to the next line of the label.

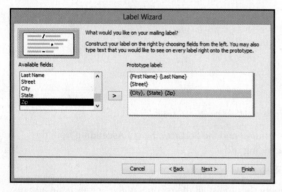

FIGURE S15-11
Fields and text are placed on the Prototype label used to build each mailing label.

Step 6.   Double-click **Street** to place the field on the second line of the mailing label. Press **Enter** to advance to the third line.

Step 7.   On the third line, place the **City** field. Type a comma and a space to place this text following the City field.

Step 8.   Double-click **State**, type a space, and double-click **Zip** to complete the third line of the mailing label. The Label Wizard dialog box should now look like that in Figure S15-11. Click **Next**.

Step 9.   On the next box, you can choose how the labels are sorted. Double-click **Last Name** and then double-click **First Name**. The labels will be sorted by last name and then first name. Click **Finish**.

Step 10.   Mailing labels appear as shown in Figure 15-23 in the chapter. Check your work and correct any problems you see.

Step 11.   Save the mailing labels as **Labels Dogs**. Close the Labels Dogs report.

On Your Own 15.11 Step-by-Step Solution   How to Create a Report from a Query

Create the DogShow Database: Part 8 of 8

Follow these steps to create the class roster report:

Step 1. Using the DogShow database, double-click the **ClassRoster** query in the left pane. The query results appear in the right pane.

Step 2. On the CREATE ribbon, click **Report**. A report is created using the selected query. Right-click the report tab and click **Save**. Name the report **ClassRosterReport**.

Step 3. To change the title of the report, click in the title box and change the text to **Class Roster Sent to Ringmaster**.

Step 4. To narrow the Class column, click somewhere in the Class column to select it. Orange boxes appear around items in the column. Press and drag the right side of a selection box, moving it to the left, as shown in Figure S15-12.

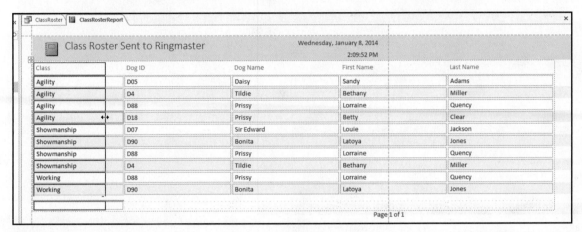

FIGURE S15-12
Press and drag a selection box to narrow the field width on the printed report.

Step 5. Narrow the other columns so that all columns fit on a single page without spilling off the right side of the page, as shown in Figure S15-13.

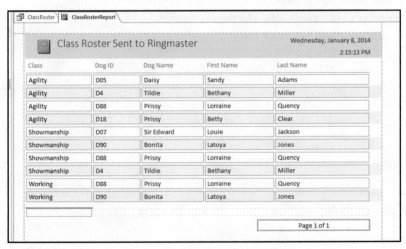

FIGURE S15-13
Narrow all columns so they all fit across one page.

Not Working? If you make a mistake as you work, click the Undo button in the title bar and try again.

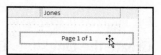

Step 6. Hover over the page number box until your pointer changes to a four-headed arrow. Then press and drag the box to the left so it doesn't spill off the page. Figure S15-13 shows a good position for the box.

Step 7. To sort the records by Class, click **Group & Sort** on the DESIGN ribbon. The Group, Sort, and Total pane appears at the bottom of the Design View.

Step 8. Click **Add a sort** and click **Class**. The records are sorted by Class.

Step 9. To group the records by Class, click **Add a group** and click **Class**. A Class Header is added to the report (see Figure S15-14).

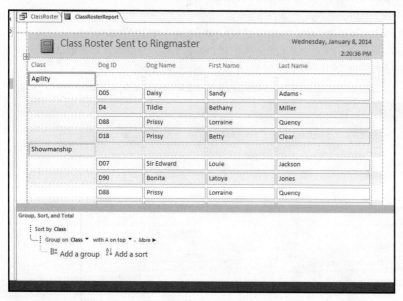

FIGURE S15-14
Use the Group, Sort, and Total pane to sort rows in the report by Class and add a group header.

Step 10. To change to Report View, right-click the **ClassRosterReport** tab and click **Report View** in the shortcut menu.

Step 11. To change to Print Preview view, right-click the **ClassRosterReport** tab and select **Print Preview** in the shortcut menu. The print preview appears. To close the view, click **Close Print Preview** on the PRINT PREVIEW ribbon.

Step 12. To save the report, right-click the **ClassRosterReport** tab and click **Save** on the shortcut menu.

CHAPTER 16 STEP-BY-STEP SOLUTIONS
Authoring Your Own Website

The solutions in this appendix are for you to use if you get stuck when doing an On Your Own activity in the chapter. To learn how to teach yourself a computer skill, always try the On Your Own activity first before turning to these solutions.

On Your Own 16.1 Step-by-Step Solution **How to Create a Web Page**

Build a Website: Part 1 of 8

Follow these steps to create the web page:

Step 1. Create a folder on your USB flash drive, hard drive, or another location given by your instructor. Name the folder **Website**.

Step 2. To open Notepad using Windows 8, go to the Start screen and start typing **notepad**. Then click **Notepad**. To open Notepad using Windows 7, click **Start**, **All Programs**, **Accessories**, and **Notepad**. The Notepad window opens.

Step 3. Type the following text and press **Enter**:

Our family vacation this year was at the beach.

Step 4. To save the file, click **File** in the menu bar. Click **Save As**. The Save As dialog box appears. Navigate to the Website folder you created in step 1. Change the Save as type to **All Files**. Change the File name to **Index.html** (see Figure S16-1). Click **Save** to save the file. Close the Notepad window.

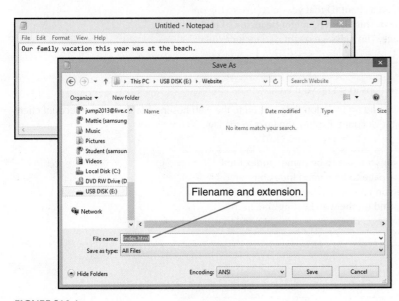

FIGURE S16-1
Save the Index.html file to your local storage device.

Step 5. Open File Explorer (in Windows 7, open Windows Explorer). Find the **Index** file on your storage device. Notice the file type is an HTML document. Double-click the file name. The file opens in Internet Explorer, which displays the one sentence on your web page.

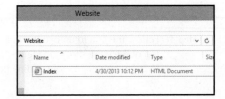

Build a Website: Part 2 of 8

Follow these steps to use Google.com to find a free web hosting site:

Step 1. In Internet Explorer, go to **google.com** and enter **free web hosting** in the search box. Click links until you find a hosting site that you like. In our example, we use awardspace.com, but your site might be different.

Step 2. To read reviews about the site, enter the site name followed by the word **review**. For example, enter **awardspace.com review**. Make sure a site gets good reviews before you select it.

To set up a website on a web hosting site, generally, you sign up for a web hosting account, select a subdomain name for your site, and upload files to your website. To set up a website on a web hosting site, follow these steps:

Step 1. Go to the home page of the site and find a link to set up an account.

Step 2. Follow the links to set up your account. You need to enter your name, mailing address, email address, and password to your web hosting account. Be sure you remember or write down your password.

> **Hint** Some web hosting sites require you to select your subdomain name at the same time you set up your account.

Step 3. An email message is sent to you. You might need to wait 15 minutes or more for the message to arrive. Click a link in the message. You can then return to the web hosting site to complete the setup.

> **Hint** During the setup process, you might be assigned a client ID that you must use to log on to your web hosting account along with your password. This client ID might be included in the email message, so be sure to save or print the message. The message might also include links to help features on the web hosting site.

After setting up your web hosting account, follow these steps to set up your website:

Step 1. Go to the home page of the web hosting site and find a logon link. Log on to the web hosting site using your account client ID or email address and your password to the account. Explore the links to manage your website.

> **Hint** Most web hosting sites allow the home page for your site to be named Index.html or Default.html. A few hosting sites require the home page to be named Index.htm or Default.htm. The names allowed for your home page on your web hosting site should be stated somewhere on the instructions for getting started on the web hosting site. In this chapter, we use Index.html as the name of the home page. However, you might need to use Default.html instead.

Step 2. Click the link to set up your subdomain name.

> **Hint** If you were required to select the subdomain name when you first set up your web hosting account, you can skip step 2. The subdomain name is already created.

Step 3. Return to the website manager page and click a link to upload a file to the website.

Step 4. Follow the link to upload the Index.html file to your website. For our example, you would click the Upload button at the top of the page shown in Figure 16-3 in the chapter, but your link might be different. Locate the Index.html file on your local computer and follow directions to upload the file.

> **Hint** If your web hosting site requires your home page to be named Default.html, rename the Index.html file to Default.html and upload that file.

Step 5. Open a new tab in Internet Explorer. Enter the URL of your website. In our example, that URL is myvacation.atwebpages.com, but your URL will be different. The web page appears in your browser window.

> **Not Working?** If your web page does not appear, make sure you entered the URL correctly in the Internet Explorer address box. Make sure the home page name is Index.html or Default.html.

On Your Own 16.3 Step-by-Step Solution   How to Add a Line Break Tag to the Page

Build a Website: Part 3 of 8

If the Index.html file is not already open in Notepad, follow these steps to open it:

Step 1. Open **Notepad**. If you need help opening Notepad, see On Your Own 16.1 Step-by-Step Solution. In the Notepad window, click the **File** menu and click **Open**. Normally, only .txt files display in the Open box. Click the drop-down list to the far right of File name and select **All Files**. All file types now appear in the list (see Figure S16-2).

FIGURE S16-2
Show All Files so that the HTML file will appear in the list of files that Notepad can open.

Step 2. Navigate to the **Index.html** file stored on your local computer, click it, and click **Open**.

> **Hint** As you build the website, keep Notepad open with the Index.html file open. Use one tab in Internet Explorer to view the local Index.html file and another tab in Internet Explorer to view the published Index.html file. When you save the file in Notepad, click the **Refresh** button ↻ in IE to view the local version of the file. When you publish a new version of the file, click the tab in IE to view the published version of the file and then click the **Refresh** button ↻.

Follow these steps to add new text to the Index.html page:

Step 1. In Notepad, go to the first blank line, type the following, and press **Enter**:

> The kids loved the aquarium we visited on the way to the beach.

Step 2. To save the file, click **File** and **Save**. Do not close the Notepad window or the Index.html file.

Step 3. Do one of the following to view the new version of the file:

- If an Internet Explorer tab is open with the local Index.html file displayed, click the **Refresh** button ↻ to see the new version of the file.

- If the local Index.html file is not currently displayed in Internet Explorer, open File Explorer (in Windows 7, open Windows Explorer), locate the **Index.html** file on your local storage device, and double-click the file.

Step 4. Notice that all text appears on one line (see Figure S16-3). To fix the problem, return to the Notepad window that is still open and type **
** at the end of the first line of text.

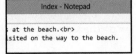

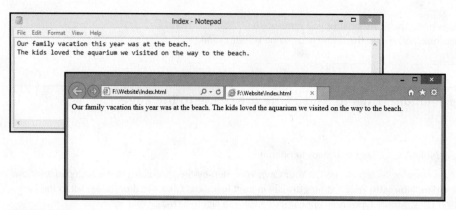

FIGURE S16-3
Internet Explorer does not recognize a hard return entered into the web page file.

> **Step 5.** To save the file, click **File** and **Save**. Return to the Internet Explorer window viewing the local Index.html file and click the **Refresh** button ↻. The text appears on two lines in the browser window.

On Your Own 16.4 Step-by-Step Solution   **How to Use HTML Structure and Formatting Tags**

Build a Website: Part 4 of 8

Follow these steps to add HTML tags to the file:

> **Step 1.** If necessary, open Notepad and use it to open the **Index.html** file.

> **Step 2.** Edit the file to include the HTML tags. Use the Tab key to indent lines in the file:

```
<html>
<head>
    <title>Our Family Vacation</title>
</head>
<body>
    Our family vacation this year was at the beach.<br>
    The kids loved the aquarium we visited on the way to the beach.
</body>
</html>
```

> **Step 3.** Click **File** and click **Save** to save the file. View the file in Internet Explorer and correct any errors reported by IE. Verify the web page title appears in the page tab of the Internet Explorer window.

> **Hint** If you don't see the title in the page tab, a mistyped tag or a missing ending tag is most likely causing the problem.

> **Step 4.** Just below the <body> tag, insert the following two lines of text. Indent the lines as shown in Figure S16-4.

```
<h2>The Aquarium and the Beach</h2>
<hr>
```

> **Step 5.** Add the <p> and </p> tags before and after the sentence about the aquarium. Add the <i> and </i> tags to format a word in italics as follows:

```
<p>The kids <i>loved</i> the aquarium we visited on the way to the beach.</p>
```

> **Step 6.** When you are finished, the Notepad window should look like that in Figure S16-4. Save the file and view it using Internet Explorer.

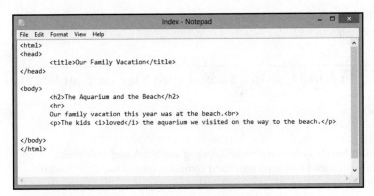

FIGURE S16-4
The page has structural tags and formatting tags added.

Step 7.   To view the source tags in Internet Explorer, first make sure the IE window is the active window and then press **F12**. The developer pane opens. On the left side of this pane, click the **Debugger** button as labeled in Figure 16-9 in the chapter.

> **Not Working?** This book assumes you are using Windows 8.1 and Internet Explorer version 11. If you are using an earlier version of IE, click **Script** in the developer pane to see all text and HTML tags.

On Your Own 16.5 Step-by-Step Solution   **How to Add a Photo to the Web Page**

Build a Website: Part 5 of 8

Follow these steps to add a photo to the page:

Step 1.   Open File Explorer (in Windows 7, open Windows Explorer) and locate the **Aquarium.png** file in the sample_files folder on the www.pearsonhighered.com/jump website and in MyITLab. Recall that you downloaded the sample_files folder to your USB flash drive in Chapter 2. If you need help finding the folder, see On Your Own Step-by-Step Solution 2.7. Copy the **Aquarium.png** file to the **Website** folder.

Step 2.   If necessary, open Notepad and use it to open the **Index.html** file.

Step 3.   Add three new lines of text below the sentence about the aquarium as follows:

```
<img src=Aquarium.png>
<hr>
Want to see our beach photos?
```

Step 4.   Save the Index.html file and display it in your browser. Correct any errors you see.

> **Hint** If the photo is missing, make sure the Aquarium.png file is in your Website folder and the <img> tag is written exactly as shown in step 3.

On Your Own 16.6 Step-by-Step Solution   **How to Use a Subfolder on Your Website**

Build a Website: Part 6 of 8

Follow these steps to use a subfolder in your Website folder that will hold the website images:

Step 1.   Open File Explorer (in Windows 7, open Windows Explorer) and open the Website folder on your local storage device. In this folder, create a subfolder named **Images**.

Step 2.   In the Website folder, press and drag the **Aquarium.png** file and drop it on the Images folder. Look in the Images folder to verify the file is there.

Step 3.   If necessary, open Notepad and use it to open the **Index.html** file. Edit the <img> tag as follows:

```
<img src=Images/Aquarium.png>
```

Step 4. Save the Index.html file and view it in Internet Explorer. The web page should look the same as it did in On Your Own 16.5. If this is not the case, correct any problems you see.

Build a Website: Part 7 of 8

Follow these steps to create the second web page:

Step 1. Use File Explorer (in Windows 7, use Windows Explorer) to copy two photos, **Zack.png** and **Shark.png**, from the sample_files folder to the **Website/Images** folder you created earlier on your local computer. (Recall you downloaded the sample_files folder to your USB flash drive in Chapter 2.)

Step 2. Use Notepad to create a file named **Beach.html**. Save the file in the **Website** folder on your local computer. Enter the following text and HTML tags in the file:

```
<html>
<head>
    <title>Beach and Sea Photos</title>
</head>
<body>
    <h2>Our Beach and Sea Photos</h2>
    <hr>
    Zack's first dip in the ocean and Joy caught the hammerhead shark!<br><br>
    <img src=Images/Zack.png>
    <img src=Images/Shark.png>
    <hr>
</body>
</html>
```

Step 3. Save the Beach.html file and view it in Internet Explorer. Correct any errors you see. The web page is shown in Figure 16-11 in the chapter.

Follow these steps to add a hyperlink to the Index.html page:

Step 1. Use Notepad to edit the **Index.html** file. Insert the <a> and </a> anchor tags around the text **beach photos** as follows:

```
Want to see our <a href=Beach.html>beach photos</a>?
```

Step 2. Save the Index.html file and view it in Internet Explorer. When you click the link on the page, the second web page displays. Correct any errors you see.

Build a Website: Part 8 of 8

This solution has two parts:

▶ How to add a link to another website

▶ How to publish a website

How to Add a Link to Another Website

Follow these steps to add a link to another website to the Index.html page we are building:

Step 1. Use Notepad to edit the Index.html file. Edit the <img> tag in the document as follows:

```
<a href=http://www.ripleyaquariums.com><img src=Images/Aquarium.png></a>
```

Step 2. The Index.html file should now look like that shown in Figure S16-5 when displayed in Notepad. Save the Index.html file and view it in Internet Explorer. When you click the link on the page, the Ripley's Aquarium site displays. Correct any errors you see.

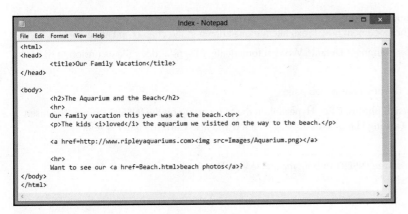

FIGURE S16-5
The Index.html file is completed.

How to Publish the Website

Follow these steps to publish the latest version of your website:

Step 1. If you are not already logged on to your web hosting site, open a new tab in Internet Explorer and log on to the hosting site using your email address or client ID and password.

Step 2. Find the link to create a subfolder under your subdomain folder. Create a new folder named **Images**.

Step 3. Upload the **Index.html** and **Beach.html** files to the subdomain folder.

Step 4. Upload the **Aquarium.png**, **Zack.png** and **Shark.png** files to the **Images** subfolder.

Step 5. Do one of the following to view the new version of your website:

- If an Internet Explorer tab is open with the URL of your website, click the **Refresh** button ↻ to see the website.

- If necessary, open a new tab in Internet Explorer and enter the URL of your website and press **Enter**.

Step 6. Your home page appears. Test the two links on the home page and check both page for errors. Correct any problems you see.

> **Hint** If a photo is missing on a page, remember that a file name is sometimes case sensitive. Make sure the upper- and lowercase characters in the file name in your <img> tag are correct.

On Your Own 16.9 Step-by-Step Solution   How to Use Word to Create a Web Page

Follow these steps to create a Word document and then a web page:

Step 1. Create a folder on your USB flash drive, hard drive, or another location given by your instructor. Name the folder **Website2**.

Step 2. Copy (don't move) the **Beach.html** file you created earlier into the **Website2** folder.

Step 3. Copy (don't move) the **Images** folder you created earlier into the **Website2** folder. (The Images folder you copy contains three files.)

Step 4. Open Word and open a new blank document. Enter this text in the first line of the document and format the text using the **Heading 1** style:

> The Aquarium and the Beach

Step 5. On the second line, type the underscore character (_) three times and then press **Enter**. A horizontal line appears in the document. Press **Enter** again to add more spacing.

Step 6. Type the three lines of text, pressing **Enter** at the end of each line:

> Our family vacation this year was at the beach.
> The kids loved the aquarium we visited on the way to the beach.
> Want to see our beach photos?

Step 7. Create two blank lines above the last line of text. Move your insertion point to the first blank line. Click **Pictures** on the INSERT ribbon. Use the Insert Pictures dialog box to locate the Aquarium.png file in the Images subfolder and insert it in the document.

Step 8. Move your insertion point to the beginning of the last line of text. Type the underscore character (_) three times and then press **Enter**. A horizontal line appears. The document now looks like the one shown in the chapter in Figure 16-13.

Step 9. Save the document to the Website2 folder, naming it **Default**. Word automatically assigns a .docx file extension to the document file.

Follow these steps to insert a hyperlink and save the document as a web page:

Step 1. To create the hyperlink, select the text **beach photos**. Click **Hyperlink** in the Links group on the INSERT ribbon. The Insert Hyperlink dialog box opens. Make sure **Existing File or Web Page** is selected and also **Current Folder** is selected.

> **Not Working?** If you don't see the Links group on the INSERT ribbon, maximize your Word window so that all items on the INSERT ribbon are visible.

Step 2. Select the **Beach.html** file in the Website2 folder and click **OK** to create the hyperlink. (Refer to Figure 16-13 in the chapter.)

Step 3. To test the hyperlink, press **Ctrl** and click **beach photos**. The Beach web page opens in Internet Explorer.

> **Not Working?** If the link does not work, right-click it and click **Remove Hyperlink**. Then try again.

Step 4. Save the Word document.

Step 5. To save the web page, click the **FILE** tab and click **Save As**. In the Save As window, select the current folder. In the next Save As window, change the *Save as type* to **Web Page** (see Figure S16-6). Click **Save**. The Default.htm file is created along with the subfolder containing the one image needed to build the page.

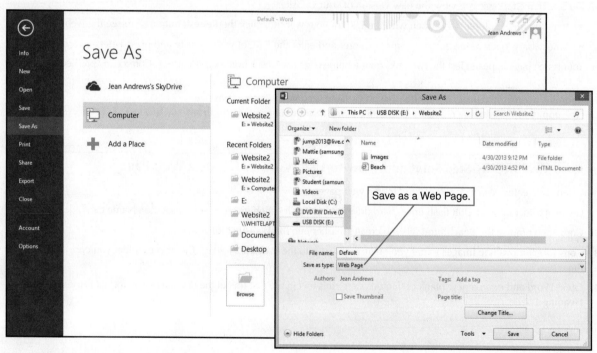

FIGURE S16-6
Save the Word document as a Web Page.

Step 6. Close the Word window. Open File Explorer (in Windows 7, open Windows Explorer), and double-click the **Default** HTML Document file (see Figure S16-7). The web page opens in Internet Explorer. To display the HTML code, press **F12** and click the **Debugger** button (in earlier versions of IE, click the **Script** tab).

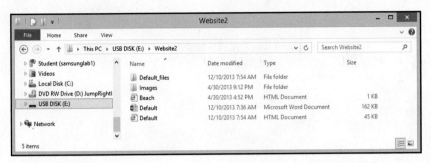

FIGURE S16-7
Word created the HTML Document and a folder containing files used by the web page.

Index

E

N

O

S

T

X

Y

Credits

Figure	Credit Line
Chapter opening photo	Goldfish jumping out of the water to escape to freedom. White background: Tischenko Irina/Shiutterstock
01-01	Keyboard: Borodaev/Shutterstock Mouse: janprchal/Shutterstock Hand holding processor: © Desintegrator/Alamy Hard drive: Kitch Bain/Shutterstock Memory module: Norman Chan/Shutterstock Monitor: Kitch Bain/Shutterstock Printer: restyler/Shutterstock Touch pad-: Joy Dark
01-02	Keyboard, monitor: K. Miri Photography Rear of PC case: Ivan Montero Martinez/Shutterstock Open optical drive: Fotocrisis/Shutterstock Ethernet port (right side of image): hfng/Shutterstock USB port: (left side of image): hfng/Shutterstock Analog video port: carroteater/Shutterstock Digital video port: Charlie Hutton/Shutterstock Computer Case: Ivan Montero Martinez/Shutterstock Green PS/2 port: Ivan Montero Martinez/Shutterstock
01-03	Laptops and netbooks: Joy Dark
01-04	A netbook computer: Joy Dark
01-05	All in one computer: Joy Dark
01-06	Tablet: vovan/Shutterstock
01-07	3.5 inch harddrive: Joy Dark
01-08 through 01-26	Windows 8 screenshots: Microsoft Office 2013, copyright © 2013 Microsoft Corporation.
01-08, 01-09	Windows preview screenshots: Microsoft Office 2013, copyright © 2013 Microsoft Corporation.
01-11	Windows Paint screenshot: Microsoft Office Paint 2013, copyright © 2013 Microsoft Corporation.
01-12	Memory module: Norman Chan/Shutterstock
01-12 through 01-16	Windows preview screenshot: Microsoft Office 2013, copyright © 2013 Microsoft Corporation.
01-17	Windows Notepad screenshot: Microsoft Office Notepad 2013, copyright © 2013 Microsoft Corporation.
01-18 through 01-20	Windows preview screenshots: Microsoft Office 2013, copyright © 2013 Microsoft Corporation.
01-20	Weimaraner dog: Joy Dark
01-24	Asian couple at computer: Microsoft Blonde male at laptop: Microsoft Isolated hand moving mouse: Microsoft
7S01-01 through 7S01-09	Windows screenshots: Microsoft Office 2013, copyright © 2013 Microsoft Corporation.
7SMargin01-01 through 7SMargin01-04	Windows Paint screenshots: Microsoft Office Paint 2013, copyright © 2013 Microsoft Corporation.
8S01-01 through 8S01-15	Windows screenshots: Microsoft Office 2013, copyright © 2013 Microsoft Corporation.
8SMargin01-01 through 8SMargin01-04	Windows Paint screenshots: Microsoft Office Paint 2013, copyright © 2013 Microsoft Corporation.
Margin01-08	USB port: AlessandroZocc/Shutterstock
Margin01-09	Network port: al1962/Shutterstock
Margin01-10	VGA video port: antos777/Shutterstock
Margin01-11	DVI video port: antos777/Shutterstock
Margin01-12	HDMI port: Joy Dark

Figure	Credit Line
Margin01-13	Display Port port: Joy Dark
Margin01-14	USB flash drive: bluebloodbkk/Shutterstock
Margin01-15	Dog: Eric Isselee/Shutterstock
Margin01-18	Man in glasses on phone in front of pie chart graph: David Lees/Getty Images
Margin01-19	African American man with Afro in front of bank of computers: Goodluz/Shutterstock
Margin01-20	Asian woman in yellow dress holding books: Pius Lee/Shutterstock
Margin01-16	Close up of Windows Key: Joy Dark
Margin01-17	Local disk, hard drive: Joy Dark
02-09	Blank software box: alxpin/GettyImages
702-01, also 7S02-01	Microsoft MSN screenshot: Microsoft MSN 2013, copyright © 2013 Microsoft Corporation.
702-03, 702-07, 7Margin	Google screenshots: Courtesy of Google.com
702-04 and 7S02-10	Prentice Hall screenshot (used twice): Courtesy of Pearson Education.
702-06	google.com screenshot: Courtesy of Google.com
7Margin02-01, 7Margin02-03	Microsoft MSN screenshots: Microsoft MSN 2013, copyright © 2013 Microsoft Corporation.
7Margin02-04	Microsoft Explorer screenshot: Microsoft Explorer 2013, copyright © 2013 Microsoft Corporation.
7Margin02-07	Dell screenshots: © 2014 Dell Inc. All Rights Reserved.
7S02-02	Windows Explorer screenshot: Microsoft Explorer 2013, copyright © 2013 Microsoft Corporation.
7S02-03	Google screenshot: Google, Inc.
7S02-04	Windows MSN screenshot: Microsoft MSN 2013, copyright © 2013 Microsoft Corporation.
7S02-05 through 7S02-10	Google screenshots: Google, Inc.
7S02-11 through 7S02-13	Windows Explorer screenshots: Microsoft Explorer 2013, copyright © 2013 Microsoft Corporation.
7S02-13 through 7S02-18, also InlinePic7S02-23	Windows SkyDrive screenshots: Microsoft SkyDrive 2013, copyright © 2013 Microsoft Corporation.
7S02-19 and 7S02-20	PayPal screenshots: Courtesy PayPal
7S02-21 through 7S02-24	Microsoft Windows screenshots: Microsoft 2013, copyright © 2013 Microsoft Corporation.
7SMargin02-01	Windows MSN screenshot: Microsoft MSN 2013, copyright © 2013 Microsoft Corporation.
7SMargin02-02	Google screenshot: Google, Inc.
7SMargin02-03	Windows MSN screenshot: Microsoft MSN 2013, copyright © 2013 Microsoft Corporation.
7SMargin02-04 through 7SMargin02-08	Google screenshots: Google, Inc.
7SMargin02-09, 7SMargin02-10	Microsoft SkyDrive screenshots: Microsoft SkyDrive 2013, copyright © 2013 Microsoft Corporation.
7SMargin02-11 through 7SMargin02-14	PayPal screenshots: Courtesy PayPal
802-01, 802-02, 8Margin02-01, 8Margin02-02, 8Margin02-04, 8S02-01, 8S02-09, 8SMargin02-01, 8SMargin02-02, 8SMargin02-07	Microsoft MSN screenshots: Microsoft MSN 2013, copyright © 2013 Microsoft Corporation.

Figure	Credit Line
802-04, 802-07, 8Margin02-06, 8S02-04, 8S02-07, 8S02-08, 8S02-10 through 8S02-15, 8SMargin02-04, 8SMargin02-05, 8SMargin02-06, 8SMargin02-08, 8SMargin02-10 through 8SMargin02-12	Google screenshots: Google, Inc.
802-05 and 8S02-14	Prentice Hall screenshots: Courtesy of Pearson Education.
802-08, 802-10, 802-11, 8S02-17, 8S02-25, 8SMargin02-13, 8SMargin02-14	Microsoft Windows screenshots: Microsoft 2013, copyright © 2013 Microsoft Corporation.
8InlinePic02-01 through 8InlinePic02-16	Microsoft Explorer icons: Microsoft 2013, copyright © 2013 Microsoft Corporation.
8InlinePic02-01 through 8InlinePic02-28	Microsoft Explorer icons: Microsoft Explorer 2013, copyright © 2013 Microsoft Corporation.
8Margin02-05, 8SMargin02-08, 8SMargin02-09	Weather.com screenshot: Courtesy weather.com
8Margin02-08	Dell.com screenshot: © 2014 Dell Inc. All Rights Reserved.
8S02-02, 8S02-03, 8S02-05	Microsoft Explorer screenshots: Microsoft Explorer 2013, copyright © 2013 Microsoft Corporation.
8S02-18 through 8S02-23, 8SMargin02-15	Microsoft SkyDrive screenshots: Microsoft SkyDrive 2013, copyright © 2013 Microsoft Corporation.
8S02-21, 8SMargin02-14	PayPal screenshots: Courtesy PayPal
8SInlinePic02-01 through 8SInlinePic02-28	Microsoft Explorer icons: Microsoft Explorer 2013, copyright © 2013 Microsoft Corporation.
InlinePic7S-01 through InlinePic7S-22	Microsoft Explorer screenshots: Microsoft Explorer 2013, copyright © 2013 Microsoft Corporation.
InlinePic02-01	Start button or circle: Microsoft Office 2013, copyright © 2013 Microsoft Corporation.
InlinePic02-02	Internet Explorer Quick Launch icon: Microsoft Explorer 2013, copyright © 2013 Microsoft Corporation.
InlinePic02-03	Windows preview screenshot: Microsoft Explorer 2013, copyright © 2013 Microsoft Corporation.
InlinePic02-04	Pointer: Microsoft Explorer 2013, copyright © 2013 Microsoft Corporation.
InlinePic02-05	Minimize button: Microsoft Explorer 2013, copyright © 2013 Microsoft Corporation.
InlinePic02-06	Maximize button: Microsoft Office 2013, copyright © 2013 Microsoft Corporation.
InlinePic02-07	Restore button: Microsoft Explorer 2013, copyright © 2013 Microsoft Corporation.
InlinePic02-08	Close button: Microsoft Explorer 2013, copyright © 2013 Microsoft Corporation.
InlinePic02-09	Back button: Microsoft Explorer 2013, copyright © 2013 Microsoft Corporation.
InlinePic02-10	IE9 tools button: Microsoft Explorer 2013, copyright © 2013 Microsoft Corporation.
InlinePic02-11	Pointer as hand when hovering over a link: Microsoft Explorer 2013, copyright © 2013 Microsoft Corporation.
InlinePic02-12	IE9 home button: Microsoft Explorer 2013, copyright © 2013 Microsoft Corporation.
InlinePic02-13	Google search results double arrow for preview: Microsoft Explorer 2013, copyright © 2013 Microsoft Corporation.
InlinePic02-14	Google search results options button: Microsoft Explorer 2013, copyright © 2013 Microsoft Corporation.
03-01 through 03-18, Margin03-01 through Margin03-09	Microsoft Word screenshots: Microsoft Word 2013, copyright © 2013 Microsoft Corporation.
03-12	Clip art of gramophone: Microsoft
03-18	Silhouette of man playing guitar—clip art: Microsoft
03-19	Guitar player silhouette: © izumi1042/Fotolia
InlinePic03-01 through InlinePic03-41	Microsoft icons: Microsoft 2013, copyright © 2013 Microsoft Corporation.

Figure	Credit Line
S03-01	Microsoft Windows screenshot: Microsoft Windows 2013, copyright © 2013 Microsoft Corporation.
S03-01 through S03-08 and SMargin03-02 through SMargin03-24	Microsoft Word screenshots: Microsoft Word 2013, copyright © 2013 Microsoft Corporation.
S03-01 through S03-4	Microsoft icons: Microsoft 2013, copyright © 2013 Microsoft Corporation. Google Logo: Courtesy of Google.com
04-01 through 04-05, 04-07, Margin04-03, S04-01 through S04-06, S04-08, S04-10, S04-12, S04-13, S04-26, SMargin04-01, SMargin04-02, SMargin04-03, SMargin04-09 through SMargin04-11	Microsoft OneNote screenshots: Microsoft OneNote 2013, copyright © 2013 Microsoft Corporation.
04-06, 04-11, 04-12, S04-07, SMargin04-06	Wikipedia screenshots: Copyright Wikimedia Foundation
04-08	Amazon screenshot: © Amazon.com, Inc. or it's affiliates. All Rights Reserved.
04-09b	Library of Congress screenshot: Courtesy of the Library of Congress
04-10, Margin04-01, Margin04-02, S04-10, SMargin04-04, SMargin04-05, SMargin04-07, SMargin04-08	Google screenshots: Google, Inc.
04-13	Journal cover: Joy Dark
04-14, Margin04-03, S04-11, S04-24, SMargin04-10	Peace Corps screenshots: Courtesy the Peace Corps.
InlinePic04-01 through InlinePic04-15, InlinePic04-17 through InlinePic04-23, InlinePic04-26 through InlinePic43	Microsoft icons: Microsoft 2013, copyright © 2013 Microsoft Corporation.
InlinePic04-16, InlinePic04-24, InlinePic04-25, InlinePicS04-16, InlinePicS04-24, InlinePicS04-25	Google icons: Google, Inc.
InlinePicS04-01 through InlinePicS04-15, InlinePicS04-17 through InlinePicS04-23, InlinePicS04-26 through InlinePicS04-43	Microsoft icons: Microsoft 2013, copyright © 2013 Microsoft Corporation.
S04-9	Carrot2.org screenshot: Courtesy of Carrot2.org
S04-14	Taunton Gazette screenshot: (also used in chapter 5, S05-09): Courtesy of The Taunton Gazette.
S04-15	Waidsworld screenshot: (also used in chapter 5, 05-08 and S05-08): Courtesy of Michael Waidmann's Waidworld.
S04-16 through S04-18, 05-02, 05-03, 05-09, S05-08	Screenshots of *The Insider's Guide to the Peace Corps* by Dillon Banerjee on Google Books, Ten Speed Press.
S04-21, S04-22	Association for Experimental Education screenshots: (also used in chapter 5, 05-11a, 05-11b): Courtesy of the Association for Experimental Education
05-04, S05-05	Microsoft OneNote screenshots: Microsoft Office OneNote 2013, copyright © 2013 Microsoft Corporation.
05-19	Long quotation taken from an article on Icouldbe.org's blog published Jan 25, 2011 by Kate Schrauth and put in a fake research paper: Courtesy of Kate Schrauth and icouldbe.org
InlinePicS05-01 through InlinePicS05-15, InlinePicS05-17 through InlinePicS05-23, InlinePicS05-26 through InlinePicS05-46	Microsoft icons: Microsoft Windows 2013, copyright © 2013 Microsoft Corporation.
InlinePicS05-16	Google icons: Google, Inc.

Figure	Credit Line
S05-03, 05-05 through 05-07, 05-10, 05-12 through 05-18, Margin05-01 through Margin05-08, S05-02, S05-04, S05-06, S05-10, MarginS05-01 through MarginS05-19	Microsoft Office Word screenshots: Microsoft Office Word 2013, copyright © 2013 Microsoft Corporation.
S05-03	Microsoft Windows screenshot: Microsoft Windows 2013, copyright © 2013 Microsoft Corporation.
06-01	Computers and servers: Joy Dark
06-02, 06-03, 06-07, S06-01, S06-03, SMargin06-01, SMargin06-02	Screenshots of Gmail inbox: Courtesy of Google, Inc.
06-03	Volvo: Joy Dark
06-04, Margin06-01, S06-06 through S06-10, SMargin06-03 through SMargin06-10	Microsoft Outlook screenshots: Microsoft Outlook 2013, copyright © 2013 Microsoft Corporation.
06-05	Microsoft Defender screenshot: Microsoft Defender 2013, copyright © 2013 Microsoft Corporation.
06-06	Microsoft Security Essentials screenshot: Microsoft Security Essentials 2013, copyright © 2013 Microsoft Corporation.
06-17, S06-11	Send a quick Tweet to your followers about what's happening now: Courtesy of Jean Andrews/twitter.com
06-19	Woman at laptop video-chatting: carlosseller/Shutterstock
06-20	Screenshot of Marc and Angel Hack Life blog: Source: Marc and Angel Hack Life blog
Figure06-08	Facebook screenshot. Courtesy of Facebook.com
Figure06-09	All personal Facebook accounts are organized the same way. The orange areas can be seen publicly: Courtesy of Jean Andrews
Figure06-10	The menu bar at the top of the Facebook window gives access to pages in your Facebook account: Courtesy of Facebook.com
Figure06-11	The menu bar contains links to my account even when I'm visiting my friend's profile: Courtesy of Facebook.com
Figure06-14	Click a friend who is online to open a chat box between you: Courtesy of Facebook.com
Figure06-16	To Like a page, mouse over it and then click Like: Courtesy of Facebook
Figure06-18	Make a connection in LinkedIn: Courtesy of Jean Andrews/LinkedIn
Figure06-19	Find a new connection through your current connections in LinkedIn: Courtesy of Jean Andrews/LinkedIn
Figure06-23	A chat session can include voice and video if both parties have a speaker, microphone, web cam, and installed software: Courtesy of Jean Andrews/Google, Inc.
InlinePic06-22	Windows Explorer icon: Microsoft Explorer 2013, copyright © 2013 Microsoft Corporation.
Margin06-03	Facebook search for Dave Dusthimer: Courtesy of Facebook.com
Margin06-05	Like a photo: Courtesy of Facebook
Margin06-02	webcam: kees59/Fotolia
Margin06-01	Headset: Joy Dark
S06-02, S06-04, S06-05	Google screenshots: Google, Inc.
S06-13 through S06-15	Microsoft Wordpress screenshots: Microsoft Wordpress 2013, copyright © 2013 Microsoft Corporation.
SMarg06-11	Twitter screenshot: Courtesy of Twitter
07-01	Search your area of interest for a job listing-Craigslist Atlanta screenshot: ©2011 Craigslist. Reprinted by permission.
07-09	Printer: Joy Dark
07-02 through 07-03, 07-07 through 07-10	Microsoft Word 2013 screenshots: Microsoft Office Word 2013, copyright © 2013 Microsoft Corporation.
07-04 through 07-05	Microsoft Word Preview screenshots: Microsoft Office Word 2013, copyright © 2013 Microsoft Corporation.
07-06, 07-11	Microsoft Office 2013 Outlook screenshot: Microsoft Office Outlook 2013, copyright © 2013 Microsoft Corporation.

Figure	Credit Line
MarginS07-06	Word screenshots: Microsoft Office Word 2013, copyright © 2013 Microsoft Corporation.
MarginS07-09	Outlook screenshot: Microsoft Office Outlook 2013, copyright © 2013 Microsoft Corporation.
MarginS07-02, S07-03	Word Preview screenshots: Microsoft Office Word 2013, copyright © 2013 Microsoft Corporation.
Margin07-01	Microsoft Office 2013 Word Preview screenshots: Microsoft Office 2013, copyright © 2013 Microsoft Corporation.
MarginS07-08	Windows preview screenshot: Microsoft Office 2013, copyright © 2013 Microsoft Corporation.
SF7-1,3	Microsoft Office 2013 Word screenshots: Microsoft Office Word 2013, copyright © 2013 Microsoft Corporation.
SF7.2, SF7.4, SF7.6	Word preview screenshots: Microsoft Office Word 2013, copyright © 2013 Microsoft Corporation.
Table07-01	Table07-01 Common File Formats Supported by Word: Created by Jean Andrews.
08-04	All hands finger pointing at a businessman: © ryanking999/Fotolia Graduates hugging: © bonniemarie/Fotolia Man surfing wave in barrell: © Sportlibrary/Fotolia
08-17	Male musician with headphones playing an electric guitar: © Ljupco Smokovski/Fotolia Father and his two sons playing on beach: Uwe Krejci/Getty Images People laying in a circle on grass: Brocreative/Shutterstock Dad and son playing videogames: © biker3/Fotolia Winter fun, snow, sledding at winter time: gorillaimages/Shutterstock
08-18	Male musician with headphones playing: © Ljupco Smokovski/Fotolia Father and his two sons playing on beach: Uwe Krejci/Getty Images Businessman hoola-hooping infront of co-workers: Deborah Kolb/Shutterstock
08-01 through 08-02, 08-04 through 08-07, 08-10	Powerpoint screenshots: Microsoft Office Powerpoint 2013, copyright © 2013 Microsoft Corporation.
08-08 through 08-09	PowerPoint SmartArt graphic screenshots: Microsoft Office Powerpoint 2013, copyright © 2013 Microsoft Corporation.
Figure08-03	Outline for What Motivates You: Pearson Education
Margin08-02 to 08-04	PowerPoint screenshots: Microsoft Office Powerpoint 2013, copyright © 2013 Microsoft Corporation.
Margin08-05	PowerPoint Smart Art screenshot: Microsoft Office Powerpoint 2013, copyright © 2013 Microsoft Corporation.
MarginS08-02 through 05, 10, 11	PowerPoint screenshots: Microsoft Office Powerpoint 2013, copyright © 2013 Microsoft Corporation.
MarginS08-07 through 08-09	PowerPoint SmartArt screenshots: Microsoft Office PowerPoint 2013, copyright © 2013 Microsoft Corporation.
Margin08-01	Projector: Istvan Csak/Shutterstock
Motivation PPT	"Motivation" PowerPoint quote: "Try not to become a person of success, but rather a person of value." 14 words: Source Albert Einstein
S08-01 to 03; S08-07	PowerPoint screenshots: Microsoft Office PowerPoint 2013, copyright © 2013 Microsoft Corporation.
S08-04 to S08-06	PowerPoint SmartArt screenshots: Microsoft Office PowerPoint 2013, copyright © 2013 Microsoft Corporation.
Table08-01	Main Purposes for PowerPoint ribbons: Created by Author
09-02	Musical group of five persons playing (used with audio in cite 350): © Pavel Losevsky/fotolia Garage door: © pyzata/Fotolia Guitar player: © micahbowerbank Crowd silhouette at a rock concert: dwphotos/Shutterstock Man singing into microphone: bikeriderlondon/Shutterstock Band playing on stage: Andrey Armyagov/Shutterstock
09-10	Cheering crowd at concert (repeat of 09-02d): dwphotos/Shutterstock
09-11	www.office.com screenshot of Image search: Microsoft Office 2013, copyright © 2013 Microsoft Corporation.

Figure	Credit Line
09-14	Labrador retriever dog on a a grassy meadow: Slobodan Djajic/Shutterstock Boston terrier (repeat of 09-18b): Eric Isselée/Fotolia Chihuahua (repeat of 09-18c): Konstantin Gushcha/Fotolia Philadelphia brownstones: © luminouslens/Fotolia Woman duck hunter portrait with labrador and decoys: Suzi Nelson/Shutterstock Child playing with puppy on grass: Getty Images
09-15	Duck hunter with retriever: Suzi Nelson/Shutterstock Philadelphia brownstones: © luminouslens/Fotolia
09-16	Chihuahua: Konstantin Gushcha/Fotolia Labrador retriever dog on a a grassy meadow: Slobodan Djajic/Shutterstock Boston retriever: Eric Isselee/Fotolia
09-17	Duck hunter with retriever: Suzi Nelson/Shutterstock Weimaraner in water: PhillipsC/Shutterstock Weimaraner playing in stream: PhillipsC/Shutterstock
09-18	Yellow Labrador retriever: Slobodan Djajic Boston terrier: Eric Isselée/Fotolia.com
Figure09-01	Figure09-01 Outline—How to Get the Garage Band out of the Garage and On the Road: Courtesy of Jean Andrews
Figure09-01, 09-08 through 9-10	PowerPoint screenshots: Microsoft Office PowerPoint 2013, copyright © 2013 Microsoft Corporation.
Figure09-02 through 09-10 and 09-12 through 09-18	PowerPoint screenshots: Microsoft Office PowerPoint 2013, copyright © 2013 Microsoft Corporation.
Margin09-16	www.office.com screenshot Image search: Microsoft Office 2013, copyright © 2013 Microsoft Corporation.
Margin09-01 through 09-04, 09-06	PowerPoint screenshots: Microsoft Office PowerPoint 2013, copyright © 2013 Microsoft Corporation.
MarginS09-01 through 10, 09-01	PowerPoint screenshots: Microsoft Office 2013, copyright © 2013 Microsoft Corporation.
FigureS10-01 through 03	Excel screenshots: Microsoft Office Excel 2013, copyright © 2013 Microsoft Corporation.
InlinePic65-72	Excel screenshots: Microsoft Office Excel 2013, copyright © 2013 Microsoft Corporation.
Margin10-01, 10-03	Excel screenshots: Microsoft Office Excel 2013, copyright © 2013 Microsoft Corporation.
Margin10-02	Excel screenshot: Microsoft Office Excel 2013, copyright © 2013 Microsoft Corporation.
MarginS10-01	Excel screenshots: Microsoft Office Excel 2013, copyright © 2013 Microsoft Corporation.
11-01 through 11-24	Excel screenshots: Microsoft Office Excel 2013, copyright © 2013 Microsoft Corporation.
InlinePic73-74	Excel screenshots: Microsoft Office Excel 2013, copyright © 2013 Microsoft Corporation.
Margin11-01 through 1	Excel screenshots: Microsoft Office Excel 2013, copyright © 2013 Microsoft Corporation.
MarginS11-01 through S11-11	Excel screenshots: Microsoft Office Excel 2013, copyright © 2013 Microsoft Corporation.
s11-01-s11-08	Excel screenshots: Microsoft Office Excel 2013, copyright © 2013 Microsoft Corporation.
Margin12-01	Internet modem: ramcreations/Shutterstock
12-01	Wide area network: Pearson Education
12-02	Local area network diagram: Pearson Education
12-03	Wireless router: Joy Dark
12-03	You can manage network connections using the Network and Sharing Center: Pearson Education
12-04	Cell phone tethered to laptop: Joy Dark Portable mobile broadband modem: Joy Dark Wi-Fi portable broadband modem: Joy Dark Stationary mobile broadband modem: Joy Dark
12-05	The lights near the network port: Joy Dark
12-05, 12-08, 12-19, 12-20	Windows 7 screenshots: Microsoft Office 2013, copyright © 2013 Microsoft Corporation
12-07	Windows screenshot: Tell Windows the network location so it can set the security level for the network: Microsoft Windows 2013, copyright © 2013 Microsoft Corporation.

Figure	Credit Line
12-08	Wifi hotspot diagram: Pearson Education
12-09	ESC button on keyboard: Joy Dark
12-10	You must agree to the terms of use before using this public hotspot: © Pearson Education, Upper Saddle River, New Jersey
12-12	Windows screenshot: You must restart the computer so Windows can install its updates: Microsoft Windows 2013, copyright © 2013 Microsoft Corporation.
12-13	The System window shows information about the system and reports Service Pack 1 is installed: Microsoft Windows 2013, copyright © 2013 Microsoft Corporation.
12-14	Control how and when Windows receives and installs updates: Microsoft Windows 2013, copyright © 2013 Microsoft Corporation.
12-15	"You can use the Windows Backup and Restore utility to back up data on your hard drive to another storage media": Microsoft Windows 2013, copyright © 2013 Microsoft Corporation.
12-16	Use the Previous Versions tab on the Properties box to recover a corrupted file: Microsoft Windows NoteBooks 2013, copyright © 2013 Microsoft Corporation.
12-17	The control Panel gives access to many Windows utilities and allows you to change Windows settings: Microsoft Windows 2013, copyright © 2013 Microsoft Corporation.
12-18	You can use this window provided by the router setup program to secure the wireless network: Courtesy of Linksys.
12-20	"Use the HomeGroup window to view the homegroup password and to manage the homegroup": Microsoft Windows 2013, copyright © 2013 Microsoft Corporation.
InlinePic12-81	Windows 8 screenshots: Microsoft Office 2013, copyright © 2013 Microsoft Corporation
InlinePic80	Wireless network available icon: Microsoft Windows 2013, copyright © 2013 Microsoft Corporation.
Margin12-03, 12-05	Windows 7 screenshots: Microsoft Office 2013, copyright © 2013 Microsoft Corporation
Margin12-03, 12-05	Windows 8 screenshots: Microsoft Office 2013, copyright © 2013 Microsoft Corporation
Margin12-04	IP address in address box: Microsoft Windows 2013, copyright © 2013 Microsoft Corporation.
Margin12-06	Security key: Microsoft Windows 2013, copyright © 2013 Microsoft Corporation.
Margin12-07	Properties in menu: Microsoft Windows 2013, copyright © 2013 Microsoft Corporation.
Margin12-08	Security box: Microsoft Windows 2013, copyright © 2013 Microsoft Corporation.
MarginS12-01 through MarginS12-04	Windows 8 Screenshots: Microsoft Office 2013, copyright © 2013 Microsoft Corporation
MarginS12-02	UAC box: Microsoft Windows 2013, copyright © 2013 Microsoft Corporation.
Margin12-01	Windows 7 screenshot: Microsoft Office 2013, copyright © 2013 Microsoft Corporation
Margin12-02	Cell card and laptop: Joy Dark
S12-01, S12-02	Windows 7 screenshots: Microsoft Office Windows 2013, copyright © 2013 Microsoft Corporation
S12-03	AppData folder: Microsoft Windows 2013, copyright © 2013 Microsoft Corporation.
S12-04	Control how and when Windows receives and installs updates: Microsoft Windows 2013, copyright © 2013 Microsoft Corporation.
S12-05	You can use the Windows Backup and Restore utility to back up data on your hard drive to another storage media: Microsoft Windows 2013, copyright © 2013 Microsoft Corporation.
S12-06	Select the storage media to receive the backup: Microsoft Windows 2013, copyright © 2013 Microsoft Corporation.
S12-07	Choose the option to make your own selections as to what to back up: Microsoft Windows 2013, copyright © 2013 Microsoft Corporation.
S12-08	Select the libraries and folders to back up: Microsoft Windows 2013, copyright © 2013 Microsoft Corporation.
S12-09	Set the backup schedule: Microsoft Windows 2013, copyright © 2013 Microsoft Corporation.

Figure	Credit Line
S12-10	The name of the standard account is Mattie: Microsoft Windows 2013, copyright © 2013 Microsoft Corporation.
S12-11	Type the password twice: Microsoft Windows 2013, copyright © 2013 Microsoft Corporation.
S12-12	This main menu window is provided by the wireless router setup program: Microsoft Windows 2013, copyright © 2013 Microsoft Corporation.
S12-13	Change the password used to access the router setup software: Microsoft Windows 2013, copyright © 2013 Microsoft Corporation.
S12-14	"Decide what to share with the homegroup": Microsoft Windows 2013, copyright © 2013 Microsoft Corporation.
S12-15	Windows suggests a strong password for the homegroup: Microsoft Windows 2013, copyright © 2013 Microsoft Corporation.
S12-16	Enter the homegroup password to join a homegroup: Microsoft Windows 2013, copyright © 2013 Microsoft Corporation.
S12-3	Select all updates before the service pack: Microsoft Windows 2013, copyright © 2013 Microsoft Corporation.
W8-12-05 through 12-10	Windows 8 screenshots: Microsoft Office 2013, copyright © 2013 Microsoft Corporation
Win8 S12-01–S12-02	Windows 8 screenshots: Microsoft Office 2013, copyright © 2013 Microsoft Corporation
13-01, 13-20, 8Figure130	Win 8 O/S Properties screenshot: Microsoft Windows 2013, copyright © 2013 Microsoft Corporation.
13-02	Win 8 O/S Disc Cleanup screenshot: Microsoft Windows 2013, copyright © 2013 Microsoft Corporation.
13-03	Windows O/S properties screenshot: Microsoft Windows 2013, copyright © 2013 Microsoft Corporation.
13-03, 13-05, 13-06	Win 8 O/S Control Panel screenshots: Microsoft Windows 2013, copyright © 2013 Microsoft Corporation.
13-04, 13-09, 13-18, S1	Win 8 O/S Task Manager screenshots: Microsoft Windows 2013, copyright © 2013 Microsoft Corporation.
7Figure13-04 through 7Figure13-10	Windows 7 OS Control Panel screenshot: Microsoft Windows 2013, copyright © 2013 Microsoft Corporation.
13-12, 13-21	Windows 7 O/S Task Manager screenshots: Microsoft Windows 2013, copyright © 2013 Microsoft Corporation.
13-19	Windows 7 Manage Add-ons screenshot: Microsoft Windows 2013, copyright © 2013 Microsoft Corporation.
13-28	Win 7 O/S Virtual Machine Connection screenshot: Microsoft Windows 2013, copyright © 2013 Microsoft Corporation.
13-29	Win 7 O/S System Info screenshot: Microsoft Windows 2013, copyright © 2013 Microsoft Corporation.
Margin13-05	Keyboard and aerosol cleaner: © Wilawan Khasawong/Alamy
Margin13-01	Surge protector: Joy Dark
Margin13-02	Dust cleaner: Joy Dark
Margin13-03	Keyboard and vaccuum: bubamarac/Shutterstock
Margin13-04	Wipes: Joy Dark
Margin13-05	Processor: Lipowski Milan/Shutterstock
14-02	Memory card reader: © Coprid/Shutterstock
14-03	DVI port to a VGA port adapters: Joy Dark
14-05	External hard drive: Joy Dark
14-06	Laptop has two SuperSpeed USB ports and one Hi-Speed USB port: Joy Dark
14-08	Motherboard: Joy Dark
14-09	SMARTPHONE: Oleksiy Mark/Shutterstock Laptop and notebook: Joy Dark Tablet PC laptop isolated on white background: Alexirius/Shutterstock Map on digital tablet: Vincenzo Lombardo/GettyImages

Figure	Credit Line
14-10	A sheet battery fits on the bottom of a laptop and enhances the charge from the main battery: Joy Dark
14-14	Graphics card: Joy Dark
14-16	A DVI to Display Port adapter to connect a DVI monitor to A Display Port on a computer: Joy Dark
14-17	"VGA to Display Port adapter to connect a VGA monitor to a Display Port on a computer": Joy Dark
14-20	Printer: restyler/Shutterstock Color printer: luchschen/Shutterstock
Figure14-11 through 13	HP Official Store screenshots: Copyright © Hewlett-Packard Development Company, L.P. Reproduced with permission.
Figure14-04, 14-07, SFigure14-01, SFigure14-02	Microsoft Windows screenshots: Microsoft Office 2013, copyright © 2013 Microsoft Corporation.
Figure14-15, 14-18	Dell.com screenshots -video card, support, monitor search: © 2011 Dell
Figure14-19, S14-05	Amazon.com shopping screenshots: © Amazon.com, Inc. or it's affiliates. All Rights Reserved.
Margin14-01	SD card: Joy Dark
Margin14-01	Graphics card: Joy Dark
Margin14-02	Memory: Joy Dark
Margin14-03	Display port: Joy Dark
Margin14-04	HDMI port and cable: Joy Dark
S14-06	AskIntel.com home page screenshot: Courtesy of Intel.com
SFigure14-09	Google.com screenshot-search desktops: Courtesy Google.com
SFigure14-03, 04	tigerdirect.com screenshots: Courtesy of Syx Technology
Table14-02	Table14-02 Manufacturers of Brand-Name Computers-weblinks to manufacturer sites: Store.acer.com; Store.apple.com/us; Dell.com/computers; Shopping.hp.com; Shop.lenovo.com; Store.sony.com; Toshiba.com: n/a
F15-01 through F15-25 and Margin15-01 through Margin15-25	Microsoft Office 2013 Access screenshots-57 pgs: Microsoft Office 2013, copyright © 2013 Microsoft Corporation.
16-10	Boy and girl: Joy Dark
16-11	Zack and Joy on boat: Joy Dark
16-15	Trip to the aquarium: Joy Dark
16-16	Jelly fish: Joy Dark
Figure16-01 through; 14 through 16	Website creation screenshots 15 pgs: Courtesy of Jean Andrews
Figure16-13, Margin16-01	Microsoft Office 2013 Word screenshots: Microsoft Office 2013, copyright © 2013 Microsoft Corporation.
SFigure16-01 through SFigure16-05 and SMargin16-01 through SMargin16-05	Microsoft Office 2013, Notepad screenshots: Microsoft Office 2013, copyright © 2013 Microsoft Corporation.
SMargin16-01 and SFigure16-01	Microsoft Office 2013, Windows screenshots: Microsoft Office 2013, copyright © 2013 Microsoft Corporation.
Cover	A goldfish jumping out of the water to escape to freedom. White background: Tischenko Irina/Shutterstock
Media-01	A goldfish jumping out of the water to escape to freedom. White background: Tischenko Irina/Shutterstock
Media-02	A goldfish jumping out of the water to escape to freedom. White background: Tischenko Irina/Shutterstock
Media-03	Gold fish isolated on white: Tischenko Irina/Shutterstock
Media-04	Question button on the keyboard: rvisoft/Shutterstock
Title	Goldfish jumping out of water: Tischenko Irina/Shutterstock Question button on the keyboard: rvlsoft/Shutterstock Goldfish isolated on white: Tischenko Irina/Shutterstock Young boy and pet dog: Morgan Lane Studios/Getty Images